1968

M

SYMBOLISM IN MEDIEVAL THOUGHT
AND ITS CONSUMMATION IN THE DIVINE COMEDY

ADORATION OF THE LAMB: DETAIL GHENT ALTARPIECE

THE BROTHERS VAN EYCK: THE CATHEDRAL OF ST. BAVON, GHENT

SYMBOLISM IN MEDIEVAL THOUGHT AND ITS CONSUMMATION IN THE DIVINE COMEDY

BY H. FLANDERS DUNBAR M.A. B.D. Ph.D.

New York

RUSSELL & RUSSELL

1961

PREFACE

THE hypothesis on which this thesis is founded is no more nor less than that Dante Alighieri was in full possession of his senses and of serious intent when, in words of supreme importance for the student of medieval thought, he defined the subject of his *Commedia*. Dante wrote: "Be it known that the sense of this work is not simple, but on the contrary it may be called polysemous, that is to say, of more senses than one; for it is one sense which we get through the letter, and another which we get through the thing the letter signifies: and the first is called literal but the second allegorical or mystic." It will be remembered that he proceeded then to analyze the allegorical meaning into its three senses, consistent with his earlier statement: "it should be known that writings may be taken and should be understood *chiefly in four senses.*"

Students of medieval thought, like the rest of mankind, group themselves in hostile camps and appear impervious to the sense of Dickens' aphorism: "There is much to be said on both sides." Only too frequently, blind to the implications in that which they themselves term the literary masterpiece of the Middle Ages, scholars dispute, arguing with assurance over alternative theories. In Dante as he appears in the *Divina Commedia* has been recognized an epitome of all that is medieval, and factions among Dante critics represent adequately the schools of interpretation of medieval thought.

There are critics for whom the *Commedia* is an aesthetic and imaginative masterpiece, as such to be appreciated; the question of symbolic meanings is waived as of no abiding import: "Dante will live as a poet; why trouble about what he meant?" Greeted with disdain by opposing schools, these critics have for comfort Dante's own statement that for those little gifted with keenness of intellect or insight, there remains yet a good: appreciation of the sheer beauty of the poem; and should not this lead their opponents to regard them with charity?

Again, there are those to whom the poem is alluring as a revelation of the poet's private life. They delight to behold in it the artistic culmination of a romance, or a cleverly contrived weapon for the discomfiture of acquaintances and of those whom Dante regarded as the cause of his personal misfortunes. Among them, the latest interest is study of the poem as revelation of a childhood neurosis. Certainly, it is with justice that they allege Dante's promise in the *Vita Nuova* to write of Beatrice "what hath never been written of any woman," and aver that judgments on individuals throughout the *Commedia* are not without their sting.

There is, on the other hand, a considerable school in whose opinion only littleness of mind could fail to perceive in the masterpiece of one of the world's greatest poets something more than the bereaved lover or the unhappy wanderer seeking compensation in dreams or satire. They see in the *Commedia* the work of a patriot and social reformer who, unable as administrator to realize his platform (revealed in the *Monarchia*), sought to present it in a poem of sufficient power to enlist the enthusiasm of princes. Their position is not difficult to defend, for of the very fabric of the *Commedia* are passages[1] of obvious political and social import.

Perhaps best known is the interpretation of the *Divina Commedia* as a prolonged tractate on ethics, in which Dante, like Bunyan's Christian, having become familiar with the wages of sin, proceeds to rid himself of the vices and acquire the virtues, that he may at last ascend to Paradise. Partisans of the ethical theory have such basis as Dante's statement of the poem's subject: "man,—as by good or ill deserts, in the exercise of the freedom of his choice, he becomes liable to rewarding or punishing justice." Related is the contention that Dante's story is an evangelical thesis to demonstrate the humble position befitting the intellect in the presence of religious experience. Dante's confession of infidelity to Beatrice (who according to this theory is interpreted as Revelation or Faith, since she reflects divine truth) becomes then a confession of sinful preoccupation with philosophy.

Finally, the *Commedia* is regarded frequently as being solely of philosophical or mystical interest; and justification for this point of view is not far to seek. For completeness' sake, mention may be made of those for whom the poem is, like the Bible, a

---

1. For example, *Par.,* vi, 97-107 and *Par.,* xxx, 137-141.

source of mysterious prophecies. Even for their position support is granted in Dante's implicit comparison of his poem to Holy Scripture.

It is the very facility with which justification may be found for diverse interpretations of the *Commedia* that has been the occasion of so much annoyance among critics. One of them, for example, published a work entitled, "The Art of Misunderstanding Dante,"[2] wherein, having demolished to his satisfaction the political theory, he predicted with sarcasm that in the future would appear an interpretation of the poem as expressing the whole history of the Roman Empire. This critic then proceeded to give "the true interpretation" in terms of German pietism and romanticism.

No Dante critic need feel himself without justification; but for the confusion of all stand Dante's words: "of more senses than one." According to the explanation of its author, the *Commedia* is polysemous, to be interpreted *at one and the same time on different levels so closely interrelated that each is corrected by the other and that all are blended into an harmonious whole.* Such interpretation demands two things: the admission (on the basis of equal truth in their respective levels) of many meanings in addition to and necessary for the correction of that which happens to be the reader's special interest; and the rejection of certain meanings as ruled out by the harmony of the whole. For example, had the meaning of polyseme been appreciated by the school of criticism here termed evangelical, the implication would never have been possible that Dante, having left Reason (Virgil) behind, was in Paradise a sort of Orlando Furioso. Disregard of Dante's words and inevitably resultant misconceptions have gained a prevalence to be checked only as it becomes the custom among critics to study Dante with reference to his *milieu* no less enthusiastically than with reference to their own.

To make matters worse, however, the medieval *milieu* itself has been considered from the retrospective of modern advance, rather than from the perspective of the great intellectual development of which it was the culmination. In consequence

2. In Karl Witte, *Essays on Dante.*

there is readily at hand no basis from which the Dante student may proceed to the more refined aspects of his task and a clearing of the ground is demanded. With this in mind the present work as first conceived was arranged in two parts: the first having reference to the function of symbolism in medieval thinking, necessary background for an understanding of Dante; the second being a consideration (from an approach given justification in the general study) of the *Divina Commedia* as illustration and consummation of medieval theory. With the working out of the problem other arrangement seemed expedient. As the book now appears: Chapters I, III Part I, IV Part I, V Part I, and VI constitute a study in broad outlines of medieval symbolism as a whole, origins and philosophy, methods, molding of the learned tradition, and relation to the activities of the people; Chapters II, III Part II, IV Part II, V Part II, and VII constitute an application of the principles of medieval symbolic usage to the specific problem of Dante interpretation. The possibility is thus left open for anyone who prefers a different arrangement to accomplish it for himself or to omit entirely the sections of more specialized reference to Dante. A similar procedure with regard to the sections dealing with medieval theory for obvious reasons is not recommended to the Dante student.

It need scarcely be stated that complete treatment of symbolism in medieval thought, and complete solution of the problem of the *Divina Commedia,* are equally beyond the scope of this work. On the other hand the purpose is not, on the ground of some accepted theory, to analyze one more minor problem. It is rather to present, not a thorough and detailed interpretation of the *Commedia,* yet a basis for it, a pattern into which detailed studies may be fitted. Many of the interpretations here suggested will require monographs in their support, some of which it is the hope at a later date to supply. It should be understood clearly that such interpretations are presented far from dogmatically, even where limited space has rendered impracticable full recognition of the controversies involved. The present work must stand or fall on the harmony of the whole, not on any one detail of interpretation.

If it be conceded that in the letter to Can Grande and in the related passages in the *Convivio* Dante probably meant what he said, and that[3] the polyseme is not only consistent with Dante's nature and traditional heritage and with the period in which he lived, but also crucial in the whole of medieval thought; then the purpose of this study will have been achieved. On such a basis it is possible to synthesize meanings already found in the *Commedia* and to suggest at least in outline that which would be involved in a complete solution. The fuller comprehension alike of Dante and of the Middle Ages can be attained only as critics cease to insist that the true solution must be a question of "either—or," and to ignore both the possibility, and Dante's assertion, of "both—and."

Elucidated by an understanding of the polysemous nature of the *Commedia,* Dante's poetry may become again, as Shelley found it, "the bridge thrown over the stream of time which unites the modern and the ancient world." The restoration of this bridge is almost a *sine qua non* if modern thought is to become truly conversant with its great ancestry in the Middle Ages.

The author wishes to express indebtedness to Dr. Irwin Edman for encouragment in the study of Plotinian philosophy; to Dr. F. J. Foakes-Jackson for direction in reading on church history and practice; to Mr. Dino Bigongiari for *explications de textes* of the *Divina Commedia;* to Dr. Lynn Thorndike for guidance in the history of thought in the Middle Ages; to Dr. William W. Rockwell for bibliographical suggestions; to Canon Winfred Douglas for a critical reading of the entire manuscript; to Miss Mary A. Ewer for assistance in the preparation of the manuscript for the press; and to Mr. William Henry McCarthy, Jr., for a checking of bibliographical details. A special debt of gratitude is owed to Prof. Jefferson B. Fletcher, whose insight into the symbolism of the *Divina Commedia* first turned the author's studies in medieval symbolism into the particular channel of Dante criticism.

H. F. D.

New York City
April, 1927

---

3. Whether or not the authenticity of Epistle X be disputed, as it was a number of years ago. The letter now is generally accepted as genuine. The subject is fully treated by Dr. Moore in his *Studies in Dante. Third series,* pp. 284-374.

CONTENTS

CONTENTS

SYMBOLISM IN MEDIEVAL THOUGHT

CHAPTER I. SCHEMA

Symbolism as a medium of expression. Symbol defined. Philosophy of symbolism. Philosophic basis of medieval symbolic usage. Method of medieval symbolic usage. Medieval search for knowledge. Summary.

CHAPTER I. SYMBOLISM AS A MEDIUM OF EXPRESSION: ITS ORIGIN AND DEVELOPMENT

Nel giallo de la rosa sempiterna,
  che si dilata ed ingrada e redole
odor di lode al sol che sempre verna,
qual è colui che tace e dicer vole,
  mi trasse Beatrice, e disse: "Mira
quanto è 'l convento de le bianche
    stole!"

Within the yellow of the eternal rose,
which doth expand, rank upon rank,
and reeketh perfume of praise unto the
Sun that maketh Spring for ever, me—
as who doth hold his peace yet fain
would speak—Beatrice drew, and said:
"Behold how great the white-robed
concourse!"

I. PROEM

THE vision that sees in a yellow rose the solution of the drama of life and death is not native to this generation. Modern culture, formed in the rise of the scientific method, and freed from cobwebs of fantasy, finds itself in a position to smile at the *naïveté* that sees in a flower at once an expression of philosophic truth, the goal of a career, and the fulfilment of social and political theory. Dante's Celestial Rose is readily banished to the realm of poetic conceit or buried among the ashes of time-worn symbolisms, while contemporary thought puzzles genially over an almost obsolete tradition: seeking in its fossils disclosures of phenomena of mind, and ignoring their living rôle organic in the enigma of genius.

No longer, as in the thirteenth and fourteenth centuries, is a rose a natural and appropriate expression of the deepest that is known. Once a luminous eternity unfolding without pause its myriad petals, each the throne of a radiance-vestured soul, it offered up perpetually as perfume the incense of creation's praise. As it mirrored, like the crystal sea, the Threefold Glory in whose radiance it was bathed, over it angelic multitudes, glowing and shadowless, like bees ascended and descended bearing blessings from the Sun. In this Celestial Rose has been discerned a statement of truth far more accurate than any possible to the unaided power of science, although demanding foundation in the most rigorous discipline of the intellect.[1]

It is of the nature of today to exile such use of symbol to the realm of poetry, where it may be harmless, charming, even em-

---

1. Cf. the closeness of Dante's scientific reasoning, for example in *Convivio*, 3, 5, and also of the reasoning in the *Monarchia*, where are analyzed those theories for which he gives consummate expression in the Rose.

blematically suggestive of a Paradise itself long since relegated
to the same region. Dante was a poet, but he was likewise a
statesman and a student of the sciences; he lived in an age in
which specialization was not yet supreme as the means of penetrating into the mystery of the universe. For him, symbolism
constituted not only the natural, but the most adequate expression. Today even poets are puzzled by the intricacy of Dante's
imagery, and scientists fail to recognize in him a kindred spirit.
Historians, although unable to ignore his thought, prefer the
more direct and lucid expression current in the literature of the
League of Nations, while lovers of utopias are more drawn to
the delicate conceits of the Houyhnhnms than to the pageant of
the *Paradiso.* The *Divina Commedia,* although an inspiration in
the Renaissance and from time to time of men of genius who
have "trusted their light bark to the waves in Dante's wake," is
so little understood that it has become the seldom-disputed prey
of scholars delighting in the obscure.

The modern reader of medieval philosophy, lore of the medieval church, early fable and allegory, Grail legends, courtly
love, mysticism, alchemy, astrology, wonders at the puerile and
contradictory extravagance of the Middle Ages. Now and then
he looks askance at the masterpiece of genius, which in some
way grew out of that perplexing period. Perhaps allured by the
suggestion that in the *Commedia* of Dante Alighieri may be
locked the solution of many puzzles, and half suspecting from
the baffling ubiquity of symbolism in medieval thought and expression that in it may lie the key, he may be challenged to the
quest for the lost secret of its use.

Should he aspire to penetrate the jungle of adversities on a
quest for an understanding of medieval symbolism, he may well
undertake, like the hero of myth and faery, several preliminary
exploits as it were for the achievement of magic cap, mirror, steed, and sword, against the perils which are to throng
the path. He should be prepared with a definition of symbol,
and he should know something of its philosophy and ultimate
origin. Not only this but there must be added a survey of the
philosophic bases of medieval symbolic usage itself, and the
method by which medieval thought in its quest for knowledge

wrought of the materials of symbolism a means of penetration into the mysteries of the universe. To win this equipment will be the task of the introductory chapter, after which the quest may well commence with a rough map (Chap. II) of the ground which it would seem that Dante intended his scripture to cover, in which may be observed, as in a microcosm, the Middle Ages itself. Next, endeavor must be made to isolate and analyze (Chaps. III to V), in the light of Dante's traditional heritage and of the thought of his time, the more important aspects of the multiplex symbolism of the *Divina Commedia,* thus to test the validity of that which has been postulated. Confirmation may then be sought (Chap. VI) in a glimpse of the varied activity of the thirteenth century, which at the same time should have been illumined by the preceding study. It will remain to ponder on the meaning of that which has been achieved.

II. SYMBOL DEFINED

"Qu'est-ce-que le symbolisme? On frisson à la pensée qu'il faudra répondre à cette question-là!" Beaunier.

THE student of symbolism nowadays follows a Siren's song; his peace of mind is the inevitable sacrifice. Let him consider well before he attempt to communicate his ideas, especially if he has ventured beyond two or three well-defined phases of his subject. If his interest be in the mathematical system, he will attain to the understanding of a restricted audience. If it be in the static arts, to the sympathy of colleagues will be added from those to whom symbolism suggests "apples and pomegranates in the hands of medieval Madonnas" such understanding as may be gleaned from *Baedekers* and glossaries. The psychologist or interpreter of dream symbols, to some degree supposedly beneath the banner of Freud, will be surrounded by the fascinated— admirers and calumniators alike. With these types of symbolist our generation is at ease; it has labeled them and their terminology has penetrated its vocabulary. Not so, however, with the symbolist who sees in his theme a fundamental impulse, essential alike in human thought and expression. Even among those of kindred interests such an alien must "run the gauntlet" in the ordeal of definition of terms.

To say that in the field of language the word "symbol" has been used loosely is an euphemism. There are books professing to deal with the subject, the authors of which seem cheerfully oblivious of the fact that definition is a useful convention. An indication of the inadequacy of current exposition of symbolism is the frequency of such questions as: How does symbol "differ from" allegory, analogy, emblem, sacrament, parable, metaphor, and the like?

Fundamentally, as far as there is any agreement among men, it is agreed that a symbol is an expression of meaningful experience. The basis in association (of course between some combination of ideas, emotions, and sensations) is indicated in the root of the word itself.[2] As to association, there is unwonted accord among philologists and philosophers, psychologists and psychiatrists, that essentially it is of two types. Following the ancient classification of knowledge, association has been defined as mediate and immediate[3] or more recently as extrinsic (association through contiguity) and intrinsic (association through resemblance).[4] Two types of symbol are thus defined, which for present purposes will be noted as the extrinsic or arbitrary-association and the intrinsic or descriptive.[5]

With these two groups of symbols[6] readily classified and explained as dependent on simple psychological laws of association, it is customary to assume the subject to have been covered. There remains to be defined, however, a group of symbols which depend on a synthetic process for which as yet psychology has no adequate description, as for the validity of its analogies philoso-

2. Symbol, from σύμβολον-συμβαλλειν, to put together (σύν + βαλλειν, to throw). For the range of variation in use of the term symbol, reference should be made to Appendix I, ii, footnotes. Consideration of the problem, in relation to the divergent statements and ideas there exemplified, has suggested the possibility and expediency of dealing with symbol under a threefold classification.

3. Among others, by Wundt, Kraepelin, and Aschaffenburg. (Cf. Leonardo Bianchi, *The Mechanism of the Brain*, p. 220.)

4. Wundt's terminology. With this classification, however, the world was already familiar as a result of the learning of Teufelsdröckh—see Carlyle, *Sartor Resartus*, Bk. III, chap. 3 (Everyman ed., pp. 167-169). Compare also C. G. Jung, *Psychology of the Unconscious*, p. 105.

5. For full differentiation of the two types of symbol, cf. Appendix I, ii.

6. Cf. Appendix I, ii, for a more detailed discussion of arbitrary-association and of descriptive symbols.

phy has no definite verdict. These are the symbols which characterize the thinking of the genius.

Language itself is rooted in sense ideas, and the most modern research has tended only to fuller establishment of Locke's anticipation that "if we could trace them to their sources, we should find in all language the names which stand for things that fall not under our senses, to have had their first rise from sensible ideas."[7] The abstract has been called but the product of a fusion of concrete images vibrating together on the threshold of consciousness.[8] Teufelsdröckh, however, became spokesman for mankind when he recognized "in the highest sensible phenomena, so far as Sense went, only fresh or faded raiment, yet ever, under this, a celestial essence thereby rendered visible";[9] and there are many (even among modern psychologists) who are of the opinion that "thought contains elements which are wholly irreducible to sensory terms."[10] Having pointed out that a sentence together with the mental image which it arouses has no meaning *per se,* a modern writer asserts "it means *through* these mental events to something else."[11] In other words, above the level of simple association and the play of fancy, man tends ever to feel that a reality is glimpsed through the datum of experience or expressed in it, which is completely beyond and beneath it and imperceptible to sense *per se.* The experience is not for its own sake described and made more vivid through the use of comparison drawn from other data of sense, as is the case with descriptive symbol, but it is given importance only as a gateway into something beyond. Such usage would make the symbol in some wise a semblance of a reality greater and truer than the symbol in all its aspects, a sort of initiation in which thought may be led through meaning to deeper meaning. In speaking of God as spiritual food, for example, God is regarded as being essential to life, strengthening, and refreshing, like food, but in an infinitely greater manner and degree. Here the

7. Locke, *Lectures on Language,* 2d ser., chap. viii, p. 345.
8. Bianchi, *The Mechanism of the Brain,* p. 235.
9. Carlyle, *Sartor Resartus,* Bk. III chap. 1 (Everyman ed., p. 156).
10. Robert S. Woodworth, "Imageless Thought." *Jour. Phil. Psych. and Sci. Meth.,* III (1906), 701-707.
11. R. M. Eaton, *Symbolism and Truth,* p. 12.

basis is a supposed intrinsic likeness, as against the extrinsic association which governs the arbitrary-association symbol even when it treats of the supersensible. The aim is apprehension of a reality greater than the symbol in all its aspects, of which indeed the symbol is but a shadow. Imagery thus used for its glimpse of a beyond may be classified as insight or interpretative symbol.

In the insight symbol is that which has been described as the union of silence and speech, infinite and finite.[12] Carlyle has said of the man who is unfamiliar with such language, that he "is but a pair of spectacles, behind which there is no eye. Let those who have eyes look through him, then he may be useful."[13] Indeed, there is a tendency among those familiar with this use of imagery to regard it as the only true symbolism. It is the symbol which deals ever with that which is just beyond man's grasp. Characteristic is the statement: "Symbolism . . . concerns itself with just those experiences that seem beyond the reach of drama. . . . In the symbol proper, what we call a symbol, there is ever, more or less distinctly or directly, some embodiment or revelation of the infinite."[14] The relationship postulated between insight or interpretative symbolism and reality is rooted in the *Weltanschauung* itself.[15]

Symbolism is, then, to be described under three headings: arbitrary (extrinsic), descriptive (intrinsic), and interpretative or insight. Symbolic usage associated with a definite object is of all these types.[16] Attention may be centered on a rock. A geologist, or navigator charting a channel, will note on the map the conventional sign, thus using an arbitrary-association symbol as

12. Carlyle, *Sartor Resartus*, Bk. II, chap. 10 (Everyman ed., pp. 154-155).
13. *Ibid.*, Bk. I, chap. 10 (Everyman ed., pp. 50-51).
14. Frederick M. Tisdel, *Symbolism in the Theatre*, p. 288.
15. For the point of view prevalent in the Middle Ages as to this problem, Cf. sec. vi of this chapter.
16. Similarly a symbol may have at different times (or even at the same time, as will be seen later) all three significations. A palm is an emblem of victory, as a result of the historical fact that palm branches were strewn before victors; that is, the palm may be an arbitrary symbol. In the *Song of Songs* the palm tree is a descriptive symbol used to describe and enhance the stature of the bride. The palm is an interpretative or insight symbol, however, when, through its flourishing growth and its characteristic position in oases, it becomes as it were a veil behind which the desert dweller may discern the faithfulness and the mercy of God and the justice of the righteous man.

a shorthand representation of the datum. The artist on the other hand may sketch the rock, or write a poem describing it in terms of other sense experience, which then becomes a descriptive symbol of the rock. Finally, the philosopher or the artist gifted with insight may look through the object to one or more deeper meanings, such as the stability of eternal law, and so use the rock itself as an insight symbol.

It will be found that not only all dictionary definitions of symbol, but even such casual definitions of symbol as are encountered in treatises, fall readily into one of the three classes defined,[17] with the exception that there is generally either a vagueness which leaves one in doubt as to which of three very separate entities is under discussion, or an arbitrary use of the term in a specialized sense as if that were the only conceivable meaning. These two factors, however, have seriously handicapped modern understanding of symbolism.

There are those who, taking up a book purporting to treat of symbolism, are astonished and disappointed if they find but slight discussion of the star on the breast of St. Thomas and the gridiron of St. Laurence. Hence the question: Are not symbols emblems? In answer it is but needed to reverse the words: Emblems are symbols. They represent, however, as generally discussed, but one type of symbol, that based on arbitrary association. The fact commonly neglected by iconographers that they are seldom so in origin and need not be so in interpretation—many would agree with Quarles that "emblem is but a silent parable"—gives them their place in medieval development. There are others who in reading of symbolism in medieval thought expect to read of allegory (for in many minds the two have become synonymous) ; yet allegory as generally understood today has its basis in symbolism of the arbitrary-association type and hence has no kinship with the allegory based on insight symbolism which dominated in the learned tradition of the Middle Ages. Allegory is symbol, but as such it is of different types,[18] conveying varying meanings in different traditions. The

17. Cf. Appendix I, ii, n. 7a.
18. Cf. Appendix I, ii. For a discussion of the distinction between the allegory of personification and the allegory of insight symbolism, see pp. 278 ff.

scholar, who in his instruction of the modern generation explains without definition that allegory dominated medieval thought, places himself on a par with the Sunday-school teacher who impresses on the minds of youth mental pictures of the Oriental king clad in purple and fine linen, yet neglects to mention that by "purple" is meant not "purple" (as grandmother wears it), but blood-red or crimson. Again, few minds today approach the subject of symbolism untouched by the pervasive atmosphere of current psychology. Hence the question: Are not symbols but projections of that which is beneath consciousness? A projection of that which is beneath consciousness is a symbol; but symbols are of different types. Symbol to Freud has a specific and esoteric meaning of its own based on arbitrary association and comparison. It is, however, through the broadening of the psychologist's understanding of symbolism to include insight usage, that there have come the most valuable hints for mental therapy and the reconstruction of the individual.[19] A symbol is an expression of meaningful experience having basis in association. As such, emblems, metaphors, parables, are all symbols, but in this sense so is all expression whatsoever. In consequence, the symbolist, setting out to discuss anything but the philosophy of expression,

19. The original school of psychoanalysis sees in the symbolism of myth, art, and involuntary fantasy, alike, no deeper meaning than the representation of a crude sense experience. Dr. C. G. Jung, however, sees in it representation of racial (i.e., universal) tendency and experience, with the (generally unconscious) object of working out the individual's relationship to his particular environmental and personal problems. Likewise M. Baudouin sees in the imagery of the "symbolist" school of literature an attempt to work out individual problems in the deeper levels of the personality. Dr. Beatrice Hinkle sees, deeper than the levels mentioned, the representation of racial experience in an attempt to work out racial problems. Mental therapy at its height, then, would consist in assisting the individual to make his utmost contribution to the successful working out of these problems. Had a medieval thinker of the first rank been equipped with modern psychological background and technique, he would no doubt have maintained that the deepest meaning behind each of the interpretations given was the attempt to make that adjustment to the Infinite which Dante represents fully accomplished in the last four lines of the *Paradiso*.

Probably nothing is more needed by the student of disorders of the human mind than a thorough study of the development of insight symbolism and the place that it filled during those centuries when in every science it held the attention of students. A study of symbolism from the objective—philosophical and literary—point of view gives basis for a more sound psychological evaluation than any study of the psychological elements antecedent to a grasp of the meaning consciously intended. The author is at present engaged on a study from the point of view of psychiatry, of the medieval tradition in general and of the *Divina Commedia* in particular.

must analyze the type of association involved in the symbolism with which he is dealing.

Although reference will be made to luxuriant subsidiary symbolisms having basis in arbitrary-association and comparison, the subject matter of this study is insight symbolism, that expression of meaningful experience which has basis in an association neither extrinsic arbitrary, nor intrinsic remaining in the realm of sense comparison, but intrinsic as expressing and reaching out toward the supersensible. Such association is constantly used, but seldom defined or even recognized except by the initiate. In the words of the Greek aphorism: "Many are the wand-bearers but few are the mystics."

III. PHILOSOPHY OF SYMBOLISM

MODERN students of symbolism cannot but gain some of their first and perhaps unconscious impressions of the subject from present-day reverberations of the theories propounded and contested in the nineteenth century by those first inspired to undertake a scientific study of the symbolic problem. In consequence, and because in them are revealed roots of present confusion over the connotation of the word "symbol," these theories demand passing notice. Owing to them, the two words "symbol" and "mystic" constitute today sufficient stimulus to send the reader delving down into his hypothetical subconscious with its wilderness of childhood experiences, or back to the infancy of the race. On the other hand, psychologists and ethnologists, for all the bitter trial they have been to conservatives, have opened vistas of human development and incidentally have made more possible the understanding of the medieval symbolic tradition in the perspective of the tremendous development to which it owed its being.

There has been too great a tendency to consider medieval culture either as inheritor of a mutilated classical tradition or else as heir of no background at all. Drawing from the great cultures in the Roman melting pot, and indirectly from the source of all of these in primitive paganism, medieval culture in addition fell heir to the rich though dim background of the unwritten history of barbaric Europe. In the life of the barbarian, symbol, more or less consciously recognized, played an integral part, and his symbolisms exerted quite as powerful an influence on the Middle Ages as did the more consciously wrought symbolic systems of Greek, Roman, Jew, and Oriental. In consequence, without a word as to the more elemental symbolisms of myth and pagan cultus, it were insufficient to suggest possibilities of symbolism as a medium of expression or to note against the background of the classic traditions in their medieval development[20] its philosophical basis and its method.

No slight contribution to the religious doubt and difficulty of the early nineteenth century was made by such students as Payne-Knight, who rediscovered for a world just emerging from frills and powdered wigs the fact familiar in the dawn of the Middle Ages, that Christianity had much in common with religions of paganism; that, indeed, its symbolisms betrayed it as sharing the common origin of religions in sun worship. This suggestion, although a contribution to knowledge, supplied in a self-centered age new weapons to those embittered and disillusioned in regard to the religions of the day. Soon, however, precursors of the psychoanalytic school declared the explanation of the whole background of Christianity as vegetation myth to be a mere *tour de force*. A little study of the reactions of men, so they said, would make clear that the real basis of religion is sex, and that the gods so confidently proclaimed as solar heroes are merely representations of the phallus. Subsequently considerable energy was devoted to the demonstration that each Christian symbol had its phallic prototype. These two factors exerted a powerful and subtle influence among the many elements of nineteenth-century skepticism.[21] It is little wonder that our Victorian ancestors became more and more uneasy about their religion, even amid movements for deepening it, and became also increasingly wary of any external representation or symbolic expression.

Psychologists[22] have pointed out that throughout the history

20. Cf. Chap. III, Pt. I.
21. For a more detailed discussion of theories of myth origin in their application to the problem of symbolism, cf. Appendix I, iii.
22. As one of many examples, cf. E. A. Ross, *Social Psychology*, p. 142.

of human culture the replacement of inner elements, whether by a borrowing or by development, goes on more rapidly than the replacement of outer elements, and in consequence civilization is full of survivals of which the original content and purpose is forgotten. Indeed, some have found the world but a "huge rag fair," with the "rags and tatters of old symbols" raining down everywhere suffocatingly. This has led even to the extreme of declaring the basis of symbolism to be in dissociation rather than in association; in other words, that the race, rather than adding to and developing that which its ancestors had enclosed within the outer covering of the word, with the passing of generations, has discarded this content as incomprehensible or useless.

Many a student of the human mind has bewailed the fact that man's developed ideas are largely detached from their perceptual foundations.[23] Whether or not this detachment has brought him nearer to truth in the abstract is again a question for philosophy. Certainly it has made understanding much more difficult, not only of the thought of the past but also of the functioning of human minds today. In recognition of this fact even the philologists are coming to adopt as their aim the restoration to present consciousness of whatever has been in the past consciousness of the race.[24a] Identical has been the constant aim of the worker with difficulties of mind, the restoration to consciousness, of the past consciousness both of the race and of the individual. This he has attempted to accomplish through recognition of the symbolical nature of words and objects and ideas, that is, their character as the outward expression of some deeper meaning. This process, because of its therapeutic value, has come to be associated with the pathological, in accord with that same fallacy which fails to recognize in illness merely the misfunctioning of normal and essential processes. Symbols may be the husks or outer shells of ideas which the world has outgrown, but "symbols are the chief means by which the human mind expresses, not so much those ideas which it has outgrown or wishes to conceal, but those which it has not yet mastered."[24b]

23. Alfred Storch, *Primitive Archaic Forms of Inner Experience and Thought in Schizophrenia*, p. 9.

24a. Dr. G. P. Krapp in lecture, Columbia University, Winter Session, 1922-23.

24b. J. H. van der Hoop, *Character and the Unconscious*, p. 119.

Ultimately, the confusion is the result of failure to distinguish the three essentially different connotations of the word symbol. Symbols of the type of arbitrary-association or comparison may be shells which once conveyed a different significance, or within which thought-kernels have shriveled, blighted in their development. Not so however is insight symbol, the meaning of which may not fade or become stereotyped without destruction of its fundamental character and so reduction to one of the other types. Its very existence as true insight symbol depends on the continual re-creation and expansion of its meaning. The meaning can never really change, because in its first apprehension it represented a fundamental truth, or psychological entity, the understanding of which may increase, but only to give to its expression a richer content, never to abrogate that content. With the first two types of symbolism dissociation is possible, but the basis of the third is in continual association.

It has been the custom to recognize only arbitrary-association and descriptive symbol, and there has come a general lack of skill in the handling of insight symbolism. The fact that man can think usefully with words of vague meaning is well known[25] and is not surprising: his actions are determined at every instant by incomplete perceptions. Occasionally, however, life compels some attempt at accuracy of observation. Similarly, eternal neglect of analysis of vague meanings is not permitted with impunity. When the mind becomes haunted by shades of long-forgotten significances of its language, it becomes subject for the psychiatrist. Its symbolism is dissociated. The genius recognizes in his language insight symbolism within which he may penetrate to level upon level of deeper truth.[26] Genius differs from insanity perhaps only in that it knows how to manage its ghosts. For the one the words shroud meanings; for the other they be-

25. B. Bourdon, "La pensée sans images," *Jour. de psych.,* XX (1923), 189-205.

26. "The analysis of the dreams or fantasies of a neuropath is curative, in that it disentangles the obscure affective troubles which underlie the neurosis. A similar analysis, when applied to the fantasies of the normal imagination, reveals the normal sensibility; applied to the creations of the man of genius, it discloses the secret soul of the man of genius. Such analysis is far from pre-supposing, as field of action, a morbid individual, toward whom the analyst assumes an air of medical superiority." Baudouin, *Psychoanalysis and Aesthetics,* p. 33.

come "lamps behind ideas."[27] In the Middle Ages the attempt was made to create a consistent tradition of insight imagery for the handling of the materials of symbolism.[28]

IV. PHILOSOPHIC BASIS OF MEDIEVAL SYMBOLIC USAGE

IN the use of insight symbol lies the secret of the intellectual tradition of the Middle Ages. Reaching far back of the beginnings of medievalism was a long cycle of development. Whereas to the primitive thinker the universe presented itself probably as a vague, little differentiated experience, advance in the process of differentiation marked the first progress in culture.[29] History of thought bears record of this development, important to the Middle Ages, in the early culture of Jew, Greek, Oriental,[30] and Roman. Gradually the universe became less and less a unity and more and more a composite of contradictory and conflicting elements, until the exigency of order forced upon the world the formulation of a metaphysic. Everywhere the essential dualism of the cosmos claimed attention; but Greek philosophy and late pre-Christian Judaism sought further for a unity underlying even this dualism, while in Roman legalism, just as truly as in Oriental mystery cults, was manifested the same aspiration toward ordering of experience.

During the first centuries of our era, in the Roman Empire, become the melting pot of the world, these widely divergent radii of search for unification were brought into violent juxtaposition. The result was definition of an attitude toward the universe, in expression increasingly articulate.[31] First, ever since the days of Plato, it had been becoming more and more clear that the meaning of the universe lay, not in isolated phenomena, but in their relationships, which constituted the "pattern of the universe." Second, as early as distinction was made between finite

27. As Maeterlinck said of the older languages of mankind.
28. Cf. Chap. III, Pt. I, ii. For this reason the period merits special investigation by the student of the human mind.
29. Cf. the development of myth, Chap. III, Pt. I, i.
30. Throughout, the word "Oriental" is used as restricted to non-Hellenic and non-Semitic Oriental influences.
31. And in articulation increasingly sun-centered. Cf. Chap. III, Pt. I, ii and iii.

and infinite, the phenomenal universe was seen as finite expression of an infinite which gave it meaning and coherence. Third, from this background it is evident that just as no scientific generalization can be made from one fact alone, so no understanding of the infinite can be gained through one finite phenomenon separated from its relationships.[32] Not only then does *scientia* (knowledge of the particular) derive its significance from *sapientia* (knowledge of universals or general ideas), but science bears somewhat the same relation to the underlying infinite that logic bears to thought, the enunciation of which it defines. As the body is a mechanism of self-expression for man, and language for thought, so the cosmos is a mechanism of self-expression for the infinite.

The conception of the cosmos as the mechanism of self-expression for the infinite has flowed through all ages of thought like a subterranean stream. Breaking forth now and again on the surface of life, it has been accorded a varying reception. Sometimes it has been welcomed as a source of untold power and used consciously to the utmost of men's ability. At other periods, however, it has been felt to bring the menace of ghosts and demons with which superstition peoples the outlets of mysterious force, and men have devoted their energy to stopping up the hole. Carlyle greeted it with circumspection, presenting it half humorously from behind the ample shield of nineteenth-century German philosophy and the name of the mythical Teufelsdröckh. "All visible things are emblems," he wrote, "matter exists only spiritually and to represent some idea and body it forth." He went on to make clear, however, that Teufelsdröckh "was no Adamite in any sense and could not, like Rousseau, recommend . . . a return to the savage state,"—"either bodily or intellectual nudity." Just here lies the paradox of insight symbolism, on which those who refuse to recognize paradoxes are doomed to founder. The symbol is but the bodying forth of the infinite, yet it is of the very life of the infinite to be bodied forth. Carlyle tried to express this in a correction of the garment

32. For the value of the sun focus in giving relationships, cf. Chap. III, Pt. I, i. Here is included interrelationships between symbolisms in hierarchic order. Cf. pp. 96 ff., 272 ff., Chap. V, Pt. I, iii, and pp. 393-394.

symbolism: "Language is called the Garment of Thought:' how-ever, it should rather be, language is the Flesh-garment, the Body, of Thought." A recognition of the true relationship of expression to that expressed is the only basis on which interpre-tative symbolism can lead to truth.[33] Their manner of union was a mystery quite as vital to later thought[34] as it had been awe-inspiring to the primitive.[35]

Symbol has been well defined as an "expression of a similar force in different material." Basic to its use is the belief that all things in nature have something in common which they are striv-ing to express, although no one alone can ever express it per-fectly. It is of the character of insight symbol to look beneath a datum of experience to its relationships in the universal pattern and in consequence to set forth, not only the particular fact, but also that fact in its fundamental relationships. Thus it came to seem the closest possible approach to the expression of truth.

33. The only means of avoiding the fallacy of the argument by analogy. Cf. also Chap. IV.

34. In consequence, men call themselves by such names as materialist, pan-theist, parallelist, and so forth.

35. This feeling appears in innumerable legends and early epics, among the northern as well as the southern races, cf., for example, the Kalevala. An interest-ing example appears on one of the Tablets of Creation. Marduk the sun god was chosen in a counsel of all the gods as their champion against the powers of dark-ness and chaos, and thus as the divine instrument in creation. After His appoint-ment their first procedure was to invest him with power that would cause his every word to be followed immediately by the effect toward which it was directed:

"They founded for him a majestic canopy,
He seated himself in the seat of kingship in the presence of his fathers, who
    said unto him:
Thou art honorable by reason of thy greatness among the gods.
Thy position is unrivalled, the words thou utterest become Anum (i.e. as
    fixed as the sky) . . .
Then a cloak was set in their midst,
They addressed the god Marduk their first-born:
Thou, Lord, shalt hold the foremost position among the gods.
Decree thou the throwing down and the building up, and it shall come to
    pass.
Speak but the word, and the cloak shall disappear,
Speak a second time and the cloak shall return uninjured.
Marduk spoke the word, the cloak disappeared,
He spoke a second time, the cloak reappeared.
When the gods his fathers saw the issue of the utterance of his mouth,
They rejoiced and adored him, saying, Marduk is King."

(*Babylonian Legends of the Creation*, publ. by the British Museum, 1921, pp. 48-49.) Cf. also Gen. 1.3: And God said, Let there be light, and there was light. Cf. further, p. 144.

Unique in its power to give perspective of relationships, and so to preserve the harmony of truth with its expression, it was unrivaled as a tool of thought. Such was the basis of the symbolism of the Middle Ages—of course not all worked out at once or without controversy, or understood equally by all symbolic writers.

V. METHOD OF MEDIEVAL SYMBOLIC USAGE

GOD was the name given in the Middle Ages to the underlying infinite which gave significance to the *disjecta membra* of experience; and failure to believe in its existence was regarded then as a sign rather of dementia than of mentality. Taking pity on man's long struggle to learn through the perceptible forms of nature alone, God gave also scripture, into which was woven the same universal pattern. Thus the medieval mind recognized a self-revelation of God not only in the world around it but also in history and the development of man himself.[36, 37]

Nevertheless, during the centuries formative for medieval thought, this kindness on the part of the Creator of the universe seriously complicated the problem of Rome as hostess in the great salon wherein peoples from all quarters of the world were given courteous if precipitous introduction to one another. In scripture Deity had revealed to each group the Truth; but these scriptures when juxtaposed exhibited anomalous and even contradictory divergencies. Held in check and gradually subdued by the presence of the Roman ideal of citizenship, men came to adjust their difficulties through a recognition of insight symbolism as the process of thought. The more meditative became convinced that, though speaking with the languages of Babel, in reality all were trying to say very much the same thing. In this situation, the rigors of logic demanded a method for the ordering of interpretation through insight symbolism, in its recon-

36. Teufelsdröckh was supposed radical because his idea was so old: "Is not God's universe a symbol of the godlike; is not immensity a temple; is not man's history, and men's history, a perpetual evangel?" *Sartor Resartus,* Bk. III, chap. 7 (Everyman ed., pp. 190-191).

37. Cf. Chap. III, Pt. I; Chap. IV, Pt. I; Chap. V, Pt. I. In the four important cultural traditions which contributed to the development of medieval thought, the idea of the revelation of God in nature was elaborated chiefly by the Greeks, that of the revelation of God in history chiefly by the Jews.

ciliation of the conflicting sacred scriptures of the world. In
answer to this need there was gradually developed the method
which was to govern the interpretation in the Middle Ages alike
of nature and of scripture.

It became clear that every fact or event in the realm of nature
or of scriptural record might be considered as conveying truths of
four kinds. These were analyzed as: the literal (including words
in their standard usage, and symbols of the arbitrary-association
and descriptive types), and three "symbolic" interpretations,
called allegorical, tropological, and anagogical, all being of
the nature of insight symbolism. The symbolical interpretation
called allegorical[38] included truths in relation to humanity as a
whole, and here the Christian of course included truths in regard to Christ as the Head of humanity. The interpretation
called tropological[39] applied specifically to the moral lesson
which might be learned from any event. The trope was of great
comfort to ethical traditions such as the Hebraic. The final truth
was that of anagoge[40]—ultimate truth, belonging neither to
time nor to space, such knowledge as had been dear to the
Greeks since the formulation of Plato's absolute Ideas. These
four meanings were sought particularly in the two sources of
external revelation, nature and scripture—the spatial, and the
historical or temporal world.

This instrument of thought was to be applied to nature, the
spatial source of external knowledge. In consequence lapidaries,
bestiaries, and all other works of so-called medieval pseudo-science were characterized by elaborate interpretations of natural
objects. To begin with a single illustration, the rock (the use of
which as arbitrary-association, descriptive, and insight symbol
has been cited),[41] must have three levels of meaning as insight
symbol, beyond its literal use as arbitrary or descriptive symbol.
It may stand for Christ, as in the familiar hymn *Rock of Ages;*
or it may exemplify that which each soul should be to its fel-
lows, as Christ himself used the symbol with reference to Peter;
or finally, the rock may mean the foundation of the heavenly

38. ἀλληγορία—ἄλλος + ἀγορεύω, to speak otherwise.
39. τροπολογία—λογος + τρόπος, from τρέπειν, to turn.
40. ἀναγωγή, elevation, a leading up,—ἀνα + ἀγωγη.
41. Cf. pp. 8-9.

kingdom. In other words, every natural object may be taken[42] allegorically as telling of the life of the Logos; tropologically, as conveying teaching as to the inner life of man; and anagogically as containing revelation of the life in glory. Every symbol should be understood at one and the same time in all of these significations. (More than this, under each heading—allegorical, tropological, and anagogical—several interpretations are generally intended, but the laws governing their relationship will be discussed later.) Each natural object, whether animate or inanimate, had its particular meaning on each of these three levels.

Ponderous catalogues of symbolic significations were demanded not only in works of specific scientific import but also in every dictionary and encyclopedia. The symbolic method essential to the understanding of nature (spatial source of external knowledge) was essential also to the understanding of *scriptura* (temporal source of external knowledge); and especially of the scripture, of which the purpose was in the last analysis clarification of ultimate knowledge mediated through life experience in the universe. Its written word told of things and events, but these things and events themselves had eternal meanings, through which lay another approach to the understanding of the universal pattern. In other words, whatever may have been the truth as to Abraham's literal sacrifice of Isaac, and however readily the story may be brought to mind through association symbols (such as the representation of a boy bearing faggots), or made more vivid through the use of comparison symbol; its true meaning can be neither gained nor conveyed without the use of it as an insight symbol. Allegorically, the story typifies Christ's sacrifice on Calvary; tropologically, it brings to each soul knowledge of the sacrifice inevitable in the life dominated by the divine will; anagogically, the story suggests the greatest height to which man can rise, the utter self-giving which takes place in eternity, in union with God.

An understanding of symbol, then, developed with the earliest medievalism, in accordance with which everything could be

42. More than this, natural objects came to mean actually the truths which they taught. Cf. Chap. IV, Pt. I, iii.

taken as an insight symbol, thus involving, in the case of earlier usages, no loss, but merely refinement and completion of meaning. With this understanding, medieval symbolism added unto itself the full power of the symbolisms of the ages. Thus endowed, Dante wrote the *Divina Commedia*.

VI. MEDIEVAL SEARCH FOR KNOWLEDGE[43]

IN eager search for knowledge, the symbolic method was applied not only to the external sources of knowledge, both temporal and spatial, but also, with equal assiduity, to inner experience, until the search for hidden meanings became veritably a deciphering of God's code.[44] Its power was tremendous; and in the early days, mediated through the preaching of Ambrose, enabled Augustine himself at last to reconcile with his reason the statements of scripture and so to become a Christian. In this connection a popular misconception of the symbolic method should be noted. The recognition of multiple meanings, in the same word or image, has been felt to lead to equivocation and to intellectual dishonesty, allowing the shift in meaning which is characteristic of the distributed middle. Such an objection is obviously irrelevant as applied to the medieval system, in accordance with which the question is never of "either—or" but always of all the meanings as true at once. The meaning on each higher level both includes and illuminates the lower, but never in any sense falsifies them. All the meanings are necessary to an understanding of the fact in its universal implications. Unless this is held in mind constantly, much of medieval thought and especially its summation in the *Divina Commedia* will remain an enigma.

Symbols are related like algebraic equations. A determined

43. For discussion with special relation to nature, cf. Chap. III.
   For discussion with special relation to scripture, cf. Chap. IV.
   For discussion with special relation to inner experience, cf. Chap. V.
44. An idea not confined to the Middle Ages. Cf.: "We speak of the Volume of Nature; and truly a volume it is—whose author and writer is God. To read it! Dost thou, does man, so much as well know the alphabet thereof? With its words, sentences, and grand descriptive pages, poetical and philosophical, spread out through solar systems, and thousands of years, we shall not try thee. It is a volume written in celestial hieroglyphs, in the true sacred-writing; of which even prophets are happy that they can read here a line and there a line." Carlyle, *Sartor Resartus,* Bk. III, chap. 8 (Everyman ed., pp. 193-194).

equation of the first degree represents but one curve. Equations of higher degrees and undetermined equations represent different curves or families of curves, related among themselves by a definite law. Such equations, experience has proven to give greater power as tools and far deeper insight into the operations of natural law than do the simple equations. Similarly the insight symbol has this greater power. But with symbols as with other tools, this very power involves an increasing danger: misuse can lead to far more serious error, even to disaster. So for medieval minds, poring over hidden meanings in scripture and in nature—herself remarkably resembling *litterae scriptae*—disaster occurred: the emphasis swung to the exaltation of the symbol over the thing symbolized. With the creation of fanciful and factitious meanings came the disobedience to the laws of symbolism, that is, the violation of the fundamental union between the truth and its expression, which marked the twilight of the tradition. Reasoning and arguing by symbols and through them, scientists, philosophers, and poets alike, after several centuries, found themselves in a labyrinth of verbal intricacies from which sooner or later inevitably a Bacon or a Descartes had to break for freedom. These initiators of the scientific method, however, stirred up such a whirlwind enthusiasm for the great advance that the world is only just beginning to rub the dust from its eyes and to look back, wondering if perhaps after all there may be something in the road behind it. A secret was lost, and as a result modern ignorance of the thought processes of more than a third of the historical world is disconcertingly general: only the mystic, through his use of the insight symbol, has retained any great degree of continuity with medievalism.

The very question of the place of mysticism in the Middle Ages, it may be noted in passing, has been one of the most perplexing. It is felt that symbolism is in some way intimately bound up with the temperament and thought—when there is any—of the mystic; also it is common to consider as a criterion some claim to the mystic vision. In reality if mysticism is to be defined in terms other than those of personal experience, that spirit is called mystical which employs insight symbols. All devotional mystics have used them, and furthermore such symbols will account for that elusive flavor of mysticism found in the writings of many not definitely numbered among the mystics. The mark of the Middle Ages was, as has been stated of the mystics, the "passionate belief in continuity of essence through ever changing form"[45] of which the only possible grasp as well as the only possible expression is through the insight symbol. It is inherent in mysticism to demand expression and at the same time to realize that the most perfect expression attainable is but a shadow of the reality.

Living in the close of the thirteenth century, Dante Alighieri accomplished in a poem consummation of the whole medieval symbolic development. Led by the sun[46] and the wealth of its symbolic associations, he penetrated deep into the mystery of the universe. Some grasp of this mystery was then thought a prerequisite to any understanding of politics and social conditions, as well as to the solution of personal difficulty in the following of the mystic way through the terrors of the *selva oscura*. Aided by symbols hoary with history, Dante has blazed his path for those who can follow. Some he realizes will see very little, and others he warns lest in ignorance of symbolic theory they be led astray, yet real understanding leaves open also the possibility that some may see even farther than the symbolist himself. Maeterlinck has said, "I am also disposed to believe that every language thinks always more than the man, even the man of genius, who employs it, and who is only its heart for the time being."[47]

Considered in the aspects of life-giving, light-giving, and heat-giving,[48] the sun supplies imagery central in the *Divina Commedia*. To anyone familiar with the *Commedia* this needs no illustration. Dante's universe depends on it: heaven is the source of light, heat, and motion; deepest hell is the dark lake of Cocytus in which Satan is frozen motionless. Essential to the seeker for Dante's full meaning is a study, not only of the sun

45. Caroline C. Spurgeon, *Mysticism in English Literature*.
46. For sun and sex as the equivalent materials of symbolism, cf. pp. 109 ff., also Appendix to Chap. III, Pt. I, i.
47. M. Maeterlinck, *Ruysbroeck and the Mystics*, p. 42.
48. For the development of this division of the sun's aspects, cf. Chap. III, Pt. I.

symbol, but especially of its relationships in a system of amazing complexity. He who plunges at any point into the symbolism of the Middle Ages will find himself as it were in a solar
vortex, his vision dazzled by unnumbered diverging rays, any
one of which he may follow indefinitely, strewing tomes behind
him as records of his progress.

VII. SUMMARY

SYMBOLISM, whether conscious or unconscious, always fundamental in thinking, became in the Middle Ages both the natural
medium of thought and expression, and an instrument consciously developed as the truest means of penetration into the
mystery of reality. It was such, in whichever branch of knowledge lay the seeker's interest: for all were united in their goal.

Always there has been demanded careful distinction between
that symbolism which is merely literal figure—the result of arbitrary association or of the perception of likenesses between
objects—and that symbolism which in conveying intimation of
fundamental relationships is interpretative of the universe. Symbolism of the latter type removes the menace from the associations with which man's long ancestry has endowed his language,
and makes them truly lamps behind ideas, guides in thinking,
rather than haunting phantoms of unsolved problems.

The symbolic method wrought by centuries of conscious and
unconscious striving was the instrument which made possible to
medieval thinking unification of the diversities and contradictions of experience. The essence of this method was the recognition of the essential simultaneous validity of levels of interpretation, which by their correction of each other might ever more
exactly express the truth.

Such was the tradition which made possible the *Commedia*
wherein the Middle Age finds its consummation. It has been
written:

Looking back on the great epochs of history we seek in vain for another period represented with comparable fullness and vitality in a
single masterpiece of art. The Homeric Age would doubtless come next
in the order of poetic interpretation; but the Iliad, with all its beauty,
shows forth only a few sides of human life in the Homeric period.

Whereas the Divine Comedy, understandingly read, evokes a picture of medieval existence in its completeness, with its great aspirations, religious, social, philosophic, artistic, with the intricacies of its politics, the rivalry of municipal interests, the hates and loves of all sorts and conditions of men. . . . But this is not all. Not only does Dante's poem reveal to us a dead age; it reveals a living man, a man who as long as our civilization shall last can never die.[49]

Yet to recognize only that the racial inheritance offers no more perfect picture of an historic period and of a man than the *Divina Commedia,* is to overlook the real greatness of the poem. It is rather the most perfect picture of man in his relationship to his whole environment. In it is harmonized knowledge of the universe with knowledge of human relationships and with knowledge of human personality. In consequence the interpretation of the poem involves an outline of all known to the medieval mind of physical science, the science of human relationships, and the science of the relationship of the individual to the universe—with, if the validity of Dante's symbolic theory be accepted, the addition of all that is known today.

One of Dante's sorest and most constant trials was "not to be able to 'gaze fixedly,' not to have vision to grasp the whole of things,"[50] yet in his poem is contained perhaps the most tremendous unification and presentation of the whole ever accomplished by the human mind. Today, the philosopher, struggling with the paradoxes inherent in the universe; the physical scientist, seeking "the way from one thing to the whole of things"; the artist, reaching out toward the fairy angel beneath the flux of appearances; and the great mass of "wanderers in the middle mist"; can find no surer rest for their troubled gaze than the sunlit rose wherein is revealed in its ultimate simplicity the solution of the drama of life and death.

49. C. H. Grandgent, *Discourses on Dante,* p. 10.
50. *Ibid.,* p. 15.

CHAPTER II. SCHEMA

Dante's only commentary on the *Commedia* relates to the *Paradiso,* canticle dedicated to Can Grande. In this canticle is given the truth-in-eternity underlying the whole *Commedia* of which it is both root and culmination. Here also is clue to the interpretation of the poem written in honor of Beatrice, the miracle who is a nine. Dante's application of fourfold method to "four sources of knowledge" results in three threefold orders of symbolism with their summary and anagoge. Truth of the first order appears against background of knowledge of natural universe, of the second, against background of knowledge of scripture, of the third, under direction of reason. To the anagoge man is raised by grace alone.

I. *First order:* Truths revealed in the Moon, Mercury, Venus, relate to three phases of Dante's personal experience: the story, the political career, the moral and intellectual development, respectively. In the Sun is shown as a foreshadowing of the Beatific Vision the anagoge of this order. The true blessedness of a man lies in his relationship to the Infinite Tri-unity.

II. *Second order:* Truths revealed in Mars, Jupiter, Saturn, relate to three phases of the Incarnate Life of Christ: his earthly life and suffering, the mystical union of all humanity, and the perfection of individual souls. In Gemini is shown as a foreshadowing of the Beatific Vision the anagoge of this order. The true blessedness of humanity lies in its relationship to the Incarnate Logos.

III. *Third order:* Truths revealed in the Primum Mobile, and in the Empyrean as seen in the company first of Beatrice, and then of Bernard, relate to three phases of the mystic quest for knowledge. The Beatific Vision, the reality of that foreshadowed in the Sun and in Gemini, is the complete anagoge of the *Commedia.* Ultimate blessedness lies in vision of things as a whole, giving union with ultimate reality and demand of a return.

CHAPTER II. SYMBOLISM BASIC IN THE DIVINA COMMEDIA: ITS ROOTS IN THE PARADISO

Guardando nel suo figlio con l'Amore
  che l'uno e l'altro etternalmente
    spira,
  lo primo ed ineffabile Valore,
quanto per mente o per loco si gira,
  con tanto ordine fè, ch'esser non
    puote
sanza gustar di lui chi ciò rimira.

Gazing upon his Son with the Love which the one and the other eternally breathes forth, the primal and ineffable Worth made whatsoever circleth through mind or space with so great order that whoso looketh on it may not be without some taste of him.

A T the close of the thirteenth century, the Sun, that planet "che mena dritto altrui per ogni calle," became guide on a pilgrimage in which the whole of medieval development was gathered up, and the dominant forces in the unfolding of symbolic theory (nature, scripture, and inner experience) were brought together in an organic relationship. The Sun which had ordered for dogma and romance the conception, as reached through nature, of a triune God[1] now ordered the progress of Dante from the terror and confusion of the Dark Wood to the peace and vision of the Celestial Rose in its illumination by triune Deity.

In the course of centuries men had come to reverence the fourfold interpretation, with its multiplex symbolism, as the means of mastery over the secrets and enigmas of experience. This key for the deciphering of the message of God as written in nature and scripture was indispensable even in expression of thought, and thus is the key to the interpretation of the medieval masterpiece,—indeed, Dante has so declared it.[2] Not only is it the part of scholarship and of intelligence to approach a problem, key in hand, but also it is the part of courtesy, in the reading of a work of art, to bear in mind the injunction of the author as to how he intended that it should be read. As in medieval literature in general, so in the *Divina Commedia,* then, many significations are to be expected for each person, object, circumstance, and emotion. The poet has warned[3] that, apart from such multiplex interpretation, though his journey may entertain, its import will remain hidden.

The history of Dante criticism contains an anomaly which is

1. Cf. Chap. III, Pt. I.
2. Cf. *Epistle to Can Grande,* 7, and *Convivio,* 2, 1.
3. Cf. *Epistle X to Can Grande.*

suggestive. Rare is the interpreter, whatever his insight, who has penetrated successfully beyond the now almost proverbial admonition:

> O voi che siete in piccioletta barca,
>> desiderosi d'ascoltar, seguiti
>> dietro al mio legno che cantando varca,
> tornate a riveder li vostri liti:
>> non vi mettete in pelago; chè, forse,
>> perdendo me, rimarreste smarriti.[4]

Very like an enchantment, guarding the portals of the third canticle, this message has remained, proving itself of greater potency than that even more forbidding portent:

> Per me si va ne la città dolente,
>> per me si va ne l'etterno dolore,
>> per me si va tra la perduta gente.
> Dinanzi a me non fuor cose create
>> se non etterne, ed io etternò duro.
>> Lasciate ogni speranza, voi ch'entrate.[5]

The reason is, however, not far to seek. Hell is proverbially alluring, whereas not only is weariness likely to overcome him who has journeyed from the depths of the Inferno to the top of the Mount of Purgatory—indeed the Terrestrial Paradise has its appeal as a resting place—but also there is a lack of incentive to further progress. The *Paradiso* has seemed static and confused in the luminous vagueness and conventionality characteristic of medieval paintings of heaven.

Nevertheless the only scrap of commentary in regard to the *Commedia,* left by Dante himself, prolix commentator of his own works, is by way of an introduction to the *Paradiso*.[6] Just

---

4. "O ye who in your little skiff, longing to hear, have followed on my keel that singeth on its way, turn to revisit your own shores; commit you not to the open sea; for perchance, losing me, ye would be left astray." *Par.,* ii, 1-6.

5. "Through me is the way into the doleful city; through me the way into the eternal pain; through me the way among the people lost. . . . Before me were no things created, but eternal; and eternal I endure; leave all hope, ye that enter." *Inf.,* iii, 1-3, 7-8.

NOTE. The text used throughout is the present standard of the Società Dantesca Italiana (*Le Opere di Dante, a cura di Barbi, Parodi, etc.,* Florence, Bemporad, 1921), even where the translations used are based on a slightly variant reading.

6. In the *Epistle to Can Grande.*

as the information he supplied as to the method of his writing has been largely overlooked, so this fact has received little attention. The oversight is the more surprising in that it is well known how essential to Dante's nature is his habit of bringing reason into every detail of his working, not to limit beauty, but to give her force. Moreover, from his premises his conclusions follow inevitably. In medieval thought, time and space depend on eternity for their reason and their upholding.[7] The scene of the first two canticles is time and space, whereas that of the third is eternity.[8] Dante's comment, beginning with his third canticle, began at the beginning, since for the Middle Ages the beginning was in eternity, not in time and space; and only in eternity was the real truth of the time-space universe contained.[9] Indeed, the final cause is logically, though not temporally, the inceptive cause.

Logical as it may seem to begin with the first canticle in the interpretation of the medieval masterpiece, modern thought beginning with time and space makes of its attempted progress to eternity an endless puzzle resembling the old antinomy of Achilles and the tortoise: it is impossible to reach infinity through the finite. Dante himself, though morally perfect at the top of the Mount of Purgatory, cannot of his own volition and power ascend to heaven. It is even apart from his knowledge that he rises, gazing on Beatrice, herself drawn by the Sun, at first through the agency of the physical sun, symbol of deity, later directly by the Sun who is God.

Further, it is the *Paradiso* and only the *Paradiso* which Dante dedicated to his hero, the inspiration of the familiar political allegory which runs also throughout the *Inferno* and the *Purgatorio*—Can Grande della Scala.[10] In eternity is not only the

7. Though eternity seem static, in it lies the power of all earthly progress, cf. p. 35.

8. It is true that the heavenly spheres are within time and space, save the Empyrean; but it is to be remembered that the beings who in these spheres appear to Dante do so merely as a condescension to his infirmity of vision. The truth of all that he sees in the *Paradiso* lies beyond temporal and spatial limits.

9. The medieval mind, with its belief in order and unity, was assured that anyone failing to grasp the system of the universe could not grasp correctly even its details.

10. The well-known fact that Dante's earlier hopes were centered in Henry does not invalidate the application to Can Grande of the entire body of references to the Deliverer in the *Divina Commedia*. Some of these, for example the

plan and reason of all of time and space, but its very existence and its consummation: in dedicating to Can Grande the *Paradiso,* Dante had dedicated the whole of his great scripture. Although his story of necessity worked through time and space to its consummation in eternity, in the *Paradiso* was contained the truth underlying the first two canticles, and at the same time the only complete solution of their polyseme.

Not only has Dante indicated that the fourfold method is to be employed for the interpretation of his *Commedia,*[11] and that the basis for complete interpretation is to be found in the *Paradiso,* but also he has left definite hints as to his symbolic pattern. Throughout the *Vita Nuova,* in which Dante set forth his ambition to say of Beatrice Portinari that which had never before been said of any woman ("di dicer di lei quello che mai non fue detto d'alcuna") there was an identification of Beatrice with the number nine. Their first meeting took place in the ninth year of his life[12] and her death occurred on the ninth day of the ninth month of the year of the century "wherein the perfect number was completed nine times."[13] Dante gives as reasons for the friendship to her of nine, first that at her birth the whole nine moving heavens were most perfectly related, but second, and he thinks more truly, that "if three is the sole factor of nine, and the sole factor of miracles is three, namely, Father, Son, and Holy Ghost, who are three and one, this lady was accompanied by the number nine to give to understand that she was a nine, that is, a miracle whose root is the wondrous Trinity alone."[14] Here is indicated a fact which becomes increasingly evident with

mention of the Veltro, *Inf.,* i, 101 (Can Grande signifies Great Dog), obviously are intended for none other. Others, although perhaps originally intended for Henry, were reinterpreted by Dante himself to refer to the predestined deliverer, whose function, after Henry's death, it seemed that Can Grande was to fulfil.

For a statement of the opinion often advanced, that Dante's hopes, centered on Henry alone until his death (1313), were not thereafter transferred to another (at least as far as influence in the *Commedia* is concerned), see Moore, *Studies in Dante,* 3d ser., pp. 253 ff.

11. Cf. Epistle XIII (X) and *Convivio,* 2, 1.

12. Cf. *Vita Nuova,* 2.   13. Cf. *Vita Nuova,* 30.

14. "Se lo tre è fattore per se medesimo del nove, e lo fattore per se medesimo de li miracoli è tre, cioè Padre Figlio e Spirito Santo, li quali sono tre ed uno, questa donna fu accompagnata dal numero del nove a dare ad intendere ch' ella era un nove, cioè un miracolo, la cui radice, cioè del miracolo, è solamente la mirabile Trinitade." *Vita Nuova,* 30.

the reading of the *Commedia:* that the number nine is fundamental in its symbolic pattern.[15]

These three important bits of information given by Dante as
to his *Commedia* have been constantly overlooked,[16] in part
probably because he stated them so briefly and axiomatically.
Dante, however, could have stated them in no other way, since
they were peculiar to him only as they were inherent in the
whole of medieval thinking, and for the medieval mind the
whole was implied in the statement of subject: the soul's journey from a state of misery to a state of bliss. Medieval ontology
demanded that a study of things-as-they-are begin and end in a
study of the eternal infinite expressing itself in time and space.[17]

15. Moreover, Can Grande, to whom the *Paradiso* was dedicated and through
whom Dante hoped for the solution of earthly political difficulties, as through
Beatrice for the solution of the whole, was also a nine. Cf. *Par.,* xvii, 76-81. For
fuller discussion, cf. pp. 326-327.

16. Or interpreted with insufficient reference to their actual meaning in
Dante's time. For example, Professor Grandgent mentions casually in his introduction to his edition of the *Divina Commedia* that "if to the literal and the allegorical we must add a moral and an anagogical interpretation, we may assume
that morally the poem is a warning against sin, an exhortation and guide to repentance, and an incentive to religious contemplation. Anagogically, the poet may
be said to portray in Hell the wicked world as he knows it, in Purgatory the
rescue of the elect, and in Paradise the kingdom which is to come."

As a matter of fact, however, that which Professor Grandgent has called "allegory" is a "moral" interpretation, in the medieval sense of the terms. That which
he suggests as a "moral" (tropical) interpretation is in no wise distinct from
that which he has termed "allegory," being merely its restatement in abstract
terms. Both represent *quid agamus*—what we ought to do. Furthermore, in his
statement of the anagoge, Professor Grandgent has been guilty of that which in
the Middle Ages would have been an impossible mingling of the temporal and
the eternal. That is, if the poet portrayed "the wicked world as he knew it" and
the "rescue of the elect," such symbolism he would have termed allegory, since
these facts are viewed in the light of the Incarnation, *quid credamus*—what we
ought to believe—rather than as anagoge, the eternity *quo tendamus*—whither
we should be moving.

Incidentally, moral interpretation of the *Commedia* from the point of view of
the trope, without regard to historical setting in medieval church and empire,
fails completely to satisfy the criteria of the medieval symbolic method. It were
no worse to interpret Christianity from the point of view of the soul's adventure,
disregarding its setting in the divine-human drama of redemption, a procedure
which as a matter of fact would have been heretical.

The reader who finds it difficult to bear in mind the philosophical definitions
of the four types of meaning as indicated in the introductory chapter (cf. p. 19)
may find comfort in the memorization of the medieval rule:

> Littera gesta docet,
> Quid credas allegoria,
> Moralis quid agas,
> Quo tendas anagogia.

17. Cf. Chap. III, Pt. I, ii, and Chap. V, Pt. I, i.

Medieval cosmology saw the universe as the effect solely of the Tri-unity, and hence as bearing the imprint of the three in the miracle which is nine.[18] In accord with medieval epistemology, knowledge is gained from the four primary sources[19] through the symbolic theory, by means of the fourfold method.[20] In accord with the medieval theory of values, human life is a journey from the Dark Wood of this life to the heavenly garden.[21] In other words, had Dante never written the letter to Can Grande, and had the *Commedia* survived, unillumined by the author's other writings, the student of medieval thought, as will appear more clearly in the succeeding chapters, would not lack the key to the interpretation of the poem. Since, however, Dante himself has supplied the key, medieval thought can be approached perhaps most easily through the *Commedia* in which is its consummation.

The "medieval miracle of song" in honor of the miracle who was a nine is then, to be interpreted in some sense on nine levels. How these accord with the fourfold method in the unity of the whole, is the problem of Dante's symbolic pattern outlined in the *Paradiso,* which it is the purpose of this chapter to analyze in brief. That no aid to the true following of Dante throughout the maze of his symbolism may be neglected, the attempt will be made to follow also his guide, "that planet which leadeth men aright on every road." As the study of the symbolism proceeds, the organizing center will become the Sun and his messengers.

DANTE'S JOURNEY IN THE DIVINA COMMEDIA

I. MOON. THE FICTIVE NARRATIVE

SEEKERS for the romance in the *Divina Commedia* have reiterated annoyance over Dante's first question to Beatrice on reaching the first of the heavenly spheres. His mind set at rest as to

18. Cf. p. 339—for example, the universe was composed of nine moving spheres. For further discussion, cf. Chap. V.
19. Nature and reason, scripture and grace.
For further discussion of nature as a source, cf. Chap. III, Pt. I.
For further discussion of scripture as a source, cf. Chap. IV, Pt. I.
For further discussion of reason and grace as sources, cf. Chap. V, Pt. I.
20. Directed by reason and grace. Cf. pp. 361, 364-365; also 263 ff., 281-282.
21. Cf. pp. 229 ff., 312-314, Chap. V, Pt. II.

the reason for his mysterious levitation, Dante's primary interest is in the moon-spots. He asks a detailed rather than a comprehensive question because himself well versed in medieval science,[22] but the question has in itself a far-reaching significance. As for man in his mortal life the first source of knowledge is the material universe, so for Dante as he finds opening before him the gateway to eternal truths, the first desire is for truth in regard to the physical constitution of things.

Without some understanding of the universe as Dante conceived it,[23] the mere structure of the third canticle will remain a mystery, not because it is difficult or elaborate, but because, as it has been so well said: "in this age we are generally unfamiliar with the skies":

We do not eat our breakfast or go to our office by the sun, nor do we watch the stars to see when grouse-shooting begins, or the summer holidays end. . . . When we think at all of the movements of the heavenly bodies, our notions are usually taken from diagrams and tables, not from what is actually seen in the skies. We only think, for instance, of the seasons as caused by the earth's journey round the sun, and the tilt of her axis: therefore, when Dante speaks of Venus as a Morning Star veiling the Fishes with her rays, or the horn of the Celestial Goat touching the sun, it conveys little, although the seasons of spring and of winter are as clearly indicated as if he had spoken of the blossoming of primroses or the fall of snow. When Cacciaguida in the heaven of Mars tells the date of his birth by counting how many times the planet had since then[24] returned to his Lion, those who only think of Mars as circling round the Sun, and have never traced his path among the stars, are at a loss, and think the method very far-fetched. . . . A little individual watching of the apparent movements of the heavenly bodies would put us in a position to realize the meaning of a large number of Dante's astronomical descriptions and allusions, without any knowledge of any theory.[25]

Dante in Paradise progressed from Moon to Mercury to Venus to the Sun; from Mars to Jupiter to Saturn to the stellar heaven; and finally to the Primum Mobile and the Empyrean, because

22. For medieval science and its close relationship to all other activities of the human intellect, cf. Chap. VI, iv.

23. Cf. Appendix II, i, for scheme of medieval astronomy.

24. An error. Cacciaguida dates his birth by telling how many times before it, but since the message of the angel to Mary (Luke 1. 26-38), Mars had returned to Leo. See *Par.,* xvi, 34-39.

25. Mary Acworth Orr, *Dante and the Early Astronomers,* p. 3.

such was the order of the spheres of the planets, which surrounded as a sort of fifth essence[26] the four concentric rings of
the world:[27] fire, air, water, earth.

Similarly, motions and positions in the *Paradiso* are not created by the fancy, but follow from the actual motions of the
spheres as conceived by medieval science.[27] The motion of the
Primum Mobile, the first moved by the Prime Mover,[28] is the
most rapid, whereas each inner sphere, being less perfect, introduces a drag, making it move less rapidly than the next outside
it.

Veramente, fuori di tutti questi, li cattolici pongono lo cielo Empireo,
che è a dire cielo di fiamma o vero luminoso; o pongono esso essere
immobile per avere in sè, secondo ciascuna parte, ciò che la sua materia
vuole. E questo è cagione al Primo Mobile per avere velocissimo movimento; chè per lo ferventissimo appetito ch' è 'n ciascuna parte di quello
nono cielo, ch'e è immediato a quello, d'essere congiunta con ciascuna
parte di quello divinissimo ciele quieto, in quello si rivolve con tanto
desiderio, che la sua velocitade è quasi incomprehensibile. E quieto e pa-
cifico è lo luogo di quella somma Deitade che sola [sè] compiutamente
vede. Questo loco è di spiriti beati . . . Questo è lo soprano edificio del
mondo, nel quale tutto lo mondo s'inchiude, e di fuori dal quale nulla
è; ed esso non è in luogo, ma formato fu solo ne la prima Mente, la
quale li Greci dicono *Protonoè*.[29]

For complete understanding of Dante's meaning here, Aristotle's theory of motion (which Hegel made familiar to the

26. Quintessence.

27. Cf. the outline of the spheres and their motion, Appendix II, i.

28. According to medieval thinking, God, though the Prime Mover, was not
himself active in causing motion. He was thought of as moving the spheres in
the sense in which a powerful magnet causes motion. The spheres were moved
directly, however, by angelic intelligences (the Primum Mobile by the Seraphim),
the impelling reason for the motion being, as Dante puts it, "the most fervid
appetite" of desire for union with the infinity of God.

29. "Beyond all these the Catholics assert the Empyrean heaven, which is as
much as to say the heaven of flame, or luminous heaven; and they assert it to be
immovable, because it hath in itself with respect to every part that which its
matter demandeth. And this is the cause of the Primum Mobile having the swift-
est motion, because by reason of the most fervid appetite wherewith every part
of this ninth heaven, which is next below it, longeth to be conjoined with every
part of this divinest, and most tranquil heaven, it revolves therein with so great
yearning that its swiftness is scarce to be comprehended. But still and tranquil
is the place of that supreme deity which alone completely perceiveth itself. This
is the place of the blessed spirits . . . This is the sovran edifice of the world,
wherein all the world is included, and outside of which there is nought, and it is
not itself in space, but was formed only in the primal mind, which the Greeks
call Protonoë." *Convivio*, 2, 3.

modern world) should be recalled. It is in brief simply that space would reach perfection could each point in it be all points at once, and that motion is the means by which it attempts to attain this goal.[30] Thus the Primum Mobile by its rapid motion seeks "to touch the Empyrean in each and every part at once with all its own parts and thus have perfect contact" with the perfect. With increasing swiftness of motion, the contacts, separated by lesser and lesser intervals of time, approach the unbroken contact which is perfection. Thus infinity was found to be the explanation of motion, and its source. This infinity Dante recognized as Supreme Intelligence radiating like light from sphere to sphere, inspiring the intelligence of each with love for God, the real motive power of all existence.

The answer to every scientific question then, if it is to be complete, must start from the knowledge which is the motif of the *Paradiso,* and the subject of its first three lines:

> La gloria di colui che tutto move
> per l'universo penetra e risplende
> in una parte più e meno altrove.[31]

It is the Prime Mover, the infinite, timeless and spaceless, that gives meaning in true proportion to every detail of the physical universe; and it is by virtue of his magnetism that each appears beautiful and attracts.

More than this, it is the love of the infinite and eternal that is responsible for all motion and life in the cosmos, and similarly within man himself.[32] As it is love that moves the heavenly spheres, so it is love that moves human beings: love rightly or wrongly directed. Thus it is fitting that in the *Divina Commedia,* wherein is set forth the scheme of things, there should occur the greatest of idealizations of love: that, indeed, such should be its motivation.

Ideally, and in noble souls (as the matter of love was discussed among the aristocracy of Dante's time), love of an ideal lady should develop human personality and draw it ever nearer to God, as Beatrice is drawing Dante:

30. Cf. W. T. Harris, *Spiritual Sense of Dante's Divine Comedy,* p. 149.
31. "The All-Mover's glory penetrates through the universe, and regloweth in one region more, and less in another." *Par.,* i, 1-3.
32. Cf. sun and sex as materials of symbolism, Cf. Chap. III, Pt. I, i.

> Quel sol [Beatrice] che pria d'amor mi scaldò 'l petto,
>   di bella verità m'avea scoverto,
>   provando e riprovando, il dolce aspetto.[33]

This she would have done long since, had he been true to her love. Instead, he had been guilty of that same imperfection which gave the moon its character.[34] This became clear in the discussion of the moon-spots initiated by Dante's first question. Beatrice showed Dante in the Moon souls who, though now loving God perfectly and rejoicing in his will, on earth had wavered in the pursuit of their ideal. Having made the high resolve to follow God's "counsels" over and above his "precepts"[35] they had allowed themselves to be diverted, albeit against their desire, from a greater to a lesser good. Thus they had failed in obedience to the law of love as expressed both for the court of heaven and for the courts of earth.[36] Dante, in the Earthly Paradise, although aware that he had wavered, had been surprised at the sharpness of Beatrice's rebuke,[37] and now again he is puzzled by her sternness in regard to the fault of Piccarda and Constance, a fault which scarcely appeared a fault. Beatrice enlightens him:

> Se fosse stato lor volere intero,
>   come tenne Lorenzo in su la grada,
>   e fece Muzio a la sua man severo,
> così l' avria ripinte per la strada
>   ond' eran tratte, come fuoro sciolte;
>   ma così salda voglia e troppo rada.[38]

Although force had torn Piccarda and Constance from the fulfilment of their vows force had not constrained them constantly

---

33. "That sun [Beatrice] which first warmed my bosom with love had thus unveiled for me, by proof and refutation, fair truth's sweet aspect." *Par.*, iii, 1-3.

34. Cf. *Par.*, v, 98-99, and *Purg.*, xxxi, 34 ff.

35. The precepts of God, according to the Catholic church, are the duties obligatory on every Christian whatsoever; the counsels are poverty, celibacy, and obedience, the duty of those only who have vowed themselves to them.

36. Cf. pp. 168-171, 226, 346-347, 386-390 ff., and especially pp. 427-430.

37. "Volgendo suo parlare a me per punta, che pur per taglio m'era paruto acro." *Purg.*, xxxi, 2-3.

38. "If their will had remained intact, like that which held Lawrence upon the grid, and made Mucius stern against his own right hand, it would have thrust them back upon the path whence they were drawn, so soon as they were loose, but such sound will is all too rare." *Par.*, iv, 82-87.

thereafter. To that love on which depends the universe, is due the unswerving dedication of will which, even if innocently diverted for a time, must swing back again like the lodestone so soon as pressure is released. Such is the responsibility of human freedom, and any lesser response to the divine love tends by the law of love to introduce repulsion into what previously has been attraction.

Because of his own unfaithfulness, Dante finds himself in such condition that when Beatrice looks on him "with eyes filled so divine with sparks of love," he becomes "as lost with eyes downcast."[39] This apparent paradox is merely illustrative of the fundamental law of love. Love, wilfully rejected, pushes back and downward from itself not in vengeance but in mercy,[40] a fact brought home to the soul before the Judgment Seat in the *Dream of Gerontius:*

> *Guardian Angel* (speaking of the soul):
>   the keen sanctity
> Which, with its effluence, like a glory, clothes
> And circles round the Crucified, has seized,
> And scorched and shrivelled it; and now it lies
> Passive and still before the awful Throne.
> O happy, suffering soul! for it is safe,
> Consumed, yet quickened, by the glance of God.
>
> *Soul:*
> Take me away, and in the lowest deep, there let me be,
> And there in hope the lone night-watches keep, told out for me
> There motionless and happy in my pain, lone, not forlorn . . .
> There will I sing my absent Lord and Love:—Take me away,
> That sooner I may rise, and go above,
> And see Him in the truth of everlasting day.[41]

Expulsion from the presence of God appears as mercy, first, because in the divine wisdom it is only so that the discipline may be undergone which can make possible to the individual the

39. "Beatrice mi guardò con li occhi pieni di faville d'amor così divini, che, vinta, mia virtute diè le reni, e quasi mi perdei con li occhi chini." *Par.,* iv, 139-142.

40. Cf. pp. 78-79, 213-215.

41. From J. H. Newman, *Dream of Gerontius.* This poem is, among English-speaking Catholics, probably the best known literary description of Christian experience after death.

blessedness of its fullest communion with the infinite; and second, because the experience of the sinful man brought near to God is such torture, even though desire of creature answer to desire of Creator, that the one impulse is to flee from the Presence in order to return purified.

Thus Dante's much-remarked question as to the moon-spots, lacking though it be for the modern reader both in significance and in romance, contains suggestion of the two truths fundamental in any quest for vision. First, knowledge of all that is, is to be sought through the physical universe, including the history and experience of man. Second, power for the seeking is supplied only through perfect faithfulness to the love which moves all things.

With the new insight into the nature of the universe comes a new appreciation of the *modus operandi* of symbolism through which nature is understood. Although it is symbolism which makes possible to man vision beyond the limitations of the physical universe, yet the laws of symbolism persist even in the heavenly spheres. The souls of Piccarda, Constance, and all the inconstant appear in the Moon, yet in reality they are in the Empyrean, no more distant spatially from God than is any other soul, albeit penetrating less deeply into his light. Their appearance in the Moon is in deference to the law of human intellect for which the only apprehension of truth is through the senses:

> non perchè sortita
> sia questa spera lor, ma per far segno
> de la celestial c' ha men salita.
> Così parlar conviensi al vostro ingegno,
> però che solo da sensato apprende
> ciò che fa poscia d'intelletto degno.
> Per questo la Scrittura condescende
> a vostra facultate, e piedi e mano
> attribuisce a Dio, ed altro intende.[42]

Further, just as all that is fact teaches of God, so may fiction, provided only that in some way it be proportionate to the

42. "Not that this sphere is given them but to make sign of the celestial one that hath the least ascent. Needs must such speech address your faculty, which only from the sense-reported thing doth apprehend what it then proceedeth to make fit matter for the intellect. And therefore doth the Scripture condescend

truth.[43] Dante in the first star has given his answer to the question which has vexed so many critics: it is made clear that
whether or not his vision represents what he wished to be
thought a literal experience is, for the purpose of the truth symbolized, a matter of little import.[44]

The teaching of this sphere of the Moon is in fine the truth
as to Dante's own life and so as to his present journey in so far
as it is a simple literal story. Having addressed Beatrice as the
love of God himself: "O amanza del primo amante, o diva . . .
il cui parler m'inonda, e scalda si, che piu e piu m'avviva"[45]
Dante says:

> Io veggio ban che giamai non si sazia
> nostro intelletto, se 'l ver non lo illustra
> di fuor dal qual nessun vero si spazia.[46]

Here again is the sun symbolism of the Trinity: Truth shining,
Love warming, both deriving from the primal Lover, Prime
Mover of the universe. Beatrice is acting in relation to Dante
with the attributes of the Holy Spirit, and so to her is transferred his symbolism.[47] Dante's literal story then is given in the

to your capacity, assigning hand and foot to God, with other meaning." *Par.*,
iv, 37-45. This insistence on knowledge as entering only through the gate of the
senses is good Thomistic, as opposed to Augustinian, psychology. Cf. Chap. V,
Pt. I, ii. The idea which Beatrice carefully avoids is that of souls, formed of
planetary fire, returning after death to those planets with which they claimed
kinship. This idea (together with a belief in the rationality of the stars, suggested by their movements) formed part of the religio-philosophical system
of the Stoics.

43. Cf. Chap. IV, Pt. I, i, also Appendix IV, Pt. I, i.

44. The question as to whether Dante did or did not wish his readers to believe that he had been granted the Beatific Vision, is as impossible of solution as
would be the question as to whether the vision in fact was granted to him. Both
lie outside the realm of reasonable investigation. The claim of having experienced the Beatific Vision would not be, *ipso facto*, heretical, since Catholic theologians have differed (Cf. Poulain, *Graces of Interior Prayer*, p. 252) as to
whether the vision can be granted to the living and if so, to other than the
apostles. Hence *Par.*, xxxiii, 52, cannot be adduced, along with *Inf.*, ii, 10 ff., as
evidence that Dante wished to conjoin his mission with that of St. Paul, though
Par., xxxiii, 73-75, would go to support such a construction. Cf. pp. 179, 294,
especially n. 156.

45. "O Love of the primal Lover, O divine one . . . whose speech o'erfloweth
and warmeth, so that more and more it quickeneth me." *Par.*, iv, 118-120.

46. "Now do I see that never can our intellect be sated, unless that Truth
shine on it, beyond which no truth hath range." *Par.*, iv, 124-126.

47. Cf. pp. 272 ff.; Professor Fletcher has devoted much space in his *Symbolism of the Divine Comedy* to establishing the thesis that Beatrice does act
symbolically with the attributes of the Holy Spirit. A striking evidence is this
passage. Cf. also pp. 99, 169 ff., 237, 327, *et al.*

Moon as that of one, able by reason of his own unfaithfulness to respond to love, only "as lost with eyes downcast," yet, subject to Primal love, a wanderer through the medieval universe on the quest of knowledge, under guidance of the Holy Spirit manifested in Beatrice and her emissary Virgil.[48]

II. MERCURY. DANTE'S POLITICAL DEVELOPMENT

THE dual allegory of Dante's political situation is elucidated in Mercury. On the night of Maundy Thursday in the year of papal jubilee 1300, as the story goes, Dante, in *medio vitae,* came to himself in a Dark Wood near the mouth of hell. It is easy to recognize in this statement an expression of Dante's situation in Florentine politics. It is likewise easy for one who has associated symbolism rather with fancy than with thought to fail completely in appreciation of the intellectual appropriateness of Dante's imagery. The wood was terrible because it was dark and sunless.

Important among the achievements of earlier centuries had been the elaboration through the aid of sun symbolism of the conception of a triune God.[49] In the sun with its three aspects of life-giving, light-giving, and heat-giving, had been found a principle of order which could give a consistent philosophical perspective to all other imagery that had been used of Deity. Dante himself gives the interpretation in another connection:

Qui è da sapere che sì come trattando di sensibile cosa per cosa insensibile, si tratta convenevolmente, così di cosa intelligibile per cosa inintelligibile trattare si conviene. E però, sì come ne la litterale si parlava cominciando dal sole corporale e sensibile, così ora è da ragionare, per lo sole spirituale e intelligibile, che è Iddio. Nullo sensibile in tutto lo mondo è più degno di farsi essemplo di Dio che 'l sole. Lo quale di sensibile luce sè prima e poi tutte le corpora celestiali e le elementali allumina: così Dio prima sè con luce intellettuale allumina, e poi le [creature] celestiali e l'altre intelligibili. Lo sole tutte le cose col suo calore vivifica . . . così Iddio tutte le cose vivifica in bontade.[50]

---

48. Cf. pp. 31 n. 15, 99 n. 251, *et al.,* for discussion of the relationship of this identification to the fact that Beatrice is a nine.

49. Cf. Chap. III, Pt. I, and its Appendix.

50. "Here you are to know that just as it is suitable to treat of an object of sense by means of a thing which is not an object of sense, so it is suitable to treat of an object of the intellect by means of a thing which is not an object of the intellect. And so, since in the literal exposition the discourse opened with the

Dante in the Dark Wood was blind to the guidance of God. The Sun, his rightful guide, for him had been obscured.

In all literature, the imagery of the sun-god distinguishes his messengers also, and those who to some degree share in his character.[51] For Dante, God's two foremost representatives on earth were pope and emperor,[52] viceregents of the Divine Sun for the state, corresponding in function toward men to the divine and human natures of the Second Person of the Trinity. Just as the utmost respect marked the relationship of the divine to the human nature, that each might maintain its own integrity,[53] so mutual recognition of each other's spheres must mark the relationship between church and state. Both derive their authority directly from God, even as both natures in Christ are directly upheld by his divine Person; each is supreme and independent in his sphere, and the appropriate symbol of each is the sun.

> Soleva Roma, che 'l buon mondo feo,
>   due soli aver, che l'una e l'altra strada
>   facean vedere, e del mondo e di Deo.[54]

Pope and emperor for Dante were the two suns of Rome.

To recall that symbolism was the process of thought in these centuries, and that change of symbol was essential to change of ideas, is to recognize the appropriateness of Dante's discussion in the *Monarchia*[55] where he devotes his attention to the breaking down of a syllogism based on the designation of pope as sun

corporeal sun, accessible to sense, we are now to discourse of the spiritual sun, accessible to the intellect, that is, God. No object of sense in all the universe is more worthy to be made the symbol of God than the sun, which enlightens, with the light of sense, itself first, and then all the celestial and elemental bodies, and in like manner, God illuminates first himself with intellectual light, and then the celestial and other creatures accessible to the intellect. The sun quickens all things with his heat . . . and in like manner God quickens all things in goodness." *Convivio,* 3, 12, comment on beginning of second stanza of Ode II.

51. Cf. Chap. IV, especially 272 ff., also Appendix IV, Pt. I, ii.

52. For a careful discussion of Dante's political theory, in relation to other theories of his time, cf. Rolbiecki, *Political Philosophy of Dante Alighieri,* 1921.

53. "Non unam, sed duas operationes esse in Christo asserendum est, cum sint in illo duae naturae, divina scilicet et humana, quarum utraque propriam formam et virtutem, per quam operatur, habeat." Cf. Aquinas, *S.Th.,* 3, Q. 19, *art.* 1, *c.*

54. "Rome, that made the good world, was wont to have two suns, which made plain to sight the one road and the other; that of the world, and that of God." *Purg.,* xvi, 106-108.

55. In book 3, chap. 4.

and emperor as moon. They are rather to be designated as two suns, in different spheres equal and autonomous. Even were it correct to call them sun and moon, he argues, the distinction would be in brightness, not in authority each within his own proper sphere. The relationship is similar to that between the two natures of Christ. As Christ's human nature is illumined by his deity,[56] so the empire is illumined by the church:

> Sic ergo dico quod regnum temporale non recipit esse a spirituali, nec virtutem que est eius auctoritas, . . . sed bene ab eo recipit ut virtuosius operetur per lucem gratiae, quam in celo Deus et in terra benedictio summi Pontificis infundit illi.[57]

Thus the empire existing, as it did for Virgil, apart from the church, had neither the glory nor the power possible to the later Christian Empire. Yet in the Donation of Constantine[58] the empire had erred in giving, and the church in taking, what lay not

56. Though each functions in its own sphere, that is, they are in no wise mingled, as was wrongly held by the Eutychians and Apollinarians.

57. "I affirm that the temporal power does not receive its being from the spiritual, nor its virtue, which is its authority . . . but it does receive therefrom the power of operating with greater virtue, through the light of grace which the blessing of the supreme pontiff infuses into it, in heaven and on earth." *Monarchia*, 3, 4. Dante was writing in opposition to the principle defined by Innocent III (pope 1198-1216), as follows:

"Even as God, the creator of the universe, has placed two great lights in the firmament of the heavens, a larger one to rule over the day, a smaller one to rule over the night, in like manner has he placed in the firmament of the universal church two great offices, a larger one to rule over the souls, a lesser one to rule over the bodies; the papal and the imperial authority. And even as the moon receives its light from the sun, so the imperial power receives the splendour of its office from the papal dignity."

It was Dante's contention that the empire as well as the church derived its office from God.

58. The Donation of Constantine was "the supposed grant by the Emperor Constantine, in gratitude for his conversion by Pope Silvester, to that pope and his successors forever, not only of spiritual supremacy over the other great patriarchates and over all matters of faith and worship, but also of temporal dominion over Rome, Italy, and 'the provinces, places and civitates of the western regions.' "

The *Donatio Constantini* formed part of a collection of forged documents entitled the *Constitutum Constantini*, dating probably from Rome in the latter half of the eighth century. In the ninth century this collection was included in a larger collection now known as the False Decretals. Two centuries later it was incorporated in the *Decretum*. Although not made the basis of papal claims till the middle of the eleventh century, its genuineness was not doubted in the Middle Ages, and from the twelfth century on, it became a powerful weapon of church against empire.

Dante was not alone in thinking the *donatio* a betrayal of trust on the part of Constantine—this being the only argument open to supporters of the claim of

within their right to take and give. Thus the two suns of Rome were in mutual eclipse, leaving Dante unlighted in the dark wood òf Guelph-Ghibelline politics.

All of this is appropriately discussed in Mercury, that planet almost always obscured by the sun. Indeed, the truth in regard to the Guelph-Ghibelline controversy had been obscured by the misuse of allegory in the sun-moon argument of the Guelphs—such is the disaster of false symbolism.

Although like all the world, through no fault of his, traveling under a cloud, Dante thus, not only in the literal meaning of his journey, but also in the allegory of his political life, had been too changeable.

> E se la stella si cambiò e rise,
>   qual mi fec'io, che pur di mia natura
>   trasmutabile son per tutte guise![59]

The truth of his personal political situation as it stood in eternity is revealed to him here by an imperial soul:

> Sì come il sol che si cela elli stessi
>   per troppa luce, come 'l caldo ha rose
>   le temperanze dei vapori spessi;
> per piu letizia sì mi si nascose
>   dentro al suo raggio la figura santa.[60]

Thus Justinian, who *was* Caesar, now hidden like a sun in his own rays, tells of the great days of the great honors of the Roman Empire. Justinian had once, he points out, held the Monophysite doctrine that Christ had but one nature, the divine; just as the Guelphs considered that God had but one vicarate, the papacy, to which the empire was subordinate. Dante too had started with this opinion, or at least had been brought up among

the empire to independent temporal dominion. Among others of Ghibelline sympathies, Walther von der Vogelweide gave interesting expression to the opinion.

The genuineness of the collection *Constitutum Constantini* was not assailed till the middle of the fifteenth century (Laurentius Valla), and a controversy raged over it from that time till the eighteenth century. Now it is universally admitted to be a forgery.

59. "And if the star was changed and laughed, what then did I, who of my very nature am subjected unto change through every guise!" *Par.*, v, 97-99.

60. "Like as the sun which hideth him by excess of light when the heat hath gnawed away the tempering of the thick vapours, so by access of joy the sacred figure hid him in his own rays." *Par.*, v, 133-137.

those who held it. Later, like Justinian, he had been turned to
the acceptance of the dual truth.

As Justinian points out, in Italy both parties are at fault. Both
are sternly rebuked:

> Perchè tu veggi con quanta ragione
>   si move contr' al sacrosanto segno
>   e chi 'l s'appropria e chi a lui s'oppone,
> Vedi quanta virtù l'ha fatto degno
>   di reverenza; e cominciò da l'ora
>   che Pallante morì per darli regno;[61]

and:

> Omai puoi giudicar di quei cotali
>   ch'io accusai di sopra e di lor falli,
>   che son cagion di tutti vostri mali.
> L'uno al pubblico segno i gigli gialli
>   oppone, e l'altro appropria quello a parte,
>   sì ch' è forte a veder chi più si falli.
> Faccian li Ghibellin, faccian lor arte
>   sott' altro segno; chè mal segue quello
>   sempre chi la giustizia e lui diparte.
> E non l'abbatta esto Carlo novello
>   coi Guelfi suoi; ma tema de li artigli
>   ch'a più alto leon trasser lo vello.
> Molte fiate già pianser li figli
>   per la colpa del padre, e non si creda
>   che Dio trasmuti l'armi per suoi gigli.[62]

It is no remedy for Guelph policies, to adopt the extreme Ghibelline position. Dante's final solution of the political difficulties
of the time is neither Guelph nor Ghibelline, it is an affirmation
of the affirmations of each of these, and a negation of the de-

61. "That thou mayest see with how good right against the sacred standard
doth proceed both he who doth annex it to himself and he who doth oppose him
to it, see how great virtue hath made it worthy of reverence, beginning from the
hour when Pallas died to give it sway." *Par.*, vi, 31-36.

62. "Now mayest thou judge of such as I accused but now, and of their sins,
which are the cause of all your ills. The one opposeth to the public standard
the yellow lilies, and the other doth annex it to a faction, so that 'tis hard to see
which most offendeth. Ply, ply the Ghibellines their arts under some other standard! for this he ever followeth ill who cleaveth justice from it; and let not that
new Charles down beat it with his Guelphs, but let him fear talons that have
ripped its fell from mightier lion. Many a time ere now have children wailed for
father's fault, and let him not suppose God will change arms for those his lilies."
Par., vi, 97-111.

nials of both of these. For the Guelph, the church was supreme, and Dante agreed; by implication the empire was not supreme, and Dante disagreed. For the Ghibelline, the empire was supreme, and Dante agreed; by implication the church was not supreme, and Dante disagreed.[63] It should be realized that for Dante the field of politics was the problem of the whole organization of humanity, whether for civil or for spiritual ends. His insight, clear as it is in the light of Mercury,[64] has not been attained by Dante without effort.

Nor, even in the historical sketch of the empire by Justinian, does sun symbolism fail to play its part. The Eagle is the symbol of empire, *l'uccel di Dio*—the sole bird which can look upon the sun, governing mankind "sotto l'ombra delle sacre penne,"[65] that is, tempering to them the light of God and sheltering on occasion even the church beneath those wings.[66] Later Dante is to perceive more deeply the truth of this Eagle-symbol of organized humanity, when he is thinking more intently of all mankind, and to see a fuller meaning in the self-sacrifice of Pallas whose death was required "to give it sway."[67] Here he is gaining insight into the truth of his own political reasoning, and his relation to the politics of his age. The time is not yet for him to sink his whole individuality in consideration of the deeper truth: humanity as the Mystical Body of Christ. This he will do in the sphere of Jupiter.

One eternal aspect of the relation between church and empire it is necessary for Dante to grasp in order that he may fully understand his own relation to the situation of the time. Dante's stay in Mercury closes, as did his sojourn in the Moon, with new

63. For an excellent modern example of this type of solution of an antinomical problem, cf. Dr. Wm. P. Montague's attempt at reconciliation of the three main epistemological theories:

"I shall try to show that each of the three theories in its original or 'naïve' form can be condensed into two propositions; that in each case one member of the pair of propositions can be proved false and the other proved true; that the true propositions constitute adequate definitions" [and that the resulting theories] "can be combined to form a complete and self-consistent solution." Wm. P. Montague, *Ways of Knowing,* p. 292.

64. It is interesting that astrologically Mercury signifies the intellect applied to earthly ends: not necessarily base ones, but the type of shrewdness that aids in getting along in the world and guides among human policies and relationships.

65. "Under the shadow of his sacred wings." See *Par.,* vi, 1-9.

66. *Par.,* vi, 94-96.   67. *Par.,* vi, 34-37. Cf. p. 71.

light concerning the nature of the triune God: this time not specifically with regard to the nature of the Prime Mover of the
universe, but with regard to the mystery of the Incarnation, in
which God by act of his eternal Love, joined to himself that nature which had gone astray from its Creator.[68] As Dante has
pointed out in the *Monarchia*,[69] the authority of the empire over
all mankind was essential to the redemption of mankind. This
Justinian indicates, speaking of the eagle-ensign of empire:

> chè la viva giustizia che mi spira
> li concedette, in mano a quel ch'i' dico,
> gloria di far vendetta a la sua ira.
> Or qui t'ammira in ciò ch'io ti replico:
> poscia con Tito a far vendetta corse
> de la vendetta del peccato antico.[70]

He explains that the empire was that tool which in God's hand
punished human nature in the person of Christ for its rebellion,
and later punished the Jews, the human instruments of that just
vengeance.[71] (Thus the central symbolism here stressed is not
as in the Moon, that of nature, but that of history, which likewise in every detail reveals the truth of the eternal divine counsel.) Regarding this paradox Dante is instructed by Beatrice, in
canto vii, in terms which have full support in Thomistic theology. Creation, Fall, Incarnation, Crucifixion, Immortality—all
are bound up in the political allegory, the relation of an individual to the party politics of his time!

68. "La natura, che dal suo fattore s'era allungata, unì a se in persona con
l'atto sol del suo etterno amore." *Par.,* vii, 31-33.
69. "Christ . . . chose to be born of a virgin mother under edict of the
Roman authority, in order that the Son of God, made man, might be enrolled as
a man in that unique register of the human race." *Monarchia,* 2, 12.
"If the Roman empire was not of right, the sin of Adam was not punished in
Christ. . . . punishment does not simply mean penalty inflicted on him who
worked the wrong, but penalty so inflicted by one who has penal jurisdiction.
. . . If, then, Christ had not suffered under a qualified judge, that suffering
would not have been a punishment, and the judge could not have been qualified
had he not had jurisdiction over the whole human race; since it was the whole
human race that was to be punished in the flesh of Christ." *Monarchia,* 2, 13.
70. "The living justice that inspireth me, granted it, in his hand of whom I
speak [Tiberius], the glory of wreaking vengeance for his wrath. Now find a
marvel in the double thing I tell thee! Thereafter, under Titus, to wreak vengeance on the vengeance on the ancient sin it rushed." *Par.,* vi, 88-93.
71. This punishment likewise was just; since the motive was evil, and since,
though human nature rightly was punished, the Person who bore the punishment
was divine and divinely sinless.

Dante in Mercury has received insight into the waverings of his own past policy, and into the fundamental bases of the "party by himself" which, after his exile, he gradually evolved. His personal political story is that of one who after disastrous dabblings in current political theories is led, through the agency of Divine Love, to the formation of a new and inclusive platform, making possible allegiance to Divine Wisdom who in his two natures established on earth a dual vicarate.

III. VENUS. DANTE'S INNER LIFE

A LEVEL of truth still more fundamental as to Dante's personal life is revealed by his sojourn in the epicycle of the fair Cyprian. Dante in the first of the planets beheld himself in the physical universe, a wayfarer under the inescapable law of love; and in the second, beheld himself in the civic community under the necessity of finding his place in the realm of human relationships. In the third epicycle of his journey, he is to see himself as an individual both determined by natural law and personally responsible to Divine Love. For Dante the principle of individuation is the influence of planets and stars, or, more accurately, of the intelligences by which they are moved.[72] The ego, created directly by God, in its connection with the body comes under stellar influence, and at birth is stamped like wax by a seal.[73] All impressions from the stars are good,[74] since there is no lovableness that does not reflect the lovableness of God. It is the harmonizing and proportioning of these good qualities in their true relationships that makes this or that person more or less perfect.

It is likely that the modern reader, with his oversimple con-

---

72. See *Par.,* viii, 127-135, comparing line 133 with 127-129.

73. Cf. *Purg.,* viii, 112-114; xxx, 109-111; *Par.,* xiii, 67-79; xxii, 112-114.

74. "The heavens are the *organum* and the *instrumentum Dei.* I must in passing note how this throws light on the nature of Dante's firm belief in Astrology. It is really 'God whose neverfailing providence ordereth all things both in heaven and earth,' but the Angels are the 'ministering spirits' through whom that providential guidance is dispensed; and the stars are the instruments by which their allotted operations are exercised. This sheds an entirely new light upon a belief which is generally associated with credulity and superstition. In this distinction between immediate and mediate creation we cannot fail to observe how closely the teaching of Dante resembles that of Plato in the Timaeus." Edw. Moore, *Studies in Dante. Fourth Series,* p. 163.

ception of astrology, will lose much of the meaning of Dante and of other medieval authors who make as casual reference to astrology as do modern writers to geology and psychology. Astrology was both more complicated and more scientific in method than the familiar birth-month pamphlets suggest. No reader of the *Divina Commedia* can afford not to realize that the birth-month is only one of three important determining elements in the horoscope, and that these three are subject to infinite modification.

The zodiacal sign in which the sun is located at birth is determined by the month. Dante was born under Gemini, the sign harboring the sun from May 20 to June 21.[75] Even more important than the sun-sign, moreover, is the "rising-sign" on the eastern horizon at the moment of birth. Only if birth is at or near sunrise will this sign coincide with the sun-sign. Thus, although a child born at sunrise between May 20 and June 21 will have both sun-sign and rising-sign Gemini, one born at sunset between the same dates will have sun-sign Gemini, but rising-sign Sagittarius (180° distant from Gemini), and thus will be "born under" two signs.[76] The rising-sign then depends not on the date of birth but on the combination of the date and the hour of the day. If the rising-sign happens to coincide with the sun-sign, of course the characteristics represented will be intensified.

The third decisive element to be considered is the "lord of the horoscope"—the planet or Light rising or about to rise (on, or within 30° under the eastern horizon) at the moment of birth.[77] This ruler, in his horoscope, it would seem that Dante believed to be Venus:

75. New Style. Dante states that his sun-sign is Gemini, in *Par.*, xxii, 115-117.

76. Similarly a child born at sunrise between July 20 and August 20, for example, will have both sun-sign and rising-sign Leo, while one born at sunset between the same dates will have sun-sign Leo but rising-sign Aquarius, 180° from Leo. For a child born at other hours than sunrise and sunset, not only date and hour must be considered, but also latitude of the place of birth, since the apparent position of the zodiacal signs varies also with latitude.

77. If neither sun, moon, or planet is in such a position, the "lord of the horoscope" becomes that which is on, or within 30° above, the western horizon; if this position also is vacant, the next choice is midheaven or 30° eastward; and the last is the nadir or 30° westward. That is, the "ruler" must be placed on an arm of the Cross of the Heavens.

da costei ond' io principio piglio
pigliavano il vocabol de la stella
che 'l sol vagheggia or da coppa or da ciglio.[78, 79]

In his later definite statement that Gemini is his sun-sign, he
failed to indicate whether or not Gemini was rising[80] at his birth,
but stated only that at that time the sun rose and set with Gemini.[81] The assumption that he was born near sunrise is justified, however, since one making such constant reference to astrology could scarcely have omitted information as to his rising-
sign.[82] Moreover, this assumption is congruous with that of
Venus as lord of his horoscope, since Venus like Mercury is

78. "From her from whom I take my start, they took the name of the star
which courts the sun, now from the nape, now from the brow." *Par.,* viii, 10-12.
   79. It is sometimes considered that the word *principio* refers rather to the
beginning of the canto than to any more fundamental beginning. If this were the
case, as is of course grammatically possible, it would be the one instance known
of Dante's use of so trivial a detail, apparently only to form his tercet. It is so
much against Dante's usual seriousness and carefulness that it seems almost incredible. Incidentally this is not the only case in modern criticism where critics
have endeavored to give to the word "beginning" a suspiciously trivial textual
meaning, in order to avoid the implications of the more obvious reading of the
passage. Cf. for example commentaries on the word ἀρχή in the first chapter of
Mark.
   Nevertheless even supposing *principio* to refer to the beginning of the canto,
the implication in view of Dante's symbolic method is unaltered, since it is in
this canto that Dante reveals most concerning his inner life. (In this connection it
should be remembered that in quoting the first line of his ode: *Voi che intendendo il terzo ciel movete,* he by implication directs attention to the whole of
that ode, with the second book of the *Convivio* his commentary upon it. He thus
refers both to his statement of the fourfold method, and to his exposition of the
influence and significance of the stars and their powers.) Again, Friday, which is
in the *Divina Commedia* the day of beginnings, is not only the day of the Crucifixion but also Venus' day. (The days of the week are Dies Solis, Dies Lunae,
Dies Martis, Dies Mercurii, Dies Jovis, Dies Veneris, and Dies Saturni. Cf.
T. O. Wedel, *Medieval Attitude toward Astrology.* Cf. also Albertus Magnus.)
   Finally, this passage is far from the only passage in the *Divina Commedia*
which would lead to the assumption that for Dante, Venus is lord of the horoscope. Indeed, the astrological implications, to his medieval confreres, of his frequent placing of himself under Venus' especial patronage or under that of her
symbolic equivalents, could scarcely be escaped.
   80. Or that the sun was rising.   81. *Par.,* xxii, 111-117.
   82. Had his rising-sign and sun-sign differed, he would have claimed the influence of two signs. As a matter of fact, he ascribed "all his genius" to Gemini—
Par., xxii, 113-114. It should be noticed that Gemini, one of the houses of Mercury, naturally bestowed a taste for learning. Furthermore, it is evident that the
sign of the divine-human Twins had been potent in shaping Dante's theories,
both political and philosophical, based as these theories were on the concept of
the "two suns" of Rome.

never far from the sun.[83, 84] It is important to realize that no contradiction is involved in saying both that Dante was born under Gemini, and that Dante was born under Venus.[85, 86]

Although for Dante astrology was the noblest of the sciences,[87] there was a very real danger of the perversion of its teaching, a danger involving the problem of determinism and free will.[88] As the melée of Guelph and Ghibelline politics could

83. The limit is about 45° in either direction.

84. Of interest is the fact that Dante seems to pay no attention to the horoscopical positions of all the other planets, and to their possible influence on minor traits of character. Possibly he doubted the expediency of studying these. In fact, it is likely that his neglect of minor positions and angular distances between planets is due to the fact that these were much used for divination, for example, by Michael Scott and Guido Bonatti, both of whom Dante places in hell (*Inf.*, xx) for their practice of that art. Knowledge of the future by means of the stars is quite possible (*Purg.*, xxx, 40-42) but seems to be regarded as usually illicit during the earthly life.

85. The 360° of the horoscopic (sky) circle are completely occupied by the twelve signs of the zodiac, within which, therefore, the planets must be located.

86. From such astrological data as have just been discussed, it has been possible to gain new information as to the probable date of Dante's birth, which it is the purpose of this writer to present in a forthcoming paper.

87. He connects it with the sphere of Saturn in *Convivio*, 2, 14, *q.v.*

88. Astrology in some form or other was in almost universal acceptance in the Middle Ages, and was supposed to have an experimental basis. It is true that most churchmen warned against that abuse of it which would lead to determinism, much as modern religious men warn against that view of science which leads to unrelieved mechanism.

Dr. Wedel, in his *Medieval Attitude toward Astrology* (p. 80), states: "Dante, condemning astrology in the *Inferno* in so far as it is a diabolic art, restores it to its proper place in Christian cosmology and ethics in the *Purgatorio* and *Paradiso*. For Dante, the influence of the stars upon human life was indeed an awe-inspiring fact."

The spirit of the best thought of the time is given clearly by "The Philosopher of the Middle Ages." Having insisted that the motion of the stars in no wise prevents free will, although capable of influencing the will indirectly, since directly moving the passions, he states the conclusion:

"Cum intellectus et voluntas, quae humanorum actuum principia sunt, corporeis organis vires alligatae minime sint; non possunt corpora ipsa caelestia humanorum actuum causae directe esse, sed indirecte, agendo per se in corpora, quae ad utriusque potentiae opera conducunt." Aquinas, *S.Th.*, 1, Q. 115, *art.* 4, *c.*

In reply to the objection that correct astrological predictions as to the outcome of wars, and other human activities, prove that human actions are caused directly by the stars, he explains:

"Quod plures hominum sequuntur passiones, quae sunt motus sensitivi appetitus, ad quas cooperari possunt corpora caelestia; pauci autem sunt sapientes, qui hujusmodi passionibus resistunt. Et ideo astrologi ut in pluribus vera possunt praedicere, et maxime in communi, non autem in speciali, quia nihil prohibet aliquem hominem per liberum arbitrium passionibus resistere. Unde et ipsi astrologi dicunt quod sapiens homo dominatur astris, inquantum scilicet dominatur suis passionibus." *Ibid.*, *ad* 3.

be ordered only with reference to the ideals of empire and church, the conflict of natural law and human will could be resolved only with reference to theology and true philosophy. Theology and philosophy were in the moral realm what church and empire were in the realm of human organization, and to these regents of God was extended the characteristic symbolism. Their identification with the sun is familiar in medieval literature. It is evident to the student of history that human liberty is enhanced rather than diminished by the proper activity of governing agencies in church and state. To the Middle Ages it was equally evident that freedom of the mind is enhanced rather than diminished by proper discipline in theology and philosophy. All of this Dante was to understand more fully in Jupiter and Saturn, where perspective was increased by the change in center of attention from the problems of himself as an individual to the problems of humanity.

Dante himself, in his comment on his ode which he here quotes, describes the time in which his attention was devoted to the wooing of Lady Philosophy, saying of her: "Iddio mette sempre in lei del suo lume," and: "sua biltà, cioè moralitade, de piove fiammelle di foco, cioè appetito diritto, che s' in genera nel piacere de la morale dottrina."[89] Interestingly enough, in the thirteenth century theology and philosophy, like papacy and empire, were in conflict, and astrology with its presentation of the problem of determinism, human will versus natural law, was an important battleground of the struggle. That theology against which Thomism stood out in contrast, held philosophy to be ancillary, useful merely for Christian apologetics, but heathen in any other sphere. Similarly in the realm of philosophy was a tendency, represented by the Averroists, to hold theology subject to its results. Thus the two suns of the moral realm were in mutual eclipse.

With regard to this conflict the fundamental truth-in-eternity is presented to Dante in the sphere of Venus, lord of his horoscope. His solution here is similar to his solution of the political dilemma, that is, acceptance of the affirmations of each theory,

89. "God ever sets of his light in her." "Her beauty, to wit, morality, rains down flamelets of fire, that is to say, right appetite, which is begotten by the pleasure of moral teaching." *Convivio,* 3, chaps. 13 and 15.

and rejection of the denials of each. Moreover, he definitely connects philosophy with empire as theology with church:

Duos igitur fines Providentia illa inenarrabilis homini proposuit intendendos; beatitudinem scilicet huius vitae, quae in operatione propriae virtutis consistit, et per terrestrem paradisum figuratur; et beatitudinem vitae aeternae, que consistit in fruitione divini aspectus ad quam propria virtus ascendere non potest, nisi lumine divino adiuta, que per paradisum celestem intelligi datur.

Ad has quidem beatitudines, velut ad diversas conclusiones, per diversa media venire oportet. Nam ad primam per phylosophica documenta venimus, dummodo illa sequamur, secundum virtutes morales et intellectuales operando; ad secundam vero per documenta spiritualia que humanam rationem transcendunt, dummodo illa sequamur secundum virtutes theologicas operando, fidem, scilicet spem et caritatem. Has igitur conclusiones et media, licet ostensa sint nobis . . . humana cupiditas postergaret nisi homines, tamquam equi, sua bestialitate vagantes in camo et freno compescerentur in via.

Propter quod opus fuit homini duplici directivo secundum duplicem finem: scilicet summo Pontifice, qui secundum revelata humanum genus perduceret ad vitam eternam, et Imperatore, qui secundum phylosophica documenta genus humanum ad temporalem felicitatem dirigeret.[90]

Like church and empire, theology and philosophy are supreme, each in its own sphere.

The relationship of philosophy and empire to theology and church is made more clear in the succeeding discussion of the practical applications of philosophy and its subsumed sciences,

90. "That unutterable Providence, then, has set two ends before man to be contemplated by him: the blessedness, to wit, of this life, which consists in the exercise of his proper power and is figured by the terrestrial paradise, and the blessedness of eternal life, which consists in the fruition of the divine aspect, to which his proper power may not ascend unless assisted by the divine light. And this blessedness is given to be understood by the celestial paradise.

"Now to these two, as to diverse ends, it behoves him to come by diverse means. For to the first we attain by the teachings of philosophy, following them by acting in accordance with the moral and intellectual virtues. To the second by spiritual teachings which transcend human reason, as we follow them by acting according to the theological virtues, Faith, Hope, to wit, and Charity. Now albeit these ends and means are made plain to us . . . yet would human greed cast them behind were not men, like horses going astray in their brutishness, held in the way by bit and rein.

"Wherefore man had need of a twofold directive power according to his twofold end, to wit, the supreme pontiff, to lead the human race, in accordance with things revealed, to eternal life; and the emperor, to direct the human race to temporal felicity in accordance with the teachings of philosophy." *Monarchia*, 3, 16. For the mutual independence of philosophy and theology, cf. also Aquinas, *S.Th.*, 1, 1, *Q.* 1, especially *art.* 1.

especially astrology. Charles, once prince of Naples, who appeared to Dante from out the brilliant throng of joyously circling souls, had died before his father the king, and the rightful
accession to the throne of Carobert, Charles' son, had been prevented by usurpation on the part of Charles' brother Robert.
This brother through his intrigues caused much ill to the country.[91] What more natural than Dante's first question: How from
sweet seed may come forth bitter ("com' esser può di dolce seme
amaro"). The stars, Charles explains, give a freedom from
heredity. Personalities receive with their bodies, through the
influence of the stars, a freedom from such great similarity to
their families as might bind them, like the Indian caste system,
to follow in the footsteps of their parents. The foundation laid
by nature is good: indeed all things move in response to the
Primal Love, and in the last analysis all the creature's abilities
come from God, the "sol che la riempie" to whom it turns
"come quel ben ch'ad ogni cosa e tanto."[92] But man must choose
and apportion his heritage:

> se 'l mondo là giù ponesse mente
>   al fondamento che natura pone,
>   seguendo lui, avria buona la gente.
> Ma voi torcete a la religione
>   tal che fia nato a cignersi la spada,
>   e fate re di tal ch' è da sermone:
> onde la traccia vostra è fuor di strada.[93]

The wise will choose his vocation on the basis of his natural
abilities, in the understanding of which astrology is of service.

Astrology may be used safely, however, only in accord with
the inspiration of the Holy Spirit, as appears cogently in Cunizza's prophecy. Inspired by the Holy Spirit, as is fitting in the
heaven of love, Cunizza states her knowledge of the future to
be from the light of God reflected from the Thrones as mirrors,

91. "Il mondo m'ebbe giù poco tempo; e se più fosse stato, molto sarà di mal,
che non sarebbe." "The world held me below but little space; had it been more,
much ill shall be that had not been." *Par.*, viii, 49-52.

92. Cf. *Par.*, ix, 7-9: "the sun that filleth it" "as to the good ample for all
things."

93. "If the world down there took heed to the foundation nature layeth, and
followed it, it would have satisfaction in its folk. But ye wrench to a religious
order him born to gird the sword, and make a king of him who should be for
discourse; wherefore your track runneth abroad the road." *Par.*, viii, 142-148.

"li quali, naturati de l'amore del Santo Spirito, fanno la loro operazione, connaturale ad essi, cioè lo movimento di quello cielo, pieno d'amore."[94] Philosophy, it is shown again, although like empire supreme in its own sphere, requires the inspiration of theology, as does empire that of the church, in order to reach the height of knowledge in a true perspective.

So closely related, however, are these four guardians of the personality, that in the meeting with Folco, Dante is brought back again to consideration of church and empire. The introduction here of Rahab, as the soul "in questa lumera che qui appresso me così scintilla, come raggio di sole in acqua mera"[95] is appropriate. Rahab had made possible that conquest of the Holy Land which was one of the beginnings of the church.[96] As Rahab had accomplished great things through her guidance of Joshua, so Dante hoped through his guidance of the great deliverer to come, to restore true church and empire.[97] At the same time, however, the mention of the adulteress recalls Dante's feeling as to the union of a corrupt papacy and the church, to which Folco here immediately gives vehement expression:

> La tua citta . . .
> produce e spande il maledetto fiore
> c' ha disviate le pecore e li agni,
> però che fatto ha lupo del pastore.[98]

In the thirteenth century the papacy, florin-fed, was heedless of the Holy Land and of its obligation to meditate on the gospels and to feed the sheep and the lambs.

94. "Which, taking their nature from the love of the Holy Spirit, make their work connatural thereto, to wit, the movement of that heaven which is full of love." *Convivio*, 2, 5.

95. "Within that light which here by me so sparkleth as the sun's ray in pure water." *Par.*, ix, 112-114.

96. The church of the New Testament and that of the Old are essentially one. Cf. p. 69 n. 154.

97. This symbolism is further developed (Cf. pp. 63 ff.) as Dante comes to understand himself as a type of Christ whose ancestress Rahab was. Joshua, himself, who led his people into the Holy Land, is for many reasons one of the important scriptural types of Christ (for example, the lifting up of his hands in battle presaged the cross) ; and in one signification Rahab is the church saved by the "scarlet thread" of Christ's blood.

98. "Thy city . . . maketh and spreadeth that accursed flower which hath set sheep and lambs astray, for it hath turned the shepherd to a wolf." *Par.*, ix, 127-132. Cf. *Purg.*, xxxiii, 37-45.

The root of the current political confusion, in regard to which Dante has seen the truth in Mercury, lay in the misuse of individual free will. Human will, undisciplined by theology and philosophy, could no more escape annihilation through conflict with natural law, than could Guelph policies escape eclipse through conflict with Ghibelline when ungoverned by the ideals of true empire and true church in their mutual autonomies. The individual came before the state, not vice versa.[99] Devil-planted Florence had produced a new kind of flower for pasturage—the devil's plan to turn the world to himself. Free will acts by choosing that upon which it will feed. Dante is not unaware of the element of determinism in the world: having fed, actions follow. Such is the law of nature. But the food may be chosen. Circe by food turned men into beasts; Florence by florin-food has turned the papal shepherd into a wolf.[100]

Finally, it is through love that there is given the power to choose, and so freedom to direct the inevitable transmutation wrought by life.[101] The modern conception of ethic as a thing in and for itself, apart from love motivation, was repugnant alike to the moral theology with which Dante was familiar, and to the spirit of courtly love, the new passion of the twelfth and thirteenth centuries. Philosophy itself was understood in its definition as the "loving exercise of wisdom"; wherein stands out clearly the distinction from modern formulations, in which the aspect of wisdom is carefully elaborated, but the love is generally omitted from discussion. It is this which renders irrelevant the criticism that Dante's praises of the Lady Philosophy in the *Convivio* are meant merely to cover up the literally amorous character of his poetry.[102] Whether or not a real girl was the original inspiration, to the medieval symbolist her interpretation as Philosophy still would be in order. Love it was, who, entering into the gentle heart by the instrumentality of the beau-

99. Cf. Maurice De Wulf, *Histoire de Philosophie Medievale.*
100. For connection of Circe and of the wolf with the sun-symbolism, cf. p. 166, and for connection of Dante with food symbolism, cf. pp. 68-69.
101. "Haec libertas sive principium hoc totius libertatis nostrae, est maximum donum humanae naturae a Deo collatum, sicut dixi; quia per ipsum hic felicitamur ut homines, per ipsum alibi felicitamur ut Dii." *Monarchia*, 1, 12.
102. For the subject of Lady Philosophy in her bearing on Dante's life, cf. also pp. 169-171.

tiful lady, guided the moral life into true nobility,[103] ordering it aright for this world and the next, for the lady's smiles and for the favor of God.

The whole moral trope of the *Divina Commedia* is to be read in the light of courtly love, and so as the fruition in Dante's life of that first glimpse of Beatrice in his young childhood. In so far as the story is to be read as typical of the moral development of any soul,[104] that soul also is expected to have a lady, to guide by her eyes through love to the perfect haven. In the thought process of symbolism earthly love derived its significance solely and supremely from the fact that it was a type and symbol of the love existing in the court of heaven, and as such, a step toward its comprehension and attainment.

It was appropriate then that the sunshine of Beatrice's smile should give to Dante his first guidance in the maze of his inner life, imperiled as he was by the fatal food of Circe. All food attracts through its element of good,[105] for all existence is in response to Primal Love. All goods however may not be chosen separately without doing violence to higher goods. That men may not interfere with each others' right to choose, there was established in man's outer environment God's dual vicarate of empire and church; for the preservation of the right of the individual to choose in accord with the light of the intellect, there was established in man's inner environment the dual vicarate of philosophy and theology. The power to make use of these two vicarates is the gift of that personal love which demands complete allegiance.

In brief, then, the teaching of Venus is appropriately of love, yet not of a love which is mere kindliness to others, but a love which is desire for oneness with the beloved object. From such love proceeds all moral action, since it alone has power to in-

---

103. Cf. Guido Guinicelli's *Ode on the Gentle Heart.*
104. For Dante as typical of any soul, cf. pp. 74 ff.
105. As Dante explains, unworthy objects of desire mislead the love of mortals only because they have in them some trace of the "eternal Light." See *Par.,* v, 11. Dante also says: "quum totum universum nihil aliud sit quam vestigium quoddam divine bonitatis." (*Monarchia,* 1, 8.) Cf. Aquinas, *S.Th.,* 1, Q. 93, *arts.* 1-4. In other words, as Thomas Aquinas states, no act can be evil in every aspect from which it may be viewed, since it is not possible to corrupt all the circumstances of virtue at once, *S.Th.,* 1, 2, Q. 73, 2, *c.fi.*

spire the human will, enabling it to remain autonomous in its own sphere without conflict with natural law.

> Nè creator nè creatura mai,
> . . . figliuol, fu sanza amore,
> o naturale o d'animo; e tu 'l sai.
> Lo natural è sempre sanza errore,
> ma l'altro puote errar per malo obietto,
> o per troppo o per poco di vigore.[106]

Quodlibet agens ex amore agit quodcumque agit, cum ex intentione finis et boni operetur.[107]

More specifically, Venus is both morning and evening star: "che 'l sol vagheggia or da coppa or da ciglio,"[108] and the principles through which she governs the moral life are twofold: the natural pagan virtues dictated by philosophy—courage, prudence, temperance, justice—through which man may live in an earthly paradise; and the supernatural virtues revealed by theology—faith, hope, charity—which are required to raise man from the earthly to the heavenly Paradise.[109] As Dante leaves the sphere of the "fair Cyprian," again he has learned more of God; this time of the Holy Spirit, Divine Love.

In the third epicycle, Dante has seen himself as a human person guided in his moral development by theology and philosophy, as directing the interaction of his will with universal law. Having chosen the food of angels as ministered by Beatrice, rather than the florin-food of Florence, he undergoes a transmutation, not like that of the evil shepherd, from man to beast, but rather from man to angel.

106. "Nor Creator, nor creature, my son, was ever without love, either natural or rational; and this thou knowest. The natural is always without error; but the other may err through an evil object, or through too little or too much vigour." *Purg.*, xvii, 91-96.

107. Aquinas, *S.Th.*, 1, 2, *Q.* 28, *art.* 6, *c.*

108. *Par.*, viii, 12. When Venus is morning star, she precedes the sun, and thus is conceived as with her back to him, going forth in his service. When she is evening star, she follows the sun, and so is conceived as facing him, in the exercise of that holy contemplation which Dante regards as specifically the privilege of old age, after the active work of life is done. Cf. *Convivio*, 4, 28.

109. Cf. *Monarchia*, 3, 16, as quoted on p. 205.

Cf. the allegory of Marcia and Cato in *Convivio*, 4, 28.

Cf. also the method of progress through purgatory, where the day is governed by the four cardinal or natural virtues, and the night by the three theological or supernatural virtues, each shining as a star in the heavens. Active progress is possible only during the day; the night is for holy meditation. Cf. pp. 204-205.

IV. SUN. SYMBOL OF THE TRINITY

DANTE, having seen the truth of his visionary journey, his political theory and his moral and intellectual development, has
explained three levels of the fourfold meaning of his life-story:
the literal, the allegorical, and the tropological. The anagoge
remains, that is, the vision of the eternal meaning of the three
as a whole. Not until he has gathered up these three threads in
such vision and adoration of the Divine Tri-unity as is now possible to him, may he go farther.

In the sun, that most complete of physical symbols of the
deity, occurs the unification of all truth known thus far. Dante's
first thought in the physical sun is of the Trinity:

> Guardando nel suo figlio con l'Amore
>   che l'uno e l'altro etternalmente spira,
>   lo primo ed ineffabile Valore,
> quanto per mente e per loco si gira . . . fè . . .[110]

The method is that of symbolism, and the opening lines of the
Paradiso are reëchoed:

> La gloria di colui che tutto move
>   per l'universo penetra e risplende
>   in una parte più e meno altrove.[111]

Scarcely has Dante described the equinoctial position of the Sun
as he reached it, before he has disclaimed any idea that the
physical sun itself is the thing which matters.

> Quant' esser convenia da sè lucente
>   quel ch'era dentro al sol . . .
>   non per color, ma per lume parvente![112]

110. "Gazing upon his Son with the Love which the one and the other eternally breathes forth, the primal and ineffable Worth made whatsoever circleth
through mind or space . . ." *Par.*, x, 1-5. Referring to Chap. III, Pt. I, and
realizing that Dante is familiar with most of the authors there quoted, it is evident that he could have had no other thought as he reached the sun.
111. "The All-Mover's glory penetrates through the universe, and regloweth
in one region more, and less in another." *Par.*, i, 1-3.
112. "How shining in itself must that needs be which in the sun . . . itself
revealeth not by hue, but light!" *Par.*, x, 40-42.

Having beheld in the first three spheres, against the background of the physical universe, the meaning of his life, he is now beyond the shadow of the earth (which according to medieval computation ended at the sphere of Venus). Although perceiving the anagoge of the first three levels in the physical symbol of Godhead, he is definitely beyond the reach of the earthly temptation to value the symbol for itself.

Within the sun are souls who make of themselves a living crown representing the "primal Worth." They are soon surrounded by a second crown and a third, for that ultimately revealed in the Sun must be, not merely blessed souls who see the Trinity, but the Trinity itself as it were mirrored in them. Beyond such a vision no individual man, as such, may go: "Sopra 'l sol non fu occhio ch'andasse."[113] Later, Dante will point out that both all humanity as one, and the individual soul aided by special mystic graces, may pass beyond even this, the normal soul-stretch of man.

Again reminding of the symbolism comes Beatrice's exhortation: "Ringrazia, ringrazia il sol de li angeli, ch'a questo sensibil t'ha levato per sua grazia."[114] The soul should, indeed, be utterly sunk in God, but not so that it fails to return to his created mirrors. This is as it were the inbreathing and the outbreathing, the tidal flow of the soul, in which Beatrice rejoices.

Indications connecting the first and second crowns with the Father and the Son are not great or obvious, in spite of the emphasis on the Trinity throughout the heaven of the Sun.[115] It would seem that Dante intended even the philosophical reader to be not quite certain as to his meaning until the appearance of the third crown, with its obvious reference to the Holy Spirit:

> parvemi lì novelle sussistenze
> cominciare a vedere, e fare un giro
> di fuor da l' altre due circunferenze.

113. "Never was there eye that could transcend the sun." *Par.,* x, 48.

114. "Give thanks, give thanks unto the Sun of the angels, who of his grace hath to this sun of sense exalted thee." *Par.,* x, 52-54. Beatrice (in the next three tercets) is pleased when Dante adores God so intensely that he forgets her (and, of course, all else); but she brings his attention back to the souls around him by the splendour of her smile.

115. Cf. *Par.,* x, 1-6; x, 49-51; x, 76-77; xiii, 25-27; xiii, 52-60; xiii, 79-81; xiv, 28-33; xiv, 67-75.

> Oh vero sfavillar del Santo Spiro!
> come si fece subito e candente
> a li occhi miei che, vinti, non soffriro![116]

Now the discourses of the prudent Doctors may be read with a new ear to hear. The truth of symbolism is not perceived without the enlightenment of the Holy Spirit—and furthermore, the doctrine of the Trinity is not complete, understandable, a consistent whole which can stand against criticism, until the doctrine of the Spirit is elaborated.[117]

Nevertheless it is with reason that Francis becomes the interest of the first crown. St. Thomas describes him:

> Non era ancor molto lontan da l'orto,
> ch'el cominciò a far sentir la terra
> de la sua gran virtute alcun conforto.[118]

Francis is sharing the symbolism of the Father, for it is the sun, not its rays or its heat, that is central, and the words used are "power" and "strengthening." Francis' career also gave spiritual life on earth, in the household he gathered.[119]

Dominic is the interest of the second crown. Like the Second Person of the Trinity, he gave light (knowledge) even before his birth:

> come fu creata, fu repleta
> si la sua mente di viva virtute,
> che, ne la madre, lei fece profeta.[120]

Furthermore he chose poverty and humility, saying "Io son ve-

116. "I there began to perceive new-come existences making a circle out beyond the other two circumferences. Oh very sparkling of the Holy Breath! how sudden and how glowing it became before my eyes, which, vanquished, might not bear it!" *Par.*, xiv, 73-78.

117. Historically as well as theoretically a fact. Cf. Chap. III, Pt. I, iii; Chap. V, Pt. I, ii.

118. "Not yet was he far distant from his rising when he began to make the earth to feel from his great power a certain strengthening." *Par.*, xi, 55-57.

119. It will be remembered that the triune sun-god is characterized as life-giving, light-giving, and heat-giving.

120. "So soon as created, his mind was so replete with living virtue, that in his mother's womb he made her prophetess." *Par.*, xii, 58-60. A similar effect of supernatural knowledge before birth is ascribed not only to Christ, but to John Baptist, in the birth narratives of the early chapters of Luke.

nuto a questo";[121] and "per amor de la verace manna in picciol tempo gran dottor si feo."[122]

It was not merely an act of courtesy that led Thomas a Dominican, to praise Francis; and Bonaventure a Franciscan, to praise Dominic; nor was it merely a tribute to the friendship believed to have existed between Thomas and Bonaventure, who were associated at the University of Paris. Though Dante himself calls it courtesy,[123] in his mind friendship and courtesy if real signify truths lying deep below the surface. The great Dominican appears first, not the great Franciscan, even though his appearance be in the crown where Francis is to be praised; for as Dante is to learn later, knowledge comes before love. The Dominican, however, turns attention not to his own master, but to Francis; since the knowledge which precedes love brings it forth. The Franciscan in turn directs attention to Dominic; since the love brought forth by knowledge brings deepening of knowledge. According to Dante and the Thomistic philosophy, however, although the courtesy would seem to be the same, Bonaventure could not have appeared first in praise of Dominic. That is, in contradistinction to Bonaventure's own theory, love is incapable of bringing forth knowledge until first stimulated by knowledge. Thus with courteous irony Dante has so placed Bonaventure that in symbol he admits his own error.

A deeper level in this symbolism now is elucidated by the appearance of the third crown. The primal Love, who is the Holy Spirit breathed forth mutually by the Father and the Son, is their mutual love and self-giving, so intense that It is a Person. Dante cannot perceive the symbol of the Holy Spirit before he perceives the mutual giving in love of the crowns symbolizing the Father and the Son, for he is still in time and space, perceiving under symbolisms as well as expressing himself through symbolism. His very vision of the Trinity, later to be instantaneous, is now consecutive.

In the light of this new vision of the Trinity, all that flows from it is reviewed and summarized:

121. "It was for this I came." *Par.*, xii, 78. Cf. Heb. 11. 7, 9.
122. "For love of the true manna [Christ] in short season he became a mighty teacher." *Par.*, xii, 84-85.
123. Cf. *Par.*, xii, 142-145.

Ciò che non more e ciò che può morire
non è se non splendor di quella idea
che partorisce, amando, il nostro sire:
chè quella viva luce che sì mea
dal suo lucente, che non si disuna
da lui nè da l'amor ch' a lor s'intrea,
per sua bontate il suo raggiare aduna,
quasi specchiato, in nove sussistenze,
etternalmente rimanendosi una.
Quindi discende a l'ultime potenze
giù d'atto in atto, tanto divenendo,
che più non fa che brevi contingenze;
e queste contingenze esser intendo
le cose generate, che produce
con seme e sanza seme il ciel movendo.[124]

Brief attention is given to the creation of the angelic intelligences; the creation of souls, including the astrological influence upon them of the intelligences; and finally the method by which Adam and Christ were formed humanly perfect and not subject to stellar influence. The duty of using the intellect for the practical ends of the position in which the individual is placed, the need of careful distinction in reasoning, and the duty of withholding of judgment,[125] are again touched upon. These considerations, followed by another hymn to the Trinity, and the sole reference to the blessedness of the reunion of friends and relatives in the heavenly kingdom, make up the rest of Dante's perception in the "sun of sense."

For Dante there has been completed in accord with the fourfold method, analysis of his personal life, against the background of the physical universe. He has seen knowledge and love in their true relation to political and moral life, specifically as governing the relationship of Guelph to Ghibelline and of

124. "That which dieth not, and that which can die, is nought save the reglow of that Idea which our Sire, in Loving, doth beget; for that living Light which so outgoeth from its Source that it departeth not therefrom, nor from the Love that maketh three with them, doth, of its own goodness, focus its own raying, as though reflected, in nine existences, eternally abiding one. Thence it descendeth to the remotest potencies, down, from act to act, becoming such as maketh now mere brief contingencies; by which contingencies I understand the generated things which are produced from seed, or seedless, by the moving heaven." *Par.*, xiii, 52-66.

125. *Par.*, xiii, 130-142. Cf. with this passage the medieval conception of the thorn as symbolizing Judaism, and the rose as symbolizing Christ.

human will to universal law. Thus he has attained basis for his personal adjustment to contemporary politics and contemporary intellectual life. But there has come premonition of a deeper truth in the relation to redemption of empire and philosophy as well as of church and theology; and with the appearance of the third circle, completing the first foreshadowing of the Beatific Vision, there is hint of the resurrection. Yet by this symbol of the Holy Spirit[126] Dante's sight is vanquished; for although the Holy Spirit teaches of the Father and the Son, there is none to teach men of himself, and he remains a mystery.

CHRIST AND HUMANITY IN THE DIVINA COMMEDIA

I. MARS. CHRIST AND THE CROSS

IN the Sun was made complete all that the story of Dante as an individual man could signify. Further he might not progress with his own story as the center of interest. His visionary journey is, however, an allegorical representation of the literal earthly life of Christ.[127] Dante must now proceed to the allegory of Christ and Humanity, if his poem is to bear that resemblance to Scripture so significantly implied.[128]

The full meaning of Scripture, Dante's model, could be perceived only through the recognition in its characters of types of

---

126. *Par.,* xiv, 67-78. Notice the three lines which follow, and cf. p. 80.

127. Cf. pp. 288-291, especially p. 291 n. 149; also, cf. Chap. V, Pt. II, i.

128. Dante, in the *Epistle to Can Grande,* discusses in regard to his poem the *"subject, agent, form* and *end,* the *title* of the work, and the *branch of philosophy* it concerns."

The *branch of philosophy,* he states, is ethics, even as is that of the Scripture.

The *title* is *Commedia,* Comedy, defining the work as one wherein the beginning is in some evil complication, but the end is prosperous. In this sense the Scripture was the greatest and most inclusive of all Comedies, beginning in the Fall of Man, and ending in the Church of the Redeemed in heaven,—those who had fallen below the proper estate of humanity raised in the end far above it.

The *end* is stated as: "to remove those living in this life from the state of misery and lead them to the state of felicity"—the exact purpose of the Scripture.

The *form,* as Dante so frequently pointed out, is directly subservient to the end in view.

Again, as to the *agent,* that is, writer, who is of course Dante himself, he indicates in *Inf.,* ii, 10 ff. (cf. pp. 178, 294) that he regarded himself in some sense functionally equivalent to St. Paul, by whose preaching knowledge of the good news of the Scriptural "comedy" was brought to the Gentile world. Furthermore, like the writers of Scripture, Dante is divinely commissioned to bear a

Christ.[129] Similarly with Dante's Comedy, to which, as he has taken care to indicate, are to be applied the rules of interpretation that were applied to Scripture.[130] Not only was Dante's conception of his office as philosophical guide to the vicar of the emperor[131] such as to make this symbolism suitable; but also there was a special significance in the symbolism with which he surrounded himself in the Comedy. Examples are the dual nature of his birth-sign[132] and the close connection of Venus with the Holy Ghost, but many more are revealed during Dante's visit in Mars. It should be recalled that Friday, the day sacred to the central mystery of redemption, was Venus' day, "ond' io principio piglio"[133] and it was the day on which his journey began.

Dante was welcomed in Mars by Cacciaguida, an ancestor revered for his participation in the crusades:

message to those who sit in darkness; and as Scripture writers set down their message at the dictation of the Primal Love, so Dante at the dictation of Love (cf. *Purg.*, xxiv, 52-54).

The *subject*, "Man as by good or ill deserts, in the exercise of the freedom of his choice, he becomes liable to rewarding or punishing justice," is plainly that of Scripture. Cf. p. 182 n. 258.

Hence, in all the six elements which, according to the author, must be considered in regard to a work of art, Dante's poem is modeled on his conception of Scripture. This picture is borne out by relevant passages in the *Commedia*.

129. Cf. for instance the long list of Old Testament characters treated as types of Christ, as given in the index of the *Patrologia Latina* (Migne).

130. The purpose of Dante's Comedy, like that of Scripture, is to lead mankind from a state of misery to a state of bliss. (Cf. footnote 128.)

The fact that in the *Convivio* Dante distinguishes between the symbolic method of the poet and that of the theologian is sometimes urged against the assumption that the *Divina Commedia* was intended to be interpreted by the rules in force for Scripture interpretation. This argument, however, rests on the ungrounded assumption that the difference between poetic and theological interpretation lies in the truth of the literal level. This Dante does not imply. Cf. references below, and Appendix IV, Pt. I, iii. The difference, which applies only to the *allegory*, or second level, would seem from his illustrations to lie in the fact that Scriptural allegory must center in Christ.

Cf. also pp. 267-268 and Appendix IV, Pt. I, i, on the verbal and functional truth on the literal level.

131. It was in this light that Dante viewed Can Grande and his own destined relation to him. Cf. pp. 326-327.

132. According to Albertus Magnus (*De laudibus B. Mariae Virg.*, 7, 1, 2) Gemini is a sign appropriate to Mary "quod est aliena negotia curare ut propria, et non sibi, sed toti gentium se credere mundo. Et hoc maxime facit virtus charitatis, quae non quaerit quae sua sunt, sed communia negotia propriis anteponit." It is possible that Dante justified his belief that he was divinely called to be in some sort philosophical guide of the Empire, by the conception of his birth-sign as causing him to place the public affairs before his own.

133. "From whom I take my start." Cf. p. 49 n. 79.

Quale per li seren tranquilli e puri
  discorre ad ora ad or subito foco,
  movendo li occhi che stavan sicuri,
e pare stella che trasmuti loco,
  se non che da la parte ond' el s'accende
  nulla sen perde, ed esso dura poco;
tale, dal corno che 'n destro si stende
  a piè di quella croce corse un astro
  de la costellazion che lì risplende.
Nè si partì la gemma dal suo nastro,
  ma per la lista radial trascorse,
  che parve foco dietro ad alabastro.[134]

In the simile comparing the welcome of Dante by Cacciaguida to that of Aeneas by Anchises[135] is reminiscence of that aspect of Dante's personal life in which his function was akin to that of Aeneas,[136] preparation for the human mission of Christ. There would seem to be at the same time suggestion of an equation of Cacciaguida to David, from whose blood Christ sprang.[137] The allegorical burden is more defined in Cacciaguida's greeting: "O superinfusa," and in his rhetorical ques-

134. "As through the tranquil and pure skies darteth, from time to time, a sudden flame setting amoving eyes that erst were steady, seeming a star that changeth place, save that from where it kindleth no star is lost, and that itself endureth but a little; such from the horn that stretcheth to the right unto that cross's foot, darted a star of the constellation that is there aglow; nor did the gem depart from off its riband, but coursed along the radial line, like fire burning behind alabaster." *Par.*, xv, 13-24.

135. *Par.*, xv, 25-27.

136. And also that of Paul. Cf. *Inf.*, ii, 10 ff., where the implication is, that since his going was urged, his function is comparable to that of his two protagonists.

137. "When the immeasurable divine goodness willed to reconform to itself the human creature . . . it was appointed in the most lofty and united divine consistory of the Trinity that the Son of God should descend to earth to effect this harmony. And inasmuch as at his coming into the world it was meet that not only heaven but earth should be in its best disposition . . . therefore that people and that city who were destined to bring this about (to wit the glorious Rome) were ordained by the divine providence. And because the abode wherein the celestial king must enter ought to be most clean and pure there was likewise ordained a most holy family from the which after many merits should be born a woman supremely good amongst all the rest, who should be the treasure house of the Son of God. And this family is that of David. . . . And it was all at the same point of time wherein David was born and Rome was born, that is to say Aeneas came into Italy from Troy, which was the origin of the most noble city of Rome." *Convivio*, 4, 5.

Even the phrasing of his poetry suggests that such ideas are in his mind. Cf. for example *Inf.*, vii, 99, with *Aeneid*, 6, 539, "Nox ruit Aenea; nos flendo ducimus horas."

tion "sicut tibi, cui bis unquam coeli ianua reclusa," which implies the answer, "Christ."[138]

The next reference to the stars would have seemed even more
strange to a medieval than to a modern reader, and this just because of the former's acquaintance with the astrological concepts to which Dante makes such facile reference. Cacciaguida
dates his birth by saying that since the birth of Christ "five hundred, fifty and thirty times did this flame [Mars] return to *his
own Lion* to rekindle him beneath his feet."[139] Astrologically,
this is incorrect. Leo is not one of the two signs (Aries and
Scorpio) ruled by Mars, but is, on the contrary, ruled by the sun.
Dante evidently is interested here in a symbolism which is not
primarily astrological. The conjecture has been made that he
was connecting Mars the war-god, or Mars the red star, with
the qualities of lions. Dante, however, was a medieval symbolist
of the first rank, and not likely to use a mere comparison symbol
with no intention or possibility of deeper meaning. It is more
likely that the connection is between Christ as the Lion of the
Tribe of Judah, and Mars as the sphere in which Dante sees the
Cross; Mars, moved by the Virtues, the *second* order of the
middle hierarchy of intelligences, who according to Dante contemplate the Son as he is in himself.[140]

In Mars, for the first time, the central attention of the poem
is directed toward Christ, Christ in his human earthly life. Like
the Milky Way, dotted with various-sized points of light, "sì
costellati facean nel profondo Marte quei raggi il venerabil
segno che fan giunture di quadranti in tondo."[141]

138. A case might be made for the implied answer, Paul; but the interpretation here given seems to dovetail better with the other symbolic indications. Of
course on different levels both may be true. Cf. p. 179.

139. "Al suo Leon cinquecento cinquanta e trenta fiate venne questo foco a
rinfiammarsi sotto la sua pianta." *Par.*, xvi, 37-39.

140. Cf. *Convivio*, 2, 6. Dante holds that the nine moving heavens are moved
each by one of the nine orders of angels, divided into three hierarchies of three
orders each; of which the first hierarchy contemplates the Father, the second the
Son, and the third the Holy Ghost. The three orders within each hierarchy contemplate different aspects of the one Person. Thus, in the second hierarchy, the
Principalities, moving Jupiter, contemplate the Son in relation to the Father; the
Virtues, moving Mars, contemplate the Son as he is in himself; and the Domina-
tions, moving the Sun, contemplate the Son in relation to the Holy Spirit. But
cf. p. 88 n. 218.

141. "So did those rays, star-decked, make in the depth of Mars the venerable
sign which crossing quadrant lines make in a circle." *Par.*, xiv, 100-102.

> Qui vince la memoria mia lo 'ngegno;
>   chè'n quella croce lampeggiava Cristo
>   sì, ch'io non so trovare essemplo degno:
> ma chi prende sua croce e segue Cristo,
>   ancor mi scuserà di quel ch'io lasso,
>   vedendo in quell' albor balenar Cristo.[142]

Nowadays the earthly life of Christ brings to mind the carpenter, the friend of fisher-folk, healings and teachings on the mountains and lake-shores and plains of Galilee; but in the Middle Ages the central fact of Christ's life was his death,[143] presented forcefully to Dante in the cross which he sees in the glow of Mars. The *Divìna Commedia* opens in the *selva oscura,* as did Christ's life on earth. He, Sun and Light, became obscured by the cloud of flesh,[144] and came to human consciousness in the Dark Wood of humanity. Among the allegorical meanings listed by Rabanus for *silva,* is *mens humana.* The signification of this earthly life of Christ was the cross, with its song of victory so far above mortal perception that neither the agony nor the triumph could be reached by human imagination.

> così da' lumi che lì m'apparinno
>   s'accogliea per la croce una melode
>   che mi rapiva, sanza intender l'inno.[145]

All of the sweet song that could be grasped by the understanding was its refrain: "Rise thou up and conquer" in the strength of Christ who has won the victory.

Dante is in three respects a type of Christ so far as this story is concerned: first, as above, in his typical human nature; second, in his destined and foretold sufferings, which Dante, having had previous forebodings and partial prophecies, sees here in the light of eternity. He hears of the coming trial

142. "Here my memory doth outrun my wit, for that cross so flashed forth Christ that I may not find example worthy. But whoso taketh his cross and followeth Christ shall yet forgive me what I leave unsaid, when he shall see Christ lighten in that glow." *Par.,* xiv, 103-108.

143. Cf. Aquinas, *S.Th.,* 3, *QQ.* 49 and 50.

144. Mary is sometimes called *Nubes,* because historically she gave flesh to the Sun of Righteousness, from whose burning rays she now shelters men through her prayers. Cf. Albertus Magnus' phrase: "flesh the cloud that hid the Sun."

145. "So from the lights that there appeared to me was gathered on the cross a strain that rapt me albeit I followed not the hymn." *Par.,* xiv, 121-123.

Nè per ambage, in che la gente folle
gia s'inviscava pria che fosse anciso
l'Agnel di Dio che le peccata tolle,
ma per chiare parole e con preciso
latin . . .[146]

He hears it, not as the Jews heard the future sufferings of Christ,
foretold in such dark sayings that they could fail to recognize
the fulfilment when it came, but as Christ himself foreknew his
own sufferings, clearly and with no concealment from the beginning. To make the type more strong, it is plotted "la dove
Cristo tutto dì si merca"[147] and the details of the suffering also
have a correspondence: the innocent is blamed,[148] all that is
loved most dearly is abandoned,[149] Dante like Christ is "numbered among the transgressors."[150] Nor is the expected result
less significant: Dante is to strike out a path for himself and
lead others from a state of misery to a state of bliss. Even the
prevision of victory, through the instrumentality of one as yet a
child, has a definite connection with the Passion.[151]

Third, in the fruits of his victory also, Dante is a type of
Christ as shown by the answer to his query as to whether, under
the foreseen conditions, he is to tell the whole truth. What is
his duty, his mission, in the midst of the predestined trouble?
Recalling Circe and the florin-pasture, recalling Beatrice and
the food of angels, the answer becomes significant:

se la voce tua sarà molesta
nel primo gusto, vital nutrimento
lascerà poi, quando sarà digesta.[152]

As Dante's external fortunes and pain of exile are to typify the

146. "In no dark sayings, such as limed the foolish folk of old, before the
Lamb of God who taketh sins away, was slain, but in clear words, and with precise discourse." *Par.*, xvii, 31-35.
147. "In the place where, day in and day out, Christ is put to sale." *Par.*,
xvii, 51.
148. *Par.*, xvii, 52-53.   149. *Par.*, xvii, 55-57.
150. *Par.*, xvii, 61-63.
151. *Par.*, xvii, 76-92. Cf. Ps. 22 (connected in the worship of the Church
with Maundy Thursday and Good Friday) in which, after a graphic recital of the
sufferings of Christ (vss. 1-21) and a declaration of the vital benefits conferred
by the death of Christ (vss. 22-30), occurs the prophecy of a people *yet to be
born* to the accomplishment of his glory.
152. "If thy voice be grievous at first taste, yet vital nutriment shall it leave
thereafter when digested." *Par.*, xvii, 130-132.

passion of Christ, so his mission, undertaken at last in knowledge and love, like Christ's, is to give food.[153] Against the background prepared by empire and church, Dante's voice, bitter at
first, is to become and to remain a source of nutriment to both
throughout the future.

II. JUPITER. HUMANITY AND THE EAGLE

IN Mars, the discussion of Christ's earthly life as it led to the
development of the church, culminates in the extension of the
Incarnation to all mankind, which is the truth presented to
Dante in Jupiter. For Catholic theology the Incarnation never
stops with historical fact, since this fact was itself to be understood in accordance with the fourfold method. The term "Body
of Christ" represents the literal human nature assumed by God
in the Incarnation, but just as truly on the allegorical and moral
levels it represents the mystical Body, formed (ideally) by all
mankind[154] and the sacramental Body given to each individual
man. There is, of course, as the anagoge, the glorified Body in
heaven.

Thus in Jupiter Dante sees the eternal truth of his political
theory, not as in Mercury, in regard to his personal function
and duty in it, but in regard to the proper organization of all
mankind in Christ. The Dark Wood is a natural symbol not

153. Cf. Ps. 22. 26, 29. It is to be noted that the sacramental body of Christ
is termed the "bread of angels," a term doubtless derived from the connection
with manna in John 6, and a comparison of Ps. 78. 25-26.

154. Christ is conceived as the Head of all humanity, whether living before
his earthly life or after it, whether believing in him or not. Thomas Aquinas
says: "Quanquam non eodem modo, omnium tamen hominum Christus caput
est." *S.Th.*, 3, *Q.* 8, *art.* 3, *concl.* And: "Illi qui sunt infideles, etsi actu non sint
in Ecclesia, sunt tamen de Ecclesia in potentia." *Ibid., ad primum.* And: "Sancti
Patres non insistebant sacramentis legalibus tamquam quibusdam rebus, sed sicut
imaginibus et umbris futurorum. Idem autem est motus in imaginem, inquantum
est imago, et in rem, ut patet per Philosophum. Et ideo antiqui patres, servando
legalia sacramenta, ferebantur in Christum per fidem et dilectionem eamdem, qua
et nos in ipsum ferimur; et ita patres antiqui pertinebant ad idem corpus Ecclesiae ad quod nos pertinemus." *Ibid., ad tertium.* Cf. also the following modern
Roman Catholic statement:

"What is the Catholic Church? To this question we might give many answers,
but if I were asked to answer it in one brief statement, I should say that the
Catholic Church is nothing less than the Mystical Body of Jesus, the Incarnation
extended across the universe and adown the centuries, Jesus Christ living in the
world today—that is what we Catholics understand by the Church." Richard
Felix, *What Is the Catholic Church?* N. Y., Paulist Press, 1922, pp. 3-4.

only for the bewildering maze within which Dante found himself in Florence, but also for the general bewilderment of mankind without central government. It is a symbol not only of the human nature which veiled the Godhead of Christ in Bethlehem, but also of the state of deformity in humanity as a whole.[155]

That which first greets Dante in the heaven of Jupiter is the aphorism from the Wisdom of Solomon: "Diligite justitiam, qui judicatis terram," pricked out by lights which in the end remain in the shape of the letter "M," symbol of human nature[156] and then become an eagle of which the "M" forms the body.[157] This vision, as judged from Dante's immediate exclamation, was deeply significant to him:

> O dolce stella, quali e quante gemme
> mi dimostraro che nostra giustizia
> effetto sia del ciel che tu ingemme![158]

Next is briefly suggested and summarized that which Dante has explained at length in other works, especially the *Monarchia*, and pictured powerfully in the early stages of his journey. Every man exists for the attainment of the "good of the intellect";[159] mankind as a whole exists that the potentiality of intellect may

155. The root of sin in the human race, which necessitates governing powers to check its greed. Cf. *Monarchia*, 3, 4, lines 107 ff.

156. An old-fashioned "M" may be seen in the outline of the skull. If, now, we imagine the eyes to form an "O" in either half ⋂ ⋒ we have the word *omo*, man. Cf. *Purg.*, xxiii, 31-33.

157. Professor Fletcher thus comments upon this sentence:

"Against the law of the 'felon folk,' 'family of the Beast,' the Deliverer shall array the Law of Jove's Eagle, defined in '5 times 7 vowels and consonants.' After the first 3 letters, DIL, there is pause, during which Dante appeals for understanding to the 'Muse' that maketh to be glorious and long-lived men and cities and kingdoms. Then is spelled out Christ's Law of Justice: *'Diligite iustitiam qui iudicatis terram.'* Thus separately presented, the first 3 letters—number of the Trinity—serve as superscription to the Law, by recognized cipher initialling *Domini Iesu Lex.* Also, product of the numerals D, I and L—500 times 1 times 50—equals that of D, X and V—500 times 10 times 5—of the Deliverer's number. His *product* will be Christ's Law of the Roman Eagle.

"For this product he must possess the authority implied in the thirty-*fifth* and last letter of the Law—the M of terram—Monarchy of earth . . ." J. B. Fletcher, *The Crux of Dante's Comedy*, p. 31.

158. "O sweet star, what and how great gems made plain to me that our justice is the effect of that heaven which thou dost engem!" *Par.*, xviii, 115-117.

159. That is, knowledge. "Good" is used in the sense of "valuable or desirable thing" in the sense in which we still use its plural, "goods" to designate desirables in the material sphere.

be reduced to actuality.[160] The individual man cannot attain the good of the intellect unless he be in a condition of peace and of freedom; peace and freedom cannot exist apart from justice (the sole protector against the *lupa,* avarice, which else would so bite all, that each would be snatching at his neighbor's goods, and defending his own from aggression); and justice demands coöperation of humankind, of which the necessary condition is one emperor governing the one humanity in the civil sphere, and similarly one pope governing the same humanity in the spiritual sphere. Thus there is basis for the old interpretation of the eagle as symbolizing "the work of all righteous governors," etc., but this is to grasp only part of its significance.

For the medieval reader, the first association with the eagle was not his significance as a patriotic ensign but his nature as the one living creature able to look with unshut eye upon the sun.[161] Only Christ can thus look on the glory of the Supreme Sun which is God, and this Christ does, not only as God, but as taking up into himself human nature, even as according to Dante's vision, the ⌒ became the body of the Eagle.[162] The suffering of the Incarnation appears here as the deeper meaning of that suggested to Dante in Justinian's words with reference to the empire: "Vedi quanta virtù l' ha fatto degno di reverenza; e cominciò da l' ora che Pallante morì per darli regno."[163] The symbolism of the Eagle, then, includes all humanity, in whichever aspect, empire or church.[164] Both alike exist for the furtherance of man in his intellectual capacity, man aspiring to the good of the intellect, which is the vision of all things in God, and is fittingly summarized in the Logos, himself the Good of the intellect. Whereas in all the other spheres individuals have spoken to Dante, as representative of a group,

160. Cf. *Monarchia,* 1, chaps. 3-4. Cf. also the note to 1, 3, lines 66-78, in the Temple Classics edition, *Latin Works of Dante,* p. 135.

161. Cf. Medieval bestiaries. The idea doubtless arose from observation of the eagle and its flight.

162. Cf. Col. 1. 18 and 2. 17-19.

163. *Par.,* vi, 34-36. "See how great virtue hath made it worthy of reverence, beginning from the hour when Pallas died to give it sway."

164. The eagle is as appropriate a symbol of the church as of the empire. For example, in the grifon of the pageant of the terrestrial paradise, which represents Christ in his two natures, the eagle represents the divine, not the human, and thus by association of symbol may represent Christ's spiritual vicarate on earth, the Church.

here the Eagle speaks as constituting the whole group: "Io vidi e anche udi' parlar lo rostro, e sonar ne la voce e 'io' e 'mio,' quand' era nel concetto 'noi' e 'nostro.' "[165]

The wreathing of the ⌒ with lilies suggests the lilies of France and of Florence, not in themselves evil, but evil when signifying national spirit overstepping its bounds and standing in opposition to the Emperor as vicar of Christ in whom is united all humanity. Predicting that which is to be when the ideal empire is restored, with a slight motion the lilies become the head of the Eagle.[166] The fleur-de-lis, flower of light, is symbol of Christ himself, and is frequently represented with a crown from which shine forth the rays of the sun.[167]

In this vision Dante seeks to understand not simply the relationship to the Body of all its members good and bad, but especially the relationship of those who have never known of Christ. How with justice can they be cut off from the Body which is all Humanity? The Eagle explains that human sight—but one of the rays of the divine mind whose many rays enlighten the universe—must remain blind to the depths of the eternal justice, which, being itself their cause, is essentially immeasurable by human ideas.

The Eagle's answer is striking here, in that it contains one of the two exceptions to its usual form of speech in the singular. The Eagle may not disavow its own perception of the divine justice, that is, the perception by its divine nature, transmitted to Man in the hypostatic union of the two natures of Christ.

165. "I saw and likewise I heard, the beak discourse and utter in its voice both *I* and *Mine,* when in conception it was *We* and *Our.*" *Par.,* xix, 10-12.

166. Professor Fletcher notes that in *Inf.,* ix, 67 ff. the spirits in Dis, in refusing to admit Virgil, are doing the exact opposite of those who change the lilies into the eagle—that is, they refuse the empire. Dr. Grandgent also gives to this incident a definitely political interpretation quite in accord with the spirit of the sphere. The standard of the Guelph Florence is the lily, similar in shape to the "M." Reluctant at first to give up this standard, the Guelph souls nevertheless readily conform to the imperial design. One is frequently amazed at the detail in which Dante's symbolism works itself out. It may be remembered that the grifon, whose eagle nature appears here wreathed with lilies, was white mingled with vermilion. In the 12th century the white lily was the party badge of the Ghibellines while the red lily was adopted by the Guelphs. Cf. Alvin C. Beal, *Gardening and the Use of Flowers in the Middle Ages.* Lecture given before the Horticultural Society of New York and the Garden Club of America . . . Mar. 6, 1925.

167. Cf. Harold Bayley, *The Lost Language of Symbolism.*

The Eagle, then, in its rare use of the plural, is speaking for
humanity as men, rather than—as is its custom—for humanity
as Man. Further, it is the injustice of earth which keeps the
Eagle from its complete formation and blessedness, not the justice of heaven; and although no one ever rose to heaven without belief in Christ, nevertheless since Trajan and Ripheus form
part of the very eye of the Eagle, it is clear that there are more
ways than man knows, of acknowledging the Christ who is the
Soul, the Head of the Body.[168]

The unification of humanity in the Eagle subsumes also the
individuality of man. The Body of Christ is composed of free
individuals coöperating, not of beings whose wills are absorbed
into a larger entity. So soon as the Eagle ceases its speech, the
individual souls each begin to sing. They sing, however, in harmony, being as far from the disunity of a crowd as they are
from indistinguishableness. This fact likewise has its symbolism
in the sun, which, when it sinks, renders visible the stars. Their
light, although subordinated to the sun's, is not submerged and
buried in it.

Moreover the Eagle is conscious of its individual members:

> La parte in me che vede, e pate il sole
>   nel aguglie mortali, incominciommi,
>   or fisamente riguardar si vole,
> perchè de' fuochi, ond'io figura formi,
>   quelli, onde l'occhio in testa mi scintilla,
>   e' di tutti i lor gradi son li sommi.[169]

Here is indicated the primacy of contemplation. The Eagle goes
on to name certain of these individual members, and of each as
he is named, it says triumphantly: "Ora conosce . . ." "Now
knoweth he . . ." On earth, man must be content not to know.
In heaven, much that has been hidden is revealed to each individual, though there remains the ultimate inability to cope with
divine predestination: "noi, che Dio vedemo, non conosciamo

168. According to Origen, all men might be saved. This idea, however, could
not be called orthodox in Dante's time.
169. "That part in me which seeth and dost endure the sun in mortal eagles,
it began to me, must now fixedly be gazed upon, for of the fires where from out
I make my figure, those with which the eye sparkleth in my head, of all their
ranks are chief." *Par.*, xx, 31-36.

ancor tutti gli eletti."[170] In this regard is to be noted again the careful avoidance by the Eagle of stating or implying "*I* do not know." As in the earlier passage,[171] there is distinction between Man and men, but here this truth is extended to the blessed in heaven.

In brief then, because Dante's journey rehearses the life of Christ as it bore fruit in the church, and also because Dante from one point of view is the typical Christian—"one of the least of the sheep on the pastures of Jesus Christ"[172]—therefore his story and vision are to be read also in the light of all humanity. In that light, place is given even to Dante's personal life and limitations: his bewilderment and failure to understand the justice of his exile, the conviction that through him is to come a triumph. *L'uccel di Dio* contemplates the drama in its entirety: church and empire, Christendom and heathendom, Creation to Final Judgment, all in one. The day will come when the Eagle will say also of Dante, "Ora conosce . . ."

III. SATURN. THE INDIVIDUAL AND THE LADDER

IN Saturn is considered the Body of Christ in its tropological significance. It will be remembered that in the Middle Ages, as with Catholics today, the term "Body of Christ" is to be understood in four significations.[173] The earthly Body of Christ, corresponding to the literal level of symbolism, is that which suffered upon the cross. The mystical Body of Christ, corresponding to the allegorical level, is ideally all Humanity, the total empire and church, including those dead in the Faith, living members, and, in a sense, the unborn. The sacramental Body of Christ, the heavenly Bread of the Eucharist, is given to each member of the mystical Body for his advancement on the way to God, and hence corresponds to the tropological or moral level;[174] while the glorified Body of Christ is that in which he

170. "We, who see God, know not as yet all the elect." *Par.,* xx, 134-135.
171. *Par.,* xix, 52. Cf. pp. 71-72.
172. *Epistle to the Italian Cardinals,* Epistle XI (VIII).
173. Cf. p. 70 and pp. 286-287.
174. "Tropologia est sermo conversivus, pertinens ad mores animi; et magis movet quam allegoria, quae pertinet ad ecclesiam militantem, anagoge ad triumphantem et ad Domini trinitatem." (Tropology is a figurative speech, pertaining to the habits of the soul; and it moves men more than allegory, which pertains

is now present in heaven. There is a mystic sense in which these four are one.

The Incarnation—made historical through the earthly Body, extended to all Humanity in the mystical Body, the church—in the tropological (sacramental) Body is extended especially to the individual soul. This is the Body of which Thomas Aquinas wrote:

> Dedit fragilibus corporis ferculum,
> Dedit et tristibus sanguinis poculum,
> Dicens: accipite quod trade vasculum,
>   Omnes ex eo bibite.
>
> .   .   .   .
>
> Panis angelicus fit panis hominum;
> Dat panis coelicus figuris terminum:
> O res mirabilis, manducat Dominum
>   Pauper, servus, et humilis.[175]

That which is true of Christ is true also of his members: not only have they a corporate life in the Body, governed by the dual vicarate of pope and emperor, in virtue of which, as one, they say "I"; but they have also a private life in the Body, directed by the dual vicarate of philosophy and theology, in virtue of which they say "we."[176] Directed by the knowledge through which Supreme Wisdom expresses himself to men, and nourished by his self-giving in the sacraments, this life by necessity points to a culmination in the mystic quest for knowledge, not reached by all on earth, but the goal of all the blessed in heaven.

Dante, "sotto il petto del Leone ardente," perceives the Ladder of Contemplation,[177] leading up from cold Saturn where he

to the church militant, while anagoge pertains to the church triumphant and to the trinity of the Lord.) Peter Comestor, *Historia Scholastica,* preface; Migne, *P.L.,* 198, col. 1056.

175. "He gave to the weak His Body as food, and he gave to the sad the cup of His Blood, saying: Receive the cup which I give to you, drink ye all of it. . . . The Bread of angels becomes the Bread of men; the Bread of heaven puts an end to types; O wondrous thing, the poor, the servant, and the lowly, feed upon their Lord." Translation from M. Britt, *Hymns of the Breviary and Missal,* p. 187.

176. The scholastic stress upon individualism is well known. Cf. the works of De Wulf on medieval philosophy.

177. *Par.,* xxi, 28-30. Cf. ladder on gown of Lady Philosophy as described by Boethius (*De Consolatione,* 1, pr. 1).

stands, to the regions where is consummated the mystic's quest. It has been suggested that the bosom of the Lion may refer to the star Regulus, known then as *Cor Leonis*. There is, however, a deeper significance to Dante's stellar arrangement in the seventh heaven. Leo, astrologically, is unique as the "sign" of the sun. The Sun is God, and Christ is the Lion of the Tribe of Judah:[178a] thus in the phrase "sotto il petto del Leone ardente" is indicated, "beneath the heart of Christ."

In heraldry an eagle is sometimes found on the summit of a ladder. The ladder is the *scala perfectionis,* and the eagle is the goal of the vision.[178b] Dante's vision of Christ has advanced from the cross which was the sign of his taking unto himself a finite nature, to the separate vision of the two natures, Eagle and Lion, represented in the Grifon of the Terrestrial Paradise. The Ladder is soon to lead him from beneath the heart of the Lion to the fuller vision in Gemini, of Christ in his glorified Body surrounded by the elect.

More than this, the ladder surmounted by the eagle is the standard of the Scaligeri, of Can Grande della Scala.[179, 180] The exile once welcomed in Verona had come to behold in this ladder the means of ascent for himself and for all men from the obscurity in which the only life was through the sacramental Body,[181] from the heart of Christ himself (*il petto del Leone ardente*),[182] to the accomplished vision of the rightful empire

178a. Medieval identification of lion with Christ based also on early conception of nature of lions. Cf. Isidore, *Etymologies,* xii, ii, 5.

178b. Bayley, *op. cit.,* chap. 5.

179. *Par.,* xvii, 70-72.

180. "Dante himself, thanks to the *Scaliger,* the Ladder-bearer, is made ready for the heaven-ascending 'plumes' with which Beatrice will fit him, and so justify interpretation of his name as the *'Alagherius,'* the Wing-bearer." J. B. Fletcher, *The Crux of Dante's Comedy,* p. 38.

181. It is important that for Dante no invalidation of the sacraments was involved in his belief that for the world of his time there was in power no true pope and no true emperor. The modern Roman Catholic doctrine that the validity of the sacraments for the conveying of grace is dependent on communion with the true pope, while not unknown in the time of Dante, became general only after the Council of Trent.

Dante's charge against the false pope is not invalidation of the sacraments, but, through facile excommunication, the withholding from many, "now here, now there,"—or *qui, or quivi*—"the bread the tender Father bars from none"— *lo pan che il pio padre a nessun serra.* (*Par.,* xviii, 128-129.) (It is interesting in this connection that both Can Grande and Dante for a period suffered excommunication. To Dante's mind, a difference of opinion with the pope on a question

and church wherein the mystical Body, the Eagle, should shed forth in its sphere the radiance which should transform the *selva oscura* into the heavenly garden wherein reigns Christ glorified.

Strange as it may seem that the ardor of contemplation should arise from Saturn, coldest and slowest of planets, this is in reality the only symbolism which would be consistent with medieval theology[183] and mysticism. In the spiritual life there must be this duality of the long coldness of discipline and obedience and the glow of devotion and contemplation, in which rest the two feet of the Ladder, philosophy and theology, declared by Dante sole basis for the attainment of blessedness.[184] Trained in such discipline Dante himself turns at a word from the highest ecstasy he has yet known, in instantaneous and unquestioning obedience:

> Qual savesse qual era la pastura
>   del viso mio ne l'aspetto beato
>   quand'io mi trasmutai ad altra cura,
> conoscerebbe quanto m'era a grato
>   ubidire a la mia celeste scorta,
>   contrapesando l'un con l'altro lato.[185]

Dante, gazing upon the Ladder as it stretches up out of the sphere on which he stands, beholds in quick preview the stages

of politics had nothing to do with the question of his loyal Catholicism,—the very point at issue between both the Ghibelline view and Dante's own, and that of the Guelphs.) The sacraments then were valid, however corrupt the representatives of Christ's mystical Body.

Moreover, grace may come direct from Christ to those deprived of physical reception of the sacramental Body, by ignorance, by circumstances, or by wrongful excommunication. This is true in virtue of Christ's eternal self-manifestation to men not only through the literal Body of his life in Judea and through the mystical Body, but also through the sacramental Body. Even those receiving grace before the birth of Christ did so as members of his mystical Body and as spiritual recipients of his sacramental Body. Cf. Thomas Aquinas, *S.Th.*, 3, Q. 80, *art.* 1, *ad primum*. Cf. p. 69, also p. 286 n. 125.

182. Cf. the sphere of Venus, the corresponding sphere in the first triad, where was stressed the primacy of the individual in the state.

183. According to Catholic theology, salvation is neither by works alone (the Pelagian view) nor by grace alone (the Augustinian and Lutheran view); but by both acting together. Similarly the mystic reaches the heights of union not by discipline alone (asceticism), and not by contemplation alone (quietism); but by the practice of both together.

184. Cf. *Monarchia*, 3, 16.

185. "Whoso should know what was the pasture of my sight in the blessed aspect when I changed me to another care, would recognize how much it was my joy to be obedient to my heavenly guide, weighing the one against the other side." *Par.*, xxi, 19-24.

of the mystic way through which it leads. He is given intimation not only of the equal necessity of discipline and grace, but also of the nature of the rational and the suprarational, through his questioning of the soul who comes down to him upon the Ladder.[186] The final teaching is the value of contemplation shown in action, since contemplative souls appear in Saturn, which is not only cold and slow, but inspirer of external rather than internal activity. Without the discipline of Saturn, no man may reach the heights of mysticism which rise as by a ladder from its foundation:

> di color d'oro in che raggio traluce
> vid'io uno scaleo eretto in suso
> tanto, che nol seguiva la mia luce.[187]

For mystic development the ladder or steps of the soul is one of the most frequent symbolisms.

This, the sixth level of symbolism (the third relating to Christ and Humanity) is, like the two preceding, dual, reflecting Christ's dual nature. It is dual in its foundation, philosophy and theology, upon which those nourished by the sacramental Body may rise in the mystic Way, and it is dual also in the aspects of that way of which it gives prevision. Love and obedience, ardor and discipline, are the two motions of the soul.

While Dante stands at the foot of the Ladder of which the other end reaches beyond time and space, of a sudden the heavens are rent as it were by thunder with the outcry of blessed souls. Stupefied by the shock of the sudden transition Dante, *figlio palido e anelo,* turns to Beatrice who in reassurance reminds him of the fundamental law: souls living a life of grace

186. When Dante asked (*Par.,* xxi, 55 ff.) why Peter Damian rather than some other soul had come to him, he was instructed that free love is the cause of obedience; and later, that both the ability to do the duty and the joy of doing it are the fruits of the divine light which raises the soul above itself to God. Nevertheless even souls perfected in love fail to see all of the secret things of God, who remains forever beyond the final comprehension of man. Thus there must be both the discipline of the reason through which man reaches up to God, and the gift of that knowledge which is beyond reason, the depth of which is inevitably beyond his grasp.

187. "Colored like gold which doth recast the ray, I saw a ladder erected upward so far that my sight might not follow it." *Par.,* xxi. 28-30. Cf. such titles of mystical treatises, as Hilton's *Scala Perfectionis,* and Richard of St. Victor's *De Quatuor Gradibus Violentae Charitatis.*

close to the Divine Sun share in the characteristics of his two aspects, creative and destructive; and that love which gives life, light, and warmth to all that responds to it, appears inevitably as destructive when it is contemned, as it was by corrupt rulers and unfaithful Christians in the world Dante knew. Souls in union with God through grace and obedience to grace, pray and are answered not only in individual matters but for the Body which is Humanity.

A further step in solar symbolism, a further lesson in the relation of men to the Sun God, remains:

> Questi altri fuochi tutti contemplanti
> uomini fuoro, accesi di quel caldo
> che fa nascere i fiori e' frutti santi.[188]

The second triad of Dante's symbolism is now complete: God the Sun, whose guidance of Dante (through Beatrice and her emissary) is evident in the Moon and illumined in Mars by his self-revelation in the earthly life of Christ; whose dual vicarate, papacy and empire, over which Guelph and Ghibelline had striven, is clarified in Mercury and illumined in Jupiter through the relationship of the Logos to all Humanity; whose dual governance through natural law and human free will is shown in Venus, appears here in Saturn as the Logos in relationship to individual souls, radiating forth "the warmth which giveth birth to the holy flowers and fruits."

Dante also, as in other places, is here a flower:

> L'affetto che dimostri
> meco parlando, e la buona sembianza
> ch'io veggio e noto in tutti li ardor vostri,
> così m'ha dilatata mia fidanza,
> come 'l sol fa la rosa, quando aperta
> tanto divien quant' ell' ha di possanza.[189]

Although the Rose traditionally represents Christ, or, as in the next canto, his mother[190]—the apostles being lilies—at this level

188. "These other flames were all contemplatives, kindled by that warmth which giveth birth to the holy flowers and fruits." *Par.*, xxii, 46-48.

189. "The love thou showest, speaking with me, and the propitious semblance which I perceive and note in all your glows, hath so outstretched my confidence as the sun doth the rose when it openeth to its utmost power." *Par.*, xxii, 52-57. Cf. also the "garland" ballata.

190. For a discussion of the rose as symbolizing the Virgin, cf. Adams, *Mont-*

in the symbolism Dante appropriates the rose-symbol to himself. Christ who is God lived a life on earth in a human body. Christ lives a permanent corporate life in the totality of humanity, which forms his mystical Body. Christ lives, further, a separate life in each of his members, since the body of each is the temple of God. Dante, in so far as he is a type of Christ, becomes in a sense representative of each of these lives.

In the triad or order of symbolic levels wherein is set forth Dante's personal career and the development of his political and philosophical ideas, complete grasp of the motivation of the first two levels (his visionary journey, his political development) is gained only when light is thrown on them by the third level (his Vita Nuova in love), which is itself not completely understood within its symbolic order. This last fact was emphasized even in its anagoge, where the nature of the triple crown, mirror of the Trinity, was clear only when there appeared in flashing radiance the third crown, of which in itself Dante learned nothing. Thus was the triune nature of God the Sun made evident in the physical sun itself.

Similarly in this second triad,[191] satisfactory meaning for the earthly life of Christ and the painful struggles of Humanity is not reached until Dante attains to the mystic Ladder, which alone leads upward even beyond the place where Christ, with his glorified church, is revealed; yet in no sphere is Dante's desire for information so little gratified as in this of Saturn. The life of the soul in Christ is hidden beneath even its own knowledge. Fundamental in the *Commedia* is this triadal pattern, in which the third of each triad, giving light to its precursors, itself remains obscure until the achievement of a deeper symbolic order,[191] just as in the pattern of the *terza rima* within each group of three is the rhyme-word which demands the next tercet.[192]

Saint-Michel and Chartres, p. 117. For discussion of association of the Rose with Christ and heaven, cf. Busnelli, *Il Concetto* . . ., pp. 233-238. This association is brought out in the ceremonial with which on the fourth Sunday in Lent, the Pope blesses a gold rose.

191. As will be seen in the succeeding chapter, a similar relation of triality exists in the manifestation of evil.

192. Considering the triads formed by the three symbolic meanings, the mystical sense of the latter, the parallel with the pattern of the *terza rima* becomes exact.

Journeying from Mars to Jupiter to Saturn, Dante has seen and represented in its inner meaning the life of Christ on earth, the dual aspect of all humanity, and the typical life of each sheep of his pasture. Dante is, then, as many commentators have pointed out, the typical Christian. The only mistake lies in supposing him to typify this alone.[193]

IV. FIXED STARS. CHRIST AND HIS REDEEMED

In Gemini the three levels of the Christ allegory are gathered up, as were the three levels of Dante's personal story in the Sun. The Eternal Twins, inseparable, though one divine and the other human,[194] are appropriate to the twofold nature of the literal Christ; to the dual aspect of Humanity, the allegory; and to the double nature of the inner life, the spiritual trope. As before, the basis of the summary is the anagoge.

The appearance of the glorified Christ is awaited eagerly by Beatrice, that he, the Sun, may give her light to seek food for Dante, as a bird for its nestling,[195] for throughout the Comedy it has been Beatrice, as the expression of Divine Love, who has inspired Dante in the choice of that on which he shall feed, and has given him the power to choose the bread of angels in pref-erence to the florin-food of Florence. The fuller revelation ap-pears at last, Christ in his glorified Body surrounded by his garden, the flowers and fruits nourished in the rays of his light. Dante had written in his letter to Henry: "All those who hun-ger and thirst shall be filled with the light of his rays, and those who love iniquity shall be confounded by his countenance all aflame." Now he beheld

> sopra migliaia di lucerne
> un sol che tutte quante l'accendea,
> come fa il nostro le viste superne;
> e per la viva luce trasparea
> la lucente sustanzia tanto chiara
> nel viso mio, che non la sostenea.[196]

193. The Pilgrim's Progress type of allegory comes a little later, and repre-sents the decadence of the type. Cf. Chap. IV, pp. 279-281.

194. Cf. *Purg.,* iv, 61.   195. Cf. *Par.,* xxiii, 1-10.

196. "Thousands of lamps surmounting, one sun which all and each en-kindled, as doth our own the things we see above; and through the living light outglowed the shining substance so bright upon my vision that it endured it not." *Par.,* xxiii, 28-33.

Here for the first time, in the full radiance of the glorified Christ, Dante is able to look upon Beatrice and behold her as she is:

> Apri li occhi e riguarda qual son io:
> tu hai vedute cose, che possente
> se' fatto a sostener lo riso mio.[197]

Though no eye may look upon the sun; yet by its light all things are seen.

All that Dante might know of the Beatific Vision on the basis of knowledge of nature alone was summed up in the physical sun. Now that he has beheld the literal truth, the allegory, and the trope of scripture and human history, he is able in the eighth sphere (traditionally identified with the church triumphant,[198]) to penetrate beneath the blinding glory of the sun of sense, to behold the glorified Form of Christ in his Garden, itself but the pale adumbration of the supreme glory of the mystic Rose.

In the "bel giardino che sotto i raggi di Cristo s'infiora,"[199] Dante beheld "la rosa, in che il verbo divino carne si fece . . . li Gigli, al cui odor si prese il buon cammino."[200]

> Come a raggio di sol che puro mei
> per fratta nub, già prato di fiori
> vider, coverti d'ombra, gli occhi miei,
> vid'io così più turbe di splendori,
> folgorate di su da raggi ardenti,
> sanza veder principio dei fulgori.[201]

197. "Open thine eyes and look on what I am; thou hast seen things by which thou art made mighty to sustain my smile." *Par.,* xxiii, 46-48.

198. Cf. G. Busnelli, *Il Concetto e l'ordine del* . . . Here it may be interesting to note that Philo considers eight a particularly sacred number, being the first number after the seven which among other significations represents the incorporeal ideas.

199. "Fair garden which flowereth beneath the rays of Christ." *Par.,* xxiii, 71-72.

200. "The Rose, wherein the Word Divine made itself flesh . . . the Lilies at whose odor the good path was taken." *Par.,* xxiii, 73-75.

The Rose of course signifies Mary (cf. p. 79), while the Lilies are the Apostles. All the flowers of the garden receive their life from the Divine Sun.

201. "As under the sun's ray, which issueth pure through a broken cloud, ere now mine eyes have seen a meadow full of flowers, when themselves covered by the shade; so beheld I many a throng of splendours, glowed on from above by ardent rays, beholding not the source whence came the glowings." *Par.,* xxiii, 79-84.

The meaning, then, of the Incarnation is primarily the rendering fertile, by the Sun, of the earth of humanity to the production of flowers and fruits. To this end Christ suffered, to this end church and empire are formed, to this end philosophy and theology are given to guide the individual soul in its individual effort and in its nourishment by sacramental grace.

Dante is next examined by Peter, James, and John, as to the three theological virtues. These virtues, in Dante's scheme, are related to the four cardinal, somewhat as contemplation is related to action, as theology to philosophy, as church to empire. In each pair both are necessary, the first has the greater honor, and sheds light on the second, but each is supreme within its own realm. Without the four cardinal virtues taught by philosophy, the fulfilment of the three theological virtues may not be accomplished;[202] without faith, hope, and charity, no attainment of heaven would be possible—the three are infused into the soul in baptism by the Divine Sun, and are, as it were, the living sap which causes the plant to flower under his rays.

After this examination in faith, hope, and charity,—conducted by the rightful officers of Christ's mystical (allegorical) Body, and in its outcome signifying that through Christ's sacramental (tropological) Body[203] Dante at last has been brought to perfection, not only in the cardinal, but also in the theological virtues,—the heavens ring with a song so glorious that it is only to be compared to the radiant smile of all the universe:

> Al Padre, al Figlio, alo Spirito Santo,
>   cominciò gloria! tutto il paradiso,
>   sì che m'inebriava il dolce canto.
> Ciò ch'io vedeva mi sembiava un riso
>   de l'universo; per che mia ebbrezza
>   intrava per l'udire e per lo viso.[204]

202. The function of the four cardinal virtues is to lead to the state symbolized by the terrestrial paradise; that of the three theological to lead to the celestial paradise. (Cf. *Monarchia*, 3, 16, quoted, p. 52.) Had Dante failed to reach the terrestrial paradise at the top of the mount of purgatory, obviously he would not have reached the sphere of the theological virtues above. Note also the tradition that the apostles and evangelists themselves symbolize the virtues. Cf. Wm. Molsdorf, *Christliche Symbolik*.

203. Cf. p. 286 n. 125.

204. "All Paradise took up the strain, to the Father, to the Son, to the Holy Spirit, glory! so that the sweet song intoxicated me. Meseemed I was beholding a

In astounding contrast to this radiance heaven is immediately
darkened and reddened in terrible reminiscence of the Inferno,
as Peter officially makes declaration of indignation and dis-
avowal against the present pope. Through the mutual eclipse of
the earthly vicarates, hindering the fulfilment of God's purpose, there has been brought even into the unspeakable joy of
heaven eclipse of the Divine Sun himself. Expression of the
Primal Love appears through storm and darkness. Peter's de-
nunciation reveals the awful truth that

> In vesta di pastor lupi rapaci
> si veggion di qua su per tutti i paschi.[205]

Dante, remembering the shattered rocks of lower hell left by
the earthquake when the universe "felt love"[206] here recalls the
"eclipse in heaven when the Supreme Might suffered."[207] The
corruption of the papacy was no less than a reenactment of the
Crucifixion. In dramatic juxtaposition the poet has beheld the
joy of disciplined and intelligent response to the Infinite Love
which in the Incarnation took unto itself the finite, and the
shock and horror of Love's denial.

After watching the lights go upward like a celestial and reversed snowstorm,[208] Dante looks for the second time at the
spheres through which he has come. His first look backwards
was possible only in the anagoge which gave the true meaning
in Christ to all his vision: it occurred as he entered the starry
heaven, just as his second occurred as he was leaving it. The
reversed snowstorm of fire gives the key to the next three levels.
In all the universe of man snow falls downward and fire moves
upward, unless there has been a breach of divine law.[209] Light-

smile of the universe; wherefore my intoxication entered both by hearing and by
sight." *Par.*, xxvii, 1-6.

205. "In garb of pastors ravening wolves are seen from here above in all the
pastures." *Par.*, xxvii, 55-56.

206. *Inf.*, xii, 34-35. Cf. p. 180. Dante draws the doctrine that love, uniting
the "elements," produces chaos in the material realm, from Empedocles.

207. "Eclissi . . . 'n ciel . . . quando patì la suprema possanza." *Par.*,
xxvii, 35-36.

208. In the rising of Christ and Mary, followed later by the assembly of the
saints, here is symbolized the Ascension of Christ and the Assumption of Mary
in a triumph which recalls the pageant of the church militant in the Terrestrial
Paradise.

209. Cf. *Inf.*, xiv, 28-30.

ning, which constitutes an apparent exception to this statement, is the weapon of the sun-storm god,[210] and as such is regarded as directed against the contemners of his law. Here Dante, who has been led from level to deeper level of meaning in the application of the fourfold method to the second source of knowledge—scripture and human history, as he is about to enter the last realm of time and space, is given a hint of the reversal there to be accomplished.

THE THREEFOLD WAY IN THE DIVINA COMMEDIA
I. PRIMUM MOBILE. MYSTIC INVERSION

ON the great journey undertaken in honor of Beatrice Portinari, the wayfarer has penetrated into the mystery of reality through six significations: two triads, each with its summation in anagoge. The first three have been beheld against the background of nature, as the story first, of Dante's visionary experience in hell, purgatory and heaven, second, of the gradual development of his theory of human government, and third, of the growth of his inner life. Their summary was an adumbration of the Beatific Vision, because in nature, could man but comprehend it, the drama of the universe is completely written. The second three against the background of scripture and history express first the life of the Incarnate Christ, second the progress of Christ's mystical Body (ideally all humanity) in its dual organization under his two vicars, pope and emperor, and third the development of the individual soul guided by philosophy and theology in its individual effort and in its reception of grace by means of the sacramental body of Christ. Their summary was an adumbration of the Beatific Vision because in scripture and history, rightly read, the drama of the universe is completely contained.[211] There remains a study of the revelation within man

210. For the significance of the sun-storm god and his weapon, cf. pp. 109, 213.

211. Dante's conception of the history of the world—including of course the biographies of individual men—as a divine drama in which was worked out the purpose of God, derived from St. Augustine and from the *Historia adversus paganos* of Paulus Orosius (a book written at the suggestion of St. Augustine, to supplement his *De civitate Dei*). Both works refute the pagan attribution of the troubles of Rome to the neglect of the pagan gods, and point out the directing agency of the Christian God in human affairs. Cf. Chap. IV, Pt. I, especially pp. 305-307 n. 187a.

himself, which from discipline and grace through the rational and the suprarational, action and contemplation, may lead to the completion of understanding of that which stands written in nature and in human history.

Just as Dante's personal story has three phases, and Christ's Incarnate Life has three phases, so has the mystical life of the soul.[212] Of the mystic way the first phase, sometimes called purgation, begins with conversion, a turning, and consists in the actualizing of that turning in habits and in life. This "conversion" is more than that which is commonly considered the initiation into the Christian life. It is more than experience or decision, being a complete reversal in perspective.

From the human point of view (as will appear in the next chapters), there is a Worm at the center of the world. Even those who turn to God are as it were turning centrifugally, as far as their perception is concerned. The center of space is the center of the earth, the motionless dark cold lake of Cocytus in which Satan, king of the fires of hell, is freezing.

Cacciaguida had described the sphere in which Dante met him as the "quinta soglia del' arboro, che vive dela cima e frutta sempre e mai non perde foglia."[213] In the Primum Mobile both space and time have their beginnings.[214] That which is apparent

212. Bernard, one of the three mystics to whose books Dante gives special reference (cf. *Epistle to Can Grande*), in analyzing the mystic progress, which to both is a matter of the love of God, finds as it were three roots or three intertwined phases of this love. "Quaerat enim homo eminentiora bona sua in ea parte sui, qua praeëminet sibi, hoc est in anima, quae sunt dignitas, scientia, virtus." Bernard, *De Diligendo Deo*, cap. II.

He goes on to explain that by *dignitas* he means free will, by *scientia* he means the consciousness of freedom given by God, and by *virtus* the seeking and loving of God. The terms are somewhat strange, to modern ears, in this connection, but the meaning is that which has been discussed on a preceding page: advance in discipline (right use of free will), advance in knowledge, and advance in union with God, are the three strands of mystic progress. The fact that Bernard, essentially Augustinian, gives his knowledge a voluntaristic turn, while Dante, a Thomist, translates Bernard's terms into more intellectualistic language, need not obscure the essential similarity of conception. Moreover, it is Bernard whom Dante has acknowledged as his master in mysticism, who stands by his side at the approach to the Beatific Vision.

It is significant also that Bernard follows his definition of the three strands by a statement that each is twofold. It did not need much in the way of insight for Dante to evolve from such statements as this of Bernard's a conception of co-ordinate "pairs" in each of the three main phases of the mystic way.

213. "Fifth range of the tree which liveth from the summit, and ever beareth fruit, and never sheddeth leaf." *Par.*, xviii, 28-30.

214. Dante has discussed at length in the *Convivio* the kinds of motion: ki-

to man in the realm of the finite is but the leaves of the great
tree which become comprehensible only after vision of its roots
in the circle of the first motion:

> Non è suo moto per altro distinto;
>   ma li altri son misurati da questo,
>   sì come diece da mezzo e da quinto.
> E come il tempo tenga in cotal testo
>   le sue radici e ne li altri le fronde,
>   omai a te può esser manifesto.[215]

Here is the first hint of that inversion of outlook which must
come to him who is to be granted vision of things as they are.
Dante came to see why this is a topsy-turvy world.

Humanity, like Circe, daughter of the Divine Sun, has lost
her first beauty:

> Così si fa la pelle bianca nera
>   nel primo aspetto de la bella figlia
>   di quee ch'apporta mane e lascia sera;[216]

because there is none to govern upon earth, "onde sì svia
l'umana famiglia."[217] This loss of perspective on the part of humanity has placed the Worm at the center of the universe, in
such a way that of it even those striving for righteousness and
knowledge must be ever conscious.

There may come, however, a point in each soul's development when the world seems turned inside out, when God instead of the Worm begins to seem (not merely to be believed
to be) the true center. This is the beginning of the mystic way.

Dante, until completely prepared for the inversion which
leads into the supreme heaven itself, was not able to look downwards to the earth. There, finally, having looked outward
toward the universe, he directs his gaze to Beatrice and per-

netic or motion in space; quantitative, or increase and diminution; qualitative, or
transmutation; substantial, or generation and corruption. He points out that did
none of these exist there would be no change and so no Time.

215. "Its movement by no other is marked out; but by it all the rest are meas-
ured, as ten by half and fifth. And how Time in this same vessel hath its roots,
and in the rest its leaves, may now be manifest to thee." *Par.,* xxvii, 115-120.

216. "So blackeneth in the primal aspect the white skin of his fair daughter
who bringeth morn and leaveth evening." *Par.,* xxvii, 136-138.

217. "Wherefore the human household so strayeth from the path." *Par.,* xxvii,
141.

ceives a strange reflection in her eyes. Turning to see its source, Dante perceives the universe turned inside out. (The symbolic connection between contemplation and vision should be recalled.) Instead of a series of concentric spheres, earth in the middle, the Primum Mobile largest in extent, he sees a point flaming with such light that none can look on it. This effulgence is surrounded by nine circles of fire, the largest being slowest. Instead of the spheres, the material embodiment of God's universe, Dante is seeing the truth of each sphere in the angelic intelligences.[218]

Immediately puzzled by this inverse relationship, described as a mirror image,[219] Dante of himself is powerless to comprehend it. The reversal has involved not merely a turning inside out of the universe, but also an inversion in the very time-space relationship in motion.[220]

> E io a lei: Se 'l mondo fosse posto
> con l'ordine ch'io veggio in quelle rote,
> sazio m'avrebbe ciò che m'è proposto:
> ma nel monde sensibile si puote
> veder le volte tanto più divine,
> quant' elle son dal centro più remote.[221]

218. The confusion as to the arrangement of the angels which Dante notes in *Par.*, xxviii, 133-135, is of interest particularly because Dante himself had altered his grouping of them since the writing of the *Convivio.* The two differing arrangements used by Dante are given below. Still different numberings were sometimes given.

	As given by: Gregory in *Moralia* Brunetto Latini in *Tresor* Dante in *Convivio*, 2, 6	As given by: Dionysius the pseudo-Areopagite Dante in *Par.*, xxviii, 98 ff.
Highest Ternary	Seraphim Cherubim Powers	Seraphim Cherubim Thrones
Middle Ternary	Principalities Virtues Dominations	Dominations Virtues Powers
Lowest Ternary	Thrones Archangels Angels	Principalities Archangels Angels

219. Cf. *Par.*, xxviii, 1-4.   220. Cf. *Par.*, xxviii, 16-22.

221. "And I to her: Were the universe disposed in the order I beheld in these then were I satisfied with what is set before me. But in the universe of sense we may see the circlings more divine, as from the center they are more removed." *Par.*, xxviii, 46-51.

The answer is in Beatrice's discourse[222] on the creation of angels: all things in the universe, form and matter, potentiality and actuality, are illumined in their origin from the divine center; and evil itself is rendered impotent. With him who has entered on the mystic way, as with Dante here, no longer may the Worm operate as central in the universe. His monarchy becomes, as Dante beheld it in Cocytus, a negation and a caricature. Such is the reversal accomplished for the mystic in the Way of Purgation through discipline and grace, loosening at last the bonds of time and space.

There follows a period of suspense in deep silence. At length Beatrice, gazing on the point "where every *where* and every *when* are focused,"[223] speaks further to answer Dante's unspoken questions as to that which he beholds. At this moment begins a vision of joy and beauty to convey which symbols themselves fail. Up to this point each mention of Beatrice has been to picture her in a greater glory and effulgence. Now:

> Se quanto infino a qui di lei si dice
> fosse conchiuso tutto in una loda,
> poco sarebbe a fornir questa vice.
> La bellezza ch'io vidi si trasmoda
> non pur di là da noi, ma certo io credo
> che solo il suo fattor tutta la goda.
> Da questo passo vinto mi concedo
> più che già mai da punto di suo tema
> soprato fosse comico o tragedo.[224]

In the Empyrean the truth here indicated is illumined.

II. EMPYREAN (BEATRICE). MYSTIC EXPRESSION

GUIDED by Beatrice, Dante issues at last into the heaven which is pure light: "luce intellettual piena d'amore, amor di vero ben

222. *Par.*, xxix.

223. "Là 've s'appunta ogni *ubi* e ogni *quando*." *Par.*, xxix, 12.

224. "If that which up till here is said of her were all compressed into one act of praise 'twould be too slight to serve this present turn. The beauty I beheld transcendeth measure, not only past our reach, but surely I believe that only he who made it enjoyeth it complete. At this pass I yield me vanquished more than e'er yet was overborne by his theme's thrust comic or tragic poet." *Par.*, xxx, 16-24.

pien di letizia, letizia che transcende ogni dolzore."[225] Here he understands that which has been taught him earlier:

> fonda
> l'esser beato nel' atto che vede,
> non in quel ch'ama, che poscia seconda.[226]

Yet even beyond time and space in the heaven of God himself Dante's perception is through symbols, frail as they have become. Disturbed and puzzled, Dante beholds reflected on the surface of the Primum Mobile, a circle of light which becomes a glowing river bordered by flowering grasses which it showers with sparks. Beatrice, still the sun of Dante's eyes,[227] must again explain. The symbolism has no longer, as he has truly felt, the necessity engendered by time, space, and matter, but retains the necessity engendered by human weakness:

> Il fiume, e li topazii
> ch'entrano ed escono e il rider de l'erbe
> son di lor vero umbriferi prefazii.
> Non che da sè sian queste cose acerbe:
> ma è difetto dalla parte tua,
> che non hai viste ancor tanto superbe.[228]

That this weakness may be taken from him—for symbols, which in time and space are the truth-revealing messengers of the deepest that may be known, are indeed here truth-concealing— Dante must drink with his eyes from the flaming river. Not till the flames have touched his eyelids may he see truly in the *lumen gloriae* without symbolic mask:

> Ad videndum Dei essentiam requiritur aliqua similitudo ex parte visivae potentiae; scilicet lumen divinae gloriae confortans intellectum ad videndum Deum; de quo dicitur; *In lumine tuo videbimus lumen*.[229]

---

225. "Light intellectual full-charged with love, love of true good full-charged with gladness, gladness which transcendeth every sweetness." *Par.*, xxx, 40-42.
226. "The being blessed is founded on the act that seeth, not that which loveth, which after followeth." *Par.*, xxviii, 109-111.
227. *Par.*, xxx, 75.
228. "The river and the topaz-gems that enter and go forth, and the smiling of the grasses, are the shadowy prefaces of their reality. Not that such things are harsh as in themselves, but on thy side is the defect, in that thy sight not yet exalteth it so high." *Par.*, xxx, 76-81.
229. Aquinas, *S.Th.*, 1, *Q.* 12, *art.* 2, resp. Cf. the whole discussion there given as to the nature of vision.

Commentators, however, too often forget that the purgation of Dante's sight has not purged also his readers from the aforesaid human weakness. Dante may suffer vicariously, but the mystic experience is not open to vicarious action. The poet then must perforce express himself to men through symbols, even though he no longer perceives symbolically. The same necessity rests upon God himself. This is the second law of mysticism, the lesson of the Illuminative Way, with its autonomies of the rational and the suprarational. The mystic, ultimately assured that he sees truly, nevertheless can communicate his vision through symbols only. Symbols being in his realm rather truth-concealing than truth-revealing, he is likely to declare his vision incommunicable.[230] The actual vision in the *lumen gloriae* to which the Celestial Rose bears witness, will remain eternally hidden, interpret as we may.

In the Purgative Way, as represented for Dante in the Primum Mobile, is learned the truth about the universe, so here in the Illuminative Way is learned the truth in regard to humanity and angels,—truth which wrings from Dante the prayer:

> Oh trina luce che 'n unica stella
> scintillando a lor vista, sì gli appaga!
> Guarda qua giuso a la nostra procella![231]

Even more overpowering than Dante's vision of the universe turned inside out is his vision of humanity in its true perspective.

Through the inward reversal of purgation and the progressive instruction of illumination, Dante has journeyed, led by Beatrice, love of his childhood and inspiration of his intellectual and spiritual growth. With his progress through the spheres, however, he has found not *one* to understand, possessing the power to read his inmost thoughts, but *many*. Strangely enough, this power possessed by glorified souls of knowing him, as it were from the inside, becomes one of Dante's greatest joys. This

230. Dante stressed the incommunicableness of his experience. Cf. p. 100 and n. 256 on that page.
231. "O threefold light, which in a single star, glinting upon their sight doth so content them, look down upon our storm!" *Par.,* xxxi, 28-30.

joy of complete and immediate consciousness of each other among the Blessed, with its tendency to heighten rather than diminish their separate personalities, is one of the mysteries of the court of heaven, where the response to Divine Love is both corporate and individual.

Although eternally Dante's inspiration, Beatrice may not guide in the Unitive Way which is to come. As symbols have lost their usefulness for perception, so creatures may no longer direct. Bernard himself, saint and mystic, although in a sense succeeding to Virgil and Beatrice, stands by Dante's side not as guide but as sponsor in the realm of the spirit, turning his gaze toward the blessed as they may be seen in God.

He who earlier could not so much as take his eyes from Beatrice, having so long mourned on earth his separation from her, in this second separation, although he perceives the distance, feels no remoteness and so no pain:

> Da quella region che piu su tona
>> occhio mortale alcun tanto non dista,
>> qualunque in mare più giù s'abbandona,
> quanto lì da Beatrice la mia vista;
>> ma nulla mi facea, chè sua effige
>> non discendea a me per mezzo mista.[232]

Having been guided by Beatrice through the ways of purgation and illumination, Dante, now prepared for the way of union, is no longer dependent on her symbolic presence. Moreover, it is only when Beatrice has left his side to take her place in the Rose, that Dante at last forsakes the *voi* of formal address for the greater intimacy of the *tu*. He prays:

> Tu m'hai di servo tratto a libertate
>> per tutto quelle vie, per tutt' i modi
>> che di ciò fare avei la potestate.
> La tua magnificenza in me custodi,
>> sì che l'anima mia, che fatt' hai sana,
>> piacente a te dal corpo si disnodi.[233]

232. "From that region which thundereth most high, no mortal eye is so far distant, though plunged most deep within the sea, as there from Beatrice was my sight; *but that wrought not upon me,* for her image descended not to me mingled with any medium." *Par.,* xxxi, 73-78. (Italics supplied for the present purpose.)

233. "Thou hast drawn me from a slave to liberty by all those paths, by all those methods, by which thou hadst the power so to do. Preserve thy munificence

These are Dante's last words to Beatrice. He adds "quella, sì lontana come parea, sorrise e riguardommi; poi si tornò a l'etterna.fontana."[234]

III. EMPYREAN (BERNARD). MYSTIC PROGRESS

OF the trope, the Unitive Way, and its culmination in the ultimate anagoge, the Beatific Vision (the perfect knowledge of God which issues in perfect love), Dante may express but little. Its law, the third of mystic perception, is the law of ascent through creatures.[235] Not God first comes to Dante's sight, but the lesser saints, each brightness strengthening his vision. In the dual governance of the Way of Union through action and contemplation, progress is thus from contemplation and service of creatures, through ever more glorious creatures, to the Uncreated.

From weakness of vision, springs moral as well as intellectual imperfection. Such imperfection can be healed through accession of light yet the full truth would dazzle and blind like the sun at noonday. The eye must be strengthened gradually through progression from truth to deeper and brighter truth. Thus the journey scheme of the *Commedia* is not merely a dramatic device but is also a symbolizing of a philosophic truth. Man may not gaze on God directly but must approach through the hierarchy of creatures. Under Bernard's tutelage, Dante, who has seen the truth of the universe and of human and angelic life (so far as one who has not yet seen God can see them), sees now the truth of spiritual progress, the law of ascent both on earth and in the realms of the dead. This law, only now clearly known, has been fundamental throughout the journey.[236]

The Blessed Virgin, most glorious of creatures, alone may prepare Dante for the ultimate vision. In this fact is more than the motive of devotion to her in whose womb "si raccese l'amore per lo cui caldo ne l' etterna pace così è germinato questo

in me, so that my soul which thou hast made sound, may unloose it from the body, pleasing unto thee." *Par.*, xxxi, 85-90.

234. "She, so distant as she seemed, smiled and looked on me, then turned her to the eternal fountain." *Par.*, xxxi, 91-93.

235. Cf. pp. 365 ff.   236. Cf. pp. 167, 394.

fiore,"[237] and the recognition of grace mediated by her.[238] Through the supreme clarity of her vision—"non si dee creder che s'invii per creatura l'occhio tanto chiaro"[239] into the eternal light—her brightness alone has power "ogni nube li disleghi di sua mortalità."[240]

Supremely personal as is the ultimate vision, of which even the revelation to another is eternally an impossibility, it is attained in accord with the law of progression from light to light, only through a union with all creatures, intimate beyond the power of the finite mind to conceive. That ardor of discipline and knowledge, which alone can make possible right relation to the universe and to men, prepares for the intimacy with the souls of the Blessed from which the soul is raised to the consummation of the mystic marriage.

Personal life culminating in the Sun, the supreme symbol of the Trinity; corporate life consummated in the Heaven of the Fixed Stars with a vision of Christ and the redeemed, both failed to give full vision of God. The mystic way is indispensable. Clear definition of mystic experience as "supernatural states containing a knowledge of a kind that our own efforts and our own exertions could never succeed in producing"[241] belongs to a later date. Nevertheless, Thomas had stated the theological truth (based on I Cor. 2. 9 and on rational considerations) that man by his own powers cannot reach to the vision of God in his essence.[242] Dante indicates that without mystic experience, some participation in purgative, illuminative, and unitive ways,[243] there is possible no approaching to the fulfilment of the lives of

237. "Was lit again the love under whose warmth in the eternal peace this flower hath thus unfolded." *Par.*, xxxiii, 7-9.

238. "Donna, se' tanto grande e   "Lady, thou art so great and hast such tanto vali, che qual vuol grazia ed a te   worth, that if there be who would have non ricorre, sua disianza vuol volar   grace, yet betaketh himself not to thee, sanz' ali." *Par.*, xxxiii, 13-15.   his longing seeketh to fly without   wings."

This feeling in the Middle Ages was carried to the extreme of belief that Mary saved souls against the word of God and all the saints. Cf. Adams, *Mont-Saint-Michel and Chartres*, pp. 272-273, also 251, 257, 261, 267, 284.

239. *Par.*, xxxiii, 44-45.

240. "To scatter for him every cloud of his mortality." *Par.*, xxxiii, 31-32.

241. Poulain, *Graces of Interior Prayer*, chap. 1 (Engl. tr., p. 3).

242. Aquinas, *S.Th.*, 1, 2, *Q.* 5, *art.* 5.

243. Cf. Chap. V, also pp. 238, 327.

personal virtue and corporate union.[244] The final truth of the Unitive Way is the hierarchical progression from light to light, and its ultimate gift, the Beatific Vision.

IV. EMPYREAN (BEATIFIC VISION). MYSTIC FULFILMENT

OF the great scripture in honor of the miracle who was a nine, symbolic meaning has been distinguished in three orders, consisting each of three levels (literal, allegorical, tropological) together with their respective anagogai, increasingly vivid projections of the ultimate anagoge which is the Beatific Vision. Moreover, these three orders are themselves related as literal story, allegory, and trope, and their anagoge is the ultimate anagoge itself, the Beatific Vision.[245] The symbolic pattern through which Dante's meaning is to be grasped, would appear, then, to be both fourfold and ninefold. By this means Dante has analyzed each of the sources of knowledge in accord with the fourfold method, and accomplished their final unification in a vision of the whole.

At first thought one would have expected the nine levels to correspond with the nine spatial spheres which Dante visits. Indeed, the author made trial of this obvious assumption, only to be convinced that an attempt thus to apportion the nine levels is but an attempt to force fact to fit theory, and can never produce a self-consistent and harmonious whole.

According to Dante's statement, a fourfold interpretation is intended in his ninefold compliment to Beatrice; yet the nine spheres are not divisible by four. Dante's own harmonization of the four and the nine, throughout the structure of the *Commedia,* has been in ten (or its square, one hundred).[246] Thus a

244. Indeed, in a sense, each of the three canticles of the *Divina Commedia* is representative of the appropriate phase of the mystic way.
245. Dante's personal story is analyzed and summarized, against the background of the physical universe, in the first four spheres. His allegorical story as he is significant of Christ is analyzed and summarized, against the background of scripture and history, in the next four. The tropological story, type of the progress of the individual in the mystic way, finds its literal level in the ninth sphere wherein are the roots of time; but its deeper meanings, allegorical and tropological, beyond time and space; and its consummation in the Beatific Vision, wherein is the anagoge of the whole, already foreshadowed in the visions of the Sun and of the Starry Heaven.
246. Cf. Chap. VII, vi.

possible harmonization of the nine and four would be through an arbitrary modification of the fourfold method, as three triads of letter, allegory, trope (the nine spatial spheres) with their ultimate summary or anagoge in the one (Empyrean). It is not, however, Dante's habit to make arbitrary modifications, and, moreover, such a solution fails to accord both with the facts of the *Commedia*[247a] and with medieval symbolic tradition.

All levels of symbolism are not logically to be allotted equal time or space: the progression is toward ultimate truth to be vouchsafed to the mystic where space and time are nonexistent. The stages of the fourfold revelation of Dante's personal life against the spatial background of nature, like the stages of the fourfold revelation of the drama of humanity against the temporal background of history, may each be allotted a sphere in time and space but the stages of the fourfold revelation of mystic progress, against the subjective background of inner experience directed by reason and inspired by grace, must of necessity be telescoped to indicate the spaceless and timeless nature of its culmination in that vision to which man is raised by grace alone. The order of symbolism relating the fourfold story of personal life leads inevitably to the second order of symbolism, by which it is illumined, its allegory, wherein is related the fourfold story of humanity, which in turn demands and is illumined by the third order of symbolism, the trope of progress in insight, springing with the roots of time itself from the Primum Mobile. Thus in the Empyrean by progressive illumination through each of the possible sources of knowledge, there is attained that vision foreshadowed in the sun against the background of nature only, and further illuminated by scripture in Gemini.

That which is beheld in the Sun is clearly the summary and anagoge of Dante's personal story, the center of attention in the first three spheres, and as such is at the same time a foreshadowing of that which is timeless and spaceless; similarly the revelation of the eighth sphere is summary and anagoge of the allegory, given in the preceding three spheres, referring to

247a. E.g., the easier schemes are denied by the content itself, i.e., that which Dante beholds in each of the spheres.

Christ and Humanity. Moreover, the scenes of these anagogai in themselves are significant. They are not in ordinary planetary spheres. Of the first triad the anagoge appears in the Sun, most perfect physical symbol of Deity; of the second, in the Fixed Stars, the background which alone renders visible all planetary motions. Thus they prepare for and indicate their oneness (as opposed to the distinctness of each level of the triads) with the supreme revelation of the Beatific Vision,[247b] for which the immediate preparation is the mystic progress, and wherein is consummated the anagoge of the whole *Commedia*. In other words, Dante has emphasized the fact that the *one* is not merely that which added to the nine makes ten, but is itself an all-pervading tri-unity.[248] Dante, having applied the fourfold method to each of the possible sources of knowledge,[249] has said the

247b. The conclusion of an analysis of an inner life-story with a vision, even though veiled, of the Trinity, would seem to imply the complete arrival of the soul at its ultimate goal. Likewise, with a study of the redemption wrought by Christ in his divine and human natures, the saving organization of man in church and empire, and the appropriation in contemplation and right action of the benefits thus extended to the individual soul,—culmination in a vision of Christ surrounded by his apostles, saints and redeemed, would indicate ultimate conclusion.

248. For a discussion of the nineness, cf. Chap. III, Pt. I.

For a discussion of the four in relation to the nine, cf. Chap. IV, Pt. I.

For a discussion of the four and the ten, cf. Chap. V, Pt. I.

249. Dante, like most students in the Middle Ages, was familiar with the *Sentences*, in which Peter Lombard treats the possible sources of knowledge as four: nature and reason, revelation and grace. A study of Dante's own writings, as well as of those of Thomas Aquinas, makes clear the emphasis given to this division of knowledge in Dante's period. Since the days of Augustine such serious attention had not been given to analysis of inner experience as was given in the thirteenth century. Although earlier the inner experience described as reason and grace was valued chiefly for its elucidation of those external sources of knowledge, nature and scripture—in the thirteenth century it came to be valued for itself; and indeed it is the sole motif of that poem from which sprang the *Divina Commedia*. Dante, in telling of his New Life, records in detail his inner experiences from his first glimpse of Beatrice till his resolution after her death to write a supreme poem in her honor. This poem, then, could scarcely fail to give to inner experience an importance equal to that given to nature and to scripture.

Further, a similar division of the sources of knowledge appears in the *Convivio*, wherein, to those Italian people who had lacked time and opportunity for study, Dante makes offering of that which is the supreme desire of man. "As saith the Philosopher in the beginning of the first Philosophy" so run the first words of the *Convivio*, "all men by nature desire to know." That with which Dante begins, however, is an analysis of his own inner experiences. It is only in the third treatise that he gives actually a kind of medley of information in regard to the natural universe (including philosophy of physical science, of psychological science, etc.), interspersed still with reflections on his relation to Lady Philosophy. From this he turns in the fourth treatise to that sphere in which human

most that can be said of the whole, on which it has been his constant endeavor to "gaze fixedly." At the same time he has obtained a ninefold pattern given eternal meaning in the one and the ten, through which to honor her who is a nine.

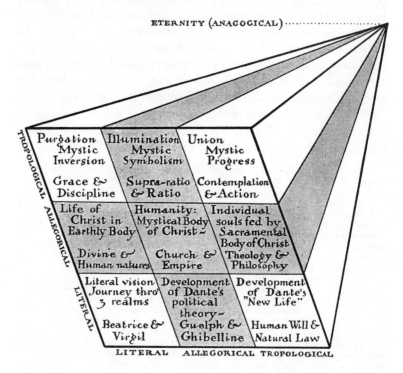

ETERNITY (ANAGOGICAL)

REALITY AS EXPRESSED THROUGH THE FOURFOLD METHOD*

In ten, the oneness, twoness, threeness, fourness, and the Miracle of Nine.

* For full explanation of this diagram and of the cross which forms its center, cf. pp. 468-469, Chap. VII.

voluntary action has its place—the sphere of scripture and history. In discussing true nobility, he presents in brief form that view of Empire which he had developed in such scholarly detail in the learned tongue of the *Monarchia*, and proceeds to discussion of the virtues proper to different ages of men. The body of knowledge presented in the fourth treatise pertains to politics, history, economics and ethics. Here the *Convivio* ends, although there are extant more odes, commentary on which it is thought Dante had intended to include in the *Convivio*. Perhaps the poet's weariness, to which the abrupt ending of the *Convivio*

The mystic significance, and appropriateness to Dante's use, of the number nine will appear more clearly in the following chapters. Nevertheless here it should be called to mind that to medieval thinking nine as the square of three is the symbol of all creation; that as the sum of three, six, and zero, it is the symbol of every circumference; and that it is that number which, multiplied no matter how many times, produces naught but itself.[250] Thus the troubadour of olden times who would say of his lady that to him she was all the world, could do so no more appropriately than by calling her a nine.[251] Dante has done more in making Beatrice symbol of God in creation, leading into the very heart of ultimate being.

Nevertheless, of failure in expression of his supreme vision of the whole, Dante is keenly aware, and now he points out not only the lack of possible symbols but the absence of the symbols of his own memory:

> Da quinci innanzi il mio veder fu maggio
> che 'l parlar nostro, ch'a tal vista cede,
> e cede la memoria a tanto oltraggio.
> Qual è colui che somniando vede,
> che dopo il sogno la passione impressa
> rimane, e l'altro a la mente non riede,

is ascribed, resulted in part from a realization that he had already covered the possible fields of knowledge. In any case, Dante, having set out to present a banquet of erudition, includes knowledge pertaining to the philosophy of objective science, to the philosophy of human relationships, and to the philosophy of inner experience in the search for reality, as he does in his one other work of similar scope, if the present interpretation be correct.

In the *Divina Commedia* is the literal order of symbolism, giving against the background of *natura* the fourfold story of Dante's life; the allegorical order of symbolism, giving against the background of *scriptura* the fourfold story of humanity; the tropological order of symbolism, giving against the background of *reason* the ways of progress in insight; leading to the anagoge, to which man may be raised by *grace* alone. It is further important that each of the orders of symbolism is fully grasped only as given inspiration by the one next higher.

250. Since the sum of the integers of 18, 27, 36, etc., are each 9.

251. Furthermore with reference to her function in the Comedy, nine is the number of the symbolic self-revelation on earth of the Holy Spirit as he appeared at the Baptism of Christ. "Therefore also the Holy Spirit came as a dove, a simple and joyous creature, not bitter with gall, not cruel in its bite, not violent with the rending of its claws, loving human dwellings, knowing the association of one home." Cyprian, *On the Lapsed*, "Ante-Nicene Library," Vol. 8, p. 384. Numerologically, nine is the number of the Dove (801 = 9). Cf. Bayley, *The Lost Language of Symbolism*. Cf. Chap. IV, Pt. II, i.

cotal son io, chè quasi tutta cessa
mia visione, ed ancor mi distilla
nel core il dolce che nacque da essa.[252]

With the initial faint foreshadowing of the Beatific Vision, in
the Sun, Dante had experienced much that followed not his
memory.[253] With the increasing revelation comes the falling
away of those very symbols through which the revelation has
been attained, until the finite mind emerges in utter nakedness
into the presence of the Infinite.[254] The Vision itself, by the ultimate law of symbolism, is devoid of physical imagery; although, the experience being over, memory may retain certain
impressions expressible in symbolic but inadequate terms.[255]
With the approach, the mind progresses not only beyond the
power of symbol to aid, but also beyond the power of symbol to
express; and in consequence by necessity the memory is gradually rendered powerless. This matter to Dante was of such importance that he made of it not only a preface to his few words
about the Beatific Vision, but also a matter of defense in his letter to Can Grande, establishing his own view through the witness of St. Augustine, St. Bernard, and Richard of St. Victor.[256]

252. "Thenceforward was my vision mightier than our discourse, which faileth
at such sight, and faileth memory at so great outrage. As is he who dreaming
seeth, and when the dream is gone the passion stamped remaineth, and nought
else cometh to the mind again; even such am I; for almost wholly faileth me my
vision, yet doth the sweetness that was born of it still drop within my heart."
Par., xxxiii, 55-63.

253. Cf. *Par.*, xiv, 81.

254. According to Thomistic psychology, it is through the progress of the
mind that the ego comes to its closest approach to the Infinite.

255. Cf. Aquinas, *Quaestiones de Veritate*, xiii, 2, and *S.Th.*, 2, 2, Q. 175,
art. 4.

256. Speaking of himself in the third person, Dante writes to Can Grande:
"And when he has said that he was in that place of Paradise . . . he goes on to
say 'that he saw certain things which he who thence descends cannot relate,' and
he tells the reason, saying that 'the intellect is so engulfed' in the very thing for
which it longs, which is God, 'that memory cannot follow.' To understand which
things be it known that the human intellect, when it is exalted in this life, because of its being co-natural and having affinity with a sejunct intellectual substance, it is so far exalted that after its return memory fails it, because it has
transcended the measure of humanity. And this we are given to understand by
the apostle, speaking *ad Corinthios*, where he says, 'I know such a man (whether
in the body or out of the body, I know not, God knoweth), who was rapt into
Paradise and heard hidden words, which it is not lawful for a man to utter.'
Behold, when the intellect had transcended human measure in its ascent, it remembered not the things that took place beyond its own range. . . . And if all
this suffices not the carpers, let them read Richard of St. Victor in his book *De*

According to the thought of the time human intelligence had just power enough to understand how far beyond the scope of its comprehension lay the vision of the ultimate.

After this final summation of the laws of symbolism, Dante suggests in a minimum of words the summation of the whole meaning of his *Commedia*. His first sight within the depths of the eternal light is of the unification of all existent things, all their qualities, all their relationships, this being necessary because

> il ben, ch' è del volere obietto,
> tutto s'accoglie in lei; e fuor di quella
> è difettivo ciò ch' è lì perfetto.[257]

All the truths of the universe and their relationships are here "legato con amore in un volume, cio che per l'universo si squaderna."[258] There is, however, no attempt at communication of his vision.

Suggestion follows of the mystery of the Tri-unity, in the symbol of the circles:

> Ne la profonda e chiara sussistenza
>   de l' alto lume parvemi tre giri
>   di tre colori e d'una contenenza;
> e l'un da l'altro come iri da iri
>   parea reflesso, e 'l terzo parea foco
>   che quinci e quindi igualmente si spiri;[259]

Contemplatione, let them read Bernard *De Consideratione,* let them read Augustine *De Quantitate Animae,* and they will cease to carp. But if they yelp against the assignment of so great exaltation, because of the sin of the speaker, let them read Daniel, where they will find that Nabuchodonosor, too, was divinely enabled to see certain things against sinners, and then dropped them into oblivion; for he 'who maketh his sun to rise upon the good and the evil, and sends his rain upon the just and the unjust,' sometimes in compassion, for their conversion, sometimes in wrath, for their punishment, reveals his glory, in greater or less measure, as he wills, to those who live never so evilly." *Epistle to Can Grande,* para. 28.

257. "The good, which is the object of the will, is therein wholly gathered, and outside it that same thing is defective which therein is perfect." *Par.,* xxxiii, 103-105.

258. "Bound by love in one volume, the scattered leaves of all the universe." *Par.,* xxxiii, 86-87.

259. In the profound and shining being of the deep light appeared to me three circles, of three colors and one magnitude; one by the second as Iris by Iris seemed reflected, and the third seemed a fire breathed equally from one and from the other." *Par.,* xxxiii, 115-120.

yet Dante immediately exclaims: "O luce etterna che sola in te sidi, sola t'intendi, e, da te intelletta e intendente te ami ed arridi!"[260] The union of the divine and human natures in Christ, indicated in the terms of Catholic theology, is illuminated in a flash which, taking complete possession of the personality, renders impossible any attempt to express it.

Such vision, Thomas teaches, is the beatitude of man, and its necessary and attendant consequence is the perfect harmony of the will with the will of God. Thus is fulfilled the aim of each and every level of the *Commedia*—Dante's miraculous journey, his political theorizing, his new life in love; the earthly life of Christ, the corporate life of humanity, the normal spiritual life of the individual soul; the reversal of world-view of the mystic, his view of the world as symbol, and his progress from light to light. This fulfilment is in the motivation of human desire and will, "sì come rota ch' igualmente è mossa," by "l' amor che move il sole e l' altre stelle."[261]

From perfect contemplation Dante returned to action, that he might "remove those living in this life from the state of misery and lead them to the state of felicity."[262] It remains now to undertake the journey from the mouth of hell to Paradise, attempting to disentangle in the story of the *Inferno* and the *Purgatorio* that web of symbolism of which the only solution is the final vision. Dante attained his goal through discipline and grace, and so as a consecrated messenger he must lead mankind in the same arduous journey, from the place where the Sun is silent, to the eternity of illumination where the Sun compels silence.

260. "O Light eternal who only in thyself abidest, only thyself dost understand, and to thyself, self-understood, self-understanding, turnest love and smiling!" *Par.*, xxxiii, 124-126.
261. "Even as a wheel that moveth equally, by the Love that moves the sun and the other stars." *Par.*, xxxiii, 144-145—the last words of the *Commedia*.
262. *Epistle to Can Grande,* para. 15.

CHAPTER III. SCHEMA

PART I

I. Materials of Dante's symbolism formed against the background of the natural universe through centuries of cultural development. Study of origin of myth and symbol reveals two focal materials of symbolism. Sun (macrocosmic) and sex (microcosmic) symbolisms for deity lead to trinitarian development. Syncretism of first centuries of Roman Empire resulted in solar pantheism.

II. Through cultural conflict, philosophy of insight symbolism assumed prominence. During period of syncretism the solar trinity of life, light, and heat was central in unification of thought. From it were drawn concepts of infinity, unity, value and limitation of symbolic expression. Through it embryonic medieval tradition was preserved to conquer and assimilate pagan heritage.

III. The orthodox definition of deity for Dante's tradition accomplished through use of this imagery. Paradox of Eternal Generation of the Son expressed without paradox in relation between Sun and Radiance. During the so-called Dark Ages interest shifted from veneration of Infinite Wisdom to dread of Divine Power and Judgment, giving way in the twelfth century to new appreciation of Infinite Love. Such was the background of the threefold light on which, as focus of Dante's symbolic materials, the structure of the *Commedia* depends.

PART II

The first order of Dante's symbolism consists of the application of the fourfold method to the materials of symbolism as they relate to the first of man's four sources of knowledge—the natural universe (spatial), given focus in the triune sun. The literal events of the vision relate allegorically the political, and tropologically the moral, vicissitudes which Dante experienced in the working out of his life as a citizen of Florence; the solution in anagoge was revealed only in the threefold light of the *Paradiso*. The method here employed is that of commentary, as being best illustrative of the progressive understanding which played so large a part in Dante's dramatic method. The pattern of interpretation, which is in harmony with the tradition to which Dante fell heir, is given on page 156, *q.v.*

CHAPTER III. SYMBOLISM IN MEDIEVAL THOUGHT: ITS CENTER IN THE SUN

Ciò che non more e ciò che può morire
non è se non splendor di quella idea
che partorisce, amando, il nostro
sire;
chè quella viva luce che sì mea
dal suo lucente, che non si disuna
da lui nè da l'amor ch' a lor
s'intrea,
per sua bontate il suo raggiare aduna,
quasi specchiato, in nova sussistenze,
etternalmente rimanendosi una.

That which dieth not, and that which
can die, is nought save the reglow of
that Idea which our Sire, in loving,
doth beget; for that living Light which
so outgoeth from its Source that it departeth not therefrom, nor from the
Love that maketh three with them,
doth, of its goodness, focus its own
raying, as though reflected, in nine existences, eternally abiding one.

THE ninefold veil[1a] which for Dante in the region of the spheres was gradually drawn aside, was the subject of the preceding chapter. This ninefold revelation through symbol has appeared not only as a veil tempering the brightness of the sun to the weakness of human vision, but also as the means of access. Each triad, with its fulfilment in the Beatific Vision, may now be considered separately against the background of the conception formed of it in the medieval world, in the detail with which Dante came to understand it on his journey through the intricacies of the time-space universe. Such will be the task of this chapter and the two succeeding.

On the basis of insight symbolism (distinguished both in definition and in philosophy from every other type of imagery), and of the fourfold method which the Middle Ages had shaped to govern its use, Dante's symbolic pattern sketched in the preceding chapter, becomes for his subject natural and inevitable. His choice of symbolic devices none the less remains a bit puzzling unless one be content to attribute it to the poetic license of the genius. Once more it must be recalled that for Dante beauty unsupported by reason was vapid. As a matter of fact, the materials of his symbolism had been shaped to his hand in the medieval tradition, just as truly as had the method.[1b]

1a. First his fictive narrative, his formulation of civic theories, and the development of his inner life; then the Incarnate Life of Christ, its extension to humanity in church and empire, its extension to the individual soul in grace and discipline; finally, the mystic inversion of the sense-world, the mystic function of symbolism, and the mystic recognition of hierarchy in the universe.
1b. Cf. Chap. IV for the development of the fourfold method.

Just as for the foundation of the symbolic tradition it was necessary to go back to the primitive origins of symbol and of language itself; so as to the materials of symbolism, information is to be sought in the earliest discernible records of primitive man, even below the horizon of history. To seek such knowledge is an appropriate labor for one who has attempted to follow Dante, for it was the whole universe and the whole of human history which Dante in his *Commedia* sought so to unify as to enable the human mind "to gaze fixedly."

PART I. THE SUN IN MEDIEVAL TRADITION (PHILOSOPHY)

I. MATERIALS OF SYMBOLISM

AMID the conflict of theories which befog modern endeavor to peer below the horizon of history, there have been indicated two fundamental oppositions: the one as to the spiritual versus the pseudo-scientific content of early myth and symbol,[2] the other as to the origin of religion in the worship of sun or of sex.[3] The former is important to symbolic method, the latter[4] to analysis of materials of symbolism, the purpose of this chapter.

As a matter of fact it were impossible that the sun should not be one of the first objects to demand the attention of primitive man. Not only was it inescapable as a subject for meditation, but it was peculiarly inspiring to imagination in the creation of a medium of expression. Repeated experience of its daily and yearly course early suggested, as is well known, comparison with the cycle of man's life, passing from activity to sleep or from the dawn or spring of childhood to the evening or winter of old age. From this it is but a step to ideas of immortality, associated with the recurrence alike of dawn and of spring. The sun, indeed, was the only object in experience, the rhythm of which consisted as it were in the recurrence of rebirth, with at the same time no discernible change in substance or in indi-

2. As mentioned in the introductory chapter, and discussed in Appendix to Chap. I, iii.
3. Cf. Appendix III, Pt. I, i.
4. Which persists in the two most modern approaches to the subject: in the historical as well as in the psychoanalytical school. With the former are associated such names as those of Dr. Rivers, Dr. G. E. Smith, and Mr. Perry; while the latter is represented by Drs. Freud, Jung, Rank, Stekel, Hinkle, and others.

viduality. Again, through consideration of the sun in its relation to man and the world of nature there comes soon its para-
doxical identification as Giver of life and light, and Destroyer.

In noting the association of lightning with the sun god, Carlyle ascribes it to the fact that a hot sultry day in summer is the
presage of a storm. However this may be, the identification of
sun and storm divinities is familiar in primitive literature, for
example in stories of Zeus (*Dyaus pitar*) and in legends of the
Irish sun heroes Curoi and Cuchulain. The description of the
riastradh or distortion of Cuchulain is especially worthy of remark: he tucks his feet behind him, shoots out streamers of
blood-red light; clouds and mists gather, and at the end he
leaps into his chariot and performs his thunder feat before going into battle.[5] Compare with this the primitive Babylonian
description:

He set the lightning in front of him.
His body was filled with a glancing flame of fire.
He made a net wherewith to enclose Tiamat.
He made the four winds to take up their position so that no part of her
    might escape:
The South wind, the North wind, the East wind, the West wind

.   .   .   .

The Lord raised up the wind storm, his mighty weapon.
He went up into his chariot, the unequalled and terrible tempest.
He equipped it, he yoked thereto a team of four horses,
Pawing the ground, champing, foaming, [eager to] fly

.   .   .   .

His brightness streamed forth, his head was crowned [thereby].[6]

Again, in an early prototype of the story of *Gawain and the
Green Knight,* Yellow, son of Fair, and Terror, son of Great

5. A letter from Abi Milki of Tyre to Amenhotep IV (as king, the earthly
representative of the All Glorious One) shows the influence of the same conception:
    "To the king, my lord, my god, my Sun. . . . My lord is the sun that riseth
over the earth day by day, according to the bidding of the Sun, his gracious
Father. It is he in whose moist breath I live, and at whose setting I make my
moan. He maketh all the lands to dwell in peace by the might of his hand: he
thundereth in the heavens like the storm-god so that the whole earth trembleth
at his thunder . . ." E. A. T. Wallis Budge, *Tutankhamen, Amenism, Atenism
and Egyptian Monotheism,* p. 101. The letter is not intended as an expression of
adulation, but as a sober appeal for help against invasion.
    6. From the fourth tablet of Creation, described in the British Museum
pamphlet, *Babylonian Legends of the Creation* . . ., 1921, pp. 50-52.

Fear, are identified as the giant antagonist. There is no difficulty in such an identification, since, like the sun god, the storm
god has his life-giving as well as his destructive aspect. His gift
being rain, he may counteract the destructiveness of the too
great heat of his other form. This recognition of sun and storm
as different aspects of one power made possible to the primitive mind a monism rather than a dualism. From the very dawn
of mind on earth there would appear to have been felt a peculiar relationship between oneness and twoness[7] appearing as a
tension which at times was an irresistible attraction and at
others a repulsion. Myths gather about one element, building
man's universe into a unity, and again dissipate, different stories
which once had told of different aspects of one power, becoming stories of a multitude of heroes. In such stories early man
has left record of his progress in the differentiation and analysis
of his experience, and in gradual reconciliation of its contradictions.

MYTH PATTERN

Throughout this flux, however, there has been a constancy of
pattern, shaping the myths of all races and of all ages. The
story in its complete form centers in the "fatal child" who is to
deal the deathblow to his parent. He is exposed, rescued, attains
the triumph of the Ugly Duckling, and in his triumph fulfils
the prenatal prophecy. He loves a radiant maiden whom he forsakes or slays; or he may have many brides. In the end the beloved of his youth returns. Occasionally there is an identification of bride and mother, to both of whom the hero inevitably
brings suffering.

Though this fated being has a capricious and malign aspect,
his character is brave, generous, and self-sacrificing, and his life
is one of suffering and toil for others. Often he is a slave, given
impossible tasks. He is a great traveler, and a destroyer of monsters and noxious beasts harmful to the fertility of the land.
He has blue eyes, sometimes only one eye, and among dark
races as well as fair, his face is always gleaming and his hair
golden. He is mantled in clouds, his garments are dazzling,

7. For the fuller development of this idea, cf. Chap. IV, Pt. I, i.

sometimes destructive, and his weapons never fail. In battle he is brilliant, and his followers are powerless without him; but his doom is early death, which can be accomplished only by his own sword. Another common feature of myths is the journey to the Otherworld, often to rescue a captive or captives. Finally, before his tragic death the hero is considered aged or maimed; the maintenance of fertility requires that he be slain and his place taken by a "young god" of fresh virility.

Most myths fit into this plot or into some section of it, either as they arose originally or as they accumulated about the person of some prominent hero: examples are the myths of Hercules, Tantalus, Adonis, Attis, Osiris, Odin, Beowulf, Krishna.[8] The process of accretion has received frequent comment, not only in the case of Arthur, but also in that of Christ.

SOLAR AND SEX CYCLES

It is maintained by those who hold to the solar origin of myth that the story just roughly sketched represents the daily and annual course of the sun. The brief infancy story corresponds to the period just preceding sunrise, the idyllic young love story to the dawn, the bride being the Dawn Maiden;[9] while the many brides are the countries (or perhaps the waters)[10] on which the sun shines, and the children all earthly vegetation. The life of toil and suffering (usually involved in slavery),[11] is

8. Others are: Belus, Ammon, Saturn, Ra, Jupiter, Pan, Serapis, Aesculapius, Mithra, Pluto, Apollo, Atys, Bacchus, Theseus, Jason, Tammuz, Manu, Buddha, Roland, Havelok, Arthurian heroes, Olger the Dane, Guy of Warwick, all the Great Fools of traditional legend. Cf. also p. 125 n. 70.

9. For example, Surya (an Aryan sun god) is the husband of the dawn, but the dawn is also his mother. Here is the germ, perhaps, of the Oedipus myth. It should be noted that the mothers of dawn maidens and sun gods frequently die at their birth. G. W. Cox, *Mythology of the Aryan Nations,* pp. 81 and 90.

10. Krishna marries 16,100 maidens *at the same time* but in separate mansions, in such a manner that each one thinks he has wedded her alone. After citing this story from the Vishnu Purana, Cox comments: "To suppose that this is the arbitrary invention of a poet living in a polygamous society is beyond measure ludicrous. The essence of the story lies in the simultaneous marriage of a countless multitude to one single being . . . when the shades have been driven away, the same sun is reflected in the thousands of sparkling drops." *Ibid.,* pp. 22-23.

11. Hercules, who in the 11th Orphic hymn is addressed as "the strength and power of the sun" well exemplifies this long servitude—"one continued self-sacrifice for the good of others, his most marked characteristic being an irresistible bodily strength, which is always used to help the weak and suffering,

the sun's journey on his fated course through the heavens, slaying poisonous and evil things in his light and heat, the weapons that never fail. Finally, the return of the young bride is evening,[12] and the descent to the Otherworld is the unseen journey at night from west to east. The period during which the hero is maimed, involving a curse on the land, corresponds to winter. During this period the sun's bride—dawn and twilight, queen of the moon,[13] goddess of fertility—also becomes ugly, often shorn of her hair (rays of brightness). The slaying of the old god by the young god, who is the same divine being with his youth restored, is the annual resurrection at the vernal equinox. The outline of the story is somewhat as follows: The young god is fated to engage in terrible combat and goes on a quest for it, spending a night with a glorious host, the old god in his sun aspect, and by him is directed onward. His next guidance is from a giant herdsman, who treats him churlishly, the old god in his vegetation aspect (Pan).[14] Ultimately, having met his

and for the destruction of all noxious things. The great harvest of myths which has sprung up round his name may be traced to the old phrases which had spoken of the glorious sun as toiling for so poor and weak a creature as man; as born to a life of toil; as entering on his weary tasks after a brief but happy infancy, and as sinking finally to his rest after a fierce battle with the storm clouds which had sought to hinder his journey." *Ibid.*, p. 101.

The less noble Samson also is a great laborer for his people. His hair, the loss of which robs him of his strength, represents the sun's rays. Dr. Jung states also that the slaying of the fish monster Mishe-Nahma by the hero of the Hiawatha legend "is the typical myth of the work of the hero, distributed over the entire world." C. G. Jung, *Psychology of the Unconscious,* pp. 336, 381.

12. This story, according to Cox, was regarded by primitive man as a drama. "The Dawn appears, full of light, life and love. For a few moments she seems to rejoice in the love of the newly risen sun; but his splendour then becomes fatal to her, and she is seen no more, while he goes on his weary way, mourning for the love which he has lost, toiling for the benefit of weak and worthless men, and hurrying on to his home in the west where he knows that he shall behold the face of the radiant maiden whom he had deserted or driven away at the beginning of his career. She too has had her troubles. Her love has been sought by those who would make her faithless to her husband, but she comes forth scathless from the ordeal, only to see the being to whom her heart is given smitten down by the blackness of death almost as soon as she is reunited to him." Cox, *op. cit.,* pp. 53-54. Cf. also, e.g., W. N. Matthews, *Navaho Legends,* especially pp. 104 ff.

Dr. Jung sees the same thought operative even in Christianity: "It can be said that in the morning the goddess is the mother, at noon the sister-wife, and in the evening again the mother, who receives the dying in her lap, reminding us of the Pieta of Michelangelo. . . . This thought has been transferred as a whole into Christianity." Jung, *op. cit.,* p. 272.

13. For different symbolism in regard to the moon, cf. p. 231.

14. For the identification of sun god and herdsman, cf. for example the fol-

terrible opponent, the old god in his storm aspect, the young
god conquers, takes the old god's house (sky) and wife (the
vegetation goddess, herself now made beautiful).[15] Fertility is
restored and the curse removed from the land. Such facts as that
the young god is always the son of the old god, reared by foster
parents,[16] bear witness to a consciousness that the god is always
the same, regenerated in suffering like the Phoenix.[17] Here
again is the tension between oneness and twoness or diversity,
illustrated in another aspect by the primitive sacrifice in which

lowing lines from the Egyptian hymn (1400 B.C.) more of which is quoted on
pp. 220.

> "Valiant herdsman who drives cattle,
> Their refuge and the giver of their sustenance,
> Who passes by, running the course of the sun-god."

15. Cf. the various tales in which the hero by his love for an ugly hag renders
her young and beautiful once more. Cf. also the Parsifal legends, discussed in
Chap. VI.

16. Dr. Loomis points out that the young god always is reared by a foster
mother. An explanation is given by Dr. Jung, who declares that the sun story
expresses the perennial desire of man for regeneration and eternal life, to be
gained by rebirth, hence the necessity of two mothers, the foster parent theme,
and also the incest theme. He says: "It is most especially the totality of the sun
myth which proves to us that the fundamental basis of the 'incestuous' desire
does not aim at cohabitation, but at the special thought of becoming a child
again . . . of coming into the mother once more in order to be born again . . .
Thus the libido becomes *spiritualized in an imperceptible manner*. The power
'which always wishes evil' thus creates a spiritual life." Jung, *op. cit.*, p. 251.

Again, in burial, "the dead are delivered back to the mother for rebirth."
Ibid., p. 264. Also, "the burial of the dead in a holy place . . . is restitution
to the mother, with the certain hope of resurrection by which such burial is
rightfully rewarded." *Ibid.*, p. 407. For the two mothers, Dr. Jung cites the
myths of Hercules, Hiawatha, Buddha, Romulus and Remus, and the second
mother of the Christian in the second birth of baptism, namely, the Cross of
Christ. *Ibid.*, pp. 356-357. Another example is Siegfried. *Ibid.*, p. 392.

17. "When the Sun-god fights against the summer heat, he fights against himself, and when he kills it, he kills himself. Most certainly! The Phoenician, Assyrian, and Lydian ascribes self-destruction to his sun-god, for he can comprehend
the lessening of the sun's heat only as a self-murder. He believed that the sun
stood at its highest in the summer and its rays scorched with destroying heat:
thus does the god burn himself, but he does not die, only rejuvenates himself."
Steinthal, in *Zs. für Völkerpsychologie*, Vol. 2, p. 133. (Cf. with this rejuvenating self-destruction the story of the Phoenix, briefly discussed on pp. 139-
140.)

Herr Steinthal continues: "Also Hercules burns himself, but ascends to
Olympus in the flames. This is the contradiction in the pagan gods. They, as
forces of nature, are helpful as well as harmful to men. In order to do good and
to redeem they must work against themselves. The opposition is dulled, when
either of the two sides of the forces of nature is personified in an especial god,
or when the power of nature is conceived of as a divine personage; however,
each of its two modes of action, the benevolent and the injurious, has an especial symbol."

each year new human victims were slain as annually recurrent incarnations of the unchanging deities of sun and fertility.

This story of the sun is embedded in the consciousness of the race and of the individual, and its impress is deep on religious ceremonial.[18] Through it, moreover, every human experience may find expression.

On the other hand, just as the sun in man's external environment was the element most powerfully attractive to his thought, and could become an organizing principle for his experience, so also was sex in man himself;[19] and indeed, it forms as good a basis as does the sun for the myths, the fundamental pattern of which has been outlined.[20] In reality, similar deductions are made from both. Sex symbolism, however, need not receive separate discussion here, since with developing culture it tends to be taken up into the symbolism of the sun. In Dante's tradition in the Middle Ages, sex symbolism added richness to solar symbolism, while existing, generally unrecognized, as an undercurrent.[21]

18. Most primitive religious custom and ceremonial fits into the typical myth pattern: a striking example is presented in the many forms of the annual vegetation sacrifice. It has been pointed out repeatedly that "The profound fundamental connection between the ceremonies of the great world religions and the facts of nature is shown by the way in which they are grouped round the story of the year." Generally the great festivals fall upon the two solstices and the two equinoxes. It is well-known that Christmas (the winter solstice) is always the birthday of the hero. Easter, the vernal equinox, marks his sacrifice and regeneration or resurrection. The summer solstice, although observed with Midsummer celebrations, especially among agricultural peoples tends to be suppressed, probably owing to the exigencies of the harvest. It should be noted however that among wandering tribes such as for example the American Indians, the date for the great Sun Dance (during which all that may pass the lips of the dancer is water made pure by the sun god) falls within the zodiacal sign (Cancer) of the summer solstice, and thus just before the entrance of the sun into Leo, the sign of his greatest power. Because of its position in the southward, or declining course of the sun (as viewed from the northern hemisphere), the autumnal equinox is less stressed. In the Christian calendar, although the winter solstice and the vernal equinox are marked by the two greatest of feasts, Christmas and Easter, the Nativity and Resurrection of the *Sol Verus,* all four critical points of the sun are marked by "Ember Days," three days each at each of four seasons, the purpose of which is special prayer for, and dedication of, the priesthood.

19. The student who prefers to see experience in the development of human organization as fundamental in primitive thought and myth-making is in reality but reaffirming the centrality of the power of generation, as any study of primitive society makes clear. Cf. also Appendix III, Pt. I, i.

20. Cf. also Sir J. G. Frazer, *The Golden Bough.* For a graphic popular presentation of the story, cf. the descriptions by Mr. F. Britten Austin in the *Saturday Evening Post* for Feb. 13 and Mar. 13, 1926.

21. Cf. Chap. V, and also Appendix III, Pt. I, i.

The ease with which the unification of the two can be accomplished is important for its bearing on the ideals of courtly love, the love quest of the mystic, and Dante's union of both in the love of the Court of Heaven. Not a few scholars have pointed out the very close connection existing between sun and sex. The cross, early connected with each, has been used often as a bridge, leading many to the conclusion that Christianity is nothing short of a perverted worship of sex. This view is supported by a modern writer[22] in the summary: "It is not difficult to discern how the cross, originating as an emblem or symbol of sexual union, became connected with the worship of the sun . . . for the attributes of the sun are the same as those of sex. For instance, the sun is a creator of life upon this planet; so is the male lingam. The sun gives warmth to the land, and sex gives warmth to the love of man and woman; the sun is capable of rebirth each day, and the soil, which it impregnates, gives birth to new life annually; even so, the phallus is capable of imparting new life, daily and annually . . . in this way, the paths of both forms of worship—Sun worship and Sex worship —did cross one another, and *the symbols of the sexual nature of all life could be used with ease to represent the Sun—its center.*"[23] Whatever may be thought with regard to the deductions, the statement of the connection of sun and sex symbolism through the idea of fertility is well founded.[24]

22. One of many: cf., e.g., A. J. Storfer, *Marias jungfräuliche Mutterschaft* . . . (Berlin: Barsdorf, 1914), *et al.;* Thomas Inman, *Ancient Pagan and Modern Christian Symbolism Exposed and Explained* (London, 1869) ; etc.
23. G. T. Hastings, *Love, Evolution, and Religion* (White Plains: Hastings, 1924), Bibl., pp. 305-308.
24. The following practice is recorded by Sir J. G. Frazer (*The Golden Bough* [3d ed.], Vol. 2, pp. 98 ff.) : "Once a year, at the beginning of the rainy season, Mr. Sun comes down into the holy fig-tree to fertilize the earth, and to facilitate his descent a ladder with seven rungs is considerately placed at his disposal . . . and is adorned with carved figures of the birds whose shrill clarion heralds the approach of the sun in the East. On this occasion . . . the mystic union of the sun and the earth is dramatically represented in public, amid song and dance, by the real union of the sexes under the tree."
The Golden Bough abounds in examples of varied uses of sexual union (or continence) to promote the fertility of the land. In connection with these there is frequently the idea of the incarnation of a divine child and more and more instances are being discovered like that pictured at Deir el Bahari, in which the cross is closely associated. In this case the frog goddess is pictured "holding out to the newly created figures the symbol of life, the *crux ansata,* in order that they may breathe and live." *Ibid..* p. 132.
Sun and sex symbolisms are conjoined in the depths of racial experience. Of this fact plant and tree myths, which reappear in so much ,even of the present

Indeed, this writer failed to point out all the paths of inter-connection. An important omission is the fact that sex, like the sun, has its destructive as well as its creative aspect.[25] Moreover, the phallus, like the sun, was associated with healing, and with both sun and sex is connected a sacrificial element culminating in a regeneration and eternal life. The individual, like the hero, whether sexual or solar, if he is to live "must fight and sacrifice his longing for the past, in order to rise to his own heights. And having reached the noonday heights, he must also sacrifice the love for his own achievement, for he may not loiter." Even as sacrifice of the parent is demanded in fulfilment of the biological law of racial development, his life given for the coming generation, so "the sun also sacrifices its greatest strength in order to hasten onwards to the fruits of autumn, which are the seeds of immortality; fulfilled in children, in works, in post-humous fame, in a new order of things, all of which in their turn begin and complete the sun's course over again."[26] Again, even as the sun hastens yearly on to autumn, so he goes down daily to his death in the west, in preparation for the rebirth of morning, a fact deeply buried in the human feeling that to "go West" is to go on to death. "This western land is the land of the setting sun, whither Hercules, Gilgamesh, etc., hasten with the sun, in order to find there immortality, where the sun and

nursery fairy lore, is an example. "Osiris lies in the branches of the tree, sur-rounded by them, as in the mother's womb. The motive of *embracing and en-twining* is often found in the sun myths, meaning that it is the *myth of rebirth*. A good example is the Sleeping Beauty, also the legend of the girl who is en-closed between the bark and the trunk, but who is freed by a youth with his horn. The horn is of gold and silver, which hints at the sunbeam in the phallic meaning . . . An exotic legend tells of the sun-hero, how he must be freed from the plant entwining around him." Jung, *op. cit.,* p. 272.

25. As the student of the human personality declares from his point of view, "the libido is fructifying as well as destroying." (Jung, *op. cit.,* p. 316.)
Dr. Jung also comments on the Book of Job:
"God is like the behemoth and the leviathan, the fruitful nature giving forth abundance—the untamable wildness and boundlessness of nature—and the over-whelming danger of the unchained power. But what has destroyed Job's earthly paradise? The unchained power of nature, . . . the God who created such monstrosities, before whom the poor weak man stiffens with anxiety, truly must hide qualities within himself which are food for thought. . . . The person, that is to say, his conscious 'I,' is like a plaything, like a feather which is whirled around by different currents of air, sometimes the sacrifice and sometimes the sacrificer, and he cannot hinder either. The Book of Job shows us God at work both as creator and destroyer." *Ibid.,* p. 70.
The hero, in the sex cycle as truly as in the solar cycle, brings suffering alike to bride and mother.
26. *Ibid.,* p. 391. Cf. p. 212.

the maternal sea unite in an eternally rejuvenating intercourse."[27] Ultimately sun and sex become indistinguishable in their fostering in man of the idea of immortality, while at the same time they unite as inspiration and the means of his inquiry into the mystery of existence, showing him as ultimate the principles of generation, enlightenment and destructiveness (which comes to be perceived as evaluation). It is little wonder then that man's ideas of God and of immortality should appear innate.

There are innumerable accounts of the solar association of the cross.[28] It is well known[29] that the great festivals of all religions tend to fall on the four points of the sun's annual course. Lines connecting these zodiacal positions form the Great Cross of the Heavens, on which at the vernal equinox the sun hero is sacrificed. Moreover, Ixion, another sun god, has his instrument of torture, to which he is bound at noontide, "the fiery cross which is seen in the sky by those who look on the noonday sun."[30] Discussion of the sex associations of the cross are equally abundant. It has been said that the association is from the wooden phallus through the tree of life to the rod given to Hermes by Apollo, the spear given to Abaris by the Hyperborean sun god, the scepter of the king, and so on. In such wise the cross of Christianity is identified with the "mystic tau which . . . de-

27. *Ibid.*, p. 275. He continues: "Our supposition of a condensation of the Hierosgamos with the myth of rebirth is probably confirmed by this."

28. In Amerind symbology, a yellow disk with inscribed cross represents the sun shining north, east, south and west, that is, all over the earth. A green disk, with white light rays, red heat rays, and an inscribed swastika, is used in ceremonies praying for rain for the corn crops.

29. Cf. p. 112 n. 18.

30. Cox, *op. cit.*, p. 98. A useful summary of the association through motion has been made by M. Ferrero (*Les lois psychologiques du symbolisme*, p. 146): "Selon l'hypothèse ingénieuse de M. Goblet, la croix gammée, aurait été à l'origine une représentation du mouvement du soleil; les branches de la croix gammée seraient des rayons qui marchent, c'est-à-dire l'instrument qui exprimerait, comme symbole métaphorique, l'action. Cette hypothèse est probable, parce que, d'un côte elle est entièrement d'accord avec les lois psychologiques de la formation des symboles métaphoriques; et de l'autre elle est appuyée par une série de preuves tirées de l'examen des monuments. . . . Il y a, dans tout la symbolisme ancien, une tendance incontestable à associer la croix gammée aux représentations du soleil et des divinites solaires." M. Ferrero also notes for example: "Les monnaies grecques offrent souvent à côté de la croix gammée la tête d'Apollon, ou la reproduction de ses attributs."

For a careful discussion of this whole subject consult, for example, Count Goblet d'Alviella, *La Migration des Symboles.*

scends to us from the gloom of an unfathomable past . . .
among races whose thoughts and feelings seem to have naught
in common, but who, with one accord, hail it as an ensign of
their faith, a type of superhuman power, an emblem of the Life
Giver and of life."[31] In brief the cross indicates essentially union
of the principles of sun and sex.

Vibrating between the great centers of sun and sex, as a help
to the minds of those little capable of a unification of their experience and thought, grew up the great wealth of animal symbolism. The bull is familiar as symbol of the "living hero, the
shining sun,"[32] just as is the serpent as symbol of the "dead,
buried, or chthonic hero, the invisible sun."[33] On the other hand
sex significations of both are familiar, an example being the
brazen serpent of the Pentateuch in which Cox notes the union
of the two emblems, cross and serpent, the quiescent and ener-
gizing Phallos.[34] Like its major sources of significance, sun and
sex, the serpent had its beneficent and its evil aspects, the evil
aspect of materialism and the good aspect of spiritual rebirth.[35]

Any adequate discussion of animal symbolism,[36] however,
would demand as much space as a thorough treatment of tax-

31. H. S. Cuming, "On the Tau or Emblem of Life," *Jour. Brit. Arch. Ass'n*,
27 (1871), 307-314.

In illustration of the same idea, Cox writes: "In a form which adhered still
more strictly to the first idea [that of generative action] the emblem became the
stauros or cross of Osiris and a new source of mythology was thus laid open. To
the Egyptian the cross thus became the symbol of immortality, and the god himself was crucified to the tree which denoted his fructifying power. Rising from a
crescent, the modified form of the Yoni [cf. the moon goddess, and the woman
in the Apocalypse—Rev. 12. 1—'clothed with the sun, and the moon under her
feet'], the cross set forth the marriage of Ouranos and Gaia, of Vishnu and
Sacti, of heaven and earth. But this cross was itself a symbol of the sun." (Cox,
Mythology of the Aryan Nations, p. 115. See also pp. 116-117.)

It should be noted however that "Sacti" is properly the innate creative energy
of a god; and in later literature becomes the feminine associate of the god as
objectifying his creativity. The above use of the term is therefore questionable.
The feminine objectification of Vishnu's life-giving power is Lakshmi.

32. Why this should be is indicated clearly in Dr. Jung's classification of
symbols, which a little study will show to be identical, with the exception of
added subdivisions useful for psychoanalysis, with that given here (Chap. I,
ii, and Appendix). He instances a form of comparison by activity: "the libido is
dangerous when fecundating like the bull, through the power of its passion, like
the lion, like the raging boar when in heat. . . . The possibilities of comparison
mean just as many possibilities for symbolic expression." Jung, *op. cit.*, p. 105.

33. Jung, *op. cit.*, p. 476.   34. Cox, *op. cit.*, p. 116.   35. Bayley, *op. cit.*

36. Horses likewise were connected with sun and sex. Although their relationship has been worked out in great detail, it is sufficient here to recall the

onomy, even were there available a logical scheme of classification by genera and species. Perhaps as good a summary as is possible in a brief compass lies in the idea as old as the mind of man "that existences and events as they appear on earth correspond to cosmic existences and events."[37] Small things and tangible, in the course of man's daily life, gain significance through some observed analogy to the greater powers of existence, and thus become venerable, alike to little minds incapable of the greater thought, and to greater minds who make of them reminders and symbols truly interpretative of the deeper reality. The sphere has always been "emblem of creative motion, because manifesting force is rotary."[38] One reason given for the veneration accorded the sacred scarab was the observed fact that it rolled a round pellet backward with its hinder part, "this in imitation of the sun, which while it moves from west to east [at night] turns the heaven the contrary way."[39] It is to be noted that the scarab was represented rayed in indication of its solar connection.[40] The fundamental characteristic of all such symbolism is stress of specific elements in the more basic symbolisms of sun and sex, with at the same time usually implication of disintegration between them or of an integration not yet accomplished.

The task of the genius is always to order, unify, and render consistent the entangled luxuriance of specialized symbolisms. That "the sun migrated through a hundred human forms in various countries: was adored as the bull Apis, as a lion, a cock, a ram, a wolf, and in half the monsters of the zodiac," is a fact.[41] Just as Amenhotep IV (father-in-law of Tutankhamen), in his far-reaching reform, united all the ram, bull, "crocodile

horses of the sun chariot and the sex significance of the horseshoe. Cf. Jung, *op. cit.,* p. 312.

Cf. also the Brahmin sacrifice for the consecration of an altar, in which a white horse representing the sun, "that thunderbolt, even yonder sun; for that horse is yonder sun," is led sunwise around the altar. While progressing east to west (daytime sun) "he makes it smell that layer of bricks; that horse is yonder sun, and those bricks are the same as all these creatures on earth; thus even as he makes the horse smell, so yon sun kisses these creatures . . . even as he makes it smell, so yonder sun strings these worlds to himself on a thread." *Satapatha Brahmana,* 7, 3, 2, 10-13 (*SBE,* 41, p. 359).

37. Storch, *op. cit.,* p. 11. 38. Cf. Ezekiel's vision of a wheel within a wheel. 39. Bayley, *op. cit.*   40. J. M. Chase, *Great Pyramid of Gizeh.* 41. Payne-Knight, *Discourse on the Worship of Priapus,* Pt. 2, x-xi.

and pile-dwelling gods into the disk of the sun, and made it clear that their various attributes were compatible with the sun's attributes,"[42] so after him, peers among men wrought similar unifications in later polytheisms. In the process is a rhythm suggesting that of the sun in drawing up moisture from over the face of the earth, which with changing atmospheric conditions is to fall again in scattered drops, later to be united anew. In human thinking the one, the two, the three, and the many are eternally in unstable equilibrium.

The great similarity and close association of sun and sex make unnecessary, as already noted, the treatment in equal detail of the other organizing center of the materials of symbolism.[43] Furthermore, whereas all the ideas suggested in relation to the sun have arisen likewise from consideration of the sex power within man himself, the sun is uniquely adequate for their objectification, and the objectification is needed to give balance and freedom in thinking. On the other hand, it is with the aid of sex symbolisms that, in the recurrent process of unification and dispersion of myths, the solar trinity becomes more and more dominant and more and more sharply defined.[44] So only has the human mind been able to attain the basis for such stability as is essential to the continued progress of thought. To such solution man is driven not only by the macrocosm of the external world, but by the microcosm of his own physical and emotional nature. Sex, moreover, leads even more rapidly and surely than does the sun to unification in a trinity;[45] and thus not only does solar imagery give needful balance to sex im-

42. Jung, *op. cit.*, p. 106.

43. For further discussion of the unification of sun and sex, cf. Jung, *op. cit.*, pp. 108, 226-229, 237, 275, 474, also p. 70.

44. Levi L. Paine has noted that the most developed trinities belong to the most intellectual and philosophic religions. He adds that Christianity is essentially a doctrine of Christ as the Second Person of a Trinity, stating his opinion that, had it not been for the natural tendency to evolution of duality into triality, Christianity would have remained dual. In Egyptian and Babylonian trinities he sees constant action and reaction: polytheism to triality to duality to unity, unity to duality to triality to "the polytheistic belief which has ever haunted the race." "The remarkable thing about it all," he concludes, "is that the idea of trinity is so persistent, holding its ground so tenaciously, while so Proteuslike in the shapes it assumes."

45. For trinity and unity as sex symbolisms, cf. Jung, *op. cit.*, p. 184. Cf. also present discussion of the Plotinian and Christian trinities, Chap. V, Pt. I, ii, and Appendix V, Pt. I, ii (1).

agery, but the symbolism of sex reinforces and gives added power to the symbolism of the sun.

It is to be remembered that throughout this discussion solar symbolism has been treated, not as the common origin of all myth and symbol, but as the inevitable center of unification as the mind of man acts on the materials of symbolism. The student of the human mind has, in his researches into the unconscious, certain advantages over the student whose approach to these questions of the deepest motivation of human living is entirely from the outside. It is worthy of attention that in those levels of consciousness to which pertain man's most primitive reactions, the imagery of sun and sex should have been found central,[46] thus corroborating that which is coming to be the consensus of opinion in anthropology, religion, and history. The materials of symbolism are the materials of the objective universe and the inner consciousness of man—the one centering in the sun, the other in sex, which two correspond point to point as macrocosm and microcosm.[47]

SYMBOLIC ELEMENTS AT THE CLOSE OF PAGAN ANTIQUITY

With as background a glimpse of the sun's rôle in barbarism, it were interesting to trace the successive stages in its accession to ultimate centrality in the great cultural traditions, noting especially the varying of the aspect stressed with the particular genius and environment of each people. Only a suggestion, however, may be given here, in regard to the four traditions, Jewish, Greek, Oriental, and Roman, which, supplemented by eastern infiltrations, became the basis of medieval development.

In Hebrew thought the sun was prominent especially where it was most needed, in the individual and nationalistic eschatologies,[48] and their final harmonization through the further de-

46. Cf. Appendix III, Pt. I, i. Although there is still wide dispute as to the material against the spiritual connotation of symbolism.

47. For the broadening of these hypotheses to include in the external world the whole firmament in its motion, rather than the sun alone, and in man's inner experience all of his fundamental instincts rather than sex alone, cf. Appendix III, Pt. I, i.

48. N. Schmidt, *Origin of Jewish Eschatology*, in *Symposium on Eschatology*. For the color lent to Hebrew thought by nomadic inheritance, cf. Appendix III, Pt. I, i.

velopment of the latter in post-Exilic times.[49] Dr. N. Schmidt thinks it more likely, however, that these traditions found their inception in the perception of JHVH as manifested in earthquake, cyclone, fire from heaven, and other such elements. These, although perhaps at first unified in the cosmic deity who spoke from the volcanic mount, underwent gradual transference to the solar god. That ceremony which marked the climax of the whole religious ritual of the Hebrew was held at the time of the sun god's sacrifice and return to life, whereas the Lamb, suggestive of the zodiacal sign of the solar sacrifice, was baked in the form of a cross, thus uniting both the cross of the heavens whereon the sun suffered, and the cross of sexual union, symbol of the inevitable sacrifice bound up with the most powerful organizing center in the nature of man.

For its place in early Hebrew experience Egyptian culture should be mentioned, and that which first comes to mind is of course the form of those great monuments to the threefold nature of the sun, the pyramids themselves—the complex symbolism of which, not yet fully understood, would demand a treatise in itself. No better witness, however, could be borne to the high development in Egyptian culture of the worship of the sun than the beautiful hymns from which these extracts are taken:

> Hail to thee, O disc of day!
> Creator of all and giver of their sustenance,
> Great Falcon, brilliantly plumaged,
> Brought forth to raise himself on high of himself,
> Self-generator without being born,
> Firstborn Falcon in the midst of the sky,
> To whom jubilation is made at the rising and the setting likewise,
> Fashioner of the produce of the soil.

> Thy dawning is beautiful in the horizon of the sky,
> O loving Aton, Beginning of Life!
> When thou risest in the eastern horizon,
> Thou fillest every land with thy beauty,
> Thou art beautiful, great, glittering high above every land,
> Thy rays, they encompass the lands, even all that thou hast made,

---

49. "Aus der Beobachtung der Präcession der Sonne erklärt sich . . . die Gleichung von Urzeit und Endzeit, die in der Eschatologie eine solche Rolle spielt." Quoted by Dr. N. Schmidt.

Thou art Re [All] and thou carriest them all away captive,
Thou bindest them by thy love.
Though thou art far away, thy rays are upon the earth,
Though thou art on high, thy footsteps are the day.

.   .   .   .

Even as thou hast made them
When thou hast risen they live
When thou settest they die,
For thou art length of life of thyself,
Men live through thee,
While their eyes are upon thy beauty
Until thou settest.[50]

The hymn to Aton represents the first literary expression of an attempt in any religion to establish a monotheistic worship.[51] This would suggest that for all the great lesson of unity taught by the steady motion of the sky, it was the power of its usurping offspring, the sun, through which was first rendered possible a successful combating of polytheism.

Of Babylonian literature with its many Old Testament parallels, suggestions in terms of sun symbolism are, for example, the descent to Sheol (Isa. 14, compare the Descent of Ishtar) and the lament over Tammuz, whose death was celebrated annually with wild outbursts of mourning. The full importance of sun symbolism here, however, is contained in the Chaldean development of astrology: "In Syria astrology lent the firmness of intelligent conviction to notions that were vague elsewhere. The Chaldean cosmology, which deified all elements but ascribed a predominant influence to the stars, ruled the entire Syrian syncretism." In this astrological system, Dr. Cumont states: "The sun was supreme because it led the starry choir, because it was the king and guide of all the other luminaries, and therefore the master of the whole world. . . . As the 'intelligent light' it was especially the creator of human reason, and just as it repelled and attracted the planets in turn, it was believed to send

50. G. A. Barton, *Archeology and the Bible,* pp. 402-406. The first quotation is from a hymn dated about 1400 B.C.; the last two are from the beautiful *Hymn to Aton,* time of Amenophis IV. In the British Museum publication, entitled *The Book of the Dead,* is to be found more concerning these remarkable hymns.

51. E. A. T. Wallis Budge, *Tutankhamen, Amenism, Atenism, and Egyptian Monotheism.*

out souls, at the time of birth, into the bodies they animated, and to cause them to return to its bosom after death by means of a series of emissions and absorptions. Later on, when the seat of the Most-High was placed beyond the limits of the universe, the radiant star that gives us light became the visible image of the supreme power, the source of all life and all intelligence, the intermediary between an inaccessible god and mankind, and the one object of special homage from the multitude. Solar pantheism, which grew up among the Syrians of the Hellenistic period as a result of the influence of Chaldean astrology, imposed itself upon the whole Roman world under the empire."[52] The writer continues with the statement that this was the last form assumed by the pagan idea of God.

In Zoroastrianism, sun symbolism received perhaps its most complete pre-Christian development, Fire, as representing the sun, was always central for its purifying power. At the sun's rising all the waters of the world and all the creatures of the Good Spirit are made clean.[53] Through sun symbolism were expressed the most advanced conceptions of the Parsi religion; indeed, the sun became a great ideal:

He who offers up a sacrifice unto the undying, shining, swift-horsed Sun, to withstand darkness, to withstand the demons born of darkness . . . offers it up to Ahura Mazda, offers it up to the Amesha Spentas, offers it up to his own soul.[54]

Mayest thou have piercing rays, like Mithra! Mayest thou be warm, like the moon! Mayest thou be resplendent, like fire![55]

Brightness and glory are attributed to all good creatures,[56] even and especially to the cow, of all earthly creatures the most essential to life in early Persia.[57]

52. F. Cumont, *Oriental Religions*, pp. 133-134.
53. *Khorshed Yast*, 2 (*SBE*, 23, p. 85).
54. *Khorshed Yast*, 3 (*SBE*, 23, p. 86).
55. *Vistasp Yast*, 4 (*SBE*, 23, p. 329). This Yast is a prayer for a young king.
56. That is, those created by Ahura Mazda.
57. The hope of the Parsi is, in the judgment after death, to pass through the paradises of good thought, good word, and good deed to final enlightenment: "the fourth step that the soul of the faithful man made, placed him in the Endless Lights." *Yast 22*, 15 (*SBE*, 23, p. 317). The Persian Sosiosh, or Saviour, is expected to come from the region of the dawn. (L. Paine, *Ethnic Trinities*, p. 14.)

Ultimately, there developed the Mithra cult in which the Persian trinity first became completely solar. The mark of him who is consecrated to Mithra is the diadem or halo, symbol of the sun's rays.[58] It should be noted that from the first the especial character of Mithra, Sun and second person of the trinity, was the highest ideal of truthfulness: "the all-powerful, all-seeing, undeceivable Mithra."[59] "Originally, Mithra was the god of the heavenly light, and in that character he knows the truth, as he sees everything: he is therefore taken as witness of truth, he is the preserver of oaths and good faith, he chastises those who break their promises and lie to Mithra, destroys their houses and smites them in battle." Here in the emphasis on truth is a link of sympathy with Greek thought in particular,[60] but truth for Zoroastrianism was conceived morally rather than philosophically.

Plato, in his allegory of the Cave, immortalized the symbolic usage of light, but indeed the quest of the Greek was always for enlightenment.[61] In Greek tradition better than any other can be seen recorded the process of philosophic and religious unification and disintegration. Greek mythology is full of evanescent trinities, forming and dissolving like shadows, with suggestion of slow kaleidoscopic motion. Aristotle himself declared trinity to be fundamental in nature, and went on to the great philosophic unification in the concept of motion, wherein he com-

58. L. Paine, *Ethnic Trinities*, p. 19.
59. *Mihir Yast*, 167.
60. Cox has discussed this peculiar character of sun gods as seeing all things and avenging all evil, especially lies. (Cf. Cox, *op. cit.*, p. 60.) It should also be noted that *Amen* (used to signify *So be it*, or solemn assent, at the end of prayers) derives from one of the names of the Egyptian sun god, Amen-ra, and signifies an unbreakable oath. Although in the Old Testament are traceable numerous parallelisms with Mazdayasnian imagery, the specific association of truth with the sun does not occur, except as JHVH, the God of Truth, is himself the God of light.
61. In the intellectual tradition culminating in the last pre-Christian centuries, fire, with its greater closeness to the life of every day, became central: "Stoic monism was emphatic on the unity of things, God was conceived as the world, or again as the spiritual element or vital fire of the world." Man's soul, as a portion of this fire, had the freedom of God himself. At last the soul would be drawn up into the greater fire and its earthly dross would be burned away. (Cf. Angus, *Mystery Religions and Christianity*, p. 70, and Murray, *Stoic Philosophy*, pp. 28 and 35.) Cf. Prudentius' Burial Hymn, "Deus ignee fons animatum." Cf. also the *Bhagavad-Gita*, where it is written: "I am the fire residing in the bodies of all things that have life."

bined the wheel or aureole with the cross (swastika).[62] The
consummation of the Greek tradition came ultimately in Plotinus, whose trinity is unique in that in it is neither myth nor history, but pure philosophy. Yet his trinity also is expressed in
terms of the sun.[63]

In the drama of the mystery cults[64] (Greek, Syrian, Phrygian,
Egyptian, and Persian) attention centered in the conveying to
man of sacramental strength[65] whereby he might so live as to
share in the resurrection for which the sun god suffered. In
brief, in the Mysteries the initiate, after experiences of death,
undertook a journey to the world beyond. His body characteristically was placed on a sloping surface facing east, waiting for
the rising sun, and typically the resurrection occurred on the
third day. Characteristic of his experience is the following:

> I approached the confines of Death and trod the threshold of Proser-
> pine; I was carried through all the elements and returned again; in the
> middle of the night I saw the sun gleaming in radiant splendor. I
> approached into the presence of the gods below and the gods celestial
> and worshipped before their face.[66]

Indeed, as Dr. Angus writes, "all ancient *epiphaneiae* were of
the character of dazzling light. Porphyry knows that 'the eye of
the body cannot bear' the brightness of divine apparitions. The
experience of Apuleius . . . refers to such an epiphany. In the
Attis cult, 'Hail, Bridegroom, Hail, new Light' announced the
epiphany." In the *Liturgy of Mithra* it is written:

> Thou shalt see a youthful god, lovely in form, with *red locks*[67] wear-
> ing a *white* tunic and *scarlet* mantle and holding a *bright crown*.[68a]

62. Cf. Dante's theory of circular motion, discussed on p. 182.
63. Cf. Appendix V, Pt. I, ii.
64. The mystery cults spread through all the boundaries of the then known
world and beyond. Mithraic remains are found for example in the Scandinavian
countries. The rites of Samothrace, which stood next in importance to those of
Eleusis, are supposed to have penetrated into Ireland, since Strabo, recording the
travels of Artemidorus (100 B.C.) speaks of an "island near Britain, where they
sacrifice to Demeter and Kore as they do at Samothrace."
65. To the word Θεωρία (contemplation) as used for "a dramatic or sacramental spectacle such as the representation of a suffering God" Pythagoras gave
a new meaning "as the contemplation, not of the sacrament, but of the underlying truths which sacraments symbolize." W. R. Inge, *Philosophy of Plotinus,*
2, pp. 178-179. For the full development of Dante's conception of contemplation, cf. Chap. V, Pt. I, iii.
66. Angus, *op. cit.,* p. 92, quoting Apuleius.
67. Dr. Roger S. Loomis points out that Cuchulain has three bands of hair,

Proclus says of all these initiations and mysteries:

The gods reveal many forms of themselves, changing their modes of apparition. There issues from them *a light,* sometimes formless, sometimes in human shape, and again transmuted into other shapes.[68a]

"As it were a marvelous light" confronts the terrified and shuddering soul in death just as "in one of the great mysteries."[68b] Sun symbolism, especially with its associated imagery, is found in these cults in the utmost intricacy, together with marked vibration between the emphases of inner and outer, sex and the sun.

Ultimately, just before the culmination in Plotinus of Neoplatonism, and the recognition under Constantine of gospel authority, Graeco-Roman paganism ended in "a pantheism, which made abundant provision for a subordinate polytheism . . . in which the sun [Sol Invictus] was the symbol of the supreme and all-embracing divinity."[69] Thus, in the first centuries of our era, the sun symbol, with the momentum of centuries behind it,[70] was a point of unification of all cultures.

In fine, the materials of symbolism, sun and sex, however interconnected, appear in man's life as two ways of approach to the same problem—the problem of the ultimate origin and continuance of life, with its implications as to the relationship of

dark red, orange, and glistening gold. He is clearly the sun (e.g., he is under a taboo never to rise later than the sun, and is described as facing ever westward). In fact he is none other than the youthful form of Curoi. His mysterious weapon, the *gae bolga,* can be no other than lightning. The weapon of the sun, Dr. Loomis maintains, is always a missile weapon, sharp and forked. (Lectures delivered at Columbia University, 1925-26.)

68a. Angus, *op. cit.,* p. 136.

68b. Cf. Angus, *op. cit.,* p. 136. Quotations are from a fragment of Themistius.

69. G. F. Moore, *Religious Thought of the Greeks,* pp. 270 ff.

70. Cf. p. 109 n. 8. Note the following gods and heroes given as sun deities on the authority of writers of the period of syncretism:

Saturn, Chronos, Jupiter, Hercules, *by* Macrobius and Nonnus.

Janus, Pan, Aesculapius, Adonis, *by* Macrobius.

Mercury, Hermes, *by* Macrobius.

Belus, Baal, *by* Nonnus.

Pluto, Aidoneus, Priapus, Vulcan, *by* the Orphic poet.

Bacchus, Dionysus (sun at night and lord of vegetation), *by* Virgil, Ausonius, Macrobius, Sophocles.

Osiris, Horus, Serapis, *by* Diodorus Siculus, Macrobius, Eusebius.

Apollo, *by* all authorities.

the individual to the community and to the universe.[71] Novalis
was spokesman for large numbers of men, when he said:
"There is but one temple in the world, and that temple is the
Body of Man. Nothing is holier than this high form. Bending
before men is a reverence done to this revelation in the flesh.
We touch heaven, when we lay our hands on a human body."[72]
Other multitudes prefer to think in terms of the question: "The
sun, the moon, the stars, the seas, the hills and the plains—are
not these, O Soul, the Vision of Him who reigns?"[73] Both fields
of investigation are necessary to him who uses arbitrary and
comparison symbol. In the realm of insight symbolism acquaintance with both methods of penetration beneath the realm of
appearances, and the recognition of their essential oneness,
marks balance in man's progress in adjustment to his environment. Through either one may be worked out all the implications of the other; yet in reality, representing two aspects of
the same thing, they are used most powerfully in conjunction.
Moreover, as man progressed through the use of these materials
of symbolism to a unification of his experience, there was inevitably developed a trinity in which sun and sex united.

It is important only to bear in mind that medieval thought
received much, fairly directly, from the symbolisms of barbarism in which the sun-sex emphasis was strong, as well as from
the more refined traditions dominated by the same emphasis in
greater unification. Suggestion has been given of the symbolic
rôle of the sun in the interplay of pre-Christian cultures which
prepared for the first five centuries of the Christian era. In these
centuries in particular, the traditions of the Middle Ages proper
have their roots, for in them was evolved the conception of the
Trinity which for medieval thought defined the underlying Infinite that gave intelligibility to all experience. Without an understanding not only of this conception, but also of the cultural
traditions out of which it grew, much will remain obscure of
that which Dante expressed through the Threefold Light which

71. Here is the primitive root for Dante's highly refined ideal of the love of
the Court of Heaven, the mystic union with the divine Sun. Cf. pp. 427-430,
36-37, 168-171, 226, 346-347, 386-390.
72. Carlyle, *Sartor Resartus*, Bk. 3, chap. 6 (Everyman ed., p. 180).
73. Tennyson, *The Higher Pantheism*.

guided him on his journey through the incoherencies of the
world, and at last, in his vision, gathered up into one the scattered leaves of the universe. Out of such a more or less inco-
herent background developed that large part of the historic
world within which Dante was a microcosm, a world which devoted itself exclusively to the systematic development of symbolism as a tool of thought and expression.

II. BASIS OF SYMBOLIC DEVELOPMENT

IN the year 313 A.D., as at the end of a chaotic day, long to be
remembered for its capricious alternations of storm, sunshine,
and fog, the sun was to be seen above the Roman Empire
through the mist, drawing up diffused vapor which, ordered
and fused, was to descend in torrents at a later day. The mor-
row was to bring forth disintegration of the Empire which for
some centuries had offered itself, a great arena, for the titanic
contest of culture against culture. Philosophies and ways of life,
nurtured by small groups of men in nearly every corner of the
then known world, were brought to trial, and in the great convention at Rome there was much of revelation and much of dis-
illusion. Yet the combat proceeding under the surveillance of
the ideal of Roman citizenship bore an air of gentlemanly ease,
and often the contestants themselves were unaware that the
battle was to the death. Under the machinery of the Roman
government, moralists meditated, philosophers debated, and
the sect called Christians flourished in obscurity except as it
stimulated the imagination of scandalmongers, while the mystery cults contributed the piquancy of adventure, proffering at
the same time a sense of security in the unknown.

Yet at the very moment storm clouds hung over the cata-
combs, and even while little Laeta was learning her Christian
prayers at her pagan grandfather's knee, thunderings reverber-
ated from Tertullian's conflict as he fought single-handed, a
toreador against the Roman consulate. It would seem that difference of potential in the atmosphere may have caused at times
a fleeting uneasiness even in those otherwise completely under
the sway of a civilization unable to bear the test of apparent
exemption from external peril. Meanwhile, man's age-long

search for intelligibility in the universe was carried on as it were in a cloud, through which were dimly discernible contours of old and new philosophies in process of syncretistic metamorphosis. It is small wonder that there were "wanderers in the middle mist" who began to doubt the supremacy of the *Sol Invictus.*

In a sunny moment Sicilius, Octavius, and Minucius wandered toward the shore and paused where children were skipping stones, a fitting scene for the courteous disagreement of which the humble occasion was a kiss thrown to a statue of Serapis, yet from which sprang the "first masterpiece of Christian Apologetic."[74] In the *Octavius* of Minucius Felix are concepts[75] which are fundamental in the development of medieval symbolism.

Of Latin Christian literature or philosophy worthy of attention the *Octavius* is almost alone, yet in its few pages as in no other work is caught the atmosphere of the period.[76] If, moreover, the present aim is to obtain an understanding of thirteenth century thought as it influenced the author of the *Divina Commedia* (which in turn became its supreme literary expression), a feeling for the atmosphere of these seething centuries in which the dominant ideas of the Middle Ages took initial form, is almost a *sine qua non.*

Rome's conquest of the world had marked the inception of decline in her literature. The Claudian period, for all the brilliance of Seneca and Lucian, had been marked by strain, affectation, and rhetoric only too revealing as to the upheaval in progress. Flavian literature claims the name of Pliny the Elder and of Statius, but was credulous and pompous to a degree that fairly compelled the epigrams of Martial. The writings of Tacitus, Juvenal, Pliny, and Suetonius show the progress of sophistication which always marks a society incapable of enduring the

---

74. The first apologist of whom we have a writing is Aristides, *c.* 140—the first worthy of note, Justin Martyr, writing about 150-160. A. Aall, *Der Logos.*

75. To be briefly discussed in the next few pages.

76. We know but little of Minucius Felix himself: what we can gather from his own work, from Lactantius and from Jerome. The possible limits of his dates are between 160 and 300 A.D., since he is mentioned by Lactantius, *c.* 260-340, and himself mentions Fronto, *c.* 100-170. Most students place Minucius between 160 and 250.

blessings of peace. Juvenal had only a sneer for Greek philosophy; and in the next period, although the culture was still Greek, men who thought were moralists rather than philosophers, as, for example, Epictetus, Marcus Aurelius, and Dion Cassian. Greek literature had in effect come to an end (exception being made of the African tradition), and Latin literature was solely practical, the few Christian writings being by way of propaganda. Drawing from the thought of a far earlier period the *Octavius* is a product of educated circles, representative of the first writings of the Italian School.[77] Modeled on Cicero's *De natura deorum,* with reminiscences of Virgil and Horace, it contains much of the philosophy of Lucretius expressed in terms of sun and fire, even though the meaning conveyed was material and not intentionally symbolic:

There is no artificer, no judge, no creator of the world. Thus, when the elements of fire have united, new and ever new suns are always shining; when the vapours of earth have been given off, the mists are continually increasing.[78]

Other earlier traditions are given. Using their vocabulary of sun and fire analogy, Minucius Felix makes a very definite attempt to transfer it to incipient Christian doctrines in which Christ was to assume the rôle of solar deity.[79]

CHRISTIAN FORMULATION OF SYMBOLIC BASES

That there is a fundamental unity underlying all things is among the strongest points of the *Octavius.* There is emphasis also on the interrelationships of all things, strongly suggestive of the thesis of the *Divina Commedia:*

All things are so closely connected, combined, and linked together,

77. This school, succeeding to the style of Quintilian as a second impulse of Ciceronianism, attempted to mold classical Latin to Christian use. It is in sharp contrast to the African School which wrote in the New Latin, bearing affinity in style to Apuleius, of which Tertullian is the early example. Finally in the fourth century the two languages were combined by Augustine. Cf. F. W. Mackail, *Latin Literature,* p. 248.

78. *Octavius* of Minucius Felix, tr. by J. H. Freese, p. 33.

79. "The Stoics firmly maintain that, when the supply of moisture is exhausted, the whole world will be consumed by fire; the Epicureans also hold the same opinion about the conflagration of the elements and destruction of the world. Plato tells us that the different parts of the world are alternately overwhelmed by flood and fire . . ." *Op. cit.,* p. 89.

that it is impossible to understand the nature of man without thoroughly examining into the nature of the deity, just as it is impossible successfully to administer affairs of state without a knowledge of this state that is common to all—the world.[80a]

Moreover, there is the long argument based on the nature of kingship, within which is an identification of the fundamental unity with the infinite.[80b]

Octavius' argument is presage of the system later developed in detail, and reflects the attitude toward the universe worked out in the redefinition resulting from the juxtaposition of cultures in the Roman Empire. There is first, insistence, in Ciceronian oratory, that knowledge of God is to be gained from the universe and especially from the sun and the course of the year:

> We, with looks erect and eyes lifted to heaven, endowed with speech and reason whereby we recognize, feel and imitate God, neither ought to nor can we ignore the heavenly brightness that thrusts itself before our eyes and senses. . . . Look at the sky itself—its vast expanse, its rapid revolution, whether studded with stars by night or illuminated by the sun by day; you will at once understand how wonderful, how divine is the equilibrium maintained by the supreme ruler of the universe. Consider also how the course of the sun makes the year, how the moon, by its increase, wane and disappearance brings round the month. I need only mention the successive recurrence of darkness and light, to provide the alternate renewal of work and rest.[81]

Here is reflection of the syncretism in progress, which was ultimately to unite, and, as Christian theology maintained, to correct, all symbolisms of deity—all the old gods whether of sun or of sex—in the triune solar God as representing their completion, that which they had been striving to express.[82]

80a. *Op. cit.*, p. 52.
80b. In a work which is primarily a reflection of trends of thought in the first Christian centuries it is not expected that philosophic ideas always shall be expressed clearly. Although the infinity of God, self-expressed in the universe, has been presupposed and even stated in the following passages, it is possible that this infinite may be either limitless extension (*Unendlichkeit*) or the absolute infinity defined by Boethius and fundamental in later thought as in the *Divina Commedia*.
81. *Op. cit.*, p. 53.
82. Among Christian theologians there were varying attitudes to the inevitable syncretism. Eusebius of Alexandria deprecated the tendency, which lasted into the fifth century, to pray toward the rising sun:
"Ah! woe to the worshippers of the sun and the moon and the stars. For I know many worshippers and prayer sayers to the sun. For now at the rising of

The linking with earlier thought is conscious. Octavius rehearses the names applied to God by Thales, Anaximenes, Anaxagoras, Pythagoras, and so on down through Zeno and Aristotle to philosophers of his own day, concluding in a tone of raillery:

Not to waste time over all these Jupiters, I will merely say that he has as many monstrous forms as names. Erigone hanged herself, that she might shine among the stars as the Virgin; Castor and Pollux die alternately that both may live; Aesculapius is struck by lightning that he may rise a god; Hercules is consumed by fire on Mount Oeta, to divest himself of his mortal nature.[83]

It is to be remembered that each of these heroes has been involved in the story of the sun god;[84] and this fact by later writers was used consciously as an aid to a syncretism in which the solar trinity was the focus. Octavius himself said: "For they, too, had learnt to know our God, for He is the God of all"[85] and "they have given us a shadowy imitation, a garbled truth taken from the divine predictions of the prophets."[86]

Octavius, however, had just made clear that which the tradition of the Middle Ages reiterated with such emphasis: since God is infinite, the meaning conveyed by the physical deity-symbol belongs to a different order and realm:

He is invisible, for he is too bright for us to look upon. He is impalpable, for he is too pure for us to touch. He is incomprehensible,

the sun, they worship and say, 'Have mercy on us,' and not only the sun-gnostics and the heretics do this, but also Christians." (Quoted by Jung, *op. cit.*, p. 114.)

On the other hand, the author of the work *De solstitiis et aequinoctiis,* attributed to John Chrysostom, feels that his Lord is the fulfilment of all that solar worship had meant:

"Moreover the Lord is born in the month of December, in the winter . . . when the ripe olives are gathered, so that the oil, that is the chrism, may be produced, moreover they call it the birthday of the Unconquered One [Solis Invicti]. Who in any case is as unconquered as our Lord, who conquered death itself? Or why should they call it the birthday of the sun; he himself is the sun of righteousness, concerning whom Malachi, the prophet, spoke: 'The Lord is the author of light and of darkness, he is the judge spoken of by the prophet as the Sun of righteousness.'" (Quoted by Jung, *op. cit.,* p. 113.)

83. *Op. cit.,* p. 69.

84. Cf. p. 109 n. 8 and p. 125 n. 70 and the many names of Parsifal, p. 437.

85. *Op. cit.,* p. 88.

86. *Op. cit.,* p. 89. The feeling that pagan religion is a degenerate form of a once pure revelation granted before the incident at Babel, is based on the literal acceptance of Genesis common at this time. Origen was almost alone in per-

for he is beyond our ken—infinite, immense, and his real greatness is known to himself alone.[87]

It is not to be thought that this statement is original with the first master of Christian apologetic. Pagan sun worshipers were constantly pointing back of the sun of sense to that which it symbolized.[88] The tendency of the human mind to centralize the symbol rather than the thing symbolized always has caused difficulty. By Christianity in these centuries it was combated with especial vigor because of the close contact with religions in that stage of decadence wherein the spiritual interpretation of myths was generally unrecognized, having become a philosophical *tour de force* or a matter of secret initiation. That for this reason there should be expressed in early Christian writings much of repugnance to external form and ceremonial in religion is natural; and proves nothing either way as to the fulness of development of Christian ritual at that time. The idea that physical things are inadequate completely to express God is repeated endlessly in the Latin theological writers of the Middle Ages.[89] Yet it is these same writers who stress the im-

ceiving the mythical nature of Hebrew tradition. This fact, however, does not alter the significance of the statement of Minucius here quoted.

87. *Op. cit.,* p. 57.

88. "Throughout the ages men have adored the sun as the symbol of that supreme intelligence which governs the solar system and all systems of solar systems. It is not believed by men who have considered the subject with unbiased minds that the sun worshippers of the past, any more than those of the present, esteemed the sun as the supreme intelligence, but as one of the great centers through which that intelligence manifests its powers, its glories and its radiances." J. M. Chase, *The Great Pyramid of Gizeh,* p. 38.

Harnack (*Expansion of Christianity,* Vol. 1, p. 376) quotes a protest by Porphyry against the charge of image worship: "Images and temples of the gods have been made from all antiquity for the sake of forming reminders to men. Their object is to make those who draw near them think of God thereby. . . . When any person gets an image or picture of a friend, he certainly does not believe that the friend is to be found in the image, or that his members exist inside the different parts of the representation. His idea rather is that the honor which he pays to his friend finds expression in the image. And while the sacrifices offered to the gods do not bring them any honor, they are meant as a testimony to the good-will and gratitude of the worshippers."

An equally cogent, if briefer, reply, is that of an old Hopi chief, who, upon being asked whether, when he went to the mesa-top each morning to pray at sunrise, he prayed to the Sun; answered, "No: to that which is back of the Sun." For this incident as well as for many valuable suggestions with regard to Amerind Symbology, the author is indebted to Canon Winfred Douglas.

89. For constant repetition of this theme there is no better illustration than Hilary of Poitiers.

portance of symbol as the sole means through which man may understand God.

External expression directed by the new attitude toward the universe in process of formation was not only sanctioned but demanded. After denying that Christians worship crosses, Octavius says:

By what image am I to represent God, since, rightly considered, man himself is the image of God. What temple am I to erect to him, since the whole of this world, which has been fashioned by him, is unable to contain him?[90]

He had said earlier:

If I should speak of him as father, you would think of him as an earthly father; if as king, you would imagine him as a king of this world; if as lord, you would certainly understand him to be mortal. Take away all additional names and you will behold his splendor.[91]

This passage has been taken to represent a conception of God philosophical rather than Christian. In reality it is but an expression of the fact recognized alike by the enlightened in all religions that both the nature of God and his relation to men are beyond the power of adequate human expression. Continuing in this argument Minucius uses one of the most frequently reiterated of medieval analogies:

Again, we cannot even look into the sun, which is the origin of vision; our powers of sight are impaired by its rays, our eyes are weakened by gazing at it, and if we look at it too long, we are unable to see at all. Could you endure the sight of the creator of the sun himself, the source of light, you who turn away from his lightnings and hide yourself from his thunderbolts? Do you expect to look upon God with the eyes of flesh, when you can neither behold nor grasp your own soul, by which you are quickened and speak? Look again at the sun; although stationary in heaven, its light is shed over every land; present everywhere alike, it mingles with all, and its brightness is never dimmed. God, the creator and examiner of all things, from whom nothing can be hid, must with far greater reason be present in the darkness, be present in our thoughts, which are as it were a second darkness![92]

On the other hand Octavius says: "Not only the man who thinks he knows the greatness of God, depreciates it," but also,

90. *Op. cit.*, p. 85.   91. *Op. cit.*, p. 57.   92. *Op. cit.*, p. 86.

continuing immediately, "He who does not desire to depreciate it, is ignorant of it."[93] Thus man, ever realizing that his best thought and expression of the greatness of God fall short, must continue thinking and expressing in the highest terms he knows. The very tradition which later met its death through the tendency to centralize the symbol, in its rise conquered, leading man through external expression to the idea.

The difficulty has always been the simultaneous and equal emphasizing of the two truths in this paradox: Through symbol is man's only apprehension and expression of truth; symbol can never reach the truth. Here is the hint that truth lies in the reconciliation of opposites—an idea developed later in much greater completeness, to become perhaps the greatest power in medieval thinking.

Thus early, then, Minucius Felix picked out as important the unity underlying all things,[94] its infinity in which all opposites are reconciled, and its expression through the discrete. Whereas no one fact can ever contain or express perfectly this unity, the significance of each depends on it, and their expression of it is rooted in their very nature. Here, then, appear against the background of some suggestion of their *raison d'être,* the emphases noted in the introductory chapter as fundamental in any philosophy of insight symbolism.

It is fitting that Lactantius should stand at the close of the Christian apologetic of this period, since he is the first Latin apologist to offer a complete, though elementary, Christian doctrine.[95] In spite of his significant divergence from the thought of his former teacher, Lactantius shared and carried further Arnobius' perception of the inadequacy of sense terms in connection with God[96] and their absolute necessity, the same em-

---

93. *Op. cit.,* p. 57.
94. An idea centralized also in early religions, especially of the Orient. Cf.:

> "There is true knowledge. Learn thou it is this:
> To see one changeless life in all the lives,
> And in the separate, One Inseparable." *Bhagavad-Gita,* 18.

A more literal translation (by M. M. Chatterji) is: "Know the true knowledge belonging to enlightenment, by which is perceived the one exhaustless Essence, undistributed, though in distributed (separate) bodies."

95. Finally, at the end of the period which gave definite form to the creed, came his dogmatic identification, for the people, of reason with faith.

96. Lactantius, *Divine Institutes,* iv, 6-8. ("Ante-Nicene Library," Vol. 21.)

phases noted in connection with the *Octavius*. Lactantius recognized, moreover, the paradox here implied, and the solution in the Infinite.[97]

The works of the first and last masters of Christian apologetic in this period illustrate sufficiently well the development. A careful study of the intervening works serves simply to reinforce the three emphases: unity underlying all things, its infinity in which all opposites are reconciled, and its expression through the discrete—all suggested in those first words extant as spoken by a Christian layman in defense of his religion. So well did

97. In the *Divine Institutes*, Lactantius discusses particularly the superiority of *Verbum* over *Filius* as a designation for Christ, because of the absence in it of sex implications. Among the great trinities brought into conflict during these centuries, one of the most striking disagreements lay in the sex of the second person of the trinity, through whom the Sun God expressed himself in man's behalf.

The embryonic Hebrew Logos appears in the Wisdom-literature as the feminine *Sophia*. (Cf. Dante's conception of Lady Philosophy, whom he equates to the Second Person of the Trinity. Cf. pp. 169-171.) That most celebrated of eastern shrines, Sancta Sophia in Constantinople, was dedicated to the Second Person of the Christian Trinity (not, as many a tourist has imagined, to a female saint named Sophie. The glorious Mithra, the final power of the religion of Persia, god of the Roman soldier, was on the other hand of virile masculinity. Among the Greeks, to Athena (translated to Rome as Minerva) fell the function of mediation, she being the Divine Wisdom, sprung full-armed from the forehead of Zeus. (The conception of Greek religion gained by those who read these myths as if, for instance, it were a subject of literal belief that a full-grown woman sprang from the head of the chief of the gods, is not unlike that which would be gained of Hebrew and Christian religion, by one reading the eighth and ninth chapters of Proverbs, and assuming that Sophia (Wisdom) was a divine woman, sister to the Lord—since she was brought up with him—who, having built a new house, proceeded to give a lavish feast, with meats and wines, to her *protégés*.)

In the mysteries, there were both sex emphases, although there was a tendency of the feminine to dominate, as for example in the very popular cult of Isis, second person of the trinity of Osiris, Isis, Horus. In Lactantius' preference, however, for a sexless word to express the Second Person of the Christian Trinity, there is not a side-stepping of the issue, but, true to the spirit of his tradition, an insistence that in the infinite God is the reconciliation of opposites. In the Logos, as later developed, were united masculine and feminine elements in a truth superseding both.

Lactantius discussed also the superiority of *Logos* over *Verbum* as a designation for Christ, because Logos means both speech and reason (making reference to Trismegistus, who, he said, had already perceived the sacredness of speech in his discussion of the mystic language). Here is established not merely reconciliation of opposites, but a hierarchy of symbolism. Both are dominant conceptions in the tradition. Thus in relation to Christ, Eternal Wisdom and the supreme self-revelation of God to man, Lactantius stressed the importance of symbol alike to thought and to expression.

"If a Unity exists, in which and toward which all energies centre, it must explain and include Duality, Diversity, Infinity—Sex!" Adams, *Mont-Saint-Michel and Chartres*, p. 261.

Octavius support his courteous raillery over the kiss thrown to
the statue of Serapis.

PAGAN FORMULATION OF SYMBOLIC BASES

In the last century of the integrity of the Roman Empire,
Latin replaced Greek as the liturgic and cultured language. Exercised in the combating of heresies and the formulation of
Christian creed, it underwent a transmutation which placed a
chasm between its medieval and its classical forms. Latin culture, encompassed by strange forms and foreign concepts, mori-
bund but revivified by Christian enthusiasm, was about to lose
its Greek pedagogue, the formative influence in its growth.
Plato himself was to be known only through the *Timaeus,* and
perhaps the *Meno* and part of the *Phaedrus,* and Aristotle was
to become little more than a name.

Throughout this troubled period, however, vitality had
poured in from Alexandria, and from the Alexandrian tradition
came the last great gift of Greece to the Middle Ages. Through
Plotinus and his pupils, Neoplatonism assumed a cast the import of which for the Middle Ages even yet is scarcely realized.
The part played by sun symbolism, moreover, in this *Weltanschauung* was to be of no small influence in the thought development of the Augustinian tradition, especially subsequent
to the ninth century.

That which had been reiterated with greater or less imperfection by chorus after chorus of voices, Plotinus stated carefully. Underlying all the world of appearance is one ultimate
reality, of which all things being manifestations,[98] not only can
be, but must be regarded as insight symbols. Among these symbols, as one would expect, the sun, which proved of such power
through the centuries, is primary. Yet nature is but a pale copy,
and above all her other imagery Plotinus prefers that of light
because it introduces the least error of time and space limita-

---

98. The common misapprehension that Plotinus regarded matter as evil, rests,
as do so many misapprehensions of philosophers, on a verbal misunderstanding.
That word of his which has been translated in English as "matter," was used by
him to denote that which receives a "form," and in its absolute sense, the abso-
lutely void, a condition answering to nothing perceived in the physical universe,
in other words, a postulate of thought. Cf. Inge, *op. cit.,* Vol. 1, pp. 128 ff.

tions. Sex imagery he uses with great effectiveness.[99] Not only are lovers among the three classes of men who have set out on the quest of the One,[100] but generation, both eternal and temporal, is the actualization of contemplation. "That which is eternally perfect begets eternally and that which it begets is eternal. . . ."[101] The words with which he continues lay the basis upon which Athanasius, with the additional aid of sun symbolism, defined the infinite nature of the relationships within the Christian trinity.[102] He goes on to say: "When the begetter is supremely perfect, the begotten must be so intimately united to him as to be separated from him only in that it is distinct from him."

Appearances, though inadequate, are never false, unless so rendered by man's impure perception. Symbols are, however, arranged in hierarchical order, and through them one may advance at last to the pure and imageless perception of the One.[103] The necessity of symbolism for spiritual advance, together with its inadequacy to take men all the way, have perhaps never been better stated than by Plotinus: "These symbols are but figures, by which the wise prophets indicate how we may seek God. But the wise priest, understanding the symbol, may enter the sanctuary and make the vision real."[104] Thus Christian and pagan

99. His sympathy with pagan symbolisms of sex as well as of sun is shown clearly in his interpretation of the myth of the ithyphallic Hermes (*Ennead*, 3, 6). He says: "That no doubt was the meaning of those ancient sages who in mysteries and initiations symbolically represented the 'ancient Hermes' with the generative organ in erection, to teach that it is intelligible reason that begets sense objects . . ."

100. The three classes of men who search for, and are to find, the One, are philosophers, musicians, and lovers.

101. *Ennead*, 6, 9. Cf. Plato's *Symposium*.

102. Cf. Appendix V, Pt. I, ii (1).

103. "We may train ourselves by contemplating noble things here on earth, especially noble deeds, always pressing on to higher things, and remembering above all that as the eye could not behold the sun unless it were sun-like itself, so the soul can only see beauty by becoming beautiful itself." Quoted by Inge, *op. cit.*, Vol. 2, p. 213.

Cf. Dante's progression through symbols in hierarchical order (see pp. 93 and 365 ff.). In one sense, Dante's poem is a dramatization of Plotinus' path of dialectic to the One. Indeed, it was the thought tradition of Plotinus which, having been lost to sight during the so-called Dark Ages, reëmerged to dominate the thought of Dante's period.

104. Quoted by Inge, *op. cit.*, Vol. 2, p. 141. "Very much of the pleasure which we find in poetry and painting arises from brilliant *translations* of an idea from one language to another, showing links between diverse orders of being, symbols of the unseen which are no arbitrary types, or evidences of the funda-

agreed on the fundamental principles which were to dominate the symbolic tradition and for their more adequate formulation Plotinus brought to bear the whole philosophical heritage of pagan antiquity.

SYNCRETISM

The struggle of the centuries of Empire had been toward some sort of cultural equilibrium. The method of progress was the recognition of similarity in apparently conflicting systems and the reinterpretation of current vocabulary and expression in terms of insight symbolism. Count Goblet d'Alviella has given a summary which applied not simply in the religious field, but also with slight difference in the philosophic:

> When the Christians and the Buddhists concentrated on the image of their respective masters the principal attributes of the sun—beginning with that halo of glory whose prototype dates back to the aureoles carved upon the Chaldean monuments—did they mean to do homage to the orb of day? In reality, they only claimed to refer to the venerated physiognomy of their founder the symbol which has not only formed from time immemorial the most radiant expression of celestial glory, but which also characterized, in an especial manner, the highest personification of the Divinity in contemporary creeds.[105, 106]

Indeed, Constantine composed for his legions a prayer, equally acceptable to the worshipers of Mithras, of Serapis, of the Sun, and of Christ.[107] Tertullian wrote to the heathen in these terms: "[You criticize us] because it is a well-known fact that we pray toward the east, or because we make Sunday a day of festivity. What then? Do you do less than this?" The constant reiteration during this period, was, as Justin Martyr himself had said: "We teach the same as the Greeks, poets and philosophers." Throughout the work of Tertullian, unique as the first Church Father[108] and Christian apologist,[109] appear the dominant em-

mental truths about creation, that the universal soul made the world in the likeness of its own principle, Spirit. Ultimately all is the self-revelation of the One and the Good." *Ibid.*, Vol. 2, p. 217.

105. Goblet d'Alviella, *Migration of Symbols*, pp. 266-268.

106. Wundt probably never was nearer the truth than when he ascribed the rise of both Christianity and Buddhism to the rank of world religions, to their remarkable capacity to assimilate auxiliary mythological conceptions.

107. According to M. V. Duruy, as noted by Count Goblet d'Alviella.

108. Irenaeus claims the title of first Church Father. A native of Asia Minor,

phases of the *Octavius,* but especially the unification of thought
through symbolism. His attempt through solar imagery to explain the relation of Christ to the Godhead, will be discussed, in
connection with the full development of such imagery for the
definition of the Trinity.[110] The imagery particularly illustrative
here is that through which he expressed the dominant preoccupation of his time, the resurrection:

Day dies into night . . . the glory of the world is obscured in the
shadow of death . . . and so over the loss of the light there is mourning. But yet it again revives, with its own beauty, its own dowry, its
own sun, the same as ever, whole and entire, over all the world, slaying
its own death, night—opening its own sepulchre, the darkness—coming forth the heir to itself. . . .[111]

After other analogies, he continues:

Forasmuch as earth receives its instruction from heaven to clothe the
trees which had been stripped, to colour the flowers afresh, to spread
the grass again, to reproduce the seed which had been consumed, and
not to reproduce them until consumed . . . by a destruction which is
profit, by an injury which is advantage, by a loss which is gain. . . .
Nothing perishes but with a view to salvation. The whole therefore of
this revolving order of things bears witness to the resurrection of the
dead.[112]

He goes on to relate, for those to whom his description is too inanimate, the story of the Phoenix (in its full form for the Middle
Ages ascribed to Lactantius). Consider, he says, the Phoenix,

which renews its life in a voluntary death; its dying day is its birthday,
for on it it departs and returns; once more a phoenix where just now
there was none; once more himself but just now out of existence;
another, yet the same . . . must men die once for all, while birds in
Arabia are sure of a resurrection?[113]

he died as bishop of Lyons, about 202. Tertullian, more purely Greek, was pres-
byter in Carthage, and died about 220. He is more usually accorded the title.

109. Although he was later convicted of heresy.

110. Cf. Chap. III, Pt. I, iii. In his work is also a hint of the development
through imagery of a doctrine of the soul and of a way of life such as was later
to be worked out in detail.

111. Tertullian, *De resurrectione carnis,* cap. xii ("Ante-Nicene Library,"
Vol. 15). For him, of course, the fundamental unity and its identification with
God was of the nature of a postulate.

112. *Ibid.*

113. Tertullian, *op. cit.,* cap. xiii. It is to be noted that Tertullian agrees with

Here is illustrated the value of animal symbolism in connection with solar symbolism, to which earlier reference has been made. The Phoenix, more tangible and more readily worshiped than the remote solar orb, became in the Far East the bird priest of the Sun, and lived in a secret wood. Every thousand years it suffered a voluntary death, burning to ashes in a nest built on a palm tree in Phoenicia to serve as its funeral pyre. Like the Sun, each time it rose again. Its ashes then were transferred to the temple of the Sun in Egypt.

On the basis of symbolic principles developed simultaneously by pagan and Christian thought, Christians presented their God as the unity on whose existence all cultures had agreed, in whom was the gathering up and the solution of all symbolisms.[114] In their very first initiation, there was unification of symbolisms. Through baptism the soul is *renatus in aeternum,* as in pagan initiations, and immortality is gained. Water symbolism was then important, while in the *Pistis Sophia* it stands written: "When a man receiveth the mysteries of the baptisms, those mysteries become a mighty fire, exceedingly fierce, wise, which burneth up all sins."[115] Thus in the first place there was union of the symbolisms of the mother and father of all things.[116] Not only, however, was there included the more abstract and fundamental symbolic elements, but there was the ever present and valuable animal symbolism. Fish imagery, similarly associated with this first initiation, was characteristic of the primitive church, and prominent even in the writings of the first Church Father. Vipers, asps, and basilisks, Tertullian suggests, may prefer deserts, "but we, little fishes, after the ex-

Jerome and disagrees with Origen in his attitude toward symbolism; since the basis of his use evidently rests on the literal truth of the story to be symbolized. Cf. pp. 267-268.

114. So general was this habit of reinterpretation of earlier worships among Christians that even today one continues to discover fresh evidence of it. Recent discoveries lead one to believe that in more than one small village of Europe there still lies hidden an ancient shrine, carved with ram's head or other astronomical symbolism, and placed with definite reference to the meridian; while in the parish church below there is held yearly, on that noontide when the sun throws a certain shadow exactly to the sacred point in the shrine of pagan worship, a high mass declared by tradition to be of supreme importance for the village.

115. *Pistis Sophia,* tr. by G. R. S. Mead, Bk. ii, paras. 299-300.

116. Cf. Appendix III, Pt. I, i, and pp. 114-115.

ample of our Ιχθυς, Jesus Christ, are born in water, nor have we safety any other way than by permanently abiding in water. And so that most monstrous creature . . . knew full well how to kill the little fishes, by taking them away from the water." (The "monstrous creature" was a heretical preacher who had prevented many from presenting themselves for baptism.) Such symbolism in primitive religions was associated with that of the sun and sex, and the fish is familiar as a sign of new life; but for the Christians in this period its use was based on the coincidence that in Greek the initials of the phrase "Jesus Christ, Son of God, Savior" spell fish.[117] The symbolism is of deep appropriateness for the mediating principle of the solar trinity: as Eisler notes, the sun himself has been conceived to be "a fish, rising from the ocean and staying with mankind during the day, to return to the ocean and remain in the deep over night emerging therefrom the next morning."[118] There could scarcely be a more ineradicable picture of the drama of the Incarnation, with its expected Parousia.

In accord then with the tradition which grew out of the titanic contest of culture against culture for which the Rome of the first three centuries presented the arena, Christianity took unto itself as insight symbolism the luxuriant imageries of pagan religions and philosophies, reinterpreting and correcting them by pointing out deeper levels in their meaning.[119] By such means occurred the amazing development whereby the faith of

117. This phrase itself may be formed by reading the initials of the first twenty-seven lines of the prophecy of the Erythrian sibyl (*Oracula Sibyllina*, VIII, 217 ff.). St. Augustine, in *De Civitate Dei*, 18, 23, relates that a learned man named Flaccianus showed him these lines, and, after pointing out that, read as an acrostic, they presented the above-mentioned phrase, added: "But if you join the initial letters of these five Greek words, they will make the word *ichthus*, that is, fish, in which word Christ is mystically understood, because he was able to live, that is, to exist, without sin in the abyss of this mortality as in the depth of waters." In the full form the acrostic (given also in Eusebius' *Life of the Blessed Emperor Constantine*) yields the full phrase: "Jesus Christ, Son of God, Saviour, Cross." There is a translation of the oracle by Neale, in the *Christian Remembrancer* for October, 1861, reproduced in B. Pick, *The Cabala*, pp. 88-90; cf. p. 435, Appendix V, Pt. I, ii.

118. Eisler, *Orpheus the Fisher*.

119. It has been noted in comparison, for example, of the Mithraic with the Christian sacrifice, that whereas in both the point of reference is the mediating sun god; with the former, stress is laid on the sacrifice of the "lower wishes" whereas in the latter the sacrifice must be of the whole personality. Cf. Jung, *op. cit.*, p. 478.

the new and obscure sect grew in power, to be defined at last as *"quod semper, et ubique, et ab omnibus."*[120]

Just as pagan religions in the second century had culminated in pantheism, in which the sun was the symbol of the universal deity, so naturally the sun was dominant even in the fragmentary and formative period of Christian doctrine throughout the contest preceding the victory, in the edict of Milan (313 A.D.), of the tradition which was to dominate medieval development. To it accrued the full power of symbolisms of the world without and of the world within, both united in the cross.

III. DEFINITION OF THE TRINITY

IN the Rome of the first three centuries, the birth of that medieval culture within which Christianity was to hold so exalted a position, would have been impossible but for the symbolic tradition.[121] Had the Fathers of the church attempted to establish Christianity as a new and independent religion, rather than as fulfilling the thought of the past in its highest aspects, their faith could scarcely have survived its first infancy in the *mêlée* of conflicting cultures and ideals, and the form medieval culture would have assumed is a challenge to speculation.

The religious background of early Christianity has been treated felicitously by Dr. Angus, whose book appeared with this blurb: "The ultimate triumph of Christianity over its rivals, the religions of symbolism, myth, allegory, and archaic ritual, existent in the remote centuries before Christ." The victory, Dr. Angus states in the words of Dr. Mackintosh,[122] was won "not by borrowing ideas or decking itself out in ancient symbols, but by the exhibition of a fact within the field of history in which were more than fulfilled the inextinguishable yearnings of the

120. The well-known Catholic rule of Vincent of Lerins.
121. For example, Payne-Knight tells us (*op. cit.,* p. 28) that the "T" cross "served as the emblem of creation and generation, before the church adopted it as the sign of salvation; a lucky coincidence of ideas, which, without doubt, facilitated the reception of it among the faithful." (When a head is added to the "T" cross, it gives "the exact appearance of a crucifix.")
Although this thought has been disturbing to later generations; as appeared clearly in the preceding section, it was the mainstay of the Fathers of the early church.
122. Angus, *op. cit.,* p. 314, quoting Mackintosh, *Person of Jesus Christ,* p. 533.

world's desire." It should be borne in mind, however, that the conquest of symbolism by this "fact," was achieved through symbolism.

Through the shaping of the materials of symbolism by the newly defined philosophy of insight imagery, Christianity had triumphed, declaring its God to be that infinite unity in whom all opposites are unified, and of whom all phenomena give those shadowy intimations which have been the inspiration of all philosophies and all religions. The task then at hand was the definition of that tri-unity claimed to be the consummation of all warring trinities. Whatever the value of symbolism in appreciation, its greatest import in medieval tradition is in the apprehension of ideas.

The whole development of thought to which the thirteenth century fell heir had been progress through symbol to more adequate symbol. This progress for Dante had provided that discipline of intellect and emotion which constitutes the approach to the mystic vision. He who would follow Dante in his realization of ninefold truth rooted, as the miracle nine must ever be, in the Trinity, must first understand something of the Trinity in medieval thought, as it became more and more the luminous unification of all symbolisms—and then accompany Dante step by step in his laborious journey to the Paradise at the summit of the Mount.

Just as through symbolism had been accomplished the victory of 313 A.D., so through symbolism was to be accomplished the great intellectual labor of the last centuries of imperial Rome. The whole development of the doctrine of the Trinity is so intimately bound up with insight symbolism that one wonders, the nature of man and of the universe being what they are, if without such symbolism exact definition would have taken place at all. One is further tempted to question which came first, the symbol's elucidation of the dogma, or the dogma elucidated. The question as to how much work the medieval system of symbolism accomplished in this way[123] for the medieval mind prob-

---

123. The situation has been given expression by M. Ferrero, who has discussed psychologically laws underlying symbolism, and the large part it plays in the working out of thought. He says:

"Remarquons avant tous que la métaphore, que nous croyons un privilège de

ably attracted attention in the Middle Ages, if the awe with which they regarded the whole matter of verbal expression may be taken as an indication.[124] Although words had been, from the days of the savage, a source of wonder, and especially of unique importance in magic, the doctrine of the Logos brought the Word into peculiar prominence. This has been remarked already in the work of Lactantius, but was fairly general throughout the period, owing to the influence particularly of Philo, Plotinus, and the writer of the Fourth Gospel. According to Athanasius,

the Son is the Image and Radiance of the Father, and Expression, and Truth. For if, when Light exists, there be withal its Image, viz. Radiance, and a Subsistence existing, there be of it the entire Expression, and a Father existing, there be his Truth, viz. the Son. . . .[125]

The idea of the Son as the Expression of the Father is developed by means of the relation of the sun and its rays. Indeed, it seems doubtful if Athanasius, the great champion of the Deity of Christ and his unity with the Father, could ever have combated Arianism without the assistance of sun symbolism.

FORMULATION OF TRINITARIAN CONCEPT

For Athanasius, as for Plotinus, the fundamental unity underlying all things is a triune God. The controversy of the period raged around the relation existing between the Father and the Son. Athanasius thus points out what seems to him their real unity:

The Saints have not said that the Word was related to God as a fire kindled from the heat of the sun, which is commonly put out again, for

la fantaisie des poètes, est par contre un processus normal de la formation des paroles." (Ferrero, *Les lois psychologiques du symbolisme,* p. 47.)
And again:
   "La métaphore n'est pas seulement un moyen d'exprimer des idées, lorsque les mots ou les signes graphiques font défaut: parfois elle est aussi une vraie forme de la pensée. Lorsqu'un phénomène naturel vient frapper nos sens, il ne réveille pas dans le plus grand nombre des cas une tendance de la volonté à diriger l'attention sur lui et à l'étudier . . . . il provoque par contre très souvent des associations involontaires d'images collatérales qui s'accomplissent par elles-mêmes." (*Ibid.,* pp. 49-50.)
   124. And the passion for etymologies (generally false) in the men of that time. Those given by Isidore of Seville are the best known. Cf. p. 17 n. 35.
   125. Athanasius, *Select Treatises in Controversy with the Arians,* p. 209.

this is an external work and a creature of its author, but they all preach of him as Radiance, thereby to signify his being from the substance, proper and indivisible, and his oneness with the Father.[126]

Further developing this unity, which it is to be noted is not an identity, he says:

Who will presume to say that the Radiance is unlike and foreign from the sun? rather who, thus considering the radiance relatively to the sun, and the identity of the light, would not say with confidence, "Truly the light and the radiance are one, and the one is manifested in the other, and the radiance is in the sun, so that whoso sees this, sees that also"?[127]

Elaborating still further the paradox of a Trinity in a Unity which is indivisible, he writes:

The radiance also is light, not second to the sun, nor a different light, nor from participation of it, but a whole and proper offspring of it. And such an offspring is necessarily one light; and no one would say that they are two lights, but sun and radiance two, yet one the light from the sun enlightening in its radiance all things. So also the God-head of the Son is the Father's; whence also it is indivisible; and thus there is one God and none other but he.[128]

All this was in accord with the usage of the period, but it was to be of incalculable significance.

Arius insisted that the Son had a beginning in time, that is, that there was a time when the Son was not. Athanasius inquires:

For who can even imagine that the radiance of light ever was not, so that he should dare to say that the Son was not always, or that the Son was not before his generation? or who is capable of separating the radiance from the sun, or to conceive of the fountain as ever void of life, that he should madly say, "The Son is from nothing" . . . ?[129]

In answer to the Arian theory that the Son was brought into being for the purpose of creating the world he remarks:

For he is the Father's Radiance; and as the Father is, but not for any reason, neither must we seek the reason of that Radiance.[130]

In this is no dogmatism, but a sifting of questions that are rea-

126. *Op. cit.,* p. 39. 127. *Op. cit.,* p. 41. 128. *Op. cit.,* p. 484.
129. *Op. cit.,* p. 20. 130. *Op. cit.,* p. 356.

sonable from those that are unreasonable. A dispute as to the reason for the existence of the Son was no more intelligent than a dispute over the purpose for which a luminous body emits light. In other words, the reason for the existence of the Second Person of the Trinity is to be sought in the nature of God himself and not in any kind of teleology. Arius' contention was based on the contemporary and erroneous translation in the Septuagint of Prov. 5. 22. Although Athanasius devoted a great deal of energy to the breaking down of errors founded on this authority, at the same time he recognized the necessary function of the Son in creation:

As the Light enlightens all things by its radiance, and without its radiance nothing would be illuminated, so also the Father, as by a hand, in the Word wrought all things. . . .[131]

For Athanasius sun symbolism was an unfailing resource,[132] not only for expression of doctrinal points, but also for keeping his own mind and the minds of his flock clear on fundamental questions, in the midst of the sophisms based on the Father-Son symbolism as used by the Arians.

Scarcely could there have been found a better basis than this controversy for Newman's comment: "The ideas gained from the earthly types are but imperfect . . . in consequence if any one of them is used exclusively of Him, it tends to introduce wrong ideas respecting Him, but . . . their respective imperfections lying on different sides, when used together they correct each other."[133] Similarly there could scarcely be a better statement of the basis of medieval symbolism than is this statement of Newman's.

Strikingly enough, yet inevitably, in view of the nature of the materials of symbolism, the Arians were not able to escape the use of the very symbol which vanquished them. Arius used it in the *Thalia*,[134] in a statement of his own position:

Understand that he is conceived to be Radiance and Light.

131. *Op. cit.*, p. 323.
132. Other examples of this use may be found in *op. cit.*, pp. 22, 34, 36, 42, 48, 49, 140, 141, 144, 150, 153, 154-155, 156, 187, 190, 192, 198, 199, 202, 204, 216-217, 220, 231, 264, 266, 284, 327, 338, 402, 410-411, 417, 421, 452.
133. *Op. cit.*, p. 140, footnote.
134. *Op. cit.*, pp. 94-128. Athanasius gives here a history of Arian opinions, with many quotations. The quotation given above from the *Thalia* is on p. 96.

Here appear even the two significant words "radiance" and "light." (His follower Asterius tried a bit unconvincingly to use the sun symbol in a different way, in an attempt to prove the Son, like the sun, to be one among many creatures.) As a matter of fact, of the nine creeds of the semi-Arians quoted by Athanasius to show their progressive changes of doctrine, all but three contain the phrase "Light from Light" or some equivalent words. Athanasius, never one to lose an opportunity, questions them in their own language:

> But if they speak concerning God and his Word, let them complete their question and then ask, Was the God "who is" ever without rational Word? and whereas he is Light, was he rayless? or was he always Father of the Word? Or again in this manner, Has the Father "who is" made the Word "who is not," or has he ever with him his Word, as the proper offspring of his substance?[135]

Such argument was a mainstay of the church in the early centuries.[136] Augustine himself took up the same thesis:

> Fire engenders a coeval brightness. Among men you only find sons younger, fathers older; you do not find them coeval; but as I have said, I shew you brightness coeval with its parent fire. For fire begets brightness, yet is it never without brightness. Since then you see that the brightness is coeval with its fire, suffer God to beget a Coeternal Son.[137]

In other words, the controversy which threatened the very existence of Christian monotheism,[138] rising partly out of the symbolism drawn from human parenthood, was met by symbolism drawn from the sun—for while a son cannot be coeval with his father, brightness is coeval with its generating luminary. Here solar symbolism was necessary to raise sex symbolism above the limitations of time and space to its true meaning of the Eternal Generation. Thus was defined the infinite Tri-unity to which the

135. *Op. cit.*, p. 209.

136. In the New Testament itself, as will be shown in the next chapter, are revealed the first stages of this differentiation of the persons of the Trinity in terms of solar symbolism, which assumed such prominence in the controversial period.

137. Augustine, *Sermons on . . . the N. T.*, p. 504.

138. The theory of Arius is not to be confused with that of later monotheistic Unitarianism. To Arius the Supreme God was so far removed above the world that of necessity he must create *lesser deities* to create the world. Thus Arius' success would have reintroduced pagan polytheism, under the guise of Christianity.

true relationship of the finite[139] was contained in the dual nature of the Second Person.

The rôle that symbolism played in the development of thought is clear. Quite naturally these early symbolists occasionally were caught unawares by implications in symbolisms as yet unchallenged;[140] nevertheless the principles to govern symbolic usage were gradually worked out in full detail. It is only in self-defense and in the testing of centuries that men win the power to say what they mean and to understand what they have said.

PHILOSOPHIC DEVELOPMENT OF IMPLICATIONS IN THE SYMBOLUM

Not only, however, was the thought of philosophers important in the development of the Trinitarian concept, but the course of history itself exercised an important influence. Al-

139. Cf. Chap. IV, Pt. I, i.

140. A symbolic system is not always proof against error, especially when its use is still in the trial-and-error stage. Tertullian had said:

"He is the Son of God, and is called God from unity of substance with God . . . Even when the ray is shot from the sun, it is still part of the parent mass; the sun will still be in the ray, because it is a ray of the sun—there is no division of substance, but merely an extension. Thus Christ is Spirit of Spirit and God of God, as light of light is kindled. The material matrix remains entire and unimpaired, though you derive from it any number of shoots possessed of its qualities; so too that which has come forth out of God is at once God and the Son of God and the two are one." Tertullian, *Apologeticus,* "Ante-Nicene Library," Vol. 11, pp. 92 ff.

Had this symbolism been fully carried out, as was that used by Athanasius and Augustine later, it would have led to a different doctrine than that which came to be held by the Catholic Church. The relation between the sun and a ray of the sun is not that existing between the first and second Persons of the Christian Trinity, but that existing between an immanent God and any human soul. On the other hand, Tertullian did not himself hold the convictions to which his symbolism would seem to commit him. He tried to correct what he himself recognized as a difficulty in his symbolism, by using the additional symbolisms of root and tree, fountain and river—"But still the tree is not severed from the root, nor the river from the fountain, nor the ray from the sun," likewise, not the Word from God. *Against Praxeas,* c. 8.

His use of psychological symbolism is more true to his own thought: "Whatever you think, there is a word; whatever you conceive, there is reason. You must needs speak it in your mind, and while you are speaking, you admit speech as an interlocutor with you." *Against Praxeas,* c. 5, "Ante-Nicene Library," Vol. 15. He concludes in substance that, in converse with his own word, a person produces thought, so that, in a sense, the word is a second person within the mind that conceives it. This correct use of psychological symbolism (whatever may be thought as to the psychology) Tertullian may have owed to Neoplatonism.

though God for Augustine was the source not only of truth, but
of love,[141] in his symbolism the emphasis is on the light-giving
aspect of the sun. Even the Old Testament has been interpreted
where possible in terms of this light imagery, and the light is
constantly identified with Wisdom[142] "for she is the Brightness
of the everlasting Light."[143] "Wisdom of God, Light of souls,"
is with Augustine a recurrent refrain.

This emphasis, perhaps to be expected in a philosopher, was
none the less inherent in the beginnings of medievalism. Echoing in the ears of the believer through the conflict of ideas,
pagan, Christian, and mystic, were the words "I am the Light
of the world; he that followeth me shall not walk in darkness,
but shall have the light of life."[144] The fiery controversies of the
preceding centuries centered in the nature of the Second Person
of the Trinity, and finally the one point on which all could
agree was the imperative need of light.

The pagans worshiped power or wisdom, and to the early
Christians, the power of knowledge gained through reason and
faith, is a natural concern. To be sure, God is the source, not
only of truth, but also of love, just as truly among Christians as
in the system of the great pagan philosopher, yet interest in God
as love is still subordinate. Whenever Augustine mentioned the
heat of the sun's rays, a thing he did rarely, it was only to em-
phasize further the power to illuminate:

> For He hath covered His light with cloud beneath; and it is difficult
> to fly, eagle-like, above every mist with which all the earth is covered,
> and to see in the words of the Lord most unalloyed light. In case then
> He may haply with the warmth of His rays scatter asunder our darkness,
> and in the sequel vouchsafe somewhat considerably to open Himself,
> let us defer these questions, and see what follows.[145]

Athanasius using sun imagery indeed mentions the Third Person of the Trinity; but even then characteristically omits to give
him any place in the symbolism. The following is typical:

> For where the Father is, there is the Son, and where the light, there

141. The terrible thirst for love exhibited, according to Angus (*Mystery Religions,* p. 276), by dying paganism, and echoed in the *amabam amare* of Augustine, was to bear fruit in a later century.
142. Cf. *Confessions* of St. Augustine, 13, 6.
143. *Wisdom of Solomon* 7. 26.   144. John 8. 12.
145. Augustine, *Homilies on the Gospel according to Saint John,* 5. 22-23,
p. 291.

the radiance; and as what the Father worketh, he worketh through the Son . . . when baptism is given, whom the Father baptizes, him the Son baptizes; and whom the Son baptizes, he is consecrated in the Holy Ghost. And again as when the sun shines, one might say that the radiance illuminates, for the light is one and indivisible, nor can be detached, so where the Father is or is named, there plainly is the Son also; and is the Father named in baptism? then the Son must be named with him.[146]

In brief, in these first centuries still in close touch with Greek philosophical tradition, sun symbolism in spite of full formulation was emphasized in life chiefly in its aspect of light-giving. It was during these centuries that man's attention was directed supremely to the question of intelligibility in the universe.

Plotinus the pagan, in the progress of syncretism, came nearer than any Christian of his time to the complete expression of a Solar Trinity in terms of life-giving, light-giving, and heat-giving.[147] Centuries of bitter experience were to precede the full development of this concept in Christian thought:

> Per solem saepius interpretatur Pater, per radium vel splendorem solis Filius qui est splendor gloriae et figura Patris, per calorem Spiritus sanctus, de quo dicitur, Nec est qui se abscondat a calore ejus . . . aliter, in sole quia circuit mundi machinam, signatur Patris potentia: in splendore qui totum illuminat, Filii sapientia: in fervore qui totum calefacit, Spiritus sancti benevolentia.[148]

Characteristic of the twelfth century are these words from Albertus Magnus expounding the solar Tri-unity which was to become the inspiration of the *Divina Commedia*.

ILLUMINATION OF SYMBOLUM THROUGH LIFE EXPERIENCE

The barbarian invasions put an end to the period of philosophic syncretism. Not only was Greek culture lost to the next few centuries, but Latin culture itself was in peril. Some of its representatives still held their place, but in the form in which they appealed to the barbaric mind many of them are scarcely recognizable. Virgil never lost his supremacy: whether or no

146. Athanasius on Prov. 8. 22, in *Treatises against Arianism*, Vol. 2, p. 338.
147. Cf. Appendix V, Pt. I, ii.
148. Albertus Magnus, *De laudibus B. Mariae Virg.*, 12, 5, I, para. 2.

anything was really known of him, he was revered as the great
sage and magician, although in the Middle Ages proper his
reputation was sadly compromised through implication in black
magic.[149]

Latin culture having come to an end, the struggle for the next
three centuries was to preserve for transmission such fragments
of classical culture as had managed to survive the invasions.[150]
It has been pointed out that while in the fourth century Christians had been forbidden to read the classics, in the fifth century
Christians were the only people who were concerned for the
classics. Gregory the Great, standing on the threshold of the
so-called Dark Ages, continued to stress the symbolism of light,
giving in his commentary on Job a more mystical interpretation.
The fact that he was the first to use the image of the sun as seen
through a cloud or mist, suggestively foreshadows the intellectual atmosphere of the next centuries.

After the *mêlée* of the barbaric invasions Europe awoke to a
Weltanschauung which had little in common with anything
that had gone before.[151] Bede, Alfred, Alcuin, Aelfric, among
the earliest of the outstanding intellectual figures of the period,
had little time for anything further than mere recording of
events and attempts at the education of their barbarian con-
temporaries. The task was not simplified by the fact that they
were cut off from the traditions of ancient culture, being themselves but a few generations from the age of the Germanic
migrations. Since Alfred's interest was thus almost perforce in
practical ethics, he and his co-workers naturally chose to em-
phasize the ascetic elements in the thought of the past,[152] for
whose philosophical intricacies they had neither leisure nor
serenity. Moral emphasis had begun, however, before the days
of Alfred, and is pronounced in the earliest vernacular literatures. The symbolic tradition is carried on, but the ideas ex-

149. Cf., e.g., Comparetti, *Virgil and the Middle Ages*.
150. More fragments of the old learning survived in Ireland and in Northum-
bria than anywhere else. Cf. *Cambridge Medieval History*, Vol. 1, pp. 502-504.
151. Cf. pp. 416 ff.
152. This may account for the traditional feeling that certain early writers,
e.g., Plotinus, Augustine, etc., were mainly ascetic, even though a reading of
their works shows asceticism not to have been the main element of their philosophies.

pressed are chiefly those of hope of healing, cleansing, and relief from an intolerable world.[153a]

This was the situation into which John the Scot brought, almost as if from the clouds, the heritage of Neoplatonic philosophy and mysticism.[153b] He was influenced importantly not only by Dionysius, but also by Gregory of Nyssa, Maximus the Confessor, and Augustine. Thus Eastern infiltration again demands attention. His greatness will be discussed in his relationship to mysticism,[154] and his contribution to theology will receive brief reference in the next chapter, after the discussion of the symbolic method necessary for its understanding.

At the beginning of the twelfth century there was a new development in medieval thought, only partially found in the increasing prominence of scholasticism. Centering, during that age of wandering scholars, in the monastery of St. Victor in Paris, were the beginnings of a renaissance of mysticism. Followers of this movement were generally attached to the Platonic-Augustinian school of philosophy, which maintained, against the Aristotelian-Thomistic school, "the primacy of will over intellect, both in God and in man. So by act of will man attains to God."[155]

All at once, as it were, the world seemed to have discovered what St. John meant in his succinct statement, "God is Love." The sun, important as usual in the development of new ideas, almost as suddenly becomes interesting no longer solely as a symbol of divine light, or of righteousness, but especially as a symbol of God's love. Does not its heat make joyful, vivify, mature fruit, and draw all things to itself?

SUMMARY

In the centuries, then, preceding the life of Dante Alighieri, sun symbolism had led in the unification of life experience. In

---

153a. Cf. pp. 420 ff.
153b. In his translations from the Greek, among which must be mentioned the following four works of Dionysius the pseudo-Areopagite: *Ecclesiastical Hierarchy, Celestial Hierarchy, On the Divine Names,* and *Mystical Theology.*
154. Cf. pp. 357 ff., Chap. V.
155. J. B. Fletcher, *Symbolism of the Divine Comedy,* p. 75. Professor Fletcher shows that Dante, in his *Paradiso,* argues "that the two schools are not antagonistic, but complementary. St. Thomas and his group communicate by

the first five centuries after the life of Christ, the philosophy which gave foundation to insight symbolism took form: Giving intelligibility to all things is an infinite unity, to be known only through nature and past events, alike understood as insight symbols, any one of which if used alone would lead to error. Throughout these centuries the desire had been for wisdom, and attention had centered in the Second Person of the Trinity, whose name alone, in early days, was sufficient for the initiation by baptism. During the Germanic migrations and the gradual recovery from them, the imperative need was for strength to live and to die. Whenever thought was possible, its focus was the power of God and his teaching and judgment through Christ.[156] Thus God had been conceived as light-giving and life-giving. With the awakening of the love element the Trinity was complete. Just at this time Thomas of Aquino was born to give final form to the theological exposition of the Trinity, and Dante Alighieri to include this final formulation as basic in the universe through which he journeyed.

Thus developed the triune Sun of the *Paradiso,* in the eternity of whose light lay the intelligibility of all finite things, as in the *Paradiso* lay the plan and meaning of Dante's journey. The infinite intelligence, of whom nothing could be known in time and space except through symbols, was nevertheless to be approached through the symbols of nature and of scripture, used in rich profusion that their various inadequacies might correct each other and so permit at last the finite to find its true relationship to the infinite. The next need was a law by which this luxuriant symbolism might be ordered and governed in its harmonization by the Sun. This law was the fourfold method of which the development will be discussed in the succeeding chapter. It was the outgrowth of the solution to the problem of the relation of truth to its expression,[157] which man had striven so long to solve, that his trinity might be stable.

science the true; St. Bonaventure and his group communicate by charity the good, . . . Both are needed" (p. 77). For love development cf. also Chap. VI, ii, and its Appendix.

156. Cf. pp. 416 ff.

157. The exact nature of this solution is to be discussed in Chapter IV. It is none the less true that this solar trinity is uniquely stable. and armed against the inroads of pantheism.

In this completion of the solar trinity, the idea of destructiveness and wickedness, frequently associated with the heat aspect of the sun in earlier usage,[158] has disappeared. The heat is still consuming, but it is consuming love—the love of the sun-storm god which, as made clear in the *Paradiso,* if contemned, must repel: the love which in mercy constructed hell, yet the love which aims to draw into the way of supreme joy.

158. Cf., for example, Loki (Scandinavian), Moloch (Ammonite), and Siva (Hindu). This destructiveness is in reality evaluation. Cf. Chap. IV, Pt. I, i.

LITERAL LEVEL	ALLEGORICAL LEVEL	TROPICAL LEVEL
Dante's vision a Comedy, begins in hell, ends in heaven	Dante's political career a Comedy, begins in turbulent Florence, is to end in Florence redeemed	Dante's moral career a Comedy, begins in internal conflict, ends in harmony directed by true philosophy
I. Dante comes to himself in Dark Wood of indescribable terror obscuring right relation between sun and earth	I. Dante comes to himself caught in the political corruption of Guelph-Ghibelline controversy	I. Dante comes to himself in perplexity of mind amid false claims in behalf of human freedom and of "necessity"
Escape barred by Three Beasts—Leopard, Lion, She-wolf	Escape barred by three factions—Florence, France, and Papal Rome	Escape barred by three vices—fraud, violence, and cupidity
Rescue, instituted by Three Ladies, Mary, Lucia, and Beatrice, offered by Virgil, emissary of Beatrice	Rescue, made possible by the Triunity of infinite Power, Wisdom, Love, offered through working out of complementary truths in Ghibelline and in Guelph theory	Rescue, made possible by the Triunity of infinite Power, Wisdom, Love, offered through working out of complementary truths in fatalistic and in voluntaristic theory
II. Progress through the agonies of hell, in increasingly clear vision of threefold evil:	II. Progress through agonies of political situation, in increasingly clear vision of manifold political menace:	II. Progress through agonies of moral situation, in increasingly clear vision of threefold moral menace:
Vestibule *Upper hell*	*Refusal* to take a stand *Failure* to solve problem caused by *gravezza* appears in:	*Refusal* to think *Failure* to solve problem caused by *gravezza* appears in:
Limbo	Change of allegiance to Ghibelline	Change of philosophy to fatalism
Upper circles	individual office-seeking in disregard of political principles	self-assertion in disregard of philosophic solution
City of Dis	*Defiance* of ideals of true empire and church, necessitating implication in the	*Defiance* of ideals of true philosophy and theology, necessitating subjection to
Upper Dis Lower Dis	violence of Valois and graft of Florentine leaders bringing him through betrayal face to face with the	violence in the emotions, and fraud in the intellect, bringing him through betrayal to understanding of the
Satan in Cocytus Turning point in center of earth gave opportunity for further progress	*avarice* of Pope Boniface Turning point in exile of Dante gave opportunity for development of new theory	*root of evil* in cupidity in the will Turning point in complete loss of freedom gave only possible mean of its recovery
Climbing out on the opposite side of the earth	Readjustment	Readjustment
Progress through the labors of purgatory	Progress through the construction of a new political platform	Progress through study and elaboration of a philosophy of life
Ante-purgatory	Offering of new political hope with the Scaligeri	Offering of new moral hope with Lady Philosophy (*Conv.*)
Terraces Terrestrial Paradise	Study and discipline "Party by himself" harmonizing claims of Ghibelline and of Guelph	Study and discipline Philosophy harmonizing the dilemma of "necessity" and of free will
III. Dante at the top of the Mount is ready to pass to the Stars and return to the fulfilment of his mission	III. Dante, master of his political platform, is able to rise to complete vision of ultimate meaning of human organization and to return to become philosophical guide of the empire	III. Dante, master of his moral platform, is able to rise to complete vision of the ultimate meaning of human knowledge, and return to bring the bread of angels again within reach of the people

CHAPTER III. SYMBOLISM IN MEDIEVAL THOUGHT: ITS CENTER IN THE SUN, CONT.

PART II. DANTE'S JOURNEY: THE SUN TRANSCENDENT

I. SITUATION—OPPOSITION OF COSMIC FORCES

IN the year 1300, Dante Alighieri, already midway in the journey of human life,[159] awoke to sudden consciousness of himself as an actor in the drama of life and death. Heir as he was to the tremendous achievement of past ages in the ordering of the inconsistencies of life experience, he yet found himself helpless in a jungle so terrible that "scarcely more is death"—"poco è più morte"—and in it the path was lost—"la diritta via era smarrita." In the fearful darkness of his sudden awakening, knowing only that, Florentine by nation, he was not so by character, he became abruptly aware of the conflict of cosmic forces, of which Florence itself contained only a pale reflection. Given brief hope by the rising of that Sun which had guided man's thinking since its birth, Dante set out to ascend the mount which the dawn disclosed to him. But the *selva selvaggia* still held him in its shadow, and at the very outset a leopard (*lonza*) appeared to bar his way, and not only a leopard, but then a lion (*leone*) and then a she-wolf (*lupa*), that bitterest of all the enemies of man. He who, filled with hope in the freshness of the morning, was mounting upward in response to the sun's power, with the appearance of the *lupa* was seized by such heaviness that, bereft of all hope, he turned back, rushing downward to where the Sun is silent. Thus dramatically in the first lines of the first canto of the *Inferno,* Dante has brought together those forces of which the conflict forms not only his *Commedia,* but the drama of the universe—the conflict of the Tri-unity of life, light, and heat, against the trinity of the beast.

At this point the reader, having glimpsed already the manifold truth as contained in eternity, of this journey undertaken in 1300, may feel himself in the position of one who, before the curtain rises, has pried into the secret of the *dénouement.* If so,

---

159. Thirty-five years of age, as Dante explains in *Convivio,* 4, 24. "Il colmo del nostro arco è ne li trentacinque." Cf. Ps. 90 (Vulgate numbering, 89), verse 10: "The days of our years are threescore years and ten."

let him but remember that the drama to be enacted is the mystery of life, concerning which the initiate cannot be told enough, and concerning which the uninitiate, though he be told all that words can tell, in reality can be told nothing.[160] A mystery was defined in the early Middle Ages as that which is everywhere revealed, but is not understood of those who have not right judgment. That which marked those who had right judgment was freedom in the tradition of insight symbolism, understanding of which it has been the aim of the foregoing chapters to facilitate. Of the three orders of the ninefold symbolism of Dante's journey—the threefold story of his own experience, the threefold allegory of the progress of Humanity with Christ as its Head,[161] and the threefold trope of the Godward journey of any soul—only the first order will be considered in this chapter. The story of Dante's own experience, visionary, political, and moral will be followed through the *Inferno* and the *Purgatorio* to the common goal of all orders of Dante's symbolism,[162] in a conception of the ideal life on earth and in heaven, with its vision of the Infinite and of the relationship to it of humanity and of the individual. Against the background of medieval study of nature with its culmination in the conception of the Triune God, the literal vision with its triple mystical interpretation may be followed to its consummation.

THE DARK WOOD

Dante came to himself in a Dark Wood near the mouth of hell[163]—a vivid description of the situation of the Florentine

160. "We are either admitted to the hidden knowledge, or we are not; and if we are not admitted, we never believe any secret of its ritual even if it be offered to us. The secrets . . . are of their very nature inviolable; for they can only be attained by personal progress; they might be plainly told to the outsider, and not be understood by him. For if anyone has been able to divine and to grasp such a secret, he will not tell it even to his dearest friend; for the simple reason that if his friend is unable to divine for himself, its communication in mere words would not confer the hidden knowledge upon him." Wm. W. Westcott, *An Introduction to the Study of the Kabalah*, pp. 66-67.

161. Cf. p. 69 n. 154.

162. In this chapter the first of the three orders of symbolism discernible in the *Divina Commedia* will be considered; the second, in Chap. IV, Pt. II; and the third, in Chap. V, Pt. II. For the nine levels, thus divided into three orders, cf. Chap. II, especially pp. 30-32, 95-98.

163. Supposedly on the night of April 7, the night before Good Friday in the papal jubilee year of 1300.

magistrate in the late thirteenth and early fourteenth centuries. Anyone who has glanced through the histories of the Italian city states will realize that the intricacies of the Guelph-Ghibelline controversy even over a brief period of time furnish better subject matter for a volume of history than for a paragraph of commentary. Weeks sufficed for such a rise and fall of *régimes* and of factions as would be expected ordinarily to occupy generations.[164] An epoch in Florentine history was made by that family quarrel of Donati against Cerchi, Black Guelph against White, which formed the tragedy of Dante's life. Pope and emperor no longer as two suns shed on Florence and on Italy their guiding light.

Similarly, the Dark Wood is poignantly suggestive of the moral dilemma of ignorant and passionate youth. The exact extent of Dante's youthful delinquencies is not of primary importance for the interpretation of the *Divina Commedia,* but rather the situation in which they had placed him. The Dark Wood signifies properly that perplexity of mind which leaves one prey to any temptation that may offer, rather than grave sin itself. The wayfarer is in darkness because caught between consciousness of freedom and experience of natural law, he is confused as to the guidance of God's two ministers in the moral realm, philosophy and theology. He tells that he was "full of sleep" when he "left the right way," and so, unwittingly insensitive to the guidance of the Sun.[165]

It is then appropriate in multiplex significance[166] that Dante's first progress from the terrible forest of moral and political chaos, where the two suns of each realm are in mutual eclipse, was initiated at dawn by an upward look toward that planet that leads men straight on every road. Here attention is centered

164. Dante addresses these words to Florence: ". . . te che fai tanto sottili provedimenti, ch' a mezzo novembre non giugne quel che tu d'ottobre fili." ". . . thee, who dost make such subtle provision, that to mid-November reaches not, what thou in October spinnest." *Purg.,* vi, 142-144.

165. According to St. Augustine the sleep of the soul is forgetfulness of God. Cf. p. 222.

166. That is, the literal, allegorical, and tropological significance in regard to Dante and his personal career. As will be shown in Chaps. IV and V, it is equally appropriate in regard to the story of Christ, of Humanity, and of the soul in grace, as well as to the stories involved in the Mystic Way.

on the Sun as Deity,[167] bringing a suggestion of the fact that after all, pope and emperor, over whom Guelph and Ghibelline were in conflict, like theology and philosophy, are only his earthly representatives.

THREEFOLD PERIL

At the dawn then to give the most obvious interpretation, having placed at some distance the terrors of the night, Dante turned back to see "lo passo che non lasciò già mai persona viva,"[168] and when after rest he took his way again, that way was barred successively by three beasts, the leopard, the lion, and the she-wolf. In other words, with perspective, Dante's political situation defined itself as one of peril through the machinations of the Florentine factions, of the House of Valois, and of the Roman Curia,[169] characterized respectively by fraud, violence, and cupidity, which vices constitute likewise the roots of moral peril.

But Dante was reasoning as well as describing through his imagery. The three beasts represent on earth the vicious foil of the Trinity, as do Satan's faces at earth's center. The leopard, "gendered in spouse-breach of a pard and of a lioness,"[170] is that one among beasts lacking in himself the power of giving life,[171] in whose impotence is the antithesis of the omnipotent and life-giving Father, while at the same time his spots[172] make him representative of fraud, of which the inevitable outcome is death. More specifically, his spots being Black and White, he suggests that political fraud arising from the strife of the Black and White factions within Guelph Florence, which defrauding her of the light of the Empire, made Dante an exile.

167. According to the *Magnae Derivationes* of Uguccione da Pisa, ἥλιος, the Greek word for sun, comes from the Hebrew *Eli*, God.

168. "The pass, that no one ever left alive." *Inf.*, i, 27.

169. Cf. comment, for example, in the Temple Classics *Inferno*, p. 11.

170. As expressed by Bartolomaeus Anglicus. In Dante's day, the panther was thought to be the female of the leopard.

171. The offspring of parents belonging to two widely differing species is commonly sterile, a type to be produced in no other way than by such unnatural union.

172. "Can the Ethiopian change his skin, or the leopard his spots? then may ye also do good, that are accustomed to do evil." Jer. 13. 23. That is, immutability is associated with the leopard in an evil sense, as in a good sense it is associated with the First Person of the Trinity.

In spite of the activity of the leopard, Dante had had good hope, because the "time was at the beginning of the morning and the sun was mounting up." Moreover, the sun was in Aries, the first astrological sign, in which it is at the time of the vernal equinox, and a new beginning was thus possible, both political and moral. The sun was in Aries at the moment of the Creation, of the Incarnation, and of the Resurrection.

The possibility of a new beginning revealed to Dante by the *bel pianeta* is revealed under the shadow of the cross. Dante, like his ancestor Cacciaguida, is setting out on crusade. Just as the paths of the two motions of the sun through which it governs and gives life to the earth (the diurnal and the annual, the celestial equator and the ecliptic), cross each other in Aries, the sign under which Dante's journey begins; so the two powers through which the Prime Mover governs each sphere of human activity, by their crossing of each other—in itself termed by Dante a reënactment of the crucifixion[173]—were responsible for the bitter cross of which Dante's life as statesman and exile bore the impress. Of all this the eternal meaning in victory was revealed to Dante in the cross of Mars,[174] that planet which governs Aries,[175] the sign of the suffering of the Lamb.[176]

At this moment there appeared the lion. It is to be remembered that Dante in the *Paradiso*, having beheld the meaning in Christ of his life crusade, and the true relationships in God's dual vicarate, found himself "sotto il petto del Leone ardente."[177] The lion in symbolic tradition has a dual significa-

173. Cf. p. 84, and *Par.*, xxvii, 35-36.   174. Cf. pp. 63 ff.

175. Astrologically, each of the twelve signs of the zodiac is "governed" by (nature of influence determined by) either the sun, the moon, or one of the five planets (Uranus and Neptune were unknown to the Middle Ages). Each of the planets governs two signs. Aries is one of the two signs governed by Mars. Since the position of the sun in Aries is one of the two necessary conditions determining the date of Good Friday, Dante's placing the cross in Mars has in this connection an interesting significance. For prominence of the zodiacal signs in medieval culture cf., e.g., *Encyclopedia Britannica* (9th ed.), p. 796.

176. Cf. pp. 66-68. Christ was crucified while the sun was in Aries. The date of Good Friday each year is determined in reference to the first time when the moon is in opposition to the sun (i.e., full moon) *after* the sun enters Aries. Moreover, Aries signifies Ram. Christ is termed the Lamb of God, the name conveying to English ears no sex significance; but it is to be remembered that *Agnus* is a male lamb, in other words, a baby ram. (This fact, indeed, rendered more meaningful to the medieval typologist, the Biblical narrative of the ram which was the substitute in the sacrifice of Isaac.)

177. Cf. pp. 75-76.

tion.[178] In medieval bestiaries he is preeminently good and especially significant of Christ, Lion of the Tribe of Judah, Light of
the world; here however he appears in an evil sense,[179] as
Christ's negation and therefore darkness—the outcome of the
ignorance of wrongful force in strife against the gentleness of
the Lamb.[180]

At this juncture appeared the she-wolf, to deprive Dante of
the last hope of ascending, and—the sun itself appearing to
give no further aid—to drive him back into the Dark Wood,
down where the very sun is silent. Dante was overcome by the
great heaviness (*gravezza*) induced by the dreadful presence,
of which the effect was attraction downward in direct opposition to the upward drawing of the sun.[181] It is little wonder that

178. "Sequitur et duo leones . . . Leo Christus, Leo diabolus. Uterque ti-
mendus. Ille, ne deserat; iste, ne rapiat. Leo a dextris diabolus, qui maxime
tentat per prosperitatem virtutum interius de inani gloria, per prosperitatem
rerum exterius de gula et luxuria; leo enim a sinistra Christus qui consolatur nos
in omni tribulatione nostra: per sinistram adversitas figuratur." Albertus Magnus, *De laudibus B. Mariae Virg.*, 10, 2, 35.

An interesting comparison is in the *Testament of the Twelve Patriarchs,* an
apocryphal writing brought to the knowledge of western Europe by Robert
Grosseteste, bishop of Lincoln. In the *Testament of Joseph,* the speaker saw a
virgin, born from Judah, "and from her went forth a Lamb, without spot and
on his left hand there was as it were a Lion; and all the beasts rushed against
him, and the Lamb overcame them and destroyed them and trod them under
foot. And because of this the angels rejoiced, and man, and all the earth." Cf.
p. 76.

179. In medieval symbology it is usual to find any symbol used for Christ
also capable of use for an evil character in a leading position (e.g., demons,
evil leaders of men), since the one draws man upward from man to angel, while
the other drags him downward from man to beast.

Cf. also the fact that pride is the *initium* of sin and the lion is proud while
Christ is the beginning of goodness, the second Adam as against the first.

180. Christ, here represented by Dante himself, is in this situation the Lamb,
to be saved, as by his ancestor David, from the jaws of the Lion. It is especially
suitable to think here of Christ as the Lamb, because the sun is in Aries at the
time of the *Commedia,* as at that of the Incarnation (Feast of the Annunciation,
actual beginning of Christ's earthly life, is March 25) and at that of the Passion
—cf. footnote (176) above. Cf. the paradox stated by Venantius Fortunatus,
"The Lamb withdraws the sheep from the jaw of the wolf." ("Ante-Nicene
Library," Vol. 22, pp. 223-227.)

181. That the wolf is a force of evil of which Dante is conscious throughout
the scenes of the *Commedia,* rather than *dramatis persona* in one scene only, is
indicated by Dante's comment as he views the purgation of the avaricious and
the prodigal (*Purg.,* xx, 10-15):

"Maledetta sie tu, antica lupa,
    che più di tutte l'altre bestie hai
    preda
per la tua fame sanza fine cupa!
O ciel . . .
    quando verrà per cui questa dis-
    ceda?"

"Accurst be thou, she-wolf of old,
    that hast more prey than all the other
    beasts, for thy hunger endlessly deep!
O heaven . . . when will he come
    through whom she shall depart?"

this brutal opposition to the force of primal love should have left him helpless and terror-stricken.

Throughout the history of thought, animal symbolism has veiled the truer imageries of reality, as here it tempers to human finitude the overwhelming truths of good and evil. The earthly sun, in Dante's story, brings the first intimation of the power of the triune center of all light, and with the appearance of the *lupa* comes his first clear consciousness of the *gravezza* of three-fold evil. It is the third circle of lights which not only completes the triple crown, but also reveals to Dante's sun-strengthened gaze the hidden meaning of the sun of sense, greatest of physical symbols;[182] here, the advent of the third beast brings not only completion of the trinity of evil, but the full force of its *gravezza.* Just as Dante is soon to receive from the sun new strength through Beatrice as the instrument of the Holy Spirit, so later, to his grief, he is to be brought close to the harlot of many forms,[183] Circe, whose power as bitter enemy of Beatrice he now feels through that beast which bears her title.[184] The she-wolf appears then as negation of the full revelation of the solar trinity, especially as opposing the Holy Spirit, the sun in its heat aspect, and her power draws from cold to more bitter cold.

In the Inferno the canine characteristics are most prominent in the circle where

> Cerbero, fiera crudele e diversa,
>   con tre gole canimamente latra
>   sopra la gente che quivi è sommersa,[185]

while *"urlar* li fa la pioggia *come cani"*[186] and in Cocytus, where even the faces of those frozen in the ice are *"cagnazzi* fatti per freddo."*[187] Throughout the *Divina Commedia* dogs,[188] foxes, and wolves, representing wicked men or principles of

---

182. Cf. pp. 58 ff.   183. Cf. *Purg.,* xxxii, 148 ff.

184. *Lupa,* she-wolf, is a term used in Italian also for harlot. Cf. pp. 223, 325. Isidore, in his *Etymologies* (18, 42, 2), states: "Lupae meretrices sunt a rapacitate vocatae, quod ad se rapiant miseros et adprehendant."

185. "Cerberus, a monster fierce and strange, with three throats, *barks dog-like* over those that are there immersed." *Inf.,* vi, 13-15.

186. "The rain makes them *howl like dogs." Inf.,* vi, 19.

187. "Made *doggish* by the cold." *Inf.,* xxxii, 70-71.

188. With the exception of the Veltro (cf. pp. 166-167). The sense is by way of a distinction between the genus Canis and species of Canis.

wickedness, manifest the root of all sin, cupidity, direct opposition to love as is cold to heat. The canine vice is constantly associated with cold and cupidity,[189] negation of love and the heat-giving aspect of the sun. The sin against the Holy Ghost is the one unpardonable sin, having the *lupa's* power to deprive of all hope and to drive men below the reaches of the sun.

Much deeper, then, was the significance of the beasts than the mere personification of the three vices which in reverse order determine the structure of hell: fraud, violence, and uncontrolled desire.[190] It is true that the spotted pard appeared to the Middle Ages as symbol of fraudulence (indeed he was so considered by two of Dante's favorite authors, St. Thomas and Richard of St. Victor), and the appropriateness of violence and avarice for the other two beasts is equally well established. Nevertheless, it is not of the nature of medieval tradition to stop with such superficial symbolism. Understanding progresses only through grasp of relationships, and as Dante is to become increasingly aware, the relationship fundamental among the manifestations of evil is a parody of the divine Tri-unity. His political perception failed to grasp the true evil of Florentine factions and of the plots of the House of Valois, until he recognized the usurped temporal power of the papacy as the root of earthly misgovernment. Similarly, in his personal life it was only with bitter experience of the fundamental cupidity rampant in Florence that there came full realization of the root from which sprang the fradulence (*lonza*) of her florin-fed life, and the violence (*leone*) of her rebellion against the empire. In

189. According to the *Summa Theologica*, 1, 2, Q. 84, *art.* 1, the word "cupidity" has three senses: (1) "uno modo, prout est *appetitus inordinatus divitiarum*, et sic est *speciale peccatum;* (2) alio modo, secundum quod significat *inordinatum appetitum cujuscumque boni temporalis*, et sic est *genus omni peccati:* nam in omni peccato est inordinata conversio ad commutabile bonum, ut dictum est . . . .; (3) tertio modo sumitur prout significat *quamdam inclinationem naturae corruptae ad bona corruptibilia inordinate appetenda;* et sic dicunt, cupiditatem esse *radicem omnium peccatorum*, ad similitudinem, radicis arboris, quae ex terra trahit alimentum; sic enim ex amore rerum temporalium omne peccatum procedit." Cf. pp. 184-185, 200-201.

190. Aristotle in his *Ethics*, specifies three main vices, κακία, ἀκρασία, θηριότης, in Latin, *malitia. incontinentia. bestialitas.* Dante saw these three as violence, incontinence, fraud. Note that this classification is according to the outward manifestation of sin, while the classification in the *Purgatorio* is according to the root of sin, since there the disease is being healed.

fine, on the allegorical and moral levels of Dante's personal story also, it was the wolf that brought the fuller revelation of the potentialities of evil. Thus is worked out in time and space the pattern of the *Paradiso*.

Owing to these vices, and especially that of the she-wolf,[191] it had been long since the voice of pope or emperor, the two suns of Rome, had been heard in Florence. Here is involved a symbolism of infinite suggestiveness. It must be remembered that in the immediate background of medievalism lay the elaboration of the solar trinity and the fulfilment in the Word, its Second Person, of that toward which philosophy had been striving. The equivalence of voice and light in the Word is of primary importance. The silence or the lack of the true voice of pope or emperor had plunged the world into a chaos from which redemption was possible only through the living Logos.[192] The wolf is in definite opposition to the sun, even in the matter of the equivalence of voice and light, for it used to be believed that if a wolf meet a man and see him first, the man is stricken dumb.[193]

Even yet, however, the meaning has not been exhausted of the triple opposition with which, as it were, Dante set the stage for his comedy. Again the significance is not by way of obscure or code meaning with which Dante, led by a poetic fancy or fashion, chose to endow creatures of the imagination, but is rather a significance bound up with the origin of language,

191. Cf. the discussion of the florins, pp. 54-56.

192. The definition of the Second Person of the Trinity in terms of the Light-Radiance of the Divine Sun created a problem for medieval commentators in the words *Fiat lux* in the first chapter of Genesis. Eternal Light, equated with the Word (Logos) must be specifically excepted from the account of creation. Thus in the *Glossa Ordinaria* (Walafrid Strabo, ninth century) it is written: " 'Et facta est lux,' id est angelica et coelestis substantia, in se temporaliter, sicut erat in sapientia quantum ad ejus incommutabilitatem, aeternaliter. Vel notatur hujus creaturae informitas scilicet et imperfectio antequam formaretur in amore Conditoris: formatur enim cum convertitur ad incommutabile *lumen Verbi.*"

Ambrose thus connects voice and light: "Fiat, inquit, lux. Unde vox Dei in Scriptura divina debuit inchoare, nisi a lumine? . . . Erat quidem Deus ipse in lumine, quia lucem habitat inaccessibilem, et erat lumen verum, quod illuminat omnem hominem venientem in hunc mundum; sed eam lucem fieri voluit, quae oculis corporalibus comprehenderetur. . . . Fiat, inquit, lux. Plena vox luminis non dispositionis apparatum significat, sed operationis resplendet effectu. Naturae opifex lucem locutus est, et creavit." Ambrose, *Hexameron*, 1, 9. Cf. also p. 194.

193. Isidore, *Etymologies*, xii, ii, 23-24. For literature, cf. George F. Black, *A List of Works Relating to Lycanthropy.*

reaching back of history itself. Although there have been many guesses, no one knows exactly when or how there was established the strange kinship between sun and wolf, yet in regard to Zeus himself it has been argued as to whether in reality he was wolf-god or light-god. The very words are related etymologically, the word "wolf" with "light," and the word "wolf-skin" with "darkness."[194] Firmly established as are the light associations of Zeus, Sir J. G. Frazer has said:[195] "The connexion of Lycaean Zeus with wolves is too firmly established to allow us seriously to doubt that he is the wolf-god."[196] Moreover, Zeus is not the only "Shining One" with whom there exists this close association with the wolf. Osiris, god of the sun, whose sign was Sirius the dogstar, was represented clad in a wolfskin. It is unnecessary to give more examples,[197] since the symbolisms of these two were fundamental in the forming of Dante's tradition; and whether or not he was aware of the facts, they had shaped the symbolisms that he found at hand. The wolf for Dante was in manifold association with the sun. Its very name brought the opposition to the sun in the form of association with the harlot[198] of Revelation, and thus well showed forth the corruption of the papacy, divinely appointed sun on earth.

This symbolism reaches out, as it were, organic filaments which penetrate deeply throughout the poem. With its mysterious union and conflict of sun and wolf, suggesting a dim apprehension in man's earliest thinking of fundamental unity and the ultimate nonexistence of evil, it is rightly the imagery through which Dante may achieve the mystic inversion and attain to the ultimate truth of the vision in eternity. More than this, the symbolism itself implies, that which Dante believed, that the de-

194. λύκος, wolf.
    λύκη, daybreak.
    λύγη, darkness.
    λυκέη, wolfskin.
    (Pausanias asserts that *Lykosura,* founded by *Lykaon,* was "the first city that ever the sun beheld.") A. B. Cook, *Zeus, a Study* . . ., Vol. 1, pp. 64-65.
195. Commenting on Pausanias, 8, 38, 7.
196. Quoted in A. B. Cook, *Zeus,* Vol. 1, p. 64, note.
197. A notable example is given in the Norse fire-god, Loki, with his three evil offspring who bring about the destruction of gods and men. The most powerful of the three (according to some authorities representing the death which is the wages of sin) was the Fenris-wolf.
198. See p. 163 n. 184.

struction of evil is a self-destruction inevitable in its very nature. The dog, enemy of fox and wolf, is remarkable among all animals for its destruction of the evil among its own kind. In the *Divina Commedia* dogs and wolves bear witness to the power of Circe, but also dogs may become watchdogs of the Lord;[199] and so the first word of cheer spoken to Dante is of a greyhound, "Veltro," who shall come to accomplish the destruction of the wolf, calling to mind that which is to be revealed to Dante in the heavenly spheres in regard to Can Grande della Scala.[200] The old tradition should be remembered, that with the *annus canicularis,* a period of Sirius the dogstar, an emperor would come to bring salvation to the world. The dogstar marks the climax of the sun's course.

Although there is reason to suppose that the three beasts assumed at first sight the guise of sources in which Dante recognized political peril (possibly the papacy, the city of Florence, and the House of Valois,[201] characterized respectively by the three sins mentioned here in their opposition to the three persons of the Trinity), Dante's comprehension of them is increased on his further pilgrimage.[202] The progressive understanding of his past experience is not only a secret of the power of Dante's dramatic method, but is also, as will be more clear later, an important element in the symbolism.[203]

THREEFOLD HOPE

To Dante, plunging downward from the beasts, hope of rescue was proffered through the appearance of a figure in the desert, whose long silence or faintness—"per lungo silenzio

---

199. In the thirteenth and fourteenth centuries, the Dominican friars were termed "Domini canes," dogs of the Lord. According to the legend, before the birth of Dominic, his mother dreamed that she brought forth a black and white dog with a burning torch in his mouth. Preachers, moreover, are described in one of the most familiar of medieval exempla as the little barking dogs of the Lord.

200. His name means literally, The Great Dog of the Ladder. Cf. p. 76. On another level, the Veltro, the Deliverer, is Christ himself. Albertus Magnus calls Christ a hunting dog, pursuing the evil to their destruction and his saved to their blessedness. Cf. p. 202 and Jung, *Psychology of the Unconscious,* pp. 268 ff.

201. Such identifications are found in various commentaries on the *Divina Commedia.* For example, cf. the "Temple Classics" ed., note on *Inf.,* i, 131.

202. Cf. pp. 184-185, 190, 200-201.   203. Cf., e.g., pp. 93 and 394.

parea fioco"—became meaningful[204] in the revelation of his identity as the sage Virgil, spirit of the empire. The rule of the rightful empire over mankind would make moral progress possible. Virgil's voice had been long unheard in Florence and in Italy; though he was praised as a poet (and still more as a magician) his counsel had been long unheeded.

In sore need though he was, Dante doubted his right to accept this deliverance until reassured that Virgil was but expressing the will of the three blessed ladies,[205] Mary, Lucia, and Beatrice, functioning in the *Divina Commedia* as an expression of the Divine Power, Wisdom, and Love.[206] Indeed, the effect of these three ladies on Dante, conveyed even by word of them from Virgil, is that of the sun:

> quali i fioretti, dal notturno gelo
>   chinati e chiusi, poi che 'l sol li'mbianca
>   si drizzan tutti aperti in loro stelo,
> tal mi fec'io, di mia virtute stanca,
>   e tanto buono ardire al cor mi corse,
>   ch'i 'cominciai come persona franca.[207]

Dante's soul touched by love straightened up and was freed to bear fruit; he, who at his first glimpse of the sun over the mountain top had understood that the political solution must be reached in the light of infinity, was reassured by the thought that he was under the direction of the Divine Sun in his attempt, with Virgil's guidance, to solve the problem. Thus also began the first step in the romance of courtly love:[208] Dante undertook the toil assigned by the beloved.

Beatrice was described in the first words of Virgil's reassur-

204. The question as to whether *fioco* is better translated "hoarse," indicating Virgil's hoarseness from centuries of silence, or his weakness and, figuratively, the disregard of his counsel, or whether it is better rendered "faint," to convey more pictorially the dramatic effect of his appearance, is unimportant, since in either case the symbol of the long silence is unchanged. Cf. Grandgent's commentary on *Inf.*, i, 63, also that of Scartazzini; and Flamm, 2, 209, and Moore, 1, 181. To understand both implications is in accord with the tradition.
205. Cf. pp. 234-237.
206. "Sciendum est quod cum in divinis sint duae processiones; una per modum intellectus, quae est processio Verbi; alia per modum voluntatis, quae est processio Amoris." Aquinas, *S.Th.*, 1, *Q.* 37, *art.* 1, resp.
207. "As flowerets, by the nightly chillness bended down and closed, erect themselves all open on their stems when the sun whitens them: thus I did, with my fainting courage, and so much good daring ran into my heart, that I began as one set free." *Inf.*, ii, 127-132.
208. Pp. 36-37, 226, 346-347, 386-390, and especially 427-430.

ance, in the imagery of light which marked her an emanation of the sun. In the trinity of the three blessed ladies through whom is made known the will of the Divine Sun, Beatrice appears as she did in the *Paradiso,* as the instrument of the Holy Spirit, and through her is revealed the will of the two, Mary and Lucia, who send her forth. It was this expression of the solar trinity which brought to Dante in his human limitation, comfort and assurance of opposition to the power of the three beasts. The opposition, however, is not properly an opposition of virtues to vices, as some readers have been inclined to suppose. That which vice opposes is not properly virtue, even such high virtue as faith, hope, and charity, but rather, as Dante has seen already and is to understand more fully, the triple cosmic principle, the Divine Trinity of Life, Light, and Love. Virtues belong to a different order of reality, representing habits which man must establish within himself in response to the cosmic principle, that he may gradually free himself from the burden of *gravezza.*

Even the identification of Mary with Divine Mercy, Lucia with Illuminating Grace, and Beatrice with Revelation, is but a partial truth,[209] and, as partial truths have a way of doing, may lead to absurdity of interpretation. The assumption has been made,[210] for example, that Dante had sinned against grace and the simple faith of his childhood, in preoccupation with Lady Philosophy, the rival of Beatrice who is Revelation. As always, the harmony and consistency of the whole symbolic system must be the decisive factor in the interpretation of the *Commedia.* Dante deliberately identified Lady Philosophy with Eternal Wisdom, the Logos, the Second Person of the Trinity:[211, 212]

In massima lode di Sapienza dico . . . che nel divino pensiero, ch'

209. Cf. pp. 278 ff. Dante's characters are never mere abstractions, like Bunyan's.

210. Based on Dante's praise of Lady Philosophy, which follows in point of time on that of Beatrice, his own statement that he had left the right way, and Beatrice's rebuke in the Earthly Paradise.

211. Note that the human philosophy which Dante declares (*Convivio,* 3, 13) to be his object is not properly to be ranked as created, but as the indwelling of the Eternal Wisdom. Cf. the dictum of Thomas Aquinas that the *knowledge by which we know* is a "certain participation in the divine nature." (*S.Th.,* 2, 2, *Q.* 23, *art.* 2, *ad* 1.)

212. Boethius, to whom Dante was devoted, had made the same identification in his *De consolatione.*

è esso intelletto, essa era quando lo mondo fece; onde seguita che Ella lo facesse.[213]

And:

Aprite gli occhi vostri, e mirate, chè anzi che voi foste, Ella fu amatrice di voi, acconciando e ordinando lo vostro processo; e poi che fatti foste, per voi dirizzare, in vostra similitudine venne a voi.[214]

If, then, preoccupation with philosophy be a sin against Beatrice as Revelation, devotion to Christ, the Word, is sin against Revelation.

Beatrice, however, appears to Dante as surrogate of the Holy Spirit in the realm of time and space no less truly than among the spheres. Obviously, devotion to the Logos is not a devotion to merit the rebuke of the Holy Spirit. Further, it is the Holy Spirit who brings men to the Logos. A devotion to Philosophy, following a devotion to Beatrice, is then, on Dante's principles, inevitable. Lady Philosophy may have been a real girl, but in Dante's unification of his life experience, she is Philosophy, and, as such, surrogate of the Logos. Beatrice was a real girl, but in the symbolism of her worshiper's life, she is Eternal Love, and as such, surrogate of the Holy Spirit. There can be no rivalry between the Persons of the Trinity, the only possibility of sin being the failure to recognize their essential oneness. Dante's sin against Beatrice, however it be interpreted,[215] involves a sin against Lady Philosophy as well, who appears here

213. "In supreme praise of Wisdom I say . . . that she existed in the divine thought, which is intellect itself, when he made the universe; whence it follows that she made it." *Convivio,* 3, 15.

214. "Open your eyes and see that, before ye were, she loved you, preparing and ordering your progress; and after ye were made, to direct you aright she came to you in your likeness." *Ibid.* This and the preceding passage will be recognized immediately as referring to the activity of the Logos. The use of the feminine pronoun in a designation of the Second Person of the Trinity entered Catholic thought from the Hebrew Wisdom Literature. Cf. *Wisdom of Solomon,* 726. For Thomistic theology compare the definition of the wisdom by which men are wise as *quaedam participatio divinae sapientiae* to which phrase the editors of the *Summa* under Leo XIII added in their index *quae Deus est.* Cf. also Thomas' discussion in *S.Th.,* 1, *Q.* 39, *art.* 8, of the propriety of the terms power, wisdom, and love to designate the three persons of the Trinity, respectively, and his use in *S.Th.,* 3, *Q.* 3, *art.* 8, of the word and wisdom terminology for the Son as showing a reason why the Son should have been the one of the divine persons chosen to assume a human form.

215. Cf. p. 229.

as Lucia, marked by her very name[216] as the Light of Eternal Wisdom.

Dante's love quest was inspired by the star eyes[217] of the fair Beatrice, representative to him of God. It will be recalled that he had used this symbolism in regard to Lady Philosophy, declaring that

li occhi di questa donna sono le sue *demonstrazioni,* le quali, dritte ne li occhi de lo 'ntelleto, innamorano l'anima, liberata da le condizioni.[218]

Similarly it may be assumed that the eyes of Beatrice, the demonstrations of divine things inspired by the Holy Ghost, who is Love, are bright as the writings of theology. This symbolism was appropriate to Dante, to whom the writing in any science was truly the star which illumed it.[219] Although Dante approached the mouth of hell trusting solely to the guidance of Virgil, representative of but two of God's four regents on earth, it was with the assurance of direction by church and theology, the Christ-ordained channels for the guidance of the Holy Spirit.

II. PROGRESSION—INSIGHT INTO COSMIC DRAMA

INSIDE THE GATES: THE GREAT REFUSAL

HAVING passed under the dark archway with its dreadful warning, Dante beheld vast multitudes of swirling, eddying souls, scorned alike of heaven and hell—souls whose very names

216. The hypothesis that Lucia, whose name means Light, represents the Eternal Wisdom, explains all that is told of her function in the *Commedia.* Beatrice, Eternal Love, is sent forth to Dante by Lucia, moved by Mary (surrogate here of the Divine Father, even as she was at Nazareth). The expression "il tuo fedele" is appropriate, both because of Dante's devotion to Lady Philosophy, and because of his character as one of the "faithful," i.e., a member of the Christian church. (The advantage in consistency of this interpretation, over the assumption that Dante had a devotion to St. Lucy which he mentions nowhere else, is plain.) Again, the one appearance of Lucia in the *Purgatorio* accords well with this hypothesis. Cf. pp. 216, 235-236. (Of course this is not to deny a possible devotion to St. Lucy on the part of Dante.)

217. Cf. *Inf.,* ii, 55; *Par.,* iv, 139; xvii, 114.

218. "The eyes of this lady are her demonstrations, the which, when turned upon the eyes of the intellect, enamour that soul which is free in its conditions." *Convivio,* 2, 15 (16).

219. Dante had said: "in ciascuna scienza la scrittura è stella piena di luce, la quale quella scienza dimostra"—"in every science, writing is a star, full charged with light, which showeth forth that science." *Ibid.*

might not be mentioned for they had forfeited not only the gift of life, but the gift of death itself. This realm of the trimmers, the Tomlinsons of humanity, was only too suggestive of the first possible attitude to political and moral difficulties, that is, the refusal to take a definite stand—and of its unspeakable nature and inevitable outcome.[220] Dante turned as quickly from thought of the Great Refusal in the dilemma of the opposition of freedom to natural law, as he did in the dilemma of the opposition of Guelph to Ghibelline. With his guide, the Florentine prior passed hastily on to the fulfilment of his labor, only to be halted by the ferryman of flame-encircled eyes.

On the shore of Acheron, where the souls of the damned gather like autumn leaves, Dante encountered in thunder and earthquake the initial manifestation on his journey of the love of the sun-storm god in the only form in which it may be felt in hell.[221] Insensible, he was borne across to the shore of eternal darkness, fire, and ice, "ne le tenebre etterne, in caldo e 'n gelo."[222]

UPPER HELL: THE GREAT FAILURE

Before him Dante beheld "a fire, which conquered a hemisphere of the darkness,"[223]—such a fire as he was not to see again in hell, in the infernal darkness of which fires do not shine.[224] Although fires still show forth the activity of love, it is a love which has been contemned, and in consequence they are separated fires, burning with a dead flame, cold to all but the sinner—the flame rather of the firefly than of the star.

The fire that enveloped the castle of pagan learning was unique because within, though there had been separation from God, there had been no opposition. Entering the castle of seven walls by the gates of the seven liberal arts, Dante found himself among the representatives of the greatest thought of the past. Here dwelt such wisdom as enlightens, leading to an understanding of the needs of the empire and of the moral life, al-

---

220. One picture here is of political slackers bled by wasplike grafters.
221. Cf. p. 37 and pp. 213-214.   222. *Inf.*, iii, 87.
223. "Un foco ch'emisperio di tenebre vincia." *Inf.*, iv, 68-69.
224. Thomas Aquinas explained that hell is among the places where fire does not shine.

though being without the grace mediated by the church, it could give a life only of desire without hope.[225] Yet those poets whose song like the eagle soars to the sun have been preparing for the coming of the double Sun of Rome, Christ himself, to complete his dual vicarates, and so in hell itself they live in the light of reason and in the fierce heat of desire, which in its very agony constitutes their differentiation from the damned below them.

Consideration of the local Ghibelline party presented no hope to the disillusioned Guelph, but rather such a picture as that of the castle of the good pagans. The best of government unillumined by an autonomous church gives birth perennially to desire without hope. Civil government exists for the sake of pro-

225. Cf. fire as indicating the spiritual principle in man, and the suggestion in its upward burning here, that these souls may not be doomed to ultimate loss of the "ben del l'intelletto." (Cf. p. 185 *et alia.*) Note that Dante equates perdition of soul to the loss of the "good of the intellect."

Even were one of these pagans, however, to be permitted to rise above the earth, he could never reach heaven itself, because limited to the regions of space by the compass of his enlightenment. Dante in the *Convivio* has interpreted the seven planetary heavens as the seven liberal arts, and the two remaining spatial heavens as metaphysics and moral science. Thus the farthest reaches of pagan learning are still contained within time and space only.

The seven liberal arts formed the standard prephilosophical course in the medieval system of education. They were divided into the Trivium and the Quadrivium. Beyond them were three types of philosophy. Below is listed this standard scheme of human knowledge as conceived in the Middle Ages, together with the authorities in each field, and the spheres which Dante likens to each (*Convivio,* 2, 14-15, *q.v.*):

Trivium:	Grammar	Priscian, Donatus	Heaven of the Moon
	Dialectic (logic)	Aristotle	Heaven of Mercury
	Rhetoric	Cicero	Heaven of Venus
Quadriv-ium:	Arithmetic	Boethius	Heaven of the Sun
	Music	Pythagoras	Heaven of Mars
	Geometry	Euclid	Heaven of Jupiter
	Astrology (astron.)	Ptolemy	Heaven of Saturn
Philoso-phies:	Physics	Aristotle	Heaven of Fixed Stars (visible)
	Metaphysics	Aristotle, Peter Lombard	Heaven of Fixed Stars (inferred)
	Ethics	Aristotle, Seneca	Primum Mobile

But to rise above the spatial spheres, into the presence of God, Theology is required, the noblest of all sciences.

Blessed souls, dwelling in eternity, merely appear in space though their existence is not therein, and to such a condition above time and space no conceivable ascension could raise man but the ascension of Christ himself. It will be remembered that in Dante's truth-revealing passage through the realm of the heavenly spheres, Christ's resurrection was reënacted at the juncture of time and eternity (cf. p. 84).

moting peace and justice,[226] and this, without the direction
toward higher ends of those kept in peace by its efforts, remains
the mere shell of material civilization, as such doomed, like the
civilizations of Greece and Rome. A change of allegiance, then,
from the Guelph party to the Ghibelline, would be no solution
for the difficulties in which Dante found himself.[227]

Similarly devoid of hope was the philosophy of fatalism to
one born among those confident in the power of free will.
Though provided with a basis for the development of the pagan
virtues, he whose determinism leaves no place for human will,
is doomed like the sages in the castle to a life of desire without
hope. Indeed, his virtue is a mere outer husk devoid of its living
soul; for to the Middle Ages a perfect ethic was far from being
the ultimate climax of the good life. Perfect earthly virtue in
harmony with natural law was made possible by the four pagan
virtues, yet the addition of the three theological virtues, faith,
hope, and charity, was necessary, not only to raise man to Paradise beyond time and space,[228] but to overcome the threefold
detriment of the Fall and so to restore him to the freedom of the
Earthly Paradise. Enshrined in the luminous place within the
castle of pagan wisdom, the seven liberal arts could teach supremely of virtuous living, yet the castle remained in hell.

Beyond this outermost of the infernal regions, Dante entered into a place where "naught shone," not even this light of
natural knowledge. Political and moral darkness was complete. Faced by the failure of both parties, he was at a loss.
There was still the possibility of the pursuance of public office
for its own sake. In spite of the fact that the Guelph *régime* had

226. See *Monarchia*, 3, 16.
227. Cf. discussion of Dante's later developed "party by himself," in the section on the heaven of Mercury, pp. 40 ff.
228. *Purg.*, iii, 34-42.

"Matto è chi spera che nostra ragione
　possa trascorrer la infinita via,
　che tiene una sustanzia in tre per-
　　sone
　. . . se possuto aveste veder tutto,
　mestier non era parturir Maria;
e disiar vedeste sanza frutto
　tai che sarebbe lor disio quetato,
　ch'etternalmente è dato lor per
　　lutto."

"Mad is he who hopes that our reason
may compass that infinitude which one
substance in three persons fills. . . .
If ye had been able to see the whole,
no need was there for Mary to give
birth; yet ye have seen such sages desire fruitlessly, whose desire had else
been satisfied, which is given them for
eternal grief."

not brought peace to the city, there was the fallacious hope that by gaining a position of command he might be able to inaugurate that civic peace which it would have been impossible to achieve by independent action. Journeying through hell under the leadership of Virgil, spirit of empire, Dante perceived, however, in many gruesome forms the confusion and anarchy which are the natural outcome of individual office-seeking. It is in point that his own actual expulsion from his native city was brought about through such anarchy, a condition which made possible the accusation of the very crime punished in and by the person of Satan. For Dante was at length accused of dishonesty in office. It was, in fine, the independent temporal sovereignty specifically granted to the pope by the Donation of Constantine, that subjected both church and empire to the greed which, fearsomely foreshadowed in the *lupa,* Dante was to behold as Satan himself.

Analogous in the moral story is the attempt by force of self-decision to override moral difficulties without intellectual solution of the problem of freewill and determinism. Dante shared in the moral problems of humanity which St. Paul so poignantly pictured.[229] The attempt to live in disregard of this fact in the service of ideals, no matter how noble, can but lead downward through the circles of that region wherein what is willed cannot be done. As Dante beheld with increasing vividness on his journey, the absolute autonomy within its own sphere of natural law provides the only possible *milieu* for the autonomy of human freedom.

In the realm where naught shone, Dante learned of sins against the God of Life, Light, and Love, such as must run riot where the sun of papacy is rendered impotent by its avaricious attempt to usurp another's power, and where the sun of empire weakened by this usurpation fails to function. Bit by bit he became aware of the horror which must result from conflict between God's earthly vicarates, rendering impossible to each, fulfilment of its responsibility.

Unlawful lovers are driven by a stormy wind in darkness.

---

229. "The good that I would I do not, but the evil which I would not, that I do." Rom. 7. 19. Cf. verse 24.

God's justice is shown in the punishment of their sin, which having been against wisdom (failure to control desire by intellect) is punished in darkness, not in cold.

More serious is the sin of the gluttons, more close to its root in cupidity, and as such it is punished by the coldness of the eternal heavy rain, which instead of preparing for the fruitage to which the sun gives life, as do earthly showers, serves only to render fetid the ground on which it falls. Here Dante learned of the three sparks, pride, envy, and avarice,[230] which in Florence have set the hearts of all on fire, with a fire likewise rooted in cupidity.[231] This fire therefore owns kinship rather with the fire of hell than with that of heaven.

To the sin of Cupidity the fourth circle brought Dante closer still, for God, source of life, light, and love, is source, likewise, of all worth possessing on earth. The avaricious and the prodigal, bound eternally to a circle of restless futile toil and mutual collision, pictured strikingly the condition of empire and church: in their mutual collisions remembering the Donation of Constantine, each might well reproach the other: "Why holdest thou?" and "Why throwest thou away?"[232] This, Virgil comments, is "the brief mockery of the goods that are committed unto Fortune."[233] Dame Fortune[234] is the angel of him "lo cui saver tutto tra scende,"[235] who, having made the heavens, gives them guides "sì ch'ogni parte ad ogni parte splende, distribuendo igualmente la luce."[236] She, imitating with her wheel in the earthly realm the motion of the heavens, apportions all according to his will. There is here the added associated symbolism of light for wealth[237]—gold and silver are

230. Cf. *Inf.*, vi, 74-75.
231. Cf. statement from the *Summa Theologica*, quoted p. 164 n. 189.
232. *Inf.*, vii, 29.   233. *Inf.*, vii, 61-62.
234. Cf. *Purg.*, vi, 97 ff. Dame Fortune is closely connected with astrology, as is suggested by the motion of her wheel. Cf. Boethius: *De consolatione*, Bk. 2, Prose 2 and Metr. 2, also Bk. 4, Prose 6; and Albertus Magnus, *Physicorum*, 2, 2, 14 ff. The matter is discussed by N. Busetto in his *Origine e natura della 'Fortuna' dantesca*, in "Giorn. dant.," 12, 129. Astrology, fortune, fate, etc., are discussed in the third sphere of Paradise, the third terrace of Purgatory, and, after Limbo, the third circle of hell.
235. "Whose wisdom is transcendent over all." *Inf.*, vii, 73.
236. "So that every part shines to every part, equally distributing the light." *Inf.*, vii, 75-76.
237. The connection is not merely through appearance. As the German prov-

the glittering metals—which in itself is good, though the desire for it contrary to the divine will is evil. Dante was to learn later that while all desire must be of a good, some goods[238] are of such nature that an individual in possessing them inevitably deprives another. Thus they are stamped as lower goods[239] and potentially disrupting. Disunion is among the characteristics of hell.

Those were in the fifth circle who in their lives had always turned their eyes away from the Sun, from God and from his earthly representatives in the rightful authorities of empire and church and the teachings of philosophy and theology, in so far as they were known. Both the angry and the sullen have carried blackness within their hearts: "Tristi fummo ne l'aere dolce che dal sol s'allegra, portando dentro accidioso fummo; or ci attristiam nella belletta negra."[240] The smoke in their hearts, which in the sweet air had blackened for them the Divine Sun, had gradually enslaved them to that blackness which the Sun alone can alleviate, and that slime which the Sun alone can purify, to battle perpetually in the black mire beyond which lies lower hell.

Such was upper hell, its lesson of increasing disunion bearing witness to the power of the three beasts. With this progress Dante had beheld, in the inhabitants of the dolorous realm, ever greater limitation of personality. Such limitation was inevitably consequent upon the gradual loss of "il ben del l'intelletto,"[241] supreme gift of God to man empowering him to answer to the upward gravitation of divine love. The third beast, through her special opposition to the sun's attraction, dooms her victims not only to the bleak coldness of desire without hope, but also to darkness and limitation. From a basis in

erb has it, "Morgenstunde hat Gold in Munde"—"the connection of gold and wealth is close enough, and early rising is a condition for acquiring it."

238. Cf. p. 70 n. 159.

239. Cf. *Purg.*, xv, 49 ff.

240. "Sullen were we in the sweet air, that is gladdened by the Sun, carrying lazy smoke within our hearts; now lie we sullen here in the black mire." *Inf.*, vii, 121-124.

241. The "good of the intellect" is the vision of truth. Implied in its possession (or hope) is the ability to distinguish the greater from the lesser good and so to choose the bread of angels in preference to the wine of Circe. Cf. Chap. II. Notice in the line "c 'hanno perduto il ben de l'intelletto" the omission of the usual elision, a device of Dante's to give emphasis.

limitation, darkness, and cold, sinks the monument to the *lupa,* to an inverted peak in ice.

DIS—THE GREAT DEFIANCE

In an atmosphere of increasing oppression Dante approached the river Styx, becoming vividly conscious of limitation, darkness, and cold narrowing in upon him. The very lawlessness of the realm through which he had been traveling had served only to sharpen in outline the stark immutability of Law—law every disrespect to which served but to unveil the impotence of its contemner. So compelling became the atmosphere that even in the words of Virgil there was reflected again to Dante ominous irresistibility, with the full force of a reflexive which English can poorly translate: "il troppo star si vieta"—by the nature of things it is not permitted to linger. The flamelets on the tower of Dis recall Dante's *città partita,* for they are disjunctive fires, having no part in the Divine Sun, although in subjection to its law they must give light even in hell, in so far as their signaled message is necessary to call the impotently wrathful Phlegyas to his appointed task as ferryman of the Styx.

Before the more secret gate of the *città dolente,* wherein the red glow of each mosque dispels no darkness but rather brands its own joylessness, Virgil himself filled with anxiety was compelled to await aid from the Divine Sun. Here in the suspense of waiting, the troubled Sage explained to Dante that the place farthest from heaven is the darkest. Much more he explained, which was blotted out from Dante's terror-stricken mind by a sudden appearance on the lurid summit of the tower: the Furies, handmaids of the Queen of Everlasting Lamentation. " 'Let Medusa come, that we may change him into stone,' they all said, looking downward; 'badly did we avenge the assault of Theseus.' "[242] Here, at the hour of midnight, Dante found himself in immediate peril of perdition: " 'Turn thee backwards, and keep thine eyes closed; for if the Gorgon show herself, and thou shouldest see her, there would be no returning up again.' Thus said the master."[243] So imminent was the danger, Dante

---

242. " 'Vegna Medusa: sì 'l farem di smalto' dicevan tutte riguardando in giuso: 'mal non vengiammo in Teseo l'assalto.' " *Inf.,* ix, 52-54.

243. " 'Volgiti in dietro e tien lo viso chiuso; chè se il Gorgòn si mostra e

tells, that Virgil, trusting not to Dante, with his own hands
covered the eyes of the younger poet committed to his charge.[244]
Just at this point, Dante calls marked attention to his symbolism:

> O voi ch' avete li 'ntelletti sani,
>   mirate la dottrina che s'asconde
>   sotto il velame de li versi strani.[245]

He has become clearly conscious of the necessity of a deeper
order of symbolism, underlying the letter, the allegory, the
trope, and even the anagoge, of his own story. On the desert
sand before the gate of hell, he had argued all day long with
the sage Virgil as to the propriety of undertaking a journey
made before only by Aeneas and Paul,[246] founders, respectively,
of empire and of church. In his final consent there was the implicit, if not fully conscious, acceptance of his rôle as type of
Christ, in whom alone the functions of the two leaders were
united. Before the gate of Dis, Dante's crusade became an actual
bearing of the cross.

This was the domain, not merely of the she-wolf's insidious
opposition to the Holy Spirit, but of the she-wolf aided by the
lion, in open insult to the Logos. Medusa, once beautiful daughter of Darkness, had defied the sun god, and, like Circe the sun's
own daughter, had suffered terrible metamorphosis.[247] As a result her very attraction had become *gravezza*. Though Dis
within itself bore ruins, dead witnesses to the inexorable law
which is love, yet it harbored the raving of rebellion. The bold
defiance became grotesque as its own secret gate swung open at
a mere touch from the wand carried by a messenger of heaven,
whose easy coming amid thunder and tempest bore witness to

tu 'l vedessi, nulla sarebbe del tornar mai suso.' Così disse 'l maestro." *Inf.*, ix,
55-58.
    244. "Non si tenne a le mie mani, che con le sue ancor non mi chiudessi."
Inf., ix, 59-60.
    245. "O ye, who have sane intellects, mark the doctrine, which conceals itself
beneath the veil of the strange verses!" *Inf.*, ix, 61-63.
    246. Cf. p. 294, especially n. 156, and p. 321.
    247. Medusa had claimed that her beauty excelled that of Minerva, Athena,
Divine Wisdom. (As has been noted, Divine Wisdom is ever the second person
of the solar trinity.) Medusa's transformation into a serpent-tressed horror, the
sight of whom turned the beholder to stone, is not unlike the transformation of
the sun's daughter Circe into a witch with the power of turning to beasts those
who succumbed to her spell.

the inevitable power of the sun-storm god, and recalled the Harrowing of Hell.[248] Christ, the Divine Sun, in his benefic journey, had released from the power of Plutus a multitude of souls. His approach to Hades is thus described by one of the rescued dead, adjured by the Sacred Torah to tell that which had transpired:[249] "When we were, along with all our fathers, lying in the deep, in the blackness of darkness, suddenly there appeared a golden heat of the Sun, and a purple royal light shining upon us. And immediately the father of all the human race with all the patriarchs and prophets, exulted, saying: That light is the source of eternal light, which hath promised to transmit to us co-eternal light." In that hour when the universe felt love, hell itself was rent, and reminder of that hour was not welcome. (The association was inevitable, for according to medieval symbolic thinking anyone in a given situation may stand

248. The legend of the Harrowing of Hell relates that, during the time between the death of Christ on the cross, three o'clock on Friday afternoon, and his resurrection the following Sunday morning (midnight or dawn), while his body lay dead within the sepulcher, he went, in spirit, to Hades, with the object of releasing from their imprisonment the souls of the righteous who had died previous to his redeeming death. At the gate of the infernal regions the devils refused him admittance, but by his divine power with only a word, he, the Logos, conquered them. The gate broke open and parts of the Inferno were shattered as by an earthquake. The souls of the righteous, including Adam, David, and the penitent thief who had been crucified by the side of Christ, were released and admitted to the Terrestrial Paradise, where they waited until the Ascension, to enter heaven itself in the triumphal train of Christ.

The basis for the legend is in such Biblical passages as Eph. 4. 9; I Pet. 3. 19; I Pet. 4. 6. St. Augustine includes also Ps. 107. 14 (Vulgate numbering, 106. 14). There is a mention in the apocryphal *Gospel of Peter*, but the complete description occurs first in the apocryphal *Gospel of Nicodemus*, from which source it penetrated the Grail cycle. It is probable that the legend ever attached to sun heroes, of a descent to the nether world for the rescue of a captive or captives, is one of the original inspirations of the tale. In the *Gospel of Nicodemus*, Christ's approach to Hades is described in the language of the sun hero. Cf. the quotation in the text.

249. The account of the Harrowing of Hell, as given in the apocryphal *Gospel of Nicodemus* (Pt. II), was as familiar in the Middle Ages as were the Christmas and Easter accounts in the canonical gospels. According to Nicodemus, after the events of the first Good Friday and Easter (while, as the canonical narrative relates (Matt. 27. 50-54), bodies of dead saints were seen walking in Jerusalem), a committee of the Jews—Annas, Caiaphas, Nicodemus, Joseph of Arimathea, and Gamaliel—ushered two of these risen dead into a room and, placing a copy of the Holy Torah within their hands, adjured them by the God who gave the Law to tell the reasons for these things. The two dead, who were unable to speak, motioned for paper and wrote. After a protestation to their Lord that they wrote only because adjured in his name, they recounted the events of the hours succeeding the Crucifixion, from the standpoint of the dwellers in Hades.

as type of anyone else in a similar situation.)[250] There was
venom in the Furies' cry, "Badly did we avenge the assault of
Theseus."[251] Theseus, himself a sun god,[252] had entered the
realm of Plutus on a mission of rescue, that he might restore to
her destitute earth mother, Proserpine, Eternal Spring; and so
his name concealed within itself the name, unnamable in hell,
of Christ, that Sun which maketh Spring forever.[253]

" 'Let Medusa come, that we may change him into stone,'
they all said, looking downwards,"[254] planning for Dante that
doom which even the blasphemy of Dis dared not utter against
Christ, the doom from which the sun god Theseus had escaped,
turning upward at the hour of midnight[255] from the depths of
his descent. Christ, in response to the law of love his nature,
had fulfilled the meaning of that cross of the heavens on which
all sun gods[256] had been privileged to suffer, and that cross
Dante in his mission was to bear.[257]

250. Cf. Chap. IV.
251. "Mal non vengiammo in Teseo l'assalto." *Inf.,* ix, 54.
252. "In the Athenian solar myth, Theseus is the sun, born of Aegeus, the
sea . . . and Aethra, the pure air. He lingers in his birthplace, Troezene, until
he has acquired strength enough to wield his invincible sword, then journeys
onward in search of his father, performing countless great deeds for the benefit
of mankind. He slays the Minotaur, the terrible monster of darkness, and carries
off the dawn, Ariadne, whom he is, however, forced to abandon shortly after on
the Island of Naxos. In his subsequent career we find him the involuntary cause
of his father's death, then warring against the Centaurs (personifications of the
clouds, through which the victorious sun is sometimes forced to fight his way),
then again plunging for a short space of time into the depths of Tartarus, whence
he emerges once more; and finally we see him uniting his fate to Phaedra, the
twilight, a sister of the beautiful dawn he loved in his youth. He ends his eventful career by being hurled headlong from a cliff into the sea—an emblem of the
sun, which often seems to plunge into the waves at eventide." H. A. Guerber,
Myths of Greece and Rome (New York: American Book Co., 1893), p. 391.
Cf. pp. 108 ff. of the present study.
    Dante follows the form of the Theseus myth in which the hero, though unsuc-
cessful as to the rescue of Proserpine, at length returns to the upper world.
253. The Eternal Rose in Paradise "redole odor di lode al sol che sempre
verna"—"reeketh perfume of praise unto the Sun that maketh Spring for ever."
Par., xxx, 126.
254. " 'Vegna Medusa: sì 'l farem di smalto,' dicevan tutte riguardando in
giuso." *Inf.,* ix, 52-53.
255. When the sun is thought of as passing beneath the earth from west to
east during the night, midnight is naturally the point of his lowest descent, the
point at which he turns his course upward.
256. The unity of all sun gods had been felt throughout Dante's tradition. For
example, Statius, at the end of the first book of the *Thebaid,* gives expression
to a prayer in which, after invocation to Apollo, Phoebus, Titan, Osiris, and
Mithra, occurs the phrase "by whichever name thou dost prefer to be wor-
shipped."
257. Dante prayed at the beginning of the *Paradiso* that Apollo would add

Although throughout the rest of the chapter, attention will be centered in the symbolic levels belonging to Dante's own story, it must be borne in mind that he journeyed with the new consciousness[258] that his mission, in its answering to love, made implicit in his story deeper orders of symbolism than could be given by the fourfold method applied with regard to himself alone.[259] Throughout lower hell, reference to the sun and its messengers becomes more frequent, in implicit reminder of the power by which he moves.[260] For Dante, motion, especially swift motion, regularly circling like the sun, is a symbol of delight,[261] and the doom of those who gaze on Medusa is in symbolic association with the joylessness of Dis.

Countless centuries ago meditation on the fated career of the sun, that god whose will was supreme on the earth, taught man as science teaches today, that only through law is freedom won.[262] Hercules was a slave, yet none among men had greater

his assistance to that of the Muses which had been amply sufficient for the first two canticles. His prayer is that Apollo will enter into him with his divine breath—a prayer for the indwelling of the sun god which is to make him type and minister of that divinity. Professor Fletcher points out further that Athena, Apollo, and Mars were the instruments of "high Jove" in overthrowing the rebel giants. Similarly Beatrice, Dante, and Can Grande are to overthrow the evil giants who have rebelled against God and sold his people into bondage, even as Christ in his mission (foreshadowed by other solar heroes) bound the emperor of hell and freed his captives. Cf. J. B. Fletcher, *The Crux of Dante's Comedy*, pp. 34-35.

258. Gradual increase in revelation of truth, the process of scripture, is the plan of the *Commedia* as well. (Cf. p. 63 n. 128.) Genesis, according to medieval theology, contains implicitly the totality of divine revelation, while the New Testament gives the explicit statement of that which Genesis implies and to which it leads. Similar is the relation of the first canto of the *Inferno* to the revelation of the *Paradiso*.

259. Cf. pp. 63-65, 85-86.

260. Cf. *Inf.*, x, 130, referred to on p. 185; *Inf.*, xi, 91, referred to on p. 186; *Inf.*, xv, 55, referred to on p. 187; *Inf.*, xvi, 83, referred to on p. 187; p. 189 n. 296.

261. Cf., for example, *Par.*, xviii, 42.

262. There has been a tendency in modern philosophy to find only fate in regularity of motion, and to seek freedom in irregularity. It has been thought that "caprice and eccentricity are the marks of freedom and spiritual activity. The spontaneity of life is supposed to show itself in motiveless diversity, while regularity—all that can be predicted—is a proof of thraldom to blind necessity and mechanism." "The assumption that regularity is a sign of undirected movement" is, indeed, "one of the strangest and most obstinate of human prejudices" (W. R. Inge, *Philosophy of Plotinus*, Vol. 1, pp. 243, 182). In opposition to it stands not only Dante, but his whole tradition. One could hardly find a better (though unintentional) exposition of the medieval attitude than the following:

"If it is a truth that the yearning of our nature is for reality, and that our personality cannot be happy with a fantastic universe of its own creation, then it

power to do that which he willed. All solar heroes have moved in response to law and so their wills have been supreme among men. It is through law and not caprice that the heroes of the modern world will accomplish that which is now their will and become masters of the air. Law defied brings limitation and destruction leaving men victims of mechanism. With such defiance independence decreases, as Dante is to behold through Dis and lower Dis, until ultimately men become incapable as is inanimate creation, of any self-motivation. Victims of Medusa, they are turned to stone and there is no returning:[263] "se il Gorgòn si mostra e tu 'l vedessi, nulla sarebbe del tornar mai suso."[264]

In upper hell Dante had seen the inevitable outcome, not of individual rebellion, but of individual weakness uninspired by vision of the real significance of law. Church and empire ruling in harmony display law as the condition of freedom. Their conflict on the other hand favors all that Dante beheld in the upper circles. In Dis is not only failure but rebellion, the actual refusal to use law as the means of freedom, and so appropriately approach to the condition of the inanimate. The loss of "il ben

is clearly best for it that our will can only deal with things by following their law, and cannot do with them just as it pleases. This unyielding sureness of reality sometimes crosses our will, and very often leads us to disaster, just as the firmness of the earth invariably hurts the falling child who is learning to walk. Nevertheless it is the same firmness that hurts him which makes his walking possible. Once, while passing under a bridge, the mast of my boat got stuck in one of its girders. If only for a moment the mast would have bent an inch or two, or the bridge raised its back like a yawning cat, or the river given in, it would have been all right with me. But they took no notice of my helplessness. That is the very reason why I could make use of the river and sail upon it with the help of the mast, and that is why, when its current was inconvenient, I could rely upon the bridge. Things are what they are, and we have to know them if we would deal with them, and knowledge of them is possible because our wish is not their law." Tagore, *Sadhana*, pp. 59-60.

And again, if man "were made to live in a world where his own self was the only factor to consider, then that would be the worst prison imaginable to him" because in it the gaining of his own ends would be impossible. "If consideration for our individuality could sway nature from her path, then it would be the individuals who would suffer most." *Ibid.*, pp. 61, 58.

263. "His Virgil, spur to the high imperialist mission, induces him without shame to keep his face hidden from the dread Gorgon, the malignant power of his partisan enemies. Else he must prematurely have been held in *stone*, imprisoned, and so kept back from his mission itself." Such is, no doubt, the interpretation of this scene as to the development of his political career. Cf. J. B. Fletcher, *The Crux of Dante's Comedy*, p. 11.

264. *Inf.*, ix, 56-67.

del l'intelletto" is inevitable. It is God's gift to men, rendering them capable of self-determination through vision of the higher good to be attained through law, by the application to the present of the experience of the past. With this gift God did not endow inanimate creation, to which it would avail as little as to those who have looked upon Medusa.

The wretched futility of rebellion was demonstrated in the advent of the messenger of heaven, whose preoccupation expressed as much of scorn as his words, with their enforcement of the motivation of Virgil's leadership, "thus it is willed there, where what is willed can be done"—"vuolsi cosi cola, dove si puote cio che si vuole." Here is a secret of Medusa's power, to be understood only of those whose intellects are sane. Lower hell harbors souls not merely guilty of the Great Failure to use law, under the control of reason, as a means of freedom, but guilty of attempted violence to law through the opposition of their wills. In Dis, that which is willed cannot be done.

Such was the city of Florence. In upper hell Dante had seen punished victims of the she-wolf alone, but in lower hell are victims of the she-wolf aided by the lion, and of the she-wolf aided by the leopard.[265] Throughout the empire Dante had seen victims of the corrupt papacy, but in Florence he found himself in a hotbed of fraud and violence, the result of the intrigues of Valois and her own corrupt leaders. Dante, having accepted office in such a city, was in sorest need of Virgil's protecting hand.[266]

Of this deeper meaning a suggestion is given in Cerberus, whose three faces may signify the three senses of the word "cupidity."[267] Stationed in upper hell in the circle of the gluttons, he prepares the way for the three supernatural creatures

265. It will be noted that at the outset leopard and lion had by themselves no power to drive below the reaches of the sun, until the she-wolf appeared. The she-wolf by herself has power to accomplish the ruin that is upper hell, but in lower hell she prowls attended by the leopard and the lion, fraud and violence.

266. The details of the political interpretation are given less attention here than those of other levels of meaning, since this level has been studied at length by Prof. J. B. Fletcher. Although the larger outline of the political story as here given is not in entire accord with that of Professor Fletcher, the details of interpretation fit into either outline.

267. Cf. statement from Aquinas, *Summa Theologica*, given on p. 164 n. 189.

who represent in hell the three beasts. The first two of these are Plutus, ruler of the whole of hell, whom Virgil called Wolf, and Phlegyas, who represents the lion, that violence by which the ends of cupidity are sometimes sought.[268] Phlegyas ferries over the Stygian marsh, connecting the sins of violence, belonging more naturally to the realm of the she-wolf alone, with those which belong definitely to the she-wolf aided by the lion. A difference is obvious, for example, between murder committed in anger, and murder committed with malice prepense, to obtain money or to remove an obstacle from one's path. This dual nature of Phlegyas recalls again the opposition of the lion to the Second Person of the Trinity, to whom, it will be remembered, special insult was offered on the further shore of Styx. Moreover, the historical Phlegyas, in the medieval understanding of history, was a king guilty of rage against the sun god Apollo, specifically the second person of a Greek trinity. Of the leopard, Dante was to learn more anon.

In the first circle of Dis were those who had set their intellects against the truth of the Logos in his redemptive revelation of the Trinity. Inevitably they burn in their sepulchers as scattered flames, not united like the one great flame of the church, and as flames of glowing heat without the light which they had refused. As Dante trembled for his own fate prophesied by Farinata, Virgil as the spirit of philosophy and of empire admonished him that he could learn truly of his fate only after Beatrice—signifying the revealing power of God and here distinguished as the Sun—had shown in their right proportion these partial messages of hell.[269] There can be no true vision among victims of the transmutation wrought by Medusa, to whose increasingly limited existence knowledge can be no longer of any service. In an atmosphere made horrible through the forfeiture of "il ben del l'intelletto," Dante himself may not hope to know, with complete soundness of intellect.[270] As he had been told already, here the inhabitants are being deprived gradually of all knowledge.[271] Even now their knowledge of the

268. Cf. pp. 199-200.   269. *Inf.*, x, 130.
270. Cf. his reference to "sane intellects," *Inf.*, ix, 61.
271. Dante's use of *mente* for "memory" is of interest here.

present is gone,[272] and their memory of the past seems to be recalled normally only by questioning.[273] At the final judgment
they will lose their remaining knowledge,[274] since time and the
future will be no more[275] and they have forfeited their right to
an existence in eternity. Such is the inevitable doom of those
who, having turned from the light of the Sun,[276] have contemned the Love which is Law.

Eager to understand more of what he saw here in hell's sixth
circle Dante turned to Virgil as to the "Sol, che sani ogni vista
turbata,"[277] the only messenger of God now close to him, the
spirit of philosophy and of imperial Rome in the abstract, sent
and inspired by God. In Virgil's realm Beatrice never inter-
feres,[278] for his guidance precedes her.[279] Beatrice on the political level appears as the Holy Ghost in his operation as divine
guide of the church; on the moral level, as the Holy Ghost, the
inspiration of theology. In the midst of the ruin of the *città
partita* came again the reminder of the autonomy of vicarates
divinely appointed to protect man from the *lupa*.

In the seventh circle, after traversing the boiling blood of
Phlegethon and passing by the Wood of the Harpies, Dante
was confronted by a snowstorm of fire, for he was in the circle
of the violent against God, against nature,[280] and against art,[281]
where fire itself does violence to its nature: instead of sweeping
upward to its sphere, it was descending in flakes upon the sand.
As in the Starry Heaven the snowfall upward marked the entrance of the soul upon the mystic way to union with God,[282] so
its caricature in the fire, which descended like flakes upon the

272. *Inf.*, x, 58-69, and 97-114.   273. *Inf.*, xviii, 52-54.
274. *Inf.*, x, 100-108.   275. Cf. Rev. 10. 5-7.   276. Cf. pp. 37, 84, 214.
277. "Sun who healest all troubled vision," *Inf.*, xi, 91.
278. Though the reader may suppose that Beatrice sent the angel who opened
Dis, that is in no sense an interference in Virgil's sphere of labor.
279. It is of interest that, as one party upheld the primacy of the church, and
another the primacy of the empire, while Dante's reasoned position was that
they were equal in authority, each within its own sphere; so one opinion upheld
the absolute supremacy of theology, with philosophy subordinated, another upheld a similar supremacy of philosophy, while Dante concluded them to be equal
in authority each within its sphere, directed to diverse ends. Cf. *Monarchia*,
3, 16. Cf. also pp. 51-52.
280. Sodomites do violence to Nature, who is God's minister.
281. Money-lenders, according to the medieval view, in taking interest do
violence to human industry, the offspring of Nature.
282. Cf. pp. 84-85.

sand, heralded the approach to that lowest region of the dreadful city where the she-wolf, aided by the leopard, holds bound the victims of her opposition, not only to Love and Wisdom, but to the Prime Mover of the universe himself. With Dante's further journey, the raving impotence of hell came to be expressed not merely in negation, and in destructive opposition (inversion in its three aspects: erratic motion, perversion—here trickiness—of intellect, and destructive burning),[283] but also in caricature.

In this circle also, Dante was vouchsafed reminder of the brightness above. From among the violent against nature, his revered teacher Brunetto Latini appeared to reassure him of a glorious outcome of his venture, should he follow his star,[284] which, as Venus and as Love of Beatrice, was his guide on his life journey.[285] With the equipment determined by the heavens at his birth, however, should he in faltering fall under the influence of Circe, he would be guided to a love, the opposition of which to the love of Beatrice he had apprehended in the Circe-like Medusa.[286] Then from three scorching, wheeling souls came a fresh reminder of the "beauteous stars" to be seen once more after escape from the "gloomy realm."[287] There was suggestion not only of the stars of the natural universe, but also of the writings of the sciences,[288] leisure for the study of which was to be his after his escape from the hell of Florentine politics, a benefit alike to his political theory and to his moral insight. The association, as was seen at the outset, continued through the eyes of Beatrice to the influence of God.

Fortified by fresh dedication to his mission, Dante approached the beast, image of Fraud, from the sting of whose tail the ideal of rightful empire and true philosophy protected

283. The opposition to the Third Person of the Trinity is expressed here, not only by destructive burning, but by the familiar perversion, *evil dogs*, the nature of dogs being to act in opposition to the *lupa*, not as her instruments. Cf. p. 167.
284. "Se tu segui tua stella, non puoi fallire al glorioso porto." *Inf.*, xv, 55-56.
285. Cf. pp. 47 ff.
286. For the opposition of Beatrice and Circe, cf. pp. 234 ff.
287. "Se campi d' esti luoghi bui e torni a riveder le belle stelle." *Inf.*, xvi, 82-83.
288. "In every science scripture is a star, full charged with light, which showeth forth that science." *Convivio*, 2, 15 (16).

him, while Virgil assured that such were the only stairs by which
further progress was possible. Virgil and Dante were standing
at the head of a torrent of waters of evil, the deafening roar of
which bore witness to the length and precipitousness of the fall
which separated the eighth circle from the seventh. Plunging
down on the back of Geryon into the abode of those who were
victims particularly of the she-wolf and the leopard, Dante was
reminded of the terrible descent of Phaeton and of the fall of
Icarus, both punished by the Sun for presumption.[289] In presumption Dante recognized a sin against God of the greatest
magnitude, partaking of the nature of fraud,[290] for both these
sins involve the perversion of man's highest gifts through an
attitude to natural law on the part of the human will, of defiance rather than of coöperation.

This passage in the *Inferno* is not Dante's only connection of
a precipice leading to destruction, with the myth of Phaeton. He
writes to the Italian cardinals (assembled at Avignon[291] to elect
a successor to Clement V) rebuking them for their subjection
of the church to cupidity through the nationalistic schemes of
France:[292]

Et, quod horribilius est, quod astronomi quidam et crude prophetantes
necessarium asserunt, quod, male usi libertate arbitrii, eligere maluistis.
Vos equidem, Ecclesie militantis veluti primi preposti pili, per mani-
festam orbitam Crucifixi currum Sponse regere negligentes, non aliter

289. For a fuller discussion of this passage, cf. Chap. IV, Pt. II, ii. The especial appropriateness of these legends may be noted in passing. Throughout this
order of symbolism Dante depicts his developing consciousness of himself as
type of Christ. Convinced in upper hell of the futility of the evil inherent in the
position both of Guelphs and of Ghibellines, he had attempted none the less, in
the Florence which was Dis, through his own power as prior to bring salvation
to the city. The descent on Geryon is the preparation for the expulsion from
his beloved city, which brought to Dante the absolute conviction that in attempting such a task in his own power he was guilty of the sin of Icarus, or that like
Phaeton he had attempted to drive the chariot of the Sun, of which the fiery
steeds could be controlled by no other voice than by that of the sun god himself.
In other words, salvation was not to be accomplished by Dante as a person in
authority. Only Dante as a type of Christ might safely undertake that journey
through the depths of evil ventured by the Sun of Righteousness in redemption
of man. For the myth of Phaeton cf. Ovid, *Metamorphoses*, 2, 227-332.
   290. *Inf.*, xi, 25-27.   291. In 1314.
   292. Not only did the residence of the pope and papal court at Avignon subject the papacy to the ambitions of the House of Valois, but, to Dante's mind, it
rendered the papacy (whose seat was ordained by God at Rome, cf. *Monarchia*)
actually invalid.

quam falsus auriga Pheton exorbitastis; et, quorum sequentem gregem per saltus peregrinationis huius illustrare intererat, ipsum una vobiscum ad precipitum traduxistis.[293]

In addition to the conflicting pairs of church and empire, Guelph and Ghibelline, theology and philosophy (including theological virtues and natural virtues),[294] Dante has here introduced liberty of the will as against natural law or "necessity" (for him synonymous with the stars, regarded in astrology as the determiners of earthly actions).[295] Even superficial study of his writing shows this conflict to have taken a prominence in his moral life. Noteworthy is the connection here made explicitly of the sun's course with the cycle of Christ's life, which was intended for daily following by his mystical Body.[296] Christ, the true Sun God, in each of his Bodies must follow the course prescribed by universal law, through coöperation with which his will renders itself effective. Phaeton, the false sun god, had set his will in opposition to this law, and in consequence had fallen to a depth from which, having forfeited his seat in the chariot, he could not reascend. Here is premonition of that greatest of all sins against the Prime Mover of the universe, wrong motion on the part of the powers of light and heat. In lower hell are princes of the Sun who, disobedient to the very law which is solar nature, have shot downward from the appointed course, like Satan that greatest of all fallen light-bearers,[297] to self-destruction and extinction in the freezing waters of Cocytus, the lake opened in the heart of wounded earth by the lightning fall of the supreme traitor.[298] With Geryon's downward plunge,

293. "And, what is more horrible, certain astronomers, crudely prophesying, declare that to be of necessity which in truth ye, making ill use of the liberty of the will, have rather chosen. But ye, as it were the officers of the first rank of church militant, neglecting to guide the chariot of the spouse along the manifest track [orbitam] of the Crucified, have gone astray no otherwise than the false driver Phaeton. And ye whose duty it was to guide the flock that followed you through the glades of this pilgrimage, have led both it and yourselves to the precipice." *Epistle* IX (VIII), para. 4.

294. Cf. *Monarchia*, 3, 16, as well as the preceding discussion.

295. Cf. pp. 47 ff.

296. Note that he uses the word "orbit" for the path of Christ which the church should follow, and "wandering from the orbit" (*exorbitastis*) for going astray. Cf. pp. 274, 304.

297. Lucifer, one of the names of Satan, means Light-bearer or Light-bringer. Bonaventure comments that from Lucifer he became Tenebrifer.

298. Cf. Luke 10. 18 and *Inf.*, xxxiv, 121-126.

Dante "saw extinguished every sight, save that of the beast."[299, 300]

As Plutus represents the she-wolf and Phlegyas the lion,[301] similarly Geryon is the form in which the leopard reappears in hell, the weapon of guile by which the ends of cupidity are sometimes sought. Support for this identification is given by the knots and circles on Geryon's skin, as well as by the fact that the cord with which Dante intended to catch the leopard actually caught Geryon. Thus, again, Dante perceived the wretchedness of hell divided and summed up in the three beasts, negations of the solar trinity: cupidity against heat (charity), cupidity using violence to gain its ends against light (wisdom), and cupidity using fraud to gain its ends against life and motion.[302] (It will be remembered that at the outset of his journey Dante found the light of the sun an assistance against the leopard only. In other words knowledge that violence, art of the lion, is meditated against one is of little assistance; but knowledge that trickery is planned is of great value.) In upper hell were sins of incontinence, springing from the Great Failure—the failure to order desire by intellect,—but in lower hell were perversions: in the first two circles the perversion of rebellion, and in the region which Dante was about to enter, the perversion of betrayal— for Dis is the city of the Great Defiance.

In the ten pockets of the Malebolge, various types of simple fraud found their depth. Among the panders and seducers, who inhabit the first pocket, Dante met Jason, solar hero who had broken faith with the sun.[303] No longer compelled by the law of his solar nature, Jason is held to his appointed course by eternal scourging. Thus is caricatured the law of the sun's career. In the doom of the flatterers, who are sunk in the fetor which is the natural condition of earth unpurged by sunlight, there is

---

299. "Vidi spenta ogni veduta fuor che de la fera." *Inf.*, xvii, 113-114.

300. Cf. the mention, by Augustine, of the "fabled threebodied Geryon."

301. The violence of the lion is represented a second time in upper Dis by the Minotaur, "quell' ira bestial," who in his fury defeats his own ends. *Inf.*, xii, 1-33.

302. The inversion of the order of these beasts in the Dark Wood and in hell should be noted. Cf. pp. 199 ff.

303. In *Metamorphoses*, 7, 95-97, Ovid relates that Jason broke an oath sworn "by the father of his father-in-law-to-be [Sol, father of Aetes], who sees all things." Tr. by John Clarke, 1755.

likewise caricature, in which however negation is more prominent than destruction. Brief consideration of the characteristic
iniquities of these first two pockets of the Malebolge shows that
they are in association as ground sin and accompanying sin, the
one furnishing soil for the other. Where panders and seducers
abound, there are found also flatterers, with their impious perversion of the light of truth.

Fraudulent representatives of the Second Person of the
Trinity were the simoniacal popes,[304] guilty of inversion of their
office, having made themselves not *servi servorum Dei,* but having turned the *servos Dei* into servants of themselves. Intellect
and heart being turned from the enlightenment and warmth of
the sun, fire tortures the soles of their feet and dense blackness
their eyes, as they writhe in a hole in a fiery rock, head downward, each upon the feet of his predecessor.

Similarly significant of inversion of proper function before
the eyes of God is the fate of the diviners, who having sought
unlawful knowledge from the stars, walk backward weeping
through an infernal chasm:

> mirabilmente . . . travolto
> ciascun tra 'l mento e'l principio del casso;
> chè da le reni era tornato il volto,
>   ed in dietro venir li convenia,
>   perchè 'l veder dinanzi era lor tolto.[305]

This condition of the diviners, the vision of which in Dante's
journey, follows close upon his experience with the simonists,
represents the result of the same defiance, even if in a different
and less radical form. It is the infection of the church with
simony, thus lessening its spiritual appeal, that gives potency to
all those sects which, with pretended power to foresee the future or to bring news from the spirit world, flourish on the
credulity of the people. In the caricature which brands the exist-

304. Their hearts were so set on the florins, bearing the image of John the
Baptist, that they have quite forgotten SS. Peter and Paul. For further discussion
of Boniface, cf. p. 223 n. 451. Simony has ever been considered an especial offense against the Holy Ghost.

305. "Wondrously distorted, between the chin and the commencement of the
chest; for the face was turned toward the loins; and they had to come backward,
for to look before them was denied." *Inf.,* xx, 11-15.

ence of these inhabitants of the third and fourth *bolge,* there is predominance first of destruction and then of negation.

In the same circle with the simonists (guilty of graft in ecclesiastical office) are the barrators (guilty of graft in civil office), for the two suns of Rome are equal. The barrators find their natural *milieu* in a pit, *mirabilmente oscura,* of pitch boiling without fire, guarded by some of the most grotesque of the demons of hell. Here, in Dante's political career, was the point where he was personally most in danger, the time when he, in office in Florence, was in the midst of a pitchy flood of graft, result of the inversion of the divine attributes of the solar trinity.[306] The doom of death had compelled his flight from Florence; the same fate was planned for him in this realm where the she-wolf plots to accomplish her ends through the leopard. The leopard, in special opposition to the source of all life in the universe,[307] of necessity threatens death.

Still under shadow of this peril, Dante journeyed under false direction through the sixth *bolgia,*[308] where dwell those who, flourishing amid graft, suffer in caricature of the attributes of the Third Person, negation being marked, as was destruction among the barrators. These hypocrites, who imitate the Sun only outwardly, wear in their glittering cloaks a leaden lining.[309] However the *lupa* may simulate the Sun, her power is *gravezza,*[310] which Caiaphas was coming to know in its full force, as, crucified to the ground by three stakes, he and others of the Sanhedrim formed the pavement for the dragging tread of those who bore bright vestures, wrought by the *lupa* into "weary mantles for eternity."[311]

The key to the symbolism of the realm, and its climax, is

306. Limitation of motion by the sticky pitchiness, and the darkness of its fireless heat, well symbolize perversion of the freedom, light, and love of the realm of the Sun.

307. Cf. pp. 160, 200.

308. Dante was saved from the ultimate outcome of the false direction, by the Jolly Friar.

309. Uguccione da Pisa defines *ypocrita* as "superauratus," deriving it from ὑπέρ and χρυσός.

310. This inversion is worthy of study. Whereas the sun mantles himself in the darkness of rainclouds which bring blessing to those beneath, those who, dark within, imitate him falsely in shining aspect, clothe themselves in a brightness which brings upon all beneath them the burden of *gravezza.*

311. "Oh in etterno faticoso manto!" *Inf.,* xxiii, 67.

given in this outstretched form of Caiaphas, caricature of Christ's suffering. As Dante was to behold in heaven, that situation which had necessitated his exile was in very fact a reënactment of the Crucifixion.[312] Yet in this chill of ruin, Dante was cheered by Virgil's smile, with its promise of escape from the power of Malacoda, renewing his hope as had the Sunrise after his night of wandering in the dark forest, and the encounter with the leopard.

In the fifth pocket of the Malebolge, with its supplement in the sixth, Dante found the lowest degree of that cupidity which subjects men to destructive caricature[313] of the Divine Tri-unity. With his further progress he was to meet those whose defiance of law had reduced them to even more debasing limitation. In their experience of increasing de-animation, destructiveness itself became swallowed up in the negation of the Divine Tri-unity, in lack of motion, darkness, and cold.

From the realm of cupidity seeking its ends by trickery, Dante entered the pit of the thieves, who take not merely by guile like the leopard, but also by force like the lion. The she-wolf as the root of all evil is yet to be seen in her lowest form, although her impress on the characters of hell now marks them as in defiance no longer of the Trinity in some one aspect, but of Godhead itself.

Here occurs a remarkable change in symbolism. The pattern of things as they are is given by the Tri-unity of life, light, and heat, Power, Wisdom, and Love, in which had been accomplished the perfect unification of the two materials of symbolism,[314] through which man's thought had advanced. To the immutable law of that Tri-unity the very incoherence of hell bore witness in its presentation of negation, inversion, caricature, and after the culmination of caricature in the caricature of the Crucifixion, the final negation in which all are combined. In the consummation of transmutation, which precedes this final negation, however, after mockery of the very cross in which the ma-

312. Cf. p. 84.
313. The progress seems to be from a foreshadowing of negation in upper hell, through perversion and caricature, to the final opposition which combines all in absolute negation.
314. Cf. Chap. III, Pt. I, i, and Appendix III, Pt. I, i.

terials of symbolism were united, a disintegration between sun and sex[315] becomes inevitable. This disintegration, in Dante's *Commedia,* as in the progress of man's thought, finds expression through animal symbolism, and more than that, through the symbolism of the serpent, in which disharmony between macrocosm and microcosm may become most striking.[316] (Indeed, it was through the instrumentality of the serpent that there was inaugurated the whole drama of human transmutation.) Thus far in the *Commedia,* animals have shadowed forth in concrete terms the powers of good and evil in the drama of the universe. Animals, however, have been recognized always as but symbols of symbols, the primary symbolism being that of the solar trinity and of its negation, in response to whose attraction and *gravezza* the drama of human transmutation moves. Now, animal symbolism has become itself the main element in that transmutation, a dreadful parody of the ultimate truth of all existence.

Enacted in a chasm swarming with reptiles, among whom ran naked human beings serpent-girdled and manacled, Dante beheld a travesty of the great truths of the resurrection and immortality, and of the story of the Phoenix, through which through centuries these truths had been taught both in the literature of learning and in the literature of the people. Before Dante's eyes a thief, assaulted and bitten by a serpent "là dove 'l collo a le spalle s'annoda,"[317] was burned to ashes, only to rise again that the agony might be repeated. From the lips of this sinner came in the same breath the blasphemy of the mention of the name of God in the *Inferno,* and the most obviously dissociated sex imagery[318] in vulgar crudeness of insult to Deity. As the awful burlesque of divine mysteries proceeded, Dante beheld the merging into one of human and serpent natures. Such a monster Church and State had become in Dante's time.[319] In Christ also two natures were assumed by one Person, but in the taking up of

315. Cf. pp. 116-117.   316. Cf. pp. 212-213.
317. "There where the neck is bound upon the shoulders." *Inf.,* xxiv, 99.
318. According to Payne-Knight, the "fig hand" originally "represented the act of generation, which was considered as a solemn sacrament in honor of the Creator." *In Worship of Priapus,* p. 28.
319. Cf. the monstrous transformation of the Car and the Tree in the Terrestrial Paradise. See p. 325.

human nature into Godhead there is not the distortion of merging,[320] but the preservation of the separate dignity of each. Then, finally, there occurred the consummation of the ruin figured in the serpentine transformations, as in horrible embrace "both forms were ready to exchange their substance"—"ambo e due le forme a cambiar lor materia fosser pronte"—and the man became serpent, and the serpent, man. In the *Inferno,* as in the *Purgatorio* and in the *Paradiso,* there is a special potency in the gaze of two into each other's eyes,[321] yet here *gravezza* makes of it one of the most dreadful caricatures in Dis of the heavenly transmutation which leads to union with the Divine Beloved.

In an atmosphere of such insult to the love which inspires the intellect with the power to choose,[322] even Dante feared lest he misuse his genius, the gift of Venus and of God whose will directs all stellar influence. Fresh from the revelation that one whose faculties are not turned to good ends is horribly deprived of them, Dante trembled lest the power of Venus might become for him enslavement of Circe.[323] The power of hell to deprive men of sanity was impressed so deeply on his mind that in the Empyrean, enveloped in the threefold light which revealed the vision of the Rose, he exclaimed in his last words with reference to his native city, that at last he had passed from Florence to a people just and sane.

The fact that readers of the *Commedia* are wont to shudder most at the scene of the serpentine transformations, in the *Inferno,* confesses them still haunted by the ghosts of their language, or still sensitive to that element in nature which is the foundation of the symbolic tradition. It was of the genius of the Middle Ages, fulfilled in Dante, to perceive also in symbolism the means of conveying truth to the intellect, and thus through symbolism to achieve simultaneous response from all elements of human nature. Here, where is offered open insult to God-

---

320. As certain heretics (Eutychians, Apollinarians) had held. In Catholic theology the two natures are distinct and perfect.

321. *Inf.,* xxv, 88-93. Cf. *Purg.,* xxxi, 121-126, where Beatrice gazes in the eyes of the grifon, and *Par.,* i, 64-72, where Dante is "transhumanized" by gazing into the eyes of Beatrice, and *Par.,* xxvi, 10-15, 76-79, where Beatrice's look has the power to dissipate Dante's blindness.

322. Cf. pp. 51, 55.   323. *Inf.,* xxvi, 21-24.

head itself, Circe's power has done its utmost, the whole being shudders, and the intellect recognizes the disintegration of the human personality to be complete.

Soon Dante found himself walking amid flame-embodied souls, gleaming like fireflies (with a light not continuous, bright, nor warm). These were the evil counselors, flourishing in the company of thieves, whose transmutations had delivered them up to fiery union with the power of evil.[324] From within a flame by which with Diomed he was embodied, Ulysses, whose only tongue was the darting flame, told Dante of his desire to place himself in a wrong relation to the Sun.[325] After his year under the influence of Circe, Ulysses, unrestrained by the sun-ward-guiding loves of parent, wife, and child, had set out once more from home, turning his back toward the morning, and venturing southwestward across the Equator, to behold the Mount of Purgatory which it was not his right to see. That Ulysses was unaware of this was no bar to his punishment, as ignorance of the law of the universe has never saved man from the consequences of his acts. Here, at the intervention of the sun-storm god whom he dare not name, yet whose anger in a storm rushing from the celestial mountain whirled his ship in three circlings, the waters closed over the head of the misguided adventurer. The poop, at first by Ulysses' will turned toward the morning, was now turned toward the heavens, while dramatically the prow "as pleased Another" was drawn downward toward the dolorous realm at the center of the earth, where that which is willed cannot be done. Dante, in Ulysses' compelling story, is again reminded of the Sun.[326] It would seem that as Dante plunged ever deeper into hell, there was increasing need for mention of that Sun which he was to see again.

In the ninth and tenth pockets of the Malebolge are the sowers of discord and the falsifiers, the former dismembered, the latter mutilated by disease, the result of their defiance of the

324. Cf. Chap. V, Pt. I, iii, for continual burning as a mystic symbol of the unitive way.

325. He is eager to explore the worlds behind the sun (*Inf.*, xxvi, 112-117); he turns the poop toward morning, that is, his back sunward (*Inf.*, xxvi, 124)— a flight which he now considers to have been foolish (*Inf.*. xxvi, 125).

326. In Ulysses' specific mention, *Inf.*, xxvi, 117. Mention of the Sun has been infrequent in the *Inferno*.

unity of Deity. One holding by the hair his severed head, which swung in his hand like a lantern, served as reaffirmation of the fact to which all hell bears witness, that perversion of the light of the intellect through its direction away from the sun, separates it from all good, even from the sinner's own.

As in the development of thought number symbolism has appeared in the closest possible association with solar symbolism, or rather, as of its very substance, so it has appeared even in the incoherence of the *Inferno*.[327] The ten *bolge* where dwell the victims of the she-wolf aided by the leopard are linked through their sins, in pairs, as duality has always opposed that monotheism of which the perfect expression is in the number ten.[328] Through the ten diverse pockets of the Malebolge, vividly expressive of the situation of a magistrate, and of an individual, in a city where parties of empire and church, teachings of philosophy and theology, are in conflict, Dante has been guided to the edge of the pit where dwells the supreme traitor.

COCYTUS: THE GREAT DEFEAT

Lowered at last by the giant Antaeus[329] to the bottom of the pit, Virgil and Dante stood upon the ice of Cocytus. In the region which is the extreme negation of motion, light, and heat,[330] Dante was astonished to feel an icy wind.[331] Not only is the wind a time-worn symbol of the Holy Spirit, through which the life of the Deity is expressed to man, but the existence of motion of any sort means also by necessity the existence of love.[332] Hence Dante's question: "Maestro mio, questo chi move? Non è qua giù ogne vapore spento?"[333, 334]

Between the question and the answer there intervened yet

327. An obvious example of Dante's care in the use of numbers is seen in the mathematical structure of each of his canticles, discussed in most commentaries on the *Commedia*.

328. Cf. pp. 337-339, 466 ff.

329. Cf. pp. 307, 325. For a discussion of the political significance, in Dante's life, of Antaeus, cf. J. B. Fletcher, *The Crux of Dante's Comedy*, pp. 15-16.

330. *Inf.*, xxxi, 123; xxxii, 22 ff.; xxxii, 72.

331. *Inf.*, xxxiii, 103. 332. Cf. *Convivio*, 3, 3.

333. "Master, who moves this? Is not all heat extinguished here below?" *Inf.*, xxxiii, 104-105.

334. Desire, in accord with the will of the Prime Mover, results in a motion which is regular and harmonious, but without desire (love of some, though lesser good) no motion of any kind is possible.

more terrible vision of the power of the beast to distort human personality. Dante spoke with one who, under the power of *gravezza,* had sunk down into the frozen lake into which is washed all the evil of the universe. Up to his neck in ice, he was bereft of motion, of light, and of all heat. By his very tears his eyelids were frozen shut. This victim of Circe's wand had suffered, even before physical death, the ultimate wages of sin, which is separation of soul and body,[335] in a transmutation of peculiar horror. Such was the nature of his union with the power of evil that in continued deception of all who had known him, his body still moved on earth, inhabited by a demon.

Close upon the shock of Dante's breach of faith with the traitorous friar to whom "to be rude was courtesy,"[336, 337] there followed outrage in the heralding of approach to the King of all evil, by a parody of the sacred ritual hymn of welcome to the Cross.[338] "Vexilla regis prodeunt inferni,"[339] announced Virgil—strange words from the lips of the sage, yet superbly expressive of the caricature and negation which is hell. God,

335. Cf. p. 166 n. 197 and p. 293 n. 153.
336. "Cortesia fu lui esser villano." *Inf.,* xxxiii, 150.
337. More detailed applications on the political and moral levels fit harmoniously into the pattern. Prof. J. B. Fletcher has thus analyzed certain elements of the allegory in regard to Dante's political career:
"The experience of the two years of his dominance in Florence . . . is the allegory of the Hell, first act of his *Comedy.* . . . While Dante held power those two years in the *parte selvaggia,* he might with a clear conscience apply the maxim: 'In church with the saints, with the gluttons in tavern.' (*Inf.,* xxii, 14-15.) He can meritoriously placate Cerberus, greedy watchdog of the stinking bog, by feeding it the mire it craves. (*Inf.,* vi, 25-33.) To keep them quiet while he needfully remains among them, Dante as Prior is justified in bribing the greedy Florentine 'dogs,' the rabble. . . . By shrewd evasion he foils the Minotaur's fury, partisan violence. So, casting off the girdle of simplicity and candor, he summons and is carried by the spirit of Deceit down to the very depths of the City of Fraud. So, riding the 'Evil-tail' (*Inf.,* xvii, 1), . . . he is accepted as one of theirs by the chief 'devil' of the City, himself an Evil-tail, a Malacoda. (*Inf.,* xxi, 79 ff.) And so, one after another, Dante dupes his enemies who are also God's. A true Christian need not be true to such, but may even meritoriously break his plighted word to them. (*Inf.,* xxxiii, 109 ff., 148-150.)" J. B. Fletcher, *The Crux of Dante's Comedy,* pp. 11-12.
338. The hymn *Vexilla regis prodeunt, fulget Crucis mysterium,* styled by the hymnologist Neale "one of the grandest in the treasury of the Latin church," was originally written by Venantius Fortunatus (sixth century) as a processional on the occasion of the reception of a relic of the True Cross sent by Emperor Justin II to St. Radegunde. Its liturgical use as vespers hymn in Holy Week and Good Friday processional, heightens the effect of the infernal parody which Dante puts in the mouth of Virgil. Cf. pp. 309, 414.
339. *Inf.,* xxxiv, 1.

the emperor of heaven, is the Prime Mover of the universe; Satan, "lo 'mperador del doloroso regno,"[340] no longer Lucifer but Tenebrifer,[341] by the motion of his wings but eternally contributes to the freezing of himself in ice.[342] In heaven that which is willed can be done, but not so in Dis. Whereas the conflict is bitter between man and the she-wolf as between Beatrice and Circe,[343] the relationship of these instruments to their movers is, by the nature of evil, inverse: the progression from minister to master on the divine side being a progression from power to greater power, on the infernal side, a regression from power to lesser power. To such solution of the problem of evil Dante was led through the symbolism of the sun.

Dante's journey had brought ever deeper insight into the trinity of evil. Halted at the foot of the mount by leopard, lion, and she-wolf, he recognized in them three vices, separate, and apparently against the Three Persons of the Trinity, respectively, yet acting as three political powers subversive of Church and State, and as three sins in opposition to the dictates of theology and philosophy. In the circles of the dolorous realm he beheld the unveiling of this threefold evil. In upper hell, suffering from lack of heat, light, and freedom of living, were the victims of the she-wolf, that cupidity and self-centeredness which, in opposition to the activity of love's attraction, had marked the Great Failure of the earthly viceregents. In Dis were victims of the she-wolf working through the lion, that violence of thought and deed which opposes the manifestation of wisdom, and of the she-wolf seeking her ends through the leopard, that fraud which is in opposition to the power of motion.[344] This twofold rebellion of violence and fraud characterized the Great Defiance in the earthly vicarates, which had made of Florence politically and morally a veritable Dis. The she-wolf works through the two powers of violence and fraud, as the Sun works through two natures, human and divine, and Christ through dual vicarates. As negation of the Trinity of light, life, and heat characterized upper hell, so destructive inversion of these attributes characterized upper Dis, and their caricature in

340. *Inf.*, xxxiv, 28.
342. *Inf.*, xxxiv, 49-54.
344. Prime Mover, cf. p. 160.

341. Cf. p. 189 n. 297.
343. Cf. pp. 234-237.

both destruction and negation, the Malebolge. In Satan is the ultimate negation, wherein is the consummation of all destructiveness and caricature.

In lowest hell the she-wolf, cupidity, in the *gravezza* of her opposition to the reaching out of the Holy Spirit, became clearly the root of all evil, and, as such, the negation of the Trinity as a whole. In her three aspects, (a) the special sin of the inordinate love of riches, (b) the *genus* of all sins, inordinate love for any temporal good, (c) the *root* of all sins, the inclination of fallen nature to love inordinately temporal goods,[345] she gives expression, not only to herself, but to the leopard and the lion. Dante then beheld beneath the machinations of the House of Valois and of the Florentine factions, the power of the corrupt papacy strengthening them for evil. The leopard and the lion, on the other hand, as Florence and Valois, fraud and violence, become here means of accomplishing her ends, comparable to the activity toward men of the Divine Trinity through the divine and human natures of Christ, the church and the empire, theology and philosophy. In his person Satan epitomizes and unites all the elements in sin and its punishment: that which is negation of the Trinity, his bat wings which freeze the lake in darkness: and that which mocks and parodies the Trinity, his three faces,[346] red, yellowish white, and black, endlessly demolishing the three traitors, respectively, Judas, Cassius, and Bru-

---

345. Cf. statement from the *Summa Theologica* given on p. 164 n. 189.

346. Prof. J. B. Fletcher has noted a more detailed identification between the present black sun of the church, Pope Boniface, and Lucifer:

"The fact that Boniface has already been presented allegorically in Geryon is no bar in Dante's allegorical method to his representment in the Archfiend, the Antichrist. Geryon, Fraud, is one type of evil abstracted from the sum of evil, which is Lucifer. And connection is established between the part and the whole when Dante says: 'That it pleased my Master to reveal to me the creature there that had the semblance fair.' (*Inf.*, xxxiv, 17-18.) Like master, like man: in the character of Geryon, Boniface had used the *Black* devil, Corso, to destroy Dante by violence, meanwhile preserving himself the appearance of benevolent impartiality. Such was Geryon: 'His face the face was of a person just, outwardly showing great benignancy, but of a serpent all below the bust.' (*Inf.*, xvii, 10-12.) But Dante now sees Boniface in Lucifer all unmasked, visible source of all present evils in the world, including Dante's own persecution. (*Inf.*, xxxiv, 34-36.) The poison that has changed Boniface to such a monster is made manifest in the vileness oozing from Lucifer's mouths, the sin of sins—betrayal of God and man alike. Boniface too 'swallows' Judas and Brutus and Cassius. All three have entered into him. He has slain again Christ and Caesar. He has thought to silence their champion, Dante Alighieri." J. B. Fletcher, *The Crux of Dante's Comedy*, p. 16.

tus.[347] In fine, the "vermo reo che 'l mondo fora"[348] is the complete parody of all good, and the image of cupidity, the root of all evil,[349] summing up all its aspects and its two means of attaining its ends. Satan, the inspiration of the wolf, is the absolute negation of the Trinity.

Evil contains within itself its own destruction, and so in the vision it was Satan's hairy ribs and the wake of his lightning descent which provided for Dante means of escape from the Inferno.[350] Allegorically, it is the factional evil of Florence by which Dante was expelled and thereby escaping the factions was given opportunity to develop a true theory of empire,[351] which should be its possibility of salvation.[352] Finally, according

347. Judas is in especial opposition to the Holy Spirit, Love, because of the betrayal by a kiss; Cassius especially opposed to Wisdom because his rebellion against Caesar involves both failure to see by intellect the divine right involved, and rebellion against the justice of God, which the healthy intellect recognizes as inscrutable (cf. *Par.*, xix, 58-63, and xxi, 94-99) ; Brutus is perhaps especially opposed to God the Father because (cf. Plutarch) Caesar was reputed to be his father.

348. "Evil worm which pierces through the world." *Inf.*, xxxiv, 108.

349. Cf. statement from the *Summa Theologica* given on p. 164 n. 189.

350. *Inf.*, xxxiv, 70-120.   351. Cf. pp. 44 ff., 207 ff.

352. Cf. the following detailed analysis on the political level of Dante's personal story, as given by Prof. J. B. Fletcher in his *The Crux of Dante's Comedy*, pp. 12-13:

"God can turn the wiles of Satan against him, and bend them to the furtherance of good. The 'ruin' declared by Malacoda impassable proves to be for Dante the one way out. (*Inf.*, xxiii, 133-144.) Thanks to it, he can realize by experience the lower depths of the city of iniquity down to the brink of the bottommost pit. From there he is brought down lower still, down apparently into the clutches of the arch-fiend himself. Yet Lucifer cannot harm him. The dread 'arms,' against which 'giants' count as little as Dante against 'giants' (*Inf.*, xxxiv, 30-31) are impotent, locked fast in the ice made by the wind of his own bat-wings. On the contrary, his 'hairy ribs' form the very 'ladder' on which Virgil may climb with Dante out of the accursed place. . . . Thus providentially, by the powers of evil whose interest was to thwart it, Dante's mission is furthered. . . . If the allegory is of Dante's career in Florence, we can, I think, recognize the meaning of the ruin, and the identity of the 'black devil.' (*Inf.*, xxi, 29.)

"In the summer of 1300, Dante had voted with the other Priors for the exile of the heads of the two contentious parties, Blacks and Whites. The motive was the peace of the city. But the perfidiously ambitious Corso Donati, chief among the Blacks, induced Boniface VIII to send Charles of Valois as an arbiter to Florence. Actually, however, Charles' deputed authority made it possible for Corso with his band of exiled Blacks to seize and sack the city, and later to exile Dante on a trumped-up charge of graft.

"Corso's perfidy thus brought to *ruin* both Florence and Dante. But Malacoda's assertion that the 'ruin'—in either sense—can bar Dante's way, temporally or spiritually, is proved a lie. If Dante had been guilty of the sin of which Corso accused him, it would have been different. Malacoda was in rightful charge of grafters; by no artfulness might one escape for long his boiling pitch. But Dante

to the tropological significance, it was the clear sight of the
root of evil by which Dante was able to mount up, disentan-
gling the perplexities of his personal life, once more to see the
Stars,[353] the truth, and the writings of truth. As he passed the
center of the earth, at the thigh of Satan, that "evil worm which
pierces through the world," Dante was turned completely
around by Virgil, in order that his head might still be upward.[354] In passing from the northern to the southern hemisphere, he passed from evening to morning, and from spring to
autumn—that is, to a complete reversal of perspective. In the
allegory, in his attempted solution of the political difficulty, he
was turned completely from use of influence within Florence, to
hope of conquest from without; and in the trope of his moral
struggle, he turned from avoidance of sin to the difficult conquest of virtue. It has been said that it is not always wrong to
look down at hell, but when one looks up at hell, a serious mistake would seem to have been made.[355] Dante, on the other side
of the earth, now saw hell in retrospect, from the right angle.
Expelled from Florence, he now saw Florence truly. Having re-
covered from the madness of youth, he now saw the truth of
moral evil. Thus Dante had acquired the basis essential to his
mission as star of philosophy, guide of the true empire which
he hoped to see inaugurated.

The fallen prince of light still stalks the earth as a werewolf,[356] but the sun is rising to the summit of its course, to the

was innocent; the 'ruin' to which the lying accusation brought him, his exile,
will prove the 'ladder' by which he climbs—back indeed into Florence itself,
when that moral *ruin* the city now is by Corso's fault shall itself be *ruined* by
the avenging *Dux,* so that out of the ruins, Phoenix-like, the ancient 'Roman'
Florence may rearise. In effecting this salutary ruin, the Avenger, sent by God,
completes the analogy. Emissary of Christ, he does for Florence what Christ's
Passion did for hell. (*Inf.,* xii, 37-45.)"

    Cf. also p. 200 n. 346.
    353. "A riveder le stelle." *Inf.,* xxxiv, 139.
    354. *Inf.,* xxxiv, 100-120.   355. G. K. Chesterton.
    356. The only solution of the problem of evil, in accord with Dante's postu-
lates, presents Satan as he appears in Cocytus as impotent, but Satan is a werewolf. Cf. pp. 165 ff. He may achieve his will by assuming the form of the *lupa,*
to wander through the world.
    This symbolic solution is based on the medieval belief in lycanthropy. Men
or women with an inhumanly evil nature did the things which in human form
they could not do (for example, killed and ate men) through the assumption at
night of wolf form. (If, however, wounded in the wolf form, the wound appeared in the human form. For example, a wound in the left fore leg would be

days of the Dogstar.[357] At last the Hound of Heaven will compass the destruction of the werewolf, negation of his nature; and
the ice shall close above the head of the fallen Seraph at the
end of the drama of earthly transmutations,[358] to still the restless flapping of the six bat wings.

ENLIGHTENMENT

On his escape from Florence and the realm of attrition Dante
was greeted in the dawn by his own star: "lo bel pianeta che
d'amar conforta faceva tutto rider l'oriente"[359] and then immediately by "quattro stelle non viste mai fuor ch' a la prima
gente,"[360] in whose "flames the heavens rejoice." These stars so
lighted the face of Cato, guardian of the terraces of purgatory,
that he seemed to be reflecting the full glory of the Sun.

A new element here is brought into the symbolism of the
Divina Commedia. All through the *Inferno* the number symbolism has been in varying arrangements of threes and twos: the
Trinity itself includes the two natures of the Second Person,
represented in the dual vicarates of God on earth, and there is a
similar twoness and threeness in the negation of these elements
in the root of evil. At the very foot of the hill of purgatory is
brought in the number four, indicating the additional idea of
that on which the solar trinity acts, primal matter, and the wills
of men in so far as these are wax for the impression of God.[361a]
This idea obviously could have no place in hell. It is first suggested in the four cardinal virtues, by which as stars, Cato (representation of God in the *Convivio*[361b]) here is so enlightened
as to symbolize God through their medium.

Though Cato, thus illumined, is symbol of God, the sphere in
which he moves is definitely restricted. Purgatory is the realm

evident the next day in a wounded left arm. That is, the two bodies were identical.)
    Dante seems to make use of the principle of lycanthropy, to enable Satan suc-
cessfully to invade both Church and State.
    357. Cf. pp. 167, 327.
    358. At the Last Judgment, with the cessation of time, space, and finite mo-
tion, hell shall be sealed up, to remain eternally as it then is, the measure of
inquity which is to flow into it completely filled. Cf. *Inf.,* x, 97-108.
    359. "The fair planet which hearteneth to love was making the whole East
to laugh." *Purg.,* i, 19-20.
    360. "Four stars never yet seen save by the first people." *Purg.,* i, 23-24.
    361a. *Purg.,* viii, 113.   361b. *Conv.,* 4, 28.

of the four virtues of paganism, albeit under the nightly inspiration of the three theological virtues, with their reminder of the
nearer approach to Beatrice, who for Dante is the channel of
that love which alone can motivate ascent to the Terrestrial
Paradise. If it seem strange to modern thought that Cato's rule
should be restricted to the four cardinal virtues, and yet include
the seven terraces of the Christian purgatory, it is because of the
different attitude toward ethics, to which reference already has
been made. To medieval thinking, although the virtuous life
was a necessary foundation for the growth of the Christian, it
was in no wise distinctive of Christianity. An inevitable product
of philosophical thinking in regard to nature and human relationships, it was the natural obligation of men. The gift of
Christianity lay in the greater power for its fulfilment, but more
importantly in the power to advance beyond it. Salvation is impossible without ethics, as the gruesome scenes of hell had demonstrated, but ethics alone is powerless to accomplish salvation:
about the castle in Limbo burns the flame of desire without
hope. Thomas Aquinas, confronted with the question whether
there are seven principal sins, is challenged by the objection that
the root virtues are only four. In his answer, instead of combining the four cardinal or natural, with the three theological
or specifically Christian virtues, to make seven, he assumes as a
matter of fact that the root virtues are four in number, giving
reasons why there should be in opposition to them not four
vices but rather seven.[362] Those who are in purgatory are there
through imperfection in one or more of the four virtues, and in
consequence must gain their strength under the stern rule of
Cato, albeit with the inspiration of the three theological virtues,
faith, hope, and charity, to comfort in the hours of rest.

Dante has taken care to explain that, guided by philosophy
alone, man can attain to the perfection of earthly virtue and
happiness. The difficulty with this conception lies in the
changed conditions after the Fall. Had the Fall never been, the
statement would have been literally true. After the Fall, under
non-Christian conditions, that is, apart from the presence of the
church, empire and philosophy can reach only to the nearest

362. Aquinas, *S.Th.*, 1, 2, *Q.* 84, *art.* 4, *ad primum.*

imitation of earthly happiness wounded nature can produce, in
other words, to Limbo. *In the presence* of the church (if both
vicarates are functioning rightly) empire and philosophy are
once more able to reach the Terrestrial Paradise by action alone
in their own sphere. If, however, empire and church eclipse each
other, nothing but chaos is possible, save that the individual
soul (Dante) may be led to true vision, by philosophy and
grace, in order that he may assist the officers of the empire in an
attempt to rectify the situation.

Duos igitur fines Providentia illa inenarrabilis homini proposuit
intendendos; beatitudinem scilicet huius vite, que in operatione proprie virtutis consistit, et per terrestrem paradisum figuratur; et beatitudinem vite eterne, que consistit in fruitione divini aspectus ad
quam propria virtus ascendere non potest, nisi lumine divino adiuta,
que per paradisum celestem intelligi datur. . . . Ad primam per
phylosophica documenta venimus, dummodo illa sequamur, secundum
virtutes morales et intellectuales operando; ad secundam vero per documenta spiritualia, quae humanam rationem transcendunt, dummodo
illa sequamur secundum virtutes theologicas operando, fidem scilicet,
Spem et caritatem.[363]

Moreover, progress through purgatory is possible only when the
four stars are in the ascendant; it is only at night during the enforced inactivity[364] that the three theological virtues rise as
stars.[365] Dante goes on to show the rôle of the empire as necessary to make philosophy effective, and similarly the necessity of
the church for theology:

Has igitur conclusiones et media licet ostensa sint nobis, haec ab
humana ratione . . . haec a Spiritu Sancto . . . humana cupiditas
postergaret, nisi homines tamquam equi, sua bestialitate vagantes, in
camo et freno compescerentur in via. Propter quod opus fuit homini
duplici directivo, secundum duplicem finem; scilicet summo Pontifice,

363. "That unutterable providence, then, has set *two ends* before man to be
contemplated by him; the *blessedness,* to wit, *of this life,* which consists in the
exercise of his proper power and is figured by the terrestrial paradise, and the
blessedness of eternal life, which consists in the fruition of the divine aspect, to
which his proper power may not ascend unless assisted by the divine light. And
this blessedness is given to be understood by the celestial paradise. . . . To the
first we attain by the teaching of philosophy, following them by acting in accordance with the moral and intellectual virtues. To the second by spiritual teachings
which transcend human reason, as we follow them by acting according to the
theological virtues, faith, hope, to wit, and charity." *Monarchia.* 3, 16.
364. *Purg.,* vii, 53-57.   365. *Purg.,* viii, 89-93.

qui secundum revelata humanum genus perduceret ad vitam eternam; et Imperatore, qui secundum phylosophica documenta genus humanum ad temporalem felicitatem dirigeret.[366]

As the empire and philosophy are sufficient for complete earthly happiness, so are the four cardinal virtues, being sufficient also to prepare for the Earthly Paradise those legally exempted by baptism from the original sin by which their right thereto had been forfeited. The real function of the church and the three theological virtues is to raise men above nature to heaven. They may inspire the empire and the four cardinal virtues, indeed, but may not intervene outside of their own proper sphere. Thus the purgative life, although inspired by the three, is directed by the four.[367]

Morally, the dawn of the light of the four pagan virtues, so bright that they seem almost to carry the full light of God,[368] represents the point of moral conversion, the turning away from the evil to the good. The first step in regeneration, as held by theology, is the realization of the true and loathsome nature of sin, and the consequent aversion for it which would correspond to the phrase "conviction of sin," but constitutes, according to Catholic theology, not even the first step in repentance, unless definitely motivated by the love of God.[369] Repentance consists

366. "Now albeit these ends and means are made plain to us, the one by human reason . . . the other by the Holy Spirit . . . yet would human greed cast them behind were not men, like horses going astray in their brutishness, held in the way by bit and rein. Wherefore man had need of a twofold directive power, according to his twofold end, to wit, the supreme pontiff, to lead the human race, in accordance with things revealed, to eternal life, and the emperor, to direct the human race to temporal felicity in accordance with the teachings of philosophy." *Monarchia,* 3, 16.

367. The question may arise at this point as to why the moral aspect of Dante's arrival at the foot of the mount appears to demand first attention, inasmuch as hitherto first attention has been given to the political aspect of Dante's growth. Dante himself however has made clear the fact that his awakening to the perils of the Dark Wood was amid the tumults of Florence. Thus, even on the political level, the natural order of his attack on the problems would be first, recognition of the chaotic condition of affairs; next, search for the root of this condition, which he found in cupidity; next, recognition of the remedy for cupidity in the four virtues; and only then the application of his new insight to the political problem.

368. *Purg.,* i, 37-39.

369. In this point is seen the chasm separating the apparently identical attitudes of Augustine and Bunyan. Both dwell at length on their conviction of wickedness, but Augustine's conviction is characterized as motivated rather by love of God, whom his sin hurts and from whom it constitutes a separation, than by dwelling on the horror of wickedness.

of contrition, confession, and satisfaction.[370] Contrition is aversion for sin motivated by charity, by the love of God.[371] Dante at the end of the journey through the *Inferno* had learned the horror of loves wrongly directed and separated from the love of God, but as yet only attrition, that is, aversion for sin from fear and dislike, not yet a true contrition. When Cato asked who was the lamp that guided them, it was the name of Beatrice, not that of Marcia,[372] which induced him to greet them favorably; that is, it is the fire of heavenly love, not earthly (separated), which as a motive among the blest is to become the environment of Dante's further journey.

Thus Dante, having placed at a distance his native Florence, saw the virtues functioning as bright stars in the direction of his dawning political theory. It is, however, to be noted that Cato was the first to welcome Dante after his exit, not from hell itself, but from the passage leading from purgatory to hell. In the story of Dante's life this climb through a narrow passage from the center of the earth, from the back of Satan himself up to the foot of the Mount of Purgatory, may well represent the period after his expulsion from Florence while he, still acting in some accord with his turbulent faction, seems to have attempted to force his return through an attack on his city from Arezzo. It was only after his complete break with all within the earth that he glimpsed the four stars and was greeted by Cato. It is to be noted, moreover, that the first greeting was with suspicion, although the final outcome was admission to purgatory.

370. Cf. Aquinas, *S.Th.*, suppl. *Q.* 1-15.
371. According to the modern view attrition would seem quite sufficient—a turning from evil actions based merely on aversion for them. The old Catholic theology would raise a doubt as to whether a man could receive absolution based on attrition alone. Dante's emphasis on fear throughout hell shows attrition.
372. Marcia, according to Lucan's story (*Pharsalia*, 2, 338-345) was the wife of Cato, given by him to Hortensius, who after the death of the latter returned to Cato. Dante, in *Convivio*, 4, 28, develops an elaborate trope by which the stages of Marcia's career signify the virtues proper to the periods of man's life, and her return to Cato signifies "that the noble soul at the beginning of decrepitude returns to God." This fact heightens the force of Dante's use of Marcia in this passage. Earthly love, even though it be so noble that it may rightly serve as an allegory of the soul's love for God, so long as it has not been transhumanized in response to the Love that moves the stars, has no power to free from *gravezza*. Under the wretched doom of Circe, who turns her creatures into her own form of *lupa*, her victim must itself act as *gravezza* in relation to those who are working out the problem of freedom under the discipline of the law of love.

These facts would make Cato the fitting representative in the political allegory of Bartolommeo della Scala, lord of Verona, and, after Dante's break with his party, the first to show him kindness:

> Lo primo tuo refugio, il primo ostello
> sarà la cortesia del gran Lombardo
> che 'n su la scala porta il santo uccello;
> ch' in te avrà sì benigno riguardo,
> che del fare e del chieder, tra voi due,
> fia primo quel che, tra gli altri, è più tardo.[373]

Cato, however, was at first inclined to view the travelers with suspicion, due to their emergence from the direction of hell. While nothing is related as to the matter, the Ghibelline Scaligeri were doubtless hesitant at first in granting opportunity to Dante, if not actually suspicious of the good faith of one fleeing from a turbulent Guelph faction of Florence.[374]

373. "Thy first refuge and first hostelry shall be the courtesy of the great Lombard, who on the ladder beareth the sacred bird, for he shall cast so benign regard on thee that of doing and demanding, that shall be first betwixt you two, which betwixt others most doth lag." *Par.,* xvii, 70-75. The identification of the "great Lombard" of this passage with Bartolommeo dates from Dante's son Pietro. Torraca and some other commentators, however, have thought his brother Alboino the one designated, basing their argument on the date of Bartolommeo's death (1304) and a supposition that Dante's break with his party may have occurred after, rather than before, that time. The question, however, would seem to be settled, for the majority of critics, not only by the statement of Dante's son, but by the slighting way in which Dante speaks of Alboino in *Convivio,* 4, 16. (Can Grande, younger brother of Bartolommeo and Alboino, was a nine-year-old child at the time when Dante took refuge with the Scaligeri.)

374. The fact that the whole outline of Dante's life is given in Cacciaguida's prophecy in the *Paradiso* implies among other things Dante's conviction that fundamental truth is to be sought in eternity. Interesting here, in view of the words of Dante's own forefather with reference to Bartolommeo's generous protection (*Par.,* xvii, 70-75) is the paternal aspect of Cato (*Purg.,* i, 33). Another interesting association is Cacciaguida's exoneration of Dante from implication among his fellow exiles (*Par.,* xvii, 66—"their temples not thine shall redden for it") and Bartolommeo's (Cato's on the political level) similar freeing of Dante from the need of blushing—of necessity upon him during his association with the Guelph malcontents—through acceptance of him.

On the political level with reference to Dante, the outline is somewhat as follows:

Adventures in hell	Political career in Florence
Passage on Satan's back	Expulsion from Florence
Tortuous passage from subterranean realms	Period of implication in the covert activities of fellow exiles
Meeting with Cato at the foot of the mount	Refuge with the Scaligeri
Progress and enlightenment on the climb to the gate	Wanderings and studies in Italy and possibly in Paris
Passage through the terraces	Vicissitudes which are to end in the establishment of true church and empire

It is certain that Dante's political theory must have been matured after this time and before Henry's election, otherwise his activities at the latter time would have been characterized by less dexterity and certainty. If Wicksteed's conjectural date for the *Monarchia* (1309) be correct, this supposition is backed by Dante's own statement.[375] Indeed, in the *Convivio*,[376] still earlier, his conception as to the nature and extent of imperial authority is set forth. What more likely then, after Dante's final abandonment of Guelph policy, than that welcome by the Ghibelline Scaligeri in Verona should have given Dante the first moment of hope that a political theory might be developed from the Ghibelline approach. Certainly it was such a hope which during the intervening years, possibly at Paris, where he was guided also by those stars, the writings of the philosophers, he developed into the settled conviction of 1310. Whether or not Boccaccio is right as to Paris, it is certain that between Dante's entertainment by the Scaligeri and his activities on behalf of Henry (and later Can Grande) lay a period of study, in which his first new hope was nourished. Finally, the meeting with Bartolommeo, as with Cato, marked the entrance upon a period of enforced delay, irritating to one who having seen a goal desires to set out at once in active preparation for it.

The moral counterpart of this period may be that time in which inertia is being overcome, which intervenes between conversion and visible signs of progress in virtue. Cato prepares the way alike for the political and the moral purgation.

The mists of hell having been washed from Dante's eyes, that is, the mists of factional policies and entangled moral standards, the sun, then rising, again became his guide. Dante had progressed from attrition to contrition, having added to his hatred of sin the motive of the love of God. As is stated specifically,[377] it is solely "light from heaven" which is the cause of repentance, penetrating the soul with desire to see God. It was at the entrance to purgatory, moreover, that Dante was astonished at the glory of heavenly ministration. In brilliant contrast to the storm-clad angel whose wand opened Dis appeared the celestial

375. *Monarchia.* 2, 1. 376. *Convivio,* 4, 5, and 4, 9.
377. *Purg.,* v, 53.

ferryman in whose "vasello snelletto e leggiero" souls gathered
at the mouth of the Tiber were borne to the shores of purgation.

At this time Dante first realized that his earthly body cast a
shadow in the sun, and so marked him out from all the souls
among whom he was then sojourning.[378] Here, among the late-
repentant and the violently slain, Dante became self-conscious
and hung back because the shades were staring at him and whis-
pering. What again more suggestive of his situation, a Guelph,
outcast from Florence, accused of treason, taking refuge in a
Ghibelline castle? His blushing answer to Virgil, "Io vegno"—
"I come," may well represent the outcome of a real inner battle
in the incipient development of a new and independent political
theory. It was the spirit of the ideal empire that had called him,
saying:

> Perchè l'animo tuo tanto s'impiglia,
> . . . che l'andare allenti?
> che ti fa ciò che quivi si pispiglia?
> Vien dietro a me, e lascia dir le genti.[379]

Here the greeting of the two messengers[380] suggests the emphasis throughout the *Purgatorio,* that Dante, unlike those among
whom he moved, was living, and was to go back to restore order
in the chaos he had left. This idea indeed was the inspiration
of Dante's long years of preparation for his great work.
Whereas in Florence (hell where naught shines), there had not
been sufficient light to distinguish a shadow; elsewhere in Italy
(well described as the place of the dead, banished from the Sun
of Empire), there was still sufficient light, in Dante's opinion, to
make possible even on the part of others, gradual realization
of his mission.

The sun from this time forth occupies a central position, during actual progress and notably when the poets sit down to rest,
their eyes turned sunward.[381] Although Virgil is still Dante's
light[382] and so his guide even on the subject of prayer, he now
refers him further to Beatrice[383] who is to be a light between the

---

378. Cf. *Purg.,* iii, 16 ff.; iii, 88 ff.; iv, 4 ff.; iv, 25 ff.; vi, 57 ff.; xxvi, 7.
379. "Why is thy mind so entangled . . . that thou slackenest thy pace?
what matters it to thee what they whisper here? follow me and let the people
talk." *Purg.,* v, 10-13.
380. Cf. *Purg.,* v, 25 ff.   381. *Purg.,* iv, 52-53.
382. *Purg.,* vi, 28.   383. *Purg.,* vi, 43-46.

truth and the intellect. While Virgil's own answer infers the action of the Holy Spirit,

> Chè cima di giudicio non s'avvalla
> perchè foco d'amor compia in un punto
> ciò che de' sodisfar chi qui si stalla,[384]

yet more specific guidance of the Holy Spirit must now be recognized. In the Ante-purgatory, furthermore, Dante learned more of Virgil. All that the sage had done had been done well. Not only had he appreciated to the full the empire as Sun of Rome, but he had given to others that premonition of the other Sun which he himself had understood too late:

> Non per far, ma per non fare ho perduto
> a veder l'alto Sol che tu disiri
> e che fu tardi per me conosciuto.[385]

On the Mount of Purgatory Dante was no longer under the power of the *gravezza* inspired by the she-wolf, because under the attraction of God the Sun; but there is still a force of evil, as Sordello pointed out: "Truly, by night one might return downwards."[386] It is only under the rays of the Prime Mover that ascent is possible. Furthermore, as Sordello informed the poets while they gazed down upon the valley of negligent rulers: Without the guidance of the Sun of Empire, real progress is impossible; negligent rulers having caused so much lost time to others, are justly appointed a period of waiting. Similarly, in the absence of the light of Lady Philosophy, moral actions are impeded, since "by following her everyone becomes good."[387] It is through those ministers on earth that God draws man to himself. The little physical sun[388] expresses as always the spiritual Sun, partaking uniquely of its nature.[389]

In purgatory all knowledge of time and of location is from the sun,[390] and more than this eyes seek the east[391] for rest and

384. "For the height of justice is not abased because fire of love fulfills in one moment the satisfaction which he owes who here is lodged." *Purg.*, vi, 37-39.

385. "Not for doing, but for not doing, have I lost the vision of the high Sun, whom thou desirest, and who too late by me was known." *Purg.*, vii, 25-27.

386. *Purg.*, vii, 52-60.   387. *Convivio*, 3, 15.   388. *Purg.*, vii, 85.

389. Cf. Chap. III, Pt. I, i and iii.   390. *Purg.*, vii, 85.

391. An exhaustive discussion of symbolism of chronology and cosmography in the *Divina Commedia* would be the subject for a separate work.

help. Dante was deeply impressed with this truth during his first night there, a night of terror in the absence of the Sun; it was through constancy to the inspiration of Mary, and the light of faith, hope, and charity visible in the sky, that he was saved. The compline hymn *Te lucis ante terminum,* sung in the valley at sunset by eastward-facing souls, is a prayer to the spiritual Sun against the temptations of the night. In the emphasis of the east is bound up all the medieval and traditional reverence for it, as the source of the sun, as representing Mary from whom the sun was born.

Recte Maria dicitur oriens lucis; nam ex ea ortus est Christus, qui est lux mundi.[392]

From her bosom[393] come the answering angels bearing swords against the nightly serpent of unchastity, or rather the serpent which like that of Eden[394, 395] persuades man to eat the evil food of cupidity.[396] Again, these angels with their two swords are a new reminder of the two suns of Rome, empire and church, who alone make possible to man assurance of innocent nightly rest and refreshment, the one protecting from outer, the other from inner, disturbance. In their green color Dante meant probably to suggest hope renewed for the solution of imperial and moral problems.

More than this, however, would seem to be implied in Dante's choice of those particular angels as messengers of the solar trinity. Such customs and ideas should be recalled as the burial of the dead facing the east, the position of the altar toward the east, the expectation of Christ's Second Advent from the east and borne on the clouds of morning, and the east as the locus of the resurrection and the judgment. Death is always toward the west with the dying sun, and the land of the dead like Dante's purgatory is under the earth—the other side of the earth—where the sun goes at night.[397] All of this has its early phase in the story of the sun god and the associated vege-tation myth.[398] Dante himself used vegetation symbolism for the

---

392. Albertus Magnus, *De laudibus B. Mariae Virg.,* 7, 7, 3.
393. *Purg.,* viii, 37.   394. *Purg.,* viii, 99.
395. For Adam's sin, cf. footnotes, pp. 292-293.   396. Cf. p. 56.
397. Christ on the cross faced toward the west. Cf., e.g., John of Damascus, *Exposition of the Orthodox Faith,* iv, 12.
398. Cf. pp. 109 ff.

offspring in human character of the influence of the spiritual Sun, for example:

Take the harrow of fair humility, and breaking up the clods caked by the heat of your wrath, make level the acre of your minds, lest haply the celestial shower, anticipating the seed ere ye have sown it, fall from on high in vain; that the grace of God leap not back from you like the daily dew from a rock; but rather, that ye conceive like a fertile valley, and thrust forth the green, *the green, that is, that bears the fruit of true peace;* that when your land is keeping spring in this verdure, the new ploughman of the Romans may with the more love and confidence, yoke the oxen of his counsel to the plough. . . . And therefore, unless hindered by the inveterate offence which oft *in serpent fashion doth twist round and turn upon itself,* ye may perceive on either side that peace is prepared for all and every, and may taste already the first fruits of the hoped-for joy.[399]

In purgatory, the angels which came in answer to the prayer for aid against the serpent, were clothed in the green of vegetation and had the fair hair of the sun. Their flaming swords broken short, are reminiscent of the lightning weapon and of the sun-vegetation-storm hero descriptions already noted[400] in some versions of the Grail romances (obviously written by those who had forgotten the ancestry of the imagery they employed). How this influence found its way into the *Divina Commedia* is not the question in this discussion, where it is now clear that the angels with broken swords, dressed in green, are the spirit of peace which Dante hoped in 1310 God would send to put to flight from princes the serpentine spirit of faction and rebellion, even as spring perpetually routs the winter.

Nevertheless, the sun-storm imagery deserves some mention in Dante. It will be remembered that storm manifestations occurred at transitions in hell, for example, at the passage of Acheron and at the coming of him who opened Dis. Satan himself, once messenger of God, when hell was first created fell down like lightning from the heavens,[401] piercing to the center of the earth. For although the solar trinity shows no brightness

399. From Epistle 5. Cf. also *Purg.,* xi, 92, and *Purg.,* xi, 115-117.
400. Cf. pp. 109 ff.
401. Luke 10. 18. The revolt and fall of the angels is referred to clearly in II Pet. 2. 4, and Jude 6, more obscurely in Rev. 12. 9. References to it occur in the writings of early authors, for example, St. Augustine, Tertullian. It is narrated in full in Cassian, *Collationes,* 8, 11 (fourth-fifth century).

in hell, hell was created by his love and is governed by his will. It is to be noted, however, that even the storm-god form of the solar deity was never made an evil aspect as opposed to a fair and good one. Both as god of sun and as god of storm he had his intentionally benign and life-giving, and his incidentally destructive, influence. Dante, true to tradition, explained that:

Lo Sole tutte le cose col suo calore vivifica, e se alcuna ne corrompe, non è de la 'ntenzione de la cagione, ma è accidentale effetto: così Iddio tutte le cose vivifica in bontade, e se alcuna n'è rea non è de la divina intenzione, ma conviene p[u]r qualche accidente essere ne lo processo de lo inteso effetto. . . . Tanta fu l'affezione a producere la creatura spirituale, che la prescienza d' alquanti che a malo fine doveano venire non dovea nè potea Iddio da quella produzione rimuovere. Chè non sarebbe da laudare la Natura se, sappiendo prima che li fiori d'un'arbore in certa parte perdere si dovessero, non producesse in quella fiori, e per li vani abbandonasse la produzione de li fruttiferi.[402]

It was inevitable that he who defied God should experience rather the celestial thunderbolt[403] than the blessing of the sun's heat, that is, charity. The will that created hell was good, was, indeed, the primal Love, yet the manifestation of love in the city of the Great Defiance was such as well-nigh to destroy it:

Ma certo poco pria, se ben discerno,
    che venisse colui che la gran preda
    levò a Dite del cerchio superno,
da tutte parti l'alta valle feda
    tremò sì, ch' i' pensai che l'universo
    sentisse amor, per lo qual è chi creda
più volte il mondo in caos converso;
    ed in quel punto questa vecchia roccia
    qui e altrove tal fece riverso;[404]

---

402. "The sun quickens all things with his heat, and if he destroys certain things thereby, that is not of the intention of the cause, but is an incidental effect; and in like manner God quickens all things in goodness, and if any of them be evil, it is not of the divine intention, but must needs be in some way incidental to the progress of the effect intended. . . . So great an affection had he to produce spiritual creatures that the foreknowledge of some who must needs come to an ill end should not nor could not hinder God from this producing; for nature would not be to praise if, well knowing that the blossoms of a tree must perish in some certain part, she were not to produce blossoms thereon, and because of the barren were to abstain from producing the fertile ones." *Convivio*, 3, 12.

403. *Purg.*, xii, 28.

404. "But certainly, if I distinguish rightly, short while before He came, who took from Dis the great prey of the upmost circle, on all sides the deep loath-

and:

> Questa lor tracotanza non è nova;
> chè già l'usaro a men secreta porta,
> la qual sanza serrame ancor si trova.[405]

The moral significance here is that if the manifested love of Christ could have gained its desired response, hell would have remained only as a central sink of evil washed away by Lethe;[406] and a similar effect of perfect response to divine love would have transformed Florence into the perfect city. Such was the law of love revealed to Dante yet more cogently in the region of the spheres.

It is interesting that in the *Divina Commedia* the first manifestation of storm[407] produced in Dante the first sleep of his journey,[408] making him unconscious of the crossing of Acheron. Sleep, throughout the poem, is the shutting of the eyes to light, as at the outset Dante's losing of the right way was while he was full of sleep.[409] In purgatory, however, sleep is not so unillumined, and in sleep Dante experienced three visions.

At the time of the lunar aurora[410] with Scorpio in the ascendant, Dante, overcome by sleep in the valley of negligent princes, was startled by a dream of an eagle[411] "with plumes of gold,

some valley trembled so, that I thought the universe felt love, whereby, as some believe, the world has oft-times been converted into chaos; and in that moment, here, and elsewhere, this ancient rock made such downfall." *Inf.,* xii, 37-45.

405. "This insolence of theirs is nothing new; for they shewed it once at a less secret gate, which still is found unbarred." *Inf.,* viii, 124-126. The reference is to the opposition of the angels of hell to the entrance of Christ at the "Harrowing." This opposition is a familiar part of the medieval legend. Cf. pp. 179 ff., notes.

406. Cf. pp. 231 ff.

407. Throughout the *Commedia* there is a significant series of quakes or convulsions, caused by love yet full of terror for the evil. Cf. the three references in the *Inferno* to the ruin left there by the earthquake which accompanied Christ's Harrowing of Hell (cf. pp. 180, 300), the quake Dante felt at the crossing of Acheron, the purgatorial quake which signified the freeing of a soul to rise upward, and the two convulsions of love and indignation among the Blessed (*Par.,* cantos xxii and xxvii) which have a spiritual effect similar to the earthly effect of the earlier quakes.

408. *Inf.,* iii, 130-136, and iv, 1-6.   409. *Inf.,* i, 10-12.

410. The interpretation of *Purg.,* ix, 1-3, as the lunar aurora dates back to Dante's son.

411. "In sogno mi parea veder sospesa un'aguglia nel ciel con penne d'oro, con l'ali aperte e a calare intesa . . . Poi mi parea che, rotata un poco, terribil come folgor discendesse, e me rapisse suso infino al foco. Ivi parea che ella e io ardesse; e sì lo 'ncendio imaginato cosse, che convenne che 'l sonno si rompesse." *Purg.,* ix, 19-21, 28-33.

with wings outspread, and intent to swoop" who, "having wheeled awhile terrible as lightning" snatched Dante "up as far as the fiery sphere." There, writes Dante, "it seemed that he and I did burn, and the visionary flame so scorched that needs was my slumber broken." The eagle was once thought to be unique among birds for its ability to fly straight toward the sun with unhurt and clear sight, and in consequence in symbolic tradition the eagle has stood for the contemplative soul gazing upon the secret things of God.[412] Its special association with the Second Person of the Trinity was made clear to Dante in the spheres of Mercury and Jupiter. Here, however, the identification is made with Lucia,[413] without whose agency Dante could not have reached the gate of purgatory, but whose radiance he could as yet endure only under a figure and in a dream. Even under such a veil, the impression Dante received was of almost intolerable burning. Yet Lucia herself is a veil, shadowing forth the functioning of God the Son, Wisdom and Light.[413] Thus through symbols of symbols was the light tempered which for Dante was even then intolerable.

In the development of Dante's political theory this dream may represent his fuller vision of the empire as inspired by Divine Wisdom, and perhaps specifically the eagle may here represent Henry VII and the indescribable joy produced by Henry's coronation.[414] As far as Dante's moral development is concerned, although the four virtues were sufficient for the climb to the terrestrial paradise,[415] yet the decisive advance from his moral and political entanglement was rather through the grace of Christ than through the effort of Dante or of Virgil. Christ makes possible the development of the true Christian life, sending his Spirit as Lucia sent Beatrice[416] to the assistance of the struggling soul. A reminder that the struggle between good and

412. Particularly the eagle was the symbol of the apostle John, distinguished by his especial closeness to Christ and by his insight into eternal truths. Cf. *Par.*, xxvi, 53.

413. For the identification of Lucia with the Second Person of the Trinity see pp. 169-171, 235.

414. Cf. the eagle of Mercury (pp. 45-46), of Jupiter (pp. 70-74), and of the Terrestrial Paradise (p. 325). Since here is considered the *development* of Dante's political hopes and convictions, the whole discussion hinging on Henry's death preceding the completion of the *Commedia*, etc., is irrelevant.

415. Cf. pp. 204-206; also *Monarchia*, 3, 16.   416. *Inf.*, ii, 100-108.

evil is still in progress is Dante's freezing with terror after the scorching heat, a fact which has its appropriate meaning on each of the levels.

PURIFICATION

At the Gate stood a Guardian Angel in brilliance far surpassing even that first messenger of Deity whom Dante had seen on the shore below, "such in his countenance" that Dante "endured him not."[417] In his hand was the weapon of the sun god, a sword dazzling beyond the power of Dante's vision, and reminiscent of the flaming sword which at the gate of Eden[418] "turned every way, to keep the way of the tree of life." From this sword Dante received seven wounds, seven *P's* cut into his forehead, before the ashen-vestured guardian drew forth his gold and silver keys[419] for the unlocking of the gate.

In vivid contrast to the examples of Pride and rebellion to be studied by souls on the first terrace is the angel of humility, like a "tremolando mattutina stella," unique among angels in that he does not dazzle.[420] He is connected with Mary (preëminent in humility as in all the virtues) and peculiarly associated with the east and with the dawn. It was through the humility of Mary that Christ was born on earth to accomplish the conquest of pride and of that sin of Adam by which the whole world was betrayed to the *lupa*. The feeling of lightness following his erasure of the burden of the first *P* further elucidates the law of ascent in purgatory, as opposed to the *gravezza* inspired by the she-wolf.[421] The soul is freed from *gravezza* as the lightening of his load frees man from the downward pull of gravity; and thus he becomes increasingly sensitive to his own natural gravitation which is toward the Divine Sun. The reversal of foci of the universe for him who is entering on the mystic way should be recalled.[422]

417. "Tal ne la faccia ch' io non lo soffersi." *Purg.*, ix, 81.
418. Gen. 3. 24.
419. Cf. Matt. 16. 19. Peter Lombard (*Sentences* 4, 18) interprets the keys as "scientia discernendi peccata et potestas judicandi de peccatis." In both church and empire right authority and right judgment are alike requisite for due exercise of power.
420. "To us came the beauteous creature, robed in white, and in his countenance, such as a tremulous star at morn appears." *Purg.*, xii, 88-90.
421. Cf. also *Purg.*, xi, 43-45.   422. Cf. pp. 87-89.

Virgil's principle of guidance here is of course the following of the Sun.[423] To Virgil's understanding, God is expressed through empire and philosophy, to be followed unless special revelation is given through Beatrice or other messenger of God. The direction in which he turns is of interest in comparison with mystery ritual in which the officiator walks around the altar in the proper direction saying, "Sunwise we go, sunwise let our sacrifice be made."[424] Of the motion in the *Inferno* it was carefully stated that the direction was from right to left.[425] Since in the northern hemisphere the sun, going from east to west, always passes to the south of the observer, Dante's motion was counter-sunwise, though beyond the reaches of the sun. In the *Purgatorio,* however, the same spiral direction, being now in the southern hemisphere, where the sun passes to the north of the observer, is sunwise.

The guiding sun, however, profits naught to the Envious of the second terrace.[426] To them, the atmosphere of peace and justice, the highest gift of the righteous empire, avails little, since they produce their own dark atmosphere of cupidity, and of the light of philosophy they are heedless. (Perhaps this is why Dante takes pains to point out the smallness of his offense in this respect.) Virgil's reproof of them, following the manifestation of thunder and lightning consequent here as below on the wilful turning away from the sun,[427] is noteworthy:

> Ma voi prendete l'esca, sì che l'amo
> de l'antico avversario a sè vi tira;
> e però poco val freno o richiamo.
> Chiamavi il cielo e intorno vi si gira,
> mostrandovi le sue bellezze eterne,
> a l'occhio vostro pur a terra mira;
> onde vi batte chi tutto discerne.[428]

The association was doubtless meant to be with Dante's interpretation of the heavens as symbolizing the sciences:

The seven heavens that are first with respect to us are those of the planets; next come two moving heavens above them; and one above

423. See *Purg.,* xiii, 10-21.   424. Cf. p. 404 n. 13.
425. *Inf.,* i, 28-30, and xiv, 126.   426. *Purg.,* xiii, 67.
427. *Purg.,* xiv, 130-135.
428. "But ye take the bait, so that the old adversary's hook draws you to him, and therefore little avails bridle or lure. The heavens call to you, and circle

them all, which is quiet. To the seven first correspond the seven sciences
of the Trivium and of the Quadrivium, to wit grammar, dialectic,
rhetoric, arithmetic, music, geometry and astrology. To the eighth, to
wit the starry sphere, answers natural science which is called physics,
and first science which is called metaphysics. To the ninth sphere answers moral science; and to the quiet heaven answers divine science,
which is called theology;[429]

and of their stars as the writings elucidating those sciences: "In
every science, scripture is a star, full charged with light, which
showeth forth that science."[430]

The angel of fraternal love, most dazzling of all angels in
purgatory, Dante met as he approached the stairway leading to
the next terrace, the terrace of Wrath. Again his attention was
called to the fact that centering affection on the things of earth
results inevitably in the drawing of darkness even from the true
light.[431]

Suddenly in the beauty of the evening Dante was recalled to
the horrors of the *Inferno*.

> Buio d'inferno e di notte privata
>   d'ogni pianeta sotte pover cielo,
>   quant' esser può di nuvol tenebrata,
> non fece al viso mio sì grosso velo,
>   come quel fummo ch'ivi ci coperse,
>   nè a sentir di così aspro pelo;
> che l'occhio stare aperto non sofferse:
>   onde la scorta mia saputa e fida
>   mi s'accostò, e l'omero m'offerse.
> Sì come cieco va dietro a sua guida
>   per non smarrirsi e per non dar di cozzo
>   in cosa che 'l molesti, o forse ancida;
> m'andava io per l'aere amaro e sozzo,
>   ascoltando il mio duca che diceva
>   pur: "Guarda che da me tu non sie mozzo."[432]

around you, displaying unto you their eternal splendours, and your eye gazes
only to earth; wherefore he who discerns all things doth buffet you." *Purg.,* xiv,
145-151.

432. *Convivio,* 2, 14.   430. *Convivio,* 2, 16.

431. *Purg.,* xv, 64-66. (For the meaning of Guido's description of the valley
of the Arno cf. pp. 231-232.)

432. "Gloom of hell and of a night bereft of every planet under a meagre
sky, darkened by cloud as much as it can be, made not to my sight so thick a
veil, nor of a pile so harsh to the feel, as that smoke which there covered us;
for it suffered not the eye to stay open: wherefore my wise and trusty Escort
closed up to me, and offered me his shoulder. Even as a blind man goeth behind

On the terrace on which is being overcome the *gravezza* of the
third of the sins of wrongly directed love, and fresh from his
vision of the radiance of brotherly love, Dante's attention was
directed to a deeper inquiry into the root of the great evil
among men. The evil, Mark the Lombard pointed out, cannot
lie in stellar influence, first because that would rob men of free
will, their possession of which is the keystone of the universal
drama, and second because the stars are good in themselves.[433]
The trouble arose in the ordering and placing in right perspective the multitudinous imprints of good. The spheres do indeed originate man's impulses, but his gradual education requires that he become acquainted first with lesser goods; and
further, that by these he be not led into the hungry maw of the
she-wolf, there are required laws and a leader with keener insight than the herd. When the heaven-appointed leader himself
yields to the attraction of lesser goods, the souls of men are left
without direction.

Here it would seem, Dante came to his first definite formulation of the foundation of his political and moral platform[434] and
to the bitter realization that the two suns of Rome had eclipsed
each other, rendering impossible that peace and order necessary
for study[435] and advance in spiritual discernment between good
and evil:

> Dì oggimai che la chiesa di Roma,
>   per confondere in sè due reggimenti,
>   cade del fango e sè brutta e la soma.[436]

Thus she has created a murky and infernal atmosphere, dimming even the light given to each to know good and evil.[437]
Dante realized that this same problem had been faced by the

his guide in order not to stray, and not to butt against aught that may do him
hurt, or perchance kill him, so went I through the bitter and foul air, listening
to my Leader who was saying ever: 'Look that thou be not cut off from me.' "
Purg., xvi, 1-15.

433. Cf. pp. 47 ff., also 177.

434. Perhaps in his personal development the point at which he wrote the
Monarchia—obviously not a point to be asserted or argued.

435. Cf. p. 377.

436. "Say henceforth, that the Church of Rome, by confounding two powers
in herself, falls into the mire, and fouls herself and her burden." *Purg.,* xvi, 127-
129.

437. *Purg.,* xvi, 75.

Jewish lawgiver[438] and supremely by Christ in his establishment of the dual vicarate.[439]

Even sufficient light whereby to see depicted examples of their sin and its opposing virtue is not permitted souls on this terrace, of which the murky atmosphere is reminiscent of deepest hell. Yet there is an important difference: although darkness shrouds the senses, light is present to the mind. (It will be recalled that to Dante's psychology, reason, fancy, and all knowing are as much dependent on the light of God as is physical vision on the light of the sun.) Dante, before he entered the cloud, saw in imagination examples of meekness, and after leaving it, examples of wrath. He entered upon a discussion in which he explained that fancy is directed by a light "che nel ciel s'informa."[440] Even the light of imagination "fell down," however, in the presence of the angel of meekness. The radiance of those heavenly messengers conquers not only the physical senses, but also the inner light.

With rhythmic reiteration[441] Dante in his progress was attacked again and again by the horror of evil, and it was always love, in natural movement like to fire, which gave him further illumination:

> Però ti prego, dolce padre caro,
>   che mi dimostri amore, a cui riduci
>   ogni buono operare e 'l suo contraro.[442]

There is no virtue in love itself, which is the universal law of man's nature; the virtue lies wholly in his choice between loves.

The identification of Virgil with reason and Beatrice with faith has been based upon the following lines:

> Ed elli a me: Quanto ragion qui vede
>   dir ti poss'io; da indi in là t'aspetta
>   pur a Beatrice, ch' è opra di fede.[443]

438. *Purg.*, xvi, 131-132.   439. Cf. Chap. IV, Pt. II.
440. "Which takes its form in heaven." Cf. *Purg.*, xvi, 13-18.
441. Cf. *Purg.*, vi, 76 ff.; ix, 42 ff.; ix, 64 ff.; xiv, 16 ff.; xvi, 1 ff.; xvi, 58 ff.; xix, 1 ff.; xxiii, 115-117; xvii, 14 ff.; xxx, 73 ff., and the vision that sums up the evil, xxxii, 103 ff.
442. "Therefore I pray thee, sweet Father dear, that thou define love to me, to which thou dost reduce every good work and its opposite." *Purg.*, xviii, 13-15.
443. "And he to me: So far as reason sees here, I can tell thee; from beyond that point, ever await Beatrice, for 'tis a matter of faith." *Purg.*, xviii, 46-48.

Nevertheless, by this time it should be clear that no one part of the *Divina Commedia* can be understood apart from its relationship to the whole. These lines are but a characteristic acknowledgment by Virgil of one of the many functions of Beatrice who is Love.[444] Dante's symbolism is multiplex and Beatrice represents the action of the Holy Ghost who is Love (who alone of the Three Persons acts directly on men) in giving, among his other graces, the redeeming light of faith and theology. Virgil represents the light of nature, likewise inspired by the Holy Ghost, but as a gift of "kind" not of grace. The rhythmic recurrence of these considerations first of evil and then of love accords well with the recognition of the act of love as spiritual movement, and with the circular motion of the sun, the poets' constant guide.[445]

The Slothful, alone among souls in purgatory, run both night and day, since their sin is unique in a lack of sufficient love or spiritual motion. It would seem that this sin gave peculiar entrance to Satan, for here, ushered in by lack of motion, the darkness of the night, and cold (Saturn is the coldest of planets), appears the Siren[446] the most noxious embodiment of Satan appearing to Dante in purgatory. Was she perhaps given opportunity by the fact that Dante *slept* on a terrace of which the law was perpetual motion? May this not suggest that Dante, whose character, as revealed in Paradise[447] is marked by wavering and infidelity, was wearying of the task of developing a new theory, or desirous of a change? The *Convivio* itself is a monument to the fact that Dante at moments wearied of that philosophic application which he came to understand as his mission.

It is Dante's look, moreover, that makes the Siren fair "come il sol conforta le fredde membra che la notte aggrava,"[448] that is, apart from wrongly directed human love, she has no power of attraction. Dante, ever conscious of his personal power, probably realized the strength that he could add to Guelph or Ghibelline parties, representing church and empire in the clutches of the she-wolf. At the same time he had come to realize the power of

444. Cf. pp. 168 ff., also 234 ff.   445. Cf. p. 182.
446. Cf. p. 236.   447. Cf. pp. 38 ff., 43.
448. "As the sun comforteth the cold limbs which night weighs down." Cf. *Purg.*, xix, 7 ff.

a right political policy and a true philosophy, under the direction of Beatrice, to reveal to them the hideousness of their cupidity. Perhaps here is an early stage in the development of
Dante's conception of his mission as that of the star of philosophy, under the direction of Beatrice, to guide the empire. Similarly the light of philosophy and the love of Beatrice had revealed to him his own sinfulness.

Yet such had been the power of the Siren that Dante was still
sensitive to her attraction. As in emerging from the Dark
Wood, he had turned from the rising sun to look back upon it,
so in emerging from the terrace of sloth he scarcely noticed the
gentle-voiced angel of zeal, such was the power with which his
gaze had been attracted downward by the *gravezza* of the she-
wolf who had appeared to him in the Siren's form. (It is significant that this is the one heavenly messenger thus far, of whom
the radiance is not mentioned.) Virgil called Dante to himself
with the reminder of the sun in its perfect motion, and Dante,
yielding to its lure was freed from both defective and perverted
motion (love) as he felt himself circling like the falcon "infin
dove il cerchiar si prende."[449]

On the fifth terrace among the Avaricious and the Prodigal
who, having fixed their eyes on earthly things, must be bound
face downward so long as it shall be the pleasure of the just
Lord, Dante again cursed the old she-wolf "che più di tutte
l'altre bestie hai preda per la tua fame sanza fine cupa!"[450] and
concentrated his attention on the need of a new leader.[451]

At this point occurred the earthquake[452] which marked the
release of a new guide for Dante, Statius, representative of
empire as at last understanding its true relationship to the
church. At the same time this quake reminds Dante of the story
in which was basis for both the wrong and the right interpreta-

449. "Up to where the circling is begun." *Purg.,* xix, 69.
450. "That hast more prey than all the other beasts, for thy hunger endlessly
deep." *Purg.,* xx, 11-12.
451. In the thought of leadership, Dante separates clearly the office from the
person who is called to fill it for a time. For example, Boniface VIII is destined
after death to be thrust head downward into the hole upon the scorching feet of
Nicholas III, who is suffering the consequence of inversion of his office (*Inf.,*
xix, 13-57); yet the insults offered Boniface the pope by Philippe le Bel are as
a second mocking and crucifixion of Christ himself (*Purg.,* xx, 85 ff.).
452. *Purg.,* xx, 127 ff.

tion of that relationship, the understanding of which made more clear the truth. Delos was tossed about in the sea[453] before her reception of the new-born sun and moon, as was the world before the advent of church and empire. Here is brought out the old symbolism[454] which Dante had taken pains to reinterpret. The twins came equally direct from their divine father; yet the two suns of Rome, "li due occhi del cielo," are not equal in all respects,[455] and there is a sense in which sun and moon express them truly (although this symbolism has been too much misunderstood[456] for Dante to advocate its use). On this level, however, the twins have sinned equally, the former in desire of temporal power, the latter in casting it away. Both sins result ultimately in the spread among men of the root sin, avarice.

Whereas before the Fall, empire *per se* might have sufficed for the terrestrial paradise,[457] after the Fall, empire apart from the presence of the church·could lead only to Limbo. This new understanding is embodied in Statius. From purgatory gate to the end of the fifth terrace, Dante, although under the direct protection of God and his angels, had no other guide than the pagan Virgil, spirit of the empire. Virgil's actual guidance, under the direction of the Divine Sun, is made clear in numerous passages[458] and the attempt should not be made to minimize this guidance on the basis of the directions Virgil asks, for he asked directions also in hell. Virgil alone saw Dante's thoughts, as did the blessed in heaven, and further gave Dante power to see the souls around him:

> l'anima sua, ch' è tua e mia serocchia,
> venendo su, non potea venir sola,
> però ch' al nostro modo non adocchia.[459]

Virgil gives instruction, although he recognizes Beatrice as superior.

453. Cf. discussion of water in the *Divina Commedia,* pp. 231 ff.
454. Cf. *Monarchia,* 3, 4.   455. Cf. p. 42.
456. Cf. p. 41.   457. Cf. pp. 204 ff.
458. Cf. *Purg.,* iii, 4-6; xiii, 13 ff.; xx, 135; xxi, 31-33; xxvii, 23-24; xxvii, 86; and xxvii, 129-130.
459. "His spirit, which is thy sister and mine, coming up, could not come alone, because it sees not after our fashion." *Purg.,* xxi, 28-30. Notice the next three lines also: "wherefore I was brought forth from hell's wide jaws to guide him, and I will guide him onward, so far as my school can lead him."

Surrounded by souls eager to give each other help, and rejoicing over the ascent of each new soul[460a] (so different a condition from that he had left behind) Dante learned something of
the blessed state that might be produced by a right and true
government, as no doubt was the effect of his association with
the adherents of Henry. The fallibility of the empire alone,[460b]
however, was indicated by the Siren, who was able to approach
Dante and from his attention to receive power to make herself
attractive, so that Virgil himself failed to perceive the danger
until he was reproved by the Lady. Before he could lay bare the
iniquity of the Siren, it was necessary that his eyes be kept fixed
on this Lady; though symbol of empire, he represents the empire at the point of expecting the church. It was only at the release of Statius that the incomplete vision of Limbo was fulfilled and Dante was given a guidance which without in any
way lessening the civil supremacy of the empire, showed also
the true function of the church.[461] It is significant that the coming of Statius suggested to Dante's mind the resurrection of
Christ.[462]

To Statius Virgil had given light[463] as he had to Dante, although he was not even then a light to himself, or perhaps had
understood the light too late.[464] He realized however that his
light with its power to guide was given him by heaven. Further-

---

460a. Cf. *Purg.,* xxi, 67-72.

460b. The Ghibellines erred in a tendency to give the empire undue supremacy.

461. Statius' use of fire imagery, during their passage through the next terrace, in expounding the doctrine of the soul, recalls again the symbolic ascription of the heat of the sun to the Holy Ghost. Cf. also pp. 150, 154.

462. *Purg.,* xxi, 7-9.

463.

"Se così è, qual sole o quai candele
  ti stenebraron sì che tu drizzasti
  poscia di retro al pescator le vele?
Ed elli a lui: Tu prima m'inviasti
  verso Parnaso a ber ne le sue
    grotte,
e prima appresso Dio m'allumi-
  nasti.
Facesti come quei che va di notte,
  che porta il lume dietro a sè non
    giova,
  ma dopo sè fa le persone dotte."
          Purg., xxii, 61-69.

"If this be so, what sun or what
candles dispelled the darkness for thee,
so that thou didst thereafter set thy
sails to follow the Fisherman? [Cf.
p. 435] And he to him: Thou first
didst send me toward Parnassus to
drink in its caves, and then didst light
me on to God. Thou didst like one
who goes by night, and carries the
light behind him, and profits not himself, but maketh persons wise that follow him."

464. Cf. pp. 210-211.

more, he was conscious that with his increasing nearness to God, his guidance became more true:

> Ricorditi, ricorditi! E se io
> sovresso Gerion ti guidai salvo,
> che farò ora presso più a Dio?[465]

Yet his will has never wakened as has that of Statius to the point of feeling freedom to go whither his desire points.

True love, which Dante has recognized as the principle of right action, is likewise that which purifies from all baseness, and so it is on the terrace of the Gluttons that Dante refers to the true ideal of courtly love. Improving on the tradition of Guido Guinicelli, the first to identify woman with the heavenly intelligences,[466] Dante wrote, among others, the ode *Donne, ch'avete intelletto d'amore*.[467] In it he foreshadowed the love motif of the *Divina Commedia:* God, though desiring Beatrice in heaven, exiled her for a time to earth for the sake of a soul in danger of perdition. Thus Beatrice throughout the *Divina Commedia* demands devotion as an expression of the love of God, and brings to Dante the sun's attraction that he may win freedom from all that draws downward. The following poem, *Amore e 'l cor gentil sono una cosa,* as Dante states, was written for the sake of a friend who, having read this praise of Beatrice, desired to know the true nature of love. In it love is identified with the gentle heart. Evil thoughts of base hearts are frozen and perish at Beatrice's presence. The usual translation of the well-known first line may fail to express the full meaning of the Italian. Another possible translation, "Ladies that have the intellect of love,"[468] would seem more true to the usual thought of Dante. This would mean, souls whose reason is guided by divine love, as philosophy should be guided by theology, and the empire by the church.[469] It is interesting that Dante in his

465. "Remember thee, remember thee . . . and if on Geryon I guided thee safely, what shall I do now nearer to God?" *Purg.,* xxvii, 22-24.
466. Guido Guinicelli Dante sees later in the terrace of the lustful, indicating a fall from that ideal of courtly love which is such love as gladdens the court of heaven. Cf. pp. 36-37, 168-171, 346-347, 386-390 ff., and especially pp. 427-430.
467. *Vita Nuova.* Chap. XIX, quoted *Purg.,* xxiv, 51.
468. Suggested by Prof. J. B. Fletcher.
469. This guidance does not compromise their mutual independence. Cf. *Monarchia,* 3, 16, also pp. 41 ff. of this study.

own analysis of this sonnet, perhaps in accord with the current theory that love poems and mystic writings should not be understood by all,[470] and perhaps anticipating the *Divina Commedia,* expresses a desire that its meaning may be hidden from all but the "courteous."

Just as the basis of the "dolce stil nuovo" is in entire subjection and obedience to love:

> I' mi son un, che quando
> Amor mi spira, noto, e a quel modo
> ch' è ditta dentro vo significando;[471]

so the journey through hell and purgatory was undertaken by Dante in obedience to Beatrice and in subjection to her will. In reality, Dante owed not only his political theory, but also his moral development and his literary excellence to Virgil first,[472] but to the inspiration of Beatrice ultimately; that is, to the Holy Spirit acting through her. Such was the motif of the great poem in which Dante, last and greatest of the troubadours, sang like a troubadour and reasoned like a schoolman.[473]

On the seventh terrace advancing between the sheer cliff and the shooting flames wherein Lust is purged, Dante, being questioned, expressed the whole aim of his arduous quest: "Quinci su vo per non esser più cieco"—"Hence upward I go to be blind no longer."[474] This also had become the aim of his life both politically and morally, that by looking upon the Divine Sun his eyes might be healed, so that he might see all things clearly.[475] Aid is still through Beatrice, messenger of Mary— "Donna è di sopra che n'acquista grazia"[476]—on whom his eyes must be kept lest a false step be taken.[477] It was the name of Beatrice that took Dante through the fire: "Or vedi, figlio: tra Beatrice e te è questo muro."[478] Only such treatment will suffice for the healing of the last wound. On the other side of the fire

---

470. Cf. p. 158, also Chap. V.
471. "I am one who, when Love inspires me, take note, and go setting it forth after the fashion which he dictates within me." *Purg.,* xxiv, 52-54.
472. *Inf.,* i, 85-87.
473. Laurie Magnus, *A General Sketch of European Literature in the Centuries of Romance* (London: Trübner, 1918), pp. 75 ff.
474. *Purg.,* xxvi, 58.   476. *Purg.,* xxvi, 59.
475. Cf. p. 421.
477. *Purg.,* xxv, 118-120. I.e., Dante more than once before had been in serious peril through failure *tenere a li occhi stretto il freno.*
478. *Purg.,* xxvii, 35-36.

he is to meet the first of a long series of brightnesses which even though his eyes are strengthened as he progresses he cannot face.

Just as Dante has passed through the fire to find himself on the very steps leading to the Terrestrial Paradise, the sun sinks again in the west, and he is compelled to rest, comforted, however, in the night by sight of the stars, especially those representing the three theological virtues,[479] "brighter and larger than their wont."[480] In the night, when Cytherea "first beamed from the east on the mount,"[481] Dante dreamed the third dream of his passage through purgatory; and this dream, since he at last was purified, unlike the others contained no element of *gravezza* or terror. Rather it was like a meditation in which, through Leah and Rachel, was revealed in true perspective external civilization and its inner purpose, the active life whose lessons he had now learned and the contemplative which had become of increasing power in his life.

At this point Dante, at the hands of Virgil, spirit of pagan empire, is crowned and mitered over himself:

> Il temporal foco e l'etterno
> veduto hai, figlio; e se' venuto in parte
> dov'io per me più oltre non discerno.
> Tratto t'ho qui con ingegno e con arte;
> lo tuo piacere omai prendi per duce:
> fuor se' de l'erte vie, fuor se' de l'arte.
> Vedi lo sol che in fronte ti riluce;
> vedi l'erbetta, i fiori e li arbuscelli,
> che qui la terra sol da sè produce.
>
> .   .   .   .
>
> Non aspettar mio dir più, nè mio cenno:
> libero, dritto e sano è tuo arbitrio,
> e fallo fora non fare a suo senno:
> per ch'io te sovra te corono e mitrio.[482]

479. Cf. p. 205.
480. *Purg.*, xxvii, 90. "Di lor solere e più chiare e maggiori."
481. *Purg.*, xxvii, 94-95. "De l' oriente prima raggio nel monte Citerea." That is, Venus was rising. Cf. discussion of Venus and astrology, pp. 47 ff.
482. "Son, the temporal fire and the eternal hast thou seen, and art come to a place where I, of myself, discern no farther. Here have I brought thee with wit and with art; now take thy pleasure for guide; forth art thou from the steep ways, forth art from the narrow. Behold there the sun that shineth on thy brow [Cf. the four stars which so shone on Cato, as if the sun shone on him.], behold

At last Dante knew how to tread the maze of contemporary politics. This point, moreover, marked his transition from that preliminary state in which the main endeavor must be the up-rooting of vices and acquiring of virtues, to that state in which the endeavor may be centered directly on the relation to God through true love. Thus far Dante's journey had been a toil laid upon him by Beatrice and undertaken for Love's sake; at last he was prepared to enter under the direct tutelage of Beatrice herself, in that place where he was to feel directly the power of the Prime Mover in the motion of the spheres,[483] reaching him as a gentle breeze from the east.

III. CULMINATION—INITIATION

THE time was sunrise, and the *selva oscura* had given place to *la divina foresta*,[484] the state of primal innocence, which Dante entered, accompanied still by Virgil and Statius, spirit of empire inspired by the church. Though no longer dependent primarily on the function of church and empire, Dante maintained his contact with them. He will do what church and empire right-fully command, but he will do it of his own motion, not in response to their compulsion, which meanwhile is necessary for those who have not been purged of sin. He was about to learn from Beatrice in the Pageant the true function of the church, and, at the same time, from her who as Love is the Spirit of True Citizenship, to suffer rebuke for his foolish triflings with false theories and for his plans for political careers that would have been socially harmful. At last he had learned that what-ever the political and moral dilemma of earth, the true city di-rected by God exists,[485] and rightly directed love is still the source of his real life. The goal is not a thing to be produced by

the tender grass, the flowers, and the shrubs, which the ground here of itself alone brings forth. . . . No more expect my word, nor my sign. Free, upright, and whole is thy will, and 'twere a fault not to act according to its prompting; wherefore I do crown and mitre thee over thyself." *Purg.*, xxvii, 127-142.

483. *Purg.*, xxviii, lines 7-12 and 97-108.

484. *Purg.*, xxviii, 2. As the dark wood with its jungle-like growths is pruned, cleared, and made more open to the rays of the sun, it is transmuted successively into the divine forest of the Terrestrial Paradise, the heavenly garden of Christ, and the rose that opens under the light of the triune God.

485. Shadowed forth in the divine forest of the terrestrial paradise, and actu-ally existent in the celestial paradise.

striving; the goal is there. The progress, on whatever level, is
but a course of realization, in which all that is essential is that
the eyes be fixed on the triune Sun, that the being may move in
response to its attraction. Of this fact, however, the full significance belongs to a deeper order of the symbolism.[486]

At the outset of his journey, Dante, haunted by the ravening
form of the *lupa,* could think only of the evil opposition to the
trinity of life, light, and heat through which the thought of ages
had given definition to the infinite which orders experience in
the finite realm. The *Inferno,* with its shifting forms in caricature of twoness and threeness, had shown him the true nature
and inevitable outcome of heedlessness or defiance of that law
wherein alone is freedom. From contemplation of the conflict
of cosmic forces Dante advanced to thought of that "fourth"[487]
on which these forces act, which, in this order of symbolism, is
the will of the creature.

The first glimpse of the heavens in the hemisphere where
rises the Mount of Purgatory had shown him four stars, and under their guidance was accomplished the journey to the Earthly
Paradise, which he had no sooner entered than he met Matilda.
This fair lady, culling flowers, made him remember "dove e
qual era Proserpina nel tempo che perdette la madre lei, ed ella
primavera,"[488] and was herself a *primaverra* or forerunner of
Beatrice.[489] Her mission was to dip Dante both in Lethe and in
Eunoe. She it was who explained to him the waters and vegetation of the terrestrial paradise.

In the life of the earth it is water that brings fruitfulness, and
water, thus identified with the female principle,[490] has always

---

486. Cf. pp. 285 ff.

487. Cf. discussion of the symbolism of four, in Chap. V, pp. 337 ff.

488. "Where and what Proserpine was, in the time her mother lost her, and
she lost the Spring." *Purg.,* xxviii, 49-51.

489. Cf. *Vita Nuova,* 24.

490. "It is not the nature of anything upon the earth to exist without a moist
essence. And this is indicated by the throwing of seed, which is either moist, as
the seed of animals, or else does not shoot up without moisture, such as the
seeds of plants: from which it is evident that it follows that the aforesaid moist
essence must be a portion of the earth which produces everything. . . . And
the earth also, as it seems, is a mother, from which consideration it occurred to
the early ages to call her Demetra, combining the names of mother, μήτηρ and
earth, γῆ or δη. For it is not the earth which imitates the woman, as Plato has
said, but the woman who has imitated the earth which the race of poets has been
accustomed with truth to call the mother of all things, and the fruit-bearer,

appeared in close association with the sun god. Such symbolism
was found useful also in the immediate background of Dante's
tradition: Mary the Mother of Christ being symbolized frequently by a river, "de quo dicitur, Flumen Dei repletum est
aquis, id est, Maria charismatibus gratiarum,"[491] and water being the source of life in baptism, "Water was the first to produce that which had life, that it might be no wonder in baptism
if waters know how to give life."[492] In earlier thought, as frequently in the *Divina Commedia,* the female principle is symbolized also by the Moon,[493] of which the special earthly effect
is the governance of the tides.[494] In this way it is connected with
Proserpine, goddess of moon and vegetation, whose return to
the light of the sun brings light and fertility to the earth, as her
disappearance in hell leaves it frozen in winter.

The water of the earth, in function like Proserpine herself, is
twofold.[495] From one and the same spring come Lethe and
Eunoe. Lethe is to flow sin-laden, at last trickling down into
hell, bearing to Cocytus the dross of pardoned sin, even as the

and the giver of all things, since she is at the same time the cause of the generation and durability of all things, to the animals and plants. Rightly, therefore,
did nature bestow on the earth as the eldest and most fertile of mothers, streams
of rivers, and fountains like breasts, in order that the plants might be watered,
and that all living things might have abundant supplies of drink." Philo Judaeus,
On the Creation of the World, Chap. 45, commenting on "A fountain went up
from the earth and watered the whole face of the earth."

491. Albertus Magnus, *De laudibus B. Mariae Virg.,* 9, 3, 1.

492. Tertullian, *On Prayer,* in "Ante-Nicene Library," Vol. 11, p. 234.

493. According to Berosus, B.C. 250, the queen of the creatures of chaos was
named Omoroca, "in Greek Thalassa, the sea; but which might equally be interpreted the Moon." Marduk, the sun god, conquered her "and cut the woman
asunder, and of one half of her he formed the earth, and of the other half the
heavens." Quoted in *Babylonian Legends of the Creation,* British Museum, 1921,
p. 11. A note on p. 65 points out that verbs concerning the struggle between
Marduk and Tiamat [Omoroca] are not properly translated as preterites, but
refer to continued action.

494. St. Thomas Aquinas and Brunetto Latini, like Dante (*Par.,* xvi, 82-83),
are aware of the relation between the tides and the moon.

495. Similarly with the Moon, which in medieval symbology might mean
Mary, the most perfect reflection of the Sun's light, or the female power of evil,
in mystical opposition to the sun and association with the evil aspect of water.
Dante has made reference to the threatening power of the Moon in *Inf.,* xx,
127-129. Cf. also p. 276.

It is of interest that in the sun myths which formed a part of the heritage of
the Grail quest, the female character, goddess of the moon and of vegetation,
whom the hero rescues after a struggle lasting the whole winter, or after a painful journey to the Other World, often is at first ugly and servant to the powers
of evil, but is made beautiful and good by her rescuer. Something of this theme
has been retained in the character of Kundry, in Wagner's *Parsifal.*

trickle from the Old Man of Crete[496] bears thither, ledge by ledge through hell, through Acheron, Styx, and Phlegethon to Cocytus, all the unpardoned evil of the world. Similarly the Arno in its course, described to Dante in the terrace of the envious,[497] flows downward first among inhabitants transformed by Circe pasturage[498] to hogs to curs to dogs and gradually into the image of the *lupa* herself; then through many deep gorges into the land of foxes "sì piene di froda, che non temono ingegno che le occupi,"[499] thus combining in themselves the *lupa* and the leopard. It was even into the Arno that the frozen body of Buonconte was swept by the devil who raging over the loss of the soul of this late-repentant, conquered in regard to the body, the redeeming warmth of the sun.[500] The waters of Lethe are in evidence wherever the she-wolf is in power, for example, even in purgatory in the terrace of the avaricious:

> la gente che fonde a goccia a goccia
> per li occhi il mal che tutto il mondo occupa,

a sight which draws from Dante the exclamation:

> Maledetta sie tu, antica lupa,
> che più di tutte l'altre bestie hai preda
> per la tua fame sanza fine cupa![501]

It may be recalled that on his first escape from the Dark Wood, Dante likened himself to one who "con lena affannata uscito fuor del pelago a la riva"—"with panting breath has escaped from the deep sea to the shore," and "si volge a l' acqua perigliosa e guata"—"turns to the dangerous water and gazes."[502] It was on such waters that he beheld Italy, "nave sanza nocchiere in gran tempesta"—"a vessel without a pilot in a mighty

496. *Inf.*, xxiv, 103 ff.   497. *Purg.*, xiv, 22 ff.   498. Cf. pp. 54-57.
499. "So full of fraud that they fear no wit that may trap them." *Purg.*, xiv, 53-54.
500. *Purg.*, v, 94 ff.
501. "The people who distill through their eyes, drop by drop, the evil that fills the whole world." "Accurst be thou, she-wolf of old, that hast more prey than all the other beasts, for thy hunger endlessly deep." *Purg.*, xx, 7-12.
502. *Inf.*, i, 22-24. In *Inf.*, ii, 107-108 Lucia refers to the death which Dante is facing "su la fiumana ove 'l mar non ha vanto"—"upon the river, over which the sea has no boast." It is the river of evil, bitter as the sea, which flows not into the sea, but into Cocytus.

storm."[503] In the opening lines of the *Purgatorio* Dante announces that now he may sing of better waters.[504]

Very different is Eunoe, sister of Lethe, source of blessed memory, symbolically identical with the good rains of earth that nourish vegetation, and with the sea of the Paradise on which may sail only those fed on bread of angels.[505] More than once Eunoe, though unrecognized, had given strength to Dante:

> Ciò che vedesti fu perchè non scuse
> d'aprir lo core a l'acque de la pace
> che da l' etterno fonte son diffuse.[506]

It is for this water that man has ever a natural thirst.

From the very beginning water symbolism has been bound up with the way in which the Divine Sun attracts souls to himself.[507] Water is among the most appropriate of symbols[508] by which to describe man's relationship to God, for by itself, in contact with the cold breath of the *lupa*,[509] it falls downward,

---

503. *Purg.*, vi, 77. He continues: "non donna di provincie, ma bordello"— "no mistress of provinces, but a brothel." That is, Italy is the home of the *lupa*, since the word means not only she-wolf, but harlot.

504.

"Per correr migliori acque alza le vele omai la navicella del mio ingegno, che lascia dietro a sè mar sì cru- dele." *Purg.*, i, 1-3.	"To course o'er better waters now hoists sail the little bark of my wit, leaving behind her a sea so cruel."

505.

"O voi che siete in piccioletta barca, desiderosi d'ascoltar, seguiti dietro al mio legno che cantando varca, tornate a riveder li vostri liti: non vi mettete in pelago, chè, forse, perdendo me rimarreste smarriti.	"O ye, who in your little skiff, long- ing to hear, have followed on my keel that singeth on its way, turn to revisit your own shores, commit you not to the open sea, for perchance, losing me, ye would be left astray.
· · · · · · ·	· · · · · · ·
Voi altri pochi che drizzaste il collo per tempo al pan de li angeli, del quale vivesi qui ma non sen vien satollo, metter potete ben per l'alto sale vostro navigio." *Par.*, ii, 1-6 and 10-15.	Ye other few, who timely have lift up your necks for bread of angels whereby life is here sustained but wherefrom none cometh away sated, ye may indeed commit your vessel to the deep."

506. "What thou sawest was in order that thou have no excuse from opening thy heart to the waters of peace, which are poured from the eternal fount." *Purg.*, xv, 130-132.

507. Cf. p. 109.   508. Cf., e.g., p. 267 n. 82.

509. Dante has given a vivid description: "Thou knowest how in the air that damp vapor gathers, which turns again to water as soon as it ascends where the cold condenses it. He [the devil] united that evil will, which seeks ill only, with

descending ultimately to the center in the frozen lake of Cocytus; but under the radiance and the heat of the Divine Sun, it is
drawn upward toward the sphere of fire.

The universe, as was noted in the discussion of the sphere of
the Moon, was regarded as made up of four elements which, as
Lactantius claimed in his *De origine erroris,* in man were so
united as to be reduced to two, namely, fire (to which air is in-
separably joined, in the soul) and water (to which earth is in-
separably joined, in the body). Hence, it is but natural that as
soon as that water is gone, which in the streams of purgatory
and hell bears the sins of earth, the fire of the soul should cause
it to gravitate upward toward God, the home of spiritual fire,
even as the life-giving waters unsullied by the *lupa* are themselves drawn upward as vapor by the Divine Sun.

Like the waters which nourish it, vegetation also is twofold,
as is all which is connected in its symbolism with man. The
floweret of *Inferno* II, destined by the Sun who awakes it to become a flower under his rays, and a petal of the Celestial Rose,
may instead, gnarled and warped, take its place in the Dark
Wood where the *lupa* roams. So the struggle progresses in
which man is in process of transmutation, by powers of opposing tendency, to beast or to angel.

Standing in the transformed forest of the Earthly Paradise,
and looking back over the perilous journey by which the height
was won, Dante might behold in perspective the operation of
that attraction and *gravezza* which at the outset he had encountered in the symbols of sun and beast. The blessed Tri-unity of
life, light, and heat had guided him on his journey, through the
ministration of the blessed ladies, Mary, Lucia, and Beatrice,[510]
of whom, in the distress of the Dark Wood, Virgil had brought
him word. Whatever may have been the individual associations
for Dante of these three living symbols, their significance is cosmic. In Mary is the perfect instrument through which the infinite life may find expression, as through her all creation has

intellect, and stirred the mist and wind by the power which his nature gave.
Then when day was spent, he covered the valley from Pratomagno to the great
mountain chain with mist, and the sky above made lowering, so that the satu-
rated air was turned to water: the rain fell, and to the water-rills came what of
it the earth endured not, and as it united into great torrents, so swiftly it rushed
toward the royal stream, that naught held it back." *Purg.,* v, 109-123.

510. Cf. pp. 168-171.

welcomed its redemption. In the name of Lucia, whatever her human identity, is the perfect surrogate of the Divine Logos, the light giver in whose name is salvation, Sancta Sophia, the guide of life. Beatrice herself, supremely personal as was her relationship to Dante, is similarly of cosmic significance, for every man who would answer to the power of infinite life, under the guidance of infinite light, can do so only through the motion of infinite love, love which must find expression to every gentle heart through the person of the ideal Lady.

The three earthly ministers of the three heavenly ladies also are of fundamental import in the drama of human life. As within the trinity of ladies Mary, Queen of Heaven, is at once least in evidence, and Prime Mover, having initiated the whole drama in her mission of Lucia, so in the trinity of earthly ministers, Matilda's activity is at once least, and most fundamental.[511] In her is the ultimate secret of the movement of the journey, the lightness consequent upon the freeing from *gravezza* through the deletion of the seven *P's*. Not only sins, but all memory of sin must go, if emancipation from *gravezza* is to be complete. Through memory of all good is empowered the response to the magnetism of the Divine Sun. Next in prominence, like Lucia, is Statius. Like Christ, Lucia was mediator of Dante's salvation, and, in the form of the eagle, she it was who raised him to purgatory gate, from whence he might hope at last to ascend beyond the reaches of time and space, to that eternity which Christ in his ascension made accessible to men. Statius, rising at the moment of Dante's traversal of the fifth terrace, to share in the joy of the Ascension, represents the empire illumined by Christ's other vicarate the church, the mediator of his life to men. Finally, Virgil is the necessary surrogate of Beatrice, as is the discipline of human government the surrogate of that love which would draw men to itself.

Virgil, to be expressed at last in the celestial Greyhound, will compass the destruction of the she-wolf, in opposition to whom he functions and from whom he rescued Dante. A similar opposition exists between Statius, who bowed to Christ on the evi-

511. The identification of Matilda with Proserpine in *Purg.*, xxviii, 49-51, bears this out, in the coincidence of the cycle of Proserpine with the cycle of the sun.

dence of a prophecy not even understood by him who uttered it, and the lion of proud and rampant rebellion against Christ. Likewise opposed are the girlish innocence of Matilda, with her life-giving power, and the fraudulent, death-dealing leopard.

TABLE OF NINEFOLD GOOD AND ITS OPPOSITION IN NINEFOLD EVIL

	Ninefold Good			*Opposed by*		*Ninefold Evil*		
Essential Principle. DEUS	PATER *whose surrogate is*	FILIUS *whose surrogate is*	SPIRITUS SANCTUS *whose surrogate is*	Opposed by " " " "	FACE III *whose surrogate is*	FACE II *whose surrogate is*	FACE I *whose surrogate is*	Esse Neg LUC
Three Blessed Ladies of Heaven.	MARY *whose surrogate is*	LUCIA *whose surrogate is*	BEATRICE *whose surrogate is*	Opposed by " " " "	CIRCE *whose surrogate is*	SIREN *whose surrogate is*	MEDUSA *whose surrogate is*	Th Accu Lad of H
Three of the Good of Earth (types of good).	MATILDA *whose surrogate is*	STATIUS *whose surrogate is*	VIRGIL	Opposed by " " " "	SHE-WOLF	LION	LEOPARD	Th Bea of E (ty of e

As there is a balanced opposition between the representatives on earth of the bitterly contending forces of the cosmos, so there is an evil opposition to the three heavenly ladies. Over against the Queen of Heaven there stands the Queen of Dis, of death, and of the west, who would have made Dante forever a citizen of her realm,[512] as Mary was to make him a citizen of the heavenly city. Her minister is the leopard, as Mary's is Matilda. Appearing to Dante in a dream, as did Lucia, the Siren, in the coldest of hours, aimed to hurl him downward,[513] even as the eagle had raised him upward in its all but intolerable flame. Through gazing on her whose earthly minister was the lion, man was doomed to eternal lamentation, as through gazing on him who came to earth as the Lion of the Tribe of Judah, he was raised to the city of eternal bliss. Finally, Circe, the harlot whose evil transmutations are opposed to the blessed transhumanizing power of Beatrice, was on earth the she-wolf, into whose form men were metamorphosed by her wand. She worked through Medusa and the Siren, as the she-wolf through the leopard and the lion.

Shadowed forth in the beasts and the three evil ladies were the three death-dealing faces of Lucifer, whose futile mockery of the Divine Sun was displayed in Cocytus. Though central in the nine appearances of evil, the king of the dolorous realm existed only as negation. Having perceived this ninefold pattern of the universe,[514] ninefold good and its negation in ninefold evil, Dante was prepared at last to stand again in the presence of her who was a nine, that miracle whose root is the Trinity alone—by her to be led yet closer to that living light "which doth . . . focus its own raying as though reflected in nine existences, eternally abiding One."

The Pageant and the meeting with Beatrice find their full significance in deeper symbolisms than that of the literal vision,[515]

---

512. Cf. pp. 178-181. Reference is to *Inf.*, ix, 43-63.

513. Dream of Lucia, *Purg.*, ix; dream of Siren, *Purg.*, xix. Cf. pp. 215 ff., 222.

514. In the Greek letter-number system Alpha and Omega make 801, which, "reduced" is 9 (Cf. p. 339, also Appendix V, Pt. I, i). Nine is also the number of the Holy Ghost, and of the circumference (360° reduced is 9). Cf. p. 99.

515. Whereas such detailed explanation of the Pageant as that of the harlot signifying a particular pope, rightfully belongs to this part of the discussion, for

in which they are little more than an astounding revelation of
Dante's own frailty. The summation of the political and philosophic theory reached as the culmination of his long journey,
through the conflicts of Guelph and Ghibelline, of human will
and natural law, is understood completely only when attention has come to center in Humanity, with its Head in Christ,
rather than in the more personal aspects of Dante's crusade.[516]
Further discussion must then proceed in relation to those truths
perfectly revealed to Dante in the spheres of Mars, Jupiter,
Saturn, and the Stars. The literal vision of which the truth was
revealed in the Moon, Mercury, and Venus, and summarized in
the Sun, culminates in the explanation to Dante of his mission,
by Beatrice appearing as the sun.[517]

In brief, as impersonation of philosophy illumined by theology, Dante was to guide empire, at last rightfully illumined
by the church, in the maintenance of its autonomy, of which the
secret had been revealed in the nature of the Second Person of
the Trinity. The old Greek maxim accepted by pagan Rome as
Nequid nimis had found fulfilment as the completest possible
development of the members of a series of pairs, the autonomy
of each one of which in its own sphere was exigent. Greek philosophy had been preparing for some such solution in a monism
expressing itself through duality, just as had much of the rest of
pre-Christian thought; but the great difficulty was the method
of its application to life. Though reality is threefold, and nine
the number of Beatrice is the number of the circumference of all
that is, the nature of things human is dual as is that of the Son
of Man. Herein is the mystery of life. Under the utmost of
Circe's power man may never become completely beast, for his
soul must suffer endlessly; and though true to Beatrice he is
never to become angel, for his body is to share eternally the joy
of the blessed life.[518] The solution of the problems of Dante's

convenience the whole treatment of the Pageant has been deferred, more especially since such specific identifications are not the central purpose of this study.

516. Cf. pp. 63 ff.

517. Cf. the description of Beatrice's arrival, *Purg.*, xxx, 22 ff. Cf. pp. 319-
321.

518. St. Thomas discusses the question of the nature of the glorified body at
some length. It is to be subject only to the spirit:

"Sicut corpus gloriosum non potest pati aliquid passione naturae, sed solum
passione animae; ita ex proprietate gloriae non agit nisi actione animae. Claritas

personal life under the guidance of the solar Tri-unity, thus culminated in the mystery of the Logos, just as had the age-long endeavor of many races to solve the problem of life through study of the natural universe in its ordering by the sun.

autem intensa non offendit visum inquantum agit actione animae, sed secundum hoc magis delectat; offendit autem, inquantum agit actione naturae. . . . Et ideo claritas corporis gloriosi, quamvis excedat claritatem solis, tamen de sua natura non offendit." *S.Th.,* 3, suppl. *Q.* 85, *art.* 1. Cf. Dante's expression of this doctrine, in *Par.,* xiv, 43-60.

Thomas speculates further as to the age, condition, etc., of the glorified body, in the last book of his *Summa contra Gentiles.*

CHAPTER IV. SCHEMA

PART I.

I. Method of Dante's symbolism formed during centuries of cultural conflict, through study of written word. In the Logos, solar Radiance, came to be sought solution of the relationship of finite to infinite, brought into relief as key problem by the conflict of trinities. Scriptural inconsistencies necessitated symbolic interpretation governed by a definite method. Gradually functional truth of letter distinguished from literal.

II. Jesus of Nazareth appeared as fulfilment of the Logos ideal. He and his apostles employed the materials of symbolism in three distinct types of insight interpretation. The first meaning lay within the realm of history, the second applied to the individual moral life, and the third to the absolute truth in eternity. Writer of the Epistle to the Hebrews used the three as simultaneously true.

III. Intellectual leaders became occupied with classification of types of symbolism. Through lack of grasp of the philosophy of insight symbolism, conflict arose over significance of the literal. From the time of John Cassian the fourfold method was completely developed in the definition later employed by Dante. Its complexity increased by associated symbolisms. Method carefully guarded from confusion (by the unlettered) with the personification allegory. Such was the background of Dante's solar duality, the Logos, through whom was the reconciliation of scriptures, and from whom sprang the method of the *Commedia*.

PART II.

The second order of Dante's symbolism consists of the application of the fourfold method to the materials of symbolism as they relate to the second of man's four sources of knowledge. Scripture (temporal) has its focus in the dual Sun. Dante's definition of aim and interpretation of the *Commedia* necessitates this order of symbolism underlying and complementary to that discussed in Chapter III in reference to his personal life. This deeper order, wherein Dante is regarded as a type of Christ, is Allegory of the first order. Within this Allegory, the letter, allegory, and trope have reference to the physical, mystical, and sacramental Bodies of Christ, given anagoge in his glorified Body. The pattern of interpretation which seems to harmonize with the tradition to which Dante fell heir, is that given on p. 284, *q.v.*

CHAPTER IV. SYMBOLISM IN MEDIEVAL THOUGHT: THE FOURFOLD METHOD

Tutti dicean, *"Benedictus qui venis!"*
  e fior gittando di sopra e dintorno,
  "Manibus o date lilia plenis!"
Io vidi già nel cominciar del giorno
  la parte oriental tutta rosata
  e l'altro ciel di bel sereno adorno;
e la faccia del sol nascere ombrata,
  sì che, per temperanza di vapori,
  l'occhio la sostenea lunga fiata.

All were saying, *"Benedictus qui venis!"* and strewing flowers above and around, *"Manibus o date lilia plenis."* Ere now have I seen, at dawn of day, the eastern part all rosy red, and the rest of heaven adorned with fair clear sky, and the face of the sun rise shadowed, so that by the tempering of the mists the eye long time endured him.

I N the early days, while, like a play of colors about the sun, trinities were becoming foci for thinking, men became possessed of a new power over the materials of symbolism. The secret lay in the development of a mysterious system of symbolic marks—like spoken words, symbols of symbols—potent to convey to the mind images which they resembled so remotely that gradually the resemblances came to be forgotten. Of even more magic than spoken words, written signs seemed able to defy the law of perpetual change to which man's universe was subject. Just as through analysis of the natural foci for thinking, there is found elucidation of the materials of Dante's symbolism, so through the tracing of man's development and appreciation of this new power lies the key to the symbolic method alike of Dante and of the Middle Ages.

Handed down however carefully from father to son, a story changed and by necessity was told from generation to generation in different words[1] from different lips. Of other magic were written signs: to the eyes of the grandson they presented in every detail the form they had presented to the eyes of the grandfather. They thus partook of the supernatural. Nature changed—landscapes and men's dwellings—only the Sun and

---

1. An extreme example of this variation, among primitives who have not yet acquired the art of writing, is given in the changing languages of those tribes to whom the pronunciation of the name of a person who has died from certain causes, is taboo. Since in these tribes personal names are those of natural (or cultural) objects, the name of any object whatsoever may become forbidden. Thus new words are constantly substituted for old, so that a person who had learned the language at any given time could be understood only with difficulty ten or fifteen years later.

The existence of a written language enormously retards language changes. A suggestive comparison may be made with modern popular slang, which varies with momentary fashions largely because it is accepted to a much less degree in the written language than is "correct" speech.

those mysterious forces which govern the universe might be relied on to remain the same, or to repeat their cyclic courses through the successive revolutions of the heavens; and scriptures—things written—so long as man could preserve them, shared in this sacred quality of permanence. Amid the baffling evanescence of his metaphysic, man might well take comfort in the apparent stability of the written word, and come to praise the Supreme Power of the universe for his revelation of himself and of his mode of action, not only through nature, but also through the records of scripture. With the passage of time, scripture came to comprehend human history.

The perplexing rise and fall of solar trinities was still in progress in all corners of the world when the Roman Empire brought together the east and the west, the north and the south, preparing to set itself over all in the name of the *Sol Invictus*. Thought was placed in the situation of him who innocently loosed at once the four sons of Eolus. In such dilemma aid is ever sought from the gods, and scripture appeared as the supreme gift of the divine on man's behalf. It became the center of attention at Alexandria, where, in an atmosphere of learning and concentration impossible at the capital, the problem of the unification of man's experience was considered and the solutions proffered by different races and cultures were subjected to critical analysis. Here conviction grew that the coherence of metaphysics was threatened less by the problem of trinities[2] than by the problem of the relation of the infinite to the finite, the attempted solution of which had been the very inspiration of scriptures.

Attention centered in the natural universe may find rest in trinity and unity, but when thought is turned on man himself it is blocked by the question of duality. The drama of human life appears in its essence as an eternal choosing between two. Man hangs suspended pitifully between pairs, the good and the evil, the beautiful and the ugly, the true and the false. Monisms are undermined not through the threeness or even through the multiplicity of things, but always through the duality introduced by value judgments. The mind can conceive a tri-unity of life, light, and heat, even a dual unity of light and darkness, sun and

2. Reviewed in the previous chapter.

storm; but the human mind was taxed beyond its power by the reconciliation of the good and the evil, the true and the false, or of the infinite and the finite, God and man. Nowhere did this conflict of duality break forth more bitterly than in scriptures and history. In order then that a consistent metaphysic be created, powerful enough to unify the one *and* the many, a trinity was necessary. Yet men had felt this for centuries, and although nature revealed trinity, no trinity had been stable, because men had not been able to define the relationship of the one *to* the many, the infinite truth to its finite expression. For the definition of this relationship, a new vocabulary was necessary, and a better understanding of the nature of scripture and speech. This in very fact was the problem with which Alexandrian thought was occupied during the contest of cultures at Rome.

Scripture is in essence dual, presenting both the story of physical and economic fortunes, and the story hidden within it of intellectual and spiritual advancement. It resembles that most elusive and perplexing of dualities within man, the duality of matter and spirit. Some oneness between dualities was demanded. Socrates himself had failed, men could not but feel, when in his life and thought he had divorced the members of the fundamental pairs. The most satisfying attempt to bridge the chasm by which experience was severed into twoness had been supplied by the mystery religions in their symbolism. These cults unfortunately, however, showed an alarming tendency to become in practice betrayal, in the name of God, of the reality to the expression.

For centuries solution had been suspected in a vicarious suffering of the infinite, coming down into the finite, or in some way becoming incarnate in it; and so from time to time there had arisen an association between the greatest of heroes and the sun.[3] This intuition philosophy expressed in the doctrine of the Logos, the Wisdom and Fire of the infinite, immanent in all creation.[4] Scriptures, inevitably dual, and in themselves veri-

3. It is to be remembered that an essential element in the solar myth was the conception of the solar king laboring and in the end being sacrificed, to bring life to his people.

4. Indeed, such was the grip of this conception on men's minds that during the period of syncretism it was necessary only to identify a god with the Logos to insure his veneration.

table incarnations of thought, became supremely important to thought in its concentration on the riddle of the relationship of reality to outward expression, the revelation of the infinite to the finite in the Logos.[5] The great scriptures[6] became common property, and thus for minds active in the period of syncretism, human history became recognized as a source of knowledge of at least equal importance with the natural universe, and its essential complement. So the first Church Father was to declare it for the Middle Ages, and so Dante was to make it in his *Commedia.*

PART I. THE SUN IN MEDIEVAL TRADITION (SCRIPTURE AND HISTORY)

I. NECESSITY OF SYMBOLIC INTERPRETATION

THE existence in the *Divina Commedia* of several well-defined levels of symbolic interpretation has been assumed more or less dogmatically, thus far, on the basis of a direct statement or two made by Dante and on the basis of the existence in the Middle Ages of a system of interpretation similar to that which he dictates. It is the purpose of this chapter to make clear that, had Dante himself left no statement in regard to the interpretation of his work, interpretation by symbolic levels was subsumed inevitably in the nature and century of his work and definitely in his statement of his aim. In the preceding chapter attention was directed to the structure and form of the *Commedia,* which

5. Lactantius later discussed the superiority of *Logos* over *Verbum* as a designation for Christ, in this very connection, because *Logos* means both speech and reason. (He made reference to Trismegistus who had already perceived the sacredness of speech in his discussion of the mystic language.) Thus in relation to Christ, Eternal Wisdom, and the supreme self-revelation of God to man, he stressed the importance of symbol alike to thought and to expression. Cf. p. 135 n. 97.

6. For the Hebrews, their scripture was not merely the incarnation of the thought of men, but actually the incarnation of the thought of the all-powerful JHVH (whose full name was known only to his high priests. Note that although *Jehovah* is known to be a wrong pronunciation, *Jahveh* is also open to objection, since the correct vowel sounds are not known. A recent writer on occultism in the Kabalah claims personally to have known twenty-two pronunciations, each held to be the true Sacred Name.)

The scriptures of the Greek were supremely the account of the life and thought of the gods, preserved in the immortal verse of an almost prehistoric poet, and commentated by the written words of great philosophers. Other nations had their scriptural fragments of greater or less sanctity.

like the structure and form of the universe through which Dante journeyed, appeared as ordered by the *sun in nature* with its solution of the threeness of things. Understanding of solar symbolism in its tri-unity was sufficient for Dante's orientation in his environment, including (treated as letter, allegory, and trope) the physical universe, his political situation, and his moral relationships—that is, the revelation in the spheres of the Moon, Mercury, and Venus, involving the nature of things as they are. For the further question inevitably raised by these considerations, however, as to Dante's place in relation to the whole, as it were his *raison d'être,* there was no answer apart from the *sun in scripture,* with its solution of the twoness of things. In scripture the Sun rose shadowed, that the human eye might penetrate more deeply into its mystery. Such was the purport of Beatrice's communion with Dante in the Earthly Paradise, in the atmosphere of their mysterious meeting at the breast of the grifon, whose two natures, reflected as the sun in a mirror, were the message of Beatrice's eyes.

Study of the sun in nature as perennial focus of the materials of symbolism has revealed the fact that for all the victory of 313 A.D.[7] there was little new in the Christian Trinity beyond the accuracy of definition given at Nicaea and Chalcedon. Exception may be taken only with regard to the Second Person of the Trinity, in connection with whose nature study of scriptural as well as of natural solar imagery is fundamental, as it is not only to an understanding of Dante's mission and the full purpose of his Comedy, but to real understanding of the method he employed. Given a philosophy of insight symbolism and a feeling of nineness as essential in the structure of the universe and as congruous in the poem written in honor of Beatrice who was a nine, Dante yet would have had no basis for his arrangement of allegory, trope, and anagoge had it not been for the world's experience in scriptural interpretation—and, further, by this experience such arrangement was necessitated. The ascendancy gained by the Sun of the Nicene formula is of this supreme importance to medieval thinking. As a result of the union of scriptural and natural imagery, in the new doctrine of the Logos, the

7. Cf. p. 142.

Divine Word, medieval symbolism was given its character of fourfold multiplicity.

THE DILEMMA OF SCRIPTURES

The problems raised by scriptural contradictions both intrinsic and in relation to other knowledge, became even more troublesome than those raised by the apparent contradictions in nature. In the glimpse given in the preceding chapter of those cultures now so suddenly and so surprisingly brought face to face, the constant tension between unity and diversity was remarked.[8] With the small and occasional contacts of these cultures one with another, there had come from time to time the momentary necessity for reinterpretation, and so a consciousness of the significance of the insight symbol as leading through the expression to the fundamental reality, in which, as infinite, was the reconciliation of contradictions. The theory of insight symbolism, however, was less readily applied to scripture than to nature, because scripture was not only symbols, but symbols of symbols.[9] In other words, the symbols of written language represented ideas and objects in the natural universe which themselves were symbols of reality. That which was studied in scripture was the revelation of the infinite, not simply through the external universe, but in some sense through the instrumentality of human personality.

Very early, difficulty was encountered with regard to such conceptions of God and of his relationship to the universe as had been inherited in the formulation given them by previous generations. That which when it was written down had seemed altogether true and noble appeared in a later age crude, immoral, and unbelievable. Then the dilemma: Either these crude statements represented literally what the race once really had

8. Cf. Chap. III, Pt. I, i.
9. When all objects and all deeds in the physical universe are habitually considered as manifestations of and veils for a deeper reality, then any scripture must be symbolic in a double sense. The words signify certain acts or objects, these acts and objects themselves signify another reality. This is one root of the interpretation by levels. Another is found in the fact that a given passage may have an obviously figurative signification, e.g., "wings of the wind." Since the wind has no wings, a bird is being used to symbolize the wind. Thus we have wings—bird—wind—reality signified by wind, perhaps the peoples of the earth. Cf. Augustine, *Enarratio in Ps. CIII*, 13.

thought, but were to be discarded with cultural progress; or else these statements had conveyed more than could then have been said literally—"symbols are the chief means by which the human mind expresses not so much those ideas which it has outgrown or wishes to conceal but those which it has not yet mastered"—and so were to be reinterpreted. The first of these two alternatives is generally chosen when the older formulation is unwritten or unauthoritative. On the other hand when mythology is the heart of the literature of a people, as it was with the Greeks, or when in its written form it is felt to have received divine sanction, as with Jews, Mohammedans, and Christians, the symbolic interpretation is inevitable. It suggests itself spontaneously to minds seeking for a means whereby to reconcile with the fruits of philosophical speculation, the legends and the poets.[10, 11] The assumption may be that of Maeterlinck, that "every language thinks always more than the man, even the man of genius, who employs it, and who is only its heart for the time being";[12] or it may be that God has been guiding men gradually into a fuller knowledge of himself; or it may be both. In any case in the reinterpretation is involved potentially a new truth for society, a new truth for the individual, and very likely a new philosophical truth. Thus the possibility of different insight significations becomes recognized.

As study of materials of symbolism makes clear that similarity of myth among diverse races is no indication of influence or racial contact,[13] so a study of thought as it developed through these materials shows definitely that influence need not be sought for the development of the philosophy and method of insight symbolism. Given the same problem and the same symbolic materials, it was inevitable that in Rome as in Alexandria,

10. This has been noted by Comparetti and others.
11. Thomas Aquinas took pains to explain that "sicut poetica non capiuntur a ratione humana propter defectum veritatis qui est in eis; ita etiam ratio humana perfecte capere non potest divina propter excedentem ipsorum veritatem; et ideo utrobique opus est repraesentatione per sensibiles figuras." *S.Th.*, 1, 2, *Q*. 101, *art.* 2, *ad* 2.
12. M. Maeterlinck, *Ruysbroeck l'Admirable*, p. 42.
13. For example, the explanation for the fair hair of all the Navajo hero-gods is to be sought neither in the influence of European mythology miraculously conveyed to the tribe, nor in the possible but hypothetical visit of a fair-haired Saxon; but rather in the fact that the sun displays a uniform character to all people whom he visits, the natural allowance being made for latitude.

the same elementary centers of emphasis should be stressed in the application of symbol to the problem in hand.

CONTRIBUTION OF PAGAN PHILOSOPHY

The contribution of pre-Christian centuries by necessity[14] pertained to the philosophy of insight symbolism rather than to the method of its use. A brief review will serve to bring into relief that which was unique in the medieval tradition, that is, its vision in the mystic interpretation of definite levels simultaneously true.[15]

Among leaders of thought a philosophy of insight symbolism had developed gradually as an intermittent tradition cropping out now and then through the centuries. Nearer the surface in Greek culture than in any other, this undercurrent of thought, so strong in Plato, became more and more an integral part of the Platonic tradition, especially of Neoplatonism, as it centered in the Alexandrian school. The Platonist has been defined as one "who sees the invisible, and who knows that the visible is its true shadow."[16] Plato had declared that myths of the gods were perilously subject to misuse, and when purely fictional, should be deleted ruthlessly. Yet with such myths as contained truth, that is, led to noble conceptions of the divine, he had declared that all education must begin. For Plato, the sun was symbol of the Absolute (Socrates himself, supposed repudiator of all gods, had prayed to the Sun),[17] and sex was symbolic of the love of the spirit, with its mingling of unspeakable joy and the bitterest pain. The recognition of these materials of symbolism as true expressions of reality was fundamental in philosophy. Two centuries before Plato, indeed, Theogenes had interpreted Homer as containing symbolic expression of philosophic truth.[18] The Pythagoreans, in attempting to fuse the thought of Plato, Aristotle, and the Stoa, in their trinity of the One, the

14. In those centuries, since the scriptures of various cultures had not been brought into juxtaposition, no problem of interpretation and harmonization had arisen, and the need of unification through the Logos was not yet felt.

15. Cf. Appendix IV, Pt. I, iii.

16. W. R. Inge, *Philosophy of Plotinus*, 1, 74.

17. Plato, *Symposium*, 220 D-E.

18. Later Metrodorus definitely identified Agamemnon with the Ether, Achilles with the Sun, Helen with the Earth, Alexander with the Air, Hector with the Moon and so on. Such identifications were to become increasingly popular.

Intelligence, and the World Soul dealt in occult interpretations, especially of numbers. Together with their development of symbolic interpretation, went absorption in the problem of duality, expressed as the relationship of the Monad to the Dyad. Among the Stoics, whose greatest contribution to thought was their elaboration of the Logos concept (in attempted solution of the problem of duality), mystical interpretation assumed the form of an exact science. In the third century before Christ, however, the four schools at Athens, the Academics, Peripatetics, Stoics, and Epicureans, resolved themselves into skepticism[19] and eclecticism, after which philosophic thought in Athens stagnated until revived in the fifth century by the school of Plotinus, which had derived its inspiration from Alexandria.

Although, as already noted, throughout this period the sun with its associated imageries of fire and light was ever present, it was at Alexandria where, within small space, the solar symbolisms of Platonism were brought into close association with the other scriptural sun imageries of great cultural traditions, that there occurred the next important development in symbolic method. Philo, a Jewish contemporary of Christ, accomplished a blend of Greek philosophy and Judaism, which was nowhere more marked than in his doctrine of the Logos.[20] To him the infinite God was ultimately incomprehensible, though revealed to man through the images of the outer world. Perhaps it was Philo's recognition of the greatness of the task which he ascribed to these images that led him to consider them independent beings. Certainly in this he was not alone.

Philo developed an elaborate allegorism, marked by the clear perception that more than one meaning is to be seen in scriptural stories and symbols.[21] It is, however, as one would expect,

19. Cf. for example W. R. Inge, *Philosophy of Plotinus*, v. 2.

20. Closest in his philosophy to Plato, the later Pythagoreans, and the Stoics, he wrote to recommend Judaism to the Greeks. The Ideas he considered, according to the Stoic modification of Plato, to be dynamic thoughts of God, comprehended in one unity called the Logos, who is mediator and creative power of God. His terminology leaves it rather doubtful whether the Logos is thought of as being in any sense personal. Yet it has been said justly that every sentence in the Fourth Gospel has its parallel in Philo, the one exhibiting the Logos in ontology, the other in history.

21. He brings out a moral quality in the scriptural incident wherein Jacob rolled a stone to the place and put it under his head, commenting on Jacob's self-control and manly hardiness. He then gives the mystical interpretation that

in a discussion of the symbolism of the sun itself that Philo's feeling for more meanings than one comes out clearly. He says, indeed:

> Do not wonder if, according to the rules of allegorical description, the sun is likened to the Father and governor of the universe; for in reality nothing is like unto God, but those things which by the vain opinion of men are thought to be so, are only two things, one invisible and the other visible; the soul being the invisible thing, and the sun the visible one.[22]

Nevertheless, he finds in scripture (though not in the same passage) four significations for the sun: first, the human mind,[23] second, outward sense which renders man impure,[24] third, the Divine Word which protects the virtuous and destroys the wicked,[25] and, fourth, the all-seeing God himself. These four significations, when analyzed, fall into three types. The interpretation of the sun as the Divine Word bears reference to the problem of the relationship of the infinite to the finite; that of the human mind and outward sense, to the problem of man's moral progress; and that of the all-seeing God to the problem of things as they are. Thus meditating on the greatest of symbols, Philo was led to a multiplex symbolic interpretation presaging that which later was to become the fourfold system.

THE WORD OF GOD

Such were the ideas of symbolism springing up throughout the Empire. The union of the finite and the infinite, the truth

Jacob caught one of the incorporeal spirits with which the air of the holy place was filled, and enclosing it in his thoughts, made it the head of his personality. Thus, though apparently he slept, in reality he was seeking rest in the Divine Logos. (*On Dreams Being Sent from God,* cap. xx-xxi. It is one of Philo's beliefs that the air is filled with spirits or angels, like the souls of men in all but their state of disembodiment.) If this particular example of symbolic interpretation seem unnecessary, one need but consider the grosser crudities to be found in all sacred scriptures.

22. Philo, *On Dreams Being Sent from God,* cap. xiii, on Gen. 28. 11.

23. *Ibid.,* cap. xiv, commenting Gen. 11. 4.

24. *Loc. cit.,* commenting Lev. 4. 31. Cf. medieval interpretation cited, p. 274.

25. "The Divine Word, the model of that sun which moves about the heavens . . . for the Word of God when it reaches to our earthly constitution assists and protects those who are kin to virtue, so that it provides them with a complete refuge and salvation, but upon their enemies it sends irremediable overthrow and destruction." *Ibid.,* cap. xv.

The selection of this function for the Logos is interesting in comparison with the Christian thought of the Word as Saviour, and with the destruction of evil as a function of the sun god. Cf. p. 108.

and its expression, had always been in some incomprehensible manner the office of the second person of every trinity, as it was the function of symbol. All of this was implied in the name Logos. Through the creative activity[26] of the Word was the reaching out of the insensible into the sensible, and through its nature, the union of the sensible and insensible. Logos, which from earliest times had signified both Reason and Expression, contained within itself duality. It was thus in the dual nature of the second person of the trinity (of whom Dante in his further symbolic progress found it necessary to consider himself a type), that discussions at Alexandria centered, while Christians were striving to convince the Roman world that the solution was at hand in Jesus of Nazareth, the Son of God. Men had never dreamed that the finite nature of man himself was to be taken up, not into some happy region of semi-divinity, but into the infinite Tri-unity itself. Before all of this could be apprehended in the world, it was necessary that the Christian God should win his place among the religions and philosophies of the day, and that the Christian trinity should be defined, as it was for Dante, in the sun.

At Rome, the philosophy of insight symbolism as applied to nature was instrumental in the *de jure* victory over other solar deities, accorded in 313 to the Christian trinity. At Alexandria was accomplished through the study of scripture, the further development of symbolic method which was to make possible to later centuries the definite victory of the cross. Dazzled and baffled by long gazing on the Sun itself, and on the perplexing Word of it in scripture, thought in the Empire wrestled with problems of symbolism, unconscious that far to the east some men had beheld the Sun "rise shadowed,[27] so that by the tempering of the mists the eye" of man might at last endure him.[28]

26. With the development of thought the creative power of the God had become more and more definitely centralized in the Word. There is a deep psychological reason why this should be so. Cf. the comments of Dr. Jung on the "idea which spontaneously produces its object" (*Psychology of the Unconscious*, pp. 61 ff.). Fundamentally, the term "Logos" signified not only "Word," but the word-making power or "Reason." Thus as symbol of the infinite it indicated the divine manifestation by which the universe was created. Cf. pp. 17, 165, *et al.*

27. "Christus est sol aeternus a quo omnes chori angelorum illustrantur; lux est vera a quo omnes animae illuminantur; qui dum hic latuit sub nube carnis," Honorius of Autun, sermon for Ascension (Migne, *P.L.*, t. 177, col. 955).

28. *Purg.*, xxx, 25-28.

II. SYMBOLIC REVELATION OF DIVINE SUN IN SCRIPTURE

IT was in Plato's cave with an entrance open to the light that the medieval mind awoke to find itself shackled, but philosophy had learned to call the light Logos and had recognized in it the means of knowing the incomprehensible. The author of the Fourth Gospel had proclaimed the Word—the true Light which lighteth every man that cometh into the world. God having made manifest to men his great expression of himself, the world to receive the revelation had sought its own expression in a renewed vehemence of symbolism. This symbolism to the initiate had been surcharged with meaning; to others it was strange, often beautiful imagery. Philosophy in Plotinus, religion in the Fourth Gospel, declared the divine revelation through light and love—the sun was an obvious analogy.

Whether or not there had been an historic Jesus, the development[29] of the full doctrine of the Logos was inevitable—indeed, independently of the Christian trinity, Plotinus had developed it. Thinking through the sun which had become central in philosophy, men could scarcely escape the significance of the rays as the bridge between the reality and its expression, between the source and the receivers of life. Thus, for medieval thought the historic Jesus had come as the fulfilment of that for which the world had been preparing, and so gave meaning to all symbolism. More than this, *in him was defined the very function of symbolism itself, as uniting eternally the infinite meaning and its finite expression.* This definition resulted from Christ's dual nature: the secret of symbolism as ultimately developed, was to be fourfold.

In scripture, God's word, Christ—the Logos (Word)—had been prefigured, and his earthly life had been recorded. Christ himself and those who left the first records of his teachings, led both in the symbolic expression of the triune God and in the development of the medieval symbolic method. Springing up amid the fecundity of symbolic usage in the encounter of traditions, the New Testament is interesting, not only for its inclusions, as Wellhausen pointed out in another connection, but for its exclusions.[30] The student of Dante symbolism can

---

29. As Dr. Aall has so ably pointed out. Cf. Aall, *Der Logos.*
30. Cf. p. 256 n. 40.

hardly proceed without a study of the symbolic materials and the symbolic method as they appear in that which was the most seriously studied and most widely circulated of all manuscripts in the Middle Ages.

MATERIALS OF SYMBOLISM IN THE NEW TESTAMENT

The language of the New Testament is the time-worn language of symbolism, and according to tradition the materials of symbolism in scripture, as in nature their ultimate basis, find their focus in the Sun. Symbolisms for God derived from man's inanimate environment[31] fall into four groups, as they center around each of the four "elements"[32] easily distinguishable by his senses, and so appear in the canon. The *Rock* (as typical of the element *earth*) in the Old Testament was a favorite symbol.[33] This imagery in the New Testament is transferred to Christ, in regard to whom it is used twice, but with little elaboration in terms of thought.[34] The chief attributes of God made vivid through this imagery are those of stability and eternity. *Water* imagery as applied to God is common, but in the Bible it is always a fountain, spring, or rain, never the sea, which to Palestine's rocky coast brought none of its blessings. This symbol was more used by Old Testament writers[35] but traces of it are to be found in the New Testament.[36] The verbal images most closely associated are life-giving and beneficence. It is clear that as soon as God is identified with spirit he is identified with *wind: πνεῦμα*.[37] From this derive quite naturally the verbal symbols of omnipotence, omnipresence, and inscrutability as applied to God. Place beside these few verses the innumerable passages in which occur *fire* and *light* imagery, and there is no question as to which of these four was found most valuable in New Testament thought.

Fire, even apart from its natural embodiment in the sun, has for the primitive mind an obvious symbolic advantage because of

31. The same lessons can be expressed by symbolisms drawn from the animate (vegetable and animal) and human realms. The former is relatively rare in the New Testament, except in the form of the agricultural and pastoral symbolisms associated with solar concepts (cf. p. 257 n. 42).

32. Fire, air, water, earth.   33. Ps. 62. 1-2, for example.

34. Rom. 9. 33; I Cor. 10. 1-4.   35. Cf. Jer. 2. 13.

36. John 7. 37-39; Rev. 22. 17.   37. John 4. 24; cf. also John 3. 8.

the aspiration of its form[38] and the consequent belief that of all the elemental spheres that of fire is the highest. Further, sun symbolism has been used to express every one of the ideas expressed through the verbal symbols already mentioned. God as the Sun in his unity is all-powerful and inscrutable, stable and eternal, and, in his trinity is the beneficent giver of life, light, and heat, just in his operation through unalterable law; while God as the Sun in his duality is the radiance which unites the finite with the infinite, the Hound of Heaven who in his compassion and his love would give himself to men and woo them to him.[39] The idea that God is enlightening is difficult to convey through other imageries; as is his aspect as a consuming fire, at first of destruction and later of the love which tests and purifies. Moreover, wind, water, fire, and rock, are all subject to him and fulfil his pleasure. The New Testament is remarkable for this systematic development of symbolism.[40]

Not only is the New Testament a living monument to the

38. The belief was that each element strove to return to its own sphere, that of "earth" being lowest, since it will sink through water; and that of fire being above air, since instead of falling like earth and water, fire rises. Cf. the Stoic belief in the affinity of souls with fire, etc., p. 123 n. 61.

39. Francis Thompson, *Hound of Heaven*. Cf. also his *Orient Ode*.

40. In the Old Testament, except for its function in apocalyptic, the development of symbolism was fragmentary. The Lord God is a sun and a shield (Ps. 84. 11) and an everlasting light (Isa. 60. 19-20). He is the sun of righteousness (Mal. 4. 2) and his garment is light (Ps. 104. 2). Light belongs to the description of good kings (II Sam. 21. 17). Light is associated with knowledge (Isa. 8. 20); with happiness (Isa. 58. 8); with comfort in desolation (Mic. 7. 8); with the word of God and the law (Ps. 119. 105; Prov. 6. 23; Isa. 50. 11). Otherwise, God is a consuming fire, an expression of the wrath of God for the destruction of the wicked. Once fire is purifying (Mal. 3. 2).

Greek usage was likewise restricted; its application being chiefly to reason and the soul, while in the mystery cults, so far as can be determined, the use was almost exclusively representative of regeneration and immortality. In Zoroastrianism the system was more inclusive and more coherent. Associated with it were spiritual enlightenment, good works, truth, immortality, cataclysmic victory of the good, destruction of evil, and testing of character. It should be remarked that the attributes of God which have been intellectualized at such great length alike in Catholic and Protestant systems, were worked out in earlier symbolic traditions. Not only the character of God, but all the problems of theology have been perceived and attacked through the symbolic method. For example, the problem of evil appears in solar symbolism with great clarity. The answer of Persian dualism is expressed in the concept of darkness and its associate storm as an evil power attempting to overcome the god of light. The monotheistic answer is expressed in the union of the sun and storm attributes in one ultimately good divinity. The frequent strife of these two attempted solutions in religious thought is recorded in the symbolism itself by the occasional confusion between the powers of darkness and the storm aspect of the sun god.

work of the insight symbol in the ordering of the materials of symbolism, but also it contains, in the teaching of Christ and the apostles, the basis of the fourfold method. Christ and his apostles appear as the first of Christian symbolists. In the tradition of insight symbolism as it had developed through the centuries, they supplied the basis for the fourfold development in method.

METHOD OF SYMBOLISM IN THE NEW TESTAMENT

The materials of symbolism are used in the New Testament to convey not only different symbolic meanings, as in the pre-Christian centuries, but also specifically three distinct types of symbolic meaning. Christ frequently made identification of himself[41] with the Sun:[42] "I am come a light into the world, that

41. There is no intention in this study of entering into the moot question as to which of the "sayings" of Jesus are due to him, and which are merely ascribed to him by the evangelists. Obviously, for the words to have influenced Dante, it is sufficient that tradition ascribed them to Christ.

42. He uses, also, associated imagery both of agricultural and of pastoral origin (Cf. p. 256 n. 40). Cf. such passages as Matt. 18. 12-14, John 6; 10; 12. 24; 16. 5.

In the scriptures, of vegetable growths tree and vine are the favorite symbols, but in the New Testament the tree is not used for God but only for his life-giving power, as in Rev. 2. 7. The vine is of course used for Christ, to develop the corporate idea: "I am the vine, ye are the branches; he that abideth in me and I in him, the same bringeth forth much fruit, for without me ye can do nothing." This is more effective, perhaps, than is the light imagery used by the same writer for the purpose.

The much discussed imagery of the bread and wine of life should be mentioned. It is one of the closest derivatives from solar imagery, representing as it does both the fruit of the life-giving activity of the sun (vegetation worship is inseparable from sun worship) and the direct support of life for man. The prominent part played by food symbolism in all earlier religions might therefore have been predicted. The point in interest is that it, unlike all other symbolisms from the agricultural realm, was not athetized but chosen for further development.

Animals as representations of God are to be found in the Old Testament (bull, serpent, etc.), but appear of use in the New Testament only where they belong to the paraphernalia of the sun god, or have become the stock in trade of the apocalyptic writer. The Lamb, or Ram, *Aries*, for Christ, has been associated with solar symbolism, cf. p. 161, but may have been used for him originally quite independently to stress the sacrificial character of his life. One other usage is the lifting up of the serpent, John 3. 14-15. The slight use in the New Testament of such symbolisms results probably from their association with idolatry, and from their more limited symbolic possibilities. It will be noted, also, that in the few instances in which such use does occur, it is for the better description of Christ in his human aspect.

In addition to the symbolism of man's inanimate environment, centralized in the sun and thus applied to Christ, there appears then in the New Testament this

whosoever believeth on me should not abide in darkness."[43]
This became a favorite symbolism with his apostles,[44] and its
importance has already been considered in relationship with the
formulation of the Christian trinitarian concept. Christ used
solar imagery in a second sense, however, as containing a definitely moral lesson, in describing those souls so open and re-

taking up of symbols of his animate environment with a similar centering. This
latter symbolism includes also the sphere of man's human contacts.

The realm of human relationships lends four concepts to assist in the expression of God—kingship, fatherhood, friendship, marriage. In the New Testament
as in the Old, kingship was a favorite ascription, as for example in Rev. 15. 3 and
I Tim. 1. 17, also "The blessed and only Potentate, the King of kings and Lord
of lords, who only hath immortality, dwelling in the light which no man can
approach unto, whom no man hath seen nor can see, to whom be honor and
power everlasting." I Tim. 6. 15-16. This passage shows how closely even sovereignty in God was associated with light imagery. Closely allied are the titles
Lord and Master (Acts 4. 24; I Cor. 2. 8; I Cor. 15. 47; Rom. 14. 4), though
the title *Kyrios* for Christ was suggested doubtless by the mystery religions. The
three terms of sovereignty in reality express little that is not expressed through
the imagery of the sun as the physical lord of the universe.

Father as applied to God occurs only eight times in the Old Testament, and
then always in a restricted sense, but in the New Testament becomes a favorite
form of expression (for example, Matt. 11. 25; Luke 11. 11-13). Fatherhood,
which, it is to be remembered, was closely associated with sovereignty, is the
second symbol from the human realm which should be noted as significant in
the New Testament, and through the power of life-giving, as peculiarly associated with sun imagery.

The friendship idea, already met in the Old Testament, occurs in the New
Testament less frequently than one would expect, and where it does appear is
associated with Christ in his human aspect, not with God. The Christian term
Elder Brother as applied to Christ derives from passages with a similar reference
(Rom. 8. 29; Col. 1. 15; Col. 1. 18).

Finally, the marriage imagery applied to God in the Old Testament (in Hosea,
Jeremiah, Ezekiel, etc.) is now transferred to Christ. Marriage, representing our
highest ideal of union, is the third symbolism of especial significance in the New
Testament, the other two being food and fatherhood. All three are noteworthy
for their close connection with the sun. Fundamental symbolic usage in the New
Testament may be summarized as: sun symbolism with its close associate of
fatherhood in regard to God, and sun symbolism with its close associate of husband in regard to Christ, with food as the gift of both. Such in the canon is the
union of sun and sex as focus of symbolism.

It is important, moreover, that these same emphases were selected and developed in the church: a combination of solar with paternal symbolism in the
development of the Trinity; with marriage symbolism in the corporate life of
the church, and with food symbolism in the sacramental system. Further, they
came to be presented vividly, that all might understand, in the Church Year,
through which runs the golden thread of solar symbolism. Cf. Chap. VI.

43. John 12. 46.

44. See Acts 26. 13; II Thess. 2. 8; and Heb. 1. 3. In the last-mentioned passage symbolism is used almost in the exact form in which Athanasius and others
(cf. pp. 144-150) used it to define the relationship between the First and Second
Persons of the Trinity.

sponsive to the grace of God that his word might be nourished within them as is seed by the sun. In strong contrast he described those who "loved darkness rather than light, because their deeds were evil":

For every one that doeth evil hateth the light, neither cometh to the light, lest his deeds should be reproved. But he that doeth truth cometh to the light, that his deeds may be made manifest, that they are wrought in God.[45]

Here, moreover, are the two types of symbolism contained within the same passage, Christ himself being the light by which character is tested. Finally, using this imagery in a third signification, Christ, Light of the Sun, spoke of the glory which was his in union with his Father before his assumption of an earthly body. This glory is in eternity to be shared also by the righteous, who shall "shine forth as the sun in the kingdom of their Father."[46] In such passages as the foregoing the medieval symbolist at once recognizes the levels of allegory, trope, and anagoge, the threefold mystic interpretation of the letter. These interpretations appear not only in the recorded words of Christ, but even more clearly in the writings of Paul, chronologically the earliest of all Christian writings.

Not only natural imageries were used by Christ in the four typical significations, but also imageries drawn from scripture. His identification of himself with the Messiah and the Suffering Servant is too familiar to need discussion. There was even identification of his own prophetic predecessor with Elias, who, according to scripture, was to come before the Messiah,[47a] and recognition of the tau cross on which the serpent was lifted up in the wilderness as a type of his crucifixion.[47b] There is scarcely an Old Testament prophecy of which either Christ or his immediate disciples did not describe his allegorical fulfilment. (For Old Testament narrative used by himself as a "type" of himself, cf. "As Jonas was three days and three nights in the whale's belly; so shall the Son of man be three days and three nights in the heart of the earth.")[48] This centralization of himself, espe-

---

45. John 3. 17-21.   46. Matt. 13. 43.
47a. Matt. 11. 14, and 17. 10-13.   47b. John 3. 14.
48. Matt. 12. 40.

cially in the interpretation of scripture, resulted in far more frequent use by Christ of allegory than of trope, which at that time
throughout the world was the most popular of scriptural interpretations.[49] Even in the moral lesson, take for example, that
for the upbuilding of the virtuous life the soul depends on God,
Christ kept himself central.[50] He is the manna of the Old Testament, the food of the faithful soul given by God who, as a pillar
of fire, had led the Israelites in the wilderness. Finally, in anagoge, it was through the marriage ceremonial of the Hebrew
that he described his ultimate relationship to the Church,[51] even
as his follower, the author of the Epistle to the Hebrews, was to
use the ritual blood sacrifice[52] as type of Calvary and reminder
of the eternal priesthood of Christ. Thus is opened a new era in
the symbolic reading of sacred writings.

Through the threefold mystical interpretation thus appearing in the earliest Christian writings, warring readings of the
world's scriptures might be ordered. As allegory could be
grouped all those stories of divine incarnation and human deifi-
cation so dear to the mystery religions; while as trope could be
grouped those symbolic stories of ethical struggle so deep
rooted in the Hebrew's philosophy of history; finally, as anagoge place was given to the highest concepts of Greek thought
in its exploration into eternity.

Little time was required for men to clinch this potential reconciliation in an insistence that these three types of interpretation might be all of them true at once. Indeed, the author of
the Epistle to the Hebrews so analyzes both the ceremonial law
of the Jews regarded as a symbol, and the priesthood of Mel-

49. Cf. the symbolic interpretation of the Old Testament which we owe to
Philo, Christ's Alexandrian contemporary. Whereas Philo used three types of
meaning in regard to the literal sun, these types fail to stand out among the rest
of his symbolic interpretations as prominently as they do among Christian symbolisms. Furthermore, Philo's interest lies chiefly in the moral interpretation,
and every character and event is given symbolic meaning in the realm of psychological attitudes, powers, and virtues. On the other hand the interpretation most
stressed by Christ and his apostles is the allegorical, wherein Christ is identified
with that power described by Philo as the Divine Word which protects the righteous and destroys the wicked.

50. It is hard to tell here whether, in using manna as a type of himself, he is
using what medieval writers would have recognized as an allegory, or as a trope
\—as bearing primarily a creedal (concerning Christ) or a moral (concerning the
soul) signification, probably both.

51. E.g., in Matt. 25. 1-13. Cf. Appendix III, Pt. I, i.   52. Cf. p. 120.

chizedech, which he regards as a more perfect symbol. The blood sacrifices of the Temple worship are allegorical types of Calvary. The moral meaning of the sacrifices is clear in that, purging ceremonial uncleanness, they signify the purging of the conscience from evil. Finally, the yearly entrance of the high priest into the Holy of Holies to offer in the very presence of God the prayers and sacrificial expiations of the people is an anagogical representation of the eternal presentation of Christ to the Father. Melchizedech, king of Salem,[53] is, however, an even truer type of the priesthood of Christ than is the Levitical priesthood. Allegory of Christ in his blessing of Abraham and in him of all peoples,[54] he is also trope in his representation of righteousness and peace,[55] and anagoge, in his eternal and un-originated life,[56] of Christ's eternal and unchanging priesthood.

SOLUTION OF DUALITY

So the Jesus of the Gospels fulfilled the function of the Logos, in his nature as at once God and man. He united, like the sun's radiance, creator and creature, infinite and finite. He bound together the warring pair, matter and spirit, and so made possible an immortality potentially satisfactory both to the Jew, who could never manage without his body, and to the Greek, who—for all his beautifying of the body—could never get along with it (because of a disturbing conviction that only apart from it could be attained the full freedom of the spirit).[57] Finally, Christ united the two sources of human knowledge, nature and

53. The original and obscure reference to Melchizedech is in Gen. 14. 18-20. The tradition of his unique priesthood is referred to again in Ps. 110. 4. (It is to be noted that Christ himself cites this psalm as inspired—Mark 12. 36; Matt. 22. 44; Luke 20. 42-43.) Upon this tradition is based the argument in Hebrews (see especially Heb. 5. 6, 10; 6. 20; 7. 1-25). It is of interest that the sentence cited three times (Heb. 5. 6; 7. 17, 21) from Ps. 110 (Vulgate numbering, Ps. 109) still forms a part of the ordination to the Roman Catholic priesthood, signifying that all priestly acts are subsumed under the Eternal Priesthood of Christ.

54. Later interpretation, expanding this incident, points out that Melchizedech is also allegory of Christ in that as priest he brought forth bread and wine. Gen. 14. 18.

55. Heb. 7. 2.   56. Heb. 7. 3, 21-25.

57. In Christianity first came a belief in that complete and blessed immortality of which earthly symbols could be the anagogical representations, as they could not of the shade-filled Sheol of the Hebrew or even of the pure Idea-world of the Platonist. The Hebrew, unable to live ideally without his body, and the Greek, unable to live eternally with his, both found their positive hopes taken

scripture, resolving the conflict of dualities by a fourfold method. His life was the dramatic presentation of that which nature declared in sex and in sun, that for which history had been preparing—the ultimate union of opposites in solution of the problem of duality.

History thus became a drama and the universe its setting. In either one alone, had man complete understanding, he might read the answer to the riddle of the universe, but in his condition of limitation through sin and ignorance, the intervention of Divine Wisdom was demanded, who, as the living Word, brought solution of the written word in scripture. Speaking according to prophecy, in parables,[58] Christ turned the literal sense of scripture into the wine of the spiritual intelligence.[59] All future history, leading to the tremendous finale in which man should attain at last to union with God, was to present gradual realization by the world of that which Christ, as the Head of humanity, had lived in his earthly life; and in this realization, according to medieval thinking, the multiplex interpretation, of which Christ became the life, was of supreme importance. Through it, men reconciled the contradictions, not only of the Hebrew canon, but of the scriptures of the pagan world. Not only Adam, Isaac, Joseph, Joshua, David, Solomon, Jonah, but also Jupiter himself,[60] to say nothing of the Unknown God of Athens,[61] had their truth as prefiguring Christ.[62]

up into the medieval doctrine of the Beatific Vision, expressed by Dante in the Blessed Rose, where joy was to be eternally deepened when it should be shared, at last, by body.

58. Cf. Matt. 13. 35.

59. "Ipse etiam mutat aquam carnalis sensus in vinum spiritualis intellectus." Albertus Magnus, De laudibus B. Mariae Virg., 12, 6, 12. The same signification of the miracle of Cana is given by Rabanus Maurus.

60. Cf. Purg., vi, 118-119. Many sun gods were seen as prefigurements of the Sun of Righteousness, for example, Baldur the Beautiful. (Cf. pp. 109, 125.) Of course, not all Christian apologists used this method. Many, for example Arnobius and Origen, poured ridicule and scorn on pagan gods and flouted the immoral tales told concerning them, even while insisting on glossing over the crudities of the Old Testament by the use of a symbolism which they denied to their adversaries; while their adversaries, especially the pagan Neoplatonists, pursued the very same policy in regard to the Christian scripture. Dante, however, clearly belongs in the tradition which was able to see in pagan myth and history a preparation and prefigurement of Christ and of his dual vicarate in church and empire.

61. Cf. Paul's sermon on Mars' Hill, Acts 17. 22-23 ff.

62. Interestingly enough, it happened that Augustine, the first to unite in his

III. DEVELOPMENT OF LEVELS OF SYMBOLIC INTERPRETATION

IN brief review, then, it may be stated as probable that symbolic interpretation of myth developed earlier among the Greeks than among the Hebrews:[63] "The Stoics deriving this method from the cynics, brought it to perfection as a theological weapon, by means of which they were able to conserve the form of popular religion while transferring its content." The method they had made prominent in the interpretation of Homer was applied by Philo to the interpretation of the Old Testament. Allegorical interpretation appears first among Christians as used by Christ himself, although the simultaneous validity of the four typical meanings was first expressed in the Epistle to the Hebrews. The great wellspring of the allegorical method was, however, Alexandria, where it has been remarked that even Christians were trying not primarily to defend dogma by Greek philosophy, but to make their opinions clear to themselves.

FORMULATION OF THE ALLEGORICAL METHOD

Origen, first great scholar of Christianity, and called "Father of the allegorical[64] method," having learned much from his teacher, Clement of Alexandria, first wrought a finished system with the three[65] levels of meaning, literal, moral, and mystical. Within the mystical, Origen seems to have included those types of meaning which were later to be distinguished as allegory and anagoge. The three levels he recognized were styled by him the body, soul, and spirit of the scripture.[66] To ignorance of sym-

person theology and philosophy, Dante's two suns of the moral sphere, and so to establish Christianity as reasonable and capable of appeal to all types of men, was won to his task by the allegorical method. Cf. pp. 268-269.

63. Cf. Angus, *Mystery Religions,* p. 49.

64. Term applied to the method by which definite levels of symbolic meaning are perceived. It should be distinguished sharply from the term "allegory" as referring to one of the levels themselves, as Dante used it; and also from the term "allegory" as later in common use for moral tales involving personification. Cf. pp. 278-281.

65. To these three meanings the fourth was added later. Cf. pp. 270 ff. and Appendix IV, Pt. I, iii.

66. He bases his analysis on the threefold nature of man as body, soul, and spirit; on a text in Proverbs of which his version ran: "Do thou portray them in a threefold manner, in counsel and knowledge, to answer words of truth to those who propose them to thee"; and on the command given to Hermas (cf. *The Shepherd of Hermas,* an early Christian writing) to write one book (the letter)

bolic method he ascribed the difficulties faced by the church of his time: the unbelief of Jews who expected the Messiah to be heralded by the literal fulfilment of Old Testament prophecies;[67] the Gnostic denial that the Old Testament Demiurge of whom anger, jealousy, repentance, and wickedness are predicated, can be the God revealed by Jesus Christ; and the ascription to God by simple-minded believers of "such things as would not be believed of the most savage and unjust of mankind."

All scripture, according to Origen, contains the spiritual sense, and some scripture contains a corporeal sense, that is, a literal sense which is true and reasonable. The corporeal (literal) sense in many cases is "capable of improving the multitude, according to their capacity," and that sense which is the "soul" of scripture (the trope or moral signification) occurs in "numerous interpretations adapted to the multitude . . . which edify those who are unable to understand profounder meanings."[68] Only in the spiritual sense are the deepest truths of Christianity to be perceived.[69]

In accord with the tradition of the East Origen felt the literal meaning of scripture to be of no particular importance: he placed the stories of Genesis as regards interpretation on the same level with those of Homer (which in this period of sophistication were represented as pure fiction, to be interpreted allegorically). God had supplemented his revelation of himself in the natural universe by a revelation through scripture, in which

for Grapte to use in admonition of orphans and widows, and a second (the trope) for Clement to send to the cities abroad, while Hermas himself is to preach to the priests (the spiritual meaning).

67. Such as that the wolf and lamb shall dwell together, the lion eat straw, and so forth (Isa. 11. 6-7).

68. The example he gives is the command in Deut. 25. 4, not to muzzle the ox that treadeth out the corn, explained in I Cor. 9. 9-10 as an admonition to hope. Cf. with this doctrine of lesser meanings adapted to the multitude, Dante's *tornata* to his ode *Voi che 'ntendendo il terzo ciel movete:* "Ode, I believe that they shall be but rare who shall rightly understand thy meaning, so intricate and knotty is thy utterance of it; wherefore if perchance it come about that thou take thy way into the presence of folk who seem not rightly to perceive it, then I pray thee to take heart again, and say to them, O my beloved lastling, 'Give heed at least how beautiful I am.' "

69. "With respect to holy Scripture, our opinion is that the whole of it has a spiritual, but not the whole a bodily meaning, because the bodily meaning is in many places proved to be impossible." *De Principiis,* 4, 20.

was recorded history (wars, kings, etc.), biography (events in the lives of individuals), and civil and ceremonial laws:[70]

Where the Word found that things done according to the history could be adapted to these mystical senses, he made use of them, concealing from the multitude the deeper meaning; but where, in the narrative of the development of super-sensual things, there did not follow the performance of certain events, which was already indicated by the mystical meaning, the Scripture interwove in the history some event that did not take place, sometimes what could not have happened, sometimes what could, but did not.[71]

Thus Origen distinguished literal and functional truth. Such relation with the whole system of the known external universe as will serve to carry the mystical meaning forward, is the only literal truth guaranteed by inspiration.[72]

The first doctor of the Latin church, St. Hilary,[73] exiled four

70. Origen had New Testament basis for the treatment of all these as types. Cf. pp. 259-261. With especial reference to laws, see I Cor. 10; Col. 2. 16-17; Heb. 9. 23-24; Heb. 10. 1.

71. *De Principiis*, 4, 15.

72. As examples of untrue statements inserted by divine inspiration to teach symbolic truth, he cites: the first day of creation had no sky; God planted a tree; life and moral qualities were acquired by eating fruit; God walked in a garden; Adam hid from God under a tree; the devil shewed Jesus the whole world from a mountain top, etc.

As examples of impossible laws with symbolic meanings, he lists: the command to offer the goat-stag (which does not exist) as a sacrifice; that a grifon (which is never caught) is not to be eaten; the command to sit in the house all the Sabbath; and the Gospel exhortations to turn the right cheek to the smiter (only a left-handed man could smite it) and to tear out a lustful right eye.

He adds: "All these statements have been made by us, in order to show that the design of that divine power which gave us the sacred scriptures is, that we should not receive what is presented by the letter alone, such things being sometimes not true in their literal acceptation, but absurd and impossible." *De Principiis*, 4, 15-18.

73. Title officially conferred upon him by the Congregation of Rites and by papal brief in 1851. Cf. Labriolle, *op. cit.*, p. 238. It should be noted that Hilary was not only the first to familiarize the Latin world with this method of symbolism, but was also the founder of the *Schola Cantorum* which continued in corporate existence to the close of the fourteenth century, perpetuating the method in the language of music known as the Gregorian chant. (The *Schola Cantorum* established by Hilary was a definite body of ecclesiastical singers, seven in number, and as such is to be distinguished from the traditional *Schola Cantorum* of the preceding century, associated with Sylvester of Rome.) It will be remembered that in Dante's *Purgatorio* (xvi, 20) the souls sang in unison in a manner suggestive of such chants. Hilary was the first also to write Latin hymns to popular melodies. Cf. Chap. VI, i. Like all else medieval, church music had its roots in the Roman synthesis, developing amid persecutions from the time of those meetings, described by Pliny, to which came Christians "before sunrise on the first day of the week (Dies Solis) to sing antiphonal hymns in praise of Christ."

years in Asia Minor, on his return familiarized the Latin world with the allegorical method. In his *De Trinitate* he tried to impress his readers with the fact that the images and comparisons he used were completely inadequate in their expression of the truths he was attempting to make intelligible; and that in consequence they could be regarded simply as distant approximations which might lead gradually from the known to the unknown.

If in our discussion of the nature and birth of God we adduce certain analogies, let no one suppose that such comparisons are perfect and complete. There can be no comparison between God and earthly things. . . . We must therefore regard any comparison as helpful to man rather than descriptive of God.[74]

In his commentary on the psalms, and especially in his *Tractatus mysteriorum,* he has made definite the first of the three symbolic levels of interpretation as applying specifically to Christ.[75]

It will be remembered that Tertullian emphasized the necessity of learning about divine things through the universe, giving as basis, however, not merely the inadequacy of our faculties, but the intention of God. He added, moreover, scripture as the second source of instruction in the mystery of the universe:

He first sent Nature to you as a teacher, meaning to send Prophecy also as a supplemental instructor, that, being Nature's disciple, you may more easily believe Prophecy.[76]

Thus is marked the transition from the philosophic to the religious foundation for the theory of knowledge,[77] and similarly for the medieval conviction that beauty and love are worthy of

74. Hilary of Poitiers, *De Trinitate,* Bk. I, cap. 19.

75. "Every word contained in the sacred volume announces by word, explains by facts, and corroborates by examples the coming of our Lord Jesus Christ, sent by his Father, and born a man of a Virgin, through the operation of the Holy Spirit. From the beginning of the world, Christ, by authentic and absolute prefigurations in the persons of the Patriarchs, gives birth to the Church, washes it clean, sanctifies it, chooses it, places it apart and redeems it; by the sleep of Adam, by the deluge in the days of Noe, by the blessing of Melchizedech, by Abraham's justification, by the birth of Isaac, by the captivity of Jacob. . . . The purpose of this work is to show that in each personage, in every age, and in every act, the image of his coming, of his teaching, of his resurrection, and of our Church, is reflected as in a mirror." Quoted in Labriolle, *op. cit.,* p. 243.

76. Tertullian, *De resurrectione carnis,* cap. xii.

77. The identification of reason with faith is to become increasingly pronounced, and with few exceptions is to dominate until the great conflict of the thirteenth century.

worship only as symbols of the fundamental infinite, who made all things to teach man of himself. Upon both foundations, in this period, was erected the superstructure of symbolism. Here is the basis for Dante's treatment of these two sources of knowledge.

Unlike Origen, Tertullian argued that interpretation of scripture by the so-called allegorical method was permissible only when the symbol was true in its literal sense.[78] His point of view is representative of that of the Latin apologists of the period. Arnobius and Lactantius, although particularly interested in the subject, differed in no fundamental manner. At the same time, Jerome, the scholar, was occupied with better literal translation of the Bible, and his commentary has been supposed to represent a complete disapproval of allegorical interpretation. In reality, in kinship with the feeling of the West, he was shocked by the apparent contempt in which the East had held the meaning of the letter.[79] He felt that truth should exist in the literal history also, as a basis for the allegory.[80] To him, therefore, an accurate translation of scripture was the primary necessity; the literal bearing the same relation to the spiritual, that the foundation of a building bears to the superstructure.[81] He is in accord, however, even with the symbolists he condemns,[82] in the importance he gives to the superstructure.[83] The allegorical

78. For example, he points out that the use of resurrection to symbolize a moral change, rests on the premise that the prophets speak in figures of speech. There can, however, be no figure without verity. If your face is not there, you cannot see it in a mirror. Hence the use of resurrection as a symbol in an inspired writing is a proof that the resurrection is a fact. *De resurrectione carnis,* cap. xx.

He also argued interestingly that allegorical interpretation was as permissible in statements regarding the soul as in statements regarding the body.

79. Cf. for example Origen and Eusebius. See the quotations from Origen given on p. 265 n. 72.

80. "An taceam et aperte hujus generis expositionem nescire me dicam? et quando tibi potero persuadere, me non potuisse magis quam noluisse; quorum alterum imbecillitatis est, alterum superbiae?" Migne, *P.L.,* t. 24, col. 158.

81. "Caeterum si aut tu volueris, aut spatium fuerit, et voluntate nostrae Christus annuerit, spiritale supra struendum est aedificium, ut imposito culmine, perfecta Ecclesiae ornamenta monstremus." *Ibid.*

82. Jerome gave many "spiritual" interpretations. For example, the fountain of Paradise is Christ: the four streams, true literally as the Tigris, Euphrates, Nile, and Phison, represent the four cardinal virtues, the Nile being chastity, the Tigris fortitude, the Euphrates justice, and the Phison prudence. Cf. also p. 337 n. 18b.

83. "Unde post historiae veritatem, spiritualiter accipienda sunt omnia; et sic Judaea et Jerusalem, Babylon et Philisthiim, et Moab et Damascus, Aegyptus

method, still valuable in the constant conflict of Christianity
with alien beliefs, was so firmly founded in the philosophic
thought of the period that it was not easily shaken. With faulty
translation of the Bible, however, there might be question of
fault not only in the literal meaning as generally understood,
but even in the functional meaning on the literal level.[84] Such an
error might mislead for a time as to the true interpretation, as
did the error, which Athanasius had combated earlier, based
on a faulty translation of Proverbs 5. 22.[85] Thus, Jerome was
probably the first in the Latin tradition to recognize possible
loss of functional truth through neglect of literal truth. Jerome
and Origen stated opposite halves of the belief that scriptural
truth was imperiled by a lack of understanding of the symbolic
method—Origen, stressing the peril of disregard of the symbolic meaning; Jerome, stressing the peril of disregard of the
literal. On the essential functional truth of the letter, both
agreed. The criterion of interpretation is always the harmony
of the whole.[86]

Finally, after a painful progress through a maze of philosophies, Christianity found in Augustine a philosopher that it
could call its own. No longer were theories and fragments of
theories to be developed as chance dictated through the aid of
or in opposition to current thought. Christian history was to be
united with a philosophic system, and for the triumph of this
tour de force the allegorical method was the occasion. In the
lack of a means whereby to reconcile with his reason scripture
and Christian tradition, Augustine, who became almost the only
philosopher whose philosophy is an expression of Christian tradition, would have been no other than a Manichaean or a Neoplatonist.[87] Of Ambrose, enthusiastic exponent of the method

et desertum mare, Idumaea et Arabia, ac vallis Visionis et ad extremum Tyrus,
et Visio quadrupedum intelligenda sunt; ut cuncta quaeremus in sensu et in
omnibus his, quasi sapiens architectus Paulus apostolus jaciat fundamentum quod
non est alium praeter Christum Jesum." Migne, *P.L.,* t. 24, col. 20. In preface
to commentary on Isaiah.

84. Cf. Appendix IV, Pt. I, i.   85. Cf. p. 146.

86. "No book of Scripture . . . must be taken apart from the entire canon.
. . . Taken by itself, the teaching of a particular book must often be inadequate,
that half truth which, if left unsupplemented, would amount to an error, though
true as far as it goes. . . . The unity and harmony of the mystical interpretation
is thus the guarantee of its truth." E. I. Watkin, *Philosophy of Mysticism.*

87. Harnack states that Thomas Aquinas was essentially Aristotelian and only

of Origen, from whom Augustine learned of symbolism, he writes "ad eum ducebar abs te nesciens, ut per eum ad te sciens ducerer."[88] Later he states that:

saepe in popularibus sermonibus suis dicentem Ambrosium laetus audie-bam: Littera occidit, spiritus autem vivificat, cum ea, quae ad litteram perversitatem docere videbantur, remoto mystico velamento spiritaliter aperiret;[89]

and that as a result,

fidem catholicam, pro qua nihil posse dici adversus oppugnantes Mani-chaeos putaveram, iam non impudenter asseri existimabam, maxime audito uni atque altero, et saepius aenigmate soluto de scriptis veteribus, ubi, cum ad litteram acciperem, occidebar.[90]

Augustine's real contribution to the symbolic method, however, was in its development in relation to the theory of knowledge and as a basis for the mystic quest, and so remains to be dis-cussed in the next chapter.

During the last days of the empire, experimentation with the symbolic method was rife among all classes of men—theolo-gians, dramatists, occultists, and rhetoricians,[91]—and, needless to say, their efforts did not tend to greater lucidity. Gregory the Great, who from his historical vantage point gave powerful ex-pression to the materials of symbolism centered in the sun, gave also (in the proemium to his *Super Cantica Canticorum Ex-positio*) the rationale of allegory[92] in a statement which lived through five hundred years to be placed by Richard of St. Vic-

accidentally Christian; while Augustine was really Christian and only accidentally Platonic.

88. "To him was I led by thee, unknowing, that by him I might be brought knowingly to thee." *Confessions*, 5, 13.

89. "With joyful heart I heard Ambrose in his sermons to the people, most diligently oftentimes recommend this text for a rule unto them: The letter killeth, but the spirit giveth life; whilst those things which, taken according to the let-ter, seemed to teach perverse doctrines, he spiritually laid open to us, having taken off the veil of the mystery." *Confessions*, 6, 4.

90. "The Catholic faith, in defense of which I thought nothing could be an-swered to the Manichees' arguments, I now concluded with myself, might well be maintained without absurdity, especially after I had heard one or two hard places of the Old Testament resolved now and then, which when I understood literally, I was slain." *Confessions*, 5, 14.

91. Anyone interested in this question is referred to Cassiodorus' division of figures of speech.

92. He says briefly that allegory "est machina per quam anima levatur ad Deum."

tor, without acknowledgment, in his commentary on the same book:

Allegoria enim animae longe a Deo positae quasi quamdam machinam facit, ut per illam levatur ad Deum. Interpositis quippe aenigmatibus dum quoddam in verbis cognoscit quod suum est, in sensu verborum intelligit quod non suum est; et per terrena verba separatur a terra. Per hoc enim quod non abhorret cognitum, intelligit quoddam incognitum. Rebus enim nobis notis per quas allegoriae conficiuntur sententiae divinae vestiuntur, et, dum re cognoscimus exteriora verba, pervenimus ad interiorem intelligentiam.

Not only is the function of symbolism here powerfully defined, but it is defined in terms which make clear its relationship to the Second Person of the Trinity: he who "abhorred not to be known" (*"non abhorret cognitum"*) by man, raises him to the unknown God, as the sensible symbol raises him to that which is beyond sense. Christ thus becomes the limit of an infinite progression of symbols.

After this significant definition of the function of symbolism came the completion of the differentiation of method. Junilius Africanus attempted in his *De partibus divinae legis* a classification of types on a time basis[93] and immediately afterward on an ethical basis.[94] Such attempts at classification as these reveal the gropings of the intellect which must precede its ultimate conclusions, although beyond doubt the full development would have taken place much earlier had it not been for the influx of barbarians and the consequent necessity of a new synthesis.

Scarcely, however, is this period over when the fourfold interpretation appears in its full form,[95] as employed unformulated in Hebrews, and as later both employed and formulated by Dante. John Cassian says:

Theoretice vero in duas dividitur partes, id est, in historicam interpretationem, et intelligentiam spiritalem. . . . Spiritalis autem scientias genera sunt, tropologia, allegoria, anagoge. . . .[96]

93. "Praesentia, aut praeteritarum, aut futurarum rerum ignotarum, per opera . . . manifestatio." *De partibus divinae legis,* 2, 16.
94. "Typorum quatuor sunt modi: aut enim: (1) gratia gratis significantur, v.g. resurrectio Christi typus nostrae resurrectionis (2) moesta moestis, v.g. reprobatio angelorum typus reprobationis malorum (3) moestis grata, v.g. transgressio Adae typus justitiae salvatoris (4) gratis moesta, v.g. baptisma typus mortis Christi." *Ibid.,* 2, 17.
95. Cf. Appendix IV, Pt. I, iii.
96. John Cassian: *Collatio xiv. De spiritali scientia,* cap. 8.

Alardus Gazaeus comments on Cassian's statement:

Aliis verbis, triplex Scripturarum sensus mysticis a theologie assignari solet, allegoricus, tropologicus, anagogicus. . . . Allegoricus dicitur qui ad Christum, vel Ecclesiam spectat; tropologicus qui ad mores, anagogicus qui ad futuram vitam seu Ecclesiam triumphantem.

This statement is quoted in full and without acknowledgment by Rabanus Maurus, who gives his own opinion:[97]

In nostrae ergo animae domo historia fundamentum ponit, allegoria parietes ergit, anagogia tectum opponit, tropologia vero tam interus per affectum quam exterius per effectum boni operis, variis ornatibus dependit.[98]

The definition was later incorporated in the ninth century *Glossa ordinaria* of Walafrid Strabo, which was assiduously transferred to the margins of monastic scriptural parchments as the authoritative commentary. In the *Prothemata Glossae Ordinariae* the definition[99] is followed immediately by the example of the four meanings for the city of Jerusalem, which Dante was to give later in the *Convivio* and in the *Epistle to Can Grande.*

By the time of Bernard and the Victorines, and still more by the time[100] of Albertus and Thomas, the method was so universally known and used that definitions and discussion no longer seemed in order.[101, 102] Attention was devoted rather to the reading of these symbolic meanings, and many ingenious ones were

---

97. Cf. also Appendix IV, Pt. I, iii.

98. Rabanus Maurus, in prologue to his *Allegoriae in Scripturam Sacram.* The "historia" is of course the literal sense.

99. "Quatuor sunt regulae sacrae Scripturae, id est, *historia,* quae res gestas loquitur; *allegoria,* in qua aliud ex alio intelligitur; *tropologia,* id est moralis locutio, in qua de moribus ordinandis tractatur; *anagoge,* id est, spiritualis intellectus, per quem de summis et coelestibus tractaturi, ad superiora ducimur. His quatuor quasi quibusdam rotis tota divina Scriptura volvitur."

100. Isidore of Seville is important for allegorical interpretation and the giving of definite form to mystical commentaries on the Old Testament. He was noteworthy, as had been both Boethius and Gregory, for the attempt to preserve classical culture, and his influence on later centuries was chiefly through the *Etymologies,* one of the earliest of medieval encyclopedias. He furnishes what is rather a digest than an original contribution.

101. Except in exhaustive theological treatises. For the statement of Thomas Aquinas as to multiplicity of interpretation, cf. Appendix IV, Pt. I, iii.

102. Occasional writers varied from the usual analysis of the levels of symbolism, though in general the three types of "spiritual intelligence" are recognizable even in variant schemes. For the classification given by Hugh of St. Victor, cf. Appendix IV, Pt. I, iii (1).

found. So much was this the case that even a man of such modern and hard-headed English tendencies as John of Salisbury considered the *Aeneid* to have been an allegory of human life, and gave the same interpretation as that which later seems to have been Dante's.[103]

SYMBOLIC MULTIPLICITY

To understand the fourfold method in the development of its definition is not, however, to understand it in the full extent of its multiplicity, and from this multiplicity there has risen sufficient confusion to warrant a brief consideration. In medieval literature sun symbolism is frequently merely implied, even where it exists. Owing to the wealth of imagery in the *Divina Commedia* and elsewhere, it has been easy to discuss as examples, instances in which the implication is obvious. In view, however, of the medieval taste for verbal subtleties, it should not be expected that this would always be the case. From the light- and heat-giving qualities of the sun a variation may be made in the imagery by the use of light and heat (often also fire and flame) as symbols, without mention of the sun. (This is particularly common in ordinary speech, due no doubt to the physical association between light and sight and between heat and passion.) But symbolism develops according to psychological laws, giving further variations in associated symbols. Such variations fall roughly into two classes—first, where the association is through similarity between the realities symbolized—second, where it is through similarity between the symbols. An example of the first is the use of the sun to symbolize one of the saints, because the saint, in his degree, is like God a source of light. An example of the second is the use of "lamp" or "lantern" to symbolize God, because they, like the sun, give light.

Symbolic expressions associated through likeness in the things symbolized result in the representation by the same symbol of different realities. It was inherent in the doctrine of the Trinity that the Three Persons should often be represented by the same symbol. God the Father expresses himself through the Son and

103. John of Salisbury, *Polycraticus*, 6, 22, also 2, 15. Cf. *Convivio*, 4, 24. An excellent, though unsympathetic, account of such interpretation is given by Comparetti. See Fulgentius, *Expositio Virgilianae continentiae*.

the Holy Spirit as light and love. But the Son, one with the Father in all his aspects, is himself both light and love; and so also is the Holy Spirit. Perhaps the best-known statement of this doctrine is in the hymn *Quicunque vult,* generally known as the Athanasian Creed.

The next step is to apply the same symbol to persons and things which share in and call to mind the glory of God. It was in this manner that Beatrice brought to Dante "the recognition that this her splendor was the radiated reflection of still diviner beings, of the saints, and of the angels above the saints, and of the Virgin above the angels, and of the Godhead above the Virgin" which "enlarged at last his love of her to love of God."[104] The use of one symbol in many senses was natural to the medieval mind, ever conscious as it was of a unity under-lying all things. If an object, for example, the Sun, represents God for its life-giving, light-giving, and heat-giving aspects; and if a human being, for example, the Virgin; or an institution, for example, church or empire; or a book; or a virtue; or a study, for example, theology, shares to some degree in God's function in one of these respects (a sharing impossible if God had not penetrated the secondary thing with his qualities), then a connection is established between the secondary object also, and the Sun.[105] If God is the Sun, all his lesser representatives

104. J. B. Fletcher, *Symbolism of the Divine Comedy,* pp. 131-132. Cf. Chap. V (of the present study) for discussion of the function of symbol in the mystic way.

105. Cf. Lactantius' discussion of the creation of the Lights, in his *De origine erroris,* II, 10 (Migne, *P.L.,* t. 6, cols. 307-308). He states:

"Nihil enim per se continet luminis, nisi accipiat a coelo, in quo posuit lucem perennem, et superos, et vitam perpetuam, et contra in terra tenebras, et inferos, et mortem. Tanto enim haec ab illis superioribus distant, quantam mala a bonis, et vitia a virtutibus. Ipsius quoque terrae binas partes contrarias inter se, diversas-que constituit, scilicet orientem, occidentemque: ex quibus oriens Deo accensetur: quia ipse luminis fons, et illustrator est rerum, et quod oriri nos faciat ad vitam sempiternam. Occidens autem conturbatae illi pravaeque menti adscribitur, quod lumen abscondat, quod tenebras semper inducat, et quod homines faciat occidere atque interire peccatis.

"Nam sicut lux orientis est, in luce autem vitae ratio versatur; sic occidentis tenebrae sunt; in tenebris autem, et mors, et interitus continetur. Deinde alteras partes eadem ratione dimensus est, meridiem ac septentrionem: quae partes illis duabus societate junguntur. Est enim, quae est solis calore flagrantior, proxima est, et cohaeret oriento. At illa, quae frigoribus et perpetuo gelu torpet, ejusdem est cujus extremus occasus. Nam sicut contrariae sunt lumini tenebrae, ita frigus calori . . . Quibus singulis partibus suum tempus attribuit; ver scilicet orienti, aestatem meridianae plagae; occidentis autumnus est, septentrionis hyems. In his quoque duabus partibus, meridiana et septentrionale, figura vitae et mortis con-

in their degrees are suns also; even as an officer of the Empire might be distinguished by the imperial eagle. Thus, in the *Divina Commedia,* God is the Supreme Sun; but church and empire are suns of Rome; theology and philosophy are suns of the intellect; Mary, Lucia, and Beatrice are three aspects of the sun; the angels are lesser suns; Virgil himself is the sun of Dante's sight; Dante is a sun to those whom his words are to enlighten (although on Geryon he is a wandering sun).[106]

Innumerable instances of such association are scattered through medieval literature. Rabanus Maurus made a catalogue in which he adduced scriptural passages to show that the sun symbolizes *Deus, resurrectio Christi, Sancta Ecclesia, Virgo Maria, praedicatio, quilibet praedicator, baptisma, ordo sacerdotalis, quilibet sapiens, charitas, laetitia, sublimis in Ecclesia, contemplatio, fervor justitiae, tentationis calor, tribulatio, accumina sapientum, praesens tempus,* and *claritas patriae coelestis.*[107] The Venerable Gerhohus also lists significations of the sun: *tentationis ardor, claritas bonis operis, lumen veritatis, praedicatorum claritas, Dominus, persecutio, sapientum intellectus.*

Not only is one symbol to be used in many senses, but its appropriateness for the expression of any given reality is manifold. The Virgin is the sun, not only through her union with the

tinetur, quia vita in calore est, mors in frigore. Sicut autem calor ex igne est, ita frigus ex aqua. Secundum harum partium dimensionem, diem quoque fecit ac noctem, quae spatia, et orbes temporum perpetuos ac volubiles, quos vocamus annos, alterna per vices successione conficiant."

He adds: "Quae duo (day and night) etiam in hoc praescius fecit, ut ex iis, et verae religionis, et falsarum superstitionum imago quaedam ostenderetur."

106. *Inf.,* xvii, 106-114.

107. These significations, occurring in an alphabetical catalogue intended for the use of preachers, are not classified into allegory, trope, and anagoge, since to a certain extent the context in which the preacher chose to use them would determine the level. Nevertheless, in general, the significations listed above may be classified as follows:

Allegorical:

  Resurrectio Christi, Sancta Ecclesia, Virgo Maria, quilibet praedicator, baptisma, ordo sacerdotalis, quilibet sapiens, sublimis in Ecclesia, Dominus.

Tropological:

  Praedicatio, charitas, laetitia, fervor justitiae, tentationis calor, tribulatio, accumina sapientum, praesens tempus, tentationis ardor, claritas bonis operis, praedicatorum claritas, persecutio, sapientum intellectus.

Anagogical:

  Deus, contemplatio, claritas patriae coelestis, lumen veritatis.

Divine Sun, but also because she outshines all other saints as the
sun does the stars,

> Sol luna lucidior
> Et luna sideribus,
> Sic Maria dignior
> Creaturis omnibus,

because she illumines the world as does the sun, because her
love for mankind is like the heat of the sun, because she put to
flight the shadows of heathendom, and so forth.

In the early English poem *Earconwald* it is written: "In the
Sun's shrine now shines Mary." Strictly speaking, Mary is not
the Sun, but, as were the divine mothers of earlier religions,[108]
the gateway by which *Deus Sol* enters the world, and therefore
Aurora, the Dawn, the sacred East whence cometh Wisdom.
Nevertheless, it is possible to think of Christ as the principle of
light itself, and in that case Mary is the means by which light is
shed forth on the world, and so truly the Sun. Here is brought
out that law through which symbolic interpretation is ordered.
Though Mary be the Sun, she is also Dawn, the East, Gateway,
Vessel, Channel—that is, the Sun not as source of light primarily, but as that brightest of created objects through which
light is transmitted to the world. On the other hand, the symbol
of Sun as used for Mary makes it clear that the meaning of East
and of Gateway is not that she was a mere physical channel for
the entrance of Light into the world, but that she has a real and
continuous function in the Kingdom of Light. In other words,
in the use of the fourfold insight symbol there is a double check
—there must be not only the harmony of the four levels, but the
mutual correction of each other's inadequacies given by symbolic multiplicity within each level. Christ, like his Mother, is
the Sun, but he is also Eternal Wisdom, the Son of God, the

---

108. The God generates himself through the chosen Mother. (Cf. Mithra,
Osiris, and other myths.) There is, moreover, a close connection between the
birth and death of the God, that is, between Mary and the Cross, between the
Dawn and the Evening Twilight, "sweet Hesper-Phosphor, double name." Mary,
in the Old English "Dispute between Mary and the Cross" (in R. Morris, *Legends of the Holy Rood*, London, 1871) at length kisses the cross in reconciliation, because both together present Christ and redemption to the world. Moreover, there is a mystic equivalence, well known in Catholic devotion, between
the manger of Bethlehem, the cross of Calvary, and the Altar of the Eucharist.

Radiance of Uncreated Light, the Bread of Life. Thus, although one or the other may shine in the sun's shrine, there is no question of the replacement or dimming of one by the other.[109] Mary illumines the church as the sun the moon, but herself becomes the moon when Christ is described as the sun. In this way Mary becomes both sun and moon, and so illustrates the second type of symbolic association, the use of different symbols for the same reality.

Representation of the same reality by different symbols results from symbolic expressions associated through likeness of symbols. Albertus Magnus, in his *De laudibus Beatae Mariae Virginis,* has discussed in considerable detail associated imagery as traditionally connected with the Blessed Virgin. In his seventh book he lists twelve separate symbolic designations "quomodo Maria designatur coelestia et superiora." All of these naturally are connected with the sun and its light. *Sol, Lucifer, Aurora, Lux, Dies,* are directly connected; and very closely *Coelum, Firmamentum, Luna, Horizon, Diluculum,* and *Mane.* Finally, if Mary is called *Nubes*[110] it is with some such meaning as that she shelters man from the burning rays of the Sun of Righteousness.[111] After considering various Marian symbols drawn from earth and water, from architecture and war, Albertus concludes, in his twelfth book, with seven "de horto concluso qui sponsus comparat Mariam in Canticis." Garden imagery has a

109. Albertus Magnus, in *De laudibus B. Mariae Virg.,* 12, 7, 4, quotes a prayer of St. Bernard's to the Blessed Virgin: "Manet in te, o Domina, sol iste, et tu in eo; vestis eum, vestiris ab eo; vestis eum substantia carnis tuae, vestit ille te sua gloria majestatis; vestis nube solem, et tu ipse sole vestiris." Albertus says later (*ibid.,* 12, 7, 7): "Cherubim et Seraphim non lucent a se, sed a Deo qui solus lux est illuminans. Et ideo ducitur *sol,* quasi solus lucens. Caetera vero sunt lux illuminata."

110. Sometimes it is pointed out that the classical goddess appeared in a cloud, and that the idea, thus associated with deity, passed on to the Virgin Mary. The association accurately stated is the cloud which obscures the sun or tempers it to man's sight. This Mary does in more than one way: first, from her he received the human flesh which, as a cloud, tempered his radiance to human vision (cf. p. 287); second, at her intercession he tempers his justice with mercy (a conception familiar to all students of medieval religious literature); third, as an object of meditation, she is closer to human conceptions and affections than is he, and those may meditate with profit on her mysteries, who would be but dazzled by the glory of his.

111. The Sun veils himself for mortal eyes in the cloud of flesh (that is, God becomes incarnate). Albertus Magnus, *De laudibus B. Mariae Virg.,* 12, 2, 10.

manifest and permanent association with the 'sun.[112] It is through such freedom of association, based on the fundamental principle of analogy,[113] that the medieval symbolic method was maintained in a vitality and self-consistency foreign to uninspired systems of secret codes, and was made alike a stimulus to thought and a power over the personality.

That multiplicity of symbolism does not mean confusion and lawlessness, was stated at the outset and has been indicated in this chapter. Not only are there the psychological laws to govern association, and the fourfold method to guide, but there are laws of language more fundamental than grammar itself. A stranger on first acquaintance with the German language is appalled by the freedom with which new sesquipedalian and multipedalian words can be made up with apparently no rhyme or reason. In reality, construction of these words is governed by the same laws which govern the construction of the English phrase; and even those who through ignorance trespass against all rules of grammar, feel a wrongness when these laws are broken and the words cease to convey meaning. So it is with symbolism, but a consideration of its deeper laws belongs to the subject matter of the next chapter.

On the other hand even in the Middle Ages some confusion in regard to symbolic significations was inevitable, owing both to the acknowledged multiplicity and to the sudden separation from philosophic theory accomplished in the so-called Dark Ages. It was to meet such difficulty that throughout this period and the recovery from it, catalogues of symbolic meanings were compiled, and the fourfold method which was to keep in place each interpretation on its own level was put in the form of a popular rhyme as an aid to the more simple:

> Littera gesta docet, quid credas allegoria,
> Moralis quid agas, quo tendas anagogia.

On this method was based the prescribed outline in the Middle Ages for the sermon through which the people were to be instructed, usually by those little less uneducated than themselves:

112. It may be remembered also that twelve and seven are numbers with especial solar significance. Cf. labors of Hercules, signs of the zodiac, number of the Amesha-spentas, etc.
113. Cf. Appendix IV, Pt. I, i.

for example, an outline of a typical sermon in the Blickling homilies is:

I. Narrative of Jesus' ride to Jericho, curing blind man on way.
II. Statement that narrative involves a mystery.
III. Symbolical exposition:

   (1) The blind man signifies all mankind after the Fall.
   (2) Christ coming to Jericho, signifies Christ coming to light the path to eternal life.
   (3) The multitude who tried to restrain the blind man, signify carnal will and unrestrained lusts, which try to keep soul from appealing to Christ for mercy.
   (4) That the blind man asks for sight, not for money, teaches that we should ask for eternal light, not for transitory blessings.
   (5) The blind man sitting by the wayside, signifies those who believe in and follow God.

IV. Exhortations to forsake certain faults and obey God.[114]

The preacher who was unable himself to think correctly in symbolism, by the use of such dictionaries, especially if supplemented by the fourfold method as a sort of rule of thumb, could succeed fairly comfortably.

Such devices as the arbitrary sermon outline and the doggerel rule for mystical meanings were required, however, not only to guide where men's intellects were incapable of grasping the philosophic theory of insight symbolism in its ordering by the fourfold method, but also to guard against perversions by an entirely different method of "allegory," which became popular especially in connection with the developing drama. The personification allegory had no ancestry in common with the fourfold allegorical method as it dominated the literature of learning in the Middle Ages.

"ALLEGORICAL METHOD" VERSUS "ALLEGORY"

Neither fourfold nor expressing ambition to unravel the riddle of the universe, and lacking a continuous development

---

114. It is obvious that in sermons, save those delivered with special reference to monastic communities (cf. the sermons of St. Bernard on the Song of Songs) or to a learned audience, stress would be placed most frequently on the moral interpretation (trope) as in the above example. On special occasions, however, allegory and anagoge were placed before the people.

from the horizon of history, personification allegory presupposed not even the philosophy of symbolism. Its most illustrious
ancestor in the medieval tradition was Prudentius, for whom,
during the disintegration of the Empire, the battle of vices and
virtues, each one of which was personified, assumed dramatic
form as set forth in his *Psychomachia.* In Dante's tradition an
event having meaning in the objective world, through study of
its relationships in the pattern of the universe might become a
means of insight into the nature of a human person or organization; or of a vice, virtue, or tendency of the soul; or of eternal
life. But this symbolism, even on the level of the trope, where it
most closely resembled the tradition of the *Psychomachia,* is
dependent on actual objective relationships of the symbols, not
on arbitrary association, fanciful likeness, or personification.

Personification allegory is rather a reading into the universe
than a reading of what is there.[115a] Many students of the Middle
Ages have been repelled by this childlike construction of an artificial code. Just so were the medieval writers in the insight tradition, and in consequence they took pains—Hugh of St. Victor, Aquinas, and many another—to point out the essential
difference between the two methods. The term "the Word"[115b]
is not a code expression of that which is known about Christ,
but a symbol, meditation on which may lead one to an increasing understanding of the nature of infinite self-revelation in the
human realm. The medieval allegorical method is a series of
interlocking symbols of multiplex and mutually essential significations, no one of which can be understood apart from the
whole. It is an initiation into the unknown with a very definite
basis in the known.

115a. "Allegory starts with an idea and creates an imaginary object as its
exponent. If one starts with an actual object and from it receives the suggestion
of an idea, one is a symbolist." In other words, "The primary difference between
symbolism and allegory is that the former sees 'sermons in stones'; the latter
from phantom stones builds sermons." C. R. Post, *Medieval Spanish Allegory,*
pp. 4-5.

115b. It is interesting that a modern student of diseases of the brain has written: "The more we recognize what the presence of the *Logos* in man implies, the
plainer becomes the reason why he stands alone in this world." Wm. H. Thom-
son, *Brain and Personality,* pp. 78-79.

Indeed, in the last century, Huxley had written: "Our reverence for the nobility of manhood will not be lessened by the knowledge that Man is in substance
and in structure one with the brutes, for he alone possesses the marvellous en-
dowment of intelligible and rational speech." *Man's Place in Nature,* p. 119.

The personification allegory on the other hand is rather the dressing out of a preconceived abstraction in garments suggested by the mood of the occasion. In consequence it is powerless, by analogy of its function, to throw new light on the nature of the thing symbolized. Imaginative personification of the parts of the soul has a value in objectification. With the personification allegory there comes a simplification which is entertaining and morally instructive. It is, however, in no wise philosophically illuminating. Pride as an actor in the drama may be given a definite and direful career which affords welcome relief from the intricacies of life in the universe of reality, where the proud man does not always fall. In a sense the personification allegory like the *Romance of the Rose,* or like a tract even of so serious a nature as Bunyan's *Holy War,* represents a flight from reality rather than the unflinching quest of it which is the characteristic of insight symbolism.

In other words, in this which too frequently has been thought all of medieval symbolism, there is actually no symbolism,[116] because no duality of symbol and thing symbolized. The character really *is* that which it represents, in so far as it is anything at all. The populace might listen with childlike delight to tales of how Sloth and Avarice were properly overcome by Zeal and Brotherly Love, or behold on the stage the antics of costumed vices and grotesque demons as they were brought to grief by the powers of good. Such was not the humor of Dante when he wrote, "It should be known that writings may be taken and should be understood chiefly in four senses." Dante himself used the personification allegory for the purpose of adornment and picturesqueness in his pageant,[117] but beneath it all ran the full insight symbolism of the two-natured grifon, and the harlot who was the *lupa*.

It was in reality confusion in spirit between these two methods which was responsible for the dispute between advocates of

116. Although, as indicated in the Appendix to Chap. I, sec. iii, the dictionary allows many derived significations for the word "symbol," clearly indicative of our confusion in regard to the subject, in symbolism strictly understood there is necessary the duality of symbol and thing symbolized implied in the origin of the word itself.

117. For example, in the seven "handmaids" of Beatrice, who are the four cardinal and the three theological virtues.

the literal and allegorical interpretation of scripture. If, as in
the personification allegory, the whole interest is in a definite
and preconceived abstraction, the validity of the letter is in
reality of no material importance. The letter, however, has its
importance, if its functional validity forms the assurance of
validity for symbolic meanings, giving them an objective rather
than a subjective basis. Such was the case with scripture, that
second source of man's knowledge, complementary to nature,
which placed man above the beasts in enabling him to build on
the wisdom of the past. Scripture is functionally true, because
everything that happens in the world is an expression of, and,
therefore, like a projection, analogous to, the unseen and intangible.[118]

SUMMARY

Upheld by the triune Deity the very structure of the universe
bore witness to him, from the miracle of nine in the heavenly
spheres, to which the Empyrean added a mysterious and all-
inclusive tenth, to the kaleidoscopic and ever changing oneness,
twoness, threeness, and fourness which assumed so much significance throughout the universe, and in sum made up the ten.
Not only did the Sun rule beyond all time and space, but impress
of his unity and his trinity, his duality and the quaternity, was
stamped on the meanest elements of earth.[119] It is the unity and
the trinity which pertain to the essence of supreme reality,
which therefore are reflected in all that is, but it is the duality
and the quaternity which hold the secret of divine self-expression in creation.

Thus in the philosophy of the ultimate reality, which worked
itself out in the definition of the unity and trinity of the solar

118. It is evident from Dante's treatment of the Troy story, of the Aeneid, and
of events in Roman legend, as well as from his vision of the Car in the Earthly
Paradise, that he does not limit the divine message of history to the Old and
New Testaments. Not only scriptural but Roman history, both pre-Christian and
Christian, if viewed in a perspective inspired by grace, forms part of the divine
drama, and teaches in simultaneous symbolism of the incarnate life of Christ, of
the inner life of the soul, and of the life eternal wherein is the solution of the
earthly drama of conflict between the solar trinity and its negation. Cf. also p.
305 n. 187a.
119. Cf. medieval treatises on alchemy. Cf. also pp. 337 ff., and Chap. VI, iv.

god, was the basis for the symbolic method; whereas in the dual nature of the Second Person lay the definition of its function. Finally, symbolism was to accomplish this function through the fourfold method—literal, allegorical, tropological, and anagogical—as Christ accomplished his mission through his earthly, mystical, sacramental, and glorified bodies.[120] Like Christ, Dante, in the *Divina Commedia,* must deal with the ninefold reality of the universe by a fourfold method. Meanings on the four levels must be true at once and mutually consistent, as the bodies of Christ are the expression of the one Person. Thus was completed the quaternity of ultimate reality.[121]

120. Cf. p. 286 n. 125.
121. This quaternity was given usually, as for example in the philosophy of Plotinus, as the Trinity and the Matter on which it acts. Cf. also Chap. V.

Literal Level*	Allegorical Level	Tropical Level
The career of Christ in his earthly Body a Comedy begins under the shadow of the Cross, ends in the triumph of the Ascension	The career of Christ in his mystical Body, Humanity, a Comedy, begins in the awakening outside Eden, is to end in Paradise regained	The career of Christ in his sacramental Body a Comedy, begins in the breaking of bread, ends union with redeemed persona ties
I. Christ comes to himself in the *selva oscura* of the *mens humana*	I. Humanity comes to itself in the wilderness where jurisdictions of church and of empire are in conflict	I. Human personalities come themselves in the moral dilemr where jurisdictions of theolo and philosophy conflict
Escape barred by three temptations native to the *mens humana* he is redeeming: to gain its desires by underhand means, to gain its desires by violence, to desire wrongful dominion	Escape barred by three principles of disharmony: an empire without complete temporal power, nationalistic ambitions, a church with temporal power	Escape barred by three vice fraud, violence, and cupidity
Rescue, instituted by the Trinity, offered through working out of autonomy of human and divine natures, in subjection to empire (validation of redemption) leading to ideal church	Rescue, instituted by the Trinity, offered through working out of autonomies of empire and church	Rescue, instituted by the T unity, offered through worki out of autonomies of philosop and theology
II. Progress through agonies of earthly life, in increasingly vivid contact with threefold evil:	II. Progress through agonies of historical conflicts, in increasingly vivid experience of threefold menace to human organization:	II. Progress through agonies ethical development, in incre ingly vivid comprehension threefold root of sin:
Experiences of the ministry, with its revelation of burden of human nature in *gravezza*, leading up to omnious triumphal Entry into Jerusalem resulting in Experiences of the Passion, leading through betrayal to ultimate contact with evil in the crucifixion, presenting opportunity for the Harrowing of Hell, the way to triumphant entry into heaven	Experiences of *gravezza* in developing empire and church, leading up to ominous triumph of 313, resulting in Experiences leading through betrayal in the Donation, to the mutual eclipse of church and state, presenting opportunity for the coming of the Five-hundred ten-and-five who is to clear way for new empire and church	Experiences of growth throu theological and philosophical cc flict, leading up to ominous t umph in union of philosophy a theology, resulting in Experiences leading throu the betrayal of reason to inner e perience, to the mutual eclipse theology and philosophy, p senting opportunity for the res ration of the autonomies of p losophy and theology
Resurrection	Reconstruction	Reconstruction
Progress through the labors of the "Forty Days":	Progress through the labors of construction of a new polity, civil and spiritual:	Progress through the labors construction of a new intellectu tradition:
Reassurance of the apostles in their uncertainty Instruction and discipline of future leaders of the church he is founding Commission of future church (Matt. 28. 19; John 21. 15-17)	Establishment of true empire and church, to the reassurance of the well-meaning Discipline of citizens and training of honest officials for church and state Ideal state and church in operation	Establishment of sound p losophy and theology, to the assurance of the perplexed Popularization of knowlec in life (cf. aim as stated Epistle X) Harmoniously developed p sonalities
III. Christ at the top of the Mount ascends to the Right Hand of the Father, to return to the dual completion of his work (instatement in heaven of his mystical and sacramental bodies) in the mission of the Holy Spirit and in sacrament	III. Humanity from the height of ideal state and church is taken up into the Beatific Vision, to return for the perfection of the Rose in the dual glory of matter and spirit	III. Personalities from the h mony of Eden are taken up in the Beatific Vision, to return the completion of redemption the dual mantle (body and so cf. *Par.*, xxv, 121-129) of the l in glory

* For review of the literal order which forms the basis for these higher levels cf. chart of symbolism of the first order, p. 156, and for the relationship of orders cf. p. 98.

CHAPTER IV. SYMBOLISM IN MEDIEVAL THOUGHT: THE FOURFOLD METHOD, CONT.

PART II. DEVELOPMENT OF HUMANITY: THE SUN IMMANENT

I. SITUATION: POSSIBILITY OF "COMEDY"

EVEN those who look for many levels of symbolism in the *Divina Commedia* have been prone to become absorbed in the levels of the first order, those concerning Dante personally in relation to the politics and temptations of his time. One unfamiliar with the rigors of the fourfold method in its multiplicity easily may forget to read more deeply; but more than this, it is perhaps only some comprehension of the whole development of the symbolic tradition that can illumine the message which, in the long-sought reunion at the summit of the mount, Dante first read in Beatrice's eyes.

As Dante's personal story centered in Beatrice, the miracle who was a nine having as root the Trinity alone, so the solution of his personal problems, as represented in the progress from Moon to Sun, took place against the background of knowledge of the natural universe, that ninefold creation of the solar Trinity.[122] The philosophical and theological formulation of this Trinity was accomplished in the first five hundred years of the Christian era, although for the complete elaboration in life experience of the concept on which the *Divina Commedia* is built, the confusion of the succeeding centuries and the budding of chivalry and romance seem to have been required. Man had learned, however, that the stability of the trinitarian solution depended on solution of the problem of duality as it was at last accomplished in the incarnate Logos who came as at once the fulfilment and reconciliation of the messages of all scriptures.

In the symbolism of ultimate reality contained in the *Paradiso,* after the revelation of Tri-unity in the natural sun, the divine Logos suddenly becomes the center of attention and the symbolism changes from that of the Sun in nature to that of the Sun in scripture. In this connection those passages have been called to mind in which Dante implied that just as the aim of his *Comedy* was that of scripture, so was to be its interpreta-

122. Cf. Chap. II, i, pp. 32 ff.

tion. Thus the fourfold meaning of his personal life became itself the letter for the allegory which, like that of scripture, is to
tell of Christ and his four "bodies." Dante's gradual picturing
of himself as a type of Christ, wherein lay the ultimate significance of the whole of his personal life, has been suggested in
his journey through hell and purgatory.[123] In the Earthly Paradise, Beatrice herself appeared to him, not in especial relation to
the Tri-unity as the third of the three blessed ladies, but in definite relationship to the Second Person, whose twofold nature
was reflected from her eyes, while before Dante the whole of
human history was passed in review. In fine, the full revelation
of personal mission, to Dante's progressive comprehension of
which the *Divina Commedia* bears witness, brings the necessity
of another order of symbolism.[124]

The medieval insight allegory was a series of interlocking
symbols, even as the meter Dante chose for his *Commedia* was
a series of interlocking tercets, each one having a message of its
own, which, however, demanded that of the next for its completion. The poem may not stop with the symbolic aspects of a
personal story, but, like scripture, must tell of Christ, Second
Person of the solar Trinity, and that which his life, like the
sun's rays, both symbolizes and in sacrament accomplishes;
that is, the allegory of the journey of humanity toward God, and
the trope of the growth of the individual soul.

Christ's function as Logos and as the limit of an infinite progression of symbols is fulfilled literally before the eyes of man
in his earthly body; allegorically to humanity in his mystical
body through empire and church; tropologically in his sacramental body, through which the gift of grace is extended to each
soul. These bodies[125] are upheld by the fundamental reality in

123. Cf. pp. 179 ff., also pp. 287 ff. Cf. also p. 63 n. 128.
124. For the meaning of the terms "order" of symbolism, and "level" of symbolism, as used in this study, cf. pp. 95-98.
125. The term "earthly body" is used to signify the incarnate life of Christ
on earth. The term "mystical body" refers to the church. Thomas says: "Sicut
enim naturale corpus est unum ex membrorum diversitate consistens, ita *tota
Ecclesia, quae est mysticum corpus Christi,* computatur quasi una persona cum
suo capite, quod est Christus." (*S.Th.,* 3, *Q.* 49, *art.* 1.) Cf. Rom. 12. 5; I Cor.
12. 12 ff.; Eph. 1. 22-23; etc. The term "sacramental body" refers to the consecrated bread of the Eucharist, believed by Catholics to be in a special sense the
Body of the Lord. See *S.Th.,* 3, *QQ.* 75, 76, 79, 80, 81.

which all are included, his glorified body, by the sight of which in the Starry Heaven Dante was blinded, only to have his sight return, at last made adequate to Beatrice's smile. Of this deeper significance of his journey Dante became keenly conscious during that stage in his development described in the Earthly Paradise, where he beheld at last the Sun "rise shadowed,[126] so that by the tempering of the mists the eye long time endured him."

THE DARK WOOD

It is fitting then that the *Divina Commedia* should begin with the Dark Wood; for *Christ* himself, the Sun and Light, had become obscured in flesh, "flesh the cloud that hid the sun," and he came to consciousness of his human mission in the dark wood of humanity.[127] *Humanity* was without guidance in the days before Aeneas and before David, having fallen from its primal state of innocence.[128] The *individual* human person before the coming of grace finds himself in confusion, of which the "threefold detriment" is disorder of mind, liability to punishment, and weakness in following the good.[129] Thus Christ, not only directly in his incarnate life, but also in his extension of that life to humanity and to the individual, finds himself in the Dark Wood.

Dante points out in the *Monarchia*,[130] that the redemption which Christ came to bring would have been of no avail had not both Christ and all humanity been rightfully subject to the Roman emperor. In the Gospels Christ is shown as acknowledging the authority over himself of the Old Jewish Law, that is, of the

126. Cf. this imagery applied to the Incarnation "Veiled in flesh the Godhead see" in the Christmas carol "Hark, the herald angels sing," now become traditional. (The carol is ascribed to Charles Wesley, who wrote in the reaction against rationalism; but it came from his pen in a different form. He wrote "Hark, how all the welkin rings Glory to the King of kings" after hearing the church bells on his way to mass early Christmas morning. The herald angels are a later and rather unfortunate corruption.)

127. *Mens humana* is given as a meaning of *silva* by Rabanus Maurus.

128. Original sin "est enim quaedam inordinata dispositio proveniens ex dissolutione illius harmoniae in qua consistebat ratio originalis justitiae." Thomas Aquinas, *S.Th.*, 1, 2, *Q.* 82, *art.* 1.

129. *Ibid.*, 1, 2, *Q.* 109, *art.* 7, and 3, *Q.* 22, *art.* 3. In this regard it is to be noted that the incarnate Christ, who, according to the faith defined at Nicea and at Chalcedon and binding on the Catholic world, is not a human person (but an eternal divine Person who has taken human nature in addition to his own) voluntarily submitted to the result (death) of the detriment of original sin, from which he was himself free.

130. Cf. p. 46 n. 69, quoting from *Monarchia*, 2, 13.

church. According to Thomas Aquinas, Christ is the Head, not only of the church of the new law, but also of all mankind, and the church of the Jewish Fathers is an integral part of the one Catholic church.[131] Thus, for Christ as for Dante, the solar Trinity is represented on earth by the two suns of Rome, which in the time of Christ as in the time of Dante were in mutual eclipse. The Roman government had interfered outside its sphere in attempting supervision of the worship of the Temple; and the Jewish principles of separation had introduced an alien element into the Roman Empire.

THREEFOLD TEMPTATION

From this Dark Wood, having come to a consciousness of his human mission, in his baptism, Christ was led by the Spirit (the sun at dawn, his most appropriate symbol) into the wilderness (Dante's desert strand) where he was tempted first to turn stones into bread (which would have been a rebellion against the divine will which led him into the wilderness, and hence equivalent to the sin typified by the leopard); second, to cast himself down from the temple as a violent attempt to gain fame and attention of the people (lion); third, to gain all the kingdoms of the world by worship of evil, thus falling prey to cupidity, the she-wolf. These three beasts are to reappear dramatically in the course of the Passion. Even as they, especially the *lupa,* deprived Dante of all hope of direct ascent of the blessed mountain and drove him instead to gain Paradise through the realm of the lost; so human sin, rooted in cupidity (the *lupa*), rendered impossible the ascent of Christ in his earthly body—that is, with his burden of humanity—to his home in glory, by any other pathway than through the gates of hell. He, the Word, Radiance of the Divine Sun, was borne down by *gravezza* to the realm where the Sun is silent.

In this thought obviously there is no implication to Christ of sinning. God the Son, the Divine Person, completely sinless, bore the full burden of all sin. The exact meaning which this statement conveyed to the scholar in the Middle Ages is almost

131. Cf. p. 69 and n. 154. There is no contradiction involved in regarding Christ, for the fulfilment of his mission, as being subject in the course of his earthly life to the same church and empire of which he is the eternal Head.

beyond the apprehension of the scholar today who may no longer call to his assistance the keen instrument of thought and expression supplied in the univocal terminology of scholastic Latin. This bearing of sins was no mere legal fiction by which Christ "paid the price,"[132] but an inner identification by which, without personal guilt, he experienced the full mental and physical burden of all possible sin. In this fact lies the horror of the Passion, not in the obvious sufferings, though these comprised every kind of suffering known to man.[133] In his assumption of human nature he had subjected himself to the full experience of *gravezza,* an experience, it may be remembered, which is lessened not increased, by personal capitulation to the power of evil. The inevitable accompaniment of such capitulation, as Dante beheld in the dolorous realm, is the deadening of sensitiveness through intellectual detriment. Moreover it is the champion who has met every skill of his opponent and come out victorious, not the fighter who has been defeated, who has experienced, and may appreciate, the full capacity of the adversary. Not only in figure, then, did Christ, guiltless on the Cross, mourn his *delicta* (transgressions),[134] but with actual identification.[135]

This voluntary bearing of *gravezza* and its punishment, Thomas Aquinas himself connects with human penitence, of which it was the only example Christ could give.[136] Since anything may be the symbol of that which is its divine Exemplar, Dante's penitence for his own actual guilt is rightly a type of Christ's pleading his willing and innocent assumption of the burden of the sins of all the world. If it seem strained to see in Dante, guilty of actual capitulation to *gravezza,* a type of the earthly life of Christ, let this fact be remembered; and the further fact that every character ever discussed in the Middle Ages as a type of Christ was himself perforce guilty of sin.[137] More than this, frequently it was in the sinful act itself that the

132. Although often popularly so designated.
133. Thomas Aquinas, *S.Th.,* 3, *Q.* 46, *art.* 5.
134. Thomas Aquinas, *S.Th.,* 3, *Q.* 15, *ad primum.*
135. Identification implied in H Cor. 5. 21 and Isa. 53. 6. Cf. Thomas Aquinas, *S.Th., loc. cit., ad quartum.*
136. Thomas Aquinas, *S.Th., loc. cit., ad quintum.*
137. Cf. p. 291 n. 149.

analogy to the earthly life of Christ was found. In typology acts
are viewed objectively, without primary regard to moral responsibility. The same external act varies as to its moral coloring
with actor and circumstances. For example, Noah, sinful in his
drunken nakedness,[138] was none the less in that sin a type of the
sinless Christ, who, naked in the Crucifixion, was in the Passion
as it were inebriated by the Cup of the Agony, and this, moreover, like Noah, in his own house, that is, among his own race
and kindred.[139] Even the jeering of Ham was not missing, nor
the later scorn of mankind visited on those who jeered.[140]

It was the custom in scripture reading to regard the characters
of the Old Testament as types of Christ, wherever possible,
for the complete written drama of their lives.[141] For example,
David's whole life was worked out in detail[142] (including an
appropriateness even to the sin with Bathsheba) as typical of
him who was to come of the House of David, to insure that for
all eternity a King of that House should reign.[143] Indeed, if life
stories, like all else in the universe, were to be interpreted in accord with the fourfold method, it was necessary that they contain, on the level of allegory, a significance in regard to human
history, with its center and culmination in revelation through
the Logos. By means of such interpretation all scriptures, at first
mere writing down of unrelated bits of chronicle, verse, moral
precept, biographical anecdote, and even fiction, became a coherent record of the manifestation of the infinite to man, of
which the fulfilment to the Christian lay in the Incarnation.
Thus, allegorical reading of the Old Testament affirmed the lit-

138. See Gen. 9. 20-23.
139. Noah's sin is thus interpreted by Ambrose, Augustine, Isidore of Seville,
Rabanus Maurus, and others.
140. See Gen. 9. 24-25, a passage used to justify the feeling that the descendants of Ham were by divine command to be held in subjection. Among medieval
Christians a similar attitude prevailed toward the Jews, who were regarded as
responsible for the crucifixion.
141. P. 478 n. 7b.
142. For example, cf. the treatment by Hilary (Migne, *P.L.*, 9: 844), Ambrose
(*P.L.*, 14: 251, 314, 861, 883; 15: 1506; 17: 833), Augustine (*P.L.*, 36: 73,
148, 154, 245, 302, 305, 315, 600, 603, 619, 628, 646, 663-664, 713, 716; and
37: 1238, 1845), Paulus of Nola (*P.L.*, 61: 248, 251), Cassiodorus (*P.L.*, 70:
35, 43, 193, 1015), Gregory the Great (*P.L.*, 79: 461, 505, 509, 642), and
others.
143. Cf. Ps. 132. 11-12.

eral sense of the Gospels,[144] so that even those who denied the importance of all literal sense as such in the scripture, found in its allegorization reaffirmation of the literal story of the Incarnation.[145] Dante's *Commedia,* then, as claiming identity of purpose with scripture,[146] and all the similarities to which reference has been made,[147] must similarly reaffirm the literal truth of the life of Christ in his earthly body. This it must do through the story of him whose Comedy it is.[148] Further, Dante's story in many details fell naturally into the pattern of that of the Galilean, whose Comedy is scripture.[149]

Herein is another difficulty for the modern student, to whom the story of the life of Christ appears anything but a comedy. Even Dante's definition of a comedy as that which from a beginning in catastrophe culminates in bliss,[150] seems scarcely to apply to the life which sprang up amid the idyllic scenes of Bethlehem to end on the cross of Calvary. Several facts must be called to assistance: first, to the thinking of the Middle Ages,

144. The reason given for the failure of those living before the Incarnation, to understand the truth of it from the types prefiguring it, was the intellectual detriment due to the Fall.

145. Here is not an argument in a circle, that is, construction of an allegory after the pattern of the gospel life, as the poet might do, and argument therefrom as to the validity of the literal story. The allegory was governed by its own laws. It made clear that an incarnation of the Logos in human history was inevitable, and that when it occurred, its circumstances must be such as were recorded in the Gospels. See n. 149, below.

146. Cf. pp. 31, 63 n. 128, etc., and Appendix IV, Pt. I, i.

147. Cf., e.g., pp. 63-64, 161, 178, 294 n. 156, etc.

148. Of course, this in no way bars the seeing in the *Commedia* of other types of Christ as well, as, for example, Beatrice in the Pageant, the Grifon, and others.

149. "Every word contained in the sacred volume announces by word, explains by facts, and corroborates by examples the coming of our Lord Jesus Christ, sent by his Father, and born a man of a Virgin, through the operation of the Holy Spirit. From the beginning of the world, Christ, by authentic and absolute prefigurations in the persons of the Patriarchs, gives birth to the Church, washes it clean, sanctifies it, chooses it, places it apart and redeems it; by the sleep of Adam, by the deluge in the days of Noe, by the blessing of Melchizedech, by Abraham's justification, by the birth of Isaac, by the captivity of Jacob. . . . The purpose of this work is to show that *in each personage, in every age, and in every act,* the image of his coming, of his teaching, of his resurrection, and of our Church, is reflected as in a mirror." (Italics inserted for the present purpose.) Hilary of Poitiers, *Tractus mysteriorum,* I, 1, to be found in *Corpus scriptorum ecclesiasticorum,* vol. 65. Translation taken from Labriolle, *op. cit.,* p. 243.

150. The wish mentioned by Dante, that one's friends might have "a tragic beginning and a comic ending," that is, that both beginning and ending might be happy, would be taken quite differently today.

the life of Christ did not begin in Bethlehem, nor did it end on Calvary. That infinite Being, whom all the world had learned under one form or another to reverence as the Logos, had possessed divine consciousness from eternity. The awakening to finite human consciousness in Bethlehem, for one still in full possession of divine consciousness, was not to be termed a happy beginning. A fit comparison is hypothetical awakening to the limited consciousness of a reptile,[151] on the part of a man under sentence of a life and death to be experienced, while still in full possession of human consciousness, completely limited by the reptilian body and by the laws of the reptilian community.

More than this, the awakening was not to the bucolic scenes of the pastoral life, but to the imminence of the Cross. He whose emotional conception of the Nativity has been molded by such carols as "Hark, the herald angels sing" and "God rest ye, merry gentlemen," knows but one aspect of the medieval feeling for Christmas. Let him study and feel the minor of even so available a carol as the "Endris Night," and he will appreciate a little of the difference. In the words of the Child spoken in answer to his mother's "Lully my child and slepe," is conveyed his consciousness of a life to be lived under the shadow of doom. "I may not slepe, but I may wepe, I am so wo-begone. . . . Adam's guilt this man has spilt, that sin greveth me sore— Man for thee here shall I be, thirty winter and more." From this catastrophic beginning in limitation and conscious anticipation of the agony of Calvary[152] with its burden of human wickedness, the comedy progressed to the triumph of the Resurrection over

151. Though such illustrations as reptile, ant, etc., were used, no animal they could choose would really give the feeling to the medieval mind. The distance between God and man, being that between the infinite and the finite, was itself thought of as infinitely greater than any difference between finites, even between man and the lowest of creatures.

152. Further light on the medieval point of view in regard to both Bethlehem and Calvary as essentially eternal and mutually related, is thrown by the "Legend of the Cross." According to this tale, as well known as was the canonical tale of Eden, Adam, two hundred years after the killing of Abel, begets Seth. When Seth is grown, Adam, ill, sends him to Eden to beg from the guarding angel the "oil of compassion" which God had promised him. Seth, arrived at Eden gate, is permitted to look within. He sees a great tree reaching to the sky and surrounded by a great serpent. In the top of the tree is a newborn babe in swaddling clothes. The roots of the tree penetrate through the ground to touch the body of the murdered Abel. Seth is told by the angel that the babe is the Son of God, weeping over human misfortunes, and that he is himself the "oil of compassion,"

the power of *gravezza,* with its reunion of matter and spirit and its promise of the reconciliation of all opposites in an eternity at last attainable by human nature. In the Ascension Christ carried with him that limited human consciousness so full of agony from Bethlehem to Calvary,[153] now made adequate even to the demands of the infinite upon it, and capable of raising with it all humanity. Thus the disordered motion inaugurated in the Fall was brought into harmony with the immutable and divinely determined action of the spheres.[154]

which Adam may not have before five thousand years have passed. (That is, he receives it at the Harrowing of Hell. Cf. p. 180, especially footnotes.)

The angel finally gives Seth three apple seeds from the tree. These he is to place in Adam's mouth when he dies. (Cf. the medieval custom of giving three grass blades to those dying too far from priest and altar to receive the last sacraments.) From these seeds in Adam's mouth grow three kinds of tree growing as one. From this strange tree Moses cuts three rods and plants them on Mt. Tabor. David, while still hoping to be permitted to build the temple, has logs cut and brought to Jerusalem, of which this tree contributes one. From it such an odor comes forth that all the people are filled with the grace of God. During the night, however, the log raises itself upright and grows roots. Later, during the construction of Solomon's temple, a beam is cut from this miraculous tree, thirty cubits long; but no cutting enables it to fit the place where it is needed. Hence Solomon directs it to be stored in the temple. While it is still lying on the ground, a woman comes into the temple, and, weary, sits on it. At once her clothes take fire, and she prophesies, worshiping Jesus by name as God. The Jews promptly burn her, the first martyr for his Name, and cast the beam out of the temple.

The beam, however, retains its miraculous powers. Queen Sebile (a reminiscence both of the Sybil and of the Queen of Sheba) on her visit to Solomon prophesies that it is to become green again through the power of holy blood. This prophecy is fulfilled, for at the time of Christ's condemnation to death, an old Jew suggests the beam as a suitable piece of wood from which to form the Cross.

The story in Malory is a combination of this version with another in which the tree grows, not from three seeds, but from a sprout of the tree of life, growing in three colors, white, green, and red.

153. The discussion as to whether the Incarnation was necessitated only by the Fall is interesting, but that which is here important is that, had there been no Fall, even if the Incarnation had taken place, it would have lacked the elements of limitation and agony. (Aquinas stated that, except for sin, there could have been no separation of soul and body.) As it was, however, the enchantment of Circe, empowered through EVA, was unspelled by reversal through her who was hailed by the word AVE. Tertullian (in *De carne Christi,* cap. xvii) points out that Eve at the word of the devil bore Cain, while Mary at the word of the angel bore Christ. Aquinas ascribes the opening of the wound of original sin to Eve, the healing of it to Mary (*S.Th.,* 1, 2, Q. 85, *art.* 3). In a similar spirit Bernard, comparing Mary to a rose (cf. p. 79 n. 190) names Eve as the thorn. Cf. the inverse relationship of threefold good to threefold evil (table, p. 236), of the structure of hell, the Mount of Purgatory, etc., and the conception of the reversal of a spell.

154. The Fall involved a wrong motion on the part of man, and was punished by the granting of independent motion to parts of man's body (Augustine's

The infinite suggestiveness of Dante's symbolism is appreciated anew through the interpretation of this order, with respect to the equivalence in the Word, of voice and light. The Word, the Radiance of the Divine Sun, is driven down to the realm where the Sun is silent. The silence or lack of voice in the earthly vicarates had plunged the world into a chaos from which redemption was possible only through the living Word. When a wolf meets a man and sees him first, he deprives him of speech. Reversing this spell: the downfall of the *lupa* can be accomplished only by the all-seeing Logos.

Humanity, which constitutes Christ's mystical Body, lost like the human Christ in the Dark Wood of a nature deformed, more prone to evil than to good, and doomed to eternal punishment[155] as a result of Adam's sin,[156] is faced by the three vicious beasts: temptation to fraud, temptation to violence, and that inordinate desire for finite and temporal goods without which the first two temptations could have little power to terrify. It is humanity's greed, as Dante points out over and over again, that drives it down to hell.

Similarly, it is the blind cupidity of the individual which subjects him to suffering, whether that suffering be efficacious to heal or only to punish. Christ's sacramental Body extended to each individual member of the mystical Body, must for all time suffer under the laws which govern the victory of the Divine Sun.

One of the deepest truths of the drama of the Redemption, to Dante's mind, is that in this situation the Divine Sun himself is powerless except as he may act through organized humanity,

---

theory of the origin of sex impulses, in his *De civitate Dei*). To right the wrong motion, an unusual motion on the part of the Divine Sun was required. Cf. p. 304.

155. Cf. the threefold detriment. Thomas Aquinas, *S.Th.*, 1, 2, *Q.* 109, *art.* 7, and 3, *Q.* 22, *art.* 3.

156. Dante, as he symbolizes the history of Christ's mystical body, fulfils also the mission of Aeneas and of Paul. Cf. p. 179.

Such a conception was consistent with the feeling of the times. Francis and his followers had lived the life of Christ and his disciples, in all its details of poverty, acceptance of alms, and vagrancy, because such was the corruption which deprived the world of the true church, that renewal seemed possible only through a reënactment of the life out of which the Christian church had been born. This same idea was carried even farther in Dante's suggested representation, not only of Christ in his four bodies, but specifically with regard to the mystical body, his fulfilment of the mission of Aeneas, who in founding Rome "prepared Peter's mantle," and of the mission of Paul, who spread the Gospel.

made his representative on earth. Humanity can be redeemed by Christ's suffering, only if that suffering be inflicted by a *de jure* governor over all mankind. As Dante was led by Virgil, symbol of the pagan empire, so Christ, under the same authority—indeed, announced by the pagan poet—was to journey to the accomplishment of his mission.[157]

The budding church and empire were guided by Virgil's writings, as the soul is guided by "prevenient grace"[158] till it comes to the sacramental grace of Christ. None is more fitted to symbolize the guide of the individual soul in its efforts toward growth in virtue than he whose writings were interpreted by the Middle Ages as portraying the growth of a soul through youth and manhood and old age.[159]

THREEFOLD RATIFICATION OF REDEMPTION

Christ's reason for accepting the overlordship of the Empire as the condition of his redemptive passage through the maze of human suffering,[160] is of course the ratification of imperial authority by the Blessed Trinity,[161] symbolized here by Mary, Lucia, and Beatrice. Similar is the ground of acceptance of Virgil's guidance by all humanity and by individual souls. Virgil, though ignorant of his prophetic mission, is sent through *gratia gratis data*[162] by the triune God; and prevenient, like all grace, is the gift of the Trinity, of whom the Three Ladies function on all levels as the surrogates. The Holy Spirit is sent by Father and Son to initiate the salvation of man by giving him first the lesser member of each of the all-important pairs—empire and church, philosophy and theology, cardinal and theological virtues, action and contemplation. Likewise, it is the Holy Ghost

---

157. Cf. Dante's argument as to the necessity of the Crucifixion taking place under an authority having lawful jurisdiction over all mankind, in order to render it valid for the redemption of all mankind. *Monarchia*, 2, 13.

158. Cf. Thomas Aquinas, *S.Th.*, 1, 2, Q. 111, *art.* 3.

159. Cf. p. 272.   160. Cf. p. 46, especially n. 69.

161. Cf. Dante's argument as to the divine origin of the authority of the Roman Empire, in his *Monarchia*.

162. Grace given to enable the recipient to act as the instrument of God in a given situation, as opposed to *gratis gratum faciens*, grace given to promote the recipient's own spiritual advancement. Evil men, and even animals (for example, Balaam's ass), may receive *gratia gratis data*. Cf. Thomas Aquinas, *S.Th.*, 1, 2, Q. 111, *art.* 1.

who guides humanity to its rightful organization in church and empire, as it is the Holy Ghost who is to preserve the church from final error. Nor does the Holy Ghost come to guide humanity apart from his "mission" by the Father and the Son.[163] Thus empire and church have been given divine ratification as guides to humanity, as have philosophy and theology as guides to the individual soul. Man has but four ways of knowing, two external and two internal: nature and revelation, reason and faith[164]—nature and reason giving rise to philosophy, revelation and faith to theology.

More than this the Holy Spirit initiator of Christ's earthly journey, through Beatrice initiated for Dante his symbolic progress. Dante's first sight of Beatrice, as stated in the *Vita Nuova,* initiated his new life in love, as the Annunciation inaugurated the supreme expression of God's love to the world. Thus the *Vita Nuova* may be taken not only as a promise, but as an organic prologue of the *Divina Commedia.* Christ's childhood and youth may be represented in those experiences of which Dante in this prologue has left us a record. It is then with real meaning that the *Commedia* opens: "Nel mezzo del cammin di nostra vita mi ritrovai per una selva oscura, chè la diritta via era smarrita."[165] The Dark Wood is not only a setting for the drama, but also carries over into it that which has gone before.

Beatrice's second mission to Dante, mediated through Virgil, is the initiation of his journey, and may well suggest those circumstances of divine intervention which marked Christ's official entry upon his mission sponsored by the Holy Spirit in the form of a dove. Interpreted on this level, then, the action of the *Inferno* subsequent to the arrival of Virgil, begins with the years of Christ's public ministry.

To many a reader it has seemed unnatural that actual en-

163. The reading of Beatrice as primarily surrogate in Dante's vision for the Holy Spirit, is the only interpretation which explains without awkwardness why she does not come to Dante's relief without being sent by Mary and Lucia. Cf. Thomas Aquinas, *S.Th.,* 1, *Q.* 43.

164. As stated by Peter Lombard in the *Sentences.* "Faith" is a supernatural interior gift, by which the individual knows spiritual things as by the reason he knows natural things.

165. "In the middle of the journey of our life I came to myself in a dark wood where the straight way was lost." *Inf.,* i, 1-3.

trance into the city of the lost could lead to the salvation of a human soul. For an individual, a clear view of sin and of the means of escape from it might have been won by a progress through purgatory alone, even had there been needed to initiate his upward climb, other vision of the sins with which he was in personal contact. From hell no medieval theologian admitted possibility of salvation except by miracle. Hence Charon's venomous taunt:

> Guai a voi, anime prave!
> non isperate mai veder lo cielo:
> i' vegno per menarvi a l' altra riva
> ne le tenebre etterne, in caldo e 'n gelo. . . .[166]

That is no one individual needs complete experience of sin in all its aspects; indeed, the effect of such experience could never be salutary.[167] When Dante is representative of humanity, or of Christ its Head, then only is the rigid necessity of the symbolism of the *Inferno* apparent. Dante representing Christ in his earthly, mystical, sacramental, and glorified lives, was of necessity compelled to experience the full reaches of hell and the peculiar power of each sin, even of those of which he had never been particularly guilty—since only thus could Christ redeem humanity; only thus could humanity, prey to cupidity, attain to blessedness under subjection to a rightful ruler. Though in the full experience of hell the individual too must share, he shares through his sacramental union with Christ—to share otherwise were perdition.

II. PROGRESSION: DRAMA OF HISTORY

AFTER entering with Dante and with Christ the gate of hell, it would be possible to undertake a detailed study of all that Dante may have read of history or in connection with the life of Christ, and then to compare texts, hoping to link the circles in hell with

166. "Woe to you, depraved spirits! hope not ever to see Heaven! I come to lead you to the other shore; into the eternal darkness; into fire and into ice." *Inf.*, iii, 84-87. Cf. the inscription on the gate.

167. It has been noted that on each level Dante's behavior reflected the sin there punished, however foreign to his personal character, and although he is, as Virgil declared him, "without fault that merits torment." *Inf.*, xxviii, 46-48.

definite events in the ministry and passion, in the history of the race, and in the experience of grace. Although, if space permitted, some light might be thrown by such a study, the method is not in accord with the spirit of the symbolism of the *Inferno*. Similarly, whereas definite periods in human history may be recognized,[168a] it is against the spirit of the *Inferno* that a consistent picture should be given. No symbolic signification in the *Inferno* is in itself decisive, since it depends on the further experience of Purgatory and Paradise for its illumination. Moreover, the Middle Ages had no coherent life of Christ. The inconsistency of the Gospels was recognized, but thorough reconciliation such as is attempted by modern criticism and by gospel harmonies had not been deemed necessary.

PREPARATION AMID FAILURE

Christ's ministry on earth was divided by medieval thought into two periods: the earthly ministry and teaching, which was of secondary importance; and the Passion, which gave to the former its significance. Hell was divided into two sections: upper hell, through which flit the shadowy forms of leopard, lion, and wolf; and lower hell, in which the beasts appear in all their loathsomeness as in complete opposition to the Trinity.

Upper hell, separate from the Tri-unity, full of darkness and inconsistency, may well represent the setting of the ministry of Christ, his Godhead unrecognized, previous to the entry into Jerusalem. Its circles, however much more they may mean, certainly represent classes of men to whom Christ preached. Indeed, he moved among victims of the Great Failure, preaching to the wealthy and to the gross, to the avaricious and to the prodigal, to the angry and to the indifferent. The story of Paolo and Francesca stands out for the tenderness of Dante's treatment, as does the story of the woman taken in adultery, among Christ's contacts with sin on earth.[168b]

168a. Cf. p. 305, especially n. 187a.
168b. The difference between the eternal loss of Francesca and the probable salvation of the woman taken in adultery, does not destroy this analogy. Dante could not, in the literal story, represent himself as having the power to forgive Francesca's sin and raise her to renewed union with God. That Dante would not consider damnation as a bar to symbolic interpretation in a good sense, is indicated in his placement of Marcia in Limbo, although he had used her in a previous writing as a type of the noble soul who seeks and receives union with God.

Humanity ideally was ever the Body of Christ, but in its own utter unconsciousness of that fact, and far from the goal of its unity as the Eagle,[169] it had wandered for centuries through such scenes as those of upper hell, where the very rain had lost its power to bring fertility.[170] It had found itself in a vicious circle from which there seemed as little possibility of escape as from the "starless realm." From the enchantment of the circling which bored deeper and deeper into hell, humanity might obtain deliverance into that circular motion which is the fulfilment of solar law, only through sharing in the life of the solar god.

Similarly, the journey of the individual is beset by conflict within and without, of so devastating a nature as to draw him toward the doleful city where that which is willed cannot be done. His rescue lies only in the realization of his sacramental union with the Logos, in whom is the harmony of action and the perfect union of all opposites. Man not unified is not a person, but merely, as Josiah Royce once expressed it, a "psychological specimen," through which flow, as through an unresisting river channel, streams of changing psychic experiences in controversy with each other.

Upper hell had differed from lower hell since Christ's harrowing of it.[171] Previous to this time, upper hell also had been ruled by devils, and its atmosphere had been that of Dis (as previous to Christ's coming ordinary earthly life had lain, as it were, in the shadow of the grave). After this time the atmosphere had been changed, and to its two upper circles at least had been regiven the gifts of desire and love for the highest they had perceived. Indeed in Limbo, realm of the good pagans and soil of Greek philosophy which was to give power to Christ's life and

169. Cf. pp. 71 ff.

170. Dante's idea would seem to be not unlike that of Mr. Kipling in his *Ship That Found Herself*. The bolts, rods, screws, pistons, etc., selfishly and with no understanding, fight each other throughout their first ocean journey and their first storm, speaking with many and discordant voices, and doing damage to themselves and to each other. At last, however, the voices merge in one, and the Ship says "I." Not until then is she truly a ship. It is evident that Mr. Kipling intended this parable to read allegorically of a nation, and it is probable that, were the idea suggested to him, he would acknowledge its tropical applicability in respect to the individual's self-discovery, and even its anagogical truth in relation to eternal life in that heaven where, as he has put it, the artist eternally shall "draw the thing as he sees it, for the God of things as they are."

171. Cf. *Inf.*, viii, 124-130.

teaching, there is constant hint of mystery and promise. Greek philosophy had been tried and found not wrong but wanting. The meaning here is that for humanity philosophy must be illumined by her sister, theology; and the intellect of the individual by grace,[172] acting normally through the sacraments of the church. Nevertheless, although man may perceive only that good pagans, not having known Christ, must dwell forever in desire, apart from God; the Eagle's answer to Dante's question in the *Paradiso*[173] suggests that on earth all may not be understood of God's plan for those who lived previous to, or geographically remote from, his supreme self-revelation.

CONFLICT AMID DEFIANCE

In Dis there is not merely separation from Tri-unity, and foreboding reminiscence of leopard, lion, and wolf, but all the odium of defiance becoming even more naked in its blatant ugliness as the cone of hell narrows throughout the lower circles. Although Christ's entry into Jerusalem was a triumph similar to the divinely accomplished entry into the infernal city, it was a triumph full of foreboding. There were demons in human nature eager to destroy him, although through his perfect obedience to law, he was destined, like the perennial sun god, to rise again unharmed, leaving ruin among the powers of darkness by the great ardor of his love.

Here is, indeed, a foreshadowing of the ultimate Harrowing of Hell,[174] to take place in fact only after Christ has come into the closest possible physical contact with Satan, as Dante's mission of rescue began only after expulsion from his city.[175] It may be recalled that, in the level of symbolism relating to Dante's personal venture, the entry into Dis was compared to Christ's whole conquest over evil. Virgil himself made the comparison.[176] In this there was no confusion for the medieval symbol-

172. Cf. Peter Lombard's analysis of the sources of knowledge, cited p. 97 n. 249.
173. Cf. pp. 72-73.
174. Cf. p. 180, footnotes, for legend of the Harrowing of Hell.
175. Cf. p. 201.
176. Obviously this is the spirit of Virgil's words, rather than any conception that (in the order of symbolism in which Dante typifies Christ) the entry into Dis typifies the Harrowing. Such a superficial reading would be impossible. First,

ist. With the triumphal entry into Jerusalem the process was definitely initiated, which was to result at last in the triumphal entry into heaven. (It is of significance that the Jewish ritual phrase of the pilgrims on approach to the temple was used in the account of the Harrowing of Hell to herald Christ's entry into the infernal region, even as it was used in the church ceremonial to herald his entry into heaven on Ascension Day.) For Christ in the Passion, as for Dante in Dis, the road to man's redemption lay through the intimate revelation and experience of all evil,[177] and to this level of interpretation most of all belongs the full meaning of Plutus, Phlegyas, and Geryon, with the cold, spiritual death beneath.

Humanity, Christ's mystical Body, shares this vision, having been taken up by Christ into union with God. Humanity, however, after Constantine, having lost its illumination through the eclipse of the two suns, lay under the necessity of experiencing in its own organization the evils of hell. This Dante frequently points out with especial reference to Florence.

Similarly each individual, through Christ's sacramental body, as he realizes his relationship to Christ, will know of evil according to the measure of his capacity. The experience however must be directed by God and accomplished under the guidance of his instruments on earth, for as Dante realizes poignantly, any other experience of hell subjects the soul to the doom of Medusa. The value of Dante's imagery here would seem to be that found by Charles Kingsley in the Book of Revelation, the grotesque and chaotic imagery of which, he said in a lecture, explained to him the condition of Rome during the barbarian invasions.

Just as Christ's life was a drama, of which the crisis was in

since in the story of the Harrowing, Christ's mission of rescue began only after physical contact with Satan, which, though taking place for him before the gate of hell, took place for Dante only in Cocytus where Christ had cast the Arch Deceiver. Second, because the initiation of Dante's mission of rescue took place only after Cocytus and not on his entry into Dis. Third, because the journey through hell itself is typical only of the mission of ministry and passion upon which Christ, having been born into the *silva* which is the *mens humana,* entered officially after the baptism by the Holy Spirit, symbolized by the Dove, as to Dante by Beatrice. (Cf. pp. 40 n. 48, 99 n. 251, 237 n. 514—both the Dove and Beatrice are represented by the number "nine.")

177. Cf. pp. 289 ff.

the betrayal; so also was the history of the world, and the crisis was similarly a betrayal, the Donation of Constantine:

> l'aguglia vidi scender giù ne l' arca
> del carro e lasciar lei di sè pennuta:
> e qual esce di cuor che si rammarca,
> tal voce uscì del cielo e cotal disse:
> "O navicella mia, com mal se' carca!"[178]

(Here is suggested Christ's mourning over Jerusalem as he was to enter the city of his betrayal.) Yet strange as it may seem to modern thought both were comedies, since both, precipitated by evil, were to culminate in triumph and joy. This triumph was to be brought within the reach of each individual, under the aegis of church and empire, through the sacraments.

In the drama of betrayal a cord precipitates the Pyrrhic victory of evil. God had given into the hands of the empire such authority to govern rightly as could compass the destruction of the leopard. This authority was, instead, to compass the descent of God incarnate into the realm of darkness. The incarnate Logos, through his inclusion of Judas in the number of the disciples, gave into the hands of the empire the means by which he should suffer the perennial doom of the sun god. Even so Dante gave into the hands of Virgil the cord which was to summon the savage reptile with human head and scorpion tail,[179] on whose back Dante was to suffer the dread descent. The tail of Geryon, striking treacherously from behind, is a veritable Judas lance, and is appropriately concealed at his first appearance. Dante describes him as sitting on the ledge of the precipice, his fair and honorable countenance raised in greeting, his venomous tail hanging down, like that of the beaver of folklore, into the abyss. There was a legend well known in the Middle Ages and

---

178. "I saw the eagle descend down into the body of the car, and leave it feathered with his plumage. And as a voice comes from a heart that sorroweth, such voice came from heaven, and thus it spake: 'O my little bark, how ill art thou laden.' " *Purg.*, xxxii, 125-129.

179. The genealogy of Geryon has been traced as follows: Solinus, copying Pliny (*Historia naturalis*, 8, 30) describes an uncouth creature Mantichora. With Albertus Magnus it becomes Marintomorion (*De animalibus*, 22, 2, 1) and eats the men it beguiles. In Brunetto Latini's *Tresor* (5, 59) it appears as an Indian monster Manticore, with a man's face, a lion's body, and a scorpion's tail. It is a devourer of human flesh. Dante calls it Geryon and makes it a symbol of fraud. The smooth and gentle countenance may have been suggested by the comment of Thomas Aquinas on Rev. 9. 7-11.

indeed current in the fables of many northern peoples, that the beaver catches fish by sitting on the bank and allowing his tail to hang into the water as a bait. Thus the Judas Geryon sat waiting for Christ, ἰχθῦς, the Fish,[180] plotting to bear him down to the realm of eternal impotence. Satan little dreamed that he himself would be the means for the triumph whereby *Ichthus* by his death provided the waters of baptism for the home of the little fishes who are his redeemed.[181] In plotting, he angled for the *Ichthus* through the Geryon Judas, the sin of whose traitorous tail was a treason, the outgrowth of peculation in office,[182] which declared his kinship with Geryon's other-self, the leopard.

Having looked upon the mild visage of the beast whose markings betrayed him as kin to the leopard, Dante was sent apart, that, in loneliness, his experience might be full, "Acciocche tutta piena esperienza." Christ, having looked upon the face of his betrayer and given him the sop, went apart to await the moment when, like Dante in the *Commedia,* he should be delivered over to fraud and treachery. At this moment of impending doom Dante, like Christ in the Garden, is definitely alone.

Even Virgil's protection of Dante from harm by the tail of the beast into whose power he was none the less given over is an appropriate symbolism. It was Roman authority which deprived the Jewish council of the right of inflicting the death sentence, and therefore insured that Christ should die, not under local Jewish authority, but under the authority of the empire. That is, in Dante's view, the Spirit of Empire, protecting Christ from the Jewish death penalty, enabled him so to suffer as to redeem all humanity.[183]

The cord has been variously interpreted, especially by those interested in pointing a moral. Politically, it may represent legitimate self-seeking, which none the less attracted the demons of hypocrisy and kindred vices; or Dante's reliance in political

180. Cf. pp. 141 n. 117 and 235 n. 100.
181. Cf. pp. 140-141, also p. 435.
182. Since the love of financial reward which proved the undoing of Judas was nourished by the fact that he was the treasurer of the little company which followed Jesus during his ministry. Cf. John 12. 6 and 13. 29.
183. Cf. p. 46 n. 69, quoting from *Monarchia,* 2, 13.

difficulties on his own strength, which when on the brink of the malodorous chasm of Geryon[184] he cast from him. Morally, it has been thought to symbolize a vow of celibacy, cast away because Dante found in it no cure, but rather a source, for the temptations of the flesh. Such interpretations have their foundation in an age in which the monastic girdle was invested with many moral significations. Study of the symbolism of the cord in Dante's tradition, however, shows it to have a meaning much more deep-reaching.

Even the initiate in a modern secret order may know that the cable-tow symbolizes new birth,[185] for he, like the devotee of the mystery religions of old, is seeking initiation into all that leads upward to the Divine Sun. Through Judas was accomplished Christ's initiation into complete experience of the agony of the world's sin, with its outcome in the glorious victory of the Resurrection and the triumphal entry of the Ascension, the climax of the "comedy" of his earthly life. Again, this second order of levels in the *Divina Commedia* illumines the symbolism. Immediately evident is the appropriateness of Dante's choice of two stories bound up with the sun, through which to describe the downward plunge of the very Radiance of the Sun itself, into utter darkness and all that is the Sun's negation. Poignantly suggested in the fable of Phaeton,[186] the chariot of the Sun was indeed in an anomalous situation in the Passion of Christ.

184. Cf. pp. 200 n. 346, and 201 n. 352. Cf. also the identification of Geryon with Pope Boniface, dragging at his tail Corso Donati and Charles of Anjou. Of the latter his ancestor Hugh Capet remarks grimly that he had succeeded not in gain, but in "making better known himself and his," even as Judas, who returned ultimately even his thirty pieces of silver, retaining from his treachery only the infamy of the ages. (The presence of Judas in Satan's mouth does not militate against the acceptation of Geryon as his symbol, any more than the part he plays in the Gospel narrative invalidates his appearance in "type" in the Old Testament.)

185. A modern writer on Masonic symbolism states that in one sense the "cable-tow" of introduction into the Entered Apprentice Lodge symbolizes birth. This concept he derives from the Brahmanic sacred cord, the visible representation of the second birth of the Twice Born. He states that the "obvious literal meaning is the cable or cord by which something is towed or drawn. Hence with the greatest aptness it represents those forces and influences which have conducted not only the individual, but the human race, out of a condition of ignorance and darkness into one of light and knowledge. With symbolical meanings of this kind the cord seems to have been employed in many, if not all, of the ancient systems of initiation."

186. Although it is not a point to be stressed, the fact that Phaeton was killed by a thunderbolt from the king of the gods is consistent with the passage.

Dante was required to traverse the horrors of upper hell and of upper Dis before intrusting himself to the back of Geryon; so in the earthly life of Christ a period of temptation and of ministry preceded the Passion. As the candidate was prepared for initiation by a long period of instruction, humanity also, as Christ's mystical body, had gone through its period of preparation before the great betrayal. Whether or not Dante intended as much detail here as he has made clear on other levels, remains for further study to determine. Certainly he has blocked it in.[187a] The Donation of Constantine was for Dante a stabbing of the

187a. A possible supplying of detail which would be consistent with Dante's tradition is as follows:

The comedy of human history was in the Middle Ages divided into six periods, extending from the Fall, and corresponding to the six days in the work of creation. These days, with the sabbath of God which forms the seventh, Dante may have intended to rehearse in the days of the week of his journey. In a narrower sense, however, the world-as-it-has-been is represented for Dante by the Inferno itself, Purgatory lying beyond, in the future. Thus association may be made with the six symbolic beasts which preside over circles in hell.

The first of the periods, which were sometimes counted as each of a thousand years ("One day is with the Lord as a thousand years, and a thousand years as one day" [II Pet. 3. 8]) extended from Adam to Noah. In its beginning it was an age of relative goodness, not an age of darkness, though no longer lighted directly by the Divine Sun of God; and hence it may well correspond to that circle within which Dante was set down by Charon, the ferryman about whose glowing eyes flashed circles of flame. Later, however, it was marked by that lust which the Bible states as the occasion of the Deluge (Cf. Gen. 6. 1-2), one great manifestation of the terror of God's judgment, of which the rainbow is the constant pledge that it shall never be repeated: "While the earth remaineth, seedtime and harvest, and cold and heat, and summer and winter, and day and night shall not cease" (Gen. 8. 22). This may correspond to the circle in which Minos metes out the sole infernal judgment, and where is punished the sin of lust.

The second age, from Noah to Abraham, was marked by the luxury and gross self-indulgence which drove the great patriarch to the solitude of the desert. Of this age the circle presided over by Cerberus, of greedy jaws, is no unfitting sign.

The third age, from Abraham to David, was the age during most of which "there was no king over Israel and every man did that which was right in his own eyes"—the very condition for the overlordship of Plutus, the "cursed wolf," and the reign of avarice and prodigality.

The fourth age, from David to the Exile, was marked by violence, and that great act of violence which brings it to a close. The Captivity under Nebuchadnezzar might well correspond to the carrying across the bitter marsh by Phlegyas, and the entry into Dis accomplished only by divine intervention, thus indicating the ultimate overruling even of Babylon to God's ends.

Within the fifth age occurred the even worse violence of the attack on the temple by Antiochus Epiphanes, which was brought to naught by the mounted angel who guarded the treasure—an attack perhaps suggested by the futile rage of the Minotaur.

The sixth age was the age of betrayal, not only of Christ, but of Humanity of which he is Head, and is appropriately indicated by the fraudulent Geryon. The cord thrown to Geryon suggests that temporal power, which had it been kept by the emperor, might indeed have bound the leopard, but which as it was used,

dual vicarate with the Judas lance of cupidity; the result was mutual eclipse of the two suns of Rome, solar eclipse as in the betrayal of Christ in his earthly Body. Comparison should be made here with the *résumé* of the drama of history given in the Pageant, where the plumes of temporal power are the sop, graciously given but evilly received. Dante in his struggle to bring victory out of this betrayal, through the establishment on earth

precipitated the downward plunge of church and state to the region of fraud, dissension, and treason.

The seventh age was to see victory and deliverance in preparation for the Sabbath of God. The suggestion has been made by Prof. J. B. Fletcher that Dante added a seventh earthly age by the symbolical means of his gaining of a day in passing through the center of the earth. Thus he means to indicate, Professor Fletcher maintains, that Christ has gained for man a day of grace, within which mankind may the better prepare for the eternal Sabbath. It is of interest that Bede in his *De temporem ratione* argued for eight ages instead of seven, thus Dante has basis for such a division. He suggests further, that, basing himself on the text above quoted, as to the equivalence of a thousand years and one day, Dante may have thought of seven ages of the world, each consisting of a thousand years. In this case the odd consequence would ensue, that the betrayal by Constantine would fall in the year 515 of the sixth age, while the year 515 of the seventh age would occur within Dante's own time, and would, on this hypothesis, be the year of the promised deliverer. (By most medieval chronologies, the birth of Christ was placed in the year 5200 of the world.) This gives a plausible explanation of Beatrice's mysterious prophecy in *Purg.,* xxxiii, 43.

If, however, Dante chanced to be acquainted with the chronicle of the ninth century Freculphus (Migne, *P.L.,* t. 106) another explanation of the 515 would be natural. Freculphus dates the birth of Christ as 5,129 years from Adam, 2,921 from the Flood, 2,011 from Abraham, 1,506 from Moses, 1,207 from Solomon's Temple, and 515 from the Second Temple. Concerning this Second Temple it was spoken that it should be filled with greater glory than the First, and that in it peace should be given (Hag. 2. 3, 6-9), a prophecy considered by Christians to have been fulfilled in Christ, the promised deliverer and desire of all nations, coming into it in the five hundred and fifteenth year, even as the deliverer prophesied by Beatrice was to come in the five hundred and fifteenth year of that seventh millennium especially prepared by Christ.

For the characteristic medieval division of ages of the world, cf.:

Ado of Vienna, ninth century, Migne, *P.L.,* t. 123.

Claudius of Turin, ninth century, *ibid.,* t. 104 (fragmentary).

Freculphus, ninth century, *ibid.,* t. 106.

Marianus Scotus, eleventh century, *ibid.,* t. 147.

Ekkehard, twelfth century, *ibid.,* t. 154. (For his dates, he cites Bede, Isidore, Abbas, Eusebius, and others.)

Honorius of Autun, twelfth century, *ibid.,* t. 172.

Nennius, in *Monumenta historica britannica,* ed. Petrie, Sharpe, and Hardy, and others.

The idea of an allegorical representation of the history of the world was not new in the Middle Ages. Cf. the passage in Dan. 2. 31 ff., and Dante's use of the same conception in his reference to the "Old Man of Crete." *Inf.,* xiv, 94 ff.

Human history, as far as detailed references are concerned, in the *Divina Commedia,* presents one of the most puzzling problems of interpretation. Richard Hooker, in the sixteenth century, speaking of the Incarnation, said: "Howbeit because this divine mystery is more true than plain, divers, having framed

of true pope and true emperor, was a type of Christ, through whose power alone the victory of evil is turned to its own destruction.

The initiation of the Christian into the sacramental life through the new birth of baptism contains within itself dedication to a share in the mission of the sun god. Upon this birth also, torment may be consequent, for although baptism frees the soul from the devil, the devil exerts his powers, not on those who are in his own safe-keeping, but on those whom through their turning to the light he fears to lose. Thus the cord of initiation and of the new birth, on every level, calls up the evil Geryon and precipitates the struggle and pain and darkness which are to end in triumph over evil.

In the ten pockets of the Malebolge,[187b] much might be seen of the events of Christ's trial, and of the manner of shifting of responsibility as he was handed back and forth from Jew to Roman. The next clear symbolism is, however, the final commitment, in the close of this period, to the evil depths of all the universe.[188] This commitment is accomplished for Dante by the giant Antaeus,[189a] as for Christ by Pilate, in a moment which Dante describes tersely as such as to make him wish to go by another road.[189b] Antaeus, having delivered his charge in all gentleness into the pit of death at his feet, quickly straightened, raising his head high above the horrors of Cocytus, as if freed

the same to their own conceits and fancies, are found in their expositions thereof more plain than true," and such at the present is likely to be the case with any detailed interpretation of this aspect of the *Commedia*. The points which seem certain, however, are the events following upon Constantine's betrayal of trust, and the initiation of the drama in the sin of Adam, of which the consequence was dual judgment: Minos, discerner of sin, was type of the violence to redeem from which Christ, likewise a discerner of sin, came as the second Adam, the heavenly judge of quick and dead.

187b. Remembering that the most gruesome scene in the Malebolge is that in the pit of the thieves, it is of interest to note that the Barabbas whom the Jews demanded in *exchange* for Christ was a robber, and also that Christ is reported to have been crucified between two thieves.

188. *Inf.*, xxxii, 7.

189a. Note Dante's use of giant as a corrupt representative of empire (cf. p. 325) which is the exact character of Pilate. An interpretation of Antaeus on the level of human history is to be found in: Jefferson B. Fletcher, *The Crux of the Divine Comedy*. His interpretation in individual life can be filled in fairly readily by analogy.

189b. "If it be possible let this cup pass from me." Matt. 26. 39. Cf. also Mark 14. 36, etc.

from all responsibility, like Pilate who washed his hands of the matter. This identification is made the more appropriate by the fact that the giant performed his mission against his will, urged by words from Virgil, Spirit of Empire, as Pilate, driven by fear of imperial censure, acceded to the demand of the people.[190]

CRUCIFIXION

There has been expressed much question as to why the *Vexilla regis* should be parodied at this point.[191] However appropriate it may be on the personal level of Dante's symbolism, to indicate to him the nature of evil as a parody of good,[192] it attains here a fuller significance as heralding the approach to Christ, of that Cross with its motto of mockery, which was to become his royal standard. The Crucifixion itself undoubtedly is represented by Dante's actual physical contact with Satan which was to become the means of his victory over the kingdom of evil, as the Crucifixion was the means of Christ's victory. It was humorously told in the Middle Ages[193] (in many a tale of the Harrowing) that had Satan only known with whom he was dealing, he would have done all in his power to prevent the Crucifixion, which was to free not only his supposed victim, but all humanity also, from his power.[194, 195] In the words of the dead, recounted in the Gospel of Nicodemus,[196] in the dawning glory which announced to the imprisoned prophets the coming of Christ to Hades, Prince Satan in glee told Hades that at last

190. Another support for this reading is Dante's theory, already described, as to the necessity of Roman authority to validate the redemption. Cf. p. 46 n. 69, also p. 295.

191. An interesting comparison is the amazing parody, in the Mephistophelian finale of Liszt's *Faust Symphony*, of the noble themes of the first movement.

192. Cf. p. 198.

193. It has been pointed out that Milton and Puritan thought were first to ennoble the Devil, who in medieval fancy was made to play a ridiculous and grotesque rôle.

194. The idea was familiar that Satan planned the crucifixion to render impotent the intervention of God among men, ignorant that the intervening Savior was in fact God the Son. Cf. the grotesque image given by Gregory of Nyssa, who says that the Devil, as an evil fish, was caught by the hook of Christ's deity, baited with the flesh of his humanity. This poor taste, not the conception involved, was regretted by Gregory Nazianzen, Athanasius, and Augustine. *Cambridge Medieval History*, p. 587.

195. Cf. p. 201, for Dante's feeling of the paradox that evil tends to bring about its own destruction.

196. Cf. p. 180.

he had won the Christ, that most dangerous of men. Of a sudden all were startled by the shout of many voices, "Lift up your heads, O ye gates. . . ."[197] Hades, shuddering, pushed Satan out to meet his victim, and shut and locked its doors. Again the thunderous cry resounded, after which "suddenly Hades trembled, and the gates of death and the bolts were shattered, and the iron bars were broken and fell to the ground, and everything was laid open."[198, 199] The Christ entered, so the story goes, delivering to Hades Satan, its quondam prince, now fast bound for its tortures, and rendered impotent as Dante beheld him in Cocytus. From this physical contact with Satan, as also by his means, for Satan was the author of the plot which had thus destroyed him, Christ turned to his task of redemption. Up the course of the rivulet which bears sin downward, Dante toiled, representative of Christ, who, having descended to the uttermost depths of evil, returned, bearing with him "again to see the stars," that human nature which he had made his own.

Similar is the progress in the second comedy belonging to this order of symbolism, Christ's life in his mystical Body After the betrayal of church and state, organized humanity went through a period of trial vividly pictured as the second act of the Pageant in the Earthly Paradise.[200] It was the mockery of the eastern schism and the increasingly blatant turning to evil of God's gifts, which made appropriate the blasphemy and the parody of the *Vexilla regis*. The outcome in Guelph-Ghibelline politics was indeed a crucifixion, yet out of it Dante hoped was to come salvation, even as he, through his apparently ruinous exile from Florence, had been placed in a position which seemed to make possible the fulfilment of his mission.

Finally, there is a third level of interpretation in the order relating to Christ and humanity. Through Christ's sacramental

197. Ps. 24. 7-10.
198. According to the second Latin version. See "Ante-Nicene Library," XVI.
199. Such was the earthquake in which, according to Dante, the universe felt love, and hell received its fourfold *ruina:* the breaking down of the outer gate, as just described (cf. *Inf.,* viii, 125-126) ; the breaking of part of the wall between Limbo and the circle of the unlawful lovers; the landslide guarded by the Minotaur, between the circle of the heretics and that of the violent (cf. *Inf.,* xii, lines 1-13 and 31-45) ; and the ruin in the *bolgia* of the hypocrites (cf. *Inf.,* xxi, 106-114, and xxiii, 133-141).
200. Cf. pp. 325 ff.

Body each individual may be assured that, like the drama of the life of Christ and of the development of humanity, the drama of his personal life is a comedy.[201] The sacramental Body, too, given to each member of the church, is betrayed whenever through fraud, that is, sophistries of the intellect, theology and philosophy[202] are made to dim each other as guides of the inner life. Geryon's rings reveal even more clearly the menace conveyed in the spots of the leopard, in their vivid portrayal of those circular arguments which have wrought such havoc in many a life. The pockets of the Malebolge may be found suggestive of the dilemma of theology and philosophy, when brought into conflict by such specious betrayal. Sharing of the experience of the race is brought to the individual soul through its union with Christ, with whom it must be crucified in order to obtain salvation. The pain thus brought on the soul is, however, one of the mysteries of mystic progress, and so belongs to the next order of symbolism.

PROMISE

After the Harrowing of Hell, it was necessary that men should be instructed further, before Christ might ascend to glory. Redemption is not accomplished by suffering merely; ascent as well as descent is required. To the forty days of Lent, succeed the greater forty days of Eastertide. Of this truth Dante is a representation in his passage through purgatory. Up the ascent over which preside the four cardinal virtues Dante moved, engaged in a formulation of ideas as to the organization of humanity and the goal of the individual soul, and able through his possession of life to bestow immortal fame upon the dead. Even so Christ moved, doubly living among the dead and empowered to bestow the supreme gift of immortality as he taught men concerning the organization of humanity,[203] and concerning the principles of the active and contemplative life. Still in the jurisdiction of the empire, Christ, during the days of Eastertide, taught of that other sun, the church, through which his life was to be brought to man more intimately than ever had been pos-

201. Cf. pp. 285 ff.   202. Cf. pp. 51, 384.
203. Cf. Acts 1. 3. The term "Kingdom of God," to the mind of Catholic theologians, meant simply the church.

sible before. Christ was born under the Roman Empire that he might transform the metropolis of humanity at last into the heavenly city, the Dark Wood into the Rose.

Through a period of instruction, of progress from light to light, similar to the development of Dante indicated in the *Purgatorio,* humanity will move when it shall have been saved out of its experience of disunion, by passing through the center of all evil to peace under new leadership. The rank soil of mankind, left so long to grow weeds, will be cultivated and purged by the rightful authority "hitching the oxen of his counsel to the plow."

There is a sense in which, in his representation of Christ, Dante signifies not merely Christ in person, but Aeneas and Paul, progenitors of Christ's dual vicarate. Through them, likewise, comes his representation of humanity. Dante the *sylvanus,* commissioned to restore Rome, is not too distant in function from the Sylvius, literal son of Aeneas, who initiated the founding of Rome. As Aeneas, type and predecessor of Christ,[204] had prepared for the foundation of the Eternal City, so Dante, type and successor of Christ, was to aid in the ultimate transformation of the Dark Wood to the Garden of Paradise. Dante shared in the expectation of his time that in this story of humanity there would be written a final chapter of which the theme would be the deliverance, to be brought, Dante thought, if not indeed by the dead lion Henry, then assuredly by the Dog who still lived.

Of this latest stage in the epic of Rome, Dante, made in Limbo the sixth among poets, is to write. Homer told of Troy,[205] whose fall left Anchises and his group homeless, as mankind was left homeless by the fall of man. Virgil told the second stage, the story of Aeneas[206] and the flight of the Trojan remnant to the Italian peninsula, there to multiply as did the sons of Noah saved in the ark. Horace pictured his own time and its need of moral reformation[207] in terms suggesting the moral environment of Abraham, who sought to found a holy race. Ovid, telling of transmutations into beasts and into gods[208] suggests

204. Dante makes his very life follow that of Aeneas. For example, each shows temperance, in leaving Dido and the Siren, respectively. Cf. *Convivio,* 4, 24-28. Cf. p. 179.
205. In the *Iliad.*   206. In the *Aeneid.*
207. In his *Satires.*   208. In his *Metamorphoses.*

the gradual transformation of the glorious kingdom of David and Solomon into that condition which necessitated the Captivity. In Babylon Israel suffered an evil metamorphosis into hybridism, while Judah was purified for closer approach to its God. Lucan relates the victory of Caesar over Pompey[209] and the establishment of the Empire for which the Republic had prepared, suggesting the victorious return with its restoration of the Temple and the heroic preparation of the Maccabees for the Divine King to come. For Dante it remained to tell the story of the empire as vicarate of Christ, and of the way in which, having proved under Constantine false to its trust, it is once more to regain, under the predestined leader to come, its sacred position. Thus the true understanding of empire is embodied in Virgil interpreted by Dante,[210] and thus the history of the empire draws into itself the history of the world. These truths Dante is to see more perfectly at the close of the Pageant.

FULFILMENT

It is possible to understand as an added symbolism, in the order of the sins of the seven terraces, the ordering of the coming transformation of the Dark Wood. Although this order was fixed for Dante by his theological tradition, it is appropriate to his theme. After the long waiting in the valley of negligent princes[211] must come the penitence of mankind at the Gate,[212] and thorough humbling beneath the representative of the emperor, a true bowing beneath stones for the proud, till grace shall reign in their hearts and they shall stand upright. Then, as the first discipline and benefit of the rightly enthroned empire, is to come the freeing from envy, from that glance cast on other's happiness which (in itself as well as in its specific representation

209. In the *Pharsalia.*
210. Note that in Dis the demons would have been willing to admit Virgil if without Dante. (According to Dante's view, it was possible to misread the *Aeneid,* as well as to misread the Bible.) Cf. the Catholic idea that true Christianity lies in the Bible as interpreted by the church, as against that of Protestants, who will accept the Bible, but refuse to admit the church as its interpreter.
211. The appropriateness of this symbolism needs no remark, since it is the negligence of their proper duty, on the part of the emperors, which has brought mankind to its present pass in the Dark Wood.
212. The Gate of Peter, longed for by Dante (*Inf.,* i, 134), has three meanings: this gate of purgatory by which mankind enters the life of purification, the gate of Heaven itself, and a certain gate in the city of Florence.

in the florins which, deprived of their hypocritical brightness, are but dirt) constitutes the nourishment of the *lupa*.[213] Next, angry passions are to be checked, and sloth is to be replaced by zeal. Only then are the three sins connected with matter[214] to receive attention—wrong valuation of gold, of food, and of sex. At last with the establishment of the blessed state of innocence, the goal of government is achieved; the *selva selvaggia* has given place to the Garden. The stages of humanity's progress through this realm of the new leader where Cato presides,[215] since they belong to the future, Dante cannot, of course, describe definitely. Attention in consequence centers no longer in human history as it did in the *Inferno*, but on the purging of the individual, which is the real goal of the whole new state.[216]

One at a time, carrying with them their limbs and branches in various evil acts, the seven root sins (mortal sins) are torn out of the nature first mercifully raised by Christ, the Eagle of Light, past all obstacles to the Gate of Purgatory. The tearing out of evil growths opens the Dark Wood to the rays of the sun, so that at last the world may become a garden, well ordered and beautiful because the sunlight has been let in. Then only may be seen within it, in true perspective, the pageant of human history, cupidity having been shorn of its *gravezza* under the double authority of the empire as guardian of all material possessions, and the papacy as possessed of none. In the *Inferno* is shown that which each soul must suffer in sacramental union with Christ, in other words, that which the sacramental Body of Christ suffers in its union with each individual soul. But it is

213. The checking of cupidity, in Dante's mind, was the one great function of government.

214. Captious criticism has been made that Dante places lust just below the Earthly Paradise, as if it were the least instead of the most disgusting of human sins. But to Dante the fleshly sins actually were of less deadly venom than the "spiritual" sins of pride and hatred and envy, wherefore it was necessary to cleanse human nature first from the ranker growth. In this regard, note the fact that Adam's sin was not gluttony, but disobedience springing from pride. Cf. St. Augustine, *De civitate Dei*, 14, 12-14.

215. Note that in one sense it is necessary to regard Cato as foreshadowing God. Cf. Dante's earlier allegory of Cato and Marcia.

216. Cf. p. 55. The scholastic idea of the state is that it exists to help the individual to reach the highest good. The prime duty is to give to life a human value, and the state should help each of its members to reach the goal of moral and religious goodness. Cf. De Wulf, *Philosophy and Civilization in the Middle Ages*.

only in the *Purgatorio* that there are discussed the stages of purification under the direction of theology and philosophy.

The moral interpretation of the *Divina Commedia,* studying primarily virtues and vices, and usually concentrating attention on the *Purgatorio,* in which Dante is regarded as typical of the human soul climbing upward, ridding itself of each separate sin through complete experience of its inevitable consequences, and through meditation on the opposite virtue, is too familiar to need repetition. In the *Purgatorio*[217] the three bodies of Christ may be seen in the one mission of redemption: the Incarnate and Risen Christ teaches; Christ in his mystic Body, that is, all organized humanity, asserts the virtues; and Christ in his sacramental Body strengthens and develops the soul in its struggle toward the acquisition of virtues, through the gift of the bread of angels which is both the Eucharist[218] and knowledge in theology and philosophy.[219] Fruitful as this interpretation is, practical omission of it would seem to be required in order that it may be replaced in fitting proportion in the setting which Dante gave it. This setting consists of the truth of redemption symbolized with reference to Christ in the *Inferno,* the final truths of humankind revealed to Dante in Mars, Jupiter, Saturn, and the Fixed Stars, of which Gemini, the twins, give the motif— where Dante understood finally the relationship of the individual to all humanity.[220]

III. CULMINATION: EPIPHANIA

AT the end of the Forty Days Christ's life under the jurisdiction of the empire was definitely completed. His redemption perfected, and validified by the empire, he rose to his own place as king and high priest. Is not the difficulty many interpreters have felt with Virgil's mitering of Dante (as expressed in the ques-

217. For the relation of Beatrice to this interpretation, cf. pp. 319 ff.
218. Cf. *Par.,* xviii, 129, also the Eucharistic hymns of Thomas Aquinas. See pp. 75, 374.
219. Cf. *Par.,* ii, 11, with *Convivio,* 1, 1.
220. His sense of especial mission is emphasized also by his connection with Gemini, cf. p. 48. With regard to this constellation and the Virgin Mary Albertus Magnus says: "quod est aliena negotia curare ut propria, et non sibi, sed toti gentium se credere mundo. Et hoc maxime facit virtus charitatis, quae non quaerit quae sua sunt, sed communia negotia propriis ante ponit." *De laudibus,* 7, 1, 2.

tion: How could a pagan have made Dante a bishop?) really a result of confusion of symbolism belonging to the order of Dante's personal life with that belonging to the order of the allegory of Christ? By crowning and mitering Dante, Virgil no more made him bishop than he made him emperor. He simply indicated that Dante had reached that point where his will no longer needed the dictation of empire and church. On the other hand, Virgil, as Spirit of Empire, in his validification of the redemption, granted to Christ in very fact[221] his rightful rank of King and High Priest.

There was, however, an interval of waiting before Christ's representatives on earth were empowered by his Holy Spirit to carry on his mission—an interval occupied cogently by that which took place in the Earthly Paradise. Matilda has been the center of much work of interpretation, partly, it may be suspected, because she unifies in herself such multiplicity of symbolism. Whether she be primarily David the royal Forerunner,[222] or the spirit of the old (Jewish) church, or John the Baptist, forerunner of Christ, or Spring, the presage of new fruitfulness on earth through Christ as Radiance of the Sun—it is probably safe to declare her all of these and much more. In this context she is most dramatic as dawn, herald of the sunstorm god in all his glory.[223] Drawn by the grifon—two-natured beast of gold and white mingled with vermilion, Christ himself appearing now under a veil—the chariot approaching outshines the chariot of the sun and is halted by a thunderclap.[224]

221. Cf. p. 295 and passage cited from the *Monarchia*, p. 46 n. 69. That critics have not recognized Dante in the *Divina Commedia* as a type of Christ is strange, not only in view of the inherence of typological interpretation in medieval thought and of Dante's paralleling of his comedy to scripture as elsewhere discussed (cf. p. 63), but also in view of the absolute necessity of such interpretation evidenced by passages like the above about which dispute and misunderstanding have been so intense.

222. Cf.: "The first is named Primavera solely for this coming today; for I moved the giver of the name to call her *Primavera*, which is to say *prima verra* (she will come first) on the day that Beatrice shall reveal herself after her liege's vision." *Vita Nuova*, 24, 53. Cf. with *Purg.*, xxviii, 51.

223. The Navajos have a ceremonial painting in which Sky Father is pictured as Night, with moon and stars accurately placed; Earth Mother appears as bearing four sacred plants, enfolded by Sky Father in glorious blue daylight; and Dawn is a strange ghostly white figure, wearing red moccasins. The Rainbow, not personified, but terminating in growing leaves, encircles the three figures.

224. Cf. *Purg.*, xxix, 117.

At this point Dante becomes a spectator, contemplating, as they pass before him, the mysteries of Christ and of the church. Such action is appropriate to Dante the statesman and citizen of Florence, having attained, through rigorous discipline of thought and emotion, to that point where, master of himself, in perfect obedience to God, he may behold the whole in a true perspective of its relationships in the universal pattern. For perfect comprehension of his mission in the history of the world represented in the pageant before him, it is appropriate and necessary that Dante should become conscious of his union with the divine will in its desire for the salvation of the world, accomplished perfectly in the Person of Christ. Nevertheless, in the order of symbolism thus created, in which Dante becomes a type of Christ, there seems to be presented here Christ in contemplation of himself. Is there, then, a break in the symbolism of the second order?

Two facts must be brought to mind: First, that expression through symbolism approaches truth as the number of symbols used in any one connection is multiplied that there may be correction of one by the other. Thus, the simultaneous presence of Dante, of the grifon, and of Beatrice, as types of Christ, occurs in the progress of the Pageant in accord with Dante's increasing clarity of vision. Further, the ultimate bliss lies in the Beatific Vision, which to the Trinity is self-contemplation.[225] It is then only appropriate that with the accession to the Earthly Paradise whence the Divine Sun, no longer opposed by the *lupa,* may raise man to the heaven of vision, there should be a foreshadowing of that which is the joy both of God and of man in the mystery of the Rose. The further appropriateness in this order of symbolism of Christ's self-contemplation, becomes apparent with a study of the Pageant.

Taken as a whole the Pageant may represent the human authors of the Bible, as the usual interpretation runs, but more

---

225. One of the inevitable implicates of an intellectual conception of the ultimate nature of the Deity is the conception of the life of the Deity as essentially self-contemplation. Himself the ultimate Reality, if he has knowledge, it must be self-knowledge. Since, moreover, he is infinite Beauty, Truth, and Goodness, he must of necessity love himself. After this manner Thomas continues with the explanation that God is his own Beatitude.

deeply it represents the church, into which the whole of religious development is gathered up.[226] The deepest meaning of the Pageant, however, lies in its representation of the Mass, that supreme drama of the church, perfect summary and extension of the mystery of the Incarnation. Resemblances in the Pageant, both to the Mass and to the Corpus Christi procession, have been suggested recently in a comparison[227] of Beatrice's sudden appearance to the miracle of transubstantiation. Had these resemblances been considered in detail on the basis of William Durand's careful analysis of the symbolism of the Mass,[228] however, they might have been set forth with still greater cogency.

The candlesticks,[229] the slow ritual order of the vested procession, and the chant to a Blessed Lady, usher in the chariot, which, brighter than that of the sun, is the vehicle of him who is source of all light. The Logos is recognized as instrument at once of the creation and of the redemption of the finite. As St. Thomas remarked, while the motion of the Primum Mobile is one, its sole desire being for union with the Empyrean, in it are the roots of the tree of Time, and to the motion of the next

226. The church was described in the early centuries by Tertullian's follower, St. Cyprian, in similar imagery:
"As there are many rays of the sun, but one light; and many branches of a tree, but one strength based in its tenacious root; and since from one spring flow many streams, although the multiplicity seems diffused in the liberality of an overflowing abundance, yet the unity is still preserved in the source. Separate a ray of the sun from its body of light, its unity does not allow a division of light; break a branch from a tree,—when broken, it will not be able to bud; cut off the stream from its fountain, and that which is cut off dries up. Thus also the church, shone over with the light of the Lord, sheds forth her rays over the whole world, yet it is one light which is everywhere diffused, nor is the unity of the body separated. Her fruitful abundance spreads her branches over the whole world. She broadly expands her rivers, liberally flowing, yet her head is one; her source one; and she is one mother, plentiful in the results of fruitfulness: from her womb we are born, by her milk we are nourished, by her spirit we are animated." Cyprian, *On the Unity of the Church* ("Ante-Nicene Library," VIII, 381).
227. By Dr. Lizette Fisher, in her *Mystic Vision in the Grail Legend and in the Divine Comedy*.
228. Gulielmus Durantis, *Rationale divinorum officiorum*. Mâle notes this as one of the ten books on the basis of which all medieval life could be understood. The *Catholic Encyclopedia* states that it is standard on the symbolism of the medieval Mass. Cf. also Chap. VI, i.
229. The sevenfold candlestick suggests the seven petitions of the Lord's Prayer, said in the preparation for the Mass; also the seven gifts of the Holy Ghost, and various other ecclesiastical sevens. The habitable part of the earth was divided into seven strips, or "climates," stretching east and west.

circling sphere it imparts the dual motion which as duality and multiplicity characterizes successively the lesser spheres of creation. Through the nature of the grifon was the unique unification of the dual nature of finite creation, symbolized in the two wheels of the car he drew.[230] Such was the Introit of the medieval Mass. The eternal pairs, divine and human, church and empire, theology and philosophy, together with their fruit the mystic consummation in contemplation and action, are suggested in the two wheels of the car, and united in the two natures of the grifon, the white and vermilion signifying the elements of the Eucharist.

The Sun, greeted with hosannas, is the "Sol che, sviando, fu combusto per l'orazion de la Terra devota, quando fu Giove arcanamente giusto."[231] The ritual turning toward the car suggests the turning toward the altar of the ecclesiastical procession after its members have reached their appointed positions. Thus the drama of the redemption is to be reënacted. In the great cathedral the altar was hung with silken coverings of symbolic colors to represent the virtues, and was consecrated with oil as a symbol of the light which surrounded it unseen.[232] In the Pageant the chariot of the grifon is closely accompanied by ladies robed in the symbolic colors of the virtues,[233] and the light, which in the cathedral is symbolized by the consecration with oil, glows dazzlingly around it.

The usual interpretation of the thirty-five figures in the procession as symbolizing the authors of the Bible, suggests in the Mass the scripture readings, entitled "Epistle" and "Gospel." The Epistle might be read not only from the books of the New Testament, exclusive of the Gospels, but also from any of the twenty-four books of the Old Testament. Thus Epistle and Gospel together cover the whole message of the thirty-five authors of scripture.[234] This interpretation is also appropriate to the en-

230. Cf. pp. 244 ff., et al.
231. "Sun which, straying, was consumed at the devout prayer of the earth, when Jove was mysteriously just." *Purg.*, xxix, 118-120.
232. These and other details of the symbolisms of the Mass and of the mass furnishings are cited from Durantis, *Rationale divinorum officiorum.*
233. Cf. *Purg.*, xxix, 121-132; xxxi, 103-111.
234. In the Middle Ages, when there were no printed books, and education was comparatively unavailable to the masses, the only knowledge of the scripture message transmitted to the people was perforce through the Epistle and

trance or Introit of the procession. The Introit of the Mass, according to Albertus Magnus, represents the Fathers of the Old Testament sighing for the advent of the True Light which the apostles of the New Testament announce. In this connection Albertus quotes many[235] scriptural expressions of longing for Divine Light. "Et ideo suspirans anima Isaiae et sanctorum, Christum lucem veram, qui tenebras fugaret, desiderauit. Et hoc est quod dicit: Anima mea desiderauit te in nocte."[236] Again, the song thrice shouted, *Veni sponsa de Libano,* is suggestive of the rubric in accord with which the priest three times kisses the altar, in reverence to the two natures of Christ, and to his marriage with that church in which are united Jew and Gentile.[237]

After the singing of *Veni sponsa, Benedictus qui venis* (the hymn sung or recited before the consecration) and *Manibus o date lilia plenis,* there appears in the car Beatrice, and her appearance is as sudden as is the appearance of Christ under the "accidents" of bread and wine in the miracle of transubstantiation.[238] Moreover, even as he, the Sun of Righteousness, is there veiled under the appearance of bread, lest his glory vanquish his worshipers, so Beatrice as the Sun appears veiled within a cloud of flowers, her glory tempered to man's vision:

> Io vidi già nel cominciar del giorno
> la parte oriental tutta rosata,
> e l'altro ciel di bel sereno adorno;
> e la faccia del sol nascere ombrata,
> sì che, per temperanza di vapori,
> l'occhio la sostenea lunga fiata:

Gospel in the Mass (exception being made of the message often conveyed through the static arts. Cf. pp. 398-403).

235. "Sol iustitiae" (Mal. 4), "hac catena tenebrarum conclusi" (Wisd. 17), "lux vera" (John 1), "Custos quid de nocte?" (Isa. 21), "induamur opera lucis" (Rom. 13), "ignis quidem nulla vis poterat illis lumen praebere" (Wisd. 17), and others.

236. Albertus Magnus, *De sacrificio Missae,* cap. 1, on the Introit.

237. Much more could be said in regard to the details of this imagery, but it belongs to the realm of mysticism. Cf. Chap. V.

238. According to this doctrine, which Dante shared with all the churchmen of his time, at the "words of consecration" (*Hoc est corpus meum: hoc est sanguinis meum*) in the Mass, the reality present under the appearance of bread and wine ceases to be the reality of bread and wine, and becomes the reality of the Person of Christ. The term transubstantiation means literally change of substance, but the word "substance" is used not in the modern sense of chemical make-up, but in the philosophic sense of underlying truth.

così dentro una nuvola di fiori
che da le mani angeliche saliva
e ricadeva in giù dentro e di fori,
sovra candido vel cinta d'uliva
donna m'apparve, sotto verde manto
vestita di color di fiamma viva.[239]

Appropriately, the procession comes from the east and returns into it. Its source is the sun. Completed within the canonical times for the Mass, before noon the whole drama of the Pageant had passed.

As it is in response to Dante's seeking that Beatrice appears at last so it is in the Mass in response to the priest who stands before the people, like Dante a type of Christ, that Christ himself appears under the form of the elements. Beatrice's appearance here, crowned with the leaves of Minerva, makes definite her identification with Divine Wisdom,[240] rather than with Divine Love, her usual character.[241] And, like the Christ,[242] she is about to appear in the sternness of judgment.

239. "Ere now have I seen, at dawn of day, the eastern part all rosy red, and the rest of heaven adorned with fair clear sky, and the face of the sun rise shadowed, so that by the tempering of the mists the eye long time endured him; so within a cloud of flowers, which rose from the angelic hands and fell down again within and without, olive-crowned over a white veil, a lady appeared to me, clad, under a green mantle, with hue of living flame." *Purg.*, xxx, 22-33.

240. The identification is borne out in her whole action at this point. Immediately after the Pageant, including her transfiguration in the chariot, Beatrice deliberately spoke to Dante in parables, at which he, failing to understand, protested and asked for explanation just as did the disciples. Although this instance is consonant primarily with Christ in his literal, earthly Body, no one familiar with Catholic devotions can be forgetful of the fact that Christ in his Sacramental Body is thought of as taking toward the soul that receives him, the attitudes he might have been expected to take to such a soul had he met it in Jerusalem or Galilee. For example, the communicant is frequently advised to think that he hears the Sacramental Christ addressing to him the words of consolation, of reproach, or of counsel, which Christ on earth addressed to those who came to him.

241. No contradiction lies between Beatrice as the Host and Beatrice primarily as Love, the Holy Spirit, since it is through the action of the Holy Spirit that all sacraments are accomplished.

Further, while the Father is named as Power, the Son as Wisdom, and the Holy Ghost as Love, actually each is Eternal Power, Wisdom, and Love. As Augustine had stated, each of the Divine Persons *is* what he *has*. Cf. Appendix, pp. 503-504, especially n. 6.

242. In the medieval tradition, the office of Judge of living and dead was considered as exercised by the Second Person of the Trinity, who as himself possessing human nature (as well as divine) was thought of as having a special sympathy and understanding in human affairs. He was, nevertheless, conceived as a Judge in no way lacking in strictness and sternness. The doctrine is based primarily on the saying in the Fourth Gospel: "And hath given him power to execute judgment also, because he is the Son of Man." John 5. 27.

With more detailed analysis of this order of the symbolism, a further appropriateness is apparent for the simultaneous presence in the pageant of the three representations of Christ— Dante, the grifon, and Beatrice.[243] Dante here is representative of Christ who in his earthly body himself received the sacred elements at his institution of the Eucharist,[244] while the grifon, drawing the car, is representative of Christ as the head of his mystical body, humanity,[245] in the midst of which the incarnate Logos appeared as at once victim and priest, offering his body and blood for men. Ever conscious of the dual vicarate thus instituted on earth, Dante included at the supreme moment in the greatest of all dramas, the Jewish welcome (springing from the pre-Christian church), *Veni sponsa de Libano;* the Virgilian or preimperial *Manibus o date lilia plenis,* spoken in grateful veneration of him whom, yet unborn and destined to premature death, Anchises revealed to Aeneas as hope of the Empire;[246] together with the fulfilment of the hope of both in the hymn of the Incarnation, *Benedictus qui venis.* Finally, Beatrice is representative of Christ in his sacramental body, appearing with the brightness of the sun under the veiling of the elements. Thus completely in the Pageant of the Mass is revealed the function of the Logos in God's seeking of men and in men's seeking of God. This, the full message of Beatrice's eyes is revealed, however, only after the crisis in which is borne the bitter burden of evil.

Immediately with the miracle by which the presence of the Divine Sun is effected, as in the Mass, the corporate action becomes tremendously personal. God and the soul speak to each other; God in rebuke, the soul in trembling awe issuing in confession.

The shock of Beatrice's first words to Dante, spoken in accusation startlingly harsh, impresses the necessity of confession

243. Cf. p. 316.
244. Augustine points out that in the Eucharist Christ is both the Priest and the Sacrifice. The development of Eucharistic doctrine in medieval times rendered this conclusion inevitable, since the Bread contains Christ himself, and the priest acts only in his Name.
245. Note that it is the transformations of the car which in the second act of the Pageant unroll to Dante human history since the Incarnation.
246. Of Marcellus as a type of Christ, cf. the medieval interpretation of Virgil's famous prophecy in the Fourth Eclogue.

before communion. For wasted talents and all misspent life God rebukes the individual, and also the corporate body. In spite of the intensely personal nature of the scene (there is not another so personal described in the *Divina Commedia,* as there is nothing more intimate in the sacramental life of the Catholic soul) the intercourse is actually corporate. Further, at this point in the Mass, angels and saints add their voices to the cry of the sinner's whole discipline in virtue, interceding in his behalf, that communion may issue in beatitude.[247] That the contemning of divine love in the turning to lesser goods from the one great Good[248] may not sever the soul from the power of divine attraction, there must be penitence and the absolution that is in Lethe. With Beatrice's rebuke, the ice, which as the last trace of *gravezza* had gathered about Dante's heart, became breath and water;[249] and in Lethe was washed away all consciousness of the *gravezza* of the *lupa.*

247. "Rogo ergo immensae largitatis Tuae abundantiam quatenus meam curare digneris infirmitatem, lavare forditatem, illuminare caecitatem, ditare paupertatem, vestire nuditatem, ut panem angelorum, Regem regum et Dominum dominantium tanta suscipiam reverentia et humilitate, tanta contritione et devotione, tanta puritate et fide, tali proposito et intentionem sicut expedit saluti animae meae . . . O amantissime Pater, concede mihi dilectum Filium Tuum, Quem nunc velatum in via suscipere propono, revelata tandem facie perpetuo contemplari. . . ."—"I implore therefore the abundance of Thine infinite Majesty, that Thou wouldest vouchsafe to heal my sickness, to wash my foulness, to enlighten my darkness, to enrich my poverty, and to clothe my nakedness, that I may receive the Bread of angels, the King of kings and Lord of lords, with such reverence and fear, such contrition and love, such faith and purity, such devotion and humility, as is expedient for the welfare of my soul . . . O most loving Father, grant me that Whom I now purpose to receive under a veil I may at length behold with open face, even Thy beloved Son. . . ." From a communion prayer of St. Thomas Aquinas.

248.

"E se 'l sommo piacer sì ti fallio
   per la mia morte, qual cosa mortale
   dovea poi trarre te nel suo disio?"
         Purg., xxxi, 52-54.

"And if the highest pleasure thus failed thee by my death, what mortal thing ought then to have drawn thee to desire it?"

249.

"Lo gel che m'era intorno al cor ristretto,
   spirito e acqua fessi, e con angoscia
   de la bocca e de li occhi uscì del petto."
         Purg., xxx, 97-99.

"The ice which had closed about my heart became breath and water, and with anguish through mouth and eyes issued from my breast."

Both breath and water are symbols of the Holy Spirit. Indeed, in Italian, as in Latin and Greek, the same word may be used for spirit, breath, and wind. Cf. the play on the words in John 3. 5-8, where also water is associated with the spirit-wind.

That absolution is given by Matilda, Beatrice's messenger, but not until Beatrice has turned to the grifon to reflect in her eyes his dual being as man's judge and advocate, "as a sun in a mirror, not otherwise."[250] Thus is won divine forgiveness. Thus only may the soul "filled with wonderment and glad" taste that "food which satisfying of itself, causes thirst of itself" thus permitting no static satiety. The soul dazzled and bereft of self-expression gazes into the face of veiled Deity for one of those moments which Dante described, as the sinking of the intellect so deep into its desire that even the memory has no power to follow back over the track—"appressando sè al suo disire, nostro intelletto si profonda tanto, che dietro la memoria non può ire."[251] It comes to itself only to find the Mass over and the recessional begun.

Prominent as is the symbolism of the first order, relating to Dante's personal experience, Dante is truly a type of Christ, who in his entrance into earthly life accepted the burden of the sin of all the world. In the narrowest sense it was upon the cross that Christ bore the sins of Adam's race, symbolized no doubt by the physical contact with Satan at the central point of all wickedness. Nevertheless, to medieval devotion the bearing of sin, the sacrifice before God, is in a larger sense coterminous with his life, and therefore is *in toto* represented in the Mass, in the action of which is set forth the whole of his life, from the Hebrew prophecies and the mysterious Annunciation on through the Childhood and Ministry and Passion to the Resurrection and Ascension.[252] Thus in the Pageant, representing the Mass, the Incarnate Life of Christ is as it were retold, and at the supreme moment Dante as type of the human Christ presents before God the sacrifice of agony for the sins of the world.[253] Christ in the Pageant is Christ in heaven and on the

250. *Purg.*, xxxi, 121.
251. Cf. *Par.*, i, 7-9; xiv, 79-81; xxxiii, 59; Epistle XIII (X), 530; also pp. 99-100.
252. Cf. almost any Catholic book of devotions for the Mass. Children's mass books frequently picture mass scenes and Bible scenes together, to form in the child's mind the association as to the parts of Christ's life represented by the different moments of the Mass.
253. Thus in the culminating point of the Mass the priest as type and representative of Christ re-presents before God the One Sacrifice of Calvary. Cf. also p. 321 n. 244.

altar, one and the same, pleading before the Father, eternally and in connection with the Mass, his propitiation for the sins of the whole world; and ideally all humanity joins, in the Mass, in the pleading of the sacrifice and the agony over sin. Beatrice's rebuke, if read as the rebuke of the Divine Spirit to all humanity, voluntarily and legally represented by Christ, is not without poignancy. The sole value of human penitence and the possibility of the gift of absolution[254] spring only from the sacrifice of the Mass, Christ's earthly sacrificial life rendered eternal, and the consequent communion. These are the two pillars of medieval theology, and the two pillars give form to the Earthly Paradise.

Illumined to share further in the divine self-contemplation through the experience of the Mass, Dante in meditation, given form in the remainder of the Pageant, looks back over the centuries. The car of the grifon is bound to the tree (humanity) which immediately bursts into leaf and flower. The church is given over into humanity's keeping, even as once was the garden of Eden to Adam. In this comparison is presage of the betrayal of the ideal in history. Yet Beatrice, surrounded by the seven nymphs, is left to guard the car, appearing now as the Holy Spirit who with his gifts and his writers is left to guide the church. The fitness of this transition has been expressed by many a writer in Dante's tradition. St. Ambrose for example states that:

> Sicut ergo Dominus Christus et Verbum, et virtus, et sapientia et justitia et margarita et lux et via et resurrectio et caetera quae de eo scripta sunt, appellatur; ita et Spiritus sanctus sapientiae, intellectus, consilii, fortitudinis, scientiae, pietatis ac timoris, ut jam dictum est, nuncupatur. . . . Isti sunt septem oculi, qui in Zacharia propheta in uno lapide, id est, Domino Christo dicuntur inesse.[255]

As humanity prepares for its eternal citizenship the Holy Spirit gives instruction as to each personal mission.[256] So with Dante

---

254. Absolution, or sacramental forgiveness of sins, following upon detailed confession of sin, confers nothing so negative as a removal of divine indignation, but a removal of that which separates the soul from God. Absolution is then the renewal of union, in which God with man bears the burden of *gravezza* which, though increased by sin, is in absolution bereft of its power to conquer.

255. Ambrose, "De xlii mansionibus filiorum Israel," cap. v (Migne, *P.L.*, 17, col. 542).

256. Cf. *Purg.*, xxxii, 100 ff.

as an individual and as type in Christ of humanity revealed at last to its own vision. That history of humanity, known first by the soul in suffering through the sacramental union with Christ in his Passion, is now reviewed under the illumination of the Holy Spirit.

The betrayal is reënacted: One sun of Rome, the Eagle of the empire, in the persecutions despoils the other, represented by the effulgent car. Heresy, the fox, close relative of the *lupa*, thus invited, attempts to take possession of the car, but is driven thence by Beatrice, for it is only the Holy Spirit who preserves the church in true understanding. The Eagle returns in the Donation of Constantine to feather the car and thus inaugurate the fateful triumph of Circe, over which Christ mourns: "O navicella mia, com mal se' carca!"[257] The spiritual integrity of the church thus destroyed, a dragon severs the car in two (East-West schism) and the western remainder is left a prey to the merciless wand of Circe, who, usurping Beatrice's rightful place, intrigues with the lustful giant (House of Valois, the corrupt empire, the violence by which the *lupa* seeks its ends). This giant binds entirely to his own ends the harlot and her prey, the car of humanity horribly transformed (very likely the transfer of the papacy to Avignon)[258] while the attendant virtues mourn over Circe's victory.

Beatrice, comforting those with her in the words of Christ, "Modicum, et non videbitis me; et iterum, sorelle mie dilette, modicum, et vos videbitis me," in the very number of her queenly steps recalls the infinite truth of reality, recollection of which in its ultimate stability brings new strength and vision out of every tragedy, however heart-rending or futile it may appear to be. Again in the nine steps of Beatrice who is a nine, is

257. "O my little bark, how ill art thou laden!" *Purg.,* xxxii, 129.

258. The harlot's mysterious glance at Dante may represent on the political level the attempt of the Guelph party to hold him in its ranks, the jealous giant representing the equally corrupt Ghibelline party. If Dante is taken as representative of Christ, however, the symbolism is plain. When the corrupt papacy turned its attention for the slightest moment to Christ, his will for men, and the needs of his individual members, the giant of the corrupt temporal power jealously dragged it to a location where the appeal of conscience would not be heard.

In some medieval illustrations for the Apocalypse is seen a figure much like the harlot of Dante's vision (cf. Rev. 17). Clothed in purple and gold, she rides a strange beast and holds a chalice within which coils a serpent.

recalled the structure of the universe upborne by the solar
Trinity; in the tenth step about to be completed as she speaks to
Dante, is suggested the salvation and completion of creation
through twoness and fourness in the ultimate ten.[259] Beatrice
speaks to prophesy the coming of the Deliverer, who is soon to
take his place in the actualization of Christ's redemption. The
destruction of the giant and Circe is to be accomplished by the
mysterious five-hundred-ten-and-five.[260]

Unfortunately, one can say little of the "hard riddle" without
devoting a monograph to the subject. That which is important
here is the aspect in which it gives ultimate significance to
Dante's mission. Five-hundred-ten-and-five is rightly symbol of
him who, as solar radiance, brings unity out of the duality of
creation, the two fives, which united make up the ten of ultimate reality. At the same time, allegorically, five-hundred-ten-
and-five is especially a symbol of Christ, and of the leader[261]
who is to come in the five hundred fifteenth year of that age,
especially given to men that they may at last prepare for the
Sabbath of the Lord.[262]

In the Logos is practical solution of all problems of the *Commedia*. Christ as Deliverer stands as one and power of union
between the two human families of Jew and Gentile.[263] Through
him is the unification of all warring pairs, not only those sin-
fully at enmity—church and empire, theology and philosophy—
but those whose discordance seems rooted in the nature of

259. Cf. p. 339. On other levels of symbolism her steps have undoubtedly also
their appropriate significance. That they represent a review of the history of the
church has been suggested by Professor Fletcher. He suggests that the three
movements of the procession represent the three centuries of the true church,
while the steps of Beatrice represent the centuries which must elapse before its
restoration. Professor Grandgent gives a different interpretation.

260. Cf., e.g., p. 306 n. 187a.

261. For attempted solutions of the "hard riddle" the reader is referred to all
the Dante commentaries, for in practically every one he will find a different suggestion. The consensus of opinion is that on the level of allegory reference is
intended to Dante's chosen hero, Henry or Can Grande. Cf. p. 29 n. 10.

In this connection Professor Fletcher's ingenuous interpretation of the DXV
as Dominus Kanis Victoriosissimus, the superscription of the letter of dedication,
seems worthy of special mention. As he himself would be the first to recognize,
however, this in no way precludes interpretation on a deeper level with definite
reference to Christ, such as could scarcely have been absent from Dante's mind.
Cf. p. 470. For justification of more intricate interpretations, cf. Appendix V, Pt.
I, ii (2).

262. Cf. p. 306, footnote.   263. Five is peculiarly the number of man.

things—good and evil, pleasure and pain. In Christ's dual nature is the fourfold solution of duality on earth. For him in the realm of scripture expression of duality is fourfold, even as in the realm of nature the action of the Trinity is ninefold. Both these symbolisms were necessary to Dante's understanding of his mission, scripture giving fuller revelation of nature. Perhaps in this connection the action of the Trinity is thought of as expressed through Beatrice, herself a nine,[264a] and guide of Dante also a nine, that he may become star of philosophy to the true emperor, and monitor to Can Grande similarly a nine. It is of interest that Dante measures his own age by the solar cycle, thus suggesting a special association with the redemptive mission of the Divine Sun; while the association of Can Grande is with the cycle of Sirius the Dogstar, the Deliverer to come. The age of Beatrice Dante measures by the Great Cycle of the motion of the fixed stars, thus suggesting her governance of his mission even as the great cycle governs the precession of the solar equinoxes. This symbolism too, then, has its place on the level wherein Dante signifies Christ.

Up to this point in the symbolism, that which stands out is the Way. The Way on earth was opened up by Christ through his union in himself of the most fundamental of all conflicting pairs, and was illumined through the fourfold method. The Way which church and empire failed to keep straight is to be restored by the prophesied leader. Such symbolism looks forward to the symbolism of the mystic way, to be discussed in the next chapter, even as Dante's personal life and mission looked forward to the larger setting of the present chapter, with its relation to all humanity. The nine of the circumference is rendered comprehensible by the division into four wrought by the Cross of the Sun God. This second order of symbolism is but

264a. A significant fact in relation to Beatrice would appear to be the ninefold division of the "fruits of the Holy Ghost" based on Gal. 5. 22. Since the fruits of the Spirit are the supernatural effects of the action of the Divine Trinity in the souls of men, this "nine" may be said to be a "miracle whose sole root is the Trinity" even as Dante said the same of Beatrice. Herein is a further corroboration of the office of Beatrice in the *Divina Commedia* as that of a surrogate for the Third Person of the Trinity. Of further interest in view of the fact that Beatrice is in a sense the "star" Dante is to follow (*Inf.*, xv, 55), is the symbolizing of the nine fruits of the Holy Ghost by a nine-pointed star. Cf., e.g., F. R. Webber, *Church Symbolism*, p. 150. Cf. pp. 40 n. 48, 99 n. 251, 237 n. 514.

another tercet, necessitated by the first, and in its turn necessitating the third.

Dante at last, having added to understanding of himself an understanding of Christ and of all humanity, is prepared for the supreme sacramental union, through which alone comes revelation of his mission—to report "to those who live" words "concerning that life which is a race unto death." Personally, even here an allegory of the Christ, Dante is about to ascend to heaven to perfect vision, and thereafter, paralleling the "mission of the Holy Ghost"[264b] to return to earth as guide and mediator of the divine attraction to humanity, borne down under the betrayal to *gravezza*.[265]

As in the symbolism relating to Dante's personal story there was a gradual shift in emphasis from the situation of Dante Alighieri to the situation of humanity, so in the symbolism relating to Christ, there is a gradual shift of emphasis from his earthly to his mystical and then to his sacramental life, of which the implication is inevitably the mystic way. Whereas the divine grace of baptism[266] was administered at the foot of the mount, where was washed away all mist of hell which could estrange from God, the full power of the sacraments was brought to Dante only in the Terrestrial Paradise. It seems probable that his confirmation[267] (in Catholic theology the ordination of the layman), implicit in Virgil's crowning and mitering of him, is given its full meaning only in Beatrice's revelation to him of his mission, after his absolution[268] in Lethe, and his communion[269]

264b. Cf. John 14. 16-18, 26; also 15. 26.
265. The tree that is rent, in the moral signification, is God's justice. *Purg.,* xxxiii, 71-72. It is also the Cross, with its fruit thus rent away, and also humanity. Cf. the words of the grifon, when he ties to it the car.
266. The first of the seven sacraments of the Catholic church, without which the others are invalid. Based on Matt. 28. 19, and John 3. 5.
267. *Confirmation,* the strengthening for the life of the Christian, based on Acts 8. 12-19; 19. 1-7; Heb. 6. 1. *Ordination,* the strengthening for and the gift of sharing in the divine priesthood of Christ, derived from various implications in the New Testament, interpreted by tradition of the church. It is a bar to *matrimony,* as matrimony is to it. For matrimony as a sacrament, cf. Matt. 19. 3-6, and Mark 10. 6-9.
268. Absolution is granted in the sacrament of *penance.* Cf. p. 324 n. 254.
269. *Communion,* the sacrament in which, through the body and blood of Christ, actual union with God is granted. See John 6, also accounts of Last Supper, etc.

in the Pageant of the Mass.[270] The last anointing before death, purifying soul and body that it may rise to God, is symbolized in Eunoe.[271]

In the Earthly Paradise glory is rendered to the unique power of the bread of angels[272] to work in man the transformation which shall rescue him eternally from the menace of Circe pasturage, and render him capable of the vision of eternity. In a sense, the whole of the *Paradiso* is but the necessarily sequential narrative of that revealed to Dante in the blinding vision of the moment of communion "la disposizion, ch' a veder e negli occhi pur teste dal sol percossi, senza la vista alquanto esser mi fee."[273] From that moment to the close of the *Commedia,* which for Dante occupies no lapse of time,[274] Dante's conscious com-

---

270. Cf. p. 322.

271. *Unction,* normally the last of the seven sacraments, preparing for death. Under certain circumstances it may be repeated, as may matrimony. Jas. 5. 14-16. Baptism, Confirmation, and Ordination are non-repeatable if validly administered. Penance and Communion normally are frequently repeated. The name Eunoe was formed by Dante from εὔνοια or from εὖ (well) and νοῦς or νόος (mind). Cf. Dante's references to mind in the *Inferno.* Cf. pp. 183-186, 195, etc.

272. Those interested in the matter of the development of the Catholic theory of the Sacraments, and particularly of the Eucharist, will find a good survey in Miss Elizabeth F. Rogers' *Peter Lombard and the Sacramental System.* Justin Martyr pictures Christianity as a sacramental cult, but has no special term for sacraments. Tertullian used the term "sacramentum" (originally a solemn oath or obligation). Cyprian, like Tertullian, used the word loosely, to include Old Testament "types." Hilary of Poitiers takes for granted the sacramental system, and considers that those who evaluate the union between Christians and God in terms of obedience and will solely, are heretics. Ambrose, in the first entire treatise devoted in the West to the sacraments, offers no definition, but gives a "very clear exposition of the sacramental idea." Augustine attempts to define the term, but uses the word in a large and vague sense. Isidore derives the name from the secret operation of sacramental grace. His source for this is unknown. The doctrine of transubstantiation, at least in explicit form, dates from Paschasius Radbertus, ninth century. He was challenged by Rabanus Maurus and others. Ratramnus and Berengar of Tours were condemned for their opposition to this doctrine. Anselm of Lucca names only three sacraments, baptism, confirmation, communion. Gratian is vague as to number. Hugh of St. Victor begins the final formulation of the definition of sacrament ("A sacrament is a corporeal or material element sensibly presented from without, representing from its likeness, signifying from its institution, and containing from sanctification, some invisible and spiritual grace"). Nevertheless, his use of the term is vague. Peter Lombard is positive but cautious. His hesitating treatment of penance and ordination shows that it is still a novelty to call them sacraments. But he definitely enumerates the orthodox seven. All later discussion is based on the foundation laid by Peter Lombard. (Dante's authority in all probability was Thomas Aquinas.)

273. "That condition of the sight, which is in eyes but just smitten by the sun, made me remain a while without vision." *Purg.,* xxxii, 10-12.

274. It is true that time is running onward while Dante is in Paradise. Nevertheless, when the blessed are thought of as being in eternity and not in time, un-

munion was unbroken, as his vision never wavering from the Sun, was strengthened to penetrate more and more deeply into its mystery.

affected by the continual progression of time in the lower universe, it is regarded as possible for a living person, under exceptional circumstances, to be transported into the eternal realm, where he experiences no time, though leaving and returning to the earthly world at different points of time. Many tales built on such a theme are known (cf. p. 426 n. 77, for a folk tale on this order). It would seem that Dante wished his experience in Paradise to be regarded in this light, though perforce narrating it sequentially.

CHAPTER V. SCHEMA

PART I

I. Motif of Dante's symbolism formed from the study of inner experience as the tendency flowered in the thirteenth century. Basis is distinction between *Infinitas* and *Unendlichkeit*. Eternal Unity, like the Sun, creates from Nothing as a *quartum quid* the continuing universe. Mystic quest concerned with the relation of the *quartum quid* to infinite Tri-unity. Its initiation in the recognition of evil as the absolute negation of the solar Trinity, hence as impotent, lacking in life, light, and heat. The first phase of the quest is purgation (but the phases are inseparable).

II. Essential to the seeker for knowledge is not only sane discipline of the emotions, in which is maintained harmony between discipline and grace, but also discipline of the intellect in which is maintained harmony between the rational and the suprarational. Augustine, although the means of triumphant union of theology and philosophy, nevertheless, left to posterity an evil gift. The Augustinian tradition in Dante's time maintained the supremacy of the light of faith and inner experience over that of reason. The Averroists made similar claim for reason over faith. Dante, following Thomas Aquinas and the more balanced mystics of his time, maintained their mutual autonomies. For him as for Neoplatonism, the suprarational was a terminus found by reason at its highest.

III. Perils of the way of union. Met through comprehension of the relation of permanence to change. Reconciliation of opposites truly accomplished only in eternity. Mystic's life of necessity in cycles like the sun's career. Progression in the way of union from light to brighter light, through which as preparation the eye of man is strengthened to behold unharmed the ultimate glory of the light faintly symbolized in the Sun.

PART II

The third order of Dante's symbolism consists of the application of the fourfold method to the materials of symbolism as they relate to the third of man's four sources of knowledge—reason, given focus in the fourfold Sun. This order leads directly to the anagoge which is dependent on grace, the last of the four sources of knowledge. Even as the second order of symbolism was demanded by the first, so the third is demanded by the second, upon which it follows as the trope. In it, the levels of letter, allegory, and trope refer to the three phases of progress in the Way to ultimate vision of things as a whole. The pattern of interpretation which appears in harmony with the tradition to which Dante fell heir, is that given on p. 372, *q.v.*

CHAPTER V. SYMBOLISM IN MEDIEVAL THOUGHT: RELATION TO MYSTICISM

Ma non eran da ciò le proprie penne;
se non che la mia mente fu percossa
da un fulgore in che sua voglia
venne.
A l'alta fantasia qui mancò possa;
ma già volgeva il mio disio e il
velle,
sì come rota ch'igualmente è mossa,
l'amor che move il sole e l'altre stelle.

But not for this were my proper wings,
save that my mind was smitten by a
flash wherein its will came to it. To
the high fantasy here power failed;
but already my desire and will were
rolled—even as a wheel that moveth
equally—by the Love that moves the
sun and the other stars.

THUS far the Divine Sun has appeared as a focus of life, maintaining in its oneness and threeness the structure of the universe, and in its twoness and fourness determining the relationship of the universe to itself. That Dante is to write of these things he gives warning in the first tercets of the *Paradiso:* he has been in that brightest of heavens wherein is taken up most perfectly the all-pervading glory of him who moves all things.[1] The interest roused by these lines has frequently turned to annoyance as the second tercet is completed: "And I have seen things which one who descends therefrom has neither power nor knowledge to relate."[2] Probably, after all, he has seen nothing, and therefore, of course, cannot tell of it. Such is the natural reaction of him who has seen less to him who, having seen more, finds difficulty in making himself understood. In this critical conjecture there is a truth not often realized.

More incomprehensible even than the mystery of the Tri-unity was the mystery of the Incarnation; and the flash wherein this was revealed carried Dante beyond the realm of symbols to the accomplishment of the mystic quest[3] ("già volgeva il mio disio e il velle, sì come rota ch'igualmente è mossa, l'amor che move il sole e l'altre stelle"). The deep mystery of the Incarnation lies less in its duality than in its quaternity,[4] wherein is contained the mystery of Infinite Tri-unity in relationship to nothingness. Within oneness and threeness perceived through study

---

1. "La gloria di colui che tutto move per l'universo penetra e risplende in una parte più e meno altrove. Nel ciel che più de la sua luce prende fu' io." *Par.,* i, 1-5.
2. "E vidi cose che ridire nè sa nè può chi di là su discende." *Par.,* i, 5-6.
3. That is, complete motivation of desire and will by the love that moves the sun and the other stars.
4. Cf. pp. 248, 281-282, etc.

of the natural universe is contained the metaphysics of Dante's tradition. Within twoness and fourness illustrated in scripture is contained its epistemology. Of these the necessary complement is that known now as "theory of values," but in the Middle Ages as the "Way."[5] The secret of the Way is determined by the relationship to Nothing of Infinite Tri-unity, and so brings in the four, not primarily as a power of two (in which sense it applies to method), but as the sum of the Tri-unity and that on which it acts, the Nothing.[6] However strangely such language may fall upon modern ears, it contains in reality nothing of the occult. It is natural to minds that ponder on the finite and on the infinite.[7]

The metaphysics and the epistemology were the subject matter of the two preceding chapters; that which is to be considered here is their complement. The concern is then not the solution of the problem of man's personal relationship to God through the universe of nature and humanity, nor even of the mutual seeking of God for man and man for God in the drama of history, but it is the Way which each must follow in his solitary Quest.

The Logos, Creator and Redeemer, his earthly mission completed, sent forth his Spirit, that the Way of knowledge might be made manifest to men. Augustine speaks in his *Confessions,* of the Platonists, who "saw whither they were to go, but knew nothing of the way" and of the Christians, to whom had been revealed "that path which leads unto that blessed country."[8] This

5. As De Wulf has pointed out, the difference between philosophy and theology in the Middle Ages lay not in their subject matter, which was identical, but in their point of view and approach. The same might be said of medieval epistemology and its belief in revelation through the Divine Word; as also of the theory of values and the devotional life of the soul (mysticism).

6. This as the complete expression of reality becomes the sum of one, two, three, and four in ten. Ten is also the sum of the One and the Nine, the Divine Unity and the Miracle whose root is the Trinity. Cf. p. 30 and Appendix V, Pt. I, i.

7. It is to be hoped that some time the historical development of the concept of infinity may be given thorough treatment. Here it is possible only to suggest the age-long struggle in man's thinking, between the concept of *Unendlichkeit*— limitless extension in time or space—and the concept of Infinity, given definition by Boethius to become classical in later thought for the inspiration of Thomas of Aquino and of Dante Alighieri.

8. Augustine distinguishes "inter videntes, quo eundum sit, nec videntes qua; et viam ducentem ad beatificam patriam." *Confessions,* 7, 20.

phase of the study leads inevitably into the realm of mysticism: that is, the attempt so to live in all phases of the personality[9] that through increasing penetration into the mystery of reality the mind may be prepared to gaze at last upon the whole. The Way is studied against the background of the inner life, in its response to God's self-revelation through the two external sources of knowledge, nature and scripture, in their illumination by the two internal sources, reason and grace. Yet complete vision of the Way such as to include its goal lies beyond the realm of expression. Dante had seen the Nothing which is the base of finite creation, in its relationship to Infinity; and could not tell of it because language and symbols themselves are but a product of this relationship.

PART I. THE SUN IN MEDIEVAL TRADITION (INNER EXPERIENCE)

I. THE INFINITE FOCUS OF CREATION

IT was in reality not so much the relationship of the Son to the Father, as the Infinity of Deity itself, that was given definition in the *Symbolum* which resulted from the Athanasian controversy and ever after distinguished initiates of the Way from those who knew merely whither they were to go. The One and the Logos were as much Generator and Generated, whether the relationship were expressed through the symbol of parenthood or through the symbol of sun and radiance. The necessity for correcting symbol by symbol is evident; for the symbol of parental relationship used alone presupposes, as Arius justly pointed out, the finitude of the Son.[10] The sun and radiance symbolism makes comprehensible at the same time with the sonship, the infinite nature. It was the infinity and eternity, alike of God as Father and of God as Son, which solar symbolism clarified for those who followed the Athanasian tradition.

9. This conception of mysticism was held not only in the Middle Ages. It has been expressed by a modern analytic student as: "la mise en oeuvre de cette croyance par l'intermédiare du cerveau des croyants, à l'aide de certaines pratiques adjuvantes (prieres, ascétisme, contemplation, initiations, méditations, contagion mentale, intoxications, etc.)." Marie, *Mysticisme et Folie*, p. 19.

10. Because of generation in time.

ETERNAL RELATIONSHIPS

Infinity, according to mathematical definition a whole of which its every fraction[11] is equal to itself, necessarily is assumed in a definition of tri-unity. Dionysius meditated on that peculiar unity without a share in which nothing exists in the world, on the existence of which all depends—the One which "is not one of the many things in the world, but is before all Unity and Multiplicity and gives to all Unity and Multiplicity their definite bounds." He adds, "if all things be conceived as being ultimately unified with each other, then all things taken as a whole are One."[12] Such was the one simple Light of the *Paradiso*.[13] The reason for this character of the unity[14] is its infinity. Infinity acting on zero, as shown in the simple process of multiplication, produces the finites. Thus in creation, God, the Tri-unity, acting on that nothingness which constitutes the *quartum quid,* eternally gives being to the continuing finite universe. Thus truly without God all creation is nothing.

In Deity is bound up the mystery of number.[15] God in three

11. Produced by division by a finite number.

12. "For there is nothing in the world without a share in the One; and, just as all number participates in unity (and we speak of *one* couple, *one* dozen, *one* half, *one* third, or *one* tenth) even so everything and each part of everything participates in the One, and on the existence of the One all other existences are based, and the One Cause of all things is not one of the many things in the world, but is before all Unity and Multiplicity and gives to all Unity and Multiplicity their definite bounds. For no multiplicity can exist except by some participation in the One: that which is many in its accidental qualities is one in its substance; that which is many in number of faculties is one in species; that which is many in its emanating activities is one in its originating essence. . . . And without the One there can be no Multiplicity; yet contrariwise the One can exist without the Multiplicity just as the Unit exists before all multiplied Number. And if all things be conceived as being ultimately unified with each other, then all things taken as a whole are One." Dionysius the Areopagite, *On Divine Names,* tr. C. E. Rolt, chap. 13, par. 2.

13. For God as the perfect Unit, cf. also Thomas Aquinas, *S.Th.,* 1, *Q.* 4, *art.* 2. Cf. also *Par.,* xxviii, 16-21, and xxxiii, 89-90. From this perfect Unit comes all multiplicity, a fact expressed by Cacciaguida in the Heaven of Mars: "Tu credi che a me tuo pensier mei da quel che'è primo, così come raia da l'un, se si conosce, il cinque e 'l sei"—"Thou deemest that to me thy thought hath way e'en from the primal Thought, as ray forth from the monad, rightly known, the pentad and the hexad." *Par.,* xv, 55-57.

14. Dionysius prefaced the passage just quoted with the statement, "And the title 'One' implies that it is all things under the form of Unity through the Transcendence of its single Oneness, and is the Cause of all things without departing from that Unity." *Loc. cit.*

15. He who is surprised or baffled by the prominence of number symbolism in medieval thought and expression should remind himself constantly that in such

aspects as the first cause, the efficient cause, and the final cause, is Alpha and Omega, with all that lies between. He is given appropriate expression in the number three, early chosen as sacred among numbers because unique in its outlining of beginning, middle, and end. To his unity, the solar unity from which radiates forth all number,[13] his very name bears witness through its initial letter.[16] God is Three and God is One; yet with four also there exists a peculiar relationship. The cross of the solar deity, on which suffered God the Son in his human nature as the Second Adam, divides the disk of the sun into four quadrants by its four arms, directing to the four cardinal points of the compass.[17] (On Calvary it was inscribed with four words: Iesus Nazar. Rex Iudaeorum.) Essentially a triple cross, into it enter four circles —equator, zodiac, equinoctial colure, and horizon.[18a] The message of the Logos was carried by four evangelists, even as the cortege of the solar god is represented by the four "fixed" signs of the zodiac.[18b] The very name of God tends always to appear

symbolism the aim was then the expression of deeper truths than those of mathematics as now generally conceived. The significance of One in religion and in philosophy is clear, in the persistent strivings of the human mind for monotheism and for monism. Two expresses the fundamental dualities of the universe, which make monism and monotheism alike seem so beset with contradictions. Three (to give one among innumerable instances of its presentation in the world of thought) expresses the great problem of modern philosophy, the knowledge relation, with its factors of the known, the knower, and the relationship between them; and Four, as Philo justly pointed out, is the mathematical number of extended matter.

16. For a further discussion of Dante's ideas as to the Divine Name, cf. D. Guerri, "Il nome adamitico di Dio," in *Di alcuni versi dotti della Divina Commedia*, 1908.

17. The east represented the head of the cross, the origin of light. The west represented the foot of the cross, the country to which salvation goes. The north represented the left arm of the cross, the realm of sin. The south represented the right arm of the cross, the seat of grace. The initials of the four corresponding winds, Anatole, Dysis, Arctos, and Mesembria, spell ADAM.

18a. Cf. *Par.*, i, 39, and p. 161. Cf. also Howard Candler, *On the Symbolic Use of Number in the Divina Commedia and Elsewhere.*

18b. There is almost a correspondence between the symbolic animal forms of the evangelists, and those of the four fixed signs of the zodiac, the four points of the cosmic cross. Taurus, the Bull, suggests the second beast of Rev. 4. 7, while Leo, the lion, recalls the first. Aquarius, the Water-Carrier, is human, even as the third beast has a face as a man. St. John, however, is represented, not by Scorpio, but by a flying eagle. It is interesting that the animals corresponding to the four types of "elemental" spirits, in popular pneumatology of the time and later, are those of the evangelists, rather than those of the zodiac. (There is also an association of the four rivers with the four evangelists. Cf. p. 267 n. 82.)

The four beasts characteristically associated with the sun god were interpreted by Irenaeus (second century) as referring to the human nature, royal character,

as composed of four letters— θέος,[19a] Deus, Dieu, Alla, Jove, JHVH—the sacred Tetragrammaton.

priestly office, and divine grace of Christ. In consequence they represented also the four evangelists, whose descriptions of Christ stress four different aspects of his character. There was some fumbling, nevertheless, before there could be well established the medieval association of the man with St. Matthew, the lion with St. Mark, the ox with St. Luke, and the eagle with St. John.

Table of the Four Winged Beasts of Ezek. 1 and Rev. 4, as interpreted in various symbolic schemes.

	WINGED LION	WINGED OX (CALF)	WINGED MAN	FLYING EAGLE
Primary Meaning (Irenaeus, 2d cent.)	Royal character of Christ	Priestly office of Christ	Human nature of Christ	Divine grace of Christ
Secondary Meaning (Irenaeus)	St. John	St. Luke	St. Matthew	St. Mark
Secondary Meaning (Athanasius)	St. Luke	St. Mark	St. Matthew	St. John
Secondary Meaning (Augustine: Bede)	St. Matthew	St. Luke	St. Mark	St. John
Secondary Meaning (later medieval tradition, with reason assigned)	St. Mark, opens gospel with "one crying in the wilderness"	St. Luke, gives full account of the sacrificial death of Christ	St. Matthew, traces the human lineage of Christ	St. John, his gospel soars on eagles' wings to heaven

With reference to Christ Jerome said:

"Homo nascendo,
Vitulus moriendo,
Leo resurgendo,
Aquila ascendo."

Adam of St. Victor wrote:

"Man—of woman generated;
Ox—in offering dedicated;
Lion—having death defeated;
Eagle—mounting to the sky."

There are discussions in Gourmont, *Le Latin mystique*, p. 289, and in F. R. Webber, *Church Symbolism*, pp. 185 ff.

19a. John of Damascus, in his *Exposition of the Orthodox Faith*, I, 9, derives the Greek term for God, ὁ θεός, alternatively from θέειν, to run (Plato's etymology), "because he courses through all things," from αἴθειν, to burn, because he "is a fire consuming all evil," and from θεᾶσθαι, because he is all-seeing. It is to be noted that all-seeingness, fiery consumption of evil, and "coursing through all things" are the time-honored characteristics of the sun god. Cf. pp. 108 ff.

Fundamental to this symbolism of Tri-unity and four is the truth that the Infinite Tri-unity *creates*.

Verily the light passeth over many . . . substances and enlightens those which are beyond them, and there is no visible thing unto which the light reacheth not in the exceeding greatness of its proper radiance. Yea, and it contributes to the birth of material bodies and brings them unto life, and nourishes them that they may grow, and perfects and purifies and renews them.[19b]

Thus is brought in the nine to express the creation of the triune light in relation with the fourth:[19c] that produced by the symbolic meaning of a number is represented by the number's square. Nine representing the circumference of all that is,[20a] given meaning by the central point, is summarized by the all-pervasive one and ten. The eternal relationships of the Godhead lie within itself, relationships between Father and Son, between each and the Holy Ghost. Then in exuberant love creation is brought forth, the finite universe in the place of nothing. Thus are established external relationships of the Godhead—of the Divine Three to a *quartum quid*. Such relationship by necessity implies duality, and the maintenance of this duality within the unity brought upon Deity itself the shadow of the Cross. Finally, from the summation of the one, the two, the three, and the four springs the sacred ten within which is contained God

19b. Dionysius, *op. cit.*, iv, 4.

19c. It is of interest that in the Kabalah, that subtle, elusive, and esoteric power which shared in the molding of medieval quests, there was a harmonization in ten of the four with the nine. Within each of the four realms brooded over by Macroprosopus are three trinities (intellectual, moral, and material) making up the nine, to which is added the tenth, Malkuth, the Queen and Bride of Microprosopus, which in the lowest realm is the earth, and in other realms becomes increasingly spiritualized as the material on which Deity acts. (In the Tetragrammaton, "J" may be interpreted as the Father, "H" the Mother, "V" the Son, and the final "H" the Son's Bride.)

All the emanations are as it were veils to hide the Trinity of the unknowable (the Negative "One" or Ain, the Ain Soph or Limitless, and the Ain Soph Aur or Limitless Light). Moreover, in the diagrammatic arrangement of the ten, emanations or Sephiroth, each becomes a part of the symbolic body, and through the ninth, the ninefold mystery is united after sexual analogy to the tenth, representing the created universe, the womb of which is in Jerusalem. Upon the continuance of union of God and the universe localized in Jerusalem, therefore, depends the joy and well-being of the universe. For Jewish mysticism accepted at last in full literalness the sex symbolism of Reality, in connection with the solar symbolism of the Limitless Light which surrounds and flows out from the Ineffable.

20a. Cf. p. 237 n. 514.

and his creation together with all their interrelationships.[20b]
This minimum of number symbolism is plain even to the novice
in solar worship: The unity of the Light which pervades all
things; the duality in the radiance which unites the sun and the
earth; the trinity of life, light, and heat;[21] and the quaternity of
the triune sun and the earthly life which it brings into being.
The world—the soul—is finite. It was brought forth by the infinite from nothing, as time and space themselves were brought
forth.

ETERNAL VERSUS CONTINUAL

Even after Ambrose's revelation of the symbolic method, it
was the inability to conceive of an infinity not extended in time
or space, that formed a last intellectual barrier to Augustine's
acceptance of Christianity.[22] Only after attainment to this concept,[23] however, was his mind freed for the solution of the mystic's question which pagan philosophy had left unsolved: How
can the individual soul, Nothing made finite, place itself in such
relation to that Infinite that his will may be moved by "l'amor
che move il sole e l'altre stelle." On such matters as these Boe-

20b. It is from the summation of the One of Deity, the Two of the Female or
Creative Principle (the Logos is feminine, for instance, in the Book of Proverbs.
Cf. p. 135 n. 97), the Three of creation in the Realm of Ideas, and the Four
of creation in the universe of time, space, and matter, that the sacred Ten
is reached, which therefore signifies God and his creation together, with all their
interrelationships. Cf. Appendices V, Pt. I, i, and V, Pt. I, ii, also pp. 465 ff.

21. It is interesting that in Philo's presentation are involved the same elements
as in any solar development, with at the same time the omission of the conscious
use of trinity for the Divine.

22. Augustine, *Confessions*, Bk. V, cap. 10-11.

23. His expression of which was to become basic: "Summus enim es et non
mutaris, neque peragitur in te hodiernus dies, et tamen in te peragitur, quia in te
sunt et ista omnia; non enim haberent vias transeundi, nisi contineres ea. Et
quoniam anni tui non deficiunt, anni tui hodiernus dies: et quam multi iam dies
nostri et patrum nostrorum per hodiernum tuum transierunt, et ex illo acceperunt
modos, et utcumque extiterunt, et transibunt adhuc alii et accipient et utcumque
existent. Tu autem idem ipse es, et omnia crastina atque ultra omniaque hesterna
et retro hodie facies, hodie fecisti." *Confessions*, Bk. I, cap. 6.

This classical expression of infinity, given support by the clearer definition of
Boethius, wove itself into the very fabric of medieval intellectual life. Cf. for
example the statement of Anselm: "In this way dost thou transcend all things,
even the eternal, because thy eternity and theirs is present as a whole with thee;
while they have not yet that part of their eternity which is to come, just as they
no longer have that part which is past. For so thou dost ever transcend them
since thou art ever present with thyself, and since that to which they have not yet
come is ever present with thee." *Proslogion*, cap. 20.

thius pondered during the disintegration of the Roman Empire while in long unjust imprisonment he awaited torture and death. He, too, found solution in the perfecting of his conception of infinity.

Although the infinity fundamental in the systems of Plotinus and Augustine had been given implicit definition at Nicaea, it was Boethius who gave the supreme definition for the Middle Ages, a definition to be quoted by "The Philosopher" himself who in the *Paradiso* is made by Dante to point out its formulator as

> l'anima santa che 'l mondo fallace
> fa manifesto a chi di lei ben ode.
> Lo corpo ond' ella fu cacciata giace
> giuso in Cieldauro; ed essa da martiro
> e da essilio venne a questa pace.[24]

In this bitter exile Boethius was consoled by Lady Philosophy, Divine Wisdom, who later, after the death of Beatrice, was to console Dante in his own eventful exile. Eternity, the Lady defined for Boethius as "the simultaneous and complete possession of infinite life." She explained:

> This will appear more clearly if we compare it with temporal things. All that lives under the conditions of time moves through the present from the past to the future; there is nothing set in time which can at one moment grasp the whole space of its lifetime. It cannot yet comprehend tomorrow: yesterday it has already lost. And in this life of today your life is no more than a changing, passing moment.[25]

The distinction between eternity and *Unendlichkeit* is brought out unmistakably in the words which follow: "As Aristotle said of the universe, so it is of all that is subject to time; though it never began to be nor will ever cease, and its life is co-extensive with the infinity of time [*Unendlichkeit*] yet it is not such as can be held to be eternal. For though it apprehends and grasps a space of infinite lifetime, it does not embrace the whole simultaneously; it has not yet experienced the future."[26]

24. "The sainted soul, which unmasketh the deceitful world to whoso giveth it good hearing. The body whence it was chased forth, lieth down below in Cieldauro, and itself from martyrdom and exile came unto this peace." *Par.*, x, 125-129.

25. Boethius, *Consolation of Philosophy,* tr. W. V. Cooper, Bk. V, prose vi.
26. *Ibid.*

What we should rightly call eternal is that which grasps and possesses wholly and simultaneously the fullness of unending life, which lacks naught of the future, and has lost naught of the fleeting past; and such an existence must be ever present in itself to control and aid itself, and also must keep present with itself the infinity of changing time. Therefore, people who hear that Plato thought that this universe had no beginning of time and will have no end, are not right in thinking that in this way the created world is co-eternal with its creator.[27]

Thus, "to pass through unending life, the attribute which Plato ascribes to the universe, is one thing; but it is another thing to grasp simultaneously the whole of unending life in the present."[28]

God is older than his creations, not "by any period of time, but rather by the peculiar property of his own single nature. For the infinite changing of temporal things . . . falls from the single directness of the present, into an infinite space of future and past. . . . Thus if we would apply proper epithets to those subjects, we can say, following Plato, that God is eternal, but the universe is continual. . . ."[29] Moreover, "God has a condition of ever-present eternity, His knowledge . . . views in its own direct comprehension everything as though it were taking place in the present."[30] This same idea was expressed later among the schoolmen, also through the simile of God as the timeless, spaceless center present in the same manner to every point of the time-space circumference.[31] So excellent, however,

27. Boethius, loc. cit.   28. Ibid.   29. Ibid.

30. "If you would weigh the foreknowledge by which God distinguished all things, you will more rightly hold it to be a knowledge of a never-failing constancy in the present, than a foreknowledge of the future. Whence Providence is more rightly to be understood as a looking forth than a looking forward, because it is set far from low matters and looks forth upon all things as from a lofty mountain top above all." Ibid.

Boethius points out that this seeing by God of "all things in his eternal present" exerts no compulsion on events of man's future. "You can change your purpose, but since the truth of Providence knows in its present that you can do so, and whether you do so, and in what direction you may change it, therefore you cannot escape that divine foreknowledge: just as you cannot avoid the glance of a present eye, though you may by your free will turn yourself to all kinds of different actions. . . . The ever-present eternity of His sight moves in harmony with the future nature of our actions." Ibid.

This concept is well pictured in the circle simile noted above. Cf. with the statement by Augustine that by Anselm, quoted p. 340 n. 23.

31. Dante has a vision of Love weeping, in the Vita Nuova (cap. 12). In response to Dante's question as to the cause of his weeping, he replies: "Ego tamquam centrum circuli, cui simili modo se habent circumferentiae partes; tu

did "The Philosopher of the Middle Ages" consider this work of Boethius to be, that with no restatement and little expansion, he simply quotes the older formulation in his compendium of Catholic theology.

It is this eternity, true infinity, of the Tri-unity, that makes possible that inversion of the world of appearances which marks the entrance of the mystic on his quest. It is, moreover, the direct taking up of finite nature into infinity through the duality of the Incarnation, that renders this experience possible to man,[32] in defining eternally the relation to the Tri-unity of the *quartum quid*. As this at-one-ment of finite and infinite was accomplished by God through the Logos, so for man it must be accomplished through a recognition of symbolism in experience and language.[33] Discipline, illumination, and union are the three strands of the Way.

INVERSION OF THE NOTHING

Only with the turning toward the Divine Sun as the infinite focus of creation does the mystic enter seriously upon his quest, and for this turning, in which is involved inversion of the world of appearance, there is demanded the utmost of discipline. Abhorrence of evil becomes recognition of its impotence, as the Worm is dethroned from the center of the universe. So completely does Dionysius reverse the world of appearance that for him even devils, in so far as they exist, are not naturally evil. In other words, evil, from the point of view of eternity, is lacking

---

autem non sic." Cf. also the discussion in Thomas Aquinas, *Summae contra gentiles,* Bk. 1, cap. 66, 6.

32. This infinity which could take up finity into itself was the model for the solution of all Dante's problems. Cf. pp. 465 ff. and diagram p. 98.

33. Dionysius the pseudo-Areopagite, whose works, as translated by Erigena, are basic in all of western mysticism, has laid stress on the ease with which man, clinging to the familiar notion of his senses, is led astray by the superficial meaning of the ultimate truth: "As I have said elsewhere, we misinterpret things above us by our own conceits and cling to the familiar notions of our senses, and measuring Divine things by our human standards, we are led astray by the superficial meaning of the Divine and Ineffable Truth. Rather should we then consider that while the human intellect hath a faculty of intelligence, whereby it perceives intellectual truths, yet the act whereby the Intellect communes with the things that are beyond it transcends its intellectual nature. This transcendent sense, therefore, must be given to our language about God, and not our human sense." Dionysius, *op. cit.,* viii, 1. Cf. the discussion of functional and literal truth, Appendix IV, Pt. I, i.

in both power and life, as Dante, from the point of view of time, beheld it in Cocytus in the process of becoming. The real meaning of Plato's allegory of the Cave is just this reversal: "The man in Plato's allegory of the Cave . . . knew that his chief task was to turn the prisoners round so that they could face in the direction of the sun."[34] True as it is that "the sun will do the rest," it will do it only if man responds to it perfectly; and that he may be capable of such response, long discipline is necessary. Dionysius has given the summary:

> This great, all-bright and ever-shining sun, which is the visible image of the Divine Goodness, faintly reëchoing the activity of the Good, illumines all things that can receive its light, while retaining the utter simplicity of light, and expands above and below throughout the visible world the beams of its own radiance. And if there is aught that does not share them, this is not due to any weakness or deficiency in its distribution of the light, but is due to the unreceptiveness of those creatures which do not attain sufficient singleness to participate therein.[35]

The attainment of this "singleness" is that which the mystic describes as the "purgative way,"[36] the first labor of him who has set out on the mystic quest.

Gradually all that distracts, and so subjects to *gravezza* as opposed to the upward drawing of the Divine Sun, infinite focus of creation, is not only eradicated, but, after repentance and its sacrament, given over to oblivion as deep as that produced by Lethe. Even the memory of *gravezza* must not remain to oppose its shadow to the redeeming Light. In this purgative phase of the mystic progress the body is necessarily subjected to discipline, not in punishment, but as a sort of military training, that it may remain subject to the intellect, and sensitive, even in crises, to each faintest sign which would indicate the way.[37]

34. C. A. Bennett, *Philosophical Study of Mysticism,* p. 168.
35. Dionysius, *op. cit.,* iv, 4.
36. Whereas this particular term, together with the terms "illuminative way" and "unitive way," did not become current till after Dante's time, the stages of progress which they signify are a permanent characteristic of the mystical life. Mystical life is not an arbitrary attempt to go through a mapped-out scheme, but a development from a certain point of origin according to a natural psychological process. It is true that many of the pioneers in analyzing mystic stages listed four, or seven, or nine such stages; but this does not alter the fact that the stages listed are but subdivisions, each of which can be subsumed under one of the three natural major divisions of mystic progress.
37. It is only through the harmonious functioning of desire as perfectly or-

Mysticism was not then, as it is so often considered nowadays, a vague dreaminess or even such perception of the infinite in all things as Wordsworth expressed in connection with his primrose. It was rather the tedious and perilous adventure of a lifetime, the least swerving from which placed the pilgrim in the environment of Dante's *Inferno,* and involved in the fulfilment of which was crucifixion. Mystics of all times have pointed out that man may not love God with impunity.[38]

The discipline of the mystic way must be, moreover, not only physical and moral, but also, and obviously, intellectual, since its aim is the Vision. Pourrat explains, paraphrasing Dionysius:

This needful purification is at once moral and intellectual. The soul must separate itself from creatures and be preserved from voluptuousness, like Moses, who, before going up Mount Sinai and entering the mysterious cloud, separated himself from his people in order to sanctify himself. It must finally strip itself of the imagination of sense and of imperfect ideas which can only hinder it in its desire to reach contemplation. The soul thus prepared will enter into the divine light and become united to God in contemplation.[39a]

Thomas à Kempis says later: "And hence we find but few contemplatives, because there are but few who can wholly disengage themselves from perishable and created things."[39b] Thus the constant tendency in man's nature to worship the symbol rather than the thing symbolized is simply evidence of insufficient discipline in the mystic way, but at the same time right use of symbol[40] is man's only means of progress in that way, until at last his vision be bathed in the river of light. This aspect of the mystic progress has been termed the illuminative way.

Through such purgation and illumination man, setting forth

dered by intellect that the intellect is given its greatest power to know. Thus one must be holy to know, even as through knowledge one may increase in holiness.

38. E.g., "The soul instinctively knows that God cannot be loved with impunity." E. Hermann, *Meaning and Value of Mysticism,* p. 134.

39a. Pourrat, P., *Christian Spirituality,* p. 219.

39b. À Kempis, *Imitation of Christ,* Bk. IV, 31, 1.

40. "I say not (as was feigned by the ancient myth) that the Sun is the God and Creator of this universe, and therefore takes the visible world under his special care; but I say that the 'invisible things of God from the creation of the world are clearly seen, being understood by the things that are made, even his eternal power and Godhead.' " Dionysius, *op. cit.,* iv, 4.

The translator, after giving the reference to Rom. 1. 20, adds as footnote, "The sun is not personal or supra-personal, but its impersonal activity is an emblem, as it were, of God's supra-personal activity."

a living ghost from nothingness with eternity around him,[41] is prepared for the fulfilment of the promise in his initiation, wherein he is *renatus in aeternum*. Medieval literature is filled with a sense that that which alone is desired by all creation is the sun, source of life, light, and heat. Dionysius, venerated by Dante as "that taper's light, which, in the flesh below, saw deepest into the angelic nature and its ministry,"[42] states:

> and like as after the Good all things do yearn—those that have mind and reason seeking It by knowledge, those that have perception seeking It by perception, those that have no perception seeking It by the natural movement of their vital instinct, and those that are without life and have mere existence seeking It by their aptitude for that bare participation whence this mere existence is theirs. . . . All material things desire the sun, for they desire either to see or to move and to receive light and warmth and to be maintained in existence by the light.[43]

The price of the threefold detriment in man is the long discipline which must precede the fulfilment of his desire.

Occasionally the soul is vouchsafed a moment of clear sight as with Dante in the Primum Mobile when, without effort, as the fruit of perfect control, the inversion of the universe is seen as inevitable and permanent. This, which is in reality experience of the unitive way, may by the mercy of God occur at any stage of the soul's progress,[44] and it is the soul's response to this vision that bursts forth in those love ardors which seem so closely akin to the love rhapsodies of the troubadours. It is a love that can be free and youthful and joyous because the fruit of discipline has been attained; and it finds expression in the love songs of the court of heaven rather than of the courts of earth. As a modern scholar has said, commenting on a mystic poem:[45]

41. Carlyle, *Sartor Resartus*.

42. "Il lume di quel cero che, giù, in carne, più adentro vide l'angelica natura e 'l ministero." *Par.*, x, 115-117.

43. Dionysius, *loc. cit.*

44. As Dante seems to claim in his own case. He writes: "But if they yelp against the assignment of so great exaltation, because of the sin of the speaker, let them read Daniel, where they will find that Nabuchodonosor, too, was divinely enabled to see certain things against sinners, and then dropped them into oblivion; for he, 'who makes his sun to rise upon the good and the evil, and sends his rain upon the just and the unjust,' sometimes in compassion, for their conversion, sometimes in wrath, for their punishment, reveals his glory, in greater or less measure, as he wills, to those who live never so evilly." *Epistle to Can Grande*, 28.

45. *The Dark Night of the Soul,* by St. John of the Cross.

In the poem before us, the passion flames forth unchecked by any limitation because it is perfectly pure—and purity is essentially freedom from limits. . . . Good people differ from saints and sinners alike in this, that they are afraid of passion, and therefore afraid of life. . . . I do not blame this attitude of the good. It is often their only safeguard. They lack the capacity to purify and spiritualize passion, and therefore must avoid it entirely. . . . Unlike these good people, the saints have not fled from passion, they have transformed it and raised it to a higher level where it is freed from the limitations of sense.[46]

Guido Guinicelli, whose art Dante perfected, reconciled in his mystical ode, *Al cor gentil ripara sempre amore,* the two conceptions of love regarded as antagonistic[47] by all but the disciplined mystic. The mystic, as Dante knew, goes a step farther, and while accepting this pure love of Woman as a symbol through which he may reach God, refuses ever to worship the symbol for itself. As with his progress he perceives more and more of ultimate reality through the symbol, at the same time the symbol occupies less and less of his attention, until ultimately it takes its place among all created things on a petal of the rose, while he gazes beyond it into the full glory of the sun.[48]

II. LAW OF KNOWLEDGE AND EXPRESSION

OF the medieval theory of knowledge, basis of illumination in the Way, the underlying philosophy is that of insight symbolism, already described as depending on the existence of an infinite unity self-expressed in all the discrete. With the gradual attainment of that singleness which permits ever more constant turning toward the Divine Sun, infinite focus of creation, the seeker is freed more and more for progress in illumination. In the *via purgativa,* desire is permanently centered on supreme reality, and thus the soul is delivered over to the divine attraction of the sun, through which it may ascend, as Dante climbed in purgatory, with ever increasing freedom from the *gravezza* of

46. E. I. Watkin, *Philosophy of Mysticism,* pp. 398-400.
47. "On the one hand we find reconciled two conceptions of love hitherto regarded as antagonistic." Snell, *The Fourteenth Century.* Cf. pp. 36-37, 168-171, 226, 386-390, and especially 427-430.
48. *Par.,* xxxi, 64-93.

evil, until at last from the top of the mountain, even without his knowledge, he ascended to the spheres. The secret of the *via illuminativa* is progress in understanding founded on the discipline of purgation, leading to the ordering of the self-contradictions of experience in the world. As the response to divine attraction becomes perfect, the soul is given that illumination through which Dante beheld, "bound by love in one volume, the scattered leaves of all the universe."[49]

Those mystics who, like Blake, have named implicitly or actually, Urizon (Your Reason) as the eternal villain in the drama of life, have added to misconceptions already too thick in the mists which becloud the threefold Way. More than this, they have been responsible for the development of a false mysticism. The basis of the *via illuminativa* is in the theory of knowledge. So strong has been the suspicion on the part of observers that the mystic is in possession of a source of knowledge mysteriously claiming no kinship with reason and sense, that some mystics in all ages have succumbed to the lure of this belief. Body and mind have been starved in the production of strange experiences. Disastrous has been misunderstanding of the purgative way, through loss of contact with the stream of mystical thought. Such loss is exemplified preëminently in Luther, Bunyan, and Loyola, whose exaggerated sense of wickedness and desire for purgation would have been counted deadly sin in the medieval tradition.[50] Yet even more subversive has been misconception of the *via illuminativa*, responsible in very fact for the controversies which formed so large a part of the intellectual history of the Middle Ages, with their outcome in the benighting eclipse of theology and philosophy, in the intellectual realm, the two suns of Rome.

49. "Even so doth the light (being as it were Its visible image) draw together all things and attract them unto Itself, those that can see, those that have motion, those that receive Its light and warmth, those that are scarcely held in being by Its rays; whence the sun is so called because it summeth all things and uniteth the scattered elements of the world." Dionysius, *op. cit.,* iv, 4.

50. John F. Howley, *Psychology and Mystical Experience* (London: Trübner, 1920), p. 15. The mystic was not encouraged to distort his perception by a morbid dwelling on his own wickedness. His attention was rather drawn to the divine love, which immediately upon repentance removed all barriers between him and the upward drawing light. Cf. also pp. 343 ff.

THE FATEFUL GIFTS

Like the betrayal which resulted in the mutual eclipse of empire and church the intellectual betrayal, also, found its initiation for the Middle Ages in the fourth century. Constantine, glorious as the first to unite to Christianity the power of empire, and so to establish the supremacy in its own sphere of the church, at the same time though unwittingly, like the Eagle in the Pageant, bestowed upon it a fateful gift. Augustine, illustrious as the first to unite to Christianity the power of philosophy, and so to establish its supremacy in the world of thought, likewise unwittingly endowed it with a disrupting gift. As Constantine gave to the church a portion of that which belonged rightly only to the temporal government, so Augustine gave to Christian experience a portion of that which belonged rightly only to the realm of sense perception interpreted by reason. Little did Constantine foresee that through his gift the papacy was to assert temporal supremacy: likewise Augustine could scarcely have foreseen, when he insisted on the primacy of inner experience, that he was giving it the power to encroach on the rightful realm of reason and so paving the way for such aberrations as the seeking in trance and ecstasy of rapturous love, for scientific detail concerning the external universe. Honoring both leaders in the *Paradiso*,[51] Dante on earth combated with all his power the fruits of their evil gifts: the theory of papal temporal supremacy and the theory of the primacy of the act of loving over the act of knowing, each of which was an infringement on the essential autonomy of the members of earthly pairs.

As Constantine in setting Christianity above the greatest of pagan institutions made an error the pagan empire had not made; similarly Augustine, in setting Christianity above the greatest of

---

51.
"L'altro che segue . . .
   sotto buona intenzion che fè mal frutto,
   per cedere al pastor si fece greco:
ora conosce come il mal dedutto
   dal suo bene operar non li è nocivo,
   avvegna che sia 'l mondo indi distrutto."

"The next who followeth . . . with good intention that bore evil fruit, to give place to the pastor, made himself a Greek; now knoweth he that the ill deduced from his good deed hurteth not him though the world be destroyed thereby."

Par., xx, 55-60 (In Sphere of Jupiter).
Augustine holds an important seat in the Rose. Cf. *Par.*, xxxii, 35.

pagan philosophies, fell into an error of which that philosophy had not been guilty. In his defense of the Christian *Weltanschauung* as opposed even to the greatest philosophy of paganism, Augustine gave stability to Christian monotheism, yet gave definite form to the haunting shadow of dualism which has always beset even the most ambitious monism.[52] From this time forth the official philosophy of Catholicism was to be dualistic, exhibiting now and then monistic possibilities. As a matter of fact, even monists, as dualists delight to point out, although they invariably salve their conscience by calling the opposite pole of being by highly negative names, never rise above the need of a foil,[53] whether it be the devil, or raw material. For Augustine, in accord with the tendency already familiar,[54] light had its foil in darkness. More than this, he pictured the dichotomy concretely in his definition of the two cities, the one good, the other evil. For Plotinus the good was identical with Being, the evil with Non-Being. For Augustine, whatever his philosophy, and for all his training in Neoplatonism, evil assumed persistent reality.

Psychological explanation for this fact is amply suggested in the *Confessions,* but there was also a philosophical reason. Living in the wake of Nicaea, while the absolute equality of the Persons of the Godhead was among the most prominent of controversial questions, Augustine turned his attention to the demonstration of errors in the Plotinian *Weltanschauung.*[55] Himself having experienced great difficulty with the concept of infinity,[56] Augustine was hampered in handling all its applications by Plotinus. That is, although to Plotinus the World Soul, like the Logos and the One, is itself infinite and divine, yet as Augustine understood Plotinus, the World Soul was created and so finite. Whereas the Christian speaks of the Three Persons as aspects

52. The problem of evil ever forms the great stumblingblock in the path of those who would define fundamental reality religiously in terms of monotheism, or philosophically in terms of monism.

53. The point here, however, for the mystic, essentially a monist, is that the One finds eternal expression in the Two.

54. Cf. Lactantius, and others, quoted in Chap. III, Pt. I, ii.

55. "Plotinus, save in very rare instances, never discusses anything, the soul or happiness, virtue or magic, God or matter, without unmistakable reference to the totality of his universe." I. Edman, *Logic of Mysticism in Plotinus,* in "Studies in the History of Ideas," II, 52. Cf. also Appendix V, Pt. I, ii, for comparison of the Plotinian and Augustinian conceptions of the trinity.

56. Cf. *De civitate Dei,* 10, 23, and 10, 29.

of and united in the Divine Sun, Plotinus' symbolism is conceived as placing the World Soul in the position of the moon:

> Plotinus commenting on Plato repeatedly and strongly asserts that not even the soul which they believe to be the soul of the world, derives its blessedness from any other source than we do, namely, from that Light which is distinct from it, and created it, and by whose intelligible illumination it enjoys light in things intelligible. He also compares those spiritual things to the vast and conspicuous heavenly bodies, as if God were the sun and the soul the moon; for they suppose that the moon derives its light from the sun.[57]

So eagerly does Augustine combat this supposed error of Plotinus that he brings about an entire separation of the world from the divine, giving to it psychologically, if not philosophically, the position of the Plotinian Non-Being.[58] The God of Plotinus was completely transcendent, but through the World Soul also completely immanent. Augustine, in his opposition to ideas of the World Soul, well-nigh stripped his God of all immanence whatsoever. Immanence remained only as the central point in each soul: the human mind was to be turned inward. Thus the realm of external nature, even contrary to the true spirit of his own theories, became at all times a distraction and frequently an evil.

For Augustine, the setting for the great drama between good and evil is the soul of man, and all things pertaining to the external world are regarded merely as necessary interruptions.[59]

---

57. Cf. Augustine's *Confessions*, Bk. V, 10-11.

58. At the same time the concept corresponding actually to the Plotinian Non-Being in the Christian philosophy tended to become focused and personified in Mary, through whose union with God all creation and the Nothing itself were taken up into the divine unity. So powerful became this tendency that Mary, who in strict philosophical terms was but human symbol of the Absolute Nothing on which Deity acts, came in fact almost to replace the concept, giving to it, through her willing assent, an actual activity.

In all philosophical theories of creation, there is a dual motion, outward from and returning to the One. The First Person generates the Second, and from this relationship springs the Third, who, in order that there may be external manifestation of Deity, broods over Non-Being, preparing it to embody the Second, whose eternal mission is revelation of the First. Through this mission the Second Person becomes the Way to mystic union, inevitably sought by the *quartum quid*—Non-Being stirred to action by his means in creation. There is no concept in any metaphysic more difficult than this of the negative Fourth, in its relationship to the Infinite.

59. "The earthly city, which does not live by faith, seeks an earthly peace, and the end it proposes, in the well-ordered concord of civic obedience and rule,

The natural response to God as he most closely touches man becomes in consequence one of loving the Immanence within, rather than of knowing the Immanence which is in all creation. The Augustinian arrives at knowledge of the Trinity by true love.[60]

> Let no one say, I do not know what I love. Let him love his brother, and he will love the same love. For he knows the love with which he loves, more than the brother whom he loves. So now he can know God more than he knows his brother, clearly known more, because more present, known more, because more within him, known more, because more certain. Embrace the love of God, and by love embrace God.[61]

Here is the basis for the medieval controversy: Is loving dependent on knowing, or is knowing dependent on loving?[62]

A kind of otherworldliness and contempt of too much interest in the data of this present world is common to both Plotinus and Augustine. Nevertheless, both are constrained by their principles to acknowledge sacredness and holiness in matter, though for different reasons—Plotinus because the visible universe is the visible embodiment of the World Soul, and the Christian because the Logos became incarnate in the flesh. Augustine praises the Platonists for their attitude toward matter,[63] and proceeds at the same time to point out an error in their account of the origin of evil. In his opinion,

the corruption of the body, which weighs down the soul, is not the cause [as the Platonists maintain],[64] but the punishment of the first

---

is the combination of men's wills to attain the things which are helpful to this life. The heavenly city, or rather the part of it which sojourns on earth and lives by faith, makes use of this peace only because it must, until this mortal condition which necessitates it shall pass away." *De civitate Dei*, 19, 17.

60. Augustine, *De Trinitate*, 8, 7.   61. *Ibid.*, 8, 8.

62. Cf. pp. 60-61.

63. Plotinus, it is true, somewhat obscures his attitude toward the physical universe by using the term "matter" for the ultimate Non-Being or zero concept of thought, and as such there is no goodness in it. But the matter of which he is speaking is not the "matter" of the physical universe, which already shares in the being of the World Soul or Third Hypostasis of the Plotinian trinity, and as such can truly be said to share in a way in the contemplation of the Logos. (Dante in a similar manner extends the love-principle to inanimate creation. Cf. *Purg.*, xvii, 91-93.)

64. "The Platonists indeed are not so foolish as, with the Manicheans, to detest our present bodies as an evil nature, for they attribute all the elements of which this visible and tangible world is compacted, with all their qualities, to God their creator. Nevertheless, from the death-infected members and earthly

sin; and it was not the corruptible flesh that made the soul sinful, but the sinful soul that made the flesh corruptible.[65]

That is, creation *ex nihilo* provides the possibility, not the actuality, of evil in the human will, and the dragging action of matter,[66] which all men experience even in innocent physical necessities, is not the cause of the will's actualization of that possible evil, but its result. The Fall of Man actually changed the nature, not only of his soul, but of his flesh. For Plotinus the detriment in man's nature was a fact in the natural universe; for Augustine the Fall of Man was drawn into the domain of history. Further, for all of Augustine's understanding of symbolism, he had little interest in checking the one external source of knowledge, scripture, by the other, nature.[67] The key to his real divergence from the great Neoplatonists is that the attention of the strongly introspective Augustine became centered in human history and in inner experience. This Augustinian tradition with its centralization of history and inner experience rather than of impersonal truth, was to bring Christianity into frequent conflict with philosophy.

Augustinian mysticism finds then its basis in the Platonic idea of eternity and Non-Being, uniquely combined with the naïve and direct narrative of Christian tradition. The philosophy of

construction of the body, they believe the soul is so affected that there are thus originated in it the diseases of desires and fears and joy and sorrow, under which four perturbations, as Cicero calls them, or passions, as most prefer to name them with the Greeks, is included the whole viciousness in human life." *De civitate Dei*, 14, 5.

65. *Ibid.*, 14, 3.

66. To no true mystic is matter evil, and no such doctrine belongs to early Christianity. Even Tertullian, with his undoubtedly extreme ascetic tendencies, regarded the separation of soul and flesh not as a relief to the soul,—the usual Greek or Gnostic view,—but as violence to nature; and the soul, not the flesh, as the source of evil. He even is forced to argue that the concomitants of birth (of which he lists some of the least agreeable) are not shameful. God loved and honored men born in all the natural filth of the birth event, he argues, even though Marcion does not so love and honor. "Loving man, He loved his nativity also, and his flesh as well. Nothing can be loved apart from that through which whatever exists has its existence." (*De carne Christi*, cap. iv.) Only those who repudiate God can hate or envy the flesh. (*De resurrectione carnis*, cap. 63.) Christianity was saved from gnostic exaltation of spirit over matter, by the incarnation and resurrection of Christ. The body that clothes the blessed Logos must be holy, and so must be the bodies which, in his mystical body the church, come in most intimate contact with his sacramental body.

67. To Augustine the sources of knowledge possessing reliable validity are scripture (i.e., human history) and inner experience.

appearance and reality is expressed in terms of grace and sin. Nevertheless, true to the thought which was later to dominate the threefold Way, Augustine conceived the sole activity rightly termed intellectual to be the seeking of God by the soul:

> For if the eye knows how to feed on light, and yet doth not diminish the light; for the light will be no less because it is seen by more; it feeds the eyes of more, and yet is as great as it was before; both they are fed, and it is not diminished; if God hath granted this to the light which he hath made for the eyes of the flesh, what is he himself, the Light for the eyes of the heart? If then any choice food were praised to thee, on which thou wert to dine, thou wouldest prepare the stomach; God is praised to thee, prepare the heart.[68]

Augustine's truly wise man seeks God through discipline of body and mind, by a seeking within, not an external seeking.

For Augustine, it is God's handiwork in nature as contemplated within the soul, which constitutes the continual divine self-revelation to man. As the soul thus progresses in illumination it penetrates more and more deeply beneath symbols to the thought expressed: it leaves the city of darkness to penetrate ever more deeply into the mysteries of the city of light:

> For the Apostle saith, Ye were once darkness, but are now light in the Lord. . . . Why light? Because by participation of that Light, thou art light. But if from the Light wherewith thou art enlightened thou go back, thou returnest to thine own darkness.[69]

In turning to the light the human will, the root of the perturbations of the soul, is brought into harmony with the divine will:

> The character of the human will is of moment, because if it is wrong these motions of the soul will be wrong, but if it is right, they will be not merely blameless but even praiseworthy. For the will is in them all, yea, none of them is anything else than will.[70]

In all of this Augustine is in complete accord with Dante's tradition; but the journey from the city of darkness to the city of light takes place within the soul. The mystic reversal comes to him, not with the perception of the conceptual Non-Being of

---

68. Augustine, *Sermons on Selected Lessons of the New Testament*, Homily on John 5 and I Cor. 2, p. 556. Cf. also *Homilies on the Gospel according to St. John*, Homilies on John 8. 13-14 and on John 3. 29-36, pp. 493, 215.
69. Augustine, *Homilies on the Gospel according to Saint John*, 5. 26, p. 349.
70. Augustine, *De civitate Dei*, 14, 6.

evil and of its tendency to self-destruction because of the lack of reality there is in it. It comes rather as the fruit of individual progress in the life of grace, and as true for the individual only, for as soon as by grace his will is made good, there is no longer any place for evil. Within inner experience for him lies the whole drama of the world.

Although the way of illumination is traveled by all mystics, and its meaning lies in the philosophy of insight symbolism, nevertheless, for different mystics it bears different aspects. For some mystics it may become a purely intellectual pathway, the road of dialectic, while for others it lies through an ever deeper sensitivity to the meaning of sense phenomena, and for still others it may be a journey into the interior depths of the soul. In the greatest of mystics there is the conscious attempt to exhaust all possibilities of knowledge, from without and from within. Although by his own greatness and by his lack of interest in the material universe, Augustine was saved from the extravagancies into which many of his followers were led, it was philosophically unfortunate that he should have given to introspection such an overwhelming authority. With Plotinus, intuition for its validity rested on the complete development of reason, autonomous within its own sphere. It has been well said: "In the mysticism of a thinker like Plotinus, reason is carried strenuously and precisely to the very heart and substance of Being. If there it finds its own terminus, it must be noted that that terminus has been found by reason itself."[71] Ultimately, the "completest thought merges into that identity of union and rapture which life and love and art sometimes provide for an instant, instants which are types and symbols of eternity."[72] Followers of the Augustinian tradition on the other hand came to distrust reason and logic and to attempt completion of the illuminative way without them. Such was the evil gift which Augustine bequeathed to later mysticism.

RECONCILIATION OF OPPOSITES

In the approach to an understanding of God through symbolism Augustine, for all his "fateful gift" was in line with the de-

71. Edman, *op. cit.,* p. 51. 72. *Ibid.,* p. 81.

velopment of the mystic tradition as it was to be understood by Thomas as well as by Bonaventure. Like all mystics, he employed images belonging to all the senses:

> Vocasti et clamasti et rupisti surditatem meam; coruscasti, splendasti et fugasti caecitatem meam; fragasti, et duxi spiritum, et anhelo tibi, gustavi et esurio et sitio, tetigisti me, et exarsi in pacem tuam;[73]

similarly, in description of his concept of God:

> Quid autem amo, cum te amo? non specium corporis nec decus temporis, non candorem lucis ecce istum amicum oculis, non dulces melodias cantilenarum omni modarum, non florum et unguentorum et aromatum suaveolentiam, non manna et mella, non membra acceptabilia carnis amplexibus: non haec amo, cum amo deum meum. Et tamen amo quandam lucem et quandam vocem et quandam odorem et quandam cibum et quandam amplexum, cum amo deum meum; lucem, vocem, odorem, cibum, amplexum interioris hominis mei, ubi fulgit animae meae, quod non capit locus, et, ubi sonat, quod non rapit tempus, et ubi olet, quod non spargit flatus, et ubi sapit, quod non minuit edacitas, et ubi haeret, quod non divellit satietas. Hoc est quod amo cum deum meum amo.[74]

Here he has apparently quite intentionally applied to God figures involving the experience of the natural world obtained through each of the five senses. These might be simply casual figures of speech did he not carefully insist that while he means everything he says, he really doesn't mean any of it, so inade-

---

73. "Thou calledst and criedst unto me, yea thou even breakedst open my deafness; thou discoveredst thy beams and shinedst unto me, and didst chase away my blindness; thou didst most fragrantly blow upon me, and I drew in my breath and I pant after thee; I tasted thee, and now do hunger and thirst after thee; thou didst touch me, and I even burn again to enjoy thy peace." *Confessions*, Bk. X, cap. 27.

74. "What now do I love, whenas I love thee? Not the beauty of any corporal thing; not the order of times, not the brightness of the light which we do behold, so gladsome to our eyes; not the pleasant melodies of songs of all kinds; nor the fragrant smell of flowers, and ointment, and spices; not manna and honey; nor any fair limbs that are so acceptable to fleshy embracements. I love none of these things whenas I love my God; and yet I love a certain kind of light, and a kind of voice, and a kind of fragrance, and a kind of meat, and a kind of embracement, whenas I love my God; who is both the light and the voice, and the sweet smell, and the meat, and the embracement of my inner man; where that light shineth into my soul, which no place can receive; that voice soundeth, which time deprives me not of; and that fragrancy smelleth, which no wind scatters; and that meat tasteth, which eating devours not; and that embracement clingeth to me, which satiety divorceth not. This it is which I love, whenas I love my God." Augustine, *op. cit.*, Bk. X, cap. 6.

quate is symbolism when the world he is trying to express is one in which time, space, increase or diminution, satiety itself, are irrelevancies.

In the method of obtaining knowledge of God through nature interpreted by reason, there is a development with Dionysius, and with his later follower John Scotus Erigena.[75] Dionysius sought to gain understanding of God through logical steps outlined as *via affirmationis* (θέσις), *via negationis* (ἀφαίρεσις), and *via superlationis* (ὑπεροχή),—that is, first, affirmation is made concerning God based on some analogy in sense experience; next, limitations and imperfections in this analogy are defined; finally, in the *via superlationis,* these two previous steps are united in a superlative: that which through them has been glimpsed, God is to a superlative degree.

Erigena applying this method of Dionysius states that God may not be called *essentia* because of its opposite *nihil* and so must be called *superessentia.*

Item bonitas dicitur, sed proprie bonitas non est; bonitate enim malitia opponitur; igitur, plusquam bonus et plusquam bonitas. Deus dicitur, sed non proprie Deus est; visioni enim caecitas opponitur et videnti non videns; igitur ὑπερθεος, plusquam videns, si θέος videns interpretatur.[76]

Thus the tri-unity of God, which is of his *essentia,* does not completely define him, because of that *nihil* on which he acts in creation, and only *superessentia*[77] can suggest that unity of which the deep mystery lies in quaternity.

The best way to describe God, Augustine had found to be through terminology developed from observation of his self-manifestation in the world of nature and in the soul of man,

75. Although the ultimate philosophy closely resembled Augustine's, in the case of each of these thinkers. For a description of the period, cf. pp. 150 ff.

76. John Scotus Erigena, *De divisione naturae,* lib. 1, cap. xiv. Migne, *P.L.,* 122.

77. And so he goes through the list of names, and qualities, applied to God in the Bible, justifying his position thus: "Essentia est, affirmatio; essentia non est, abdicatio; superessentialis est, affirmatio simul et abdicatio. In superficie etenim negatione caret; in intellectu negatione pollet. Nam qui dicit, superessentialis est, non, quid est. dicit, sed, quid non est; dicit enim essentiam non esse, sed plusquam essentiam. Quid autem illud est, quod plusquam essentia est, non exprimit, asserens, Deum non esse aliquid eorum quae sunt, sed plus quam ea quae sunt esse; illud autem esse quid sit, nullo modo definit." Erigena, *op. cit.,* lib. 1, cap. xiv.

and yet had insisted that no term applied to him was true in its physical meaning. That truth lay in the reconciliation of opposites became an axiom through the work of Erigena[78]—an axiom relating not only to the superessential nature of God, but to the steps by which the soul and all things may return to him.[79] Its corollary in thought is that all symbols must be used; Christ must be not only the Son of God and the Sun of Righteousness, but the Lion of the Tribe of Judah, the second Adam, the Tree of Life, the Corner Stone, the Sparrow sitting alone upon the housetop, the Lamb of the Paschal Sacrifice, the Rose of Sharon, and the Lily of the Valley.[80a]

The fundamental principle of this method of the mystics is contained in the following from Dionysius:

> The highest of the things perceived by the eyes of the body or the mind are but the symbolic language of things subordinate to him who himself transcendeth them all. Through these things his incomprehensible presence is shown walking upon those heights of his holy places which are perceived by the mind; and then It breaks forth even from the things that are beheld and from those that behold them, and plunges

---

78. The system of Erigena is briefly summarized as follows:

$$\text{Deus itaque} \begin{cases} \text{per seipsum amor est,} \\ \text{per seipsum visio,} \\ \text{per seipsum motus,} \end{cases} \text{et tamen} \begin{cases} \text{neque motus est,} \\ \text{neque visio,} \\ \text{neque amor,} \end{cases} \text{sed} \begin{cases} \text{plus quam amor,} \\ \text{plus quam visio,} \\ \text{plus quam motus.} \end{cases}$$

$$\text{Et est per seipsum} \begin{cases} \text{amare,} \\ \text{videre,} \\ \text{movere,} \end{cases} \text{nec tamen est per seipsum} \begin{cases} \text{amare,} \\ \text{videre,} \\ \text{movere,} \end{cases} \text{quia est plus quam} \begin{cases} \text{amare,} \\ \text{videre,} \\ \text{movere.} \end{cases}$$

$$\text{Item, per seipsum} \begin{cases} \text{amari est,} \\ \text{viderique,} \\ \text{moverique,} \end{cases} \text{non tamen per seipsum} \begin{cases} \text{moveri est,} \\ \text{nec videri,} \\ \text{necque amari,} \end{cases} \text{quoniam plus est quam ut possit} \begin{cases} \text{amari et} \\ \text{videri et} \\ \text{moveri.} \end{cases}$$

Amat igitur	seipsum et amatur a seipso,	in nobis et in seipso;
nec tamen amat	seipsum nec amatur a seipso,	in nobis et in seipso;
sed plusquam amat	et amatur	in nobis et in seipso;
videt	seipsum et videtur a seipso,	in seipso et in nobis;
nec tamen videt	seipsum nec videtur a seipso,	in seipso et in nobis;
sed plusquam videt	et videtur	in seipso et in nobis;
movet	seipsum et movetur a seipso,	in seipso et in nobis;
non tamen movet	seipsum nec movetur a seipso,	in seipso et in nobis;
quia plus quam movet	et movetur	in seipso et in nobis.

Op. cit., cap. lxxvi. The arrangement is due to the present author. In the text it appears in simple paragraph form.

79. Here then is the philosophic basis of the statement of Cardinal Newman quoted on p. 146.

80a. In the index to Migne's *Patrologia Latina* are five pages listing such names of Christ.

the true initiate into the Darkness of Unknowing wherein he renounces all the apprehensions of his understanding and is enwrapped in that which is wholly intangible and invisible, belonging wholly to him that is beyond all things and to none else (whether himself or another) and being through the passive stillness of all his reasoning powers united by his highest faculty to him that is wholly Unknowable, of whom thus by a rejection of all knowledge he possesses a knowledge that exceeds his understanding.[80b]

Thus from one sense concept to another man attains to knowledge of God, and the intellect is prepared for that union of all opposites which the mystic is to know in the unitive way which is beyond all knowledge.

Guide us to that topmost height of mystic lore[81a] which exceedeth light and more than exceedeth knowledge, where the simple, absolute, and unchangeable mysteries of heavenly Truth lie hidden in the dazzling obscurity of the secret Silence, outshining all brilliance with the intensity of their darkness, and surcharging our blinded intellects with the utterly impalpable and invisible fairness of glories which exceed all beauty![81b]

Herein lies the meaning of Dionysius' much disputed statement, "Our highest knowledge is mystic ignorance," which, though innocent in itself, has been the cause of such endless confusion. The unity underlying all things is infinite, ultimately incomprehensible to the finite, and inexpressible even through all symbols used together (although through such use of symbols lies the nearest approach). By "mystic ignorance" is meant, not ignorance (although some in the later less intellectual tradition were so to interpret it), but the terminus found by reason itself when developed to its utmost. Similar is the meaning of the divine revelation chronicled by St. Mary Magdalen of Pazzi: "In proportion as My immensity renders Me clear and knowable in Myself, so I become more incomprehensible to My creatures, because of their incapacity. And in this I resemble the sun, which is never less visible than when it shines the most brightly."[82] Finally, this is the principle of the *docta ignorantia,*

80b. Dionysius, *Mystical Theology,* chap. 1, tr. C. E. Rolt, p. 194.
81a. Implication is exercise of reason in study illumined by grace. Cf. Rolt's note to this word.
81b. *Ibid.,* chap. 1, tr. C. E. Rolt, p. 191.
82. Cf. Poulain, *The Graces of Interior Prayer,* chap. xviii, para. 66, p. 273.

in the statement of which Nicholas of Cusa declares that in God all contraries are unified.[83] The Middle Ages said with Job: I walk in darkness toward the light.[84]

The development through Dionysius and Erigena was precursor of the intellectual mystical tradition, which in the time of Dante was to maintain the primacy of knowing as against the more emotional mysticism developed through Augustine's "fateful gift" to maintain the primacy of loving.[85a] Throughout the centuries consequent upon the disintegration of the Roman Empire, the attention of western Europe became concentrated on problems of moral readjustment,[85b] involving interest in human history. Erigena, bringing back the Greek heritage, in his insistence on the use of many and opposing symbols for the reality of the divine, vigorously reinstated the way of illumination through sense impressions and reason, and in so doing prepared for the scholastic development with its reiteration of the primacy of knowledge. With the incipient return of classical culture the tendency increased steadily to study and to use to the fullest degree symbolisms of the external universe. The gradual reënfranchisement of reason was to keep pace with the return of Aristotle to the western world.[86]

83.

"Vergine madre, figlia del tuo figlio umile ed alta più che creatura, termino fisso d'etterno consiglio, tu se' colei, che l'umana natura nobilitasti sì, che 'l suo fattore non disdegnò di farsi sua fattura. Nel ventre tuo si raccese l'amore per lo cui caldo ne l'etterna pace così è germinato questo fiore."	"Virgin mother, daughter of thy son, lowly and uplifted more than any creature, fixed goal of the eternal counsel, thou art she who didst human nature so ennoble that its own Maker scorned not to become its making. In thy womb was lit again the love under whose warmth in the eternal peace this flower hath thus unfolded."

Par., xxxiii, 1-9, being the invocation of Bernard's prayer to Mary. In Mary all contraries were perfectly unified.

84. This conception becomes clearer if we realize that the Middle Ages thought of themselves, not as going through a dark passageway toward a faint light at its end, or through a dark night toward a mountain top tinged with the dawning, but as walking directly into the blinding rays of the sun. This discipline, though resulting in the darkness of temporary blindness to eyes weak through sin, was thought of as being their only cure.

85a. Cf. pp. 61, 349 ff.   85b. Cf. Chap. VI, ii.

86. The return was not, even then, of Aristotle in his original setting, but of rewritings of Aristotle, often made with a Platonist slant. Even Platonism, moreover, does not necessitate the type of mysticism which centralizes inner experience, although Augustine derived that type of mysticism from it. Plotinus, likewise on the basis of Plato, built up the most perfectly intellectual mysticism the world has ever known.

THE SOLUTION OF THE PHILOSOPHER

Whereas Augustine knew little of Aristotle, Dionysius and Erigena knew more of him, and it is supposed that "The Philosopher of the Middle Ages,"[87] under the direction of Albertus Magnus, was responsible for a new and more accurate translation of "The Philosopher" of Greek antiquity. Harnack wrote that Thomas Aquinas was essentially Aristotelian and only accidentally Christian; while Augustine was essentially Christian and only accidentally Platonic. It seems probable that the comparison on the basis of Christianity is of greater effect than accuracy, but the respective allegiance to Plato and Aristotle[88a] of these two formed the basis for that controversy through which, in the time of Dante, the two suns of the moral realm were still dimming each other's light, for all Thomas' vigorous assertion of their mutual autonomy.

It will be remembered that in the assertion of a mutually autonomous vicarate of philosophy and theology, the rational and the suprarational, Thomas opposed equally Averroism,[88b] which asserted the supremacy of reason as did the Ghibelline that of the empire, and Augustinianism, which maintained the supremacy of faith as did Guelphs that of the church. The quarrel was in reality over the four sources of knowledge.[89] The Averroists asserted the supremacy of reason and of knowledge through nature, and thus of philosophy; whereas the Augustinians maintained as supreme, faith and knowledge through revelation, and thus theology. For Augustine, although external nature taught of the Creator, the human soul oriented toward God knew self and God directly with a certainty greater than that of any knowledge through creatures. Therefore, faith was greater than, and because of the Fall prerequisite to, reason.

87. Cf. also the analysis of the Thomistic philosophy by De Wulf in his *Medieval Philosophy*.

88a. It should be remembered that Augustine himself was strongly influenced by Aristotle, but that the emphasis of the Augustinian tradition was Platonic.

88b. Averroës was a Spanish Moor of the twelfth century, celebrated as a scholar and philosopher. He composed three commentaries on the works of Aristotle, which he knew in a Syriac translation. St. Thomas made use of one of these commentaries. In the thirteenth and fourteenth centuries, however, Averroës was regarded as a dangerous freethinker, spreading doctrines of pantheism and materialism. In the face of this difficulty St. Thomas found the path of philosophy not always easy.

89. Defined by Peter Lombard. Cf. p. 97 n. 249, also p. 296.

Augustine the philosopher, clear as was his recognition of the autonomy of the two natures of Christ each in its own sphere, nevertheless, failed to maintain a similar autonomy of the rational and the suprarational, reason and faith,[90] just as the Averroists, without a doctrine of the two natures of Christ, acknowledged no relation between the two. Such mystics as Bonaventure, following the Augustinian tradition, thought philosophy such a danger that they demanded faith only.

For Thomas, on the other hand, there was approach to knowledge only through matter and reason, and reason is the rightful guide for him who has set out on the search for knowledge along the threefold way. Man might understand the lower natures of inanimate creation, plants and animals, infinitely more truly than those higher natures of angels and God, to whom direct abstract knowledge is possible. The suprasensible is to be known only through the things of sense; the suprarational only through reason.

Thus, the problem of universals, primary in medieval philosophy and recurrent in modern thought under the head of the "epistemological problem," found in Thomas' compromise the only answer which is in harmony with symbolic tradition and with Boethius' conception of infinity. The emphasis of the Augustinian tradition had always been on the existence of the archetype in eternity before the thing. Discussion had arisen with the rebirth of scientific inquiry as to whether the idea were not merely in the thing, or perhaps even after the thing, that is, nonexistent save in the analytic mind. To deny *post rem* is to be untrue to the facts of psychology; to deny *in re* is to be false to common experience; to deny *ante rem* is to abstract the very bases of medieval mysticism. Thomas includes them all; the universal psychologically is *post rem;* yet the mind finds, it does not create, hence the universal is truly *in re;* and in view of the relationship of the universe to the Infinite which makes analogy a sound basis for symbolism, the universal must be also in a certain sense *ante rem,* not in time, but in the hierarchy of being, in eternity.

The student of literature may not well forget that the turmoil

90. Natural in his time.

of the thirteenth century was the outcome of more than the tumults of love. It was a period of intellectual tumult such as the world had not known since the days of the Empire, of which it was the true daughter. The new philosophy had come from old Greek sources by way of the pagan Orient to rob men's minds of peace as love had come to rob their hearts. Pantheism was in it, and denial of individual free will, and denial not only of the Christian God, but of the God of the Jews. In this atmosphere Maimonides published his *Guide to the Perplexed,* which is still a Jewish classic, even as the great synthesis wrought by Thomas Aquinas is a monument of Christian thinking.

One familiar with the universal scope of Dante's intellectual curiosity and with the tradition that he had a friend among the Jews of Rome[91] must recognize in the Hebrew reaction to this crisis a potential element in the shaping of the *Commedia.* One who has paused to study the intellectual conflicts of the time must recognize in Hebrew thought an actual element in the molding of all that was medieval[92] and so inevitably of the *Commedia.* Hebrew thinkers, having been spared the comfortable tradition of Augustinian psychology, were even more prone than Christians to rise to the crisis, and they too sought solution through a far-reaching unification of symbolisms.

The new philosophy given definite form in scholasticism and reinforced through the influence of Hebrew thought was generally considered the enemy of mysticism; in reality it supplied the possibility of balance and strengthening.[93] Involved in the objection made by those influenced by the Augustinian tradition was a misapplication of mystical principles, only too natural in a period marked by fresh discovery of the love ideal. The unitive way has no validity apart from purgation and illumination.

91. Emanuel ben Salomon. Dr. Moore makes the definite suggestion that Dante gained some knowledge of cabalistic numerology from this friend. Cf. Edw. Moore, *Studies in Dante. Third series,* pp. 253 ff.

92. Cf. Appendix V, Pt. I, ii (2).

93. How frequently this is true of a new and disturbing philosophy perhaps no one knows better than the student of the history of thought. In every age there are those only too eager to use the new as a ready weapon for the ruthless demolishing of the old, to the horror and chagrin of those whose life cannot be extricated from tradition. Between these opposing forces the multitude remains bewildered. That age is fortunate which has produced one capable of a synthesis in which the truths of the new and the old may find their places in a more perfect whole.

The purgative way must involve discipline both of intellect and of emotions, and progress in the illuminative way must be through symbols which can be understood truly only through the exercise of sense and reason. Yet this beginning, apparently from the finite, was in reality from the infinite, even as Dante made it in his *Commedia*. Though knowledge is primarily from the senses, "every visible and invisible creature is a theophany or appearance of God."[94] By the great law of analogy fundamental in knowledge and expression,[95, 96] the meaning of the infinite is hidden or revealed. Each sees what he has eyes to see. This conception was as fundamental in the thought of Thomas as in that of the Augustinians whose theory of knowledge he combated.

There is, moreover, in Thomas' theory nothing to deny the Augustinian claim of direct unsymbolic knowledge after passage through the discipline of the perception and of the reason through symbols. Indeed, Plotinus had shown reason itself to demand such a terminus.[97] This knowledge, however,

94. Erigena, as translated in Underhill, *Mysticism*, p. 311.

95. Hugh of St. Victor, a mystic, pointed out that the truth of *lion* as a symbol of Christ, depended on the literal meaning of the word. Cf. Appendix IV, Pt. I, i. Moreover, Erigena had made clear for all time the necessity of supplementing one sense analogy by another.

96. Considered philosophically, analogy is of two types, that which rests on likeness of relationship, for example, a king is like a pilot because he stands in relation to his kingdom as does the pilot in relation to the ship—and that which rests on the "participation de l'être créé à l'être incréé." For the use of these two types by Thomas and by Bonaventure, cf. B. Landry, *La notion d'analogie chez Saint Bonaventure et Saint Thomas d'Aquin* (Thesis, Louvain, 1922).

97. Hilary of Poitiers expressed this in words which might have been written in the twentieth century: "If we assume that an event did not happen, because we cannot discover how it was done, we make the limits of our understanding into the limits of reality." Hilary of Poitiers, *De Trinitate*, Bk. 3, chap. 20.

Thomas Aquinas, together with many other mystics, all his life insisted on that which has been expressed in a recent newspaper comment on the work of the occultist William Kingsland, entitled *Rational Mysticism*, that while in the rational pursuit of knowledge "sooner or later we reach the limit, the thus-far-and-no-farther, either in the form of a self-contradiction or as a complete absence of data" and while "we may agree that there is nothing irrational in the attitude of a mind which finds comfort in an experience transcending rational interpretation," nevertheless, "it is an altogether different position when the mystic claims by this illumination to be qualified to expound rationally and in mathematical and logical terms the conditions of transcendent reality."

In other words, just as Dante conceived it, the rational and the suprarational move in different spheres and demand different expression. To think of expressing fully with scientific exactitude the content of that which is seen in the *lumen gloriae* is nonsense. (This, however, in no way relieves the mystic of his responsibility for the expression of his vision.)

would not be the natural knowledge of the soul, as Augustine thought, but a special act of God's grace. Reason alone, autonomous in its own sphere, is rightful guide on the quest of the vision, though reason must be illumined by grace, as empire by church. Beyond the sphere of reason, grace alone has power to raise to the ultimate beatitude. Yet the mystic, even should he be permitted perception without symbols, is bound eternally to self-expression through them; and no one had felt more keenly than Thomas their inadequacy or could better sympathize with Dante's opening lines:

> Nel ciel che più de la sua luce prende
> fu' io, e vidi cose che ridire
> nè sa nè può chi di là su discende.[98]

Thomas at the end of his life, it is told, received so intense an intuitive perception of divine truth that he, the scholar, refused to write any more, even to complete the *Summa,* since in the light of the new revelation all he had written seemed to him, though not untrue, so utterly inadequate to Truth.

III. PROGRESSION FROM LIGHT TO LIGHT

THE unitive way, third of the three strands which, intertwined, make up the Way to the Beatific Vision, is of all the most hazardous. Consisting essentially of glimpses of things as a whole, each glimpse a foretaste of the Beatific Vision, it is so grateful that the soul is tempted to try to hold it and to rest in it, and to value its moments alone of all the events in the mystic progress. Man is further tempted through this experience, which pierces beyond the reach of symbolism, to discredit the weary growth from symbol to symbol, and to forget the discipline of life and illumination of intellect through which true experience of the unification of opposites has been safeguarded and at the same time rendered possible. Dante and the Middle Ages were familiar with the story of Semele,[99] daughter of Cadmus and mother of Bacchus, who, regardless of the weakness of

---

98. "In that heaven which most receiveth of his light, have I been; and have seen things which whoso descendeth from up there hath nor knowledge nor power to re-tell." *Par.,* i, 4-6.

99. Cf. Ovid, *Metamorphoses,* 3, 253-315, and *Inf.,* xxx, 2.

her still untrained vision, wilfully insisted on beholding her lover Jupiter in all his heavenly glory, only to be burned to ashes in his splendor.

The unification of opposites is accomplished only in eternity. Man in this world, though granted glimpses of eternity, must live under conditions of time. Thus, although Dante in vision may behold the ultimate nonexistence of evil, yet Dante on his journey, like all those in the *Inferno,* may experience but the ceaseless flapping of the six bat wings. Over those wings the ice will close only on the Judgment Day, when time and space shall be no more.[100] Fundamental as is a true conception of infinity to an understanding of the purgative and illuminative ways, it is even more essential to the mystic of the unitive way.

SOLUTION OF DUALISM

Of all the opposing pairs that have puzzled the minds of men, perhaps none is more puzzling than permanence and change,[101] chosen as the contradictory bases of two of the earliest of Greek philosophies, the mutually incompatible systems of Heraclitus and Parmenides. One of the earliest solutions of this problem which could have contributed to medieval development is suggested non-philosophically in the ritual of the Passover. After the familiar pattern of that modern relic of antiquity, the House that Jack Built, it is told that the father bought a kid which was eaten by a cat in turn killed by a dog which was beaten by a stick which was burned in the fire. The water that quenched the fire was drunk by an ox, promptly killed by the butcher, who himself fell under the stroke of the Angel of Death. In this folk song, year by year impressed upon worshipers, is pictured change and impermanence: death everywhere, a world in which everything,

100. The conception of Plotinus involves not only opposites in the realm of time and space, but the necessity of different coördinates. In the divided world of time and space it is true that items listed in a descending scale of Being, range from the highest conceivable condition of true Being down to all but zero, but can never be minus or negative; while the same items on a descending scale of Value, range from the highest conceivable down through zero (the morally indifferent) to negative quantities. It is only in infinity that Being and Value become related to the same set of coördinates, thus depriving evil of existence.

101. It will be remembered that the twoness to be resolved only in eternity was the solution. Thomas, commentating Aristotle's *De caelo et mundo,* 2, 10-18, states that the Primum Mobile has one unchanging motion, while the other spheres, having two or more motions, generate change. Cf. pp. 33-35, 482.

animate or inanimate, rational or irrational, lies under the
power of destruction and lasts but for a time. In the last verse
is a real triumph which for the mystic is of deeper significance
than that there shall be no more death:

> Then came the Holy One, Blessed be He—
> *And slew the Angel of Death,*
> That slew the butcher,
> That killed the ox,
> That drank the water,
> That quenched the fire,
> That burned the stick,
> That beat the dog,
> That killed the cat,
> That ate the kid,
> That father bought for two zuzim,
> One kid, one only kid.

It is the Eternal and Unchanging—Blessed be He—who initiates the whole process of change.[102] Source alike of permanence and change, in Him is the infinite and eternal meaning
beneath the world of Time. Had Israel been able to give philosophical statement to this folk song transformed into mystic
vision,[103] it is possible that monism rather than dualism might
have become dominant in the Christian tradition. As it was,
Athanasius himself failed to escape completely the dualism
which was the real basis for the Arian insistence that Christ
could not be truly very God, since spirit (God) and matter were
so diametrically opposed that it was impossible for them to
touch.[104] As it was, the achievement of a monism was vouchsafed only to the mystic of the medieval Christian tradition.
Dante in the spheres found matter and spirit everywhere

102. Aristotle gives us reason to suppose that "the Heraclitean doctrine,
learned from Cratylus, that the world disclosed to us by our senses is a scene of
incessant and incalculable mutability and variation, was one which Plato never
forgot." Plato, however, drew the conclusion not that genuine and stable knowledge was impossible, but that since genuine knowledge (science) is possible and
existent, therefore that of which this "science" treats must be something other
than the never ending flux of sense data. See A. E. Taylor, *Plato, the Man and
His Work*, p. 3.

103. The fact that this rhyme may bear for the Jew a political interpretation
also, referring to the final divine vengeance upon the enemies of Israel, in no
wise invalidates the mystic anagoge of divine triumph over the whole process of
finite change.

104. In modern times, this view is held by Christian Scientists.

united,[105] he beheld all things in the one light, even as Julian of Norwich was one day to see "all thing that is made" lying in the hand of its Creator no bigger than a hazelnut, and to hear a Voice telling her that its nature is that God loveth it and keepeth it.

THE TEST OF ATTAINMENT

Yet Dante, through his understanding of infinity and its relationship through symbolism to time and space, was able to return to a world in which "the beginning, middle, and end, the birth and perfection of all we see, arises from contraries, through contraries, in contraries."[106] Such is the realm where the she-wolf roams. For the span of life in the finite realm reason must guide, although for that which lies beyond its sphere grace may be given. The whole of life may not be lived in the moments of completest vision, even though contained therein. Following the career of the sun, the mystic's life is a cycle. Drawn upward to the summit of the heavens, to vision of the infinite whole, he must descend again to fulfilment of his part in the redeeming work of the sun, through long discipline in the finite.

Progression, not only in the ways of purgation and of illumination, but even in the way of union, is progress from light to light, the lesser to the greater, until the Divine Sun is attained, in whom darkness and light, knowing and unknowing, existence and nonexistence, are one. As Dante progressed from the foreshadowing of anagoge in the Sun to that in the Heaven of the Fixed Stars to that in the Rose, it is important to notice which symbols are the last to be discarded. Whereas the symbols of the progress levels of the mystic way were those associated with quest, such as warfare, chemical purification, weeding and plowing, loosing from bonds, appropriate to the *via purgativa,* and especially the symbols of the five senses, appropriate to the *via illuminativa;* the symbols here are those of union, the union of achievement, the union of burning, the union of feeding, and

105. Cf. Grandgent's commentary on *Par.,* xxix, 36. Cf. also many discussions as to the nature of the glorified bodies of the saints after the general resurrection —for example, by Augustine in *De civitate Dei,* and by Thomas Aquinas in *Summae contra gentiles,* especially as quoted, p. 238 n. 518.
106. Giordano Bruno, quoted by Bianchi, *op. cit.,* p. 220.

supremely the union of marriage.[107] This latter symbolism is the only symbolism except that of the sun—which includes it—that contains within itself the test as to whether the mystic has truly attained.[108] The mystic troubadour, no longer content with the phrases of courtly love only, includes also mystical marriage and its responsibilities to the children of God.[109]

THE LOVE THAT MOVES THE SUN AND OTHER STARS

Perhaps the most comprehensive picture of the unitive way has been given within a small compass by Jan van Ruysbroeck,[110] who flourished slightly later than Dante:[111] "When we have learned to open our eyes in the interior light we can contemplate in joy the continual coming of the Bridegroom. It is a perpetual genesis, an ever-recurrent dawn that knows no setting."[112] In his description of the consummation of the spiritual romance is reflected all that the world had learned of love: "The soul opens to God its powers, longing to receive the Divine substance and to give its own."[113] On the other hand, Meister Eckhart, during the same years, wrote: "Earth cannot escape the sky; let it flee up or down, the sky flows into it, and makes it fruitful whether it will or no. So God does to man. He who will escape him only runs to his bosom; for all corners are open to him."[114] True to

107. Such analysis of mystic symbols is worked out more fully in an unpublished paper by Miss Mary A. Ewer.

108. It will be remembered that these were the two symbolisms which through elimination were given prominence in the New Testament. Cf. pp. 255-256, also Appendix IV, Pt. I, ii. In this connection the influence of the Kabalah is not to be omitted. Cf. Appendices, pp. 505-506. The progression into reality, here also, was a progression through symbol to higher symbol, dominated by the symbolisms both of sun and of marriage. The author of the *Zohar* is termed in the work itself the "Holy Light-bearer," and into his nuptials in heaven all faithful followers were to enter. Cf. p. 339 n. 19c.

109. Of the mystical writers Dante knew, this symbolism was worked out the most completely by Richard of St. Victor (cf. his "De quatuor gradibus violentae charitatis," in Migne, *P.L.*, t. 196, especially col. 1216), although in great detail didactically by St. Bernard (in his *Sermons on the Song of Songs*, especially sermon ix. See the Eales translation of the Mabillon version of the works of St. Bernard).

110. Ruysbroeck possessed, however (to quote from Maeterlinck), "one of the wisest, most exact, and most subtle philosophic brains which have ever existed" and, like Plotinus, he tried "to extend the paths of the ordinary intellect into the very heart of these desolations."

111. The dates of Dante are 1265-1321; of Ruysbroeck, 1293-1381.

112. Jan van Ruysbroeck, *Flowers of a Mystic Garden*, selections, p. 47.

113. *Ibid.*, pp. 62-63.   114. Sermon lxxxviii.

his tradition Ruysbroeck stresses equally the infinite and the finite quests: "The tempests of love have differing effects: sometimes a light shines forth. . . . Then the soul and the spirit moving toward the light experience in this encounter an intolerable bliss, and there are times when the man is burnt up in the radiance. This is ecstasy, the bliss that can never be described. . . ."[115] It is, moreover, the vision of the mystic Rose of which Dante is forever powerless to tell.

The life of ecstasy for him who is prepared, is, as Ruysbroeck declares the sanest of all lives. It maintains the balance of perfect freedom in the will which has become moved entirely by love.

He only is a contemplative who is the slave of nothing, not even of his virtues . . . he must lose himself, without confusion of substance, in the holy darkness, where joy delivers him out of himself, never again to find himself according to the human mode.[116]

This balance is maintained of course through the unification of opposites:

the interior man . . . is struck by a light flashing forth from the Divine Unity. This lightning flash is the surface of darkness. . . . For when he enters the nudity he is destitute of his own light, bereft of his powers of seeing, and is wholly impregnated, penetrated, and transfigured by light itself.[117]

Man "pledged brother to every creature" is to "dwell on the summit of his soul, between essence and power, between joy and activity, essentially abiding in God in the abyss of fruition and in the depths of the darkness; for the holy darkness is not only the supreme beatitude of spirits; it is the supreme bliss of God."[118]

SUMMARY

In fine, the true life, as revealed to the initiate in the Way of purgation, illumination, and union, is not the purely contemplative, although the ladder of contemplation rises to the Empyrean; but highest is the contemplative life which bears fruit in

---

115. Ruysbroeck, *op. cit.*, p. 22. 116. *Ibid.*, pp. 44-45.
117. *Ibid.*, pp. 36-37. 118. *Ibid.*, p. 139.

action. Thus is maintained the eternal cycle uniting the finite and the infinite. From unspeakable vision the mystic, superior alike to quietism and pantheism, returns to the accomplishment of a divine mission among men.

CHAPTER V. SCHEMA: Part II, CONT.

Literal Level*	Allegorical Level	Tropical Level
The quest of the seeker on the Way of Purgation, a Comedy, begins in impotence of the will, ends in perfected nature	The quest of the seeker on the Way of Illumination, a Comedy, begins in brutish ignorance, ends in perfect vision	The quest of the seeker on the Way of Union, a Comedy, begins in infinite separation from the object of his desire, ends in union
I. The seeker comes to himself in the chaos of nature deformed through lack of discipline and sacramental grace Escape barred by threefold detriment due to Fall	I. The seeker comes to himself in the darkness of conflict between the rational and the suprarational Escape barred by three hindrances to knowledge: sacraments withheld through corruption of church, lack of peace for study due to corruption of empire, vice in the soul	I. The seeker comes to himself in a struggle between the demands of action and contemplation Escape barred by three vices; fraud, violence, cupidity
Rescue, made possible by the Trinity, offered through working out of autonomies of discipline and grace	Rescue, made possible by the Trinity, offered through working out of autonomies of *ratio* and *supra-ratio*	Rescue, made possible by the Trinity, offered through working out of autonomies of active life and contemplative life

II. Progress through agonies of initiation in the Way of discipline, in increasingly vivid appreciation of the nature of threefold detriment:
    Experiences of the corruption of natural good, leading up to dangerous triumph of appreciation of Immanent Presence, resulting in
    Tumultous experience of deformity of mind, leading through betrayal, a wrong gift from discipline to grace, to irrevocable *reatus poenae* in their mutual eclipse
out of which may come the mystic inversion, giving opportunity for restoration
	II. Progress through agonies of initiation in the Way of knowledge, in increasingly vivid comprehension of the threefold bar:
	
	    Experiences of vice in soul, leading up to dangerous triumph in foreshadowing of vision, resulting in
	
	    Tumultous experience of revelation false through neglect of study leading through betrayal to mutual eclipse of *ratio* and *supra-ratio*
	
	out of which may come opportunity for restoration of their autonomies
		II. Progress through agonies of initiation in the Way of contemplation, in increasingly vivid comprehension of the threefold root of separation:
		    Experiences of separative result of cupidity in soul, leading up to dangerous triumph in foreshadowing of union, resulting in
		    Tumultous experience of divine possession, leading through betrayal to mutual eclipse of action and contemplation (quietism)
		out of which may come opportunity for restoration of their autonomies

Reorganization of personality	Reorganization of personality	Reorganization of personality

Progress through the labors of: construction of disciplined life
    Formulation of a rule of life
    Acquiring of disciplined habits
    Perfection in habits
	Progress through the labors of: construction of sound body of knowledge
	    New plan of study
	    Practical living of knowledge
	    Perfection in illumination
		Progress through the labors of: the active life
		
		    New dedication to service
		    Practice of the active life
		    Perfection of union

III. The seeker at the height of the disciplined life is ready to rise to the realm of grace, to return to the fulfilment of his mission, moved by the Will of the Prime Mover	III. The seeker at the height of the illuminative way is ready to rise to the perfect Vision, to return to the fulfilment of his mission in expression of the Vision	III. The seeker at the height of the unitive way is ready to rise to the divine union, to return to the fulfilment of his mission in spiritual fruitfulness

* For review of the literal order which forms the basis for these higher levels, cf. chart of symbolism of the first order, p. 156, and for the relationship of orders cf. p. 98.

PART II. THE THREEFOLD WAY: UNION OF SUN AND UNIVERSE, CREATOR AND CREATED

I. SITUATION: UNIVERSAL QUEST

IN the nine-sphered Paradise of ultimate truth revealed to Dante through his communion at the summit of the Mount, it was Christ's ascension that raised him from the Heaven of the Fixed Stars to that circle wherein are the roots of time. Of all that had pertained to such knowledge as may be derived from the external universe Dante had beheld the consummation, projected in condescension to the weakness of his vision, in the sphere of the Sun. Of all that pertained to such knowledge as may be derived from human history and organization, with its center in Christ, Dante had beheld the consummation projected in condescension to his weakness, into his own sign of Gemini. At last prepared for that which should complete his vision of personal and corporate responsibility, the full revelation of each creature's relationship to the One, he is raised from Gemini by the Radiance of the Divine Sun, Christ, who had completed the revelation to men of God, not only as Father, but as Bridegroom—as the sun is both to the earth.

Complete interpretation of the first order of symbolism—of that revealed in the passage from the Moon to the Sun—was impossible until Dante had understood his relationship to organized humanity, and the sense in which his life might become an allegory of that which Christ accomplishes through his four bodies.[119] So also the deepest mysteries of the second order of symbolism—of that revealed in the passage from Mars to the fixed stars—could not be understood until Dante had grasped something of that mystic progress by which the individual soul meets God in loneliness.

THE DARK WOOD

Dante, setting out toward this goal, suggests in outline the vicissitudes of every adventurer along the threefold way. With the awakening to consciousness of catastrophe every seeker comes to himself. Deeply impressed upon him is a realization of some particular obstacle, its nature varying with his *Weltanschauung*. Impelled by a sense of the reaching out of the infinite

119. Cf. pp. 285-286, also pp. 74-75.

through the finite, and of the endeavor of human nature to reach through the finite to the infinite, he sets out upon a quest of which the nature is determined by the proportionate strength of these two forces. To the quest of the infinite through the finite, the obstacle is ignorance in some one of its many forms, whether purely intellectual or whether characterized by undue self-reliance (the form in which it is dreaded by St. Francis of Assisi, by Luther, and others) or by illusion of separateness (as generally viewed by Hindu mystics). To the reaching out of the infinite, the obstacle is human failure to provide for its reception.

The theme for the quest molded by consciousness of man's search for God, becomes God's self-revelation through the sources of knowledge; the theme for the quest molded by consciousness of God's coming to man, becomes the Real Presence. In the most balanced of mystics both themes are found, as, for example, the Real Presence is the theme of the poetic works of the great intellectual adventurer, Thomas Aquinas. The wayfarer, dominated by either one of these themes to the complete exclusion of the other, is doomed to failure; for him the beckoning goal is unattainable and recedes like a mirage into the distance. There is necessity for both activity and receptivity, and the balance between action and contemplation is to be maintained. Dante, ever insisting on the equal importance each within its own sphere of the members of pairs, gives prominence to both in the same relationship as that which governs the relation of empire to church or philosophy to theology.

Dante, the seeker for vision of things as a whole, comes to himself in the Dark Wood, which has its appropriate terrors for each phase of the mystic progress, as impotence, avoidable ignorance, and separation. On his escape from the Wood at dawn the Mount of Vision is displayed to him under the Sun of all Power, Wisdom, and Love. This goal, described in the imagery of sight, although subsuming that of all the senses,[120] stands witness to the fact of frailty, ignorance, and distance as fundamental difficulties. Of this there was premonition at the close of that work in which the *Commedia* is promised, to ac-

120. Cf. p. 356.

complish which he tells that he must study to the utmost: "E di venire a ciò io studio quanto posso, sì com' ella sae veracemente."[121]

One need but read the story of Dante's journey from the point of view of the mountaineer to realize his keen interest in the interplay of effort and of adventitious assistance, necessary for the seeker in the Way. Indeed, Dante describes as alpine— alpestro—portions of the descent into hell.[122] Clambering over the rocks and precipices of the Inferno in a pitchy blackness relieved only here and there by the dull red of torture, Dante frequently experienced the flagging of his strength, only to be exhorted by Virgil to greater effort. Even the sage refers to the climb up from the center of the earth in the wake of Satan's fall as "sì aspra e forte, che lo salire omai no parrà gioco."[123] Yet Dante, fresh from regions where "la via e lunga e 'l cammino è malvagio,"[124] was to experience the ascent up the Mount of Purgatory as anything but play. Soon "the ground beneath required both feet and hands" ("e piedi e man volea il suol di sotto")[125] and, indeed, after the first sharp climb, Dante was forced to cry for mercy, entreating the sage to wait. Yet Virgil's answer was but to point to a ledge above with the demand that his charge at all costs drag himself to its height— infin quivi ti tira." Dante, creeping upward in the footsteps of his guide, was permitted rest and the seeking of strength from the east, only with the attainment of this goal.

On the other hand, human effort strained to the utmost, suffices not for the journey, and there is constant dependence on supernatural assistance. It is present, even though scarcely perceptible, in the obscurity of the Inferno. An angel opens the gate of Dis, and Virgil himself carries Dante on more than one occasion, in virtue of the strength which empowered his whole guidance of the poet. It is to be remarked that apart from the infusion of *virtu* from outside himself for the accomplishment of his journey, the sage could not have stepped beyond the bounds of Limbo. In the *Purgatorio,* however, the infusion of grace be-

---

121. *Vita Nuova,* XLII.   122. *Inf.,* xii, 2.
123. "So rough and hard, that the climbing now will seem but play to us." *Purg.,* ii, 65-66.
124. *Inf.,* xxxiv, 95.   125. *Purg.,* iv, 33.

comes more spectacular. Dante is raised miraculously to the gate of purgatory by Lucia, surrogate of Divine Wisdom. Furthermore, the whole ascent is perilous in its governance by more than physical laws. (In this connection Dante's meticulous cosmological references may be studied.) By no possible effort can man mount upward in the nighttime, and during those hours in which the sun is absent, descent is but too easy.

THREEFOLD DETRIMENT

Virgil then as spirit of discipline, preparing for the grace of Beatrice, surrogate of the Holy Spirit, the Help of man, offers the first escape from the beasts, which, as here representative of the threefold detriment in human nature, would drive him back into the wood of impotence. The leopard, spotted and nimble, principle of death, is the *reatus poenae* remissible by God alone.[126] Man is only too ready to pursue his way, light-mindedly dismissing from consciousness the sentence under which he walks. With the appearance of the lion in opposition to Divine Wisdom, comes experience of the deformity of mind which all men bear as the mark of initial rebellion. Only the wisdom of the Logos can restore clarity of vision, yet the blind man is proverbially unconscious of his blindness, and Dante is still full of hope until that beast appears which is the corruption of natural good, human nature so disordered that it is no longer responsive to divine attraction, and in inability to choose the greater good, falls helpless prey to *gravezza*. Divine love in mercy sends discipline to prepare man for the reception of that supernatural grace through which alone he may attain the ultimate conquest of *gravezza*, be it by however perilous and tedious a path. Here in the *Commedia* is a story completely apposite to the mystical tradition of progress through the way of purgation.

Superseding even Dante's interest in effort and grace is his interest in progress and illumination. Indeed, he has written at

126. For this threefold detriment, caused by the Fall and inherited by each human child, together with the reasons why the detriment cannot be overcome, in any of its phases, without divine assistance, cf. Thomas Aquinas, *S.Th.*, 1, 2, Q. 109, art. 7, c. For the *vulneratio naturae* see Thomas Aquinas, *S.Th.*, 1, 2, Q. 85, art. 3.

some length on those defects which hinder man's attainment of knowledge, the height of human blessedness. Two of these are pardonable, pertaining to the condition of finite existence. Of these, one pertains to the environment in which a man lives, being the limitation involved in the fulfilment of duty: family responsibility and civic care. The other pertains to the man himself, being the limitation of physical defects such as deafness and blindness. Two, however, are pernicious, and likewise one of these pertains to the environment (the "luogo ove la persona è nata e nudrita") : lack of facilities for study, library, companionship, and so on; while the other pertains to the man himself: vice within the soul.[127] The place where Dante was born and nourished was Florence, a veritable city of Dis, wherein the conflict of church and state opposed a double barrier to the pursuit of human blessedness. The state had eclipsed the church, and in consequence imposed a barrier to the sacramental reception of the Infinite in his reaching out toward man. The leopard, already seen in his opposition to the Father, as the fraudulence which pervaded church and empire, on the unitive level of the symbolism defrauds mankind of the supreme Gift of the Father —the sacramental Body of the Son. Similarly the church had eclipsed the state, thus robbing the citizens of both peace and facilities for study and contemplation. The lion, already seen in his opposition to the Son, the Prince of Peace, as the violence which seizes and takes by force, on this level tears from the citizen the leisure essential for and the atmosphere conducive to thought. Florence had robbed her citizens of the "bread of angels" which is both knowledge and the Eucharist, each being the embodiment of the Eternal Wisdom for man's reception. Such is the significance here of lion and leopard, yet from both of these the seeker has hope of deliverance through the guidance of the sun himself, until the wolf appears, that vice within the soul which subjects to distraction from the goal through the delusion of vain delights. Thus hindered man is powerless to maintain the autonomy of *ratio* and *supra-ratio*.

Even as the seeker in the purgative phase of his journey is barred from attainment by the threefold detriment of fallen na-

127. Cf. the opening chapter of the *Convivio*.

ture, and as he is barred in the illuminative phase by the three-fold hindrance to the pursuit of infinite wisdom, so he is barred in the unitive phase by the threefold vice in his own nature. This vice, stressed here with reference to progress in the unitive way, was a hindrance according to the symbolism of the first order, in Dante's moral development,[128] and according to the symbolism of the second order, in the growth of individuals within the church and empire of Christ[129] though they were strengthened against it by the sacramental Body. The beast of "fame sanza fine cupa"[130] is the very spirit of separateness, enflaming such desires as set every man's hand against his brother, and lead downward in increasing distance from the sun. Assisted by her two companions she blocks the acquisition of all virtues, those natural which are acquired through effort, and those theological which are the gift of grace. Natural law and human will[131] in their conflict appear to have given her power in Dante's personal life, as, in a larger sense, the conflicting claims of philosophy and theology were her opportunity to overcome individual participants in Christ's sacramental Body. Stated generally for every seeker for union with God, the opposition is of the active life to contemplation. The solution of Thomas Aquinas here again was maintenance of mutual autonomies, as Dante beheld it in his dream on the steps leading into the Terrestrial Paradise,[132] faint foreshadowing of the ladder which rises from Saturn into the Empyrean.

Whereas leopard, lion, and she-wolf, constitute a threefold detriment in each phase of the mystic progress, there is a further symbolism in which each in turn dominates in one phase of the threefold way. The opposition of the she-wolf is a force especially in the way of purgation, although she has her special perniciousness, not only as innate corruption in natural good, but also as the vice which blocks knowledge and the cupidity which turns love through self to the Nothing in its opposition to Re-

---

128. Cf. pp. 162 ff.   129. Cf. pp. 288 ff., especially p. 294.
130. *Purg.*, xx, 12, referring to the wolf, with her "hunger endlessly deep."
131. Cf. pp. 47 ff.
132. *Purg.*, xxvii, 97 ff. Dante sees Leah as the active life, Rachel as the contemplative. This symbolism was usual. Richard of St. Victor, however, uses, not Rachel, but her beloved son Benjamin, as the symbol of contemplation, in his works, *Benjamin Minor* and *Benjamin Major*.

ality. The lion, deformity of mind, lack of peace for study, and the sin of violence as tool of the root of all sin in cupidity,[133] blocks especially the illuminative phase of the mystic progress, though he aids the *lupa* in rendering discipline difficult and sense of union well-nigh impossible. The leopard, subjecting to *reatus poenae,* is as always harbinger of death. Fraudulent in deprivation of the true sacraments of the church, the bread of life which Christ would bar to none, he is of especial malignance in the way of union; nevertheless the leopard, like the lion, assists the *lupa* to oppose all three phases of the soul's progress. Blocked by the she-wolf, the seeker may advance not one step along the way, but is driven backward into darkness.

THREEFOLD MERCY

In this dilemma there is sent, by the grace of God acting through her whose loveliness had inspired Dante's quest, the vision of discipline, of practical reason, of action. This vision is represented in Virgil, who is to guide to that point where at last, through habit working harmoniously with sacramental life, revelation, and contemplation, he may free the advanced soul for the ultimate accomplishment. The practical ordering of life releases the confused mind to realization of the forces upon which it may rely for aid: the three Ladies, each the surrogate for one of the Persons of the Trinity. They appear as: Mary, Queen of the Church, whose special care was that the sacraments of her divine Son might not be lacking to her human sons;[134] Lucia, illuminer of vision, concerned to provide peace for study even to those who live in the midst of battle; and Beatrice the Blessed, lover of wisdom and enemy of all turning from the sun, through whose inspiration Dante as a candidate for the love of the Court of Heaven, may take up his labor.

Beatrice thus opposes the she-wolf especially in empowering the mystic reversal which marks entrance on the purgative way, but she opposes the she-wolf also as that ravening beast appears in the ways of illumination and union to distract from study and to distort love from the Infinite to the Nothing. Lucia, similarly,

133. Cf. p. 164 n. 189.
134. Cf. the numerous legends in which Mary brings the sacraments to one of her devotees imprisoned or wounded in a place far from priest and altar.

opposes the lion especially as he dominates the illuminative way, but she opposes him also as he appears in the ways of purgation and union as deformity of mind and the sin of violence. Finally, Mary opposes the leopard not only, though especially, as he dominates the way of union, but also as he appears throughout the threefold way. It was Mary through whose humility was offered release from *reatus poenae* and the possibility of new life in the very face of the harbinger of death.

Here there may be added a word of caution well supported by the symbolism just described: Throughout this order of symbolism, that which Dante's time-space pilgrimage reveals in regard to eternal truths cannot be dated in respect to the mystic way, or even divided into temporal stages. This is one reason for the unsatisfactoriness of the many attempts which have been made to equate stages of the mystic way as worked out by Bonaventure, by Richard of St. Victor, or by some other mystic whom Dante may have known. The mystic way itself had not been charted with the accuracy later displayed in the Spanish school; and, moreover, it is *par excellence* that journey into eternity which, though it may be related to the time-space journey of social, moral, or sacramental development, exists in reality all at once.

Those mystics who have been most meticulous in analysis of the mystic way into sub-subdivisions of purgation, illumination, and union, nevertheless always add that the three main phases are but different meanings of the same progress, though emphasis may swing from one to another. The attempt to equate *Inferno, Purgatorio,* and *Paradiso* to the three phases of the mystic way is thus (except in a very restricted sense) contrary to the meaning of the way itself, as Dante beheld it in eternity. Indeed, there are probably few critics who would attempt to equate the *Inferno* to the whole of Dante's visionary journey, the *Purgatorio* to the story of his political development, and the *Paradiso* to the story of his moral life. The *Paradiso* is regarded as having properly no part in the journey itself, even though through the peculiar plan of appearances in the time-space spheres, of that which is not in time and place, there is given suggestion of progression. Knowledge of the mystic way as it ultimately exists

must be given, as Dante represents, only in the Empyrean beyond time and space where although he must tell of it as progression, no progression can exist. Only purgation belongs
really to time and space, and thus it is summarized in that last
most swift of the spheres of motion,[135] which to the mystic's vision becomes the first, so mightily is it moved by the point of
flame its true center.

II. PROGRESSION: INEVITABLE TRANSMUTATION

"COME, in sì poc'ora, da sera a mane ha fatto il sol tragitto?"—
"How, in so short a time, has the Sun from eve to morn made
transit?" In the *Inferno,* at the end of a long journey among
Circe's creatures, Dante comes to the sudden realization of the
reversal which marks the entrance upon the mystic quest. At
the outset of his journey, thrown into confusion by the beasts,
Dante hesitated to follow that which Virgil, as practical and
active reason, pointed out as the only road. Whereas this hesitation might have been interpreted as true humility, Virgil termed
it craven fear, the result of faulty vision, characteristic of one
still under the power of that *gravezza* which makes the Worm
the center of the universe:

> L'anima tua è da viltate offesa;
> la qual molte fiate l'omo ingombra
> sì che d'onrata impresa lo rivolve . . .[136]

Such fear is betrayal to the power of Circe and her hellish metamorphoses, the true character of which Dante is soon to see, in
the inversions and gruesome parodies of hell, where fire, image
of Divine Wisdom, falls downward to extinction in slow flakes
like snow. Hell's very shape is an inverted cone, to him whose
vision centers in the Worm; but he whose vision centers in the
Divine Sun sees the same law is potent in both hell and purgatory.[137] One need but recall Virgil's reiteration: "Vuolsi così

135. Cf. pp. 85 ff.
136. "Thy soul is smit with coward fear, which oftentimes encumbers men, so
that it turns them back from honoured enterprise." *Inf.,* ii, 45-48.
137.

"Giustizia mosse il mio alto Fattore;	"Justice moved my High Maker; Di-
fecemi la divina potestate,	vine Power made me, Wisdom Su-
la somma sapienza e 'l primo	preme, and Primal Love."
amore."	

Inf., iii, 4-6.

colà dove si puote ciò che si vuole."[138] Had the sun become for Dante permanently the center of the universe, he might have climbed "il dilettoso monte," and risen to the spheres from any point on the earth's surface. In reality, however, the reversal is an ever recurrent motif throughout the whole of the *Commedia* —finite expression of the eternal reversal in the Primum Mobile.

INSIDE THE GATE

Withdrawing attention from the drag of the great refusal, the mystic in increasing awareness of failure takes his place in the cosmic drama wherein the Dark Wood becomes, by the transmutation of mystic development, the *divina foresta* of the Terrestrial Paradise, and ultimately the Celestial Rose, as Dante himself progresses from a tangled jungle of conflict to the sturdy oak of the Terrestrial Paradise, and finally after death is to take his place among the petals of the Rose. The beasts on the other hand, three vices in opposition to Father, Son, and Holy Spirit, under transmutation become the Worm at the center of the universe. They are represented in Upper Hell by Charon, Minos, and the threefaced Cerberus. In the approach to lower Hell the transmutation becomes inversion; there where sin of will had been more than failure, is the mockery of fire and the negation of cold. Plutus, the cursed Wolf, is followed by Phlegyas the violent, and the coiled and knotted Geryon.[139] The symbolism of Charon, with eyes like wheels of fire, is appropriately the thunder manifestation; that of Minos the mockery of judgment; and that of Cerberus first the doggishness earlier discussed as the unpardonable sin,[140] and second, the three faces which sum up in cupidity the opposition to the Tri-unity.[141] At last, in Satan, parody and negation of the Sun, approach to whom is prefaced by that most horrible of all transmutations, the snake union which parodies the mystic marriage—is the summary of the whole.

---

138. "Thus it is willed there, where what is willed can be done." *Inf.*, iii, 95-96. Cf. *Inf.*, V, 23-24, and IX, 94-96.
139. Geryon's coils and knots suggest the spots of the leopard. Cf. p. 190.
140. Cf. pp. 163 ff.   141. Cf. pp. 199 ff. and p. 164 n. 189.

SEARCH AMID FAILURE

Beneath the drama of transmutation to conscious experience of which the mystic is committed, lie the vicissitudes of the threefold way, which, although never marked out in temporal stages, are cast in a universal mold. Passing out from the Dark Wood through the fateful gate and turning his back on the possibility of refusal, the seeker progresses through a period of testing characterized by vision of failure accomplished through that vice which, blocking knowledge[142] and separating it from its good, has corrupted nature. In the pattern outlined with reference to the first and second orders, each detail in the symbolism of Upper Hell is pregnant for the initiate in the way.

EXPERIENCE OF DEFIANCE

At the point where it seems that further progress is irrevocably barred, the gate is suddenly opened as it were by a miracle of supernatural power, and the traveler enters in a triumph which is ominous. In the triumph is a new sense of divine power both immanent and transcendent: which in the dolorous realm with its tumultuous deformity of mind and soul delivers the traveler through betrayal into peril of perdition.

Though in the experience of divine transcendence is a foretaste of the ultimate goal, the way to betrayal is laid open through the surrender of reason to experience of the suprarational. Furthermore the experience following the triumphant revelation of entry is a tumult which leaves no peace for study. The seeker is thus placed in such confusion that, apart from knowledge and sacrament, he tends to seek direct guidance in trance and ecstasy after the fashion of the false mystics, followers of the *Everlasting Gospel*[143] and others, who roamed through Paris, through Italy, and through Provence in Dante's

142. The importance of this conception in the Middle Ages, suggests yet another reference to Dante's philosophical background, with reference to the relationship of sin to the inability to see straight intellectually. According to Thomas Aquinas, "Peccatum non potest esse in voluntate, nisi cum ignorantia intellectus." Cf. *S.Th.*, 1, *Q.* 63, *art.* 1 *ad* 4; 1, 2, *Q.* 58, *art.* 2, *c.* and *Q.* 77, *art.* 2, *c.*; 2, 2, *Q.* 20, *art.* 2, *Q.* 51, *art.* 3 *ad* 2, *Q.* 53, *art.* 2, *c.*, etc.

143. Ascribed to Joachim of Flora. The book, which represented extreme views sponsored by certain Franciscans, was a storm center for a time at the University of Paris.

time. Such is the *sacrificium intellectus* (one of the three great perils of mysticism), which even today renders the word "mystic" slightly akin to "mentally unbalanced." Again rendered impotent in the power of the vice within the soul, the wayfarer may escape only through absolute reversal.

Similarly the experience of divine immanence within was in reality a foreshadowing of the ultimate harmonization of the will of the traveler with the will of the Prime Mover. Yet such is the threefold detriment that in the presence of the gift of grace there comes betrayal in temptation to pantheism (the second of the perils of mysticism), and a presumptuous reliance on grace for that which lies within the sphere of discipline. Thus the *reatus poenae* becomes absolute as both discipline and grace are rendered impotent, and the only escape is the mystic reversal, piercing through the utter corruption of nature.

Finally, from the point of view of development in union, there comes at the moment when despair seems imminent the miracle of sudden unitive experience. The lion, still satellite of the *lupa,* enters into experience of divine union, and through the leopard there is given to contemplation the gift of energy that should be spent in action. Thus in ensuing quietism (which is the third peril of mysticism), is destroyed the balance between activity and receptivity, man's seeking of God and God's seeking of man, and both means of progress are rendered impotent.

DEATH AND REBIRTH

The seeker for the Beatific Vision depends for his progress on the Logos, who in his union of the finite and the infinite is in fact the Way, potent to maintain the balance between effort and grace, reason and revelation, action and contemplation, and so save from peril of the *sacrificium intellectus,* pantheism, and quietism. In company with him the seeker, through some experience of these three perversions, is led to the mystic death beyond which lies the resurrection in the mystic reversal. In the passage through the center of the earth there is premonition of the reconciliation of opposites obtaining in eternity, yet the subsequent progress is the weary maintenance of opposing autonomies. Though Dante passed instantaneously from night to morning, from spring to fall, as Virgil clambered up Satan's ribs, yet he made his way up the rivulet, by effort, reason, and action, acting as autonomous in relation to grace, revelation, and contemplation. As the pantheist comes to see himself in God rather than God in him; as the supernaturalist comes to see God's gift of knowledge in the exercise of reason, rather than the best exercise of reason in acceptance of an independently given gift of knowledge; as the quietist comes to see that *laborare est orare* as clearly as he sees that *orare est laborare:* so each no longer misled by the truths of divine immanence, transcendence, and love, is freed from the fetters of a false mysticism. Even Tenebrifer may appear as if turned once more into Lucifer, or at least into a flight of stairs by which the stars of the morning once more may be regained.

THE REVERSAL STABILIZED

The center passed, the mystic must reorganize his life and whole personality on all levels or phases of the Way.[144] Emerging to see the stars of the morning, the wayfarer passes from the painful seedtime to the laborious harvest, being required before the work of the day to wait below the gates for supernatural help. In the presence of Cato, who shines as the sun of effort, reason, action, under the stars of the cardinal virtues, he must formulate a new rule of life and discipline, a new plan of study, a new dedication to service. When it shall please Lucia, the Eagle of Divine Wisdom, to end his waiting, he will be placed before the gate of true progress, which even effort, reason, action, cannot enable him to reach.[145]

INTEGRATION

In purgatory, Circe's enchantments must be unspelled, through the twofold activity of grace and the discipline it empowers. Those whom she had lured through pride must work their transformation bowed down to earth, as must the glutton,

144. Modern studies of the psychology of mysticism and religious experience, all reiterate the fact well known to men as skilled in introspection as Augustine and Dante, that the crisis of inner experience consists in a point of inversion followed by a reorganization of the personality around a new center.

145. It is as fatal to overemphasize one member of a pair, as it is the other. This is true on the mystic levels, as it has been on the six preceding.

lean and thin through fasting. Their penance, then, is not punishment, but the working out of the law of love. Even in purgatory, in the dream wherein Circe again proves her power over him who will look toward the Worm, Dante is again reminded of the unswerving devotion of his will, through which alone Beatrice can accomplish in him progress beyond the human.

Accompanying this purgation, of which the law is the perfect simplicity of intention stressed by Dionysius, comes an increasing power to perceive in symbols their true meaning. It is not enough to use reason to the fullest, reason must become a practical force in living. Even as Circe's spell of impotence is slowly and painfully unspelled through the discipline of the terraces, so her spell of ignorance is slowly and painfully unspelled through study not now unorganized but orderly, for the illumination of the lessons learned in the disorder of previous experience.[146] In this process the veil of symbolism becomes increasingly more transparent, or, more truly, substance and accidents and their relations become fused. Throughout the phase of illumination also, except in moments of unitive experience, it is Lady Philosophy reflected in Virgil (ultimately Lucia, unseen except in the symbol of the Eagle) who is guide.[147]

The way of union, most perilous of all phases of the mystic's journey, likewise receives in the purgatory its positive development. Practice of the active life is now unhampered by the confusions of hell. Though painful in the step by step unspelling of failures in love, the burden of *gravezza* is gradually removed. At length, even as at the heights effort has led to grace and reason to revelation, so action leads to contemplation, and the fruition of all the pairs is placed within the grasp of the seeker. For the attainment of the reconciliation of opposites, of which there was premonition in the mystic inversion, the seeker has been thus guarded and strengthened through the maintenance of the mutual autonomies of pairs, in the ways of purgation, of illumination, and of union itself.

The full significance of this symbolism in its relationship to the problems of the time in which Dante lived can be shown

146. The fundamental division of evil is that in the *Purgatorio*. In the *Inferno* men are punished, not for the root vice, but for the fruit to which it led.
147. Lady Philosophy is not a rival to Beatrice. Cf. pp. 169-171.

most clearly through a contrast. Among all the writings of ancient or more modern times, primitive, Jewish, Roman, or Oriental, which have afforded such a fertile field for those whose
interest is in tracing similarities,[148] the mystical works of Ramón
Lull stand out with peculiar interest. It is indeed possible that
this "Spanish Jacopone da Todi" was in Paris during those very
years in which Boccaccio tells that Dante studied there. Moreover, during a previous stay he wrote his novel-like *Blanquerna,*
within which was contained a complete mystical treatise, the
"Book of the Lover and the Beloved, teachings given to Blanquerna by Ramón the Fool"; and the allegorical "Tree of
Love." In the latter Ramón Lull set forth his failure to achieve
his aim: "to work great good by means of knowledge"; and his

148. A word of caution may not be out of place here as to the tracing of similarities as proof of literary dependence, within the field of symbolism. Perhaps
in no other field is this always hazardous occupation more likely to lead into
absurdity. The work of Fr. Miguel Asin y Palacios on Mohammedan sources of
the *Divina Commedia,* one of the greatest monuments of Dante scholarship to
appear within recent years, is deserving of comment in this connection. With no
wish to controvert Fr. Asin's conception of a great debt owed by Dante to Islamic
visionaries, one yet cannot but question, as proof of this debt, symbolisms inherent either in the definite teachings of Christian patristic theology, or in ideas so
fundamental that they appear in the minds of all mystics, modern and primitive,
whether in Greece, Rome, India, Scandinavia, or Peru. The following example
is characteristic of much of his argument:
    "The feature . . . that shows most conclusively the affinity between the two
stories is the one that is repeated *ad nauseam* in the Mahometan Ascension. At
each stage of heaven Mahomet is dazzled by the lights, and each time he is fearful of being blinded. Repeatedly he raises his hands to his eyes to shield them
from the intense radiance, and in the end he becomes dazed. . . . This scene is
reproduced, often with the same words, in more than ten episodes of Dante's
Paradiso. . . . In the eighth sphere the refulgence of Christ in the image of a
sun blurs the poet's vision. . . ." Asin, *Islam and the Divine Comedy,* p. 27.
    Had Professor Asin based this argument on the idea of a journey through the
spheres to God (as indeed he argues elsewhere), it might be accepted as a possibility; but anyone familiar with older literature would be aware that the idea
of increasing dazzling of vision with increasing nearness to God was "repeated
ad nauseam" long before Mohammed ever existed. (Cf. pp. 124 ff.) (It should
be remembered that Mohammedanism, like post-Christian Judaism and Christianity itself, is inheritor both of the Old Testament and of the Greek tradition.
In all three, in medieval times, the authority of Aristotle listing nine physical
heavens was accepted. This being so, Christian theology could not but add the
tenth heaven (cf. pp. 34-35) and the use of this conception in the *Divina
Commedia* is scarcely to be termed a literary artifice, even though Fr. Asin considers it to be such in the Ascension of Mohammed.) When the learned critic
later, compelled by his Catholic theology to trace Dante's conception of the
lumen gloriae (the unique light in which the soul may see God) to Thomas
Aquinas, then declares that Thomas could have gotten the conception from no
other than a Mohammedan source, one wonders whether his wide scholarship
has omitted a glimpse of the mystery cults. Quite apart from the biblical basis of

decision to adopt a new aim: "to work great good by means of love." To the furtherance of the new aim he is to write a book on the philosophy of love. Meditating on this decision in a forest somewhat resembling that of the Terrestrial Paradise, he meets a lady who is Philosophy-of-Love, sorrowing over the fewness of her lovers in contrast to those of her sister, Philosophy-of-Knowledge. Her words suggest the conflict between discipline and grace: when men, she says,

have mastered the sciences, they grow to love the philosophy thereof, and make many books and many arts. So their love goes wholly to the sciences, and they have none for me, nor for that love which is my essence and nature. . . . Therefore do I weep and lament, not from envy and pride, but because few men in this world have knowledge how to love.[149]

At once those ladies who have *intelletto d'amore* are recalled, among them Lady Philosophy, and Beatrice herself, whose essence and nature is Love. Here is also an idealization of the system of courtly love, giving intimation of its very problems, both real and artificial,[150] and a picture of the dilemma of the illuminative way:

Two lovers met; the one revealed his Beloved, and the other learned of Him. And it was disputed which of those two was nearer to his Be-

the idea, common alike to Mohammedanism and Christianity, there is the unbroken tradition of the Church Fathers. In the Middle Ages, as all mental seeing took place only in the presence of the *lumen intellectus,* and as all sensory seeing took place only in the presence of the *lumen solis,* so spiritual seeing required the *lumen gloriae* of which both were symbols. Fr. Asin's discovery that a comparison of many scenes in Mahomet's Ascension "with numerous similar descriptions in the *Paradiso* makes it clear that in both stories the element of light reigns supreme" (*op. cit.,* p. 25), is hardly a safe basis on which to rest his conclusion of literary influence on the *Divina Commedia* from the Spanish Moslem mystic school of Ibn Masarra and Ibn Arabi.

Even more surprising is Fr. Asin's ascription to hyperbole and affectation Dante's protestation that as the vision increases he is less and less able to tell of it. There is probably in existence no account of the mystic vision in which this has not been said, whether the vision were produced by spiritual meditation or even by the use of drugs. (Cf. Dr. Leuba's citation of the drug vision experimentally produced, of which the subject states that he has perceived the unutterable.) In brief, arguments can hardly be drawn from the fact that the psychological effect of the Beatific Vision is the same in the study of Mahomet and of Dante, since human nature remaining constant, it could not be, and indeed never has been described as, otherwise.

149. Ramón Lull, *Tree of Love,* tr. E. Allison Peers, p. 4.

150. Accused by Power-of-Love, Wisdom-of-Love, and Will-of-Love (the personification is nominal only; they have no human lineaments) for insufficient

loved; and in the solution the Lover took knowledge of the demonstration of the Trinity.[151]

Description of the mystic progress in terms of light and darkness, the attraction of the sun and its negation, dominates the whole of Lull's treatment:

> They asked the Lover in what manner the heart of man was turned towards the love of the Beloved. He answered them and said: "Even as the sunflower turns to the sun." "How is it, then, that all men love not thy Beloved?" He answered: "They that love Him not have night in their hearts, because of their sin."[152]

The way of union with its foreshadowing of anagoge is characteristically described through the combination of the supreme symbolisms of sun and courtly love:[153]

> Love shone through the cloud which came between the Lover and the Beloved, and made it as bright and resplendent as is the moon by night, as the day-star at dawn, the sun at mid-day, the understanding in the will; and through that bright cloud the Lover and the Beloved held converse.[154]

Lull is as conscious as is Dante of the danger to union of the abuse of insight symbolism, that is, the resting in creatures rather than the constant ascent from "fair to yet more fair" until ultimately strengthened for the love of the Beloved:

> And he said that he had sinned many times with the eyes in looking upon creatures of God that were fair, and rejoicing rather in their beauty than in the beauty of the Beloved, who created them to show forth his beauty and goodness, that his lovers may delight therein.[155]

use of them, and by the Virtues for neglect, the Lover appeals to Love; only to be accused freshly by Truth, Glory of Love, Difference of Love, Concordance of Love, and Contrariety of Love. Then is inserted an episode in which the Lover is ill, attended by the Physician of Love who merely attempts to aggravate the illness. Whereupon the Lover fled from Love together with Contrariety and Minority, only to be captured and thrown into jail by two angels. The Beloved wishes to condemn the Lover to death, but the Lady of Love intercedes. A trial ensues, with Life of Love the advocate for the defense, and Death of Love the advocate for the prosecution. Between them they carry on a long dispute after the tedious fashion of the courts of love. The result is that the Beloved condemns the Lover to die. Cf. pp. 428 ff.

151. Lull, *Book of the Lover and the Beloved*, tr. E. A. Peers, p. 113, § 361.
152. *Ibid.*, p. 107, § 342.
153. For medieval treatment of sex symbolism, cf. Appendix III, Pt. I, i.
154. Lull, *op. cit.*, p. 53, § 118.
155. Lull, *Tree of Love*, p. 46. Cf. Augustine, quoted on p. 356.

Like Dante, also, Lull commits his spiritualization of the ideals of courtly love to the vernacular[156]—for him, Catalan.

Ramón Lull lived and disputed on theological questions at a time when the fourfold method was in full prominence. In complete agreement with Dante's mysticism in the matter of courtly love, he failed, through an allegiance to Augustinianism in contradistinction to Thomism, to maintain the autonomy of pairs through the time-space progress of the Way. That which is remarkable is the fact that while using in his mystical works individual symbols in constant interpretation on all four levels, he has so used them in his story that more than one mystical interpretation is rarely possible. In other words, it would seem that Lady Philosophy-of-Love, suggesting Beatrice, when she is served in contradistinction to Lady Philosophy-of-Knowledge (Lady Philosophy, or Lucia) is unable to give that clearness of vision which alone makes possible the arrangement of symbolic interrelationships necessary for the complete truth of the four levels. It is to be remembered that for Dante, allegiance to Beatrice demanded also allegiance to Lady Philosophy,[157] sent forth from Mary. In reality Lady Philosophy-of-Love and Lady Philosophy-of-Knowledge are one and the same,[158] and in separating them Lull has separated the Persons of the Trinity. In creation's progress toward God, the seemingly natural order for men of reaching the Son through the Spirit and the Father through the Son (that is, from Love to Wisdom to Power) is impossible. Catholic theology could never escape the fact that man might reach union with God by way of the Primal Love, only after Eternal Wisdom had descended to earth to initiate and maintain in his own dual nature contact with men.

156. Many more similarities could be traced between the mystical work of Lull and the *Divina Commedia*.

157. Cf. pp. 169-171.

158. "Tandis que le mystique, s'élance impèteusement, le regard fixè sur le but qu'il veut attendre, le scholastique s'avance avec lenteur et précaution; il sonde le terrain, il écarte doucement les obstacles; sa démarche n'est pas rapide, mais elle est sûre. L'idéalisme de Platon est le fondement du mysticisme, et la dialectique d'Aristote l'instrument necessaire de la scholastique. . . . Elles ne s'excluent donc pas l'une l'autre . . . l'une est plus analytique et l'autre plus synthétique. . . . Saint Thomas et saint Bonaventure furent à la fois mystiques et scolastiques. . . . Il y a une vraie et une fausse scolastique, un vrai et un faux mysticisme." Mgr. Hugonin in his "Prolegomena" to the works of Hugh of St. Victor, in Migne. *P.L.*, 175.

In Dante's "dolce stil nuovo" was reflected the sternness of mystic discipline, and conventional birds and ladies and disputes had no place. Francis, when he is separated from Dominic, though still able to lead deeply into the ecstasies of love, cannot give the complete illumination which is the Beatific Vision; and this is the full significance of the *via mystica* as Dante saw it in his *Commedia.* Those loves which course around the Sun all have their delight

> quanto la sua veduta si profonda
> nel vero in che si queta ogni intelletto.
> Quinci si può veder come si fonda
> l'esser beato ne l'atto che vede,
> non in quel ch'ama, che poscia seconda.[159]

Again is made exigent the balance between the members of the pairs and, as Dionysius and John the Scot made clear in their theory of knowledge, progress is possible only through full resolution of their conflict. Love is reached only afterward, in that which surpassing both unites them. He who attempts immediate attainment of union goes upward to remain still blind, not, like Dante, to be blind no longer.

III. CULMINATION: NEW MOTION

WITH the consummation of Dante's quest in the all-revealing moment of communion at the summit of the mount,[160] the solar symbolism becomes strongly reënforced through the symbolism of marriage. There is in the anagoge of Dante's personal life[161] a suggested comparison of Dante's union with Beatrice to the marriage of Francis with Lady Poverty and of Dominic with the Faith.[162] This has its appropriateness in the order of symbolism

159. "In measure as their sight sinketh more deep into the truth wherein every intellect is stilled. Hence may be seen how the being blessed is founded on the act that seeth, not on that which loveth, which after followeth." *Par.,* xxviii, 107-111. This is the Thomist view, as against the Augustinian and Franciscan.

160. Cf. Chap. IV, Pt. II, iii, especially pp. 320 ff.

161. As seen by him especially in the sphere of the Sun. Cf. pp. 58 ff.

162. Cf. *Paradiso,* cantos xi and xii. In addition to the mystic marriage of the soul, and of all humanity to God, certain individuals chosen for a special office are conceived of as bringing forth fruit in particular mystic marriages of the kind mentioned. Even as Francis and Dominic each brought a numerous progeny to the service of God and the salvation of church and Faith, so Dante expects that by his work, inspired by Beatrice (as Francis and Dominic by Poverty and the

where Dante journeys as type of Christ, whose marriage with the church took place on the Cross.[163] To this marriage all the baptized in Christ's mystical Body owe their new birth, as on the more personal level each soul, through its relationship to the sacramental Body, is itself bride of Christ.[164] In the order of symbolism relating to the mystic quest, truly represented in the spheres in the Ladder rising from Saturn, is the final significance of this symbolism. Jacob's Ladder[165] was interpreted by Rabanus Maurus as *Charitas* which unites and couples.[166] Up the ladder of contemplation the soul journeys to ultimate union with the object of its quest.

No fact is made more evident in the symbolism of both earthly and heavenly Paradise than that he who in the culmination of the mystic progress shrinks from expression, fails in fruitfulness, and so annuls the mystic marriage itself. Expression of that to which the ecstasy of love has led, must be through the power of intellect[167] and good works, indeed, a reflection of the Trinity in all its aspects. For example, Ramón Lull, in the words of Lady Philosophy-of-Love, pointed out the barrenness of those who in union with knowledge failed to express it in good works, but then, like so many a Franciscan of his time, he sought the remedy in a union with love which failed to bear fruit in the intellect.

Faith, respectively), he will bring a numerous progeny "from a state of misery to a state of bliss." Cf. *Epistle* XIII (X).

163. Cf. Eph. 5. 25-32 and other passages.

164. It is in virtue of this marriage-union with the Logos, fruit of his suffering, that the mystic must go through the agonies of hell, since the essence of marriage consists in the making of two as one to share the same experiences. The bride of Christ shares his sufferings and his joys.

165. The ladder is a timeworn symbol for sexual congress.

166. "Quod charitas nos et per compassionem sociat proximo, et per desiderium copulat proximo." Rabanus Maurus, commenting on *scala* in Gen. 28. 12.

167. Mary, the supreme example of the mystic marriage, alone among creatures uniting the heights of virginity and of fruitfulness, is said by Albertus Magnus to have been supreme also intellectually. It is ever to be remembered that her Child was Eternal Wisdom. In fact, medieval theology itself implied the necessity of giving a high place to the intellect even in the exercises of devotion, though it is true and necessary that in practice the ignorant rely on faith in many spheres belonging properly to the domain of reason. Thomas points out that the data of revelation rightly understood no more conflict with the findings of reason than do the data of sense experience. (In both fields there are many superficial conflicts, for example, between the real and apparent size of the sun.) Faith is knowledge of a type inferior to reason. Its value lies in its greater reach. Cf. Gilson's work on Thomism, chapters 2 and 3.

How Giacomo da Todi, lawyer, became Jacopone, minstrel, is a story full of significance. After years spent in a shrewd and intelligent practice of his profession Giacomo, on the death of his wife, succumbed like so many another to the lure of the mystic way. Unprepared through discipline for its perils, he was swept from his feet in the love enthusiasm which spread like a fire through the Europe of his day. In the glory of initial triumph in a vision of the love of the Court of Heaven he hastily relegated to the court of Satan not only his former sins, but also the intellect by the light of which he had lived. Wandering about the countryside, singing songs of love, Giacomo, lawyer of Todi, became Jacopone, the simple.

The defects of such "erotic mysticism" as that of Jacopone have been the subject of frequent comment, of which the outcome is generally to place them under the ban of sex perversion. As a matter of fact a source of motivation of such power as that of love can scarce be absent from a quest which is coterminous with the whole of life, demanding the utmost of the whole personality. That which subjects the verses of such mystics as Jacopone to censure, is in reality not sex but the lack of balance resulting from the *sacrificium intellectus*. Even the uninitiate is likely to feel a sense of wrongness in a love poem to Eternal Wisdom, with its urgent supplication for union, from one who spends his days speaking scorn of all that pertains to the intellect. Although the symbolism of love and generation was chosen equally with that of the sun for preëminence in the New Testament, it is like an edged tool in the hands of children when unsafeguarded by solar imagery. In general the symbolism of the sun expresses for the intellect that which the imageries of love express for the emotions, although both are subject to either treatment.[168]

Bearing witness to his maintenance of the primacy of the act of knowing, Dante's progress on every level is from light to light, that is, from lesser to greater insight, made possible alike by his increasing discipline and his increasing illumination. In

168. Angela of Foligno, whose early life was that of a pampered lady of society, became by no means a distinctly intellectual mystic. Yet her work taken as a whole presents the balance between the two symbolisms and the two motifs which Dante makes essential in his *Commedia*, and her mysticism was fruitful

the *Paradiso* he is shown at last the function of each element of his education.[169] There is a hierarchical progression of symbols. Thus in hell the progress of Dante is from darker and grosser sights to scenes even darker and more gross, until at last, empowered to endure with Christ the full horror of evil, he ascends, greeted at first by the pale light of dawn and by an angel who causes agony to his unaccustomed eyes. Then on from brighter to brighter angels, from clearer to clear vision, he mounts, gradually lightened of sin until in the Earthly Paradise, his transmutation accomplished and his quest achieved, the miracle of nine is completed: that has been said of Beatrice which before has never been said of woman, that through her eyes is revealed the whole secret of the universe.

Dante has seen the development of himself as an individual in personal, civic, and moral life; he has seen the fourfold life of God incarnate in which is bound up the twofold corporate life of humanity; he has been granted in a flash vision of the threefold truth of the mystical life of each soul alone with God. Yet with perception of nineness in the universe—or even of the threeness of the divine nature, the sole root mathematically and theologically of the nineness—it is impossible to stop.[170] To the interlocking tercets must be added the fourth line which gives

in disciplined wisdom in her life. Cf. the atmosphere of the following selections, the first of which is a poem of Jacopone's, the other the last vision of Angela, before her death in 1309:

"Love! Love! lovely Jesus!
Love, I will die
Embracing thee.
Sweet Love, Jesus my Bridegroom,
Love, Love, Jesus thou Holy One,
Give me thyself, transform me into thyself,
Think, that I am in rapture,
That I have lost myself,
Jesus my hope,
Come, sleep in love!"

"And then he showed unto me the Bridegroom, the Eternal Word, so that now I do understand what thing the Word is and what it doth mean—that is to say, this Word which for my sake was made Flesh. And the Word entered into me and touched me throughout and embraced me, saying, 'Come, My love, My bride, beloved of Me with true delight—come, for all the saints do await thee with exceeding great joy.'"

169. To the seven heavens nearest the earth "correspond the seven sciences of the Trivium and of the Quadrivium, to wit grammar, dialectic, rhetoric, arithmetic, music, geometry, and astrology. To the eighth, to wit the starry sphere, answers natural science which is called physics, and first science which is called metaphysics. To the ninth sphere answers moral science; and to the quiet heaven answers divine science, which is called theology." *Convivio*, 2, 15.

170. Cf. p. 339 n. 19c.

completion; to the nine which is the circumference of all reality must be added the point which gives it being. It is the one ana- goge of each and all of the threefold three that binds in one volume the scattered leaves of all the universe—that which ulti- mately must be seen without symbols and so may not be told.

CHAPTER VI. SCHEMA

THE *Commedia,* like Chartres, a Speculum, gathering up the great quest motifs of the people.

I. *Liturgy:* The cathedral as a setting for the drama of the Mass presents the pattern of ultimate truth. In the Mass is represented the orbit of the Divine Sun, borne out in the daily cycle of the Hours and the annual cycle of the Christian Year.

II. *Popular literature:* Fragmentary and inconsistent reflection of the cultural development which culminated in the thirteenth century in the worship of woman and the sun-guided quest for the love of the Court of Heaven.

III. *Grail cycle:* Quest in which the hero, knighted survival of Celtic heathendom, and the Christian motif itself, are solar manifestations.

IV. *Alchemy:* The story of transmutations in which the transmuting power and the ultimate product are alike manifestations of the Divine Sun.

Thus men were trained in the quest for the Infinite, answering to the quest of the Infinite for man. To this dual quest unified in the Cross, Dante gave supreme expression.

CHAPTER VI. SYMBOLISM IN MEDIEVAL POPULAR USAGE: LITURGY, ROMANCE, SCIENCE

S'io ti fiammeggio nel caldo d'amore
  di là dal modo che'n terra si vede,
  sì che de li occhi tuoi vinco il va-
    lore,
non ti maravigliar; chè ciò procede
  da perfetto veder, che, come ap-
    prende
  così nel bene appreso move il piede.
Io veggio ben sì come già resplende
  ne l'intelletto tuo l'etterna luce,
  che, vista, sola e sempre amore ac-
    cende;
e s'altra cosa vostro amor seduce,
  non è se non di quella alcun ves-
    tigio,
  mal conosciuto, che quivi traluce.

If I flame on thee in the warmth of love, beyond the measure witnessed upon earth, and so vanquish the power of thine eyes, marvel not; for this proceedeth from perfect vision, which, as it apprehendeth so doth advance its foot in the apprehended good. Well do I note how in thine intellect already doth reglow the eternal light, which only seen doth ever kindle love; and if aught else seduce your love, naught is it save some vestige of this light, ill understood, that shineth through therein.

IT is told that when Dante, during the last years of his life, appeared in city streets of early fourteenth-century Italy, small boys were wont to gather on the corners to gaze in awe on that grave figure who had been in hell. To whisperings and the pointings of many fingers, Dante had been inured on his journey and whatever their share in deepening those lines of sorrow and of pain revealed by the death mask, in contrast to the proud courage of the early portrait by Giotto, the exile was no longer deterred by them. Walking among men for whom the separated mocking lights of hell had always held such fascination he pondered on that mission of which the Celestial Rose held the ultimate revelation: reinstatement of the suns of Rome that through them men might be brought to know the glory of the source of light in response to whose attraction all creation moves.

Dante's mission was not to leaders only, but to all people that they might know "if aught else seduce your love, naught is it save some vestige of this light, ill understood, that shineth through therein." For the sake of this mission, not only had Dante journeyed where no living man but the founders of church and state had walked, but also he had dared to intrust to the vulgar tongue the masterpiece of his life, a consummation of learning which in its import was to rival the greatest scriptures of the past.

To those undisciplined in the way of vision, and so unable

even to distinguish symbol from reality, the beauty of his poem would bring the effulgence of Supreme Reality softened and made tolerable to the weakness of their vision. This Dante expressed at the close of an ode in which as in the *Commedia,* he beheld Lady Philosophy reflected in the heaven of love:

> Ode! I believe that they shall be but rare
> who shall rightly understand thy meaning,
> so intricate and knotty is thy utterance of it:
> Wherefore if perchance it come about
> that thou take thy way into the presence of folk
> who seem not rightly to perceive it;
>
> Then I pray thee to take heart again,
> And say to them, O my beloved lastling;
> "Give heed at least how beautiful I am."[1]

Thus, for the first time a supreme expression of the deepest mystery of the universe was submitted to the world, clad in imagery *vulgaris eloquentiae.* Previous to Dante's act of daring, the deepest mystery and the highest knowledge had received for the people no other translation than translation in stone.

Indeed, the tremendous rhythms of the *Commedia* and of Chartres claim so much of kinship that real insight into the poem is scarcely possible to one unacquainted with the gargoyles and rose windows in those great forests of stone within which all men might find the terrors of the Dark Wood of medieval life softened and transformed beneath the power of the living Sun into at least a momentary semblance to the Celestial Rose. The Cathedral also was a book. Victor Hugo remarked that during the Middle Ages men had no great thought they did not write down in stone. It was soon discovered that static art was the expression to the community at large of the whole best thought and experience of medieval life. Whereas some cathedrals were chapters only, Chartres,[2] like the *Divina Commedia,* expressed all that was apprehended, dimly or clearly, through emotion or intellect, in regard to the whole universe. In later centuries, the masterpiece of the static arts, into which

---

1. *Convivio,* second treatise, Ode.
2. For a readable discussion of Chartres as an expression of the struggle of mankind to grasp the infinite, cf. Adams, *Mont-Saint-Michel and Chartres.*

had been built the full scope of medieval life, from castle to hovel, was to aid in rendering that life once more appreciated and understood.

Modern culture is full of dead symbols, for the most part ignored or treated as curiosities; but a cathedral is with difficulty ignored, and its symbolism carries conviction of persistent vitality. Perhaps, then, it is little wonder that those whose interest is in the static arts have led all groups of modern symbolists in the understanding of medieval thought. The point of view of the logician, mathematician, philologist, and philosopher is abstract, whereas that of literary symbolists has been marked by vagueness and confusion. Modern mystics have lacked discipline and an understanding of their antecedents, while the interest of ethnologists and psychologists has been confined to one aspect of symbolic usage. The artist, however, especially the artist in France with its wealth of medieval art and architecture, is fairly compelled to make a systematic study of symbolism for its meaning to the Middle Ages. To be sure at the coronation of Louis XVI, eighteenth-century screens were employed to conceal in the Cathedral of Rheims, the "crudeness" of Gothic decorations, but perhaps it became piquing to pride to live amid the masterpieces of an art the meaning and inspiration of which remained a mystery. In any case, those who have attempted to elucidate "l'histoire iconographique de la France" have led in awakening an understanding of medieval symbolism.

Taking his cue from the fact that mirror or *imago* was an ever recurrent title in medieval literary expression, M. Male has studied art as mirror, especially in the thirteenth century, of nature, science, ethics, and history. M. Millet also, with a more careful study of eastern influence and of the church in relation to the drama of Calvary, has developed this function of art as an expression of life in all its aspects. There is, however, an aspect of symbolism which the static artist and the interpreter of the medieval cathedral neglects almost entirely—its function in the development of thought itself. Would this be true, one wonders, if the cathedral were more often recognized as a forest like the forest of the *Commedia* under constant transmutation as the setting for a supreme drama enacted within it—the drama of the eternal Quest. In cathedral as in *Commedia* the source of life is the moment of communion, in the corporate intimacy of which is focused and revealed the eternal meaning of the whole. Thus is realized man's deepest and most secret longing, vision in which no symbol intervenes to dim the union with reality, though symbol still remains as the only path of attainment and the eternal expression.

I. THE SUN OF THE CHURCH

IN the symbolism of the Mass was constant stimulus for every temperament to deeper thought and deeper feeling. In the letter of its beauty and rhythm, it had its message for the artist; in allegory it reviewed for the people the life of Christ and the whole cultural development which lay back of their tradition, at the same time extending to each Christ's life; in trope its symbols taught of discipline and the acquisition of virtues and understanding; while in anagoge it contained the knowledge and inspiration of the mystic way and the means of man's nearest earthly approach to the Beatific Vision.

The church services, it is to be remembered, were not public meetings in the cause of religion, but were expression and maintenance of a vital relationship between man and God, in which the whole created universe was included. "The Mass was not devised to make an impression on the beholders. It was not primarily a meeting for propaganda or appeal or instruction; it was a union of faithful souls to adore and commemorate their God, a meeting of the Church Militant with the Church Triumphant, an attempt to realize the communion of saints in heaven and in earth."[3] The gaze of all eyes was both toward the sun, as the church faced toward the east, and toward the cross or monstrance:[4] the cross symbol of the Sun in creation and suffering,[5] the monstrance symbol of the Sun in glory. (In this connection

3. B. L. Manning, *The People's Faith in the Time of Wyclif*, p. 16.
4. The monstrance as a receptacle for the Host, came into use owing to its necessity in Corpus Christi processions. Cf. Y. Hirn, *The Sacred Shrine,* pp. 147 ff. Cf. also J. Hoppenot, *La messe dans l'histoire et dans l'art.*
5. It should be noted that only in the rood is the element of suffering emphasized. The cross on the altar represents primarily Christ in glory as Prophet, Priest, and King—the "Lamb *as it had been* slain." From this solar cross proceeds the life ministered to man in the sacraments.

it is interesting that sometimes the sun and moon are represented on the cross itself to show the sun as suffering an eclipse.) Thus the constant emphasis of the service was Godward, but there was also the constant stimulus to man for the strengthening of his vision and his love that he might be drawn, not to Negation, but ever closer to the primal Power, Wisdom, and Love.

From this point of view then, the function of church services was to give knowledge of God involving, as that must, a goal for man's life, together with a motivation and a technique for the attainment of that goal. In other words, in order to worship God man must know him. This knowledge must be more than the knowledge of the philosopher; it must become an integral part in the unification of the personality. Thus only, motivation can be supplied. Given both the goal and the desire to attain it, a definite technique is necessary. Finally, as it has been said, one must know to be holy and one must be holy to know. In other words, these three aims which for convenience' sake have been distinguished, in reality are intimately bound up with one another, and are to be strengthened by the church simultaneously.

Such being the case, it is easy to see why symbolism should have been prominent. Of course, symbolism is essential for the expression of all knowledge, indeed for the formation of any concept, especially in the realm where the finite is seeking the infinite; but more than this, symbolism of the kind used in the church services involves an inner spiritual meaning, an intellectual appeal, and an emotional stimulus received through as many as possible of the five senses. In other words, symbolism unites aspiration of the soul, the mind, and the body, and so is a tool peculiarly well suited for the unification of the personality in the search for reality. Not only this, but the God on whom all attention centered was seeking man through symbols. Through symbols was his self-revelation, and in symbolism of the kind involved in the sacramental system, his special gift of grace.

For the unification necessary that man may respond to the divine love, the outward and inward must be bound together. Symbols through which reason and faith or aspiration may function must be drawn from the created universe and from doctrine. Here again appear the four sources of knowledge. It is significant that medieval writers use the terms scripture and doctrine interchangeably, as one of these four. Although the medieval churchman asserts[6] his belief to be in that which the Bible teaches, yet as has been pointed out, he is never under the necessity of going to the Bible to discover what that may be; he knows it beforehand. The real source of his faith is the Person of Christ—interpreted to the mind and conveyed to the soul through his mystical body the church and his sacramental body mediated therein.

There was no educative factor in the life of the Middle Ages more powerful than the Mass, attended daily by the leisured class, while the poorest laborer was fined if he failed to be present on Sunday. The Mass and the church were intended to be a "toke and a boke to the leude peple that they may rede i' imagery and painture that clerkes rede i' the boke." The pictures, images, curtains, and ornaments were the lessons and scripture of the laity.[7] At the same time there was taught a mnemonic couplet similar to that used for the fourfold method[8] that there might be no confusion of these "lessons" with the God about whom they taught:

> Nec Deus est nec homo, quam praesens cernis imago,
> Sed Deus est et homo, quam sacra figurat imago.

A full discussion of the symbolism of the Mass, in which each accessory, each motion, and each word was to be interpreted on the four levels, would demand a treatise in itself.[9] On the other hand no one should venture into the symbolism of the *Divina Commedia* unfamiliar with some of the symbolism of the Mass, which, ubiquitous and omnipresent, formed the atmosphere of the Middle Ages.

6. As did Dante. Cf. for example *Par.*, xxiv, 91 ff.

7. It should be pointed out that there was consciousness, even in medieval times, of the psychological as well as of the educational effect of liturgical symbolism. For example, Cabasilas (Migne, *P.L.*, t. 150, col. 372) analyzes the psychological effect "avec toute la subtilité d'un psychologue." G. Millet, *Recherches sur l'iconographie de l'évangile . . .*, p. 28.

8. Cf. p. 277.

9. For the full symbolism of the church, cf. Gulielmus Durantis, *Rationale divinorum officiorum*, and *Church Symbolism, Being the First Book of the Rationale . . .*, tr. Neale and Webb.

The symbolism of the church itself is fairly familiar. In structure it represents the human body, the chancel being the head and the transepts the arms. It represents similarly the cross of Christ and much more, for example: that Christ saved the four quarters of the world; that charity is fourfold, to God, self, friends, and enemies; and that the cross is to be borne in four ways: "meditation in the heart, confession in the mouth, discipline in the body, and impression in the face." In the consecration of the church there occur such ceremonies as the threefold sunwise circuit to show that Christ came down to earth, descended into hell and ascended into heaven; and also to symbolize the Trinity and the threefold state of the saved. There is, moreover, the threefold knock at the door to show that Christ has a threefold right to come in: creation, redemption, and promise of glory. Throughout the Mass there is reminiscence of the threeness in the universe, as also of the twoness and fourness bound up in its unity.[10]

The symbolism was carried out into amazing detail, for example, the very cement which held the stones together was made of the lime of charity, the sand of social service, and the water of the spirit. The altar represents the ark,[11] the table of

10. For example, in the *Kyrie eleison* mercy is implored three times in remembrance of the Trinity who forgives sins by virtue of the Incarnation, while the *Gloria in excelsis* suggests the peace which Christ brought at his birth to a world in which there were three enmities, that between God and man, that between angels and men, and that between man and man. This is reminiscent of the Tri-unity which gives structure to the universe, and of its threefold negation.

11. The tabernacle of the covenant and the temple of the Old Law were regarded, likewise, as having symbolical meaning. The tabernacle is, according to Richard of St. Victor (Migne, *P.L.,* t. 196), the state of perfection, since "ubi perfectio animi, ibi et inhabitatio Dei." He says further: "Per atrium intellige disciplinam corporis, per tabernaculam disciplinam mentis. Ubi exterior disciplina deest, interior pro certo observari non potest. Disciplina vero corporis inutilis certe sine disciplina mentis." This accords with the fact that the tabernacle must be in a temple, and yet the temple is given its *raison d'être* only by the tabernacle. Nor can man remain ever in the tabernacle: "Exit homo de tabernaculo in atrium per operis exercitium. Intrat homo tabernaculam primum, cum redit ad seipsum. Transcendendo sane seipsum elevatur in Deum. In primo moratur homo per considerationem sui, in secundo vero per contemplationem Dei." Richard analyzes the sacred articles within (altar of sacrifice, candelabra, table, altar of incense, etc.) in several ways. This whole interpretation belongs to the order of trope, but the fourfold interpretation of the Old Law given genesis in the Epistle to the Hebrews (cf. pp. 260 ff.) was fundamental in the Middle Ages, even where, as here, only one order was under consideration.

the Last Supper, the heart,[12] and so on, there being the definite allegory of the corporate church, the trope in its application to the individual soul, and the anagoge in the relation to the heavenly intercession of Christ. Furthermore, not only does each accessory have its own independent appropriate signification according to the levels, but also it is given additional meanings appropriate to its relation to the course of the Mass—meanings which reflect, moreover, the alteration in emphasis throughout the yearly cycle. Thus, for example, in relation to Christ the altar is sometimes the manger, sometimes Calvary, and sometimes the tomb; whereas on the level of human history there are also appropriate meanings, such as that the priest in moving away from the right side of the altar indicates Christ's necessary transfer of the center of the church from Judea which has not received him,[13] while the final replacement of the Bible on the right side presages the ultimate forgiveness of the Jews.[14] The priest goes from the left to the right side of the altar to show, furthermore, that Christ took humanity to the right hand of God. Another meaning given to the motion in this connection is the movement of Christ from his passion to life eternal.[15]

In the consecration of the altar the water represents tears, the people made fruitful by the Divine Sun, and the Spirit through

12. The orfray is a crown in a circle on the front of the altar. If the altar is taken in the sense of the heart, then the orfray is the "taking in hand of a good occupation wherewith we ought to adorn our foreheads that we may give light to others." In the sense in which the altar represents Christ, the orfray is charity.

13. In the medieval rite in England the priest in censing, circled the whole altar sunwise, whenever the construction of the building made this possible. It is of interest to remember also that in certain oriental mysteries the priests in performing sacrifice circle the altar sunwise. Cf. p. 116 n. 36, and p. 218.

There is the same ritual in Hebrew esoteric cultus with which modern readers have been made familiar in the classic play by S. Ansky, the *Dybbuk*. Note in the scene of the solemn summoning of the dead, the stage direction which demands a sunwise circle drawn for protection, to be removed only by a counter-sunwise motion. Scottish peasant usage of a similar protective circle has been mentioned by Sir Walter Scott; innumerable such instances could be cited.

Motion in purgatory as described by Dante is especially to be remembered, as is the motion of mystical progress. Cf. Dionysius, *Mystical Theology*, on the circular motion of souls.

14. The priest's lingering at the center of the altar suggests the long sojourn in the desert.

15. "On sait que les mystiques voient dans le symbole non point un signe conventionnel, mais une manifestation réelle des essences suprasensibiles. '. . . Cette église est la figure de cette caverne. Bien plus, elle est presque la caverne même, car elle contient le lieu où gît le corps du Seigneur.' . . ." G. Millet,

whom he acts; the wine means spiritual exaltation, spiritual knowledge, and God; the salt, discretion, divine law, and faith; and the ashes, penitence, humility, and the Passion. The two candlesticks upon the altar represent the joy of two peoples, Jews and Gentiles, over the Incarnation of Christ, and recall the dual division of Dante's Celestial Rose. Their light signifies the faith of two peoples: "For ye were sometimes darkness, but now are ye light in the Lord: walk as children of light";[16a] and the progression from light to light. These two candles also represent Jesus Christ in his two natures—the Light of the World, while the snuffers of the candles are "divine words by which men amputate the legal titles of the law and reveal the shining spirit."[16b] Usually in discussion of church symbolism, however, the four levels of meaning are given only for the more important elements. It is assumed that he who is trained in the symbolic habit, when given one interpretation will without hesitation supply the others.

The drama of the Mass like all that deals with the method of man's progress to God (the historic, mystical, sacramental, and glorified body of Christ; the literal, allegorical, tropological, and anagogical levels of symbolism, and so forth) is divided into four parts. From the introit to the offertory is represented the preparation of the world for the Incarnation, and the Annunciation and Birth. In Part II (by far the longest, being from the offertory to the Agnus Dei) is represented the Ministry and Passion of Christ; in Part III (from the Agnus Dei to the kiss of peace) is represented the Resurrection; and in Part IV (from the Communion to the end) the days of waiting and the coming of the Holy Spirit. To each of these are joined, moreover, such tropological and anagogical meanings as are appropriate thereto.

The procession with which the Mass begins[17] represents the going out from Egypt and various other scriptural processions,

Recherches sur l'iconographie de l'évangile . . ., p. 26. The original of the passage quoted may be found in Migne, *P.L.,* t. 151, col. 272.

In brief, "L'église figure le lieu de la Passion et de la resurrection; la liturgie, ces événements eux mêmes." G. Millet, *loc. cit.*

16a. Eph. 5. 8.

16b. Durantis, *op. cit.,* tr. Neale and Webb.

17. Cf. the procession in the Pageant, and discussion pp. 315 ff.

such as, for example, when Joshua was victor, as was Christ later. In it is unconscious reminiscence, not only of the Jewish preparation for Christ, but also of the ancient mystery processions representing the people's waiting for the young Sun God to arise and free the goddess of fertility and vegetation. An attendant at Mass familiar with symbolisms may behold in epitome the whole history of humanity, historic and prehistoric.

After the introit, which represents the advent, the priest goes to the altar[18] to signify Christ's birth from a virgin like a bridegroom coming forth from his chambers, the invariable method of appearance of the Sun God.[19] The incense shows prayers ascending to God—"golden vials full of odours, which are the prayers of saints,"[20] even as the fires of sacrifice[21] once rose, and as the mists are drawn up by the sun. The censer has three chains, because the union of two natures in Christ involves three unions; that of flesh and soul which is common to all mankind; and that of the divine nature with each of the two components of the human nature, flesh and soul.[22] (One chain is of gold for the flesh of Christ, one of copper for the mortality of Christ, and one of iron for the fortitude of Christ.) This is important as one of those details which served to keep before the people the orthodox conception: that one of the divine Persons (the Logos) accepted human body, mind, and soul as his equipment, but did not assume simply a human body in which his eternal

18. "The East is the direction that must be assigned to his worship." John of Damascus, *Exposition of the Orthodox Faith*, IV, 12. Cf. p. 212.

19. "Ad altare accedit significans q. Christus expectatio gentium carne sacrosancta assumpta ex virginis carne incorrupta et secreto habitaculo coelorum egressus est in mundum vel de secreta ede videlicet et virginiali ubero egressus est tamquam sponsus de thalamo suo." Durantis, *op. cit.*

"In them hath he set a tabernacle for the Sun, which is as a bridegroom coming out of his chamber, and rejoiceth as a strong man to run a race." Ps. 19. 4-5.

20. Rev. 5. 8.

21. Jewish priests used to bring blood and coals in a censer for prayers. More specifically, according to Christian practice, prayers, given new meaning through union with Christ's sacrifice and holiness, first ascend to God, then in the censing in order of clergy and lay folk, descend to sanctify the members of his mystical body.

22. The implications of this theory as to the nature of the Incarnation lead to curious results as to the period between the first Good Friday and the first Easter. Death had severed the human union of body and soul, but not the incarnate union of God and Man. Wherefore the incarnate life of God was present in two places, in the tomb where lay the dead Body of Christ, and in the place of departed spirits, where the Soul of Christ was opening the gate of bliss to the souls of Old Testament saints and of the repentant thief.

divine nature became the soul. This latter theory, recurrent in recent Protestant thinking, was known as the Apollinarian heresy.

Because the church is joined to Christ in holy marriage[23] and because Christ came willingly and gladly to the altar of his passion, the priest kisses the altar. Here is recalled the sun as the source of all life on earth, and the secret of the mystic way, as the soul which has enjoyed the union of spiritual marriage in the Beatific Vision returns to bear fruit in good works.

After various moral significations to impress the fact that the second division of the Mass refers to the public ministry of Christ, comes the second censing of the altar, reminder of Mary Magdalene's anointing of the Lord in preparation for his Passion. Further ritual actions and prayers represent the stages of the Passion, till the Lord's Prayer reminds of the death cry from the cross: "Father, into thy hands I commend my spirit." The Agnus Dei declares Christ Lamb and sacrificial victim. (The connection existing, between the Lamb and Aries, the one of the twelve signs of the zodiac in which the sun is at the time of the Passion, should not be forgotten.)

In the third section of the Mass the priest re-takes the paten as a sign of the re-surrection, and breaks the host over the chalice to signify the rolling away of the stone from the sepulcher. (Morally, this is interpreted that good works must be united to the Passion of Christ to prevail; and anagogically that the fruit of the Passion is eternal Beatitude.) Through the fourth section the symbolism continues until in the last prayer is reflection of the prayers of the apostles in the period between Ascension and Pentecost,[24] and the blessing signifies the coming of the Holy Spirit. In all of this is but the barest suggestion of the significance of the four parts of the Mass. In them is concentrated and reviewed the complete story of the solar year.[25]

23. "In osculo siquid os ori coniungitur et in Christo non solum humanitas est unita divinitati verum etiam sponsa copulata est sponso iuxta. . . ." Durantis, *op. cit.*

The priest after the introit kisses the altar twice, in honor of the two natures of Christ.

24. Acts 1. 9-11.

25. "As we reckon four seasons in the solar year, so likewise four mystical seasons are distinguished in the liturgical year. The first mystical season, or Ad-

The story however was enacted daily, not only in the tremendous symbolism of the Mass,[26] but also in the seven canonical hours[27] which follow the shorter of the cycles of the sun.
The life of Christ is again suggested in this cycle with its follow-

vent, corresponds to winter. . . . The sun sheds his light and heat sparingly
and does not succeed in completely dispersing the gloom and darkness. Similarly, Advent is for souls the season of cold . . . and of waiting, . . . the
time of the spiritual labor of prayer, of penance, and of trial. . . . In nature,
spring marks the return of life, after the apparent death of winter. . . . This
is the image of the second mystical season which embraces Christmas and the
Epiphany, the true springtime of souls in which all seems to be born again to
the life of grace, in which all hastens to grow with Christmas, and to blossom
with the Epiphany. Summer is the time of hard labor. Under the action of an
ardent sun the great heat accelerates the maturing of the crops and prepares an
abundant harvest. Such is the third mystical season which includes the Septua-
gesima weeks, the austerity of Lent, the joys of Easter. It corresponds with the
most laborious time in the life of our divine Saviour. . . . In the natural order
autumn is the time of harvest. So is the fourth mystical season which includes
the whole time after Pentecost. The seed which was sown in Advent, germinated
and blossomed at Christmas and the Epiphany, and ripened during Lent and
Paschal time, is now fit to be harvested by the care of the Holy Ghost, and the
Church, the great reaper of souls." Leduc and Baudot, *Liturgy of the Roman
Missal,* pp. 42-43.

26. For a much fuller, though rather unsympathetic, treatment of this vast
subject, cf. Y. Hirn, *The Sacred Shrine.* There is an excellent bibliography.

27. Prime, Lauds, Terce, Sext, Nones, Vespers, and Compline. These monastic
offices were kept in the minds of the people by the monastery bells, often their
only timepiece. (Cf. Dante's reference in *Convivio,* 3, 6.)

Tertullian recommended the addition to daily morning and evening prayers,
of remembrance of the coming of the Holy Spirit at the third hour, of Peter's
vision at the sixth, of Peter and John in the temple at the ninth, and of the
Trinity at least at three other hours. Later assignments of the Hours varied:

York Hours (from *Lay Folks' Mass Book*)	Franciscan Office of the Passion*
Matins—Betrayal	Lauds—Scourging
Prime—Mockery	Prime—Before Pilate
Terce—Scourging	Terce—Way of the Cross
Sext—Crucifixion	Sext—Crucifixion
Nones—Death	Nones—Death
Evensong	Vespers—Descent from the Cross, body received in arms of Virgin
Compline—Burial	Compline—Placing in the tomb

The following lines written in the fourteenth century give a summary in brief:

Hora prima ductus est Jesus ad Pilatum.
"Crucifice!" clamitant hora tertiarum.
Jesu hora sexta est cruci conclavatus.
Hora nona dominus Jesus expiravit.
De cruce deponitur hora vespertina.
Hora compleotii datur sepulturae.

To be found in Remy de Gourmont, *Le Latin mystique,* p. 287.

* Given by E. Gilson, "Saint Bonaventure et l'iconographie de la passion," in
Revue l'histoire franciscaine, directeur Henri Lemaitre, t. 1, 1924, pp. 405-431.

ing of the sun as man rises each morning from the death of
sleep to the life of the new day. In nearly every one of the breviary hymns for Lauds there is some reference to the advent of
the Sun of Righteousness to revivify souls:

Splendor paternae gloriae   Laetus dies hic transeat
De luce lucem proferens,   Pudor sit ut diluculum;
Lux lucis, et fons luminis,   Fides velut meridies;
Diem dies illuminans: Crepusculum mens nesciat.

Verusque sol illabere,   Aurora lucem provehit,
Micans nitore perpeti: Cum luce nobis prodeat
Jubarque sancti Spiritus   In Patre totus Filius,
Infunde nostris sensibus.   Et totus in Verbo Pater.[28]

Day by day the Divine Sun, like the physical sun, rises and goes
his journey of life-giving, light-giving, and heat-giving, for the
sake of men, killing the noxious monsters of evil and making
the heart glad. Night by night he journeys beneath the earth
"to give light to those that sit in darkness and the shadow of
death" and to bring to them the hope of a future resurrection.
In this scheme it is clear why Mass, in which Christ the Divine
Sun comes to shed anew within the church the glory of his presence, could be said only between dawn and noon.[29] In the heat

28. Verses 1, 2, 7, 8 from the hymn for Lauds on Mondays. Author, St. Ambrose. "O Splendor of the Father's glory, bringing forth Light from Light, O
Light of Light, and Source of Light, Day illuminating Day. O Thou, true Sun,
descend, shining with everlasting brightness, and infuse into our hearts the radiance of the Holy Spirit. . . . Joyfully may this day pass by; may our modesty
be as the dawn, our faith as the noonday sun, and may our souls know no twilight. The aurora leads on the light; with the light may there appear to us the
whole Son in the Father, and the whole Father in the Word." M. Britt, *Hymns
of Breviary and Missal*, pp. 55-58.
29. With the exception of certain mystical occasions in which there is especial
reason for signifying the presence of the Divine Sun at midnight, for example,
the Midnight Mass of Christmas. For the spirit which seems to underlie the
diurnal worship of the sun, and especially the thought of the sun at midnight,
Mr. Kipling's "A Song to Mithras" in *Puck of Pook's Hill* (Doubleday, Page
& Co., 1906) is suggestive:

"Mithras, *God of the Morning*, our trumpets waken the wall!

.   .   .   .

.   .   .   .

Mithras, also a soldier, give us strength for the day!

"Mithras, *God of the Noontide*, the heather swims in the heat,

.   .   .   .

of the noonday (Terce to Sexts) is remembered especially the crucifixion[30a] and at Nones the actual death upon the cross. Prudentius gives it:

> Sol refugit et lugubri sordidus ferrugine
> Igneum reliquit axem seque maerens abdidit:
> Fertur horruisse mundus noctis aeternae chaos.[30b]

In the hymns and prayers of Vespers with memory of the deposition is reflected the setting of the sun:

> Jam sol recedit igneus:
> Tu lux perennis Unitas,
> Nostris, beata Trinitas,
> Infunde lumen cordibus.[31]

These offices also have their symbolism on the moral level as was indicated in the last two verses of the hymn quoted for Lauds. At Compline is said the prayer suggesting the experience of Dante in the valley of negligent princes, where the compline hymn is sung and receives its symbolic answer.[32]

.   .   .   .

Mithras, also a soldier, keep us true to our vows!

"Mithras, *God of the Sunset,* low on the Western main,
Thou descending immortal, immortal to rise again!
.   .   .   .

Mithras, also a soldier, keep us pure till the dawn!

"Mithras, *God of the Midnight,* here where the great bull lies,
Look on thy children in darkness. Oh take our sacrifice!
.   .   .   .

Mithras, also a soldier, teach us to die aright!"

30a. The use of the Angelus with these emphases seems to date only from the fourteenth century.
It may be remembered that with pagan religions using the symbolism of the cross, the cross is seen in the midday sky.
30b.
> For the Sun in garb of mourning veiled his radiant orb and passed
> From his flaming path in sorrow, hiding till mankind aghast
> Deemed that o'er a world of chaos Night's eternal pall was cast.

Prudentius, *op. cit.,* tr. R. Martin Pope (cf. Bibliography), pp. 104-125.
31. Verse 1 from the hymn for Vespers on Saturdays. Author, St. Ambrose. "The fiery sun now sinks to rest, O thou light eternal, O Unity and blessed Trinity, infuse thy light into our hearts." Britt, *op. cit.,* pp. 84-85.
32. Cf. pp. 212 ff.

With reference both to the life of Christ[33] and to the story of the solar year, the cycle is enacted in the greatest detail throughout the annual course. The latter, a modern Catholic writer has explained completely in the mood of the medieval conception:

The connection with the solar year consists in the harmony existing between the succession of the days, weeks, and months of the solar year and the course of events by which it has pleased God to ransom mankind, ruined by sin. Equal in length, enclosed within the same circle, illuminated, the one by the material sun, the other by the divine Sun of Justice, these two years afford man the means of attaining the end for which he was created, the solar year by the development of his material life, the liturgical year by that of his spiritual life. The first governs the natural, the second the supernatural world.[34]

Advent is the period of waiting for Christmas: "O Oriens, splendor lucis aeternae, et sol justitiae: veni, et illumina sedentes in tenebris et umbra mortis."[35]

Vox clara ecce intonat   Obscura quaeque personans;
Procul fugentur somnia   Ab alto Jesus promicat.[36]

33. Cf. the rhyme to assist children in remembering the church seasons:

"Advent tells us Christ is near;   Christmas tells us Christ is here!
In Epiphany we trace   All the glory of his grace.
Those three Sundays before Lent   Will prepare us to repent,
That in Lent we may begin   Earnestly to mourn for sin.
Holy Week, and Easter, then   Tell Who died and rose again:
O that happy Easter day!   'Christ is risen indeed,' we say.
Yes, and Christ ascended too,   To prepare a place for you,
So we give him special praise,   After those great Forty Days.
Then he sent the Holy Ghost,   On the day of Pentecost,
With us ever to abide,   Well may we keep Whitsuntide!
Last of all, we humbly sing   Glory to our Lord and King,
Glory to the One in Three,   On the Feast of Trinity."
                    (Episcopal Hymnal, 348)

Furthermore, in the Catholic system, "three parts of the liturgical year correspond with three great epochs which mark the history of mankind . . ., 1st, Advent, or the four thousand years which prepared the way for the coming of the Messias; 2d, Christmas and the Epiphany, Lent and Easter, or the time of the Incarnation and the Redemption, which were accomplished during the thirty-three years of our divine Lord's life on earth; 3d, Pentecost, or the course of centuries which began at the moment of the descent of the Holy Ghost upon the apostles and which will end at the last day." Leduc and Baudot, op. cit., pp. 41-42.
    34. Leduc and Baudot, op. cit., p. 42.
    35. The seven Great Antiphons are said, one each day, at Vespers, from December 17 to December 23, inclusive. "O Oriens" is the fifth. "O Orient, Splendor of the Eternal Light, and Sun of Justice, come and enlighten them that sit in darkness and in the shadow of death." Britt, op. cit., p. 93.
    36. Verse 1, hymn for Lauds during Advent. For liturgical use, the first line

The date of Christmas, as is well known, was fixed by the turning of the sun to return northward, after he has touched the tropic of Capricorn.[37] Christmas is consciously associated with solar imagery in the hymn for Vespers and Matins of Christmas Day:

Jesus, Redemptor omnium	Tu lumen, et splendor Patris,
Quem lucis ante originem	Tu spes perennis omnium,
Parem paternae gloriae	Intende quas fundunt preces
Pater supremus edidit.	Tui per orbem servuli.[38a]

is altered to "En clara vox redarguit." Date, fifth century. "Lo, a clear voice exhorts, penetrating everything darksome. Let dreams be banished afar, Jesus shines forth from heaven." *Ibid.,* p. 99.

37. In regard to Christmas it has been pointed out that "the necessity for such a festival arises from the fact that in both north and south Europe existed from prehistoric times the great old feasts of the winter solstice. In Scandinavia, the great feast of Yule, with all its various ceremonies, had celebrated the birth of the winter sun-god. In the Latin countries there had reigned *Saturnalia,* a cult of the god Saturn. The date December 25th coincided also with the birth of Attis, a Phrygian cult of the sun-god, introduced into Rome under the Empire. The popular feasts attached to the births of other sun-gods such as Mithras, were also invariably celebrated at the time of the winter solstice. So that a general consensus of popular feeling contributed to place the birth of our Lord, not distinctively associated in the gospels with any particular time of year, in midwinter, and by the middle of the fourth century, when the Emperor Julian went to church in state to celebrate the birth of Christ, the festival as we know it became established. . . ." The date was formally determined by the church, and a festival in honor of the Nativity decreed in the fourth century.

The traditional accessories of Christmas gaiety have roots likewise in ancient sun worship: "The Christmas tree, originating in the world ash of Scandinavia (erroneously termed Ygdrasil), is closely connected with Christmas flowering trees of all kinds—the Glastonbury Thorn being one example. . . . It recapitulates the idea of tree-worship, and the universe-tree—lights, flowers, and gilded nuts and balls symbolizing the sun, while red and golden apples are a survival of the myth of Iduna, the Goddess of Youth and Health, with her world apples keeping the gods ever young and immortal."

Like the name Easter, the name Yule has a pagan (Teutonic) origin. "In Scandinavia, England, and North Germany, there was a festival—Yule—towards the close of December in honor of Freyr, the God of Golden Sunshine. . . . Freyr represented light, love, peace, goodwill, and fertility—his shining sword was brandished against the frost-giants. His sacred animal was Gullinbursti, the goldenbristled boar, symbolical of the sun-rays or the furrows of the golden grain, ploughed by his tusks. Mounted on Gullinbursti, fabled to be swifter than a horse, the sun-god made his daily course east and west." Ethel L. Urlin, *Festivals, Holy Days and Saints' Days.*

38a. Verses 1-2, hymn for Vespers and Matins on Christmas Day. Date, sixth century. "Jesus, the Redeemer of all, who, being the equal of the Father's glory, was begotten of the sovereign Father before the beginning of light. Thou light and splendor of the Father, Thou never failing hope of all, give ear to the prayers which Thy servants throughout the world pour forth." Britt, *op. cit.,* pp. 100-102.

Again, more definitely:

Quid est, quod artum circulum	Caelum nitescat laetius
Sol iam recurrens deserit?	Gratetur et gaudens humus,
Christusne terris nascitur,	Scandit gradatim denuo
Qui lucis auget tramitem? . . .	Iubar priores lineas.[38b]

The sun comes as savior to a race lost in sluggishness, darkness, and cold; captive as, in the old stories, was the sun maiden, symbol of all the fertility and happiness of the earth. The Epiphany, likewise, is marked by appropriate symbolism:

Ibant Magi, quam viderant	Lumen requirunt lumine:
Stellam sequentes praeviam:	Deum fatentur munere.[39]

The rescue of earth from captivity to gladness, however, as always in the sun story, is no slight labor for the God. Through temptations, sorrows, and difficulties he must pass, while the earth languishes;[40] hence, during Lent, gloom increases even in the adornments of the church, until on Good Friday all is blackness.[41] Moreover, no bells of joy are rung during the period, and Alleluia is never sung. As the date of Christmas was fixed by the winter solstice, so that of Easter is fixed by the full moon of the vernal equinox.[42] Its meaning and obvious connection

---

38b. From Prudentius, *Liber metricus Cathemerinon*. Tr. R. Martin Pope, pp. 124-125.

Why doth the Sun re-orient take	Now let the sky more brightly beam,
A wider range, his limits break?	The earth take up the joyous theme:
Lo! Christ is born, and o'er earth's night	The orb a broadening pathway gains
Shineth from more to more the light! . . .	And with its erstwhile splendour reigns.

John Mason Neale, in his volume of translations of medieval hymns and sequences, compares with the first verse of the above, the statement of Peter Chrysologus, "The days begin to lengthen, because Christ, the True Day, hath arisen"; and the sequence of Notker, "This the present shining day testifies; increased in its length, because the True Sun, born on earth, hath with the ray of its light dispersed the darkness."

39. Verse 2, hymn for Vespers on Feast of the Epiphany (January 6). Author, Sedulius. "The Magi proceeded, following the star, which they saw leading the way; by the aid of light, they seek the Light, by their gifts they acknowledge him to be God." *Ibid.*, pp. 113-114.

40. Much of this is due to the length of winter in northern zones.

41. Verse 1 from the hymn for Lauds during Lent, altered from sixth-century hymn "Jam Christe sol justitiae" is "O Sol salutis, intimis, Jesus refulge mentibus, Dum nocte pulsa gratior Orbi dies renascitur." *Ibid.*, pp. 121-122.

42. That is, Easter is the first Sunday to occur after the full moon which happens next after the vernal equinox. It has been pointed out that this expresses

with the regiving of life to vegetation, and with the older tales of the dying and risen god[43] mourned and hailed under the light of the vernal equinoctial moon, is now generally familiar:

> Vexilla Regis prodeunt:
> Fulget Crucis mysterium,
> Qua vita mortem pertulit,
> Et morte vitam protulit.[44]

> Paschale mundo gaudium,
> Sol nuntiat formosior,
> Cum luce fulgentem nova
> Jesum vident Apostoli.

> In carne Christi vulnera
> Micare tamquam sidera
> Mirantur, et quidquid vident
> Testa fideles praedicant.[45]

A complete separate treatment is needed in regard to the reflection in liturgy of the development of doctrine. Sufficient here is mention of the echo in the hymns down through the centuries of the emphases already noted in regard to trinitarian doctrine;[46] or, on the other hand, of such a ceremony as the Elevation, adopted to combat the heresy of Berengarius.

Probably the most venerable of all ceremonies, comparable for age only to the ablaut in language, is the blessing of the

the redemption from winter by the *united* Sun and Moon, that is, by the masculine life-giving force of the Sun responded to by the feminine life-receiving and nourishing force of vegetation. The spiritual application emphasizing the need of the soul's response to God's grace, is plain.

43. Cf. also the resurrection hymn of Venantius Fortunatus, quoted in translation in "Ante-Nicene Library," vol. 22, pp. 223-227: ". . . The gloomy chains of the infernal law yielded, and chaos feared to be pressed by the presence of the Light. Darkness perishes, put to flight by the brightness of Christ, the thick pall of eternal night falls on earth. . . . Give back thy face that the world may see the light; give back the day which flees from us at thy death!" Cf. the underworld journey of rescue undertaken by the solar god, referred to on pp. 109-110.

44. Verse 1 of Vespers hymn, from Passion Sunday (two weeks before Easter) to Wednesday in Holy Week. Author, Venantius Fortunatus. "The banners of the King come forth; brightly gleams the mystery of the Cross, on which Life suffered death, and by his death, obtained for us life." Britt, *op. cit.*, pp. 123-124. Cf. also pp. 198, 309 for Dante's use of a parody of this hymn.

45. From hymn for Lauds on feasts of Apostles in Eastertide. Ambrosian. "A more beauteous sun proclaims to the world the joys of Easter, when the Apostles beheld Jesus resplendent with a new light. They wonder to see the wounds in the flesh of Christ shine like stars, and what they see, as faithful witnesses, they proclaim." *Ibid.*, pp. 154-155. Cf.:

> " 'Tis the Spring of souls today;   Christ hath burst his prison;
> And from three days' sleep in death   As a Sun hath risen;
> All the winter of our sins,   Long and dark, is flying
> From his Light, to whom we give   Laud and praise undying."
>   St. John Damascene, tr. J. M. Neale.

46. Through hymns doctrine was wedded to emotion in the lives of the people.

New Fire preparatory to Easter. From the downward plunge of Light into darkness on Good Friday until the hour of this service, Light lies in the tomb; and during the time, no light or fire remains in the church. More than this no sacraments are celebrated, for the sacraments are the channels of light.[47] The people wait for that spark from flint and tinder that shall kindle first the triple candle to indicate that from the light of Christ proceeds revelation of the Trinity, and then the Paschal Candle and all the lights of the New Year. An epitome of human history is in the joyous greeting of the first flame: *Lumen Christi, Deo gratias!*[48]

Such hymns as the following in which in simple terms the very thesis of the present work is stated were everywhere familiar:

> "En, pater omnipotens, proles cum flamine sacro,
> Simplex et trinus; jam veneratur homo
>   Lux, calor et motus persistunt semper in igne;
>   Invariabiliter tres deitate manent. . . .
>   Ut radius sole procedit, splendor ab igne,
>   Verbum de patre nascitur omnisciens."
>   *Analecta hymnica medii aevi,* vol. 52, no. 30, p. 32.

Furthermore, throughout the centuries, the development of philosophical and emotional emphasis was reflected. Cf. Appendix VI, i.

47. Cf. "bread of angels" as both wisdom and the Eucharist, discussed p. 377. It should be noted that whereas all sacraments must of necessity be symbols, few symbols are sacraments, that is, actual channels of Light. Analogies, through which man may progress in his search for God, are written from eternity in all things. In those however which are true sacraments is an extension of the Incarnation in a special manifestation of God's search for man. (Cf. p. 490 n. 7.) As channel of Light, Mary, the instrument of the Incarnation, thus has a special association with the sacraments. Upon this obvious fact M. Hirn has constructed his whole treatment of the "sacred shrine."

It should be noted that Light, here central in the macrocosm, has its parallel and appropriate symbolism in the life of sex, which, together with all new marriages, is discouraged during the season of Lent, to be renewed in joyfulness with the return of the new Light, after the festivities of Easter are over. Cf. Hugh of St. Victor: *De sacramentis,* 8, 13 and 9, 2. (Migne, *P.L.,* t. 196).

48. The impressiveness of this service as celebrated among the Orthodox, Armenians, Copts, Jacobites, in the rotunda of the Church of the Holy Sepulcher in Jerusalem, receives discussion in an article in the magazine section of the New York *Times,* April 17, 1926:

"It is moving beyond belief . . . the annual miracle of the bringing down of flame from heaven." Followed by a crowd carrying tapers in their hands, the Patriarch and the Armenian bishop pass into the Sepulcher. "The rest happens more quickly than the eye can take it in. A confused impression remains of the thrust of a flaming torch from the hole; of a great roar of exultation drowned by the furious clangor of the bells; of half naked runners dashing away with blazing torches held high over heads; of fire dawning from taper to taper until the entire rotunda glows with a million wavering points of brightness; of the aged patriarch staggering from the Sepulchre holding aloft three blazing bundles of tapers—an unforgettable figure of gleaming white against a background of

Thus, through liturgy was transmitted to minds in the thirteenth century the experience and the culture of past ages. Many, perhaps still barbarian at heart, could see in it only their own primitive practice, and so received it as a superb basis for charms and black magic.[49] At the same time heirs of the tremendous intellectual search for unification and consistency in experience found, in this same liturgy and its vast associated symbolism, an instrument of thought made ever more keen through the use of many generations. In this manner the vast literature centering around the twofold quest, man's search for reality and the reaching out of God for man, found a thread of unification in the daily drama of the Mass and its monumental mirrors in stone which, perhaps more than anything else, prepared the Middle Ages to receive, and Dante himself to write, the *Divina Commedia*.

II. THE SUN IN POPULAR LITERATURE

IN the thirteenth century liturgy itself bore the imprint of new experience. Into its stern fiber of moral discipline and intellectual search was infused a new idealization of the real. Fundamental as was the liturgical heritage in the structure of Dante's poem, it was this new experience which supplied not merely the motivation, but the vibrant life of the *Commedia* and of its century.

The preceding epoch of gloom presented a striking contrast to the temper of the new age. More than once this gloom[50] has been ascribed to ecclesiastical oppression from which man's in-

dark faces and dancing fire." Finally, there are "processions circling the Sepulchre rejoicing in the possession of the redeeming fire."

49. Cf. such tales as those told by Caesarius of Heisterbach, etc.

50. That the tradition of gloom, even in the so-called "Dark Ages," has been seriously overdone, is well maintained by Dr. E. K. Rand in his article, "Medieval gloom and medieval uniformity," in *Speculum,* vol. 1, pp. 253 ff. He points out further that much of the gloom that did exist was an inheritance, not from strictly medieval sources, but from classical sources:

"If young and old in the Middle Ages saw visions and dreamed dreams, if they sometimes looked gloomily on the pleasures of the present, it was partly because they read the work of Cicero, glossed by Macrobius. They might have felt far less dismal had they not been so well read in the great classics of antiquity."

Moreover, the medieval definition of man, was *animal risus capax.* To clinch his point, Dr. Rand translates the joyous spring poem of Sedulius Scottus (ninth century) entitled, *The Battle of the Lily and the Rose.*

domitable soul burst forth at last. Some idea as to what actually happened in those centuries is invaluable to him who would interpret rightly the luxuriant symbolisms of the Middle Ages proper. In his summary of the earlier age, M. Faure has said:

Had Christianity remained as Saint Paul desired it and as the fathers of the Church defined it, it must needs have turned its back upon the plastic interpretations of the ideas which it introduced. But as it wished to live, it obeyed the law which compels us to give to our emotions the form of the things that we see.[51]

No outlook on life is afforded—the soul alone has the right to life, on condition that it never breaks through the continuous circle of stone in which it is held by dogma. Rome has cemented the thought of Saint Paul in the material of the churches.[52]

It was clearly impossible that in this universe which had been closed for ten centuries, the monk sculptor of the Romanesque churches, the theologian armed with a chisel, should discover any more, at first, than a meager type of nature—emaciated, compressed, and suffering, like himself. Long figures, which make a tragic effort to break the mold of the Byzantine, were flattened against the new façades, mechanically expressing an arrested symbolism.[52]

The question as to whether St. Paul and the Church Fathers were iconoclasts, is really one of great moment in medieval symbolism.

To begin with, the people who came under this harsh and repressive rule of the church were barbarians. M. Faure himself would scarcely have expected the migrating ancestors of the Greeks to have continued the Cretan and Mycenean art development they found in progress in their new homeland, instead of beginning with the flattened and emaciated forms which have always marked the initiation of a new racial art. Why, in the case of medieval art, should such forms be ascribed to enforced asceticism? M. Faure speaks, moreover, of arrested symbolism. It is true that the development of symbolism initiated by scholars steeped in the long heritage of Graeco-Roman thought was arrested in the so-called Dark Ages, but it would seem that the mentality of the barbarian were sufficient explanation without recourse to the strictures of the church.

St. Paul's attitude was, however, in a sense iconoclastic. Like

51. E. Faure, *Medieval Art*, p. 262.   52. *Ibid.*, pp. 271-272.

all great prophets he felt keenly a reality beneath and revealed through the world of sense, and he recognized in symbol the most adequate expression of this reality possible to human language built up as it is of concrete elements with a basis in physical experience. Obviously, when a symbol came to be valued purely for itself, thus obscuring the reality it was intended to reveal, it defeated its own purpose. This is the very battleground in medieval symbolism where the conflict is sharpest between Reality and its Negation.[53] Always it has been the task of those who have penetrated more deeply into reality than the rest of mankind, to restore and to develop further the real significance of sense imagery.

Certain psychological laws have been stated by M. Ferrero by which he explains the tendency on the part of the less gifted among men to lose their hold on the reality in favor of the expression. He says of their results:

> Le symbole n'est q'un signe; sa seule fonction est de représenter quelqu'élément psychique, une image, une idée, une émotion; mais si telles sont sa nature et sa fonction considérées en elles mêmes, le symbole finit souvent au contraire par remplacer entièrement la chose qu'il devrait représenter; il absorbe la réalité, et aquiert une importance exagérée, l'importance de la chose représentée.[54]

Again:

> Il est notoire que dans la religion, presque partout et dans tous les temps, l'adoration, qui devrait s'élever jusqu'à Dieu dans le ciel, s'arrête bien plus bas, aux images qui représentent la divinité. Qu'il s'agiase des sculptures grossières des sauvages ou des chefs-d'œuvres de l'art grec, des portraits des saints catholiques ou des étranges statues chinoises, c'est toujours à ces symboles que s'adressent les prières c'est sur eux que s'appuie l'espoir des croyants, sans aucune considération de l'être qu'ils devraient représenter.[55]

53. St. Augustine, than whom no one is more typical of the "Fathers of the Church" and to whom incidentally is to be traced much of later asceticism, was in his teaching merely a good psychologist. Modern educators would scarcely recommend the theater as it flourished in his time, and are completely in accord with his objection to compelling small children to memorize certain passages of unexpurgated versions of the classics. Augustine, nevertheless, though insisting like all true mystics on the proper discipline of the senses, used all types of sense imagery to express reality. Cf. p. 353. His task was like that of St. Paul.

54. Ferrero, *Les Lois psychologiques du symbolisme,* p. 93.

55. *Ibid.,* p. 111. This tendency M. Ferrero finds to exist in social as well as in religious ceremonial: "Le cérémonial n'est donc pas seulement un sys-

But of the struggle of leaders against this tendency there are innumerable examples, all showing an urgent insistence that the insight symbol shall not degenerate into mere comparison, still less into a meaningless form. Augustine, commenting on certain anthropomorphic conceptions of the Deity, says:

> If, then, he that formed the eye be the Word, seeing all things are by the Word, and he that planted the ear be the Word, seeing all things are by the Word, we cannot say, The Word doth not hear, the Word doth not see, lest the psalm chide us and say, Ye fools, at length be wise. Consequently, if the Word does hear, and the Word does see, are we however to look even in him to find, diversely placed, eyes and ears? Doth he by some one part hear, by some other part see, and hath ear not the ability which the eye hath, and the eye not the ability which the ear hath? Or, is he all sight, and all hearing? . . . yes; always understood, however, that the act of seeing in him, and the act of hearing in him, exists in far other sort than in us. To see, and to hear, exists together in the Word; nor is it in him one thing to see, another to hear; but hearing is sight, and sight hearing.[56]

Obviously, there is danger in symbols worshiped for themselves or exaggerating sensuous elements. Imagery is invaluable, but only when it serves to render the inner reality less vaguely incomprehensible, and to keep it central and supreme. So taught the leaders, yet although tradition of insight symbolism grew constantly in power among the intellectual, its laws could never quite regulate the luxuriant complexity of the symbolisms of the people. Examples of the misuse of symbolism are multitudinous, as well in the often pedantic and artificial literature as in the visions and trances so heartily mistrusted by mystics of real vision. The decline was inevitable.

The centuries so often described as the age of gloom and church oppression comprehended in reality an age in which a race new to civilization was creating a culture of its own on the basis of such fragments of the glorious cultural heritage of the Roman Empire as those devoted to the religious life could save, at no small pain, from fire and sword. What more natural than

tème de signes ou de symboles auxquels nous attribuons une certaine signification, sans savoir le pourquoi; nous leur donnons aussi une importance plus grande encore qu'aux sentiments qu'ils devraient représenter, car nous confondons presqu'entièrement ces sentiments et leurs symboles." P. 123.

56. Augustine, *Homilies on the Gospel according to Saint John,* 5. 19, p. 283. Cf. p. 354 n. 69.

that the brightness of the sun should have gathered round the
cross, and glorified the life of the blest?

There shall sinful men, sad at heart, behold the greatest affliction.
Not for their behoof shall the cross of our Lord, brightest of beacons,
stand before all nations, wet with the pure blood of heaven's King,
stained with his gore, shining brightly over the vast creation. Shadows
shall be put to flight when the resplendent cross shall blaze upon all
peoples, But this shall be for an affliction and a punishment to men, to
those malefactors who knew no gratitude to God. . . . For all this will
he righteously exact recompense when the red rood shall shine brightly
over all in the sun's stead.[57]

There is song of angels, joy of the blest; there is the dear presence
of the Lord, brighter than the sun unto the blessed; there is the love of
dear ones; life without death . . .[58]

Was it not inevitable also that the thought of the Lord of Light
as a means of escape from the trials of the world not only
should have become dominant among those who retired to the
religious life, but should have penetrated even into the folklore
of the common people?

In much of the earlier religious literature exhortations to a
consecration of life to God's service, which then meant retire-
ment to convent or monastery, are based not on considerations
of a positive nature, but on such facts as the uncertainty and
transitoriness of human love, the manifold chances of misery in
life, the ease with which riches may be stolen, and so forth. In
A Love Rune[59] eleven out of twenty-six stanzas are occupied
with such motives. The next six contain descriptions of the joy
of heaven. The eighteenth reads:

> And never man his face shall see,
> E'en as he is, enthroned with Might,
> But all with bliss fulfilled shall be,
> Beholding him, our Lord, with sight.
> To look on him is joy and glee,
> For he is Day, that knows not Night.
> Methinks, sweet Maid, right blest is she
> That hath her home with such a Knight!

---

57. Cook and Tinker, *Select Translations from Old English Poetry,* p. 89,
Selections from the *Christ,* 7.
58. *Ibid.,* p. 91, Selections from the *Christ,* 9.
59. Cf. Jessie L. Weston, *Chief Middle English Poets.*

The remainder of the poem exhorts the Maid to dedicate her life to this "Knight."[60]

A typical medieval bestiary[61] contains an elaborate account of the manner in which the *Eagle,* grown old, renews his youth by flying upward toward the sun. The sun though renewing his sight scorches him so that he falls down into a well over which he has chosen to fly, and ultimately he escapes with youth restored. The *Significatio* of course interprets the eagle as a human soul, old in sin, its spiritual sight dimmed; the sun is God, and the well is Baptism. The soul

> Doth on Jesus Christ believe,
> Priestly lore doth learn,
> So the mist his eyes shall leave
>
> .   .   .   .
>
> All his hope to God doth run,
> Learns his love so true,
> This I trow shall be the Sun,
> Gives him light anew!
> Naked, falls he to the font,
> There renewed is he. . . .

It was at this time that such customs as that of burying the dead facing eastward (that is, toward the quarter in which Christ, as a rising Sun, was expected to appear on the Day of Judgment) assumed to the great majority far more importance than any great philosophical tradition of the church. Of matters of doctrine the Day of Judgment engaged attention:

> Then suddenly upon Mount Zion a blaze of the sun, shining clear from the southeast, shall come forth from the Creator, gleaming more brightly than the mind of man can conceive, when the Son of God shall appear hither through the vault of heaven. All glorious from the eastern skies shall come the presence of Christ, the aspect of the noble King, gentle in spirit toward his own, bitter toward the wicked, wondrously varied, diverse to the blessed and the forlorn.[62]

What wonder, indeed, that the story of the Phoenix,[63] based on

---

60. This Middle English poem is entirely in the spirit of the tenth-century Anglo-Saxon *Hali Meidenhed.* A comparison with the poem entitled "Sweetness of Jesus" is suggestive. Weston, *op. cit.,* pp. 343, 353.
61. Middle English version of the *Physiologus* of Theobaldus, translated by Miss Weston, *op. cit.*
62. Cook and Tinker, *op. cit.,* p. 86. Selections from the *Christ,* 6.
63. Described also by Ovid and Pliny, and in Dante's time by Brunetto Latini.

the poem of Lactantius, had become familiar in the hands of some Cynewulfian poet, as symbolizing the journey of the soul to "that blessedness where, fair above the hosts in the City of glory, shines the Sun"—not of wisdom, but—"of righteousness."[64] The light of the Sun is here no longer desired chiefly to illumine the mind, but to penetrate the cloud of sin.

Lo! Thou splendor of the dayspring, fairest of angels sent to men upon earth, Thou Radiance of the Sun of Righteousness, bright beyond the stars, Thou of thy very self dost illumine all the tides of time! . . . Thine own handiwork in its present need imploreth Thee with confidence that Thou send us the bright sun, and come in Thy very person to enlighten those who have long been covered with murky cloud, and sitting here in darkness and eternal night, shrouded in sins, have been forced to endure the shadow of death.[65]

At the same time, it is to be remembered, the church was reflecting this development in her hymns.

This period had been a stage of progress in cultural development, rather than a time of oppression and constriction. From the point of view of the medieval tradition, it is best compared to the discipline of the *via purgativa,* that first strand which must be woven into the life of the mystic. Indeed, the period eventuated in a typically mystic discovery. To this discovery the church, far from inhibiting, had contributed no small share alike through its constant stimulation of symbolic thinking and through its courageous endeavor to teach those lacking not only mystic but cultural discipline, to distinguish between symbol and reality.

At the time in which Dante wrote there had developed welldefined mystic movements in Italy, Germany, the Low Countries, and England. The Spanish and French schools became important only at the close of the Middle Ages, when the tradition was becoming isolated and less and less an integral part of contemporary thought. Yet they, even more than the schools first mentioned, have served to preserve the mystic spirit beneath the varying degrees of modern indifference.

The troubadour of divine love *par excellence* is, of course, St. Francis of Assisi. His biographer says: "Of the ardent love

64. Cook and Tinker, *op. cit.,* p. 160.
65. *Ibid.,* p. 80. Selections from the *Christ.* 6.

that glowed in Francis, the friend of the Bridegroom, who can avail to tell? He seemed utterly consumed, like unto a coal that is set on fire, by the flame of the love divine. For, at the mere mention of the love of the Lord, he was aroused, moved, and enkindled, as though the inner chords of his heart vibrated under the bow of the voice from without."[66] Naturally, he could not escape the sun symbol. He says himself in what is perhaps the most characteristic of his utterances, the *Canticle of the Creatures,* called by him the Canticle of Brother Sun:

Praised be my Lord God with all his creatures, and especially our brother the sun, who brings us the day, and brings us the light; fair is he, and shining with a very great splendor; O Lord, he signifies to us Thee![67]

The compiler of the *Mirror of Perfection* comments: "Above all other creatures wanting reason, he loved the sun and fire with most affection."[68] Indeed, Francis himself has been symbolized by the sun, and he is so termed, as will be remembered, by Thomas Aquinas in canto xi of the *Paradiso.*[69] "The comparison of Francis to the rising Sun is ancient and widespread. 'Glowing as the light-bearer and as the morning star, yea, even as the rising Sun, illuminating, cleansing, and fertilizing the world like some new luminary, was Francis seen to arise,' says the Prologue of one of the earliest lives."[70]

Another paean characteristic of the new age rises from the early English school in the famous "Luf es lyf that lastes ay" of Richard Rolle of Hampole. In the midst of this great love enthusiasm it was to be expected that attention should be called to

66. *Life of St. Francis,* edited with the *Little Flowers* in the Everyman ed. Chap. ix.
67. *Mirror of Perfection,* chap. cxix (in the Everyman ed. with the *Little Flowers*).
68. *Ibid.*
69.   "Di questa costa, là dov'ella frange
              più sua rattezza, nacque al mondo un sole . . .
          Però chi d'esso loco fa parole,
              non dica Ascesi, chè direbbe corto,
              ma Oriente, se proprio dir vuole.
          Non era ancor molto lontan da l'orto,
              ch'el cominciò a far sentir la terra
              de la sua gran virtute alcun conforto."
                                          Par., xi, 49-57.
70. Note to *Par.,* xi, 49 ff. in "Temple Classic" ed. of the *Paradiso.*

the physical reactions accompanying emotions. In his *Incendium Amoris* Rolle tells of his puzzle over the question:

> More have I marvelled than I showed when, forsooth, I first felt my heart wax warm, truly, and not in imagination, but as if it were burned with sensible fire . . . ofttimes, because of my ignorance of such healthful abundance, I have groped my breast seeking whether this burning were from any bodily cause outwardly. But when I knew that it was only kindled inwardly from a ghostly cause, and that this burning was nought of fleshly love or concupiscence, in this I conceived it was the gift of my Maker.[71]

Comparison of such passages with the attitude of St. Augustine shows clearly what has happened. Augustine searched through scripture and nature for knowledge of God, and, for all the importance he gave to inner experience, when he came to his own nature his attitude was that of the theoretical psychologist; his interest centered in those faculties which are bound up with reason, such as memory and imagination. Rolle, on the other hand, in his search for God looks first to his own nature, and especially to the reaction of his emotions.

The shift in the very aim of spiritual life is pointed out in a modern comment on the three properties of God—Life, Love, Light, as mentioned by Julian of Norwich.

> Here the thought seems to be centered in Light as the manifestation of Being . . . the Triune Divine Light which in man is corresponding Reason, Faith, Charity; Charity keeping man, while here, in Faith and Hope; Charity leading him from and through and into the Eternal Divine Love.[72]

Still the sun is the guide, as was seen throughout the *Divina Commedia,* but guide to a heaven of love. The earlier mentions of the love of God had been as an escape from life[73] but now men are saying that "all the life of a good Christian man is nought else but holy desire."[74] Suso and Tauler are among the many examples in Germany of this so-called "erotic mysticism."

71. From the first paragraph of Rolle's preface to the *Incendium Amoris,* as translated by Richard Misyn.

72. *Revelations of Divine Love,* by Julian, anchoress at Norwich, ed. by Grace Warrack. Note to the beginning of chap. lxxxiii.

73. Cf. pp. 151, 420.   74. *The Cloud of Unknowing,* p. 415.

The love emphasis[75] involved, moreover, not only the raptures of man, but the "inexorable following love of God, impossible to escape. . . . 'Earth,' said Meister Eckhart, 'cannot escape the sky; let it flee up or down, the sky flows into it, and makes it fruitful whether it will or no. So God does to man. He who will escape Him only runs to His bosom; for all corners are open to Him.' "[76] Thus keenly were men beginning to feel the power and attraction of the underlying Reality.

The love element as the great addition to sun symbolism in the Middle Ages proper, is outstanding in all forms of literary expression. In the search for beauty and joy even the trials of life were disguised or swallowed up in the greater whole of chivalric and love ideals expressed largely through the romances. No service was too arduous to be undertaken for a lady's favor. Here again, as with liturgy, some turned the external expression to the ends of Circe, whereas for others it was true insight symbol. Symbolism in the love motif appeared in the Middle Ages in all phases of transmutation.

It is a striking fact that all of medieval literature, from *fabliaux* and ballads to homilies and debates, could well be classified with reference to the function and levels of the symbolism. In such poems as the *Confessio Amantis* and the *Roman de la Rose* there is no more than comparison and arbitrary association symbol. Yet such symbolism as Dante used is frequent. For example, the symbolic value of certain solar elements in a Middle

75. Perhaps the culmination of mysticism from the twelfth to the fifteenth century is in Jan van Ruysbroeck, mentioned already for his inclusion of the highest of mystic symbolisms, that of marriage, with the final and most complete development of the sun symbol of the Trinity.

Such passages as these are worthy of attention:

"There the single eye is penetrated and illuminated by the eternal light, as the air is penetrated and illuminated by the sun."

"The naked intelligence is penetrated and illumined by Divine Light, and the single eye draws from its contact with this radiance power to contemplate eternal verity."

"This is why the Christ-Sun, from the summit of his ascent, seated at the right hand of the Father, sheds countless rays of light and glory into the depths of the penitent."

"This action of God glorifies, and there are those in whom it has operated who become men of light."

"We are one with the Father and Son in the unity of the Holy Ghost, the eternal fire."

    Flowers of a Mystic Garden, pp. 105, 77, 64, 16, 22, 87.
76. Translation from Underhill, *Mysticism,* p. 162.

English allegorical description of Life has been pointed out as follows:

> Life is a beautiful woman, a medieval queen. Her description in its various details resembles closely that of other women in the literature of the Middle Ages—Dame Nature, Lady Anima, Idleness, Helen, the Virgin Mary of the religious lyrics, and Venus and Flora of the Court of Love debates and Dunbar. Her countenance "brighter than the bright sun," "her rudd redder than the rose," her lighthearted joyousness and mirth, her relation to nature, are appropriate to her character as Queen of Life. The effect of her approach upon the flowers and branches . . . is especially symbolic.[77]

Furthermore, poems written primarily to tell a story or to set forth the manners of the Age of Chivalry frequently were given subsequent allegorization. The great poems of Ariosto and Tasso are among these, and Tasso, indeed, has left an allegorized interpretation of his *Gerusalemme liberata* devised by himself.

As would be expected, there is a less noble side. Nowhere is this shown better than in the so-called Goliardic verse. Symonds says: "The literature of the Wandering Students . . . owes nothing to chivalry, and emanates from a class which formed a subordinate part of the ecclesiastical militia. It is almost vulgar in its presentment of common human impulses; it bears the mark of the proletariat, though adorned with flourishes betokening the neighborhood of Church and University."[78] As is natural, this sensuous poetry connects the sun with love through

---

77. E. Scamman, *The Alliterative Poem, Death and Life,* p. 111. Cf. also the tale of three monks who saw a branch coming downstream with leaves of gold, silver, blue, and green, and fruit of wondrous sweetness. The monks set out to find the garden from which the branch came, but forgot to notify the abbot of their going. They went through beautiful woods, on the grass they found delicious manna, later they scaled a mountain one hundred miles high, then they reached the gate of Eden guarded by an angel with a flaming sword whose face was like unto the light of the sun. They sat looking at him for five days and nights and then he let them in. While hearing the sound of sweetness, softness, and delight—-the wheels of heaven revolving—two venerable patriarchs, Enoch and Elijah, came to guide them. On their journey they saw the Fountain of Youth, Tree of Knowledge, Tree of Life (from which the wood for the cross was taken), etc. When the elders asked them to leave they exclaimed, "We haven't been here a week"; the elders replied, "You have lived here seven hundred years." Returning to the monastery they proved their identity by an old missal.

78. J. A. Symonds, *Wine, Women, and Song,* p. 5.

the passionate excitements of spring, and much of it is unquotable.

On the other hand, the "religion of beauty in women" had its symbolism, identical in kind with that associated with the Divinity.

> Lady, since I conceived
> Thy pleasurable aspect in my heart,
> My life has been apart
> In shining brightness and the place of truth;
> Which till that time, good sooth,
> Groped among shadows in a darkened place
> Where many hours and days
> It hardly ever had remembered good.[79]

And:

> Love, taking leave, my heart then leaveth me,
> And is enamour'd even while it would shun,
> For I have looked so long upon the sun
> That the sun's glory is now in all I see.[80]

Again:

> Who is she coming, whom all gaze upon,
> Who makes the air all tremulous with light,
> And at whose side is Love himself?[81]

The language of courtly love is evident. But writers of the *albe* and the associated poetry of *l'amour courteois*[82] gave utterance now and then to the higher ideal of divine love,[82] if not always with sincerity, then as the result of an occasional scruple, ill fortune in a love affair, or simply imitation of a tradition. For example, Fra Guittone d'Arezzo writes, in a sonnet to the Blessed Virgin:

> Behold this earthly Love, how his darts glide—
> How sharpened—to what fate—throughout this earth!
> Pitiful Mother, partner of our birth,
> Win these from following where his flight doth guide.
> And, O, inspire in me that holy love
> Which leads the soul back to its origin,
> Till of all other love the link do fail.[83]

79. Panuccio dal Bagno Pisano. Tr. Dante Gabriel Rossetti.
80. Maestro Migliore da Fiorenza. Tr. Dante Gabriel Rossetti.
81. Guido Cavalcanti. Tr. Dante Gabriel Rossetti.
82. For a brief discussion of courtly love and its idealization, cf. Appendix VI, ii.
83. Guittone d'Arezzo. Tr. Dante Gabriel Rossetti. To Guido Guinicelli's canzone "Of the gentle heart," reference has been made previously.

Ramón Lull again refers the symbol to Christ:

> Love shone through the cloud which came between the Lover and the Beloved, and made it as bright and resplendent as is the moon by night, as the day-star at dawn, the sun at midday, the understanding in the will; and through that bright cloud the Lover and the Beloved held converse.[84]

And:

> They asked the Lover in what manner the heart of man was turned toward the Love of his Beloved. He answered them and said: Even as the sunflower turns to the sun. How is it, then, that all men love not thy Beloved? He answered, They that love him not have night in their heart, because of their sin.[85]

Here in other terms is the struggle of Beatrice and Circe, the sun and its opposition. Phineas Fletcher has used similar erotic symbolism with considerable audacity in his long poem *The Purple Island,* while the anonymous author of the *Cursor Mundi* declares his work to be a "religious romance"—openly in competition with tales of earthly love.[82]

At the same time, resolution of this competition was offered in the Court of Love itself, which was such as to admit a constant possibility of mystical interpretations. In a generation which had so glorified virginity that the married were sometimes told the love of God was not for them, there is a special pertinence in even the famous first rule of the Court, "Marriage is no good excuse against loving." The second rule, too, voiced one of the deepest laws of mystic experience, the requirement that, unless revelation were divinely bidden, the soul keep secret its most intimate commerce with God. So one might continue through the whole list of thirty-one. Even such rules as might be questioned with reference to the earthly ideal receive their full appropriateness as applied to the heavenly. The code declares, "Real jealousy always increases the worth of love"; and God, demanding complete and unique allegiance, is verily a jealous God. Furthermore, the mystic gives constant stress to such themes as are expressed in the following: "The true lover thinks naught good but what he believes pleases the co-lover";

---

84. Lull, *The Book of the Lover and the Beloved,* tr. E. A. Peers, no. 118.
85. *Ibid.,* no. 342.

"The true lover is haunted by the co-lover's image unceasingly"; "The lover cannot be satiated by the delights of the co-lover." Though as far as is known the code bound but few, its influence spread rapidly through all the courts of Europe, inspiring to the quest of love. By it expressions of crude love and inert religion were given the possibility of new interpretation. Here, again, it may be recalled that, according to medieval theory "free choice is given to man between his loves, sacred and profane. . . . So choice and following of sacred love is the 'ground of merit' by which man attains beatitude."[86] The basis of judgment is in man's recognition of the underlying reality which gives both meaning and sacredness to every outward expression. Human love, understood in its literal meaning only, may become an implement of the *gravezza* of the *lupa,* but not so if it be insight symbol. Although probably no one else accomplished a transmutation of the earthly into the heavenly Court so complete and full of daring[87] as did Dante in honor of Beatrice, the identification was an ever present potentiality throughout the medley of medieval love-song.

In brief then, symbolism, made glowing with the love motif, permeated the literature of the thirteenth century. The tales of the Middle Ages, pious and profane, were likely to be given symbolic meanings both because of their primitive origins and because of their general popularity. In this, parish priests helped not a little: in such tales was an excellent means of enlivening the sermon, and all that was necessary was to add a moral at the end. Saints' lives and sermons and pseudo-history, as belonging to the lower levels of literature of learning, shared perforce in its symbolic tradition. Of course, love was a favorite theme for debates and lyrics, and these were symbolized more or less as fancy of author or hearer dictated.[88] Since, however, all these

---

86. J. B. Fletcher, *Symbolism of the Divine Comedy,* pp. 146-147.

87. It is of interest that Virgil speaks of spiritual love (*Purg.,* xxii, 10) in the same terms in which Francesca spoke of carnal love (*Inf.,* v, 103). Cf. pp. 35, 168-169, 250, 346-347, 387 ff., Appendix VI, ii.

88. The ballad, because of its terse and direct narrative character, is not considered here; although a little later poems in ballad form were written with definite symbolic intention, and some carols were formed on the ballad model. Cf. for example such a ballad as "The falcon has borne my mate away," in which the speaker is evidently Mary, mourning over the crucifixion of Christ.

were intended for the populace, usually one of the mystical meanings was considered sufficient to stress at a time, and frequently there was degeneration to mere arbitrary and colorless personification.[89] In contradistinction, nevertheless, to the relative newness and triviality of much of this exuberant literature, represented, for example, in only one phase of the long tradition of liturgy, there was in medieval literature a romance cycle as old in experience and as well traveled, if not as highly educated, as liturgy itself.

III. THE SUN OF THE QUEST

THERE has never been a time when men have not engaged in some sort of mystical quest and adventure. Ranking rather with liturgy than with *Commedia* and Cathedral into both of which it penetrated, the Quest romance had its root in all aspects of life. It drew from folklore and epic, from customs of courts, from travel lore of the crusades, oriental infilterings, from theology, philosophy, politics, pageantry, mysticism, and even, as some have suspected, from a secret tradition to which there is no longer access even through the great initiatory societies themselves.

In the Middle Ages the Grail, the Chalice of the Mass,[90] had become central in that heterogeneous wealth of prose and verse now termed the Arthuriad. The unity of this cycle is, however, broken and blurred so that it presents none of the clear outlines of the other three medieval masterpieces.

Arthurian romance taken as a whole is like a great tapestry on which countless forgotten hands have worked. The weave is loose, no thread is held all the time, bulk and detail obscure the pattern. No one person ever saw the entire design, yet it has grown under their labors. One of the extraordinary things in literary history is this emerging of a syn-

---

89. Cf. Appendix IV, Pt. I, iii (2).

90. Much has been made of the probable origin of the Grail in magic cauldron or other vessel of Celtic folklore, and the fact that there are many extant tales and romances in which it appears, not only not as a Christian relic, but not even as a cup. The fact remains, however, that at the height of the tradition there was an inextricable interweaving of associations gathered around the magic vessel, around the Cup of the Last Supper (supposed to have been preserved by Joseph of Arimathea), and around the sacred chalice and the miracle of transubstantiation.

thetic vision, and image of a civilization on quest, from the unrelated and spontaneous activities of many minds through many generations.[91]

Nevertheless, the Morte Darthur, of which Caxton's colophon states that "here is a story chronicled for one of the truest and holiest that is in this world," is in many ways similar to the medieval *Commedia* to which was prefixed, not by the author, the adjective *Divina*.

In Arthuriad as in *Commedia* there are possible interpretations belonging to the levels of allegory, trope, and anagoge, together with centralization of Christ. An ideal in both is political unity: in the one for all the world under Italy; in the other for all of England under the House of Plantagenet.[92] Moreover, in the *Divina Commedia,* which upholds scholastic philosophy with all the clear-cut precision of Thomas Aquinas himself, is evidence of two great trends in the thirteenth century: the wedding of theology to Aristotelianism, and the increase in devotion to the sacramental presence in honor of which was established the festival of Corpus Christi. (The prayers and hymns of this office were written by The Philosopher, who appeared to Dante in the Sun.) Similarly, there is some evidence that it was at least partly under the inspiration of the monks of Glastonbury, interested in the new Eucharistic devotion, that the Grail elements of the Arthuriad assumed their Christian and sacramental form.

Arthuriad and *Commedia* alike, in their development of the quest represent the world under constant metamorphosis in varying response to the sun.[93] Knights wandering through the same forests, visiting the same castles, stopping at the same

91. Quoted from Dr. Scudder, who thus writes after having discussed the transition of early episodic tales to the expansion in the prose romances tending toward the absorption of wider and wider aspects of life, in her *Le Morte Darthur of Sir Thomas Malory and Its Sources,* p. 183.

92. This is not the place to enter into the question whether or no the Norman-English court deliberately fostered these romances; but it is at least interesting that Arthur, historically no more than a Celtic chieftain fighting a guerrilla warfare against Saxon invaders, became the great hero of the Anglo-Saxon-Norman kingdom.

93. There is not only a similarity in theme between the Grail Quest and the other medieval quests, but also, as would be expected, similarity in minor symbolic devices. Arthur, the Grail hero, and various other characters have solar significance. (A possible example: "Arthur's twelve victories are obviously a re-

wayside shrines, met with strangely different adventures; because some were feeding on the light of divine wisdom, the bread of angels, and others on the pasturage of Circe. The strengthening of vision through purgation and illumination is striking in the experience of those adventurers who, having in their quest arrived at the castle of the Grail, all unknowing journey on, only to discover their mistake and wearily journey back at last to find the castle metamorphosed through their purified vision.

Finally, however, the Arthuriad is in a sense unique among medieval masterpieces. Both *Divina Commedia* and liturgy in the setting of the cathedral, end in the triumph of vision and joyous dedication to a noble mission, but the quest of the Grail, perhaps more true to life, certainly more true to Dante's experience, ends in a lapse from an ideal too high for earth. At the last, king and knights of the Round Table confess their inability to build the kingdom of Christ in the land of Logres.

From the point of view of symbolism, also, the Arthuriad stands out among the monuments of the medieval period. In *Commedia,* Mass, and Cathedral, the symbolism is definite. Dante labored meticulously that his every line might help to convey the fourfold message of the scripture. In the Arthurian romances, on the other hand, there are long passages with no symbolism at all other than arbitrary or comparison imagery

production of the twelve labors of Hercules or the Sun; and the statement that the peerless knight never died at all, and that he who had been king should still be king again, proves Arthur to have been" one in symbolic origin with Barbarossa, Sebastian of Portugal, the Tells, Harold the Saxon, and the Moor Boabdil. Smith, *Symbolism of Science,* p. 24.) In Nennius, Arthur carries the cross of Christ on his shoulder, and tradition is recorded that Christianity was introduced into Britain by a king called Lucius, which means "Light-bringer." There is a Grail version in which Percyvale kills the (evil) Red Knight while in wolf's garb. (Cf. p. 202 n. 356.)

Guenevere of necessity had numerous rescuers, because each character of solar significance played the part of the rescuer of the sun's female counterpart. Guenevere's vegetation significance is suggested, among other scenes, in her Maying party before one of her abductions.

In the Middle English *Gawain and the Green Knight,* the fateful meeting between the two heroes (both solar derivatives) occurred at Christmas, the winter solstice. The vacant chair at the Round Table is another device which is significant. It reminds also of Dante's use of the vacant chair in *Par.,* xxx, 133. (Cf. further the vacant chair in heaven in the Syriac *Visio S. Pauli,* in the vision of Tundal, and in Caesarius of Heisterbach's *Dialogus miraculorum.*)

which, purely fanciful, appears amid vague, haunting reminiscences of old symbolisms. Dante made clear and definite in the harmony of the whole even that which he took from pagan sources, but in the Arthuriad layer upon layer of Celtic and Christian folklore are to be found, so veiled in allusion or altered and retouched, as to suggest that in the original stories outlines were intentionally blurred, perhaps to prevent understanding on the part of Christian zealots.[94] The process of tracing origins in these stories calls to mind the toil now demanded to recover on monastery and podestal walls great paintings concealed beneath plaster and the adornments of a later day.

An important and structural origin is probably, however, sacred tales of the Celtic sun-storm god, in his enactment of the resurrection drama of the year—that drama enacted by all sun gods of all races in all countries from all time, which in the Middle Ages had its locus in the cathedral and its form in liturgy. The hero, triune as sun god, storm god, and vegetation god, moves through romance after romance, revealed only by such hints as golden hair, miraculous birth, unquenchable heat of body, the marvelous weapon, or the revolving castle from which he rises at dawn. He is, moreover, bound to go on perilous expeditions, often by night, for the benefit of mankind or to rescue a lady. The names of Grail heroes are frequently traceable, with a high degree of probability, to Celtic hero-names with such significations as "Shining One, Son of the Permanent," "Gray Hero" (storm god), "Fire," "Golden Hair, Lord of Light," and so forth. The hero as the sun, loves flower ladies and moon ladies, ladies who must be rescued from imprisonment. Gawain, Peredur, Lancelot du Lac, Galeschin, and Galahad each rehearse some part of the sun drama. Galahad, indeed, reigns in the spiritual city just one year, the term of the sun god, and then is swallowed up in eternity.[95] Nor is solar imagery lacking in the Grail symbolism itself. The Grail may not appear

94. Stories of pagan deities, when Christianity gains power, must become reinterpreted and fitted into the Christian scheme, either as relating to Christ or to some saint; or they must be transformed to fairies or to devils; or they must be hidden away in some form of secret tradition.

95. Miss Weston states in her *From Ritual to Romance*, p. 154, that "the root origin of the whole bewildering complex of [the Grail legend] is to be found

without the gleam of solar radiance and the redness of the covering (red samite), before it fully manifests itself.[96]

Complete development of the solar Trinity, although strongly suggested, is not, however, to be found in these stories: First, because popular faith lacks the interest of theology in fine distinctions, and, second, because the matter in hand is really an initiation, to be concealed from him who has not achieved the Quest. All the non-initiate may know, is that there is to be achieved an *epiphania,* a manifestation of the radiance of God.

Thus, this complex of romance attracted to itself the most sacred theme of Christian art and story—the Last Supper, in the form of a sacrament administered by Christ himself within the

in the Vegetation Ritual, treated from the esoteric point of view as a Life Cult, *and in that alone."* That is, she allows no Christian origins for the legend. This statement in no wise excludes, but rather presupposes, the whole case for the solar symbolism of the creative forces, both in the primitive origins and in the medieval Christianized forms of the Grail Quest.

It is of some importance to recall the fact that solar theories of the origin of ritual customs are not opposed to "vegetation" origins. Possibly nothing is more puzzling in recent study of comparative religion than the assumption that a vegetation theory could displace a solar one or *vice versa.* Modern city civilization may see no obvious connection between solar and vegetation concepts, but the connection is clear in the experience of primitive agricultural communities. The prominence given to sexual fertility magic in vegetation theories is no argument to the contrary, since the sexual significance of the sun is clear in primitive religion, and may be expressed in brief thus: Both sun and phallus give life; they are the only creative forces known to unsophisticated man. Cf. pp. 113 ff., and Appendix III, Pt. I, iii.

96. The solar symbolism as always, and especially in the lore of the people, contains within it the symbolism of sex. Galahad arrives at the Spiritual City in the Ship of Solomon. To say nothing of the mystic meaning of his companions on that ship, or of the ship's furnishings, the Ship itself is of manifold significance. Obviously it represents the church (cf. use of ship as symbol of church by Augustine, Rabanus Maurus, etc.), primarily the church of the Old Testament, but that church as prefiguring, as symbolizing, the church of the New Testament of which indeed, in the larger sense, it was a part (cf. p. 69 n. 154). But the Ship has had a long history as a symbol. According to Cox, it is a step in the progression of ideas by which the Yoni or female principle of generation was symbolized: the ark of safety in which life was preserved, the Argo, the shell of Aphrodite, the ship of Isis, the mystic lotus of the earth's fecundation, cups and inexhaustible vessels of which the pagan original of the Grail was one.

Hence, not only in the Sun God, represented by character after character in the story—just as in Dante's vision—is there analogy between the Grail quest and the quest of the *Divina Commedia,* but also in the relation between the sacred and unspeakable vision, and the duty which ensues upon it. Even as Dante, having seen the truth of universe, Trinity, and Incarnation, returns as a wheel moved by the Divine Sun who controls all stellar orbits; so Galahad, having refound the Holy Thing and having been communicated from it by Christ himself, goes at once to his year's duty in the orbit of the Sun God, setting sail in the sacred Ship whose symbolic origin was that of the Grail itself.

walls of Corbenic[97, 98]—even as if some instinct in the mind of the people insisted on giving Christ, the Logos, his place in the framework of inherited fragments of ancient solar mythology. Indeed, such syncretism had had precedent back even of the reaches of history when early crosses bore also the wheel of the sun.[99] Who, moreover, was more logically lord of the Castle of the Fisher King than Christ, *Ichthus?*[100]

Although Dante's two direct references to the Arthuriad seem merely illustrative, in the mystic pageant, pageant of the Sun God and of the Mass, Beatrice appears as suddenly and as dramatically accompanied as does the Grail.[101] This vision is in

97. In this device is a symbolism similar to that used by Dante at the summit of the Mount. Here Dante, like Galahad, is a symbol of Christ, yet is given communion by Christ symbolized in another form. Cf. p. 321.

98. Christ's administration of the mystery within Corbenic is not the only hint of this. The writer who Christianized the Galahad quest found in his source the name Galaain (corruption of Balin), and being a pious man, thought it a corruption of Galaad (the Latin form of Galahad). Galaad is the Vulgate form of Gilead, which Gillebert, the Cistercian abbot, in his commentary on the Canticles, interprets as "hill of testimony," which, he says, can be nought else than "Christ, on whom all the testimonies of the prophets" and of his own merits and his disciples' powers, are heaped up. This hill, he continues, is the head of the church.

Thus, though there is no sign in the Grail literature of a definite statement that all is to be interpreted by the fourfold method, yet, as in the New Testament example quoted (cf. p. 259), the three types of interpretation actually are used. (It may be remembered that Caxton in his colophon termed the Grail legend one of the truest and holiest stories in the world.)

The Grail story, in its finally Christianized form, is likewise a moral tale, in which tropes are seen. Finally it deals with the vessel of the Last Supper and its contents not only as they were historically in Jerusalem, not only as they strengthened the moral lives of individuals in the sacrifice of the Mass, but also as they were in Eternity, the final goal of Quest.

99. For the consideration of the influence of the Quest motif in medieval thought, it is possible to lay too much stress on the question of origins. The early connection of the Grail with Celtic solar and fertility cults, demonstrated by Miss Weston, Dr. Loomis, and others, is no indication of awkwardness and unnaturalness in its medieval connection with the *Sol Verus,* as St. Patrick himself termed Christ. The physical feeding function of the Grail, by the laws of symbolism, enriched rather than invalidated its function in transmitting spiritual food. The achievement of the Quest as the reëstablishment of physical fruitfulness was not incompatible with the same achievement as spiritual creativity. It is the law of insight symbolism that the symbol is the natural basis of the truth which in turn gives it its meaning.

100. Fish imagery was characteristic of the primitive church and prominent even in the writings of the first Church Father. Cf. pp. 140-141.

Cf. also Eisler, *Orpheus—the Fisher.* He mentions that the Sun is equated symbolically to the Fish or has fish companions.

101. Two further points of likeness between Dante's quest and the Quest of the Grail are deserving of special attention. The Grail is carried by a beautiful woman; Dante's attainment of the Beatific Vision depends on the continual aid and inspiration of a woman. In each case blessedness is mediated by a figure of

very fact the achievement of his Quest, initiating his blessedness, as that of its hero is initiated by the Grail. The Grail, likewise, is attained only after the endurance of dire adventure and the overcoming of grievous obstacles, through which at last entrance is obtained into the sacred precincts of castle or of garden.[102] The Quest of the Grail was too tremendous and too powerful in medieval symbolism not to have left its mark in many places. Even today its symbolic power through associations running far back of history and happily free from all flavor of pietism, draws to it an ascription of sacred character: the great Wagnerian *Parsifal,* in which the music itself carries out the imagery of the seasons, is performed customarily on Good Friday,[103] its appropriate place in the solar drama of the Chris-

supreme feminine beauty, who in neither case becomes the earthly bride of the hero whom she guides to the heights of attainment.

Second, in both quests complete outward vision of the sacred symbol of blessedness is possible without attainment, and is followed by expulsion from the presence of the symbol. Gawain, during his perilous night at Corbenic, actually sees the Grail twice. In the evening the Grail is carried past the table, feeding all present except Gawain. After the bitter adventures which follow, the Grail-bearer and attendants worship before the holy vessel in Gawain's presence. This time he shares in its benefits, for it heals the wound given him by the fiery lance. Yet the outcome of his experience is to be bound in a vile cart drawn by a decrepit horse, and pelted out of town with mud and filth. Perceval's uncomprehending vision of the Grail mysteries, ending in his expulsion from the castle, is too familiar to need recounting. Similar mischances befell most of the Grail questers.

Dante's experience is not dissimilar. In the *Vita Nuova,* although behaving toward Beatrice with the utmost reverence of which he is then capable, he is scorned by her and refused her salutation. Again, in the Earthly Paradise, the mere vision of Beatrice brings not blessedness, but rather rebuke. None the less, without outward vision, in the one case of the Grail, in the other of Beatrice, no true attainment of the Quest is possible. Thus appears, in the form peculiar to the Quest-motif, the fundamental law of symbolism: successful attempts at spiritual insight must pass in every case through the channel of the symbol; yet the symbol interpreted in a literal, formal, or descriptive sense only, without the insight which penetrates to the underlying meaning, is void and barren.

102. Or full experience of their mystic meaning. Cf., for example, the adventures of Boors and of Gawain at Corbenic, as related in the Vulgate *Lancelot.* The perils include a mysterious storm, wounding by a fiery lance, encounters with lion, leopard, dragon, and armed knight, and a vision of the Grail in brilliance as if it were the sun; yet in spite of the undergoing of these trials neither Boors nor Gawain attain the ultimate goal of the Quest. Similar perilous adventures of the hero are recounted in Chrétien de Troyes' *Conte del Graal,* in Heinrich von dem Türlin's *Diu Krone,* and in Wolfram von Eschenbach's *Parzival.*

103. Dr. Loomis has suggested that, were an initiate of one of the old mystery cults to be recalled to life on Broadway on Good Friday, and, after his bewilderment by the confusion and hurry of modern civilization, were he to wander into the Metropolitan Opera House—he would feel that at last here was something which he understood, and among the significations of which, with its secret mys-

tian year. In the spring is portrayed the triumph of the Christ—and of all heroes who have shared in sun imagery—over the motionless, dark, cold blight of evil. There is something deep within even the unlettered that shows him more than farce in the confusion of the simple Parsifal when asked his name: "I have had many names." Truly, he had.

IV. THE SUN OF METAMORPHOSIS

IN constant support of the love motivation of the quest in medieval thinking is the perception of metamorphosis. Fascinating and perturbing in its mystery, transmutation is a theme with a history extending far back into antiquity. From the shape-shifting of primitive folklore to that transhumanizing which may not be told in words ("trasumanar significar per verba non si poria"[104]) this mystery aroused men to thought and to strange experience. Those in the Middle Ages most irresistibly lured by the mysteries of the natural universe became absorbed in the study of transmutation. The quest for the Philosopher's Stone motivated the initiation of modern science.[105]

Alchemists, like other knights of the Quest, worked under the spell of solar symbolism. *Sol* with its attendant lion, eagle, king, and sex symbolism, was omnipresent, and its use by alchemists is reflected in much of medieval literature from romance to bestiary and is suggested in the *Divina Commedia* itself. There was a continual discovery in nature of the new reflections of the solar Trinity and of its associated numbers,[106] in the light of

tic meanings, he was at home. It is interesting further, since many of the elements reminiscent of sun-worship and of the mysteries had been lost from the sources of the *Parsifal*, as Dr. Loomis points out, that Wagner, simply from his sense of the artistic rounding out of a whole, should have restored so many such elements.

104. *Par.,* i, 70-71.

105. "There is not the slightest doubt that chemistry owes its origin to the direct labours of the alchemists themselves, and not to any who misread their writings." H. Stanley Redgrove, *Alchemy, Ancient and Modern*, pp. 3-4. See also the excellent two volume history of experimental science, by Dr. Lynn Thorndike.

106. A summary of the principles of alchemy is given in the *Smaragdine Table:*

"1. I speak not fictitious things, but what is true and most
   certain.

2. What is *below* is like that which is *above,* and what is   *Analogy*
   above is like that which is below, to accomplish the
   miracles of one thing.

which these symbolisms in the *Commedia* should be studied. The field of medieval alchemy is, however, rather a tangled thicket than either a dark forest or an ordered garden,[107] and in it many fall prey to the powers of darkness. Its basic hypothesis was, nevertheless, that of all medieval creativity:

La matière concrète de la nature est notre seule base tangible, la seule preuve sensible de toute affirmation. . . . L'esprit et la matière, dans le

---

3. And all things were produced by the meditation of   *Unity*
   one Being, so all things were produced from this one
   thing by adaptation.

4. Its father is the *Sun*, its mother the Moon; the wind *Sun-sex central*
   carries it in its belly, its nurse is the earth.

5. It is the *cause of all perfection* throughout the whole *First Mover*
   world . . .

8. *Ascend* with the *greatest sagacity from the earth to*
   heaven, and then *again descend* to the earth, and *unite*   *Quest cycle*
   together the *powers* of *things superior* and *things in-*
   ferior. Thus you will obtain the glory of the whole
   world, and all obscurity will fly far away from
   you . . .

12. Therefore I am called Hermes Trismegistus, possessing *Achievement in*
    the three parts of the philosophy of the whole world.   *knowledge*

13. That which I had to say concerning the *operation of* *Solar deity*
    the Sun is completed."

(Words characteristic of all medieval symbolic thinking have been *italicized*.)
See Redgrove, *op. cit.,* pp. 40-41.

Cf. with (8) above, Boehme's statement of the desire of the hermetic philosopher "to arrive at the unity of vision" "by entering fully into the will of our
Saviour Christ, and therein bringing the eye of time into the eye of eternity; and
then descending by means of this united through the light of God into the light
of nature." J. Boehme, *Of the Signature of All Things,* etc. Everyman ed., p.
250.

107. Cf., for example, such an alchemical statement as:
"The spirit of Sol may tincture Mars and Venus, and change them into the
highest metalline perfection, viz. into gold; which cannot so easily be effected
in silver, unless it be reduced into the first materia, where Saturn, Mars, and
Mercury are together in the Sulphur, and then it can be done; Venus receives
its toughness from Saturn, and its redness from Mars as the fire. Now the desire
of Venus is only eager, and longing after Sol, as after her first mother, from
whence she springs forth in her birth in the first original; for the love comes
forth originally from God, and so it is likewise in the eternal Birth in the figure:
The desire of Venus goes into Sol, into the Sun, and receives in its desire the
property of the Sun, and shines from Sol. . . . For God the Father generates
the love through his heart; now the sun, by way of similitude, betokens his
heart; for it is a figure in the outward world according to the eternal heart of
God, which gives strength and virtue to every life and essence. And understand
it right; all things proceed from the word and heart of God (which is the divine
Sulphur) in the birth of the Holy Trinity, and manifest themselves in and
through the proceeded (or egressed) essence, which is God's wisdom; and they
again do eagerly force and press out of the egress, in and toward his heart and
power, and vehemently long after it, as Paul saith, all creatures groan and pant
with us to be delivered from vanity." Boehme, *op. cit.,* p. 41.

monde et l'humanité, sont entièrement liés. Les séparer, c'est amoindrir l'art. L'art est, comme la poésie, comme la philosophie et la science, et comme notre vie matérielle même, une attraction vers la création, qui à nos dans bornés manifeste le Créateur.[108]

For the Middle Ages the only possible creation was in symbolism. Craftsmen and scholars, artists in stone or in language, worked alike with the *verba Dei*.[109, 110]

It is to be regretted that the study of medieval science is too often undertaken by those who fail in appreciation of its dual nature, of which the basis is analogy, the basis of all symbolism. The scientific, like all other phases of medieval thought, becomes intelligible only with the comprehension of the symbolic method. Though brevity forbids dallying in the chaos of alchemical lore—and the greater chaos of attempted elucidations—interest in the medieval quest demands recognition of its genius. Whether the secret code descriptions of alchemical experiments represent actual laboratory directions, unsafe to publish openly, or whether they represent rather the hidden secrets

108. Baes, *Le symbole et l'allegorie*, p. 3.

109. Cf. with the statement by M. Baes given above, the *five principles of mysticism* listed in M. Hugonin's *Prolegomena* to the works of Hugh of St. Victor (Migne, *P.L.*, t. 175):

"1. Toutes les oeuvres extérieures de Dieu sont la manifestation de sa pensée et de son verbe, comme la parole est la manifestation de la pensée de l'homme. Nous sommes associés à cette grande révélation, et c'est le but de la loi du travail imposée à tous.

2. Cette manifestation s'est faite par la création: c'est le monde naturel; par l'incarnation, c'est le monde surnaturel.

3. Pour arriver à la vraie science de Dieu par ses oeuvres, il faut avoir le coeur pur, parce que la vraie science unit l'âme à Dieu, et que la péché est un obstacle à cette union . . .

4. Le but de la science étant la perfection de l'homme, c'est-à-dire le plein développement de son activité et de sa vie . . .

5. La science est toujours imparfaite sur la terre; ce n'est qu'au terme de notre pèlerinage que nous trouverons, dans notre fin, cette pleine et paisible possession de la verite par l'intelligence et par l'amour."

110. Lactantius points out this view in the words of "Hermes Trismegistus": "For Trismegistus, who by some means or other searched into almost all truth, often described the excellence and majesty of the word . . . he acknowledges that there is an ineffable and sacred speech, the relation of which exceeds the measure of man's ability." "Ante-Nicene Library," XXI, 226.

The doctrines of the occult sciences, including alchemy, are based on the ancient writings ascribed to "Hermes Trismegistus" (cf. p. 437 n. 106), for which see the translations by G. R. S. Mead. The name of the supposed author, meaning Thrice-greatest Hermes, is obviously mythical. It is not known to whom the Hermetic writings are to be ascribed, if indeed they are not the work of many hands.

of the spiritual quest, is no longer a subject of discussion. That both types of alchemical writing and thinking existed has been well established. Confusion will remain, however, so long as the student of the Middle Ages fails to recognize that for all those in the tradition of the fourfold method both types, of necessity, were valid *in the same treatise*.

On the basis of the mystic hypothesis of essential unity in the universe, just as all creation is of the Sun and ultimately unified in it,[111] so all metals are potentially gold:

Since . . . the substance of the metals is *one,* and common to all, and since this substance is (either at once, or after laying aside in course of time the foreign and evil sulphur of the baser metals by a process of gradual digestion) changed by the virtue of its own indwelling sulphur into GOLD, which is the goal of all metals, and the true intention of Nature—we are obliged to admit, and freely confess that in the mineral kingdom, as well as in the vegetable and animal kingdoms, Nature seeks and demands a gradual attainment of perfection, and a gradual approximation to the highest standard of purity and excellence.[112]

The search for the stone that should accomplish this perfection in nature was undertaken with as great ardor and enthusiasm as ever was the quest for the Grail;[113] though its literature is of necessity far less readable. In no magic forests and lakes of the Land of Faery, but in the very elements of the universe, took place the mystic marriage and the mystic death and burial recounted in alchemical lore.

In a series of pictures a drama of this strange realm is represented. In the first a noble king, Gold, is beheld enthroned in state surrounded by his son Mercury and five servants—Silver, Copper, Tin, Iron, and Lead. The son, incited by the servants, stabs his father, catching the blood in his robes. Immediately a grave is dug, and the son, in an attempt to throw his father into the grave, falls in with him. The sixth picture shows him in vio-

111. So states Irenaeus Philalethes, in the *Golden Tract Concerning the Stone of the Philosophers.* See the *Magical Writings of Thomas Vaughan,* edited by A. E. Waite. Thomas Vaughan, George Starkey, and others used the pseudonym of Irenaeus Philalethes. The identity of the author here quoted remains a subject of dispute. Cf. Redgrove, *op. cit.,* p. 79, and footnote.
112. Quoted by Redgrove, *op. cit.,* p. 28.
113. Even the equipment of the alchemist had its symbolic significations like the armor watched by the youth on the eve of his knighting (and like the habit of modern initiates in the secret orders).

lent but unavailing struggle to escape. In the seventh picture, however (note the mystic number seven), the father is restored to life completely purified; and son and all five servants are exalted to kingship by his power. In this strange comedy of medieval life is represented under figure the preparation of an amalgam[114] of gold and mercury; the former, apparently dying, covers the paler metal with its blood. The grave is the furnace in which the preparation must remain sealed until a change is observed. This story is purely and simply an allegory, a code to conceal from those of alien mind that which through lack of understanding might be confused with practices judged illicit. But both the story and the process it represents had at the same time mystic interpretation by the fourfold method.[115]

It is very likely that early ideas of transmutation within the realm of the inanimate were the outgrowth of accidental chemical experiments, probably with mixtures. When the alchemist first mingled the elements of the universe he was generally in a state of delightful uncertainty as to whether the result would be an inert and innocent mess, a new and surprising substance unlike either of its generators, or an upheaval which would effectively end his earthly experiments, sending him to render account in the presence of the Great Alchemist. More than one experimenter, hiding from the stake and faggots ever in readiness for his reception, spent within his cavern considerable periods prone in unconsciousness from the learning of the lessons which nature had to teach.

It was early discovered that gold was of all known metals the least subject to the action of any acid. Through its permanence it was in character as well as in appearance a fit symbol for him whose symbol was the Sun, and for all that was like him. The quest for the secret of the golden touch, the philosopher's stone which should make of base metals gold, was then of significance for moral progress also, the transmutation of fallen man into the likeness of God. To the alchemist philosopher, analogy ex-

114. The origination of this term is ascribed to Thomas Aquinas. The ascription to him, and to Albertus Magnus, of alchemical works, is, however, probably mistaken.

115. Cf. the mystical and psychoanalytical interpretation of a similar story by Dr. H. Silberer in his *Problems of Mysticism and Its Symbolism*.

isted between the transmutation of base metals into gold, the perfection of man physiologically, and the transfiguration[116] of spiritual man. "These three problems were one; the same problem on different planes of being; and the solution was likewise one. He who held the key to one problem held the key to all three, provided he understood the analogy between matter and spirit."[117] The secret of moral progress, however, lay in the Incarnation and its sacramental extension. Here was the great alchemical experiment in the realm of the soul—by the touch of water and of oil properly applied, a man received "character,"[118] that mysterious change in the soul which could never be lost, whether in hell or heaven; and by feeding on the bread of angels, he became transhumanized.[119] It was a foregone conclusion then that whenever the agent of chemical transmutation should be discovered, it would be a symbol of Christ, acting in its sphere as he in his.

Characteristic is the alchemical statement in regard to Christ, that he

had no need to die but he died voluntarily and rose again to make us live eternally with him as his brethren without sin. Thus gold is without stain, fixed, glorious, and able to undergo all tests, but it dies for its imperfect and sick brethren, and soon, rising glorious, it delivers them and colours them for life eternal; it renders them perfect in the state of pure gold.[120]

The transmuting principle was appropriately named the Philosopher's Stone, Stone of the Lover of Wisdom, the Spiritual Rock which is Christ.[121] In the *Sophic Hydrolith* it is written:

116. Cf. Chap. V.   117. Redgrove, *op. cit.,* p. 12.
118. The assertion that certain sacraments, and in particular baptism, confers "character." is not to be taken as meaning that a moral change is produced by a physical or non-moral means. The word character denotes in this connection rather a metaphysical change, by which the soul is made other than it was, possessing powers which it previously did not possess. Thus the moral possibilities are greater, and the responsibility likewise greater.
119. According to Athanasius, "God must be made man that man may be made God."
120. Basil Valentine, to be found in John E. Mercer, *Alchemy, Its Science and Romance.*
121. Similarly the Elixir of Life, quintessence composed of Gold and Light, the perfect medicine for all bodily ills, must bear symbolic relationship to him who as Truth was cure for all mental ills, and as Reason and Justice was cure for all ills of the soul,

"Thus . . . I have briefly and simply set forth to you the perfect analogy which exists between our earthly and chemical and the true and heavenly Stone, Jesus Christ, justly termed 'the stone which the builder rejecteth' whereby we may attain unto certain beatitude and perfection, not only in earthly but also in eternal life."[122] It was explained by many writers that "stone," even in its physical signification as applied to this principle, was a figurative not a literal term.[123] Some alchemists even named it definitely as a powder:

> Know then that it is called a stone not because it is like a stone . . . in species it is gold, more pure than the purest . . . very fine powder, impalpable to the touch, sweet to the taste, fragrant to the smell, in potency a most penetrating spirit.[124]

There was, however, in all this no confusion of thought through an intermingling in the same sphere of the spiritual and the physical. The autonomy of each was maintained. Philalethes for example goes on to say: "If we say that its nature is spiritual, it would be no more than the truth; if we described it as corporeal, the expression would be equally correct."[124] The modern interpreter who attempts to see the Stone's spiritual significances as in the same order of truth as its physical qualities, commits an absurdity. Not a few students have puzzled their heads over what chemical substance could be described as equally spiritual and corporeal, bringing "all metals to the perfection of gold and silver . . . and that by natural methods which yet in their effects transcend nature."[124] It is surprising that one familiar with the ecclesiastical tradition[125] should fail to recognize here a perfect description of the sacramental mode of action. In regard to the bread of angels, such a one would scarcely stigmatize as an exaggeration Lull's[126] statement that the smallest

---

122. Redgrove, *op. cit.,* pp. 12-13, quoting from the *Sophic Hydrolith.*
123. Compare, for example, the following statement: "Stone which is not a stone, precious thing which has no value, thing of many shapes which has no shape, unknown which is known of all." Zosimus, cf. Mercer, *op. cit.*
124. Philalethes, excerpt in, *op. cit.*
125. As, for example, Bishop Mercer, author of a standard work on alchemy.
126. The identity of the alchemist who wrote under the name of Ramón Lull is uncertain. That he is the same as the mystic writer to whom earlier reference has been made (cf. pp. 387-428) is usually doubted. It was, however, the earlier assumption.

amount of the Stone can transmute an ocean full of base metal into itself, and Salmon's claim that its transmuting power is infinite. Christ's efficacy is not diminished by the number of souls who receive of his transforming power.[127]

It is necessary then to distinguish from the literal sense of alchemical writings the spiritual analogy to be given man should he discover a physical power through which the natural universe should openly declare its unity with the sun. One must, moreover, respect the scientific temper which could expect such transformation of the physical universe to be accomplished not by vaguely miraculous powers, but only by a physical substance, acting in accord with natural laws.

In brief, that the details of scientific experiment should fail to have a spiritual meaning was inconceivable to medieval thinking. Albertus Magnus might find interest primarily in the actual physical experiment, but it was an interest comparable to that of Jerome in the textual exactitude of scripture. Every symbolist must rightly comprehend the literal before he proceeds to spiritual interpretation. On the other hand, just as it would have occurred to no one to reject physical sequences as demonstrated by experiment, so it would have occurred to no one to reject the spiritual analogies of those sequences in the soul of man. It is declared in the *Sophic Hydrolith* that "the practice of this Art enables us to understand, not merely the marvels of Nature, but the nature of God himself, in all its unspeakable glory. It shadows forth, in a wonderful manner . . . all the articles of the Christian faith, and the reason why man must pass through much tribulation and anguish, and fall a prey to death, before he can rise again to a new life."[128] In the medieval tradition divorce of physical expression from spiritual meaning was impossible. The physical was the means of the quest for wisdom.

The quest motif dominated all aspects of medieval expression, learned and popular. The object of the quest was the ultimate anagoge within which was contained the pattern of the

127. Interestingly enough, modern science has presented the world with physical substances sharing in this apparently unlimited efficacy of the Philosopher's Stone. The activity of small amounts of radioactive substances seems to be practically inexhaustible.

128. Excerpts in Redgrove, *op. cit.,* p. 12.

whole, apprehensible to man only through study of nature and scripture in the light of reason and the inspiration of the infinite. The study demanded, moreover, consideration of particulars in their interrelationships, with ultimate reference to the whole. The function of the *Speculum* in the Middle Ages, whether it were tome or cathedral, was to display within apprehensible compass the tremendous range of the known, through the unification of which the quest progressed. Of all *Speculae* the greatest in its reflection of the divine light was, as Dante had declared it, the sun itself.[129]

Thus for the Middle Ages man's age-long search for consistency in experience, fused in the Roman Empire under the power and the lightning flashes of the *Sol Invictus,* had defined the quest for the Infinite in whom all opposites found unification. This definition was given expression and brought within the reach of the people chiefly through the symbolism of the liturgy. The quest was a dual quest, not only of man for reality, but of God for man, involving an inevitable metamorphosis. Of this the people were made aware and in it they were trained by the *Significationes* of cathedrals, sermons, bestiaries, and of their own varied experimental literature; while the more aristocratic were charmed by the troubadours' discovery of the power of metamorphosis resident in the love of woman. In the fresh idealization of reality, which grew out of medieval social development and love awakening, was the motivation of the quest. For alchemists in vicissitudinous search, the metamorphosis was accomplished by the Philosopher's Stone, symbol of Christ acting through love; for the Knights of the Quest achievement lay in the Grail with its gift of mystic union with the sacramental Christ, mediated by the Holy Spirit; for Dante on pilgrimage, attainment came in that all-revealing communion with Beatrice in which she, as symbol of Love, manifests herself sacramental symbol of Christ at the consecration of the Eucharist. Such, also, was the supreme moment in the drama which is the heart of the cathedral. The desire of the individual became the placing of himself in such right relationship to the powers of attraction in the universe that the inevitable metamorphosis and the ultimate

129. Cf. *Purg.,* iv, 62.

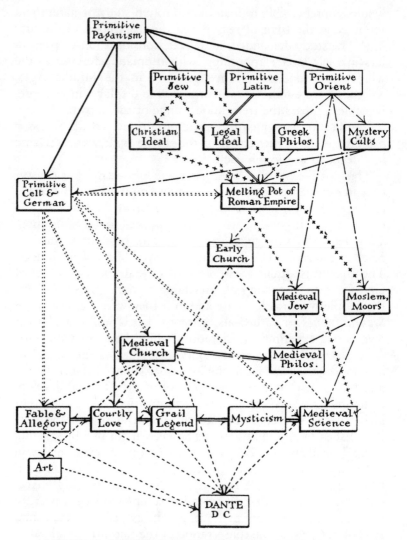

MEDIEVAL HERITAGE AND CULTURAL DEVELOPMENT
SCHEMATICALLY REPRESENTED AS CONSUMMATED
IN THE DIVINA COMMEDIA

union and spiritual marriage might take place in the Beatific Vision amid the music of the spheres, rather than in the loss of the *ben del l'intelletto* amidst mockery and negation of fire and cold.

In the intimate relationship of individual and Infinite was consummated the mystic marriage, the activity of the Infinite on the Nothing; spiritual fruitfulness was essentially individual in its accomplishment and social in its effects. Such was the experience which brought forth the *Commedia,* to present in ninefold symbolism given unity in the ten,[130] not only solution of the specific problem bound up with each source of human knowledge, as interpreted through the fourfold method, but fulfilment of the medieval quest for wisdom. Dominating both the work of the learned and the great quests of the people, in the Mass, in their literature, in the Grail cycle, and in the esoteric venture of the alchemists, the quest demanded from each his utmost in creativeness. Motivated and achieved through the Solar Tri-unity, all creativeness, whether of carpenter and mason, or of poet and philosopher, was primarily for the all-seeing eye[131] and had its *raison d'être* not in its effect on man, however great might be its economic or aesthetic value, but in its direct expression of that Reality which is truth and beauty: truth in Itself, and, since harmonious expression is the law of Its nature, inevitably beauty.

130. Cf. p. 339 n. 19c.
131. For example, the many beauties of the cathedral which are, by position and interest, invisible to human observers.

CHAPTER VII. SCHEMA

Terminus *ad quem*. Modern medievalists. Quest of knowledge. Essential duality in symbolism. *Mysteria*. The pattern of the whole. Terminus *a quo*.

CHAPTER VII. SYMBOLISM IN LETTER AND ANAGOGE: ALPHA AND OMEGA

Oh abbondante grazia ond' io presunsi
    ficcar lo viso per la luce etterna,
    tanto che la veduta vi consunsi!
Nel suo profondo vidi che s'interna,
    legato con amore in un volume,
    ciò che per l'universo si squaderna;
sustanze e accidenti e lor costume,
    quasi conflati insieme, per tal modo
    che ciò ch' i'dico è un semplice
    lume.

Oh, grace abounding, wherein I presumed to fix my look on the eternal light so long that I consumed my sight thereon! Within its depths I saw ingathered, bound by love in one · volume, the scattered leaves of all the universe; substance and accidents and their relations, as though together fused, after such fashion that what I tell of is one simple flame.

I. TERMINUS AD QUEM

DANTE ALIGHIERI died in Ravenna in 1321, in his lifetime having beheld ingathered and bound by love in one volume, the scattered leaves of all the universe; and their eternal meaning in a sunlit rose. He died in exile because Florence shared not in his character. Having chosen that the leaves of the universe should remain scattered, she was held separated by her florin pasturage, not only from the Rome of the Empire, but from that Rome where Christ is a Roman. One vision for Dante had included, against the background of the universe, the long history of humanity from Eden to the Last Judgment; the sweep of its varying transformations under allegiance to Christ or to Satan; and, in the drama of human history, the organic position of all aspects of contemporary life in their interrelationships—from mathematics to courtly love, from mysticism to politics. All had their place in the search for reality of which the most complete intellectual formulation was in the conception of Infinite Tri-unity expressed through duality and quaternity, bound up in the One and the Nothing of the mystic Ten.

Of all this the story is told in the journey of Dante's troubled life, yet even with his death he ceased not to be a figure in political controversy, and men were not inclined to allow his body rest. While Florence strove with her sister state for the body of her exiled prior, a band of cowled figures removed it stealthily in the night from the stone under which it lay, leaving Florence, Ravenna, and the pope himself, to continue a dispute of centuries over an empty tomb! Even more a center of age-long dispute than the body which his spirit left silent, has been the *Com-*

media, the body from which his spirit still might speak. While the first commentators were engaged in altercation, the spirit of a new age took surreptitiously from beneath the monument of the words they prized, that which had given those words their meaning, and left the poem as it were a cenotaph. So, like the contents of the tomb in Ravenna, the philosophy of insight symbolism was hidden away. It was only after the secret for a time handed down from initiate to initiate had been forgotten, and the walls of the monastery had begun to crumble, that a chance workman on a mission of repair revealed to the astonished inhabitants the body of the Florentine exile which had lain so long concealed within their walls. With similar discovery on the part of those absorbed in the strengthening of the civilization of the new age, may come the fulfilment which will make Dante's death like the anagoge of his journey, not only a terminus *ad quem,* but a terminus *a quo.*

II. MODERN MEDIEVALISTS

FOR centuries modern medievalists, ignorant of the philosophy and method of medieval symbolism, have labored in a confusion even worse than that of Babel. The builders of the tower, speaking in many tongues, knew that they failed to understand each other; but those today whose interest is in medieval literature, because elements of the vocabulary are familiar, are inclined naïvely to suppose that they understand. Whittier, for example, said that nature speaks in signs and symbols. This, although a true statement of the medieval position, was made without the slightest comprehension of that position, or sympathy with it. As a matter of fact, understanding is impossible until words are recognized as symbols, each bearing its heritage from the past[1] and governed by laws of interrelationship in present life.

As to the fundamental truths in the *Divina Commedia,* it may be noted by way of exemplification, there has been dispute even among the greatest of Dante critics. One scholar, criticizing a triad already suggested as light, music, and motion, insists that

1. "A word has a symbolic association with its own history, its other meanings, and with its general status in current literature." Alfred North Whitehead, *Symbolism, Its Meaning and Effect,* p. 84.

Dante's three and only leading ideas in the *Paradiso* are Light, Life, and Truth. He sees truly that motion is but a symbolic expression of life, and adds:

> With rare artistic skill and spiritual discernment he [Dante] chose his materials; the religious life is the life with God, and God is light, life and truth . . . the spiritual life is to know God, and to receive his light, life and truth. Surely there was no other material than these three elements out of which the divine poet could construct his stately paradise.[2]

Yet a child in the tradition of Catholicism would realize that just as motion and life are aspects of the same Person of the Trinity, so are truth and light (indeed, the writer just quoted, himself apparently unconsciously used "light" as symbolical of truth). Thus from both triads—that criticized and that suggested—there has been omitted the third element, which is the Primal Love. The omission of an element such as love, which is as fundamental in the universe as both truth and life, was impossible even to the least educated among those brought up in the symbolic tradition, and in no sense harmonious with the atmosphere of medieval thought or congruous with its method. But more than this, love was the very motif of Dante's century. The sun, most perfect symbol of deity, all knew, gave heat as well as life and light.

In ignorance not only of the philosophy and method of medieval symbolism, but even of the great scripture in which it centered, even more astonishing mistakes are made. For example, a recent critic speaks in shocked censure of the "medieval legend" which made Rahab an ancestress of Christ. The statement in Matthew's genealogy of Christ: "And Salmon begat Booz of Rachab; and Booz begat Obed of Ruth; and Obed begat Jesse; and Jesse begat David the king" is scarcely a medieval legend.[3] The only salvation for the student of the *Divina Commedia* lies in the visualization of Dante in his setting amid the thought currents of his time, and against the background of all that had produced them.

2. Charles Allen Dinsmore, *Aids to the Study of Dante* (Boston and New York: Houghton Mifflin, 1903), pp. 341-345.

3. Even the more radical of higher critics do not date any portion of Matthew, even the genealogical material, later than the second century.

The researches of the most careful scholarship will multiply confusion unless a framework is realized in which each detail may be given its proper position. In an age of specialization this fact causes difficulty. The expansion of knowledge having made it impossible that anyone should know all of its every phase, the assumption has arisen that to know anything, more than superficially, outside one's chosen field, is unnecessary. Dante wove his *Commedia* on a background of understanding, not only of the principles of every field of knowledge, but of every phase of life, using symbols which had increased in meaning since the time when, back of the horizon of history, man first began to walk erect and direct his gaze toward the sun.

III. QUEST OF KNOWLEDGE

As the modern world reviews past cultures, it has that degree of sympathy with classicism suggested by the pilgrimage of tourists to Olympia to worship according to their lights before the shrine of the Praxitelean Hermes. Those who, with apologies to Puritan ancestry, are gently disengaging themselves from the bonds of the Roman virtues, turn often for relief to Greek paganism, but overlook the Middle Ages, or, more literally, glance hurriedly past. It was an age of Christianity, with which is associated asceticism, and superstition with its fruit in magic.

As it happens, the human sense of humor is so constituted that that which is unfamiliar is likely to appeal to it as absurd. The first impression gained in a study of the medieval quest for knowledge is likely to be one of childishness and inconsistency. The quest cannot appear otherwise to one ignorant of the hypotheses with which it was consistent. On the other hand, firmly convinced of the seriousness and logic of the modern search, the critic is left little perspective for the smile of kindly indulgence. Strange as it may seem, however, the dominant ideas of this much descried period are cropping out in various fields of modern inquiry. Perhaps strangest of all, it is in the development of science that the recurrence of medieval principles is most marked.

Biology has long pointed out the unity underlying all forms of life, and now it "discloses the organism partaking of its en-

vironment and the environment interpenetrating the organism
. . . becoming not merely elementary material of its sustenance
and growth, but part and parcel . . . of its life."[4] At the same
time, physical science has demonstrated that every atom in the
universe is impressed with the pattern of the spheres. The all-
pervading unity has been given striking expression in a description of the whole physical universe as but "differentiated sunshine."[5] Furthermore, after decades of scientific experiment
with reconstruction of the world from empirically analyzed details, men are coming to realize that whether or not the unity
underlying all things be infinite, at least their task in the study
of it in the discrete is endless. Physicists among others are
struggling at present with the reconciliation of opposites, having found themselves dependent on two mutually contradictory
theories of light. Until a few decades ago, they had discarded
one of them in favor of the other; now they use both frankly:

No known theory can be distorted so as to provide even approximate
explanation. . . . For the present we have to work both theories. On
Mondays, Wednesdays, and Fridays we use the wave theory; on Tues-
days, Thursdays and Saturdays we think in streams of flying energy,
quanta, or corpuscles. That is, after all, a very proper attitude to take.

4. H. O. Taylor, *Freedom of the Mind in History* (London: Macmillan,
1923), p. 6.
5. Phrase used by John Fiske in his *Cosmic Philosophy*. A recent article by
Dr. Pupin well illustrates such use of symbolism:
"'The prosy modern piston,' said I, 'imitates the Olympian deities; it trans-
forms a chaos into a cosmos.' . . . Yes, the modern inventor may be said to
have stolen a secret from golden Helios, the sun-god. His steam-engine imitates
the operation of the central star of our planetary system. Where the ancient worshippers of Helios saw a resplendent sun-god radiating his breath of life to the
terrestrial waters, the modern inventor saw a celestial fire, and imitated its action
upon the terrestrial waters by fire under the boiler. Where the ancients saw the
blessings of the sun-god manifesting themselves by the rising vapors lifted on
high from rivers, lakes, and oceans, and forming clouds which, journeying to
higher elevations of the terrestrial globe, carry the waters to the thirsty conti-
nents, there the modern inventor saw the motion of steam from the boiler to the
condenser and on its journey driving the piston."
He continues: "But neither the poets of ancient Greece nor the modern inventor detected in this cyclic motion of water a fundamental process of nature.
. . . This beautiful cyclic process is a transformation of a solar chaos into a
terrestrial cosmos by the co-ordinating forces which reside in the primordial
granules of water, in its atoms and molecules, and it was revealed by modern
science." Michael Pupin, "Creative Co-ordination," in *Scribner's* for August,
1927.
As a matter of fact, this revelation of modern science is but a fulfilment of
that which Dante's symbolism taught. Cf. p. 460 n. 14.

We cannot state the whole truth since we have only partial statements.
. . . Some day we shall piece all the maps [i.e., statements] together.[6]

Not only this, but in the application of statistics to the quantum
theory, they have found themselves obliged to admit the operation of chance! More than this some tend to retrograde so far as
to perceive in chance, if not the law-abiding revolutions of
Dame Fortune's wheel, nevertheless the operation of a law.

In the modern quest for knowledge, while science is working
out anew a philosophy of interpretative symbolism, the people
are using relics of interpretative symbols left by the earlier tradition. Had the understanding persisted which showed the
name "Father" with reference to God to be but an insight symbol, under necessity of correction not only by other equally true
symbolisms from the realm of human relationships, such as
Lover or Babe, but also by the whole nexus of solar symbolism
in its majesty, thinking men of the present generation would
have been spared an embarrassing task—the necessity of ousting
from the most sacred precincts of their minds the hoary-headed
and arbitrary dispenser of rewards and punishments who, for
all his benignity, they cannot but feel unfit to preside there.

Although it is in the sciences that today is to be found the
closest approximation to the medieval symbolic spirit, through
the belief in such elements as unity, reconciliation of opposites,
and meaningfulness of total environment, yet it was the growth
of the scientific method which made impossible further hold
on the symbolic method among the people. The literal-minded
scientist is no better off than the literal-minded artist, and science itself gives its choicest gifts of insight only to the very few.
To the average man, science means practical inventions and the
life of action, shutting out contemplation altogether. Thus, in a
materialistic age, those unable to share in the joys and glory of
the scientific method, tend to seek the lost values in reactionism,
in vagaries and fads, or else in the great secret orders, where
truth is "veiled in allegory and illustrated in symbols." This
would suggest that symbolism, with or without basis, is with
difficulty ousted from life.

Although in modern literary movements now and then there

6. Sir William Bragg, in *Discovery*, September, 1921.

is displayed an uneasiness over the loss of the symbolic tradition of the past, the attempt is to recover its emotional power in disregard of its intellectual basis. Of this there could be no better example than the symbolist school in France, nourished on the writings of the Latin decadence. A writer of this school in discussing important features of symbolism in opposition to naturalism, states that symbolism discards mathematical precision in description of events, and stiff and dry exactness in their development, and second that it shakes off the yoke of the law of cause and effect.[7] When it did so, symbolism lost its grip. In accord with the philosophy which gave symbolism its greatest development, it was felt not only that there could be no more precise statement of truth than the symbol, but that the immutability of the law of cause and effect was the only basis for its use.

Another writer of the same school, however, in discussing the difference between the primitive poet and the symbolist of today, writes with more penetration: "Le poète primitif se sentait en contact perpétuel avec le surnaturel, tandis que le poète d'aujourdhui proteste contre l'opinion de ce temps que les choses sont 'toutes naturelles.' . . . . Aussi le rôle du poète symboliste consiste-t-il, en quelque sorte, a reconstituer dans l'esprit moderne une faculté perdue: le sens du mystère."[8] This passage would imply a decrying of the modern tendency to dismiss a fact with such simple understanding as is involved in a knowledge of its name, untouched by the mystery of its relationships in the unity of the universe. Yet this writer, too, like most of those newly awakened to the power of symbolism, is more interested in the aesthetic or emotional than in the thought value which is necessary to complete its power as a tool for the furtherance of human development and the ordering of human minds.

While science, albeit without intent, is engaged in a reformulation of the philosophy which once gave meaning to the symbolisms of the people, its newest child, modern psychology, with full intention is pointing out principles which underlie such en-

7. Albert Schinz, "Literary Symbolism in France," *Modern Language Association Pub.*, Vol. 18, pp. 273-307.
8. André Beaunier, *La poésie nouvelle*, p. 22.

deavors as those of the French symbolist school. From observation of the place of symbolism in the thought processes of the perennial twins, the genius and the madman, students of the human mind have sought for its roots in human nature. Although the first students saw mainly materials of symbolism as centered in sex, the microcosm, much time was not required for some to see also the macrocosmic center in the sun. With this new conception came the attempt to see in symbolism not only the expression of elemental instincts, but also the means of solution of personal problems. With appreciation of the necessity of studying the materials of symbolism as they appear in history and before it, came a recognition that the most careful analysis of the problems of the individual falls short unless in them be recognized also the problems of the race. Thus, like Dante, from an analysis of individual problems against the background of the natural universe, some psychologists are finding the necessity of a deeper order of symbolism. At present their philosophy of humanity and their symbolic method are still in process of formulation, and in consequence they can scarcely penetrate to the deeper level, the analysis of inner experience with reference to the ultimate quest. Yet that toward which they are working is clearly a philosophy of insight symbolism through which, in the bringing together of thought and emotion, unification of personalities may be accomplished. From the increasing prevalence in this field also of solar symbolism it would seem apparent that barring some cosmic catastrophe the sun is not likely to lose its symbolic prominence. For scientists the sun still, through the shadows which it casts, makes possible the measurement of high mountains and objects otherwise practically nonmensurable. For the psychologist the sun is becoming an aid in the sounding of the most inaccessible depths of human personality through the shadows which it casts in symbols. By these shadows the Middle Ages hoped also to grasp the inapprehensible.

One could go on at length to point out similarities between the medieval and the modern quest for knowledge. Until, however, existent groups of specialists become inspired with a desire not only to know thoroughly their fragments of the totality of human knowledge, but also to understand them in their interrelationships, modern thought will lack that integration through which its prophets may be understood.

IV. ESSENTIAL DUALITY IN SYMBOLISM

THROUGH this very lack of integration in the modern quest for knowledge, multiplicity of symbol now seems a Dark Wood from which escape, even through hell, is a blessing. Relief is sought in the cold clear light beneath which is never meant other than that which literally is said, or if other meaning become expedient, then one definite unchanging significance. If an eagle always represents St. John, and if St. John is represented always (if not in his own form) as an eagle, then all is well. But if an eagle may be St. John or the empire or contemplation in the abstract or a sinner seeking baptism, then symbolism becomes apparently a wilderness in which anything may mean anything, in a shape-shifting as lawless as that of any fairy tale.

This feeling results in part from the verbalism of modern learning. The word itself is not the symbol, but merely a symbol of the symbol. As Hugh of St. Victor warned, that which signifies Christ is not the word "leo" but the animal, so also it is not the word "eagle" but the soaring bird that is the source of eagle symbolism. Whatever, wherever seeks to look directly upon the sun is symbolized by the eagle, whether a great saint, an organization, a sinner seeking the waters of baptism, or contemplation itself. Such levels of symbolism are not unconnected, nor are they arbitrary. The discerning reader passes in rapid association from one meaning to the next, finding each enriched through the presence of the others.

The meaning of all human language is given by a grammar which lies back of the words, made by no one yet governing and ordering all that words express. Similarly, the meaning of the language of the universe lies back of its symbols in a nexus of laws beyond individual power of determination, yet governing the message which is perceived and conveyed. Through these laws men may grasp fundamental relationships in the universe long before they can express them in the language of science. The frequent anticipation of the findings of science as it were by instinct, in some apparent fairy tale or bizarre symbol of primitive man, is a source of constant comment:

What instinct was it led ancient peoples to worship the sun as the giver of all life? Are savages and primitive peoples endowed with strange powers that enable them to anticipate the findings of modern science? These ultra-violet rays now prove to be the life principle of the earth. Without them there would be no vegetation, and therefore no food, no animals, no men.[9]

A study of the function of insight symbolism in human development leaves this no matter of marvel. The hypothesis of a correspondence between the sensible and the supersensible, the finite and the infinite, has given birth to many anticipations of modern science much more surprising than that just noted. In order to understand the functioning of the hypothesis that the infinite or supersensible is represented in the finite and the sensible according to laws of relationship as definite as those which govern mathematical projection,[10] there is necessary only a constant distinction between the literal symbol and the anagoge which gives meaning to all that is symbolized.

It is not true that one thing representing another thing can be, in the strict sense, insight symbol. In dreams and in poetry, unconsciously and consciously, man may symbolize the external events of his life with their effect on him (Dante's personal political level). He may also symbolize the movements and developments of his inner life (Dante's personal moral level). So to interpret the *Divina Commedia* is as it were to psychoanalyze the poem in the simplest sense. Either of these interpretations is of little practical value, whatever its value to the diagnostician.[11] In this fact lies the reason for the medieval conviction that the root of reality is not the letter but the anagoge. In the same fact lies the rationale of the demand made by the primary order for a second order of levels. That is, to interpret the *Divina Commedia* as a story of no more than Dante's political

9. Waldemar Kaempffert, "Invisible Light Is Put To Work for Man," article in magazine section of New York *Times* for May 8, 1927.

10. "Chez les scolastiques, l'analogie ne designe nullement une ressemblance plus ou moins imparfaite entre plusieurs êtres; elle porte exclusivement sur des rapports." Bernard Landry, *La notion d'analogie chez St. Bonaventure et St. Thomas d'Aquin*, p. 1.

11. As Dr. Hinkle points out of symbolisms traced merely to their origin.

adventures and doings or of his inner life, lacks the spirit of insight symbolism characteristic of the Middle Ages unless there is first, constant remembrance that his life is directed by the Triune Sun God and has meaning only in that light, and second, application to all humanity. The medieval idea is not inaptly illustrated by cryptographic codes. The solver, indeed, starts with the puzzling, complex, superficially meaningless and confused letter of the cryptogram. The maker, however, started with the solution, whence he then constructed the outward form as expression; and the origin as well as the value of the cryptogram lies in the meaning, by which the letter was determined. Allegory and trope both receive their full significance only with consideration alike of the letter and of the anagoge, between the balance of which they lie.

So eager were men of the Middle Ages in their quest of knowledge through symbolism that philosophic thought centered interest in things not in and for themselves, nor even in and for man, but as revelation of universal unity. The place of fire in thought, for example, was primarily dependent not on its chemical nature as a process of combustion, and not on its economic utility, but on its value as an expression of aspiration to God. Nevertheless, fire was to be studied in all its physical attributes, for only by such knowledge of the letter could man attain to a true knowledge of the figure.

As soon as man ceases to reverence the physical—not as apart from the spiritual, but as the form through which the spiritual manifests itself—there occurs a dichotomy in his life from which springs the necessity of choice between two irreconcilable and eternally warring philosophies: materialism, and a spiritualism divorced from reality and taking refuge in fancy. Insight symbol becomes meaningless.

As soon, on the other hand, as man ceases to reverence the spiritual, coming to feel that the physical act of building a fire, for example, in itself constitutes and accomplishes prayer and divine union, the ruin of the symbolic tradition is imminent.[12]

12. Ozanam has commented on the two methods used in criticism of medieval thinking, according to one of which the argument is from the symbolized against the symbol, according to the other, from the symbol against the symbolized. He says: "Both these methods begin with a vicious circle, since the two elements

It were better to conclude that the act has none save its physical and economic significance.

In this balance between the symbol and the symbolized, for the intellectual tradition of the Middle Ages, lay the solution of the problem of duality which made of human experience such a torture of inconsistency and contradiction. Yet so delicate was this balance and so difficult of maintenance that only through the Logos could it be accomplished. Such was the significance of the Cross. As it has been seen, such was the basis for Dante's solution of all the warring opposites of his experience, the *crux* of the *Commedia*. Had medieval symbolists in general realized, as did Thomas Aquinas and his great teacher Albert,[13] the necessity of accurate experimental knowledge of the discrete, as the *materia* of their symbolism, a modification of the symbolic method might have paralleled and assisted the development of the methods of science.[14] In the actual course of events, how-

whose incompatibility they assume, to wit, the ideal and the real, on the contrary, form by their union the essence of true symbolism. The robust intelligence of the men of yore readily admitted the presence of two conceptions under one and the same sign. Our analytic habits of thought scarcely allow us fully to grasp either one." Ozanam, *Dante and Catholic Philosophy*, p. 406.

13. It is not meant to infer that Thomas Aquinas was himself of the temperament which is drawn irresistibly to personal experimental inquiry, as were his teacher Albertus Magnus, and the somewhat later founders of the empirical method. But Thomas' philosophy was built around a concept of the infinite, for whose existence and nature he saw proof not in an analysis of human ideas and inner experience, but in the data of the material universe as furnished by the senses—such as the existence of motion, and the individuality of perceived objects. Such a shift in philosophical emphasis was a true harbinger of the new experimental era.

14. There are endless examples of the fact that the symbolism of the mystic, when given free play, leads to scientific truth, even though starting from an untrue conception. For example, medieval astronomy corresponded to the Dark Wood in which the Worm is still the center of the universe. To the mystic for whom the Divine Sun was the center, the apparent position of the physical sun and the physical structure of the universe as then conceived must have required explanation, in order to accord with the laws of analogy. Yet the mystic maintained the centrality of the Divine Sun, because the other laws of his symbolism demanded it; and however difficult of justification was the belief that the earth moved around the sun, no other was consistent with the harmony of his system. That mystics failed to develop a heliocentric astronomy showed their respect for the scientific thought and the physical facts regarded as true in their day; a respect in which they differed from many modern mystics.

Indeed, in this possible interplay with the scientific imagination might be an added validification of the symbolic method, *when exercised in accord with its own laws*. For example, had the alchemists, following the mystic principle, returned always from contemplation to active analysis and observation, it is possible that the alchemical quest (to which modern chemistry promises essential fulfil-

ever, the medieval symbolist grew to understand less and less
the function of the literal level in his symbolism, and modern
thought in its revolt has come to consider that the truth of the
literal level invalidates all symbolic meanings. That is, each has
reverenced one member of the opposing pair, in disrespect to
the other. Both courage and genius are required for the maintenance of that position which politically made Dante a party
by himself.

V. MYSTERIA

IT is lack of understanding of the letter, with its possible trope
and allegory, in its relation to the anagoge, which has restrained
modern interest in the Middle Ages to its popular rather than
its learned tradition, and modern study of the *Commedia,* to the
Inferno and the *Purgatorio.*[15] To one unfamiliar with the anagoge, the *Commedia* must appear static, lacking, except in the
Purgatorio, any real progression[16]—progression being the basis
for the usual modern preference for this canticle. To appreciate
the *Paradiso,* it has been said, a state of quiescence and submission is necessary. It is true in a sense that progress has no place
in the *Paradiso,* which in its representation of infinity, contains
the ground of all progress; on the other hand, neither,has quiescence and submission, except as one of two opposites which
there are unified, where contemplation and action are as it were

ment) might have found earlier an achievement. It is a familiar fact today in
scientific circles that some scientists have become so familiar with analogies that
they can anticipate experience.

   Cf. also Harris, *Spiritual Sense of Dante's Divina Commedia,* p. 160.

   15. Even in the current revival of interest in mysticism, there has not been
realized the importance to it of its medieval prototype. The medieval prototype
itself is known only in the works which constitute its popularization; for example, the work of so little learned a mystic as Rolle has been translated for
modern thought from a Middle English rendering in which, moreover, much of
the symbolism has been altered. Latin *scripturae,* in which are both the root and
the trunk of medieval literature, remain only untranslated, but to a large extent unknown, while the attempt is made to learn from the scattered leaves. Yet
medieval Latin is unique among the languages of the world in being practically
univocal. In it a writer can scarcely avoid saying what he means. In this literature there is no such thing as "mystic vagueness." It is little wonder that modern
mysticism is not only strikingly lacking in all that was fundamental to the medieval tradition, but often greatly adds to the confusion concerning it.

   16. The basis of this difficulty lies in the perennial confusion between *Infinitas*
and *Unendlichkeit.*

the inbreathing and outbreathing of the soul, equally exigent to life and to each other.

There is a picture by Henri Martin in the museum at Bordeaux which may well arrest attention for the quality of its movement—*À chacun sa chimère.* Out of the mists of the distance comes a dense procession, in the full blaze of the sun, marching westward in the noonday. In the fore is a monk in habit, gazing upward toward the source of light, and beside him walks a naked wrestler in the games, eyes fixed on the symbol of victory in his outstretched hand. Back in the procession of humanity in its varied preoccupations, appear shapes of angels and of beasts. So, as life progresses into death, the endless transmutation is in progress. Had Henri Martin been attempting an illustration of Dante's *Commedia,* scarcely could he have achieved greater success. Yet that which he would have been representing is the progressive transformation of individuals, with no intimation of the anagoge other than that hinted in his shadows with their suggestion of the sun.

In such a picture as *l'Adorazione dell'agnello,* by the brothers Van Eyck, in which the same metamorphosis is indicated, the quality of dramatic motion is not perceived, because of the attempt to bring together the letter with its symbolism relating to progress, and the anagoge which supplies their meaning. Against the background of the beauty of natural landscape and the suggestion of the spiritual city, there is in progress the worship of the Lamb through whom is mediated the Divine Sun in all his aspects (cross and dove being present, amid various forms of the life he gives). On one side of the fountain of life kneel catechumens, and on the other hand those who, with varied interests as indicated by their postures, reveal their attraction toward sun or *lupa;* while beyond, around the sacrifice, kneel angels. Here the reciprocal forces of God's search for man and of man's search for God are in creative equilibrium. Because this is not understood, that which is presented appears static. Dr. Grandgent has written:

We of the present generation are so devoted to perpetual betterment that a state of perfection is almost abhorrent to us. It is the approach that concerns us, not the attainment. An eternity of absolute but unchanging and unproductive happiness does not attract mankind now as it did of old.[17]

So Henri Martin rested content with a superb detail of the metamorphosis of the approach, perhaps, like Dr. Grandgent, really believing that the attainment could be but an unchanging and an unproductive happiness. To believe, however, that such an attainment could have been satisfying to men of old, though unsatisfying in this generation, is to believe in a complete subversion of human nature. A devotion to perpetual betterment with no tolerance for a state of perfection was, to the initiate in the symbolic tradition, a mark of immaturity. Only with some degree of attainment did adult activity begin. It was the primal force of creativity in the anagoge which caused the symbols that approached it most nearly, to manifest themselves in the simplicity of the most elemental symbolism.

Mystery, it will be remembered, St. Chrysostom defined as that which is everywhere proclaimed, but is not understood by those who have not right judgment. He who has never considered things in their interrelationships in the fundamental unity, and he who has never meditated on the nature of the infinite, will have no grasp of reality. But this is not all. The experience of unification is not rare, and in it ultimately is not the greatness of Dante or of anyone else. That which is rare is definition of the experience, the ability with no sense of disappointment, regret, or anticlimax, to return from the supreme vision to the limitations of expression, not merely through suggestive imagery, but likewise in terms of intellectual consistency and of practical action. Than symbolism, culminating in anagoge, there is known no form of expression of greater potency for drama and for progression. It is symbolism which is regarded as arbitrary and not understood in its levels of meaning, which never escapes a static quality.

In modern life perhaps there are none more capable of realizing this truth than those initiates of the secret orders who have been admitted to higher degrees. In this very fact there is much of significance. Not only did the secret orders first come into prominence amid the collapse, through abuse in church and

17. Grandgent, *La Divina Commedia*, p. iii, note.

laboratory, of the medieval tradition, but the whole symbolism of these great orders draws from the same sources of inspiration, finding its unification in the sun, its quest in the Logos. There are, then, close resemblances to the thought with which Dante was familiar: for example, the miracle nine of which the root is the three of the trinity, the symbolization of the points of the compass, the use of symbolic positions as in the Mass, and of symbolic furnishings. Fundamentally, those of lesser progress as in the Middle Ages understand only the moral signification of the ritual forms and ceremonies in which they participate, whereas with admission to the higher degrees there comes usually deeper penetration into the farther levels. It is the existence of the "thirty-third degree" that gives meaning to the symbolic progress in initiation.

It is the dual reverence alike for the inviolability and for the essential peril of the anagoge which has engaged all true symbolists (whether of the tradition of medieval mysticism or of the modern Mason) in the solution of the same problem—the guarding of symbolism from abuse and misunderstandings. Because the center of the life of symbolism in the Middle Ages was on principle open, in the Mass, to all who could perceive, the sole means for avoidance of abuse was warning and education.[18] There is necessary, however, to bring in the atmosphere of the secret order, no recourse to esoteric writings, but only the recall of such a typical medieval preface as:

In the Name of the Father and of the Son and of the Holy Ghost! I charge thee, and I beseech thee . . . whatsoever thou be that this book shall have in possession, either by property, either by keeping, by bearing as messenger, or else by borrowing, that as much as in thee is by will and advisement, neither thou rede it, nor write it, nor speak it, nor yet suffer it to be read, written, or spoken, of any or to any but if it be of such one, or to such one, that hath by thy supposing in a true will and by an whole intent purposed him to be a perfect follower of Christ not only in active living, but in the sovereignest point of contemplative living the which is possible by grace for to be come to in this present life . . . and thereto that doth that in him is, and by thy supposing hath done long time before, for to able him to contemplative living by the virtuous means of active living. For else it accordeth nothing to him.

18. Except among alchemists, who to guard their lives and reputations adopted code.

And over this I charge thee . . . that if any such shall read it, write it, or speak it, or else hear it be read or spoken, that thou charge him as I do thee, for to take him time to read it, speak it, write it, or hear it, all over. For peradventure there is some matter therein in the beginning, or in the middle, the which is hanging, and not fully declared where it standeth; and if it be not there, it is soon after, or else in the end. Wherefore if a man saw one matter and not another, peradventure he might lightly be led into error; and therefore in the eschewing of this error, both in thyself and in all other, I pray thee for charity do as I say thee.[19]

In such various sun-illumined forms as liturgy, cathedral, Grail legend, and the *Divina Commedia,* the Middle Ages gathered up its symbolic heritage. Liturgy has ceased to be the force in daily life that once it was; the cathedral without its drama loses its power; the Grail cycle is a jungle of romances little understood; while the *Divina Commedia* is prized for the moral lessons which may be drawn from it rather by example than through symbolism. All this has resulted from the downfall of the symbolic tradition. Perhaps the secret orders have been right in guarding their symbolism through secrecy.

VI. THE PATTERN OF THE WHOLE

THE ultimate revelation of symbolism is essentially esoteric, as Dante explained at length to Can Grande in his letter of dedication. Insistence on the unspeakable yet dynamic and productive nature of the anagoge has marked both symbolic traditions, that which sought its protection in secrecy and that which strove for self-revelation. In Dante's tradition bound up with essential productivity was expression of the vision beneath the form of beauty, that others might be lured from beneath the spell of the *lupa.*

To reveal anything of the supreme venture into the unknown demands the utmost of symbolism—the central symbolism of the universe in the sun, corrected by the central symbolism of human life in love and marriage, both supported in the inevitable framework of the symbolism of number. Dante in the symbolism of his *Commedia* gave especial attention to the symbolism of number. The poem wherein all the knowable universe

19. Prologue of the *Cloud of Unknowing,* ed. Evelyn Underhill.

was to be set forth in its ultimate relationships as the stage whereon is enacted the drama of life, of necessity in its very structure must bear witness to the mystery of number on which alone depends the harmony of all that is. Not only does Dante tell of number in the very construction of his tercets and his cantos, within the canticles of the *Commedia,* but he renders that number perceptible in the music of his tercets and in the increasing of celestial harmony as he penetrates deeper into reality.[20]

The deepest mystery of reality is its quaternity, the three of the Trinity plus that on which it acts, while within the ten is the totality of all that is. In Dante's system that produced or expressed by the symbolic meaning of a number was represented by the number's square, and Dante's *Commedia,* which was to be the expression of the totality of reality, was composed of one hundred cantos, the square of the ten.[21] Again, the life of Christ being central as in scripture, each canticle represents the thirty-three years of Christ's life on earth, which, multiplied by the three of the Trinity, makes ninety-nine, to which then there must be added for the complete expression of reality, the all-pervading One and Nothing. Finally, in the ten divisions of each of the three regions is the miracle nine (whose only root is the Blessed Trinity) plus the fourth. Thus, fittingly, Beatrice as a nine dominates the three realms of Dante's journey to the Beatific Vision, where beyond her he perceives the Ultimate Truth. It is then appropriate that the interpretation should include nine levels, united and summed in one (triune) pervasive anagoge.

Thus, not only does the eternal basis of the universe analyze itself into a threefold Reality, Giver of life, light, and love, and therefore imply the essential "nineness" of the universe of which this threeness is the sole "root"—but the problems of the temporal world demand the solution of innumerable dualities (of which the most familiar are good and evil, pleasure and pain), and in the solution tend to evolve a quaternity in two

20. The closest derivative of mathematics, in medieval thinking, was music. (It is of course true that harmony depends on mathematical ratios between notes.)

21. For the symbolism of ten, cf. pp. 339 ff., also Appendix V, Pt. I, i, and V, Pt. I, ii.

ways, first by setting the universe as a fourth after the Three of the Trinity, second by seeing in written scripture four meanings. Within the Ten is bound up the full significance of the One, the Two, the Three, and the Four. To a symbolist of Dante's caliber such apparent details[22a] as the number of letters in a word may become significant. In the closing lines of that poem from which the *Commedia* was born, Dante declared his goal to be ultimate communion with her who is *benedetta* (a nine), absorbed in contemplation of him who is *benedictus* (in whom is the ultimate ten of all that is).

Though reality be fourfold and the problem of existence be threefold, the problem of living is twofold, and Dante has declared the aim of his *Commedia* to be practical. The means of relief for humanity in the agony of the tension between Beatrice and Circe, Dante finds in the eternal Logos, Radiance of the Divine Sun, whose symbolism is like a keystone in the *Commedia*. It is the two natures of Christ in their autonomy and their relationship[22b] which to Dante form the pattern for the solution of the problems inherent in the warring pairs in whose conflict he is involved. Reflecting in the coöperation of their guidance the perfect harmony of opposites in Christ, Virgil and Beatrice guard Dante through the bitter struggle between Guelph and Ghibelline, leading him to solution in a theory of ideal church and empire. The same pattern is the key to the dilemma of free will and mechanism. Moreover, the dual nature of the Incarnate Logos is not only pattern for the compromise of rival claims, but the only possible means of understanding the true relationship of empire to church and philosophy to theology. Finally, the same pattern governs the three phases of the mystic way making of it, like the other stories, a comedy with its initial catastrophe and ominous triumph. Here the stern pattern is shaped partially by the sin of the individual, but even more significantly it is the fruit of his union with the Logos. Of

22a. Details have not been stressed throughout the preceding pages because the object has been to give the broad outlines of Dante's symbolic pattern. Nevertheless, one among innumerable minor points of interest in connection with the dominance of Beatrice as a nine, is that her name ends a line nine times throughout the *Commedia*.

22b. A matter of faith, determined at Nicaea and at Chalcedon.

all these comedies the story of Christ is unique in that, in it, the conflicting pair are in perfect harmony from the beginning. But the whole of this comedy was written through the Word of God solely to resolve the age-long conflict. The cross is inevitably the *crux* of the *Commedia*.

With this solution of the perennial conflict between finite and infinite, is given potentially the solution of all rival claims. On every level the conflict formed by a pair of which the more heavenly or spiritual member, under the frailty of human conditions, tends to encroach on the territory of the more earthly member, receives ideal solution in their harmonization as autonomous in independent spheres. It will be noted, moreover, that those warring pairs which appear on a level pertaining to allegory stand out as distinct from all the rest. They have their places within the realm of history and are enacted in a sphere external to as well as internal to any individual self. The allegorical level of Dante's personal story has reference to the conflict between Guelph and Ghibelline. The three levels pertaining to the symbolism of Christ, which constitute the allegory of the whole of the personal order, refer to the conflicts between divine and human natures, church and state, theology and philosophy, all of which have their setting in history. Finally, in the order which follows as trope, after Dante's personal story and the allegory centering in Christ, the level which is allegorical has reference to the conflict between the suprarational and the rational, revelation and reason. Though they reflect conflicts which are historical, the remaining levels have their setting not in history, but within human minds: their pairs are Beatrice and Virgil,[23] human will and natural law, grace and effort, contemplation and action. If reference be made to the diagrammatic representation of symbolic levels[24]—or if the reader but write them out for himself, holding to the order of the fourfold method and recognizing that no spatial representation of the

23. As in the story of Christ the conflict was unique in that no disharmony existed within him, his effort being directed to restoring the cosmic harmony between divine and human; so in the personal story of Dante the conflict is unique. Beatrice and Virgil in themselves never conflict; it is within the arena of Dante's life that harmony must be made between his attitudes toward the one and toward the other.

24. Given p. 98.

anagoge is possible other than as a point, perhaps the apex of a pyramid the square base of which is made up by the spatial levels—it will be observed that these allegorical historical levels form a cross in the center of the square. They are thus marked as of special reference to the Incarnate Logos in whom is the meaning both of allegory and of history. The earthly life and suffering of Christ, perfectly presented in the cross, is both pattern for the solution of all conflicts and catastrophes and key to the symbolic pattern of the *Commedia*.

The pattern for the explication of the *Commedia* then becomes one in which all possible interpretations take their appointed places.[25] That it should be ninefold seems appropriate alike to Dante's honoring of Beatrice and to medieval thinking in regard to the sources of knowledge and the ways of knowing. Yet the aim of this study in so far as it relates to Dante has been no more to assert a new interpretation than to exhaust the infinite meaning of the *Commedia*, but simply to remind that according to the poet's own words it is only through multiplicity of interpretation that approach to the truth is gained. Any single line of reading unparalleled and uncorrected by many others marked by the same pattern is, like all fractional truths, pernicious. Yet, corrected by the pattern all must be included. By no other method than the polyseme could one in the intellectual

25. As was noted in the preface, a number of interpretations (e.g., the comedy as merely poetical fiction, as symbolizing Dante's political fortunes, his struggle with philosophy and religious faith, the history of church and empire, the moral development of the typical Christian) have been at one time or another suggested and partially elaborated. The elaboration has been undertaken, however, in the main apart from (1) consideration of the implications with which Dante's heritage had weighted the materials of his symbolism; (2) consideration of the method shaped by tradition to his use and employed by him with full intent—according to his own declaration; and (3) recognition of the unification of the multiplex whole dictated by the nature of the medieval search for knowledge. In consequence, (1) even the fundamental opposition of the trinities of light and darkness which forms the background for the entire drama, however interpreted, has been incorrectly grasped (cf. pp. 450 ff.) ; (2) the various interpretations have not been worked out as mutually corrective in a definite scheme and all essentially true at one and the same time; and (3) the triple strand of the mystic way has not been given its appropriate place in a pattern determined by the bases of the medieval quest for knowledge. In the development of such previously stressed factors as the above there has appeared, furthermore, as central in the whole multiplex pattern an interpretation overlooked in the past perhaps because so obvious, Dante as type of Christ, Logos, and Solar Radiance. Cf. p. 98.

tradition of the Middle Ages have hoped to bring "men from a state of misery to a state of bliss." Such was the verdict of centuries of philosophic conflict in a syncretism formed under the surveillance of the ideal of Roman citizenship by thought from all corners of the world.

VII. TERMINUS A QUO

STRANGELY was completed the *Comedy* of Dante Alighieri, through those stars so potent in his thought, which in the eyes of Beatrice and in the demonstrations of philosophy had inspired his journey and had marked the completion and the promise of each canticle of his vision. Frustrated at every turn and to the last an exile, though in contemplation of the Rose, Dante met his death among those who could see but scattered lights. Born under Gemini and the protection of Venus, on Good Friday entered on his crusade, he died under Virgo on the day of the Exaltation of the Holy Cross. As in his vision so in his life he had progressed from paler to truer symbol—from the symbol of Primal Love to the virgin symbol of Divine Power exercised in Mercy, from the foreshadowing of Christ in the divine-human Twins to the full revelation of the Logos in the exaltation of the fiery cross of the sun god.

Not only is the solar cross the pattern upon which Dante's ninefold drama is built, but upon the cross all the elements in his tradition depend. Through the cross of the Logos, in whom is the very existence of insight symbol, was won in the period of syncretism the triumph of the tradition that was to be medieval. In this cross is the solution of all personal problems, as through it is accomplished the union of the great materials of symbolism. Through the radiant Life lived beneath its shadow men were given the fourfold method for the solution of the problems of humanity whose prophets know the way of knowledge as the way of the cross. The cross is the mark of the knight on quest. Inevitably it impressed itself on the medieval comedy—cross against sun's disk yielding, in the poem which aimed to apprehend the whole, a ninefold pattern: nine which is number of the whole circumference and very self ("questo numero fue ella medesima") of Her who mediates the Courtly Love of Heaven;

a ninefold pattern to be interpreted by fourfold method, as the circumference itself is cut by the cross of the Logos.

Yet the vision of the cross was fraught with peril to all who gazed upon it with eyes unstrengthened by long gazing on the sun. Dazzled by its glory, even Constantine had erred, leaving humanity in a darkness which was to last a thousand years, till the coming of the five-hundred-ten-and-five. In this hard riddle, propounded by Beatrice, is perhaps cipher for Dante's title of dedication, *Dominus Kanis Victoriosissimus*,[26] given meaning through the ultimate truth "Deux Xristus Vincit, in hoc signo Dux."

The stars, Dante believed, in harmonious expression of the will of the Prime Mover, had arranged for Christ that he, the true Sun God, should be born at the winter solstice, and that his death should be accomplished, through the instrumentality of a legal symbol of the eternal Cross of the Heavens, at the vernal equinox the time of the solar sacrifice. Dante's own star-directed life from birth to death in its very natural setting marked him also as solar mediator. In the fictive passage through the center of the earth was shadowed forth the union and solution within the Threefold Light, Alpha and Omega, of those most antagonistic of all opposites, birth and death, the end and the beginning. The Poet of the Middle Ages, in life as in vision, passed from seedtime to the autumnal equinox of harvest and fruition, symbol of absence and return in accord with the circling of the spheres.

26. *Epistle* VIII (X), superscription.

APPENDICES

TYPES OF ASSOCIATION: DEFINING EXTRINSIC OR ARBITRARY-ASSOCIATION SYMBOL, AND INTRINSIC DESCRIPTIVE SYMBOL

ASSOCIATION may be arbitrary, a kind of shorthand, as is the case on the one hand with symbols of science and with literal language; and on the other hand with personifications, conventional symbols like insignia, and emblems. Whereas in the development of such emblems as are invested with a strong affective factor, perhaps the anchor for hope or the olive branch for peace, there is involved more than invention or arbitrary choice, yet fundamental are such mechanical laws of mind as depend on observation of contiguity and succession. The symbolism is dependent, not on intrinsic or objective similarity, but on extrinsic, often fortuitous association, although the association may be so deeply buried beneath consciousness and so heavily shrouded by emotional tone as to be scarcely distinguishable from similarity.[1]

When objection is made to the classification of emblems as arbitrary-association symbols, the reason is that frequently they are felt to have deep appropriateness and powerful emotional connotation. It is true that with the symbol which is purely an arbitrary sign[2] there is recognized no meaning except through previous agreement to understand by it some definite object or idea. Yet it should not be forgotten that although the artist may find in such a symbol as *epsilon* (ϵ) nothing to capture his imagination, to the mathematician it may hold the highest emotional content, as a result both of its associations since the time the mind of man first used it, and of the fact that it has become an emblem of that unique quantity of which the rate of change is equal to itself, on which the harmony of all natural law depends. Here is a real likeness to those emblems which because of the wealth of their traditional associations or the nobility of that which they denote have great emotional and pictorial value. It remains true, however, with all these symbols that, although they may give atmosphere, they are not intrinsically descriptive. In spite of the subjective nature of all emotional connotations, there is an obvious distinction between the symbolism involved when a sensation or an element of sense data is brought into fortuitous relation with a personal emotion, and that involved when two objects of sense data are compared because of likeness between them. For example, white lilacs and calla lilies have become associated with funerals in the experience of some persons in such a way as of themselves to arouse all the emotions connected with death and grief.[3]

---

1. The much-discussed dream symbols of psychoanalysis are frequently of this type, although many depend rather on an objective similarity.

2. It has been said of such symbols: "None of these symbols attempt to produce the original, or have any other meaning than to suggest it. They are signs which have meaning because we agree to understand them beforehand."

3. Here the emotion has attached to itself external objects fortuitously present, but not essentially related to it. Ribot has pointed out that "Joy, sadness, love,

In brief, then, even though at first sight it may seem anomalous to class emblems with the symbols of mathematics and science, yet in reality their origins and their functions within their respective spheres are similar. Arbitrary-association symbolism is to be distinguished by its basis, which is extrinsic, and by its aim and function[4] which are apt representation, or expression of *multum in parvo,* rather than descriptive enhancement of either symbol or symbolized.

When, on the other hand, the aim and function is enhancement of that which is symbolized, through a comparison of qualities, to give vividness and individuality,[5] the symbol is to be classed as comparative or descriptive. Basic to the association will be such laws as depend on the observation of similarity and contrast. Here the literary device is typical. The artist uses comparison or descriptive symbol when his interest is in some datum of experience for its own sake, and his desire to communicate his impression of it. Obviously the reality which is described is thought of as being less great, less true in kind (even if not intrinsically) than the figure which is to enhance it. In calling a man a tiger, the intention is to enhance the impression of his ferocity. Although intrinsically superior to the tiger, the man is not greater in tigerhood, he is not a supertiger. Thus, the reality described is less great in kind: the meaning above is neither that the man has all the qualities of the tiger nor that he surpasses the tiger in ferocity. Descriptive symbols have then as basis, an intrinsic likeness rendering possible a comparison, and as aim, the description of something else for the purpose of its enhancement or adornment.

ALTHOUGH objects appearing commonly in these two classes may themselves become or suggest interpretative symbols (see text, pp. 6 ff.), the distinction between them is definite. For example, the sail in ancient watermarks is properly emblem (arbitrary-association symbol) of the Holy Spirit, through its association with the wind.[6] The wind, however,

---

hatred, surprise, boredom, pride, fatigue, etc., can each become a center of attraction, grouping representations or events which are devoid of any intellectual interconnexion, but which have the same emotional tinge,—joyful, melancholy, erotic, etc." Ribot, *Essai sur l'imagination créatrice,* 1900, p. 31.

Very different from this is the description of a lady's eyes by comparison with the blue of the sky, or of her lips by the red of the rose. If an emblem is discovered to have a real similarity to that which it signifies, then it really is a descriptive or an interpretative symbol.

4. The fact that many symbols now used conventionally or even arbitrarily, had originally another significance, is irrelevant, since in present usage the aim is that of this class.

5. Johnson says: "A simile to be perfect must both illustrate and ennoble its subject; must show it to the understanding in a clearer view, and display it to the fancy with greater dignity; but either of these qualities may be sufficient to recommend it."

6. Cf. Harold Bayley, *The Lost Language of Symbolism.*

is an interpretative symbol of the Holy Spirit, due to such similarity as that expressed in the Fourth Gospel: "The wind bloweth where it listeth, and thou hearest the sound thereof, but canst not tell whence it cometh, and whither it goeth: so is every one that is born of the Spirit." Thus, interpretative symbol, like descriptive symbol, is distinguished from arbitrary symbol by the existence of an intrinsic and objective similarity.[7a]

7a. Brief study of dictionary definitions of symbol brings out these same three types. Of dictionaries, the *New English* (Murray's) is the most thorough in its presentation of definitions of symbol, and although all of the other important dictionaries have been consulted, in them were found no valuable additions to the definitions there listed:

I. (a) "A formal authoritative statement or summary of the religious belief of the Christian church, or of a particular church or sect; a creed or confession of faith."

   (b) "A brief or sententious statement; a formula, motto, maxim; occas. a summary, synopsis." (Obsolete.)

Brief analysis will show that symbol, even in this restricted usage, can be discussed according to the classification just given. (For example, the Creed may be either an arbitrary association symbol in the sense of a coat of arms or standard, or insight symbol in that it is considered the most adequate verbal symbol of an inexpressible reality.)

II. (a) "Something that stands for, represents, or denotes something else (not by exact resemblance, but by vague suggestion, or by some accidental or conventional relation); esp. a material object representing or taken to represent something immaterial or abstract, as a being, idea, quality, or condition; a representative or typical figure, sign, or token; occas. a type (of some quality)."

   (b) "An object representing something sacred; spec. (absol.) either of the elements in the eucharist, as representing the body and blood of Christ."

   (c) "A small device on a coin, additional to and usually independent of the main device or 'type.'"

   (d) "Symbols collectively; symbolisms (rare)."

In this definition is included meanings of symbol belonging to three classifications. In (b), an object representing something sacred is properly insight symbol (specifically, in Catholic usage it differs from other symbols by conveying that which it symbolizes, and in Protestant usage it differs from other symbols by its use in connection with sacred service).

III. (a) "A written character or mark used to represent something; a letter, figure, or sign conventionally standing for some object, process, etc."

Such symbols as the letters of the alphabet, arabic or Roman numerals, astrological signs of the planets, characters denoting chemical elements and compounds, characters denoting operations and quantities in chemistry or in mathematics, characters denoting the faces of a crystal, letters as used in algebra, dots and dashes in the Morse code, etc., are obviously arbitrary-association symbols, although not necessarily so in origin. But cf., e.g., pp. 326, 470, Chap. VI, iv, Appendices V, Pt. I, i and ii (2).

Allegory, as defined by the *New English Dictionary*, is:

I. "Description of a subject under the guise of some other subject of aptly suggestive resemblance."

II. "An instance of such description, a figurative sentence, discourse, or narra-

When experience of a physical object has suggested a suitable comparison through which to describe it, comparison symbol is used. On the other hand, insight symbol is employed when the physical object[7b] has suggested something larger and more abstract which that object may help to express. For example, the sight of a river may suggest description of it as a silvery ribbon flung across the green tapestry of the countryside; or, on the other hand, use of it to express man's life flowing like a river from its source to its known yet unknown end. That is, a river may be described by a lesser object such as a ribbon (which still may be superior in the quality compared) ; or it may be used to express a deeper meaning in such a way that it becomes a symbol of that meaning. In the first instance it is comparison symbol, in the second it is interpretative.

---

tive, in which properties and circumstances attributed to the apparent subject really refer to the subject they are meant to suggest; an extended or continued metaphor."

III. "An allegorical representation, an emblem."

Although the mark of the allegory may be suggestiveness of resemblance (as in definition I), it may be purely conventional (as in definition III). Allegory as in these definitions, according to the present classification may be of any one of the three types, having as distinguishing mark chiefly the narrative or time element. The dictionary includes, indeed, examples of allegory used in each of the three ways. Cf. also p. 500.

7b. In this discussion there is made no such arbitrary distinction as that (cf. Webber, *Church Symbolism,* pp. 243-244) of confining the word "symbol" to "animals, birds, and inanimate objects" and using the word "symbolic types" when human beings are in question. In the broad sense an insight symbol is any physical object, living being, or event which is used to convey a deeper meaning. Within this general field, however, is a twofold division. A symbol is called a *type* when it gains its symbolic value from some event, historical or supposedly historical (roughly scriptural vs. natural). Types are almost but not quite invariably human beings, since history deals in the main with the deeds and fortunes of human beings. (Cf. pp. 288-291 and n. 149.) Symbols which gain their symbolic value from their nature and invariable activities (e.g., the sun in its daily and yearly cycles, gems with their distinctive properties, animals with their customary habits) are not called types. The author quoted actually uses the terms in these senses rather than according to the distinction stated formally in his book. For example, he states twice that the brazen serpent uplifted upon a tau cross in the wilderness is a "type" of the crucifixion (*op. cit.,* pp. 61, 104). Thus, although types are usually human beings, yet animals and inanimate objects are termed types whenever the symbolic value is connected with a definite event rather than with nature and recurring activities. Similarly symbols which are not types are usually animals or inanimate objects, yet the human body and certain of its parts when used as symbols belong to the non-typical class.

APPENDIX I, iii.

THEORIES AS TO SYMBOLIC CONTENT OF MYTHUS

WHILE a world soberly literal, desiccated by rationalism, was being refreshed by romanticism with its exuberant imagery, and while at the same time conservative minds were holding tenaciously to the literal Bible and a worship purged of idolatrous admixtures, a significant discussion was in progress. Paralleling the philosophic preoccupation with epistemology, was a renewed interest in the source of religious knowledge. Did the beginnings of non-Christian religion lie, as had been understood from St. Paul, in an original and later perverted revelation, or did they lie in the struggle of primitive man toward knowledge and expression of life experience? The first position was taken by such men as Jacob Bryant in England and Creuzer in Germany. On the other hand, scientific and historic foundation was given to the study of mythology by C. Ottfried Müller.[8] As the adherents of the naturalistic interpretation gained standing, comparative religion, gradually established with a scientific basis, became bold enough to include within the field of its investigation Christianity itself.

Interest soon centered on the irrational aspects of myths, such as the immoral and zoömorphic elements.[9] A number of suggestions as to their origin were offered, many of them echoing theories propounded centuries before. Among these, Euhemerism, a theory of some two thousand years' standing, won great popularity[10] and éclat for its daring and novelty. It seemed logical that the gods should have been originally folk kings and heroes.[11] Unfortunately, this theory fails to answer the real question as to the origin of the irrational elements in the stories gathered about them.[12] The Euhemerist obviously is right in identifying the central figure of the greatest of modern mythical cycles, the Arthuriad, with the petty Celtic chieftain who defended the Welsh fastnesses against the oncoming Anglo-Saxons. The question remains whence came the Grail, Merlin, Morgan le Fay, the ship of Solomon, and many other elements[13] which, whatever their ultimate origin, are known to

---

8. C. O. Müller, *Introduction to a Scientific System of Mythology*. The English translation appeared in London in 1884.

9. It seemed incredible that, unless the hypothesis of a period of insanity of the whole race were to be admitted, peoples could have connected with the beings for whom they felt the highest reverence the forms of even the lowest animals, and immoral acts which would have been censured in any individual. Thus the problem as to the source of Jupiter's love affairs, as well as of the animal forms of Osiris or of Pasht, became acute.

10. It had indeed been popular in the early Middle Ages. St. Cyprian, for example, assumed the king origin of gods.

11. By a kind of extension of this theory, some modern criticism treats folk heroes and leaders as symbolizing tribal groups and movements.

12. "The euhemerists, as Cox expresses it, have rationalized Jack the Giant Killer by leaving out the giants; and have thrown away good myth to obtain bad history." F. C. Prescott, *Poetry and Myth* (New York: Macmillan [1927]), p. 96.

13. These factors scholars like Lang derive from a stage of culture in which

antedate the historical Arthur. Stories that gather around a popular hero present an almost universal similarity of incident and outline.[14]

The other theories agree in treating of myth as symbol and close to the origin of symbolism, regarding it as representative of man's earliest attempt at expression of his experience in the endeavor to find beneath it some fundamental truth.[15] There is, however, disagreement as to whether in myth is symbol of physical experience or of an imagined deeper reality glimpsed through it. On the one hand, myth has been thought to symbolize facts observed about the physical universe, such as the behavior of sun, water, winds, and the like, or the more or less conscious impulses of man, such as his nutritional and reproductive desires.[16] On the other hand, myth has been thought to symbolize crude explanations of the origin and development of the universe; or human moral and social struggles; or the psychic and dream life, including intuitions as to life after death; or finally that ill-defined body of experience which is termed mystical.[17] Sponsors of these two groups of symbolic theories have little patience with one another. A myth for them must represent *either* the material experience *or* the philosophical or religious abstraction,[18] that is, its basis must be in arbitrary or descriptive symbolism. These theories have been criticized as crediting the savage with more intellectual curiosity than anthropological study warrants. Myth, therefore, is regarded as formulating legal charters, expressing or justifying social organization, and directing coöperative enterprise.[19] The medieval thinker was spared all such conflict. In accord with his understanding of symbolism and his use of it as interpretative of reality, since every element in man's physical and social experience, whether of the surrounding world or of himself, is symbolic of the infinity underlying all experience, myth is as it were a symbol of the second order: it is man-made expression of an experience, itself by hy-

---

their rationality was taken for granted. Indeed, the assumption is made that the primitive mind works on different principles from the modern, and psychopathologists are at present pointing out similarities between the thought processes of the mentally diseased and those belonging to the so-called "pre-logical level" of primitive man. Cf., for example, Levy-Bruhl, *Primitive Mentality,* and Alfred Storch, *Primitive Archaic Forms of Inner Experience and Thought in Schizophrenia.* Even this as an explanation simply pushes the problem a step farther back.

14. Cf. pp. 108 ff. 15. Cf. pp. 15 ff., 106 ff., 243 ff.

16. Compare such writers as (a) Cox, Nicole; (b) Goldsmith, Freud, Storfer, Crawley. The subject is treated in sec. iv of Chap. I.

17. Compare such writers as (a) Max Müller; (b) Durkheim; (c) Lang, Wallis; and (d) Marie.

18. Although an occasional psychologist has gone so far as to assert that a dream symbol may be at the same time a wish fulfilment and a serious attempt to solve a moral problem. For example, van der Hoop.

19. Theory of Bronislaw Malinowski. It should be noted that not all symbolic theories imply intellectual curiosity or "armchair activity" on the part of the savage.

pothesis symbolic of fundamental truth. Myth thus represents *both* the material *and* the philosophic or religious fact. This fact should be borne in mind by the student of medieval thought.

Closely related to those theories which agree in treating of myth as symbol was the philological hypothesis which gained considerable prominence in the nineteenth century, and is popularly expressed: "A world grown grey has learned to regard the gods as diseases of language, conceived it may be in fevers of fancy, perhaps originally they were but deified words."[20] Lang has given a summary: "People had originally said something quite sensible—so the hypothesis runs—but when their descendants forgot the meaning of their remarks, a new and absurd meaning followed from a series of unconscious puns." Basic to philological theories is the well-known fact that the physical (including verbal) embodiment of an idea or emotion lasts longer than the meaning originally conveyed. It has been said that a general idea becomes stable in the word which symbolizes it. This stability is, however, relatively transient. Indeed, the word serves a little as a portfolio, which succeeding generations choose to employ as covering for ever changing material.

Critical discussion of this last theory brings in a further implication in the definition of insight symbolism as opposed to symbolisms of the other two types. In myth regarded as insight symbol there is represented not only both the material and the philosophical or religious fact, but also a definite relationship between them in a universal pattern. For this reason, although the word be considered but a portfolio which succeeding generations choose to employ as covering for ever changing material, there is a perfectly definite evolution governing the materials so included. As a result there is never falsification, but always inclusion and fuller elucidation of earlier meanings. If, on the other hand, myth be regarded as fundamentally arbitrary or comparison symbol in contradistinction to insight symbol, such is not the case. This is the second point to be borne in mind by the student of the medieval symbolic tradition for which the handling of its heritage in mythus constituted a major problem.

---

20. Edgar Saltus, *Lords of the Ghostland* (New York: Brentano's, 1922), p. 7.

COMPARISON OF MEDIEVAL AND MODERN ASTRONOMICAL SYSTEMS[1]

	Actually Seen	Apparent Motions	Medieval Explanation	Modern Explanation
THE SKY	Daily revolution, noticeable only at night.	East to West in 24 hours.	Rapid revolution of great sphere, the Primum Mobile, around earth.	Daily rotation of earth on its axis.
FIXED STARS	No apparent change other than above; records show slow retrograde motion.	East to West 24 hours. West to East in 36,000 years.	Sphere containing stars fails completely to follow Primum Mobile; a lag or W. to E. motion.	Precession of the equinoxes: motion of solar system among stars.
ZODIAC (The "signs" are star groups within zodiac.)	Sun, moon and planets move among stars, but always within a belt extending from 8° north to 8° south of the ecliptic. Ecliptic forms angle of 23° with celestial equator.	Winter solstice sun 23° south. Vernal equinox sun on equator. Summer solstice sun 23° north. Autumn equinox sun on equator.	Sun, moon, planets, each fixed on a sphere. Spheres fail completely to follow P.M. around earth: lag more than stars: motion vs. star background.	Revolution of earth and planets. Sun changes apparent direction. Orbit of earth inclined to that of sun 23°.
SATURN	Changes position in reference to the fixed stars.	East to West 24 hours. West to East in 40 years.	Lag of sphere next within that of the stars (around earth).	Revolution of Saturn around sun in 40 years.
JUPITER	As above.	East to West 24 hours. West to East in 12 years.	Lag of sphere next within that of Saturn (around earth).	Revolution of Jupiter around sun in 12 years.
MARS	As above.	East to West 24 hours. West to East in 2 years.	Lag of sphere next within that of Jupiter (around earth).	Revolution of Mars around sun in 2 years.
SUN	As above.	East to West 24 hours. West to East 1 year.	Lag of sphere next within that of Mars.	Revolution of earth around sun in 1 year.
VENUS MERCURY	As above, but always within 45° of sun,[2] being either Evening or Morning Stars.	West to East 7 months. West to East 3 months.	Lag of spheres within that of Sun. Motion of planet on epicycle upon sphere.	Revolution around sun with orbits within that of earth.
MOON	"Rises" nearly one hour later each night and near different stars.	East to West 24 hours. West to East 28 days.	Lag of sphere next within that of Mercury (motion around earth).	Revolution of moon around earth in 28 days.

1. For purposes of calculation, accurate results can be obtained with either system. The numbers in the above table are approximate only.

Fresh insight into the apparent behavior of the heavenly bodies in the detail with which it was analyzed in medieval times may be gained from the *Elementa astronomica* of Alfraganus, which Dr. Moore among others has stated to have been Dante's chief astronomical source. Of its thirty chapters, four are occupied with the spherical shape of heavens and earth, the centrality and minuteness of the earth, and the dual motion of the stars, all of which every twenty-four hours, are carried in a complete east to west revolution by the heavens, in regard to which they nevertheless slowly recede west to east. Another six chapters are concerned with the "climates" of the habitable earth, and with the relation of the length of day and night to the time of year and the distance from the equator (discussed by Dante in *Convivio,* 3, Chap. V, where it is of interest that he names the poles *Mary* and *Lucia*). The next seven chapters deal with the eight spheres (the earth is the strict center only of the eighth sphere—fixed stars —the others being slightly eccentric) ; and with the special motions of the stars. The longitudinal (east-west) motions of sun, moon, and fixed stars are first considered, then that of the five "wandering stars" (that is, planets)..This involves an analysis of the meaning of the occasional backward (retrograde) motion of the planets in respect to the Signs of the Zodiac. One chapter deals with the latitudinal (north-south) motions of sun, moon, fixed and wandering stars.

The succeeding chapter lists the fifteen stars of greatest magnitude by their Arabic names, and states that the total number of stars is 1022. The next lists the division of the zodiacal circle into twenty-eight "houses of the moon," favored by the Arabs; after which two chapters deal with the size and distance from the earth of the heavenly bodies, and the next with rising, setting, and passage of the meridian. Further subjects for consideration are the "occultation" of stars by the rays of the sun; the waxing and waning periods of the moon; the "conjunctions" of planets with the sun; and the correction to be made in relation to eccentricity of the inner spheres. The final three chapters deal with eclipses of moon and of sun, and of the length of time elapsing between eclipses. This treatment, although untrue as to basic scheme in space, is far more detailed as to the appearances, the data on which astronomical knowledge is founded, than is the (schematically truer) knowledge possessed by the modern non-astronomical student.

Cf. Alfraganus, *Il 'libro dell' aggregazione delle stelle.*

2. Mercury is seldom visible, since always within 25° of the sun and therefore obscured by its light. Cf. *Par.,* v, 129.

MATERIALS OF SYMBOLISM AS THEY VARY IN THE TRADITIONS
OF AGRICULTURAL AND NOMADIC PEOPLES

THE wide prevalence of solar imagery indicated in Chapter III is less evident to the student of comparative mythology than at first thought one would expect, and has been subjected frequently to well-warranted questionings.[1] The situation of the inquirer into problems of symbology resembles that of the explorer in a forest which is sometimes a dense jungle. That which first demands his attention is the varied foliage and fruit, and the scarcely less varied types of growth. Moreover, that which is first explained to him by the native, at home in the forest, relates likewise to this luxuriant overgrowth. The very character of solar symbolism, as root and life of lesser imageries, results in its obscuring of itself.

Just as few Christians are conscious of the solar implications of their religion,[2] not merely as origin away from which it has developed, but as the unifying power which has ordered its ritual and made possible its most philosophical conceptions, so it is frequently with the savage. This was expressed effectively by a modern writer of fiction, in a conversation between a maiden educated by a Mayan priest, and a youth of the Church of England. The latter, with a keen sense of his religious superiority, questions her as to whether the sun, which plays such a rôle in the religion of the Mayans, forms also a large part of her own religion. Her response is simply to assert that the sun plays a large part in the religion of everybody, and to refer him to his prayer book, especially in regard to the time of Easter.[3]

Man has hesitated to leave records of the deepest probings of his thought into the mystery of reality, just as he has been loath to name God in anything but vaguely suggestive code. He has been more free in the handling of superficial symbolisms. This quality of the human mind has complicated the task, not only of him who would penetrate below the horizon of history, but also of the student of primitive tribes today. The alien will tell first the exceptions, not the rule, in his religious life, and superficialities of his symbolism rather than its abiding presuppositions.[4] Not only this, but as has appeared already minds of

---

1. "The worship of the sun has been by no means so widely diffused among primitive peoples, as on purely abstract grounds, we might at first sight be tempted to suppose." Sir J. G. Frazer, *Worship of Nature,* I, 441.

2. Cf. Chap. III, Pt. I, iii, also Chap. VI, i.

3. As the story proceeds, the youth, for the first time in his life, and in a tense situation, being required to spend a whole night out of doors in complete darkness, discovers deep within his own nature the significance of solar worship. Just before dawn, he hears "loud cries and chantings and intoned prayers . . . to let the sun rise once more. Light, light, the universal cry—the cry that a short time since had almost broken from his own lips." From Alice Duer Miller, "Sunrise," in *Saturday Evening Post,* March 27, April 3, and April 10, 1926.

4. One may wonder how true an idea of the deeper presuppositions and phi-

lesser grasp will worship creatures near at hand, which their instinct and their leaders have made precious through some pale analogy to, or symbolic representation of, great truths in the fundamental mystery. Although conscious that such mystery exists, it is for them either inexpressible or axiomatic. True apprehension and use of sun symbolism demand sufficient mentality to desire and to attempt a real unification of experience. Sir J. G. Frazer has well said:

> Whatever the reason may be, a solar religion appears to flourish best among nations which have attained to a certain degree of civilization, such as the ancient Egyptians, and the Indians of Mexico and Peru at the time when they were discovered by the Spaniards. . . . A higher degree of intelligence is needed to ask whence comes the marvellous uniformity of those operations of nature whereof the courses of the heavenly bodies are at once the most easily observable and the most splendid examples.[5]

Many attempts have been made, during the conflict of the sun-sex hypotheses, to broaden each by giving as its basis in the external world the whole firmament in its motion rather than simply the sun, and in man's inner experience all of his fundamental instincts rather than sex alone. The fact still remains that the sun seems to be the most appealing center for the organization of external experience, and similarly, although hunger and self-preservation may be the more fundamental, these are more frequently in imagination associated with and subordinated to sex, than given the primary position.

Whatever be the reasons, even where in the mythology the god of the heavens is recognized as ultimate,[6] and the sun god is but one

---

losophy of the Christian religion was obtained by the Chinese student who, on his visit to a Christian chapel service, asked of a chance worshiper the meaning of the song to "God's little goat" (O Lamb of God, I come). Through its habit of proselytizing, Christianity has acquired in the matter of self-expression a decided advantage over primitive religions; yet it is fairly safe to assume that the Chinese inquirer from the minister himself would receive but a dissertation on ethics, or an admonition to model his life on the noblest life ever lived on earth, instead of an answer to his real question as to what Christians thought to be the nature of the universe and the meaning of existence. Were Christians now as little able to voice abstract and exact spiritual concepts as was man in the early days of civilization, one hesitates to conceive the travesty of religion which this inquirer might have presented to his people as the result of his researches into goat worship among Christians. Mr. Kipling, in *Kim*, has given an illustration of such a misunderstanding, in the meeting of the saintly Tibetan lama with two British clergymen. One of these ministers of God was trained in symbolisms, and understood the significance of the lama's search for a river that should wash away sins; yet the other, able to see in it nothing but insanity or imposture, desired to have him put under guard.

5. Frazer, *op. cit.*, I, 441-442. Cf. Renan's statement. "Before religion had reached the stage of proclaiming that God must be put into the absolute and ideal, that is to say, beyond this world, one worship alone was reasonable and scientific: that was the worship of the sun." Renan, *Dialogues et fragments philosophiques,* translated in Jung, *Psychology of the Unconscious,* p. 501.

6. Cf. Ouranos and Dyaus pitar. Not infrequently descriptions of a god leave

among many children, he is the fated child, and invariably accedes to power. Sometimes he is the favorite son, the only son, the chosen representative of the gods,[7] and sometimes by continuous access of strength he at last slays his father and usurps his throne—indeed, not merely his throne, but his personality. The tendency has been to regard the revolving firmament as the dwelling of the god rather than as itself a more fundamental entity. The god is more likely to be a hero represented by the sun, dwelling in a great house, the sky (which, during his absence at night, revolves, since the apparent motion of the heavens is visible at night), than to be represented by the overarching sky itself.

Study of the origin of religions, however, reveals facts which in this connection are significant. Among nomadic peoples, the sky father and earth mother[8] are more likely to appear dominant. Among herdsmen and hunters, frequently abroad at night, it is the cosmic phenomena of storm and sunshine, fair weather and foul, and the motion of the heavens visible at night, which claims most attention, making possible consideration of the sun-storm combination as expression of the sky god himself. Night and winter for the hunter are not, as for the agriculturist, times of enforced idleness and dependence on the harvest of the preceding summer, but conditions favorable to his livelihood. Certain animals are abroad only at night. Conditions of storm unfavorable to the agriculturist are favorable to the fisherman. Winter is the time for trapping, and its storms may facilitate the capture of animals. It is of significance that these peoples are slow to develop a refined or philosophical conception of immortality, while in their thinking there persists tension between the one and the many, leading to duality with but very late solution in ideas of trinity.[9] The supreme example lies in Hebrew monotheism, with its tardy reconciliation of its ideas in regard to individual and national continuance of life. Although even here sun symbol is frequent, it but late becomes important in unification.

On the other hand, agricultural tribes whose attention follows eagerly the changing seasons and their relation to seedtime and harvest soon feel the power of the dramatic career of the Lord of the Heavens, and advance quickly from fanciful tales of quest and rebirth to an increas-

---

one at a loss as to whether he is sky god or sun god. For example, many of the terms applied to Zeus, on which Mr. A. B. Cook relies to establish his identity as sky god, seem even more naturally to apply to a sun god. (Name "Bright One" from root meaning to shine, term "rays of Zeus" for light of day, etc. Cf. A. B. Cook, *Zeus, a Study in Ancient Religion,* pp. 1-68.)

7. For example, Marduk, to whose election as representative of the gods reference has been made, was called "firstborn son," "only-begotten," and "only Son." Mithra and Vishnu-Krishna are other examples. It is invariably these sun gods who become saviors or incarnate.

8. For example, the first ceremonial painting of the main rite of the Navajo (Mountain Chant) represents Sky-Father and Earth-Mother as the begetter of all things.

9. Cf. pp. 118 ff.

ingly abstract conception of eternal life. As thought progresses toward definition, the sun appears as giver of life on earth (realized first perhaps in connection with the growth and ripening of fruit, but soon generalized), giver of light which makes possible all noble activity, and source of heat, associated with which there is an element both of beneficence and malignity as in the storm aspect are both the beneficence of life-giving rain and the terror of the lightning flash. Consideration of the sun both in his nature and in his career shows him to be lord of vegetation, lord of storm, and lord of the underworld itself. Through the manifold nature and career of this glorious being, man finds the supreme expression of his every experience. While the worshiper of the sky god must wander in the wilderness of polytheism, able only through wearing discipline to preserve the supremacy of the unity, the worshiper of the sun god finds taken up into his deity all the creatures of which humanity has stood in awe, as well as all the human heroes whom it has worshiped. With him, the inevitable process of apotheosis leads not to a devastating polytheism, but to a constructive theory of the god's incarnation for the sake of men, as the *one* in its struggle against the *many* readily finds solution even of duality, through the solar trinity.[10]

For all the stable grandeur of the skies, the sun exhibits a persistent vitality far more potent to supply dynamic in the thought of man.[11] Meditation limited to the overarching heavens may well supply such impetus to living as is demanded by the rock on the hillside, but man has found his life harrowingly subject to sudden change, too stirring a vibration between comedy and tragedy, not to seek a more dramatic inspiration for his living. Though he find necessary, likewise, such stability as characterizes the heavens, he finds its values in the character of the usurper sun, through the development of some such concept as that of Ananke, the inevitable destiny (that power which holds the sun to his course),[12] or through the unity back of the trinity in the sun's nature. There would appear, then, to be truth both in Cox's observation that the deities of the wandering Semites were cosmical, whereas those of the more settled Aryans had been phenomenal, and in Nicole's assertion that the sun myth is basic both in Aryan and Semitic religions.[13]

For man's first differentiation of the indefinite heterogeneous homogeneity of his experience, sun or sky may equally well assume power over the multitudinous demons of the natural world—which one will become central in his thought may depend on the manner of his life. In the general rendering coherent of life experience, that is, in the progress toward definite homogeneous heterogeneity, philosophic thought de-

---

10. Cf. Chap. III, Pt. I, iii, Chap. IV, Pt. I, i.
11. Cf. the myth pattern, discussed on pp. 108 ff.
12. Cf. Cox, *op. cit.*, p. 123.
13. Nicole states that JHVH is an old god with the attributes of other gods added. Among all the rest, he is the god of light.

mands some unification of the values of both of these. To this fact the gradual usurpation by the sun god of the throne of his father and the inclusion within himself of the strongest elements in the sky god's personality, bear witness, as does the unanimous development of trinities by each of the great cultural traditions.

Among the Hindus the great impersonal god of the skies was Brahma and the gloriously personal god of the sun was Vishnu. Yet there was demanded a religion which contained the possibility of becoming general, the trinity of Brahma-Vishnu-Siva, while an ultimate Brahma remained in the background as a symbol of the all-pervading unity.[14] Similar has been the development of all of the great ethnic trinities.

Similar facts are to be noted in the development of sex symbolism, the complement of solar symbolism. That which becomes most deeply impressed upon the mind of the nomad is veneration not of fertility, but of the power of killing. His livelihood depends not on giving life, but on taking it. Plants and animals breed by themselves. Some years there are plenty, some years not enough, but to this very day, it never occurs to the primitive hunter to regulate the supply by breeding and care.[15] Moreover, in the human community that which is demanded is men of warlike temper, hardy and keen to kill. Women become temptations only too likely to sap man's strength, leaving him unprepared for the moment of sudden danger. Their social position is thus one of degradation, unless, as frequently becomes the custom with the progress of culture, they are vowed to virginity to tend the sacred fires of the war god.[16] God comes to be revered not as creator and life giver, but as mighty Ruler and dealer of death—the Lord, the Lord of Hosts is his name.

When such nomadic tribes as the Beni Israel are brought into contact with agricultural peoples in a fertile land, the sudden shock to their moral code finds immediate expression in the attempt to exterminate these depraved and effeminate worshipers of fertility. As a matter of fact, just as the hunter to live must kill, the agriculturist to live must give life, and his highest ideal becomes that of fertility in regard to plant, animal, and the human family itself. His deity becomes the Life Giver, frequently in female form (cf. the Great Mother, and other goddesses of fertility). Since woman with her lure to the fulfilment of sex desire and her nourishment of the child both before and after birth,

---

14. Cf. Paine, *Ethnic Trinities;* R. E. Hume, lecture at Union Theological Seminary.

15. The pastoral stage of herd keeping is a transition from hunting to agricultural life, and contains elements of both.

16. For example, the Vestal Virgins of Rome, vowed to the service of the sacred flame of Mars. Even among Indians, the Sun Dance is formally initiated by a woman who must be a virgin, and who, if proved not to be such, is slain by the warriors for polluting a religious ceremony.

becomes the embodiment of the ideal on which all life depends, religion urges not to virginity, but to fruitfulness.[17] Its symbolisms become those not of cataclysm, but of generation, in which connection the generative organs themselves, endowed with apparently independent life, become the objects of special veneration. Their association is not with weakness and effeminacy, but with strength and prosperity; not with pleasure and sin, but with the mysterious power of life incarnate in them. The advent of the nomad with his keenness for death and his morbid perversion in regard to the mysterious source of life, can be regarded by the worshiper of fertility as nothing less than demoniacal. As a matter of fact, a different sex code on the part of either agriculturist or nomad, without a corresponding change in life conditions, would threaten the extinction of the race.

Out of the conflict of the two, however, may be born the love ideal, as it was for Israel, tenderly loved bride of the great JHVH. Whereas with the agriculturist the tendency was to stop with the fact of fertility, the nomad, still horrified by such an attitude, developed none the less a sex ideal, characterized in his case by the devotion and companionship of man and woman.

In the medieval tradition, the compromise between agriculturist and nomad wrought in the period of syncretism, found expression in solar symbolism dominated by the attitude of the agriculturist and sex symbolism dominated by the attitude of the nomad, each ultimately enriched and given balance, beneath the levels of conscious thinking, by the opposing ideal. Such were the materials of symbolism out of which Dante wrought his ideal of the love of the Court of Heaven. In the learned tradition of the Middle Ages, the symbolism of sex is readily considered as the sublimated complement of the symbolism of the sun. Only in hidden byways lurked the magician and the witch, terrible and tragic reminders of the agricultural insistence on the sacredness of fertility,[18] in a society dominated by the Lords of War.

---

17. Cf. the discussion on this whole matter in John Langdon-Davies, *A Short History of Women*, New York, 1927. He tells of a savage tribe, for example, who, when asked by a missionary for a word for *Virgin*, to use in the translation of the Gospel into their language, suggested *Nolumba*, which means a woman who has lost her characteristic virtue. The natives were "quite incapable of imagining that 'virgin' could be anything but an opprobrious epithet; the great god Bunzi believes too strongly in the virtue of fruitfulness." *Op. cit.,* p. 111.

18. As Payne-Knight, in the nineteenth century, and Miss M. A. Murray, more recently, have shown, the worship of the generative powers in the Middle Ages, though furtive, had considerable vigor. Statues of priapus are to be found at Aix, Nîmes, etc. In Martene and Durand, *Vet. scrip. ampl. coll.,* t. 7, p. 35, is printed an eighth-century ecclesiastical tract against incantations before the fascinum (phallus). Adam of Bremen, eleventh century, relates that the Teutonic Freya was represented in Upsala with an immense priapus.

For a discussion of the witch cult, viewed as an organized religion of the worship of fertility, cf. Margaret A. Murray, *The Witch Cult in Western Europe.*

APPENDIX IV, Pt. I, i.

BASIS OF SYMBOLISM IN FUNCTIONAL TRUTH OF LETTER

FOR all the unanimity with which insight symbolism came to be sponsored in different schools of thought, it became subject of bitterest controversy as a result of a misunderstanding which has persisted to the present day. The assumption was made by those alien to the development of the philosophy of insight symbolism[1] that in the matter of interpretation only two possibilities existed, those two possibilities being diametrically opposed. Either the literal truth is absolute, exact in itself, and of sole importance, or the literal sense is a deliberate veil for hidden meanings. It cannot be too frequently reiterated that these to the insight symbolist[2] are not oppositions, but two aspects of one truth. The literal sense, even though true, can never be exact and adequate in itself, and similarly it must always be a medium through which deeper meanings may be perceived.

"The eyes of the Lord run to and fro throughout the whole earth."[3] "His hand is stretched out still."[4] "The Lord hath his way in the whirlwind and in the storm, and the clouds are the dust of his feet."[5] Thinking men were not so naïve as to believe the infinite prime mover of the universe actually possessed eyes, hands, and feet as men were familiar with eyes, hands, and feet. Even greater *naïveté* would be required of him who would interpret literally the Greek religious myth.[6] The most literal-minded of theologians hastens to explain that "hands, feet, arms, eyes," and other physical organs as referred to Deity, are figures not to be taken as literally true. On the other hand the symbolist declares them to be not figures literally untrue, but figures conveying the supreme truth of analogy.[7] Analogies, moreover, are defined by the symbolist in

---

1. For the relationship of insight symbolism to the personification type of allegory of which Bunyan's *Pilgrim's Progress* and *Holy War* are the household examples, cf. pp. 278 ff.

2. Cf. Appendix I, ii.   3. II Chron. 16. 9, and Zech. 4. 10.

4. Isa. 5. 25; 9. 12; 10. 4; 14. 27.   5. Nah. 1. 3.

6. Cf. the argument of Arnobius, an early Christian writer, against the common pagan ascription of male-ness to the deity.

7. Father Poulain explains analogy: "With the mystics, the words to *see* God, to *hear,* and to *touch* Him are not mere metaphors. They express something more; some close analogy. . . . By metaphor, we mean either a distant or a restricted resemblance to a single quality; as when we speak of a warrior as a *lion,* or say that we are recipients of a *torrent* of abuse. Analogy, on the other hand, is a very close resemblance, as when we say that God has intelligence, will, justice, etc. Primarily, it is true, the words are confined to the mental representation of things that we have observed in the creature. Then we apply them to God, although they are not verified in Him in exactly the same way. . . ." *The Graces of Interior Prayer,* p. 90 and footnote.

Cf. also the medieval statement: "All the statements made about God that imply body have some hidden meaning and teach us what is above us by means of something familiar to ourselves, with the exception of any statement concerning the bodily sojourn of the God-Word." John of Damascus, *Exposition of the Orthodox Faith,* I, 11.

accord with the biologist's formula: "cases in which organs have identity of function, but not identity of essence or origin." Insight symbols are functionally, not necessarily literally true, but they are true functionally as well as figuratively, that is, it is only through study of true functional relationships of such symbolisms in the natural universe that any grasp may be gained of their figurative sense.

Like the sun, to whose rays the whole world is exposed, the eyes of the Lord pass to and fro throughout all the world, having vision not only of the eternity of things as they are, but also of the intimate life of each soul, a power which, like the sun, he expresses in man's world through earthly agency.[8] Like the sun, the Lord is ruler of the natural world and lord of men, becoming their suffering redeemer and their judge—his hand is stretched out still. Like the sun, he is present to the whole world, of speed surpassing that of the wind, bringing aid and punishment, and extending even his life to men through prayer and sacrament—his way is in the whirlwind and the clouds are the dust of his feet.

A writer of the tradition[9] placed emphasis on the true and necessary function of the literal meaning (even where the literal statement is not necessarily true). The lion, he illustrates, represents Christ; not, however, as a matter of secret convention, by which the word *leo* denotes Christ. On the contrary the word *leo* must always denote a certain animal. It may represent Christ never in itself, but only through this literal signification. "Intelligit igitur quod cum leo Christum significare dicit, non nomen animalis, sed animal ipsum significat"—"It should be known therefore that when Leo is said to signify Christ, not the name of the animal, but the animal itself signifies him." Thus there would be no advantage in substituting for allegorical method a plain statement of meaning, although such is likely to be the recommendation of the critic in response to the assertion that allegory means *something other* than what is said in literal terms. Because of the unity of essence underlying all things, the animal means something in regard to Christ that all the abstractions which might be used to convey the same thought, nevertheless could not quite convey, since they lack the associations from all aspects and levels of racial experience which are called into play by the word "lion."

The literal truth, however, in any other sense than of truth in func-

---

8. For example, Boethius says: "Homer with his honeyed lips sang of the bright sun's clear light; yet the sun cannot burst with his feeble rays the bowels of the earth or the depths of the sea. Not so with the creator of this great sphere. No masses of earth can block his vision as he looks over all. Night's cloudy darkness cannot resist him. With one glance of his intelligence he sees all that has been, that is, and that is to come. He *alone* can see all things, so truly he may be called the *sun*." (There is a pun involved in the original Latin, between the words *alone* and *sun*.)

9. Hugh of St. Victor.

tion, is of minor importance.[10] The theology of Dante's tradition has never had a theory of the literal truth of the Bible[11] and has never been disturbed when this or that aspect of its literal meaning has been proved contrary to the highest that is known.[12] Social development under the empire, enlightened by the church, guides man in his understanding alike of the message of scripture and of the message of nature. The church under the guidance of Christ's sacramental life, may decide for the literal-minded which part of scripture is to be interpreted literally, and which figuratively only; but in this there is never conflict with that far more important truth, that the literal meaning is essential, and forever functionally true as basis for the insight interpretation.

Although it is not the present purpose to maintain that there were none who were literal-minded among medieval symbolists, it is true that among those in sympathy with the development of the tradition which Dante used, no question of "either—or" could arise in connec-

---

10. Cf. this typical utterance of a modern Roman Catholic scholar:

"It is undeniable that the literal meaning and truth of the Old Testament is today clouded by the difficulties raised even by a moderate historical criticism. To what degree the Old Testament is historical truth of the letter can only be decided, if at all, by the consensus of competent scholars. Without anxiety we may abandon to them a question devoid of religious significance. The mystical interpretation is the primary sense intended by the Holy Spirit . . . we can leave the minor matter of the letter to the solution of future scholarship. Whatever be the final verdict, if a final verdict be attainable, on the literal sense of the Old Testament writers, the sense of the Divine Author, the mystical or typical sense, remains unaffected. And it is this sense which possesses religious value for us. It is certain from authority and reason alike, that every event, whether or no it be historical, is certainly an allegory, that the Old Testament history is a series of inexhaustibly significant types of Christ and His mysteries. Christ and His mysteries are thus the substance of the Old Testament." Watkin, *Philosophy of Mysticism*, p. 364.

A similar spirit pervaded medieval utterances, though less explicit, since biblical criticism was not then to the fore. But cf. Origen as quoted on p. 265.

11. Catholic persecutions for heresy have been in all cases not because the literal sense of scripture was contradicted, but because definite church doctrine was thought to be imperiled; as could be shown by an analysis of cases. Cf. also p. 264 n. 69.

12. "There is no trace in Dante of that crude anthropomorphism which even in our own day cried out against the recognition of Evolution as an agency in the creative or providential energy of God, as being a doctrine which could 'not be taught without arrogancy and impiety.' Dante would not think God dishonoured by the discovery or by the belief that he had chosen some *modus operandi* other than that of an actual δημιουργός for the execution of his purposes. We have seen that even in the operations of creative power attributed immediately and directly to him no outward act is assumed, it was 'solo intendendo,' merely by an act of thought. . . . I am not one of those who seem to think that Dante was infallible . . . or that he anticipated . . . the discoveries of Copernicus, Newton, or Harvey, still less those of Darwin. But I do say there is nothing in his theory of Creation which would constitute such a barrier to his acceptance of some form of evolutionary teaching such as we have seen operating in our own day." Edward Moore, *Studies in Dante, Fourth series*, pp. 164-165.

tion with symbolic levels of meaning. Beatrice is not *either* a real girl *or* a symbol of Love, but a real girl *and* a symbol of Love *and* of the Holy Spirit *and* of the Divine Sun.

The symbolist maintains the supreme truth in function at the same time of all these levels of emphasis. The fact that in a passage which is to be understood figuratively the literal meaning generally is assumed *ipso facto* to be untrue, is the result of different understandings of symbolism. To return to the definitions given in the introductory material, with arbitrary and comparison symbols there can be no question of literal truth or untruth. But the insight symbol is by definition in some sense true in itself, as a basis for the truth of all its meanings. With insight symbol it is not a matter of saying one thing and meaning another, as in cryptograms and secret codes. "Either—or" comes more easily to the adolescent mind than "both—and" but "both—and" states the truth of traditional insight symbolism.

There was question, especially in regard to the Bible, as to which of two possibilities on the literal plane should be accepted; but this question was never vital in the method. Whether Beatrice, for example, was a real girl, or that which in life experience fulfilled her function, such as, for example, an ideal of Dante's imagination—whether the literal level was literally or only functionally true—whichever of these two alternatives were accepted, the truths, allegorical, tropological, and anagogical, remained unaffected. Thus Dante, in his *Divina Commedia*, though it be fiction, may hope to fulfil that same mission which was the mission of scripture, to bring men from a state of misery to a state of bliss.

APPENDIX IV, Pt. I, ii.

IMAGERY OF THE SUN-STORM GOD IN THE NEW TESTAMENT

In the synoptics and Acts, the conception of the sun-storm god is prominent as a means of expression,[13] and was particularly suited to the incidents in the life of Christ which were to be noted. For Matthew, Christ's birth is announced by a star in the east, and for Luke his coming is compared to the dawn:

> The day-spring from on high hath visited us, to give light to them that sit in darkness and in the shadow of death. Luke 1. 78-79.

Again, in all of man's experience there is no symbol with so great power to express the glory of the Transfiguration as that of the sun; and similarly the subjective experience of Christ's followers at the time of the Crucifixion belonged to the realm of the storm god.

Mark, in his account of the Transfiguration, gives but a hint of the

---

13. Cf. pp. 255 ff., also Count Goblet d'Alviella, *La migration des symboles.*

symbolism (Mark 9. 3) which Luke elaborates (Luke 9. 29) and Matthew makes explicit:

> Jesus . . . was transfigured before them, and his face did shine as the sun, and his raiment was white as the light. Matt. 17. 2.

All three, moreover, associate with this scene the cloud out of which comes the divine voice, in Luke's account striking terror into the hearts of the disciples. (In this connection the voice from the cloud, after the Fourth Gospel account of the raising of Lazarus, should be remembered for the association with thunder [John 12. 28-29].) Similar imagery describes for Luke Paul's experience on the Damascus road:

> Suddenly there shone from heaven a great light round about me. . . . And when I could not see for the glory of that light, being led by the hand of them that were with me, I came into Damascus. Acts 22. 6-11.

> At midday, O king, I saw in the way a light from heaven, above the brightness of the sun, shining round about me. Acts 26. 13.

This description, making the sun a mere object of comparison, indicates the significance of the spiritual experience as far greater than can be conveyed in any physical terms.

In the description of the Crucifixion the imagery of the sun god is still implicit, as opposed by the more tumultuous aspects of the power of darkness (Luke 22. 53). The Parousia is described in the traditional terms of Hebrew eschatology through language deriving from the storm-god aspect.[14]

Such description as this has led to the declaration that the whole story of Christ is but the ubiquitous and perennial myth of the sun god retold.[15] (The Fourth Gospel leads even more readily to such interpretation.) So long as the instrument of human expression is human language, terminology containing solar suggestion is unavoidable. The part played by the universe in the formation of man's vocabulary is beginning again to be realized, as it was in the Middle Ages. Although all language in the final analysis is symbolic, definite symbolic levels may be discerned, and on these depend the significance conveyed.

Through association (which will be discussed later) sun-storm god imagery attaches itself in the New Testament, not only to God, but also to his messengers, angelic and human, and to virtues and good works, in fact to practically every aspect of the relationship between God and

---

14. Cf. Matt. 24. 27-30; Mark 13. 24-27; Mark 14. 62.

15. Reaction to the evident solar elements in the life of Christ has ranged from the extreme of denying his historicity on that ground, to the opposite extreme of assertion that no one around whom sun myths failed to gather could be considered a true ambassador of God to men. Of interest in this connection is the fact that solar elements in the story of Troy caused people to consider the Trojan city and war alike fictitious, till archaeological evidence for them was unearthed.

man. Such association was to be especially prominent in the *Divina Commedia.*

Paul himself, first exponent of Christianity, in recognition of his skill in the method of allegory, was given like his rival Apollos the epithet mighty in scriptures. Against the background of his personal experience and of such facts as he had gleaned as to the life of Christ he made forceful use of symbolism. He is remarkable first of all for the complete omission of storm-god characteristics in his use of sun symbolism. His interest being preëminently the life lived in God's service, his greatest elaboration of light symbolism appears in this connection. Nevertheless, in some passages is a foreshadowing of the identification of Christ with God's enlightening power. All the other epistles of the canon treated as a group exhibit the same omission of storm-god imagery. Furthermore, attention is called to this omission of the volcanic character of God:

For ye are not come unto the mount that might be touched and that burned with fire, nor unto blackness and darkness and tempest. Heb. 12. 18.

It will be remembered that later thought, and ultimately Dante, returned to the complete sun-storm imagery transforming as did the author of the Fourth Gospel, that which some of these writers had omitted, probably as not in the spirit of the God Christ revealed. This transformation of the storm-god aspect was accomplished through the recognition of it as the inevitable expression of infinite love contemned. These writers allow themselves greater elaboration of sun-god imagery than did Paul, although again the imperfection of the symbol as against the thing signified is made clear. God is more than the physical sun.

Every good gift and every perfect gift is from above, and cometh down from the Father of lights, with whom is no variableness neither shadow of turning. Jas. 1. 17.

In Hebrews, Paul's foreshadowing of the identification of Christ with the sun's brightness is developed:

God who at sundry times and in divers manner spake in time past unto the fathers by the prophets, hath in these last days spoken unto us by his Son, whom he hath appointed heir of all things, by whom also he made the worlds, who being the *brightness of his glory* and the express image of his person, and upholding all things by the word of his power, when he had by himself purged our sins, sat down on the right hand of the majesty on high. Heb. 1. 1-3.

The importance of this passage is obvious in view of later trinitarian development, and the symbolism through which it triumphed.[16]

Savoring, even more than the later epistles, of the melting pot from which it came, the Johannine Apocalypse has turned many heads with the riotous wealth of its symbolism. The sun-storm god reigns in cata-

---

16. Cf. pp. 144 ff.

clysmic splendor, but the silken thread to guide through the maze of associated symbolism is here difficult to find. Usually descriptions of the god include, in accordance with the mythological tradition, attributes of both aspects:[17]

A throne was set in heaven and one sat on the throne. And he that sat was to look upon like a jasper and a sardine stone, and there was a rainbow round about the throne, in sight like unto an emerald. And round about the throne were four and twenty seats, and upon the seats I saw four and twenty elders sitting, clothed in white raiment, and they had on their heads crowns of gold. And out of the throne proceeded lightnings and thunderings and voices, and there were seven lamps of fire burning before the throne, which are the seven spirits of God. And before the throne there was a sea of glass like unto crystal, and in the midst of the throne, and round about the throne, were four beasts full of eyes before and behind. And the first beast was like a lion, and the second beast like a calf, and the third beast had a face as a man, and the fourth beast was like a flying eagle. Rev. 4. 2-7.

Here the sun-storm god sits enthroned amid reverberation of thunder, a rainbow around his head, and at his feet the sea reflecting his glory.[18] He is surrounded by seven planets and four mythological beasts.[19] Nowhere in the New Testament is there greater confusion of associated sun imagery or greater complexity of alien influence. To trace such influence or to argue as to interpretation in the light of symbolic traditions a tome would be inadequate. The number symbolism alone would demand a dissertation, and could be treated only against a background of Chaldean astrology.[20]

The writer of the Fourth Gospel retains sun-storm god symbolism.[21] Immediately attention is called to the main thesis of the gospel, the identification of Christ with Light: that is, the Logos has become the Radiance of the Divine Sun:[22]

That was the True Light, which lighteth every man that cometh into the world. John 1. 9.

---

17. Cf. Dante's use.

18. Cf. also Rev. 15. 1-2, and *Par.*, xxx, 61-63, 88-90, 100-105.

19. For the seven spirits, cf. the Zoroastrian Amesha Spentas. The four beasts are associated with the sun god (cf., e.g., the work of Goblet d'Alviella), although by the author of this apocalypse they were derived probably from the Book of Ezekiel. For later interpretations cf. text p. 338. Cf. also the description in Rev. 1. 12-18, where the two-edged weapon of the sun-storm god appears (cf. p. 213). Cf. also the description in Rev. 19. 11-16; also 21. 22-25, and 22. 5.

20. Cf. also pp. 119 ff. of this study. It may be mentioned here that Dr. Arthur S. Peake has a theory concerning the woman clothed with the sun, that her story is a variant of the same myth which gave rise to the birth-stories of Apollo and of Horus, "describing how the god of light was successfully born in spite of the attempt of the dragon of darkness and chaos to prevent his birth." *Commentary on the Bible* (New York: Nelson, 1919), p. 936.

21. John 12. 28-29.

22. A development foreshadowed in the Stoic tradition.

He is enlightening and life-giving:[23]

> In him was life, and the life was the light of men. John 1. 4.

> I am the light of the world, he that followeth me shall not walk in darkness, but shall have the light of life. John 8. 12.

> Yet a little while is the light with you. Walk while ye have the light, lest darkness come upon you, for he that walketh in darkness knoweth not whither he goeth. While ye have light, believe in the light, that ye may be the children of light. . . . I am come a light into the world, that whosoever believeth on me should not abide in darkness. John 12. 35-36, 46.

Of the phrase "children of light" more is made by this author than by any other New Testament writer. The life-giving and light-giving character of God is the preoccupation of this gospel, and there is little interest in elaboration to include minute teaching as to God's service in the world.

Light imagery in the Fourth Gospel, however, cannot be dismissed with a treatment of this nature. Solar symbolism is the basis for the motion of the whole—a fact understood and powerfully expressed by Godet:

> Imagine a spring day with the sun rising in a bright sky. The ground, moistened with the snows of winter, greedily absorbs his warm rays; everything which is capable of life awakes and is renewed; nature travails. Yet, after some hours, vapors rise from the damp earth, they unite and form an obscure canopy. The sun is veiled; a storm is threatened. The plants, under the impulse which they have received, nevertheless accomplish their silent progress. At length, when the sun has reached the meridian, the storm breaks forth and rages; nature is given over to destructive powers; she loses for a time her quickening star. But at eventide the clouds disperse; calm is restored; and the sun, reappearing in more magnificent brilliancy than that which attended his rising, casts on all those plants—the children of his rays—a last smile and a sweet adieu.[24]

The full significance of this gospel is indeed in the victorious power of light: "The light shineth in darkness, and the darkness comprehendeth it not," giving to the whole a triumphant sweep unequaled even by the more lurid and compelling symbolism of the celestial drama of the apocalypse.

APPENDIX IV, Pt. I, iii (1).

THE DEVELOPMENT OF THE FOURFOLD INTERPRETATION

As has been noted in the text (pp. 263 ff.) the method of reading under the letter of scripture not one but three types of "spiritual" meaning (relating to events in the historical revelation of God, to factors in the moral development of the individual, and to the heavenly life) was

---

23. Cf. the implied symbolism in John 11. 9-10, and 9. 4-5.
24. Frederic Godet, *Commentary on the Gospel of St. John,* tr. Crombie and Cusin, I, 312.

used in practice by the author of the Epistle to the Hebrews, and to a less extent by others of his time. The first clear statement of the method, however, is that of John Cassian's (fifth century; quoted on p. 270). By the time of Rabanus Maurus (ninth century) statement of the method is made as of a commonplace.[25]

The usual rule given for the four meanings of each text was to the effect that the letter told of past events, while in allegory was to be found instruction as to belief, in trope as to duty, and in anagoge as to the eternal goal toward which led the faithful keeping of creed and commandments. These four meanings were not considered as of equal depth and value; for example, Rabanus Maurus writes:

> Has namque quatuor intelligentias, videlicet historiam, allegoriam, tropologiam, anagogiam, quatuor matris sapientiae filias vocamus. . . . Mater quippe Sapientia per hos adoptionis filios pascit, conferens *incipientibus* atque teneris potum in lacte *historiae:* in fide autem *proficientibus,* cibum in pane *allegoriae;* bonis vero et strenue *operantibus,* et operibus bonis insudantibus, satietatem in sapida refectione *tropologiae;* illis denique qui et ad immis per contemptum terrenorum suspensi, et ad summa per coeleste desiderium sunt provecti, sobriam theorieae contemplationis ebrietatem in vino *anagogiae.*[26]

This statement expresses one of the roots of Dante's stress on the value of esoteric meanings intelligible only to the few.

In the Middle Ages proper, the fourfold method had come to be so widely known that definitions and discussions either are omitted or follow the familiar lines already laid down. In exhaustive theological treatises, however, the subject is considered. For example, Thomas Aquinas thus discusses the question as to whether in Holy Scripture the Word has several interpretations:

> The author of Holy Writ is God, in whose power it is to signify his meaning not by words only, as man also can do, but also by things themselves. . . . Therefore that first signification whereby words signify things belongs to the first interpretation, the historical or literal. That signification whereby things signified by words have themselves also a signification is called the spiritual interpretation, which is based on the literal interpretation and presupposes it. This spiritual interpretation has a threefold division. As the Apostle says, Heb. 7, the Old Law is a figure of the New Law and the New Law itself, Dionysius says, is a figure of future glory. In the New Law, whatever our Head has done is a type of what we ought to do. Therefore so far as the things of the Old Law signify the things of the New Law, there is the allegorical interpretation. So far as the things done in Christ or so far as the things which signify Christ are types of what we ought to do, there is the moral interpretation. So far as they signify what relates to eternal glory, there is the anagogical interpretation. Since the

---

25. An interesting analysis of the fourfold interpretation occurs likewise in the Zoharic tradition, where the Sacred Law, with its multiplicity of meaning, is compared to a woman in love. She reveals herself to her lover, first, by signs (*ramez* or literal meaning); next, by whispered words (*derush* or allegory); third, by converse with her face veiled (*hagadah* or moral signification); and, finally, grants the full revelation of the *sod,* or anagoge.

26. Rabanus Maurus, prologue to his *Allegoriae in Scripturam sacram.*

literal sense is that which the author intends, and since the author of Holy Writ is God, Who by one act comprehends all things by his intellect, it is not unfitting if even according to the literal sense one word in Holy Writ should have several interpretations.[27]

In response to the first objection he adds that multiplicity produces no ambiguity or equivocation:

seeing that these interpretations are not multiplied, because one word signifies several things, but because the things signified by the words can be themselves types of other things. Thus in Holy Writ no confusion results, for all the interpretations are founded on one, the literal. . . .

The insistence was general throughout the medieval tradition that in symbolic interpretation words signified things exactly as in ordinary usage, but that these things in turn had significations. Not the word *leo*, but the animal *lion*, in the allegorical interpretation of the phrase "Lion of the Tribe of Judah," signifies Christ.

Variation from the usual threefold subdivision of the spiritual interpretation was uncommon, but not unknown. For example, Hugh of St. Victor returned to a threefold classification much like that of Origen (cf. pp. 263-264) save that he included anagoge by subdividing allegory. Moreover, he included Junilius' time classification (see p. 270) as a subdivision under allegory. His scheme follows:

(a) Historical or literal:
"Habet enim sacrum eloquium proprietatem quamdam ab aliis scripturis differentem, quod in eo primum per verba quae recitantur, de rebus quibusdam agitur, quae rursum res vice verborum ad significationem avarum rerum proponuntur."

(b) Allegorical:
"Cum per id quod ex littera significatum proponitur, aliud aliquid sive in praeterito sive in praesenti sive in futuro factum significatur."

I. Allegory "simplex":
"Et est simplex allegoria, cum per visibile factum aliud invisibile factum significatur.

II. Anagoge:
"Anagoge id est sursum ductio, cum per visibile invisibile factum declaratur."[28]

It would seem that to Hugh the trope, which he omits from his list of interpretations, was rather a moral lesson drawn from the passage than a symbolic interpretation of it. It is clear, however, that Dante used the more generally accepted fourfold division (cf. his statement in the Epistle to Can Grande).

---

27. Aquinas, *S.Th.*, 1, *Q*. 1, *art*. 10, respectively. The second quotation is from the same article, *ad primum*.
28. Hugh of St. Victor, *De scripturis et scriptoribus sacris*, cap. ii.

APPENDIX IV, Pt. I, iii (2).

ALLEGORY *VERSUS* PERSONIFICATION

THE difference between allegory as the second level of the fourfold interpretation, and allegory in the sense of personification of psychological abstractions, is fundamental, and depends on the medieval criterion that in symbolism, not the word, but the thing represented by the word, is to be regarded as the symbol. Even suppose, for example, that Matilda was not a real person. Still, like a fictional character in a novel, she *might* be a real person. One might know her; and on what she is as a woman, real or possibly-real, depends her revelation of the manner of the soul's progress. The better one knows her, the deeper one can read into her symbolic meaning. The sun is apprehensible by the senses. The more that is known about the sun's course and relationships, the more intelligent basis is given for meditation on the relationship of the universe to that power on which it depends. This symbolism has, then, for foundation, objective or possibly-objective (functional) realities, not fictions of the imagination. The personification allegory, on the other hand, lacks this basis in the world of scientific reality. One does not meet on the street such figures as My Lord Understanding and Captain Patience,[29] nor does one expect through study of their personalities to learn more of understanding and of patience, because that which constitutes their personalities is that which is known already about understanding and patience. Their relationships to each other, moreover, are not such relationships as are either literally or functionally existent in the universe. Their relationship is rather a fictitious one based on that which might or should happen, could Understanding and Patience be abstracted completely from living human beings.

In the *Faery Queene* the two methods appear side by side. The first book, with its action concentrating in the real Una, is a Renaissance form of the medieval allegorical method. The symbolism of the subsequent books, however, is related to the personification allegory, although here the form appears not as simple personification, but as the representation of real or fictional persons, not primarily in their whole characters, but in their action illustrating some abstract vice or virtue which may or may not have been actually their most prominent characteristic.

---

29. The same is true of such figures as Giant Despair, etc.

BASIS OF NUMBER SYMBOLISM*

PYTHAGOREAN philosophy gives the first theory of numbers, making three, seven, and ten outstandingly sacred. Philo developed this theory in great intricacy, making three and four stand for the incorporeal or intellectual creation of God and the corporeal or earthly creation, respectively. He bases this on a truth stated in higher mathematics as: One point determines itself alone;[1] two points determine a straight line; three points determine a plane; whereas four points in general require a solid. Philo, living before the elaboration of modern mathematical methods, used more words to explain:

> There is also another power of the number four which is a most wonderful one to speak of and to contemplate. For it was this number that first displayed the nature of the solid cube, the numbers before four being assigned only to incorporeal things. For it is according to the unit that that thing is reckoned which is spoken of in geometry as a point, and a line is spoken of according to the number two, because it is arranged by nature from a point, and a line is length without breadth. But when breadth is added to it, it becomes a superficies, which is arranged according to the number three. And a superficies, when compared with the nature of a solid cube, wants one thing, namely depth, and when this one thing is added to the three, it becomes four. On which account it has happened that this number is a thing of great importance, inasmuch as from an incorporeal substance perceptible only by intellect, it has led us on to a comprehension of a body . . . which by its own nature is first perceived by the external senses.

It is of interest also that the cube, or typical example of matter extended in space as distinguished from abstract intellectual concepts, is said to have been sacred to the sun god Apollo, probably because it looked in all directions, and in its nature combined the three and the four. (There were also four "elements" of which three, earth, water, air, belonged to the material world, and one, fire, to the spiritual. The distinction is real, stated in modern terms as three states of matter, solid, liquid, and gaseous, plus the mysterious chemical processes, of which combustion is typical, by which their alterations occur.) It is from the summation of the Three that signify the Realm of Pure Ideas, and the Four that signify the World as we know it, that the sacred number Seven is formed.

It is to be noted that much of this number symbolism, which seems so puerile to the chance reader, represents really an attempt to express facts fundamental in the universe and in the number system. Facts in theory of numbers were often discovered by number symbolists. Philo states, for example (in a necessarily roundabout way, since algebra was not within his knowledge), that in a geometrical progression whose first term is one, with any ratio, the seventh term will be both a cube

---

* Cf. Appendix V, Pt. I, ii (2) for Hebrew number symbolism.
1. It has been suggested that a point, with neither substance nor extension, but merely indicating a focus, is the most spiritual conception of Being. Cf. *Par.*, xxviii, 16, 41-42.

and a square. (Let the ratio be k, and the first term one. The seventh term is then k^6, which is the square of the cube of k, and the cube of its square. Philo suspected, without being able to prove, the universality of this rule, which he tried out with some numerical ratios.)

Number symbolism aimed at the expression of deeper truths than those of mathematics as generally understood today. The significance of One in religion and in philosophy is clear, in the persistent strivings of the human mind for monotheism and for monism. Two expresses the fundamental dualities of the universe, which make monism and monotheism alike seem so beset with contradictions. Three (to give one among innumerable instances of its presentation in the world of thought), expresses the great problem of modern philosophy, the knowledge relation, with its factors of the known, the knower, and the relation between them; and Four, as Philo justly pointed out, is the mathematical number of extended matter.

When Arabic numerals were introduced, new possibilities were seen in number symbolism. To give but one example: if it be assumed as the rule of operation, that a number less than ten is to be equated to the sum of itself plus all units less than itself, and that a number greater than ten is to be equated to the sum of its digits, the process being carried out as far as possible, then, no matter how many times three is added to unity, the result is unity. That is,

$$1 + 3 = 4; \quad 4 + 3 + 2 + 1 = 10; \quad 1 + 0 = 1$$
$$4 + 3 = 7; \quad 7 + 6 + 5 + 4 + 3 + 2 + 1 = 28; \quad 2 + 8 = 10; \quad 1 + 0 = 1$$
$$7 + 3 = 10; \quad \text{which reduces to unity as has been shown (in the first line)}$$
$$10 + 3 = 13; \quad 1 + 3 = 4, \text{ which reduces to unity (see first line)}$$
$$13 + 3 = 16; \quad 1 + 6 = 7, \text{ which reduces to unity (see second line)}$$

and so on throughout the number series. That is, in mystical interpretation, whenever trinity is added to any unity, a higher and more inclusive unity is reached.

It is uncertain whether Dante was familiar with this interesting trick of Arabic numbers, but it would have accorded well with his symbolism, since it is grounded in the fact that ten, the base of our number system, is not only the sum of 4, 3, 2, 1 (that is, the equivalent of four in the above rule), but is also the sum of unity and Dante's miracle nine.

APPENDIX V, Pt. I, ii (1).

PLOTINIAN AND AUGUSTINIAN CONCEPTIONS OF THE TRINITY

THE philosophic trinity of Plotinus, including, as already noted, nothing of myth and nothing of history, nevertheless for its expression was dependent on those same materials of symbolism through which other trinities had been developed. Further, these materials were employed in accord with that philosophy of symbolism, which the conflict of earlier trinities was bringing to increasingly conscious definition. In the One of Plotinus, superb definition is given to the infinite unity underlying reality, in which all opposites are unified. Plotinus declared one identical essence to be everywhere entirely present,[2] and, moreover, that this essence is divisible only if thereby not diminished. For all the carelessness of Plotinus' writing, the infinity of the One was not more accurately expressed until the time of Boethius. Dean Inge, albeit with enthusiasm, gave a true explication of Plotinus' position, when he wrote:

In the relations of νοῦς and νοητά we see a complete reconciliation of the One and the Many, of Sameness and Otherness. . . . . Reality is not to be identified either with Thought, or with a kind of transcendental physical world which is the object of Thought: nor can we arrive at it by forming clean-cut ideas of these two, and saying that they are "somehow" joined together. Reality is eternal life; it is a never-failing spiritual activity; it is the continual self-expression of a God who speaks and it is done, who commands, and it stands fast.[3]

The trinity of Plotinus is a series of emanations which, though not coequal, nevertheless bear striking resemblance to the Christian trinity.[4] As Augustine, after his conversion to Christianity, stated: The Neoplatonists voiced all spiritual truths except the supreme truth of the Incarnation. The significance of this statement was appreciated fully only centuries later in the reawakening of the Middle Ages proper. During the early period of thought evaluation neither Christian nor Neoplatonist made much reference to the system which inspired the other, although presumably conscious both of the similarities and of the differences in the Neoplatonic and Christian conceptions of the universe.[5]

For both, the One (τὸ ἕν) is self-manifested in trinity. Plotinus, however, describes this Trinity as subordinate to the One, in the contemplation of whom it receives its being. Augustine describes the Trinity as completely identical with the One.[6] The real confusion, however, resulted from the Plotinian designation of this triune manifestation as the Logos,[7] a term which to Christians meant the Second Person with

---

2. *Ennead,* 6, 4.   3. W. R. Inge, *Philosophy of Plotinus,* II, 48-49.
4. Cf. text, pp. 150, 350 ff.
5. Plotinus is strangely silent concerning Christianity, although he had been a fellow student of Origen's, and must have been in reasonably intimate touch with Christians. Augustine gives great praise to Plotinus as a philosopher, considering him as it were another Plato, although disagreeing sharply on some points.
6. Augustine states that the Trinity is simple and unitary, "because it *is* what it *has,* with the exception of the relation of the persons to one another. For in regard to this relation it is true that the Father has a Son and yet is not himself the Son, and the Son has a Father and is not himself the Father. But as regards himself, irrespective of relation to the other, *each is what he has;* thus, he is in himself living, for he has life, and is himself the life which he has." *De civitate Dei,* 11, 10.
7. Plotinus places the eternal archetype of that trinity involved in the knowl-

his two natures. The difficulty was increased with regard to the realm of the World Soul, most nearly analogous in the Christian system to the impress of the Trinity on the world in goodness, truth, and beauty, although understood by Augustine and by Christians generally to be the analogue of the Holy Spirit.

Plotinus, according to Augustine's understanding, speaks first of God the Father, second of God the Son,—whom (ignoring the Incarnation) he terms the intellect or mind of the Father,—and third of the Soul of Nature.[8] Augustine comments: "But we assert that the Holy Spirit is the Spirit not of the Father only, or of the Son only, but of both."

---

edge relation, that is, "the dichotomy of thinker and thought and their inescapable noëtic connection" (Irwin Edman, *Logic of Mysticism in Plotinus*, p. 58) within the realm of his Second Hypostasis, the Logos. It is this fact which renders his Three Hypostases not analogous to the Christian Trinity, which as a whole serves as the eternal archetype, not only of this, but of every other trinity involved in Subject and Object, for example, lover, beloved, and love. Cf. Augustine, *De Trinitate*, 8, 10, and 9, 1.

The Three Hypostases of Plotinus, in so far as they are analogous to elements in the Christian *Weltanschauung*, correspond not to the Three Persons of the Christian Trinity, but to the Unity, the Trinity, and the Divine imprint on the world of nature. This is readily seen in the diagrams subjoined:

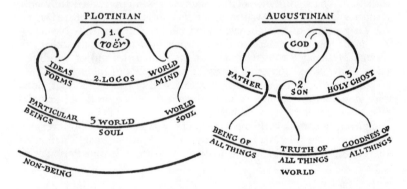

It must be borne in mind that these two diagrams are not equally true to the conceptions they picture. The first, while not complete, is true as far as it goes to the conception of Plotinus. The diagrammatic form of the Augustinian theory, however, does not give a true picture of the Catholic universe, in that wrong implications result from the omission of the inter-Trinity relations on the second level. The Greek form of the Nicene Creed tends to picture a universe more nearly of the Plotinian form, but the western church, especially subsequent to the time of Charlemagne, has been strenuously insistent on its own *schema* of the divine. A difficulty was felt in the realm of deity, comparable to the problem in our world of the relation of being, truth, and goodness, or of physics, psychology, and ethics—which, indeed, Augustine makes its counterpart.

8. Cf. *De civitate Dei*, 10, 23, and 10, 29.

APPENDIX V, Pt. I, ii (2).

HEBREW MYSTICISM AND NUMBER SYMBOLISM

THE *Zohar* or Book of Splendor, based more or less on the earlier *Sepher Yetzirah* (attributed to Abraham in the usual manner of apocryphae) and its commentaries, was attributed to R. Simeon ben Jochai of the Antonine period. It was first generally known, however, in the latter half of the thirteenth century,[9] and on both internal and external evidence it is assumed to date from that time and (by some) to have been the work of Moses de León or perhaps of someone whom he, in circulating it, represented.[10] To the universality of the reaction which this work represents, there could be no better witness than the number of authors to whom it has been ascribed.

As in the Christian solution, numerical relationships were fundamental. The four and the ten were the numbers of reality, and the stamp of solar symbolism was on it in conscious association with the correlate in sex. Much, however, was included with a definitely esoteric bearing. Through four realms the unknown ineffable Name was manifested (in accord with the Neoplatonic theory of emanations) in a series of ten principles. The first or divine realm contains the ten Sephiroth, the second contains ten Archangels, the third, ten angels, and the fourth or spatial heavens contains the heavenly spheres (the same through which Dante journeyed). In the schematic arrangements in which these were diagramed, the central position (number six, Tiphereth or Beauty) is occupied in the four realms, respectively, by the sacred Tetragrammaton (JHVH), Raphael, Michael, and the *Sun*.

Three cryptographic methods of scriptural interpretation came into use in the Kabalistic system: the *Gematria*, the *Notarikon*. and the *Temura*. According to the *gematria*, or Hebrew numerology, verses in the scripture are given new meanings through the numerical values of their letters in the Hebrew alphabet. The principle is that for any word or phrase there may be substituted another word or phrase which adds to the same number. According to the *notarikon*, a new text is formed from a single scriptural word, through the use of each letter as the initial of a new word, in a manner similar to that by which the Greek Ιχθὺς was read by the early Christians.[11] Again, the initials or finals of sentences were used to form words after the manner of the acrostic. The

---

9. The Latin version of the *Zohar*, in which (and in its translations) it is easiest for modern English-speaking people to gain a knowledge of the work, is imperfect and somewhat confused, being the translation made by a Lutheran Kabalist with propagandist intentions—Knorr von Rosenroth. Cf. A. E. Waite, *The Doctrine and Literature of the Kabalah*, pp. 380 ff.

10. Cf. Waite, *op. cit.*, pp. 103 ff., and 115 ff.

11. Cf. p. 141. For a discussion of this example of Christian use of *notarikon*, with a transcript of Neale's translation of the prophecy of the Erythrian Sibyl, see Bernhard Pick, *The Cabala*, pp. 87-90.

temura was a kind of cryptography in which, according to fixed rules, certain letters were substituted for others, in some twenty-two combinations. Whereas only those skilled in the Kabalah read the Bible chapter after chapter according to numerological methods, their application to individual texts of especial difficulty was common among all philosophers and theologians of the period, Jewish or Christian. It is thus a possibility for the solution of Beatrice's "hard riddle."[12]

The Kabalah contained more of the oriental than the western world had known for centuries.[13] Into it penetrated but little of the clear-cut thinking of Maimonides, and its meeting of the problems raised by the new philosophy was in a language which failed to meet the intellectual demands of the day. After a brief but far-reaching influence on Christian mysticism,[14] during which certain of its symbolisms were ordered by scholastic philosophy, it fell into disrepute alike in Christian and in Jewish circles.

---

12. Cf. pp. 326, 470.

13. Of necessity the Jews were more sensitive to Islamic influence than were Christians, who opposed strenuously the unrelieved, non-trinitarian monotheism of both Mohammedanism and Judaism. To orthodox Christianity it was heretical to speak of the Father, or even of the Trinity, as *solus Deus*—"God alone,"—unless the context made it clear that the meaning was not that God is a "lonely God." Christianity insisted in finding social relationships in the very nature of God himself. Cf. Thomas Aquinas, *S.Th.*, 1, *Q.* 31, *art.* 3.

14. Among Christian mystics contemporary with Dante and supposed to have been influenced by the Kabalah is Ramón Lull. Even after it had fallen into general disrepute, it influenced Picus de Mirandola (1463-94), Cornelius Agrippa, Paracelsus, and many later students. There are still occultists who establish themselves under the mantle of Kabalism, which in its development became connected with alchemy and affected the "Cambridge Platonists," the "Rosicrucians," and many others.

DOCTRINAL DEVELOPMENT REFLECTED IN SYMBOLISM IN ME-
DIEVAL HYMNS

LUMEN DE LUMINE noted earlier as the dominant emphasis during the period of philosophic synthesis, was during the first six
centuries, the favorite concept of hymnographers, likewise. It is
stressed in all hymns wherein the sun symbol is used directly and in
many more in which the imagery is implied. An instance from the third
century, or earlier, is the following:

> O gladsome Light, O grace
> Of God the Father's face,
> The eternal splendour wearing;
> Celestial, holy, blest,
> Our Saviour Jesus Christ,
> Joyful in thine appearing.[1]

In the fourth-century hymn "Lucis largitur splendide" of St. Hilary, is
a favorite form of expression:[2]

> Lucis largitor splendide,
> Cuius serens lumine
> Post lapsa noctis tempora
> Dies refusus panditur,
>
> Tu verus mundi lucifer,
> Non is, qui parvi sideris
> Venturae lucis nutius
> Angusto fulget lumine

> Sed toto sole clarior
> Lux ipse totus et dies,
> Interna nostri pectoris
> Illuminans praecordia
>
> Adesto, rerum conditor,
> Paternae lucis gloria,[3]

Reference should be made also to the hymn by St. Ambrose, "Splendor
Paternae gloriae" (quoted, p. 409).

Finally, for the doctrine of the Trinity as a whole, note may be made
of St. Ambrose's hymn "O Lux Beata Trinitas" (quoted on p. 510).
The Trinity here symbolized by the sun is a Trinity of light. God's light
is, moreover, nearly always associated with his knowledge, and both
with his power.

---

1. Translation from the Greek taken from the *English Hymnal,* No. 269. The
English Hymnal was edited by a committee of English liturgiologists, including
W. J. Birkbeck and Percy Dearmer, and was compiled with especial intention to
include ancient hymns written for use in religious services.

2. *Analecta hymnica medii aevi,* Vol. LI ("Feria secunda ad matutinas laudes,"
Cluniac MS, ninth century, No. 6, p. 9).

3. Translation of last lines quoted from *Great Hymns of the Middle Ages,*
compiled by E. W. Brainerd:

> Far brighter than our earthly sun,
> Thyself at once the Light and Day,
> The inmost chambers of the heart
> Illumining with heavenly ray;
>
> Thou Radiance of the Father's Light,
> Draw near, Creator Thou of all. . . .

Eternal Glory of the sky,
Blest hope of frail humanity,
The Father's sole-begotten One. . . .

Uplift us with thine arm of might. . . .[4]

The pagan worshiped power or wisdom, and to these early Christians, concern with the power of knowledge is a natural step in the elaboration of the doctrine of the Trinity. But interest in God as Love is still subordinate. One of the few instances of the use of light or flame imagery for the Third Person of the Trinity occurs in the fourth-century hymn, "Jam Christus astra ascenderat":

From out the Father's light it came,
That beautiful and kindly flame,
To kindle every Christian heart,
And fervour of the Word impart.[5]

Characteristically, even though this was written for Whitsuntide, interest is still rather in the Word than in the Spirit.

The darker temper of the succeeding centuries, furthermore, was at once apparent in the hymns. It is not surprising that in that time of trial, Fortunatus and some anonymous writers of the sixth century should add to the idea of pure joy in the light of God for his Wisdom, the idea of rescue from spiritual death: "Jesus has harrowed hell; he has led captivity captive; Darkness and chaos and death flee from the face of the Light," is the theme of an Easter processional ascribed to Fortunatus.[6] As has been said, brightness gathers round the cross. (Cf. the familiar hymn "Vexilla Regis.")[7] The interest in the Day of Judgment is expressed in another hymn of Fortunatus:

Judge of all! when Thou descendest
Throned in awful majesty;
When aloft Thy Cross effulgent
Beams amid the Milky Way,
O be Thou, Thyself, our refuge,
And the dawn of endless day![8]

In apprehension of the Day of Judgment the idea of purification became dominant, as in Gregory's hymn, "Primo dierum omnium,"[9]

Let all before the dawn arise
And seek by night th' Eternal Light,
As bids the prophet, timely wise. . . .

---

4. A sixth-century hymn, "Aeterna caeli gloria," tr. J. M. Neale, contains these words. *English Hymnal*, No. 56.
5. *Ibid.*, No. 150.   6. *Ibid.*, No. 624.
7. *Ibid.*, No. 94.
8. From *Great Hymns of the Middle Ages*, compiled by E. W. Brainerd, p. 24.
9. From *ibid.*, p. 27.

> Father of might, enthron'd in light,
> Thee with o'erflowing lips we pray,
> Oh, quench the fire of low desire,
> Each deed of ill drive far away.

Anatolius, in the eighth century, shows the Divine Light freeing men from trials.

> Sorrow can never be,
> Darkness must fly,
> Where saith the Light of Light,
> "Peace, it is I."[10]

With this hymn it is interesting to compare a similar hymn taken from an Irish MS:

> Christe, qui lux es et dies,   Precamur, sancte Domine,
> Noctis tenebras detegis,   Defende nos in hac nocte . . .[11]
> Lucifer, lucem praeferens,
> Lumen beatum praedicans,

In the same century, St. John Damascene associates the symbolism of the sun and the seasons with the feast of the Resurrection, interpreting winter as the state of sinfulness to be banished by the Sun which is Christ (hymn quoted, p. 414 n. 45). All through these centuries the ideas of healing, cleansing, and redeeming become associated with the Divine Sun who is now appealed to as the "Light of souls distressed."[12]

> O Unity of threefold Light,   Trinity sacred, Unity unshaken;
> Send out thy loveliest ray,   Deity perfect, giving and forgiving,
> And scatter our transgressions' night,   Light of the angels, Life of the for-
> And turn it into day.[13]   saken,
>   Hope of all living.[14]

In short, the Light of the Trinity is desired to free the soul from transgressions, rather than to illumine the understanding, and so, as in the earlier period, there is a summing up of the feeling of the age.

Finally, in the hymnology of the Middle Ages proper appears the preoccupation of the time:

> Sweet Jesu, now will I sing
> To thee a song of love-longing;
> Make in mine heart a well to spring
> Thee to love above all thing.
> Sweet Jesu, mine heart's true light,
> Thou art day withouten night;
> Give to me both grace and might
> That so I may love thee aright.[15]

---

10. *English Hymnal,* No. 388. Tr. J. M. Neale.

11. *Analecta hymnica medii aevi,* Vol. LI (*ad completorum,* No. 22, p. 21), ninth century.

12. From St. Bernard's "Rosy Sequence," given in the *English Hymnal,* No. 238.

13. *Ibid.,* No. 163. Tr. J. M. Neale.   14. *Ibid.,* No. 160.

15. *A Song to Jesus and Mary in the Passion.* From early English sources. Given on p. 72 of Benson's *A Book of the Love of Jesus.*

The Holy Ghost is known as Love, and symbolized by heat. Bianco da Siena says, in a hymn ("Discendi, Amor sento") to the Holy Spirit:

Come down, O Love divine,
Seek thou this soul of mine,
And visit it with thine own ardour
   glowing;
O Comforter, draw near,
Within my heart appear,
And kindle it, thy holy flame bestow-
   ing.

O let it freely burn,
Till earthly passions turn
To dust and ashes in its heat consum-
   ing;
And let thy glorious light
Shine ever on my sight,
And clothe me round, the while my
   path illumining.[16]

Hymnography abounds in praises of Mary and of saintly women:

De stella sol oriturus
Stellae matrem profert prius
Ut radium lucis novae
Summae Deus clementiae

Annam, filiam Abrahae
Quae fulsit ex Aaron stirpe
Quasi stella matutina
O gloriosa domina,

Ex qua caelorum degina
Mundique clemens domina
Ut haereses interimat
Aurora lucis rutilat.[17]

Often, however, in the same hymn are used all the ideas previously associated with the sun:

Jesu, joy of hearts, most bright,
Spring of truth and inward light

With us stay, Redeemer dear,
On us shed Thy brightness here;
Chase the darkness of the night,
Fill the world with sweetest light.

Oh what sweet and holy fire,
Oh what ardent blest desire,
Oh what rich refection,
Loving Thee, eternal Son.

King of glory, King of might,
King of victory most bright. . . .

Thou, the Truth, the Life, the Way—
Thou, the Sun of endless day.[18]

Furthermore, the sun symbol of the Trinity finds now its fullest development. Three hymns which show roughly the stages which have been pointed out are:

O Trinity of blessed light,
O Unity of princely might,
The fiery sun now goes his way,
Shed Thou within our hearts Thy ray,[19]

---

16. *English Hymnal*, No. 152. Tr. R. F. Littledale.
17. *Analecta hymnica medii aevi*, Vol. LII (No. 104), p. 100.
18. These selections are from the "Jesus Dulcis Memoria" of Bernard of Clairvaux, tr. Alfred Edersheim. In *Great Hymns of the Middle Ages*. See also the "Hora Novissima" of Bernard of Cluny, included in the same collection.
19. *English Hymnal*, No. 164.

of which the author is St. Ambrose, 340-397 A.D., and

> O Unity of threefold light,
> Send out thy loveliest ray,
> And scatter our transgressions' night,
> And turn it into day,[20]

written about the year 900 A.D., and

> There the Trinity of Persons
> Unbeclouded shall we see;
> There the Unity of Essence
> Perfectly revealed shall be,[21]

from the hymn, "Quisquis valet numerare," ascribed to Thomas à Kempis, who wrote in the fifteenth century. Earlier there was the emphasis on one phase or another of the Trinity; but here an age intensely interested in personal relations indicates its consciousness of the Three Persons as distinct.

APPENDIX VI, ii.

THE IDEALIZATION OF COURTLY LOVE

IT has been said by M. Faure that "everywhere in the Middle Ages, and whatever the aspect of the revival, the peoples were ignorant of the real object they were pursuing; everywhere their conquest of the life of the universe was accomplished under the pretext of religion, always with the support of the letter of the dogma, always against its spirit. It is this which emphasizes so powerfully, in the art of the Middle Ages, its confused liberty, its drunken and fecund plunges into the fields of sensation, . . . its disordered mixture of feelings springing from the contact of the soul with the world in the naked strength of instinct." Many passages in Ruysbroeck and others might seem to lend themselves to such an interpretation, but it is to be remembered that Loki and his knavery no longer belong to the heat or love symbolism of the sun. At this time the world was in the travail incident to the birth of a new social morality.

The relation between the sexes, like that between thane and overlord, was ceasing to be a property relation. Crusades and changed economic conditions were bearing their fruit. It had been long since the world had been able (if, indeed, it ever had) to spiritualize marriage. But now marriage was becoming a symbol of the union between God and the soul. The illicit amours of the period were a veritable advance toward a higher moral plane, on which marriage was no longer to be contracted on a business basis between father and husband. Of course, but few realized what they were doing in making the lover the ideal of the age.

---

20. *Ibid.*, No. 163. Tr. J. M. Neale. See also No. 160.
21. *Ibid.*, No. 250.

Still, whatever the practice undoubtedly was, the ideal was never an undisciplined love.

Courtly love, then, may be regarded as an idealistic revolt against a social system in which marriages were contracted in childhood and for political and economic reasons. The medieval marriage was essentially an immoral relation.[22] The natural revolt against such a condition was the prevalence of extra-marital love-relations.

The troubadours and their patronesses, of whom the greatest were Eleanor of Aquitaine (granddaughter of the cynical old William) and her daughter Marie de Champagne, developed extra-marital love into a cultural system, idealizing constancy, sacrifice, bravery, and defense of women and of the oppressed. Andreas Capellanus, probably at the court of Marie de Champagne, wrote *De arte honeste amandi,* in which are given the famous thirty-one laws of love, of which the following are typical: (1) Marriage is no proper excuse for not loving; (10) Love is always accustomed to avoid the domiciles of avarice; (13) Love that is revealed and subject of rumor rarely endures; (15) Every lover is in the habit of turning pale at sight of his beloved; (23) He whom the contemplation of love harasses sleeps and eats less; and (26) Love can deny nothing to love.

Even when this love was frankly physical, it was the source not of the worst, but of the best in the lovers' lives. Indeed, it has been said, and with much probability, that the superiority of modern marriage over feudal marriage is the direct result of the ideals of courtly love.

The connection between this exuberant human passion and religious devotion has been well expressed by Mr. Chesterton, in his discussion of St. Francis of Assisi:

As St. Francis did not love humanity but men, so he did not love Christianity but Christ. Say, if you think so, that he was a lunatic loving an imaginary person; but an imaginary person, not an imaginary idea. And for the modern reader the clue to the asceticism and all the rest can best be found in the stories of lovers when they seemed to be rather like lunatics. Tell it as the tale of one of the Troubadours, and the wild things he would do for his lady, and the whole of the modern puzzle disappears. In such romance there would be no contradiction between the poet gathering flowers in the sun and enduring a freezing vigil in the snow, between his praising all earthly and bodily beauty and then refusing to eat, between his glorifying gold and purple and perversely going in rags, between his showing pathetically a hunger for a happy life and a thirst for a heroic death. All these riddles would easily be resolved in the simplicity of any noble love; only this was so noble a love that nine men out of ten have hardly even heard of it. . . . The reader cannot even begin to see the sense of a story that may well seem to him a very wild one, until he understands that to this great mystic his religion was not a thing like a theory but a thing like a love-affair.[23]

---

22. According to the principles of the church, strictly interpreted, a forced marriage is held invalid, that is, nonexistent. Needless to say, this principle was not pushed to its logical conclusion in the day of feudal marriages.

23. G. K. Chesterton, *St. Francis of Assisi,* pp. 21-22.

Such writers as Dante and Ramón Lull, like St. Francis, notably spiritualized the conception of courtly love.[24] Beatrice, though she be a real girl, is as ethereal in her guidance of Dante as is Lady-Philosophy-of-Love in relation to Lull. Both these heavenly ladies, representative of the Holy Spirit, in a deep sense signify the earthly presence of him toward whom was directed the love of St. Francis and of all the great mystics—the Eternal Wisdom, Radiance of the Divine Sun.

---

24. Cf. pp. 428 ff. *et al.* The whole love motif in all of its elements is well summarized in the following: "There appeared in the world, after a long and complex transition, the elements of a new kind of love; something not without sex, yet directed in a new way to the inward essence of the individual. In this kind of love there is a metaphysical element; to be seen, under its various modes, in Dante. . . . This metaphysical element, which communicates a new excitement to the emotion of love, seems to appear first in the late Middle Ages, and to arrive at an expression not yet exhausted in modern times." T. Whittaker, *Macrobius,* p. 3.

BIBLIOGRAPHY

FOR the sake of convenience this bibliography is divided into two sections of which the first contains the principal medieval texts consulted, and the second modern studies dealing with the problems considered. In neither section has it been possible to list all the works of which use has been made.

Those who may desire to delve further into medieval material are referred to the collections and series listed as introductory to Bibliography I. Small space has been given to the more popular literature of the middle ages both because for this phase of medieval literary development selected bibliographies are readily available, and because much of it is well known to students in the field (to whom only too frequently it comes to represent the whole intellectual activity of the middle ages). Throughout this work endeavor has been made to consider the convenience of the student in giving reference to the more available editions of works cited. In general there has been departure from this rule only when from the point of view of symbolism such editions in some way seriously misrepresent the original.

As to modern studies many of the most valuable have appeared in periodicals: *Review of english studies, Romania, Revue de l'art chrétien, Giornale dantesco,* and the newly established *Speculum*—to mention but a few in differing fields. Very little of the periodical material, however, has been included in this bibliography since to make adequate reference to the relevant articles consulted would increase the list beyond manageable compass. Reference has been made also to the encyclopedias, especially: *The Catholic Encyclopedia, Encyclopaedia of Religion and Ethics,* edited by Hastings, the *Jewish Encyclopedia,* and the encyclopedias of philosophy and psychology, together with the *Cambridge Medieval History* and standard works on the early literatures in the several European tongues, especially Italian, French, Provençal, Spanish, German, Dutch, English.[1]

Furthermore, in selecting the titles for Bibliography II there has been an attempt to list the more important works together with a few of lesser import but significant of the development of interest in symbolism,[2]

---

1. Suggestions for the student are: *Cambridge history of English literature,* ed. A. W. Ward and A. R. Waller, New York, 1907. vols. 1-3; Lanson, Gustave, *Histoire de la littérature française.* 19 éd. Paris, Hachette [1926]; Flamini, Francesco, *A history of Italian literature,* 1265-1907, tr. E. M. O'Connor, with an introduction by W. M. Rossetti. New York, 1907, and Petrocchi, Policarpo, *La lingua e la storia letteraria d'Italia dalle origini fino a Dante,* Roma, 1903; Lamprecht, *Deutsche Geschichte.* 6 ed. 1920. 20 vols.; Vooys, C. G. N. de, *Middelnederlandse legenden en exempelen. Bijdrage tot de kennis van de prozalitteratuur en het volksgeloof der middeleeuwen. Herziene en vermeerderde uitgave.* Groningen, Wolters, 1926; Dozy, Reinhart Pieter Anne, *Recherches sur l'histoire et la littérature de l'Espagne pendant le moyen âge;* 3. éd. rev. et augm. Leyden, Brill, 1881. 2 vols.; Hurst, George Leopold, *An outline of the history of Christian literature,* New York, Macmillan, 1926. Certain useful works of smaller scope are listed in Bibliography II lettered G.

2. Many, for example, of the nineteenth century treatises cited in Bibliography

rather than every book consulted. A bibliography compiled for the purpose of presenting material representative of the widely different approaches to the study of symbolism (no one or two of which apart from some knowledge of the others can give the student a true conception of the symbolic tradition) by necessity must be extensive. To lessen this factor certain cuts have been made. Because most work has been done in the field of the static arts, as well as for the sake of brevity, many valuable references with regard to this phase of medieval symbolism have been omitted. These may be found in the bibliographies of the works cited, especially those of Mâle, Didron, Molsdorf, Webber, Auber. A similar omission has been made of much valuable material with regard to the mystics which is to be found in the bibliographies of Underhill and Waite (these studies of course being not primarily from the point of view of symbolism). Again, reference has been made to the official missal, breviary, and Holy Week office book of the Roman Catholic Church (which the student may consider with profit in connection with the titles listed under Catholic church. Liturgies. in Bibliography I), and to much liturgical material not listed, although working through the titles lettered E in Bibliography II the student interested may find most of it for himself.[3] The works of the classical authors used extensively by Dante have not been included in the bibliography. What these are, should be clear from the footnote material, and various lists are available.[4] Considerable omission has been made in the field of Dante criticism which the reader may remedy for himself by reference to Moore, Grandgent, Toynbee, Scartizinni, and many others. The Annual Reports of the Dante Society (Cambridge, Wilson, 1882-date) and especially the bulletins of the *Societa dantesca italiana* (Firenze 1890-date) are worth consulting. For a comprehensive listing of Dante literature see Cornell University, *Catalogue of Dante collection* and *Supplement.*

For the convenience of students who may wish to refer more particularly to works on a given phase of the subject, each title in Bibliography

---

II have been supplanted, yet they are included in order to facilitate an understanding of the gradual recurrence of interest in symbolism.

3. Of interest in addition to the Roman Catholic material are: Church of England. *Liturgy and ritual.* The ancient liturgy of the Church of England according to the uses of Sarum, York, Hereford and Bangor, and the Roman liturgy, arranged in parallel columns with preface and notes by W. Maskell. 3d ed. Oxford, Clarendon press, 1882; Greek church. *Liturgy and ritual.* Service book of the Holy orthodox-Catholic apostolic church, comp., tr. and arranged from the old church-Slavonic service books of the Russian church, and collated with the service of the Greek church, by Isabel Florence Hapgood. Rev. ed., with indorsement by Patriarch Tikhon. New York, Association press, 1922; Greek church. *Liturgy and ritual.* The liturgies of S. Mark, S. James, S. Clement, S. Chrysostom, S. Basil: or, according to the use of the churches of Alexandria, Jerusalem, Constantinople. Ed. by the Rev. J. M. Neale. 4th ed. with preface by Dr. Littledale. London, R. D. Dickinson, 1896.

4. Cf., for example, Charles H. Grandgent, *Divina Commedia,* introduction, xxiv-xxvi. For fuller discussion see Edward Moore, *Studies in Dante. First series.*

II is followed by a key letter or letters denoting in general the aspects in which its treatment has been of interest for the present study.

KEY LETTERS

A Dante criticism
B Philosophical discussion and criticism
B' Symbolist School
C Psychological discussions
D Mysticism
E History of worship; liturgiology
F Medieval and ecclesiastical art
G General discussions of medieval conditions and literature
H Discussions of Arthuriad and Grail cycle
I Discussions of medieval science and pseudo-science
J Comparative religion and anthropology*
K Some works suggestive for interpretation of symbols

---

* Considered for bearing on materials and development of medieval symbolic tradition.

BIBLIOGRAPHY I. MEDIEVAL MATERIAL

A. USEFUL COMPILATIONS AND SERIES WITH ABBREVIATIONS HERE USED

Analecta. Analecta hymnica medii avei . . Leipzig, 1886-1922. 55 vols. Ed. G. M. Dreves, C. Blume. Certain sub-series within the larger compilation:

Historiae rhythmicae: liturgische Reimofficien des Mittelalters. v. 5, 13, 18, 24-26, 28, 45a.

Hymni inediti: liturgische Hymnen des Mittelalters. v. 4, 11, 12, 19, 22, 23, 43.

Hymnographi Latini: lateinische Hymnendichter des Mittelalters. v. 35, 50.

Psalteria rhythmica: gereimte Psalterien des Mittelalters. v. 35, 36.

Sequentiae ineditae: liturgische Prosen des Mittelalters. v. 8, 10, 34, 37.

Thesauri hymnologici hymnarium: die Hymnen des Thesaurus hymnologicus Hermann Adalbert Daniel und anderer Hymnen-Ausgaben. v. 51, 52.

Thesauri hymnologici prosarium: die Sequenzen des Thesaurus hymnologicus Hermann Adalbert Daniel und anderer Sequenzen-Ausgaben. v. 53-55.

Tropi graduales. v. 47, 49.

Boll. Analecta bollandiana. Paris etc. 1882-date. 30 vols. (Lives and legends of saints and liturgical notes. Still in process of publ.)

Acta.[5] Acta Sanctorum, collegit, digessit, notis illustravit J. Bollandus, etc. Ed novissima curante J. Carnandet. Paris etc. 1863-1925. 65 vols. (Still in process of publ.)

AN. Ante-Nicene Christian library, translations of the writings of the fathers down to A.D. 325, ed. A. Roberts and J. Donaldson. Edinburgh, 1867-73. 24 vols.

Cod.Lit. Codex liturgicus ecclesiae universae in quo continentur libri rituales, missales, pontificales, officia, dypticha etc. ecclesiarum Occidentis et Orientis. Nunc primum prodit Joseph Aloysius Assemanus. Ad mss. codd. vaticanos, aliosque cantigiavit, recensuit, latine verit, praefationibus, commentariis, et variantibus lectionibus illustravit. Editio iterate, ad editionis principis exemplum, ab Huberto Welter. Parisiis & Lipsiae, Welter, 1902. 13 vols.

Beiträge. Beiträge zur Geschichte der Philosophie des Mittelalters. Hrsg. von Dr. Clemens Baeumker. Münster i.W.: Aschendorff, 1891-1923. 23 vols.

Coll. Collections de documents pour l'histoire religieuse et littéraire du Moyen Age. Paris, Fischbacher, 1898 ff.

Corpus. Corpus scriptorum ecclesiasticorum latinorum. Vindobonae 1866-1926. 65 vols. (Kaiserliche Akademie der Wissenschaften, Vienna.)

---

5. For further hagiographic material cf.: *Bibliotheca hagiographica latina antiquae et mediae aetatis. Ediderunt Socii Bollandiani.* Bruxellis, 1898-1901. 2 vols.

Deut. Deutsche Texte des Mittelalters, hrsg. von der k. preuss. Akad. d. Wissenschaften. Berlin, Weidemann, 1904 ff.

EETS. Early English Text Society, London, Publications. London, 1864-date. 148 vols. (Still in process of publication.)
  For contents see "Academies. London. Early English Text Society" in British Museum. Catalogue of printed books. Checklist also in Early English Text Soc. Publications extra series, no. 65.

EETS-e. Early English Text Society, London. Publications, extra series. London, 1867-date. 124 vols. (Still in process of publication.)
  For contents see London Library Catalogue, 1903. Checklist also in no. 118.

Hittorp. Hittorp, Melchior, ed. De divinis catholicae ecclesiae officiis ac ministeriis, varii vetustorum aliquot ecclesiae patrum ac scriptorum libri . . . Coloniae, 1568.

Mart. Martène, Edmond, ed. De antiquis ecclesiæ ritibus libri tres ex variis insigniorum ecclesiarum pontificalibus, sacramentariis, missalibus, breviariis, ritualibus editis. Antverpiæ, Novelli, 1763-64. 4 vols.

Mon. Monumenta ecclesia liturgicae. Ed. F. Cabrol, H. Leclercq, and M. Ferotin. Paris, 1900-

NPN. Schaff, Philip, and Henry Wace, eds. A select library of the Nicene and Post-Nicene fathers of the Christian Church, 2d series. Translated into English, with prolegomena and explanatory notes. New York, etc., 1890-1900. 14 vols.

PG. Migne, Jacques Paul, ed. Patrologiæ cursus completus. Patrologie greque comprenant les pères, docteurs et écrivains de l'Eglise greque depuis les temps apostaliques juqu'au dela du concile de Florence. Parisiis, Migne, 1857-66. 161 vols.

PL. Migne, Jacques Paul, ed. Patrologiæ cursus completus; sive, Bibliotheca universalis, integra, uniformis, commoda, œconomica, omnium SS. Patrum, doctorum, ecclesiasticorum, qui ab aevo apostolico adusque Innocentii III tempora floruerunt. Patrologie latine. Parisiis, Migne, 1844-5. 221 vols.
  Author and title indices in t. 218.
  Subject indices (including indices to Biblical symbolisms) in vols. 219-221.
  For table of contents, see: Index to the catalogue of books in the upper hall of the Public Library, Boston, 1861, pp. 533-535.
  For author index see: Catalogue of the Astor Library, v. 3, 1859, pp. 1139-48.

SBE. Sacred Books of the East; translated by various oriental scholars and edited by F. M. Müller. Oxford, 1879-1910. 50 vols.

Schaff. Schaff, Philip, ed. A select library of the Nicene and Post-Nicene fathers of the Christian Church, 1st series. Buffalo, 1886-90. 14 vols.

Vet. Scrip. Martène, Edmond and Ursin Durand, eds. Veterum scriptorum et monumentorum historicum, dogmaticorum, moralium amplissima collectio. Parisiis, 1924-1733. 9 vols.

B. MEDIEVAL TEXTS

ABAILARD, PIERRE, 1079-1142. Sic et Non. *PL*, 178.

ADAM *de Saint-Victor, d.* 1192. Adami a Sancto Victore sequentiae. *PL*, 196.

ALANUS *de Insulis, d.* 1202. De sex alis cherubim. *PL*, 210.

—— Liber de planctu naturae. *PL*, 210.

ALBERTUS *Magnus, bp. of Ratisbon*, 1193?-1280. Opera omnia, ex editione lugdu- nensi religiose castigata, et pro auctoritatibus ad fidem vulgatæ versionis accu- ratiorumque patrologiæ textuum revocata, auctaque B. Alberti vita ac biblio- graphia operum a P. P. Quétif et Echard exaratis, etiam revisa et locupletata, cura ac labore Augusti Borgnet. Parisiis, Vivès, 1890-99. 38 vols. *See especially:* De laudibus Beatae Mariae Virginis; De sacrificio missae; De sacramento eucha- ristiae; Paradisus animae; De adhaerendo Deo libellus.

—— De animalibus libri xxvi, nach der Cölner Urschrift. hrsg. von Hermann Stadler. Münster i. W., Aschendorff, 1916-20. 2 vols. *Beiträge* xv-xvi.

ALCUIN, 735-804. De divinis officiis liber . . . *Hittorp.* pp. 37-100.

ALFRAGANUS. Il 'libro dell' aggregazione delle stelle, secondo il Codice Medico- Laurenziano pl. 29-Cod. 9 contemporaneo a Dante, publicato con introduzione e note da Romeo Campani. Città di Castello, Lapi, 1910.

AL GHAZZALI. The alchemy of happiness. Translated by Calud Field. London, Murray, 1910.

AMBROSIUS, *Saint, bp. of Milan. 4th cent.* Opera. *PL*, 14-17. *See especially:* Hexameron, and De xlii mansionibus filiorum Israel.

—— Some of the principal works, tr. H. De. Romestin. *NPN*, 10.

ANDREAS CAPELLANUS. De amore libri tres; recensuit E. Trojel. Hauniae, Gat, 1892.

ANGELA, *of Foligno*, 1448-1509. The book of divine consolation of the blessed Angela of Foligno: tr. from the Italian by Mary G. Steegmann: introduction by Algar Thorold. London, Chatto & Windus, 1909.

ANSELM, *Saint, abp. of Canterbury*, 1033-1109. Opera. *PL*, 158. *See especially:* Proslogion; De fide Trinitatis; Cur Deus homo; Dialogus de libero arbitrio.

—— Devotions of Saint Anselm. Edited by Clement C. J. Webb. London, Methuen, 1903.

Apocalypse of Sedrach. In: *AN* additional vol., ed. Allan Menzies, 1903.

—— *See also* Sydrach.

Apocalypse of the Virgin. In: *AN* additional vol., ed. Allan Menzies, 1903.

Aquinas. *See* Thomas Aquinas.

ARTHUR, KING (*Romances, etc.*) Die Abenteuer Gawains, Ywains, und Le Morholts mit den drei Jungfrauen, aus der Trilogie, des pseudo-Robert de Borron, die Fortsetzung des Huth-Merlin; nach der allein bekannten hs. nr. 112 der Pariser national bibliothek hrsg. von H. O. Sommer. Halle, Niemeyer, 1913.

—— Les romans de la Table ronde, mis en nouveau langage et accompagnés de recherches sur l'origine et la caractère de ces grandes compositions, par Paulin Paris. Paris, Techener, 1868-77. 5 vols.

—— The vulgate version of the Arthurian romances, ed. from manuscripts in the British museum by H. Oskar Sommer. Washington, Carnegie institution, 1908-16. 8 vols.

—— *See also* Chretien de Troies, Cuchulain, Gospel of Nicodemus, Gottfried von Strassburg, Lovelich, Mabinogion, Malory, Marie de France, Le roman de Merlin, Wolfram von Eschenbach, Weston; and in bibliography ii: Bruce, Loomis, Scudder, Sommer, Weston (in addition to titles appearing in this bibliography other works with regard to Arthur are worth consulting).

ASSUMPTIO MARIÆ. Poem on the Assumption, ed. by J. P. Strachey. Poem on the day of judgment, ed. by H. J. Chaytor. Divisiones mundi, ed. by O. H. Prior. Cambridge [Eng.] University press, 1924.

ATHANASIUS, *Saint, patriarch of Alexander, d.* 373. Select writings and letters.

Ed., with prolegomena, indices, and tables, by Archibald Robertson. Oxford, Parker; New York, Christian literature co., 1892. 4 vols. *NPN.*
—— Select treatises of St. Athanasius in controversy with the Arians. Freely tr., with an appendix, by John Henry cardinal Newman. 6th ed. London & New York, Longmans, Green, 1895. 2 vols.

AUGUSTINUS, AURELIUS, *Saint, bp. of Hippo, 4th-5th cent.* Opera omnia *PL,* 32-47. *See especially:* De civitate Dei; De quantitate animae; Enarrationes in Psalmos; De Trinitate.
—— The Enchiridion, tr. A. H. Haddan. *Schaff* 3, pp. 237-276.
—— Expositions on the Book of Psalms by St. Augustine, bishop of Hippo, ed. A. C. Coxe. *Schaff* 8.
—— Sermons on selected lessons of the New Testament. Oxford, Parker, 1844-45. 2 vols.
—— Homilies on the Gospel according to Saint John. Oxford, Parker, 1848. 2 vols.
—— On the Holy Trinity, tr. A. W. Haddan. *Schaff* 3, pp. 1-228.
—— St. Augustine's Confessions; with an English translation, by William Watts, 1631. London, Heinemann; New York, Macmillan, 1912. 2 vols. Latin and English.
—— The confessions, tr. by E. B. Pusey. London, Dent; New York, Dutton [1909]

BARTHOLOMÆUS *Anglicus.* Mediæval lore, from Bartholomew Anglicus, by Robert Steele, with a preface by William Morris. London, Chatto & Windus, 1924. (Selections from De proprietatibus rerum, a typical and immensely popular mediæval encyclopedia, together with an analysis of the sources, valuable from the point of view of mediæval science.)

BARTSCH, KARL FRIEDRICH. Chrestomathie provençale, accompagnée d'une grammaire et d'un glossaire. 2. éd., augm. et entièrement refondue. Eberfeld, Friderichs, 1868.

BELETH, JOHN. *12th cent.* Rationale divinorum officiorum. *PL,* 202.

BENSON, ROBERT HUGH. A book of the love of Jesus, a collection of ancient English devotions in prose and verse. St. Louis, Herder; London, Pitman, 1917.

BERNARD *de Clairvaux, Saint,* 1091-1153. Opera. *PL,* 182-185. *See especially:* De consideratione libri v. *PL,* 182 col. 727 ff.
—— Life and works of St. Bernard. Ed. by J. Mabillon. Tr. and ed. with additional notes, by S. J. Eales. London, Hodges, 1889-96. 4 vols.
—— On consideration. Tr. by George Lewis. Oxford, Clarendon press, 1908.
—— The book of Saint Bernard on the love of God, ed., with translation and notes, by Edmund G. Gardner. London, Dent [1916] Latin and English.

BIBLE. *O. T. Apocryphal books. Enoch.* The book of Enoch, translated from Professor Dillmann's Ethiopic text, emended and revised in accordance with hitherto uncollected Ethiopic mss. and with the Gizeh and other Greek and Latin fragments which are here published in full; ed., with introduction, notes, and appendices, and indices, by R. H. Charles. Oxford, Clarendon press, 1893.
—— —— *Testaments of the 12 patriarchs.* The testaments of the twelve patriarchs, tr. by Robert Sinker. *AN,* 22.

BIBLE. *N.T. Apocryphal books. English.* The apocryphal New Testament, being the apocryphal gospels, acts, epistles, and apocalypses, with other narratives and fragments, newly translated by Montague Rhodes James. Oxford, Clarendon press, 1924.
—— —— *See also* Visio Sancti Pauli, Apocalypse of Virgin, Apocalypse of Sedrach, Gospel of Nicodemus, Harrowing of Hell, Legend of the Cross.

BÖHME, JAKOB. Theosophia revelata. Das ist: Alle göttliche Schriften. Amsterdam, 1730-31. 7 vols. Although Bohme lived outside of the Middle Ages proper his works are invaluable to an understanding of the development in alchemico-mystical symbolism.

—— Sein Leben und seine theosophischen Werke in geordnetem Auszuge, mit Einleitungen und Erläuterungen. Allen Christgläubigen dargeboten durch Johannes Claassen. Stuttgart, Steinkopf, 1885. 3 vols.

—— Six theosophic points and other writings. Newly tr. into English by John Rolleston Earle. New York, Knopf, 1920.

—— The signature of all things, with other writings. London, Dent; New York, Dutton [1912]

BOETHIUS, d. 524. Opera. PL, 63.

—— The consolation of philosophy; translated by W. V. Cooper. London, Dent, 1902.

BONAVENTURA, originally GIOVANNI FIDANZA, Saint, cardinal, bp. of Albano. Opera omnia, editae a P.P. Collegii S. Bonaventurae. Ad claras aquas, 1882-1902. 10 vols. See especially: Breviloquium; De triplici via, alias Incendium amoris; Itinerarium mentis in Deum; De reductione omnium artium ad theologiam; Vitis mystica; etc.

—— Opera omnia Sixti v, jussu diligentissime emendata; accedit sancti doctoris vita, una cum diatriba historico-chronologico-critica. Editio accurate recognita, cura et studio A. C. Peltier. Parisiis, Vivès, 1864-71.

—— Meditations on the Supper of Our Lord, and the hours of the passion. Drawn into English verse by Robert Manning of Brunne (about 1315-1330) Ed. from the mss. in the British museum and the Bodleian library, Oxford, with introduction and glossary by J. Meadows Cowper. London, Trübner, 1875. EETS. Note: Although as yet there are no accurate English translations there is a good French one.

BRENDAN, Saint. Legend. Ein lateinischer und drei deutsche Texte herausgegeben von Carl Schröder. Erlangen, Besold, 1871.

—— Les voyages merveilleux de saint Brandan à la recherche du paradis terrestre. Légende en vers du xiie siècle publiée d'après le manuscrit du Musée britannique avec introduction [and "Observations sur le texte"] par Francisque-Michel. Paris, 1878.

—— St. Brendan: a mediæval legend of the sea, in English verse and prose. Ed. by Thomas Wright. London, Printed for the Percy society by T. Richards, 1844.

CAESARIUS HEISTERBACENSIS. Dialogus miraculorum. Textum ad quatuor codicum manuscriptorum editionisque principis fidem accurate recognovit Josephus Strange. Coloniae, Heberle, 1851, 2 vols.

CASSIANUS, JOANNES, 5th cent. Collationes. PL, 49. See especially: Collatio xiv: De spiritali scientia.

CASSIODORUS, 6th cent. Historia tripartita. PL, 69.

CATERINA da Siena, Saint, 1347-1380. L'opere della Seraphica Santa Caterina de Siena. Lucca, 1721.

—— The dialogue of the seraphic virgin, Catherine of Siena, dictated by her, while in a state of ecstasy, to her secretaries, and completed in the year of Our Lord 1370. Together with an account of her death by an eyewitness; translated from the original Italian, and preceded by an introductory essay on the life and times of the saint, by Algar Thorold. London, Burns, Oates & Washbourne, 1925.

—— Saint Catherine of Siena as seen in her letters, tr. & ed. with introduction by Vida D. Scudder. London, Dent; New York, Dutton, 1905.

CATHOLIC CHURCH. LITURGIES. Missa latina. 10th cent. PL, 138.

—— Liturgies and other documents of the Ante-Nicene period. AN, 24.

—— Sacramentarium Gelasianum, (5th cent?). PL, 74.

—— For other ancient liturgical material cf. Adam of St. Victor, Albertus, Alcuin, Beleth, Durantis, Florus, Hildebert, Honorius, Hugh of St. Victor, Innocent

III, Lay Folks', Micrologus, Mirk, Missa latina, Pietrus Damian, Radbertus, Ratramnus, Reinerus, Sicardus, etc.

The cell of self-knowledge: seven early English mystical treatises printed by Henry Pepwell in 1521: ed. with an introduction and notes by Edmund G. Gardner. London, Chatto & Windus; New York, Duffield, 1910.

CHRESTIEN *de Troyes, 12th cent.* Christian von Troyes sämtliche Werke; nach allen bekannten Handschriften hrsg. von Wendelin Foerster. Halle, Niemeyer, 1884-99. 4 vols.

—— Arthurian romances; tr. by W. Wistar Comfort. London & Toronto, Dent; New York, Dutton [1913]

CLEMENS, TITUS FLAVIUS, *Alexandrinus.* Opera omnia. Recognouit Reinholdus Klotz. Lipsiae, Schwickerti, 1831-34. 4 vols. *See especially:* Paedagogus.

—— Christian doctrine and practice in the second century. London, Pickering, 1844.

THE CLOUD OF UNKNOWING. A book of contemplation the which is called the cloud of unknowing, in which the soul is oned with God. Edited from the British museum. With an introduction by Evelyn Underhill. 2d ed. London, Watkins, 1922.

—— The cloud of unknowing, and other treatises by an English mystic of the fourteenth century, with a commentary on The cloud by Father Augustine Baker, O.S.B.; edited by Dom Justin McCann. London, Burns, Oates & Washbourne, 1924.

CONSTANTINUS I, *the Great, emperor of Rome, d.* 337. [Life, laws, letters, etc.] *PL,* 8.

COOK, ALBERT STANBURROUGH, & CHAUNCEY B. TINKER, *eds.* Select translations from old English poetry; ed. with prefatory notes and indexes. Boston, Ginn, 1902.

Cross, Legend of. *See* Morris, Napier.

CUCHULAIN. The Cuchullin saga in Irish literature; being a collection of stories relating to the hero Cuchullin, translated from the Irish by various scholars; comp. and ed. with introduction and notes, by Eleanor Hull. London, Nutt, 1898.

CURETON, WILLIAM, *ed.* Spicilegium syricum. With English translation. London, Riv, 1855. *See especially:* Key of Melito, which is an encyclopedia of nature with symbolic meaning and scriptural passage for each subject.

CURSOR MUNDI. Cursor mundi. A Northumbrian poem of the XIV century in four versions. Ed. by the Rev. Richard Morris. London, Trübner, 1874-93. 5 vols. *EETS.*

CYNEWULF. The poems of Cynewulf, translated into English prose by Charles W. Kennedy, with an introduction, bibliography, and facsimile page of the Vercelli ms. London, Routledge; New York, Dutton, 1910.

CYPRIANUS, *Saint.* Writings. Translated by R. E. Wallis. Edinburgh, 1868-69. 2 vols. *AN,* 8, 13.

DANTE ALIGHIERI, 1265-1321. Le opere di Dante; testo critico della Società dantesca italiana, a cura di M. Barbi—E. G. Parodi—F. Pellegrini—E. Pistelli—P. Rajna—E. Rostagno—G. Vandelli. Con indice analitico dei nomi e delle cose di Mario Casella, e tre tavole fuor di testo. Firenze, Bemporad, 1921.

—— Tutte le opere di Dante Alighieri, nuovamente rivedute nel testo dal dr. E. Moore; con indice dei nomi propri e delle cose notabili comp. dal dr. Paget Toynbee. 3 ed., più estesamente riv. Oxford, Stamperia dell' Università, 1904.

—— Divina commedia, ed. Casini. 5 ed. Florence, Sansoni, 1903.

—— La divina commedia. Edited and annotated by C. H. Grandgent. Boston & New York, Heath [1913] 3 vols.

—— La divina commedia, commentata da G. A. Scartazzini. 7 ed. in gran parte rifatta da G. Vandelli, col rimario perfezionato di L. Polacco e indice dei nomi proprii e di cose notatili. Milano, Hoepli, 1914.

—— Divina commedia. Ed. Torraca. 3 ed. Segati, Rome, 1915.

—— La divina commedia. Il testo Wittiano rived. da Paget Toynbee. London, Frowde, 1900.

—— The Inferno, Purgatorio, and Paradiso. Text, with translation by Caryle, Okey, and Wicksteed. London, Dent, 1900. 3 vols. (Temple Classics.) Italian and English.

—— The Divine comedy of Dante Alighieri; the Italian text with a translation in English blank verse and a commentary, by Courtney Langdon. Cambridge, Harvard university press. 1918-21. 3 vols.

—— The vision of Dante Alighieri; or, Hell, purgatory and paradise, tr. by the Rev. H. F. Cary. London, Dent; New York, Dutton [1908]

—— The Divine comedy of Dante Alighieri; Cary's translation, revised with an introduction by Marie-Louise Egerton Castle. London, Bell, 1914.

—— The Convivio. Tr. P. H. Wicksteed. London, Dent, 1924. (Temple Classics.)

—— The Vita nuova and Canzoniere of Dante Alighieri. [Translated by Thomas Okey and P. H. Wicksteed.] London, Dent, 1924. (Temple Classics.)

—— The new life (La vita nuova) by Dante Alighieri; tr. by Dante Gabriel Rossetti, with an introduction by Charles Eliot Norton. One hundred sonnets, by Francesco Petrarch. La Fiammetta, by Giovanni Boccaccio. Poems, by Michelangelo Buonarroti. [New York] The National alumni [1907]

—— The New life of Dante Alighieri; tr. by Charles Eliot Norton. Boston & New York, Houghton, Mifflin, 1892.

—— De monarchia. London, Dent, 1924. (Temple Classics.)

—— De monarchia; the Oxford text ed. by Dr. E. Moore, with an introduction on the political theory of Dante by W. H. V. Reade. Oxford, Clarendon press, 1916.

DENIS the Carthusian, 15th cent. Doctoris Ecstatici D.Dionysii Carthusiani opera omnia in unum corpus digesta. Cura et labore monachorum S. Ordinis Carthusienis. Monstrolii, 1896. [Latin commentary on the works of Dionysius the pseudo-Areopagite.]

DIEZ, FRIEDRICH CHRISTIAN. Die Poesie der Troubadours. 2 verm. Aufl. von K. Bartsch. Leipzig, Barth, 1883.

DIONYSIUS AREOPAGITA. 5th? cent. Opera omnia. PG, 3-4.

—— Opera. (Translated from Greek into Latin by John Scotus Erigena.) PL, 122. See especially: Ierarchia caelestis; Ierarchia ecclesiastica; De divinis nominibus; Mystica theologica.

—— The works of Dionysius the Areopagite. Now first translated into English from the original Greek, by the Rev. John Parker. London, Parker, 1899. 2 vols.

—— On the divine names and the mystical theology. Tr. from the Greek by C. E. Rolt. London, S.P.C.K.; New York, Macmillan, 1920.

—— See Sharp, A. B., Bibliography ii.

DU MÉRIL EDELESTAND PONTAS, ed. Poesies populaires latines du moyen âge. Paris, Franck, 1847.

DURANTIS, GULIELMUS, bp. of Mende, ca. 1237-1296. Rationale divinorum officiorum. Rome, 1473.

—— The symbolism of churches and church ornaments; a translation of the first book of the Rationale divinorum officiorum; with an introductory essay and notes by the Rev. John Mason Neale and the Rev. Benjamin Webb. 3d ed. London, Gibbings, 1906.

ECKHART, Meister, d. 1327. Meister Eckhart's Schriften und Predigten. Aus dem Mittelhochdeutschen überstezt und herausgegeben von Herman Büttner. Jena, 1909-12. 2 vols.

—— Mystische Schriften, an unsere Sprache übertragen von Gustav Landauer. Berlin, Schnabel, 1903.

—— Meister Eckhart, by Franz Pfeiffer, Leipzig, 1857; translation, with some omissions and additions, by D. de B. Evans. London, Watkins, 1924.

ERIGENA. *See* Joannes *Scotus, Erigena.*

ERMENGAUD, *Maitre, 13th cent.* Le Breviari d'Amor, suivi de sa lettre à sa sœur; publié par la Société archéologique, scientifique, et littéraire de Béziers; introduction et glossaire par Gabriel Azaïs. Béziers, Benezech-Roque [1862-81] 2 vols.

ETIENNE DE BESANÇON. An alphabet of tales. An English 15th century translation of the Alphabetum narrationum, from add. ms. 25,719 of the British museum. Edited by Mrs. Mary Macleod Banks. London, Trübner, 1904-05. 2 vols.

EUSEBIUS, *Pamphili, bp. of Cæsarea. 4th cent.* Vita Constantini. *PL,* 8.

—— The life of the blessed Emperor Constantine, in four books, from 306 to 337 A. D. London, Bagster, 1845.

FIGULUS, BENEDICTUS, *pseud.?* A golden and blessed casket of nature's marvels. Now first done into English from the German original pub. at Strasburg in the year 1608. London, Elliott, 1893.

FLORUS DREPANUS LUGDUNENSIS, *9th cent.* Opusculum de expositione missae. *PL,* 119. Also *Vet. scrip.* 9.

FOLIOT, GILBERT, *12th cent.* Expositio in Cantica canticorum. *PL,* 202.

FORTUNATUS, VENANTIUS HONORIUS CLEMENTIANUS, *6th cent.* Opera. *PL,* 88.

FRANCESCO D'ASSISI, *Saint.* Opuscula S. Patris Francisci Assisiensis. Ad claras aquas, 1904.

—— Speculum perfectionis seu S. Francisci Assisiensis legenda antiquissima, auctore fratre Leone. Nunc primum edidit Paul Sabatier. Paris, Fischbacher, 1892.

—— I Fioretti di S. Francesco e il Cantico del Sole. Milano, 1907.

—— The writings of Francis of Assisi, newly tr. into English with an introduction and notes, by Fr. Paschal Robinson. Philadelphia, Dolphin press, 1906.

—— "The little flowers" & the Life of St. Francis with the "Mirror of perfection." With an introduction by Thomas Okey. London, Dent; New York, Dutton [1908?]

FULGENTIUS, FABIUS CLAUDIUS. *5th cent.* De aetatibus mundi et hominis. *See:* Fulgentius, Fabius P., Opera, p. 129-179.

FULGENTIUS, FABIUS PLANCIADIS. *5th cent.* Opera. Recensuit R. Helm. Lipsiae, 1898. *See especially* Expositio Virgilianae continentiae secundum philosophos moralis, p. 83-107.

GAUTIER DE METZ. L 'image du monde de Maitre Gossouin, rédaction en prose, avec, notes et introduction par O. H. Prior. Lausanne, 1913.

—— Image du monde. Caxton's Mirrour of the world, ed. by O. H. Prior. London, Trübner, 1913. *EETS-e.* A medieval encyclopedia in French verse.

GEHEIME WISSENSCHAFTEN. Geheime Wissenschaften. Eine Sammlungselтener älterer und neuerer Schriften über Alchemie, Magie, Rosenkreuzerei, Freimauerei, Hexenund Teufelwesen etc. Unter Mitwirkung namhafter Autoren herausgegen von A. v. d. Linden. Berlin, Barsdorf, 1913-

GERHOH VON REICHERSBERG, 1093-1169. Opera omnia. *PL,* 193-194.

The gnôsis of the light; a translation of the untitled apocalypse contained in the Codex Brucianus, with introduction and notes, by Rev. F. Lamplugh. London, Watkins, 1918.

Gnosis. *See also* Pistis sophia, and Meade, Bibliography ii.

GODEFRID ADMONTENSIS, *12th cent.* Liber de benedictionibus Jacob patriarchae. *PL,* 174.

Gospel of Nicodemus. *See* Harrowing. *See also AN,* 16.

GOTTFRIED VON STRASSBURG, *13th cent.* The story of Tristan & Iseult. Rendered into English from the German by Jessie L. Weston. London, Hutt, 1899. 2 vols.

GREGORIUS, I, *the Great, Saint, pope,* 540 (*ca.*)-604. Opera. *PL,* 75-79. *See especially:* Moralia; De cura pastoralis; Liber sacramentorum; Liber antiphonarius.

—— The book of pastoral rule, tr. with introduction notes and indices by James Barmby. *NPN*, 12.

GUIGO (*Carthusian*), *12th cent.* Scala paradisi, seu, Tractatus de modo orandi et de vita contemplativa. *PL*, 153.

GUITTONE D'AREZZO. *See* Viva Guittone del.

HALI MEIDENHAD. Hali Meidenhad, ab. 1200, ed. Rev. O. Cockayne, 1866. *EETS*.

HARROWING OF HELL. The Middle-English Harrowing of hell and Gospel of Nicodemus. Now first ed. from all the known manuscripts, with introduction and glossary, by William Henry Hulme. London, Trübner, 1907. *EETS*.

HELINANDUS, *Cistercian monk at Froidmont, d. ca.* 1229. De bone regimine principis. *PL*, 212.

Hermas. The Pastor of Hermas. *AN*, 1.

HERMES TRISMEGISTUS. Thrice-greatest Hermes. Studies in Hellenistic theosophy and gnosis. Being a translation of the extant sermons and fragments of the Trismegistic literature with prolegomena commentary, and notes, translated by G. R. S. Meade. London, 1908. 3 vols.

HIERONYMUS, *Saint.* [Commentaries on the scriptures.] *PL*, 22 ff.

—— Principal works, tr. by W. H. Fremantle, G. Lewis, and W. G. Martley. *NPN*, 6.

HILARIUS, *Saint, bp. of Poitiers, d.* 367? De Trinitate. *PL*, 10.

—— Select works: On the councils; On the Trinity; Homilies on the Psalms. *NPN*, 9.

HILDEBERTUS, *abp. of Tours,* 1056?-1133. Physiologus. [A bestiary] *PL*, 171. *See also:* De mysterio missae; and De operibus sex dierum.

HILDEGARDE, *Abbess, 12th cent.* Scivias seu visiones. Physica, i.e. subtilitatum diversarum naturarum creaturarum libri novem. *PL*, 197.

—— Scivias, ou les Trois livres des visions et révélations, de l'édit. princeps Henri Étienne, 1553, traduits littéralement du latin en français [by R. Chamonel] Paris, Chamonel, 1912. 2 vols.

HILTON, WALTER, The scale of perfection. Newly edited from ms. sources with an introduction by Evelyn Underhill. London, Watkins, 1923.

—— The scale (or ladder) of perfection. With an essay on The spiritual life of mediaeval England, by the Rev. J. B. Dalgairns. A new ed. Westminster, Art and book co., 1908.

—— The Song of angels. *In* The cell of self knowledge, Part II. *q.v.* (Hilton's only other authentic work.)

HIPPOLYTUS, *Saint,* Philosophumena; or, The refutation of all heresies, formerly attributed to Origen, but now to Hippolytus, bishop and martyr. Translated from the text of Cruice, by F. Legge. London, S.P.C.K.; New York, Macmillan, 1921. 2 vols.

HONORIUS AUGUSTODUNENSIS, *12th cent.* Opera. *PL*, 172. *See especially:* Scala coeli major; Scala coeli minor; Gemma animae, sive de divinis officiis et antique ritu missarum, deque horis canonicis et totius annis solemnitatibus; Speculum ecclesiae.

HRABANUS MAURUS, 776-856. Opera. *PL*, 107-112. *See especially:* Allegoriae in scripturam sacram and De universo. *PL*, 112.

HUGH OF ST. VICTOR. *12th cent.* Opera. *PL*, 175-177. *See especially:* De arca Noe morali; De arca Noe mystica; De nuptiis carnalibus et spiritualibus; De bestiis et aliis rebus [scriptural symbolism]; Speculum de mysteriis ecclesiase; De ceremoniis ecclesiasticis; De canone mystici libaminis.

Image du monde. *See* Gautier de Metz.

INNOCENTIUS III, *pope, d. 1216.* Opera. *PL*, 217. *See especially:* Mysteriorum evangelicae legis et sacramenti Eucharistiae, seu, de sacro altaris mysterio.

ISIDORUS, *Saint, bp. of Seville, d.* 636. Isidori Etymologiae. Codex toletanus (nunc matritensis) 15, 8 phototypice editus. Praefatus est Rudolphus Beer. Lugduni Batavorum, Sijthoff, 1909.
—— Isidori Hispalensis episcopi Etymologiarum sive originum libri xx; recognovit brevique adnotatione critica instruxit W. M. Lindsay. Oxonii, e typographeo Clarendoniano [1911] 2 vols. *See also PL,* 81-84.

JACOB'S WELL. Jacob's well, an Englisht treatise on the cleansing of man's conscience. Ed. from the unique ms. about 1440 A.D. in Salisbury cathedral, by Dr. Arthur Brandeis. London, Trübner, 1900- *EETS.*
JACOBUS *de Varagine, 12th cent.* Legenda aurea, volgo historia Lombardica dicta; ad optimorum librorum fidem recensuit T. Graesse. ed. Lipsiae, Arnold, 1850.
—— The golden legend; or, Lives of the saints, as Englished by William Caxton. London, Dent, 1900. 7 vols.
JACOBUS *de Vitriaco, cardinal, d.* 1240. Die Exempla aus den Sermones feriales et communes des Jakob von Vitry, hrsg. von Joseph Greven. Heidelberg, Winter, 1914.
—— The exempla or illustrative stories from the Sermones vulgares of Jacques de Vitry. Ed., with introduction, analysis, and notes, by Thomas Frederick Crane. London, Nutt, 1890. Latin with free English translation in notes.
JACOPONE *da Todi,* 1230-1306. Le laude, secondo la stampa fiorentina del 1490, a cura di Giovanni Ferri, Bori, Laterza, 1915.
JAMBLICHUS, *of Chalcis.* On the mysteries of the Egyptians, Chaldeans, and Assyrians, tr. from the Greek by T. Taylor. London, 1821.
—— Theurgia; or, The Egyptian mysteries: Reply of Abammon, the teacher, to the letter of Porphyry to Anebo, together with solutions of the questions therein contained, tr. from the Greek by Alexander Wilder. New York, Metaphysical pub. co. [1911]
JEROME. *See* Hieronymus.
JOANNES *of Damascus, Saint.* Exposition of the Orthodox Faith. Tr. [from the Greek] by S. D. F. Salmond, 1898. *NPN,* 9.
JOANNES *de Sancto Geminiano.* The legend of the holy Fina, virgin of Santo Gimignano: now first translated from the trecento Italian of Fra Giovanni di Coppo; with introduction and notes by M. Mansfield. London, Chatto & Windus; New York, Duffield, 1908.
JOANNES *Scotus, Erigena, 9th cent.* Opera. *PL,* 122. *See especially:* De divisione naturae; also translations and commentaries on the works of Dionysius Areopagita.
JOHN *of Salisbury, bp. of Chartres, d.* 1180. Ioannis Saresberiensis episcopi Carnotensis Policratici sive De nvgis cvrialivm et vestigiis philosophorvm libri viii; recognovit et prolegomenis, apparatv critico, commentario, indicibvs instrvxit Clemens C. I. Webb. Oxonii, e typographeo Clarendoniano, 1909. 2 vols.
JUAN *de la Cruz, Saint,* 1542-1591. Obras del mistico Doctor San Juan de la Cruz; edición crítica . . . con introducciones y notas del Gerardo de San Juan de la Cruz. Toledo, 1912. Important for a systematic analysis of the phases of the mystic way, and belonging in the medieval mystical tradition which developed late in Spain.
JULIANA, *anchoret,* 1343-1443. The shewings of Lady Julian, recluse at Norwich, 1373. (Previously entitled "Comfortable words for Christ's lovers") Transcribed and edited from the earliest known ms. (Brit. mus. addit. 37,790) by the Rev. Dundas Harford. 3d ed. London, Allenson; Chicago, Blessing [1925]
—— Revelations of divine love, recorded by Julian, anchoress at Norwich, anno Domini 1373. A version from the ms. in the British museum, ed. by Grace Warrack. 5th ed. London, Methuen [1914]
JUNILIUS *Africanus, 5th cent.* De partibus divinae legis. *PL,* 68.

JUSTINUS, *Martyr, Saint, 2d cent.* Opera. Item Athenagoræ atheniensis, Theophili antiocheni, Tatiani assyrii, & Hermiæ philosophi tractatus aliquot. Quae omnia græcè & latinè emendatiora prodeunt. Ed. nova juxta parisinam anni MDCXXXVI. Coloniæ, Schrey, & Meyerum, 1686.
JUSTUS *Urgullensis, 6th cent.* In Cantica canticorum Salomonis explicatio mystica. *PL,* 67.

Kabbalah. *See* Zohar, and Cabala Bibliography ii.
Key of Melito. *See* Cureton

LACTANTIUS, LACTANTIUS LUCIUS CAECILIUS FIRMIANUS, *4th cent.* Opera. *See especially:* De origine erroris. *PL,* 6.
—— Works, tr. W. Fletcher. *AN,* 21-22.
LANFRANC, *abp. of Canterbury,* 1005?-1089. De corpore et sanguine Domini. *PL,* 150.
LATINI, BRUNETTO. Li livres dou tresor. Pub. pour la première fois d'après les manuscrits de la Bibliothèque impériale, de la Bibliothèque de l'arsenal et plusieurs manuscrits des départments et de l'étranger, par P. Chabaille. Paris, Imprimerie impériale, 1863.
—— Il tesoretto e il favoletto ridotti e illustrati dall'abate Zannoni. Firenze, 1824.
LA TOUR-LANDRY, GEOFFROY DE, *14th cent.* The book of the knight of La Tour-Landry, compiled for the instruction of his daughters; tr. from the original French into English in the reign of Henry VI, and ed. for the first time from the unique manuscript in the British museum, Harl. 1764, and Caxton's print, A.D. 1484, with an introduction and notes by Thomas Wright. < Rev. ed., 1906 > London, Paul, Trench, Trübner, 1906 (1868) *EETS.*
Lay folks catechism. Ed. Simmons & Nolloth. London, Trübner, 1901. *EETS.*
The lay folks mass book; or, The manner of hearing mass, with rubrics and devotions for the people, in four texts, and offices in English according to the use of York, from manuscripts of the xth to the xvth century, with appendix, notes, and glossary by Thomas Frederick Simmons. London, Trübner, 1879. *EETS.*
Lay folks' prayer-book. *See* Prymer.
LEO, FRATER. Speculum perfectionis, seu S. Francisci Assisiensis legenda antiquissima, ed. Paul Sabatier, Paris, Fischbacher, 1898. *Coll.,* 1.
LEO IX, *Saint, pope,* 1002-1054. De conflictu vitiorum atque virtutum libellus. *PL,* 143.
LIBER EXEMPLORUM. Liber exemplorum ad usum praedicantium saeculo XIII compositus a quodam fratre minore anglico de provincia Hiberniae secundum codicem dunelmensem editus per A. G. Little. Aberdoniae, typis academicis, 1908.
LOVELICH, HERRY. Romance of Merlin, ed. E. A. Kock. London, Trübner 1913. *EETS-e.*
—— The history of the Holy Grail, Englisht, ab. 1450 A.D., from the French prose of Sires Robiers de Borron. London, Trübner, 1874-1905. 2 vols. *EETS.*
LUDUS COVENTRIAE. Ludus Coventriae or the Plaie called Corpus Christi, ed. K. S. Block. London, Trübner, 1922. *EETS-e.*
LULL, RAMÓN, *d.* 1315. Blanquerna, maestro de la perfección cristiana. Con un prólogo de D. Marcelino Menéndez y Pelayo. Madrid, 1883. 2 vols. Spanish translation of Catalan original.
—— The book of the lover and the beloved; tr. from the Catalan, with an introductory essay by E. Allison Peers. New York, Macmillan, 1923.
—— The tree of love, translated from the Catalan with an introductory essay by E. Allison Peers. London, S.P.C.K.; New York & Toronto, Macmillan [1926]
—— De secreti di natura o della quinta essentia libri due; Alberto Magno de cose minerali e metalliche libri chinque, il tutto tradotto da Pietro Lauro. Vinegia, 1557.

MABINOGION. Mabinogion; from the Llyfr coch o Hergest and other ancient Welsh ms; with an English translation and notes, by Lady Charlotte Guest. London, Longman, 1849. 3 vols.

—— The Mabinogion, tr. by Lady Charlotte Guest. London, Dent; New York, Dutton [1906]

MACARIUS, *Saint, the Elder, of Egypt, 4th cent.* Macarii anecdota; seven unpublished homilies of Macarius; ed. by G. L. Marriott. Cambridge, Harvard university press, 1918.

—— Fifty spiritual homilies, tr. A. J. Mason. New York, Macmillan, 1921.

MACROBIUS, *4th cent.* Macrobius. Franciscus Eyssenhardt iterum recognovit. Lipsiae, Teubneri, 1893.

MALORY, *Sir* THOMAS, *15th cent.* Le morte Darthur by Syr Thomas Malory; the original edition of William Caxton now reprinted and edited with an introduction and glossary, by H. Oskar Sommer. London, Nutt, 1889-91. 3 vols.

—— Le morte d'Arthur. London & Toronto, Dent; New York, Dutton [1923] 2 vols.

MANNYNG, ROBERT, *of Brunne, fl.* 1288-1338. Robert of Brunne's "Handlyng synne," A. D. 1303, with those parts of the Anglo-French treatise on which it was founded, William of Waddington's "Manuel des pechiez," re-edited from mss. in the British museum and Bodleian libraries, by Frederick J. Furnivall. London, Trübner, 1901- *EETS.*

—— *See* Bonaventura.

MARBODE, *bp. of Rennes, fl.* 1067-1101. De gemmarum lapidumque pretiosum formis, naturis, atque viribus. Cum scholiis Pictorii Villingen. Coloniae, Alopecius, 1539.

MARIE *de France.* Poésies de Marie de France, ou, Recueil de lais, fables et autres productions de cette femme célebre, par B. de Roquefort. Paris, Chasseriau, 1820.

—— French mediaeval romances from the lays of Marie de France, translated by Eugene Mason. London, Dent; New York, Dutton [1911]

—— Guingamor, Lanval, Tyolet, Bisclaveret; four lais rendered into English prose from the French of Marie de France and others by Jessie L. Weston. With designs by Caroline Watts. London, Nutt, 1900.

MERLIN. Le roman de Merlin; or, The early history of King Arthur, faithfully edited from the French ms. add. 10292 in the British museum by Prof. H. Oskar Sommer. London [Ballantyne, Hanson] 1894.

—— Merlin legend. On the early history of King Arthur, a prose rhyme about 1450-1460. Ed. Henry B. Wheatley. London, Trübner, 1899. 2 vols. *EETS.* Introduction contains outline of the history of Merlin.

Micrologus de ecclesiasticis observationibus opusculum ante annos sexcentos conscriptum ab homine antiquitatis ecclesiasticae . . . *PL,* 151; col. 973 ff.

MINUCIUS FELIX, MARCUS, *3rd cent.* Octavius. *PL,* 3.

—— M. Minucii Felicis Octavius. Recognovit, praefatus est, appendicem criticam addidit Aloisius Valmaggi. Augustae Taurinorum, Paraviae [1916]

MIRK, JOHN, *fl.* 1403. Instructions for parish priests. Ed. from Cotton ms. Claudius A. II., by Edward Peacock. London, Trübner, 1868 [revised 1902] *EETS.*

—— Mirk's festial: a collection of homilies. London, Trübner, 1905- *EETS-e.*

Mirrour of the blessed lyf of Jesus Christ; a translation of the Latin work entitled Meditationes vitae Christi, attributed to Cardinal Bonaventura. Made before the year 1410 by Nicolas Love, ed. by Lawrence Powell. London, Frowde, 1908.

MORRIS, RICHARD, *ed.* Legends of the holy rood; Symbols of the passion and cross-poems. In Old English of the eleventh, fourteenth, and fifteenth centuries. Ed. from mss. in the British museum and Bodleian libraries; with introduction, translations, and glossarial index. London, Trübner, 1871. *EETS.*

The myroure of Oure Ladye, containing a devotional treatise on divine service, with a translation of the offices used by the sisters of the Brigittine monastery of Sion, at Isleworth, during the fifteenth and sixteenth centuries. Ed. from the original black-letter text of 1530 A.D., with introduction and notes, by John Henry Blunt. London, Trübner, 1873. *EETS.*

NAPIER, ARTHUR SAMPSON, *ed.* History of the holy rood-tree, a twelfth century version of the cross-legend, with Notes on the orthography of the Ormulum (with a facsimile) and a Middle English Compassio Mariae. London, Trübner, 1894. *EETS.*

ORIGENES, *3rd cent.* Contra Celsum, tr. Frederick Crombie. *AN,* 23.
—— De Principiis, tr. Frederick Crombie. *AN,* 10.
OROSIUS, PAULUS, *5th cent.* Adversus paganos historiarum libri septem, ut et Apologeticus contra Pelagium de arbitrii libertate. Recensuit suisque animadversionibus nummisque antiquis plurimis illustravit Sigebertus Havercampus. Lugduni Batavorum, Potvliet, 1738. *See also PL,* 31.

PARADIS DER FORNUFTIGEN SELE. Paradisus anime intelligentis. Aus der Oxforder handschrift Cod. Laud. misc. 479, nach E. Sievers' Abschrift hrsg. von Philipp Strauch. Berlin, Weidmann, 1919. *Deut.* 30.
PARMA, G. B. Ascesi e mistica cattolica nella Divina commedia. Subiaco (Monastery) 1925. v. 1 pt. 1.
PAULINUS, *Saint, bp. of Nola,* 353-431. Opera; ex recensione Guilelmi de Hartel. Vindobonae, Tempsky, 1894. 2 vols. *Corpus.*
—— Divi Pavlini episcopi Nolani opera. Item vita eiusdem, consummatam perfectionem ac prorsus mirabilem sanctitatem continens, ex ipsius operibus & veterum de eo elogijs concinnata. Accedunt notæ Amoebææ Frontonis Dvcaei & Heriberti Ros-vveydi e Societate Iesv. Antverpiæ, Moretum, 1622.
PEARL (Middle English poem). Pearl, an English poem of the 14th century; ed., with a modern rendering, by Israel Gollancz. London, Nutt, 1891.
PERLESVAUS. The high history of the Holy Grail. Tr. from the old French, by Sebastian Evans. London, Dent; New York, Dutton [1910]
PETRUS COMESTOR, *12th cent.* Historia scholastica. *PL,* 198.
PETRUS LOMBARDUS, *bp. of Paris.* Sententiarum lib. iiii. Parisiis, Audœnum Parvum, 1543. *See also PL,* 192.
PHILO *Judæus.* Opera. Recog. L. Cohn et P. Wendland. Berlin, Reimer, 1896-1906. 5 vols.
—— The works; tr. from the Greek, by C. D. Yonge. London, Bohn, 1854-55. 4 vols. *See especially:* On the creation of the world; On the allegories of the sacred laws; On dreams being sent from God.
—— Philo on the contemplative life. Edited by F. C. Conybeare. Oxford, Frowde, 1895.
PIETRO DAMIANI, *Saint, 11th cent.* Opera. *PL,* 144-145. *See especially:* Expositio canonis missae. Hymnus de gloria paradisi.
—— Iter Gallicum; expositio canonis missae; Collectanea N.T. (In. Mai's Scriptorum veterum Nova Collectio, vol. 6.)
PISAN, CHRISTINE DE. The book of the Duke of true lovers: now first translated from the Middle French: with an introduction: by Alice Kemp-Welch. The ballads rendered into the original metres by Laurence Binyon & Eric R. D. Maclagan. London, Chatto & Windus, 1908 [1907]
PISTIS SOPHIA. Pistis sophia; a Gnostic miscellany: being for the most part extracts from the books of the Saviour, to which are added excerpts from a cognate literature; Englished (with an introduction and annotated bibliography) by G. R. S. Mead. New and completely rev. ed. London, Watkins, 1921.
PLINIUS SECUNDUS, CAIUS. The natural history of Pliny. Translated, with copious notes and illustrations, by John Bostock and H. T. Riley. London, Bohn, 1855-1857. 6 vols.
PLOTINUS. Plotini Enneades, praemisso Porphyrii de Vita Plotini deque ordine

BIBLIOGRAPHY

librorum ejus libello. Edidit R. Volkmann. Leipzig, Teubner, 1883-1884. 2 vols.
—— Plotinus, tr. from the Greek by Stephen Mackenna. London, Medical society, 1917-26. 4 vols.
—— Complete works, in chronological order, grouped in four periods; with biography by Porphyry, Eunapius, & Suidas, commentary by Porphyry, illustrations by Jamblichus and Ammonius, studies in sources, development, influence; index of subjects, thoughts and words. By Kenneth Sylvan Guthrie. London, Bell; Grantwood, N. H., Comparative literature press [1918] 4 vols.
PLUTARCHUS. Isis et Osiris. Traduction nouvelle avec avant-propos, prolégomènes et notes par Mario Meunier. Paris, L'artisan du livre, 1924.
PROCLUS, *Lycius, surnamed Diadochus.* The philosophical and mathematical commentaries of Proclus on the first book of Euclid's Elements. To which are added a History of the restoration of Platonic theology by the latter Platonists, and a translation from the Greek of Proclus's Theological elements. London, Printed for the author, 1792. 2 vols.
PRUDENTIUS CLEMENS, AURELIUS, *4th cent.* Liber metricus Cathemerinon. *PL,* 59.
—— Psychomachia. *PL,* 60.
—— Hymns, tr. R. Martin Pope. (Latin and English) London, Dent, 1905. A translation of the *Cathemerinon.*
The Prymer or Lay-folks prayer book. Cambridge university M.S., 1420, ed. Henry Littlehales, London, Trübner, 1895-97. *EETS.*

RABANUS MAURUS. *See* Hrabanus Maurus
RADBERTUS, PASCHASIUS, *9th cent.* Liber de corpore et sanguine Domini. *PL,* 120.
RAMBALDI, BENVENUTO, *da Imola.* Comentum super Dantis Aldigherij Comœdiam; nunc primum integre in lucen editum, sumptibus Gulielmi Warren Vernon curate J. P. Lacaita. Florentiae, 1887, 5 vols.
RATRAMNUS, *9th cent.* De corpore et sanguine Domini. *PL,* 121.
REINERUS, *12th cent.* Commentatio in novem ante-natalitas antiphonas ab ordientes. *PL,* 204.
REYNARD THE FOX. *English.* The most delectable history of Reynard the Fox; ed., with introduction and notes, by Joseph Jacobs; done unto pictures by W. Frank Calderon. London & New York, Macmillan, 1895. Although the text adapted for children "the introduction and notes attempt to give the adult reader a condensed account of the latest results of research in folk-lore and literary history."
RICHARD *of St. Victor, d.* 1173. Opera omnia. *PL,* 196. *See especially:* De praeparatione animi ad contemplationem, seu Benjamin Minor; De gratia contemplationis, seu Benjamin Major; Allegoriae tabernaculi foederis; Mysticae adnotationes in Psalmos; Expositio in Cantica canticorum; De Trinitate; Quomodo Spiritus sanctus est amor Patris et Filii; De comparatione Christi ad florem et Mariae ad virgam; De statu interioris hominis; De gradibus charitatis; De quatuor gradibus violentae charitatis.
—— Benjamin minor, an old English translation in The cell of self-knowledge, Part II. *q.v.*
ROCABERTÍ, HUGUES BERNARD DE, *fl.* 1461. The Gloria d'amor, a Catalan visionpoem of the 15th century, ed., with introduction, notes and glossary, by H. C. Heaton. New York, Columbia university press, 1916.
ROLLE, RICHARD, *of Hampole,* 1290?-1349. Works of Richard Rolle of Hampole and his followers. Edited by C. Horstman. London, 1895. 2 vols. Bibliography.
—— The fire of love, and The mending of life; or, The rule of living. The first Englisht in 1435, from the De incendio amoris, the second in 1434, from the De emendacione vitæ of Richard Rolle, hermit of Hampole, by Richard Misyn, bachelor of theology, prior of Lincoln, Carmelite. Ed. with introduction and glossary from ms. CCCXXXVI in Corpus Christi college, Oxford, by the Rev. Ralph Harvey. London, Trübner, 1896. *EETS.*

—— The fire of love, or melody of love, and The mending of life, or rule of living, tr. by Richard Misyn from the Incendium amoris and the De emendatione vitae of Richard Rolle. Edited and done into modern English by F. M. M. Comper, intro. by E. Underhill. 2d ed. London, Methuen, 1920.

—— English prose treatises. London, Trübner, 1866. *EETS.*

ROMAN DE LA ROSE. Le roman de la rose, par Guillaume de Lorris et Jean de Meun, pub. d'après les manuscrits par Ernest Langlois. Paris, Firmin-Didot, 1914-24. 5 vols.

—— The romance of the rose, by W. Lorris & J. Clopinel; Englished by F. S. Ellis. London, Dent, 1900. 3 vols.

Romance, vision, and satire. *See* Weston, Jessie L.

ROSSETTI, DANTE GABRIEL. Poems & translations; including Dante's "Vita nuova" & "The early Italian poets." London, Dent; New York, Dutton [1913]

ROTH, FRANZ WILHELM EMIL. Lateinische Hymnen des Mittelalters. Als Nachtrag zu den Hymnensammlungen von Daniel, Mone, Vilmar und G. Morel aus Handschriften und Incunabeln hrsg. von F. W. E. Roth. Nebst Beschreibung der benützten Handschriften und Drucke und alphabetischen Register der Liederanfänge. Augsburg, Schmid, 1887.

RUYSBROECK, JAN VAN. Werken, ed. David & Snellaert. Maetschappy der Vlaemsche Bibliophilen. Publications, 3d. ser. 1, 4, 7, 9, 12. Ghent, 1858-68.

—— Oeuvres de Ruysbroeck l'Admirable, traduction du flamand par les Bénédictins de Saint-Paul de Wisques. Bruxelles, Vromant, 1920-

—— Adornment of the spiritual marriage; the sparkling stone; the book of supreme truth. Trans. from the Flemish by P. Wynschenk Dom. Ed. with introduction and notes by Evelyn Underhill. London, Dent, 1916.

—— Flowers of a mystic garden, tr. from the French of Ernest Hello by C. E. S. London, Watkins, 1912. (Out of print.)

—— The kingdom of the lovers of God. Now tr. for the first time from the Latin of Laurence Surius, the Carthusian; together with an introduction by T. Arnold Hyde. London, Trübner, New York, Dutton, 1919.

—— Love's gradatory; tr. with preface by Mother St. Jerome. New York, Dutton, 1919.

Note: The French translations from the point of view of symbolism are much better than the English (themselves usually taken from the French), but consultation of the original is well rewarded.

SABATIER, PAUL, *ed.* Actus Beati Francisci et sociorum ejus. Paris, Fischbacher, 1902. *Coll. 4.*

SCAMMAN, EDITH. The alliterative poem: Death and Life. (In: Radcliffe college monographs no. 15, 1910, p. 95-113)

SECRETA SECRETORUM. Secreta secretorum, three prose versions ed. with introduction and notes by R. Steele, 1898. *EETS.* This work in the Middle Ages was attributed to Aristotle.

Sefer, Yezirah. *See* Zohar.

Sepher ha-zohar. *See* Zohar.

SEVEN SAGES. *Middle English.* The seven sages of Rome; ed. from the manuscripts, with introduction, notes, and glossary by Killis Campbell. Boston, New York, Ginn, 1907.

SICARDUS, *bp. of Cremona, d.* 1215. Mitrale, sive Summa de officiis ecclesiasticis. *PL,* 213.

STRABO. *See* Walafridus Strabus.

SUSO, HENRICH, *1300-1360.* Die Schriften des seligen H. Seuse. Hrsg. von Fr. Heinr. Seuse Denifle. München, Literdrisch Institut, 1876.

—— Henrich Seuse: Deutschen Schriften. Hrsg. von Dr. Karl Behlmezer. Stuttgart, Kohlhammer, 1907.

—— Little book of eternal wisdom. To which is added the celebrated "Parable of the pilgrim," by Walter Hilton. London, Norwood [1910]

SYDRACH. Das Buch Sidrach. Nach der Kopenkagener mittelniederdeutschen Handschrift v. j. 1479, hrsg. von H. Jellinghaus, Tübingen, Gedruckt für den Litterarischen Verein in Stuttgart, 1904.

SYMONDS, JOHN ADDINGTON, *ed. and tr.* Wine, women and song; mediæval Latin students' songs now first translated into English verse, with an essay. London, Chatto & Windus, 1925. "Books on Goliardic literature": p. 206.

TAULER, JOHANNES D. Joannes Thauleri, *ca.* 1300-1361. Sermones de tempore et de sanctis totius anni, plane piissime: R. F. Laurentio Surio in Latinum Sermonem translata, etc. Cologne, 1603.
—— Sermons de J. Tauler et autres écrits mystiques, précéde d'une introduction et annoté par A. L. Corin. Liége, Vaillant-Carmanne, 1924. Vol. 1.
—— The inner way: being 36 sermons for festivals. New translation with introduction by Rev. A. W. Hutton. 3d. edition. London, Methuen, 1909. (Library of Devotion.)
—— Die predigten Taulers; aus der Engelberger und der Freiburger handschrift sowie aus Schmidts abschriften der ehemaligen Strassburger handschriften hrsg. von Ferdinand Vetter. Berlin, Weidmann, 1910. *Deut.* 11.

TERTULLIANUS, QUINTUS SEPTIMIUS FLORENS, *3rd cent.* Opera. *PL,* 1-2. *See especially:* Apologeticus; De resurrectione carnis.
—— The writings of . . . Tertullianus. *AN,* 11, 15, 18.

THEOLOGIA DEUTSCH. Theologia deutsch, die lerst gar manchen lieblichen underscheit gotlicher warheit, hrsg. von F. Pfeiffer. 2. verb. verm. Aufl. Stuttgart, 1855.
—— Theologia germanica: which setteth forth many fair lineaments of divine truth, and saith very lofty and lovely things touching a perfect life; ed. by Dr. Pfeiffer from the only complete manuscript yet known; tr. from the German by Susanna Winkworth. With a preface by the Rev. Charles Kingsley, and a letter to the translator by the Chevalier Bunsen. London & New York, Macmillan, 1901.

THOMAS AQUINAS, *Saint* 1225?-1274. Summa theologica, diligenter emendata de Rubeis, Billuart, et aliorum. Turin, Marietti, 1922. 6 vols. incl. indices.
—— Summa theologica. Editio altera Romana ad emendatiores editiones impressa et noviter accuratissime recognita. Romae, Forzani, 1922-23. 6 vols. incl. indices.
—— The "Summa theologica" of St. Thomas Aquinas; literally translated by Fathers of the English Dominican Province. London, Cates & Washbourne, 1911-22. 20 vols.
—— Summae de veritate catholicae fidei contra gentiles quae supersunt ex codice autographo qui in Bibliotheca Vaticana adservatur cetera vero ex probatissimis codd. et editionibus cura et studio Petri Antonii Uccellii edita et Leoni XIII. P. M. dicata. Romae, ex Typographia polyglotta, 1878.
—— Summae contra gentiles libri iv. Rome, 1924.

LE TOMBEOR NOSTRE DAME. Of the tumbler of our Lady & other miracles now translated from the Middle French: introduction and notes by Alice Kemp-Welch. London, Chatto & Windus, 1908.

TURBA PHILOSOPHORUM, OR, ASSEMBLY OF THE SAGES. Turba philosophorum, or, Assembly of the sages, ed. A. E. Waite. London, 1914.

TURMEL, JOSEPH. La descente du Christ aux enfers. Paris, Bloud, 1905.

VAUGHAN, THOMAS. Magical writings: a verbatim reprint of his first four treatises: With the Latin passages translated and with a biographical preface and essay on the esoteric literature of Western Christendom, by Arthur Edward Waite. London, Redway, 1888.

VICES AND VIRTUES. Vices and virtues, being a soul's confession of its sins, with Reason's description of the virtues. A Middle-English dialogue of about 1200 A.D. Ed., with an introduction, translation, notes, and glossary, from the

Stowe ms. 240 in the British museum, by Ferd. Holthausen. London, Trübner, 1888-1921. *EETS.* 2 vols.

VILLANI, GIOVANNI. Cronica . . . a miglior lezione ridotta coll' ajuto de' testi a penna con note filologiche di I. Moutier e con appendici storico-geografiche comp. da Franc. Gheradi Dragomanni. Firenze, Coen, 1844-45. 4 vols. in 2.

—— Villani's Chronicle; being selections from the first nine books of the Croniche fiorentine of Giovanni Villani; tr. by Rose E. Selfe, and ed. by Philip H. Wicksteed, 2d ed. carefully rev. New York, Dutton, 1907. (Contains an account of Dante's life).

VINCENT *de Beauvais, d.* 1264. Speculum majus. [Called Speculum universale.] Strasburg [Mentelin?, 1476?] Rare.

VINCENTIUS LERINENSIS, *Saint, 5th cent.* Commonitorium adversus profanas omnium haereticorum novitates. *PL,* 50.

—— A commonitory for the antiquity and universality of the Catholic faith against the profane novelties of all heresies. *NPN,* 11.

VISIO PAULI. Visio S. Pauli, ein Beitrag zur Visionslitteratur, mit einem deutschen und zwei lateinischen Texten, von Herman Brandes. Halle, Niemeyer, 1885.

—— Vision of Paul, ed. A. Rutherford. In: *AN* additional vol., ed. Allan Menzies, 1903.

VIVA, GUITTONE DEL, *called Guittone d'Arezzo.* Rime. Firenze, 1867. (Biblioteca dei classici, serie 1, t. 1)

WALAFRIDUS STRABUS, 809-849. Glossa ordinaria. *PL,* 113-114.

WESSELSKI, ALBERT. Mönchslatein: Erzählungen aus geistlichen Schriften des XIII. Jahrhunderts. Leipzig, Heims, 1909.

WESTON, JESSIE LAIDLAY. Romance, vision & satire; English alliterative poems of the fourteenth century, newly rendered in the original metres. Boston & New York, Houghton Mifflin, 1912.

——, *ed.* The chief Middle English poets; selected poems, newly rendered and ed., with notes and bibliographical references. Boston, New York Houghton Mifflin [1914]

WILLIAM OF MALMESBURY, *12th cent.* Liber de antiquitatis Glastoniensis Ecclesiae. *PL,* 179.

WILLIAM OF WADDINGTON. Le manuel de pechiez. *See* Mannyng, Robert of Brunne.

WOLBERO, *Saint Patuleonis Coloniensis, 12th cent.* Commentaria in Canticum canticorum. *PL,* 195.

WOLFRAM *von Eschenbach.* Wolfram von Eschenbach, hrsg. von A. Leitzmann. Halle, 1902-06. 2 vols.

—— Parzival, a knightly epic, for the first time translated into English verse from the original German, by Jessie L. Weston. London, Nutt, 1894. 2 vols.

WRIGHT, THOMAS, *ed.* Popular treatises on science written during the middle ages, in Anglo-Saxon, Anglo-Norman, and English. Ed. from the original manuscripts. London, Taylor, 1841.   *I*

—— *ed.* Early mysteries, and other Latin poems of the twelfth and thirteenth centuries: ed. from the original manuscripts in the British museum, and the libraries of Oxford, Cambridge, Paris, and Vienna. London, Nichols, 1838.   *G*

ZOHAR. Kabbala denudata, the Kabbalah unveiled, containing the following books of the Zohar. 1. The book of concealed mystery. 2. The greater holy assembly. 3. The lesser holy assembly. Tr. into English from the Latin version of Knorr von Rosenroth, and collated with the original Chaldee and Hebrew text, by S. L. MacGregor Mathers. London, Redway, 1887.

—— Sepher Yezirah: a book on creation, or, The Jewish metaphysics of remote antiquity. With English translation, preface, explanatory notes and glossary by I. Kalisch. New York, Frank, 1877.

—— Sepher ha-zohar. (Le Livre de la splendeur); doctrine ésotérique des Israélites, traduit pour la première fois, par J. de Pauly, Paris, 1906-11. 6 vols.

BIBLIOGRAPHY II. MODERN STUDIES

THIS BIBLIOGRAPHY DOES NOT LIST BOOKS PUBLISHED AFTER 1927

AALL, ANATHON AUGUST FREDERIK. Der Logos. Geschichte seiner Entwickelung in der griechischen Philosophie und der christlichen Litteratur. Leipzig, Reisiland, 1896-99. 2 vols.   *B*

ABRAHAMSSON, DAVID. Solkult i nordisk bebyggelse. *Ymer*, 44: 239-59, 1924.   *J*

ADAMS, HENRY, Mont-Saint-Michel and Chartres. Boston & New York, Houghton Mifflin, 1913.   *F, G*

ALLCROFT, ARTHUR HADRIAN. The circle and the cross, a study in continuity. London, Macmillan, 1927-   *F, J*

ALLEN, JOHN ROMILLY. Early Christian symbolism in Great Britain and Ireland before the thirteenth century. London, Whiting, 1887.   *F, J*

ANCONA, ALLESANDRO D'. I precursori di Dante. Firenze, Sansoni, 1874.   *A, G*

ANGUS, SAMUEL. The mystery-religions and Christianity, a study in the religious background of early Christianity. New York, Scribners, 1925.   *D, J*

Arte, scienza e fede ai giorni di Dante. Conferenze dantesche tenuto nel MDCCCC a cura del comitato milanese delle Società dantesca italiana. Milano, Hoepli, 1901.   *A, G*

ASIN PALACIOS, MIGUEL. El Averroismo teologico de Sto. Tomas de Aquino. In: Homenaje a D. Francisco Codera. Saragossa, Escar, 1904. p. 271-331.   *B*

—— Islam and the Divine comedy; translated and abridged by Harold Sunderland. New York, Dutton, 1926.   *A, D, J*

AUBER, CHARLES AUGUSTE. Histoire et théorie du symbolisme religieux avant et depuis le christianisme. Paris, Franck, 1870-72. 4 vols.   *F, J*

—— Another ed. Paris, Féchoz & Letouzey, 1884. 4 vols.

AUDSLEY, WILLIAM JAMES & GEORGE ASHDOWN AUDSLEY. Handbook of Christian symbolism. With illustrations in chromo-lithography and wood-engraving. London, Day [1865]   *F*

AUGER, A. Etude sur les mystiques des Pays-Bas au moyen age. In: Académie royal des sciences, des lettres et des beaux-arts de Belgique, Memoires, vol. 46, 1892.   *D*

BAES, EDGAR. Le symbole et l'allegorie. Brussels, 1899-1900. In: Académie royale des sciences, des lettres et des beaux-arts de Belgique. Memoires, v. 59, no. 8.   *B, K*

BAEUMKER, CLEMENS. Die christliche Philosophie des Mittelalters. In: Die Kultur der Gegenwart, I, 1. Berlin, 1906.   *B*

BAKER, AUGUSTIN. Holy Wisdom; or, directions for the prayer of contemplation by forty treatises . . . methodically digested by R. F. Serenus Cressy, new ed. from Douay ed. of 1657, by Rt. Rev. Abbot Sweeney. London, Burns & Oates, n.d.   *D*

BARRE, ANDRÉ. Le symbolisme; essai historique sur le mouvement symboliste en France de 1885 à 1900, suivi d'une Bibliographie de la poésie symboliste. Paris, Jouve, 1911.   *B', K*

BARTON, GEORGE AARON. Archæology and the Bible. Philadelphia, American Sunday-school union [1916]   *J*

BASTARD D'ESTANG, AUGUSTE, *comte de.* Études de symbolique chrétienne. Rapports sur les crosses de Tiron et de Saint-Amand de Rouen, faits, en 1856 et 1857, au Comité de la langue, de l'histoire et des arts de la France, section d'archéologie. Paris, Imprimerie impériale, 1851.   *F*

BAUDOUIN, CHARLES. Le symbole chez Verhaeren. Essai de psych-analyse de l'art. 4. ed. Genève, Mongenet, 1924.   *C*

—— Psychoanalysis and aesthetics. Translated from the French [of Le symbole chez Verhaeren] by Eden & Cedar Paul. New York, Dodd, Mead, 1924.   *C, B', K*

BAUR, FERDINAND CHRISTIAN. Symbolik und Mythologie, oder, Die Natur-religion des Alterthums. Stuttgart, Metzler, 1824-5. 3 vols.   J
BAYLEY, HAROLD. The lost language of symbolism; an inquiry into the origin of certain letters, words, names, fairy-tales, folk-lore, and mythologies. London, Williams & Norgate, 1912. 2 vols.   D, F, K
BEAUNIER, ANDRÉ. La poésie nouvelle. Paris, Mercure de France, 1902.   B'
BECKER, FERDINAND. Die Darstellung Jesu Christi unter dem Bilde des Fisches auf den Monumenten der Kirche der Katakomben. Breslau, Mälzer, 1866.   F
BENHAM, ALLEN ROGERS. English literature from Widsith to the death of Chaucer; a source book. New Haven, Yale university press, 1916.   G
BENNETT, CHARLES ANDREW ARMSTRONG. A philosophical study of mysticism, an essay. New Haven, Yale university press, 1923.   B, D
BERNARD, THEOPHILE. Cours de liturgie romaine; au, Explication historique, littérale et mystique des cérémonies de l'église à l'usage du clergé. Paris, Berche et Tralin, 1887-1908. 11 vols.   E
BERNHART, JOSEPH. Die philosophische Mystik des Mittelalters, von ihren Antiken Ursprüngen bis zur Renaissance. München, Reinhardt, 1922.   B, D
BISOGNO, EUGENIO DI. S. Bonaventura e Dante; studii. Milano, Cogliati, 1899.
                                                                          A, D
BLOCHET, EDGAR. Les sources orientales de la Divine comédie. Paris, Maisonneuve, 1901.   A, J
BOETTGER, HEINRICH. Sonnencult der Indogermanen, insbesondere der Indoteutonen. Breslau, Freund, 1890.   J
BOISSONNADE, PROSPER. Life and work in medieval Europe (fifth to fifteenth centuries). Translated, with an introduction, by Eileen Power. London, Trübner; New York, Knopf, 1927.   G
BOND, FREDERICK BLIGH & THOMAS SINCOX LEA. A preliminary investigation of the cabala contained in the Coptic Gnostic books and of a similar gematria in the Greek text of the New Testament. Oxford, Blackwell, 1917. 96 p.   D, I
BORCHARDT, LUDWIG. Gegen die Zahlenmystik an der grossen Pyramide bei Gise; Vortrag gehalten in der Vorderasiatisch-ägyptischen Gesellschaft zu Berlin am 1. Februar, 1922. Berlin, Behrend, 1922. 40 p.   D, I, J
BOURDON, B. La pensée sans images. Journal de psychologie normale et pathologique, 20: 189-205, 1923.   C
—— La perception et la pensée verbales. Journal de psychologie normale et pathologique, 22: 721-7, 1925.   C, K
BOYLAN, PATRICK. Thoth, the Hermes of Egypt; a study of some aspects of theological thought in ancient Egypt. London, New York, Milford, Oxford university press, 1922.   D, J
BRAUN, JOSEPH. Die liturgische Gewandung im Occident und Orient nach Ursprung und Entwicklung, Verwendung und Symbolik. Freiburg im Breisgau, St. Louis, Mo., Herder, 1907.   E
BRÉHIER, ÉMILE. Origine des images symboliques. Revue philosophique de la France et de l'étranger, 75: 135-55, 1913.   C, F, K
BRÉHIER, LOUIS. L'art chrétien, son développement iconographique. Paris, Laurens, 1918.   E, F
—— L'église et l'Orient au moyen âge: les croisades. Paris, Lecoffre, Gabalda, 1907.   F, G
BREMOND, HENRI. Histoire littéraire du sentiment religieux en France dupuis la fin des guerres de religion jusqu'à nos jours. Paris, Bloud et Gay, 1916. 6 vols. Begins 1580; interesting from the point of view of modern trends in mysticism.
                                                                          D
—— La Provence mystique au XVIIe siècle. Paris, Plon-Nourrit, 1908.   D
BRITISH MUSEUM. Dept. of Egyptian and Assyrian antiquities. Babylonian legends of the creation. London, British museum, 1921. 67 p.   J
—— The Book of the Dead. London, British museum, 1922. 43 p.   J
BRITT, MATHEW, ed. The hymns of the breviary and missal, ed. with introduction

and notes. Preface by Rt. Rev. Msgr. Hugh T. Henry. New York, Cincinnati, Benziger, 1922.   E
BROERS, BERNARDA CONRADINA. Mysticism in the neo-romanticists. Amsterdam, Paris [1923] Thesis.   D
BRUCE, JAMES DOUGLAS. The evolution of Arthurian romance from the beginnings down to the year 1300. Göttingen, Vandenhoeck & Ruprecht; Baltimore, Johns Hopkins press, 1923. 2 vols.   H
BUDGE, Sir ERNEST ALFRED THOMPSON WALLIS. Tutankhamen, Amenism, Atenism and Egyptian monotheism, with hieroglyphic texts of hymns to Amen and Aten, translations, and illustrations. London, Hopkinson, 1923.   J
BUSETTO, N. Origine e natura della 'Fortuna' dantesca. Giornale dantesco, 12: 129 ff., 1904.   A
BUSNELLI, GIOVANNI. Cosmogonia e antropogenesi secondo Dante Alighieri e le sue fonti. Roma, "Civiltà Cattolica," 1922.   A
—— Il concetto e l'ordine del 'Paradiso' dantesco; indagini e studii, preceduti da una lettera di Francesco Flamini. Città di Castello, Lapi, 1911-12. 2 vols.   A
—— La concezione del Purgatorio dantesco. Roma, "Civiltà cattolica", 1906.
                                                                                      A
BUTLER, EDWARD CUTHBERT. Western mysticism; the teachings of SS Augustine, Gregory and Bernard on contemplation and the contemplative life; neglected chapters in the history of religion. London, Constable, 1922.   B, D

CABALA. See Bond, F. B.; The Canon; Franck, Adolphe; Myer, Isaac; Pick, Bernhard; Westcott, William Wynn.
CANDLER, HOWARD. On the symbolic use of number in the Divine comedy and elsewhere. (Royal Society of Literature, Transactions. London, 1910, ser. 2, 30: 1-29.)   A, I, J
The Canon: an exposition of the pagan mystery perpetuated in the Cabbala as the rule of all the arts. London, Mathews, 1897.   I, J
CARLYLE, ROBERT WARRAND, & ALEXANDER JAMES CARLYLE. A history of mediæval political theory in the West. Edinburgh & London, Blackwood, 1903-22. 4 vols.   G
CARPENTER, WILLIAM BOYD. The spiritual message of Dante. London, Williams & Norgate, 1914.   A
CARUS, PAUL. Solar worship. Open court, 32: 564-68, 1918.   J
CASEL, ODO. Die Liturgie als Mysterienfeier. Freiburg im Breisgau, Herder, 1923.   E
CASINI, TOMMASO. Scritti danteschi, con documenti inediti. Città di Castello, Lapi, 1913.   A
CASSIRER, ERNST. Philosophie der symbolischen Formen. Berlin, Cassirer, 1923-25. 2 vols.   B, C, K
CHAMBERS, Sir EDMUND KERCHEVER. The mediæval stage. Oxford, Clarendon press, 1903. 2 vols.   G
CHASE, GEORGE DAVIS. Sun myths in Lithuanian folksongs. In: American Philological Association Transactions, 1900. 31: 189-201   J
CHAYTOR, HENRY JOHN, ed. The troubadours of Dante; being selections from the works of the Provençal poets quoted by Dante, with introduction, notes, concise grammar and glossary. Oxford, Clarendon press, 1902.   A, G
CHEETHAM, SAMUEL. The mysteries, pagan and Christian. London, Macmillan, 1897. (Hulsean lectures).   E, J
CHURCHWARD, ALBERT. The signs and symbols of primordial man; being an explanation of the evolution of religious doctrines from the eschatology of the ancient Egyptians. London, Sonnenschein; New York, Dutton, 1910.   J
COLLINS, STANLEY T. The interpretation of Vergil with special reference to Macrobius. Oxford, Blackwell, 1909.   B, D, G
COMPARETTI, DOMENICO PIETRO ANTONIO. Vergil in the middle ages; tr. by

E. F. M. Benecke, with an introduction by Robinson Ellis. London, Sonnenschein; New York, Macmillan, 1895. *A, G, I*

CONYBEARE, FREDERICK CORNWALLIS. Myth, magic, and morals; a study of Christian origins. London, Watts, 1909. *J*

COOK, ARTHUR BERNARD. Zeus; a study in ancient religion. Cambridge [Eng.] University press, 1914-1925. 2 vols. in 3. *J*

CORNOLDI, G. M. La filosofia scolastica di San Tommaso e di Dante, ad uso dei licei. 8. ed. Roma, "Civiltà Cattolica", 1899. *A, B*

COULTON, GEORGE GORDON. Five centuries of religion. Cambridge [Eng] University press, 1923. Vol. 1: St. Bernard, his predecessors and successors, 1000-1200. *D, G*

——— From St. Francis to Dante; a translation of all that is of primary interest in the chronicle of the Franciscan Salimbene (1221-1288); together with notes and illustrations from other medieval sources. London, Nutt, 1906. *D, G*

COX, GEORGE WILLIAM. An introduction to the science of comparative mythology and folklore. New York, Holt, 1881. *J*

——— The mythology of the Aryan nations. London, Longmans, 1870. 2 vols. *J*

COX, GEORGE WILLIAM & EUSTACE HINTON JONES. Popular romances of the middle ages. London, Longmans, 1871. *G*

CRAM, RALPH ADAMS. The substance of Gothic; six lectures on the development of architecture from Charlemagne to Henry VIII, given at the Lowell institute, Boston, in November and December, 1916. Boston, Marshall Jones, 1917. *F*

CRAWFORD, ALEXANDER WILLIAM CRAWFORD LINDSAY, 25th earl of. Sketches of the history of Christian art. London, Murray, 1847. 3 vols. *See especially:* vol. 1, chapters on symbolism and mythology. *J*

CRAWLEY, ALFRED ERNEST. The mystic rose; a study of primitive marriage. London & New York, Macmillan, 1902. *J*

CREUZER, GEORG FRIEDRICH. Religions de l'antiquité considérées principalment dans leurs formes symboliques et mythologiques. Traduit de l'allemand par J. D. Guigniaut. Paris, 1825-41. 4 vols. *J*

CROCE, BENEDETTO. La poesia di Dante. 2. ed. riveduta. Bari, Laterza, 1921. *A*

——— The poetry of Dante; tr. by Douglas Ainslie. New York, Holt, 1922. *A*

CUMONT, FRANZ. La theologie solaire du pagenisme romain. (In: Institut de France Academie des inscriptions et belles-lettres. Memoires. Paris, 1923. 12: 447-79) *J*

——— After life in Roman paganism; lectures delivered at Yale university on the Silliman foundation. New Haven, Yale university press, 1922. *J*

——— The oriental religions in Roman paganism; with an introductory essay by Grant Showerman. Authorized translation. Chicago, Open court pub. co., 1911. *J*

CUTHBERT, *Father*. Life of St. Francis of Assisi. London, New York [etc.] Longmans, 1912. *D*

CUTTS, EDWARD LEWES. History of early Christian art. London, S.P.C.K., 1893. *F*

CYPRIAN, JOHANN. De nomine Christi ecclesiastico acrosticho Ιχθὺς, Piscis. Lipsiae, Goezianis, 1699. (Diss. Georgius Ludovicus *resp.*) *D, J*

DARÍO, RUBÉN. Los raros. (2. ed., corr. y aum.) Barcelona [etc.] Maucci, 1905. *B'*

DAWKINS, *Mrs.* MURIEL (BACHELOR). Mysticism an epistemological problem. [New Haven, Tuttle, Morehouse & Taylor, 1916] 100 p. *B, D*

DEANE, WILLIAM JOHN. Pseudepigrapha; an account of certain apocryphal sacred writings of the Jews and early Christians. Edinburgh, Clark, 1891. *D, J*

DELACROIX, HENRI. Études d'histoire et de psychologie du mysticisme; les grands mystiques chrétiens. Paris, Alcan, 1908. Bibl. pp. 465-70.   C, D
—— Essai sur le mysticisme spéculatif en Allemagne au quatorzième siecle. Paris, Alcan, 1900. Bibl. pp. ix-xvi.   B, D
DIDRON, ADOLPHE N. Histoire de Dieu, Iconographie des Personnes Divines. Paris, 1843.
—— Iconographie chrétienne. Histoire de Dieu. Paris, Imprimerie royale, 1843.   F
—— Christian iconography; or, The history of Christian art in the middle ages. Translated from the French by E. J. Millington. London, Bohn, 1851-91. 2 vols.   F
—— Paganisme dans l'art chrétien. Paris, Didron, 1853, 22 p.   F, J
DÖLGER, FRANZ JOSEF. ΙΧΘΥC Das Fischsymbol in frühchristlicher Zeit. Rom, Spithöver, 1910-22. 3 vols.   F, J
DÖRRIES, HERMANN. Zur Geschichte der Mystik: Erigena und der Neuplatonismus. Tübingen, Mohr, 1925.   B, D
DUCHESNE, LOUIS MARIE OLIVIER. Christian worship: its origin and evolution. A study of the Latin liturgy up to the time of Charlemagne. Translated from the third French ed. by M. L. McClure. London, S.P.C.K.; New York, Young, 1903.   E
—— Origines du culte chrétien; étude sur la liturgie latine avant Charlemagne. 3. éd. rev. et augm. Paris, Fontemoing, 1902.   E
DUHEM, PIERRE MAURICE MARIE. Le système du monde; histoire des doctrines cosmologiques de Platon à Copernic. Paris, Hermann, 1913-17. 4 vols.   I
DURANTEL, JEAN. Saint Thomas et le Pseudo-Denis. Paris, Alcan, 1919. Thesis.   B, D

EATON, RALPH MONROE. Symbolism and truth; an introduction to the theory of knowledge. Cambridge, Harvard university press, 1925. Bibl. pp. 317-21.   B, K
EBNER, JOSEPH. Die Erkenntnislehre Richards con St. Viktor. Beiträge, 19: 4, 1917.   B, D
EDMAN, IRWIN. Logic of mysticism in Plotinus. (In Columbia University Dept. of Philosophy, Studies in the history of ideas. Vol. 2.) New York, 1925.   B, D, K
EHRENREICH, PAUL MAX ALEXANDER. Die Sonne im Mythos. Aus den hinterlassenen Papieren hrsg., bevowortet und mit Zusätzen versehen von Ernst Siecke. Leipzig, Hinrichs, 1915.   J
EICKEN, H. VON. Geschichte und System der mittelalterlichen Weltanschauung. Stuttgart, 1887.   B, G
EISEN, GUSTAV. The great chalice of Antioch, on which are depicted in sculpture the earliest known portraits of Christ, apostles and evangelists. New York, Kouchakji, 1923. 2 vols.   F
EISLER, ROBERT. Orpheus—The fisher; comparative studies in Orphic and early Christian cult symbol.sm. London, Watkins, 1921.   J, K
ELDERKIN, GEORGE WICKER. Kantharos; studies in Dionysiac and kindred cult. Princeton, Princeton university press, 1924.   D, J
EVANS, EDWARD PAYSON. Animal symbolism in ecclesiastical architecture, with a bibliography and seventy-eight illustrations. London, Heinemann, 1896.   F

FABRIS, GIOVANNI. Il simbolismo nel prologo della Divina commedia. Vicenza, Rumot, 1921.   A
FARBRIDGE, MAURICE HENRY. Studies in Biblical and Semitic symbolism. London, Kegan Paul; New York, Dutton, 1923.   J
FAURE, ÉLIE. History of art; translated from the French by Walter Pach, illustrated from photographs selected by the author. New York & London, Harpers, 1921-24. 4 vols. (Vol. II, Mediaeval art.)   F

FAX, A. U. Des nombres mysterieux, et en particular du nombre trois. Paris, Ledoyen, 1850.

FEASEY, HENRY JOHN, Ancient English Holy Week ceremonial. London, Baker, 1897.   E

FERRERO, GUGLIELMO. Les lois psychologiques du symbolisme. Traduit de l'italien avec de nombreuses modifications. Paris, Alcan, 1895.   C, K

FEWKES, JESSE WALTER. The winter solstice ceremony at Walpi. Washington, Reprinted from the American anthropologist, volume XI, 1898. 38 p.   J

FICKER, GERHARD. Der Mitralis des Sicardus nach seiner Bedeutung für die Ikonographie des Mittelalters. Leipzig, Seemann, 1887.   E, F

FISHER, LIZETTE ANDREWS. The mystic vision in the Grail legend and in the Divine comedy. New York, Columbia university press, 1917.   A, D, H

FLAMINI, FRANCESCO. I significati reconditi della Commedia di Dante e il suo fine supremo. Livorno, Giusti, 1903. 3 vols.   A

—— Introduction to the study of the Divine comedy, tr. by Freeman M. Josselyn. Translation rev. and augm. by the author. Boston, New York, Ginn, [1910]   A

FLETCHER, JEFFERSON BUTLER. Symbolism of the Divine comedy. New York, Columbia university press, 1921.   A

—— The religion of beauty in woman, and other essays on Platonic love in poetry and society. New York, Macmillan, 1911.   D, G

—— The crux of Dante's comedy. Repr. from Romanic review v. 16, pp. 42 ff., 1925.   A

FRANCK, ADOLPHE. The kabbalah; or, The religious philosophy of the Hebrews. Rev. and enl. translation by Dr. I. Sossnitz. New York, Kabbalah pub. co., 1926.

FRAZER, Sir JAMES GEORGE. The golden bough: a study in magic and religion. 2d ed., rev. and enl. London, New York, Macmillan, 1900. 3 vols.   J

—— The golden bough, a study in magic and religion. 3d. ed. London, Macmillan, 1907-15. 12 vols.   J

—— The worship of nature. New York, Macmillan, 1926-   J

FROBENIUS, LEO. Das Zeitalter des Sonnengottes. Berlin, Reimer, 1904, Bibl. pp. 415-420.   J

GARDNER, ALICE. Studies in John the Scot (Erigena); a philosopher of the dark ages. London, New York, Frowde, 1900.   B

GARDNER, EDMUND G. Dante's ten heavens; a study of the Paradiso. 2d ed. rev. London, Constable, 1904.   A, D

—— Dante and the mystics; a study of the mystical aspect of the Divina commedia and its relations with some of its mediaeval sources, with three photogravure plates. London, Dent; New York, Dutton, 1913.   A, D

GASPARY, ADOLF. The history of early Italian literature to the death of Dante, translated from the German, together with the author's additions to the Italian translation (1887) and with supplementary bibliographical notes (1887-1899) by Herman Oelsner. London, Bell, 1901.   A, G

GAUTIER, LÉON i.e. ÉMILE THÉODORE LÉON. La chevalerie. Paris, Palmé, 1884.   G

—— Histoire de la poésie liturgique au moyen âge: les tropes. Paris, Palmé, 1886.   E

—— Chivalry, tr. by Henry Frith. London, New York [etc.] Routledge, 1891.   G

GEBHART, ÉMILE. Mystics and heretics in Italy; a history of the religious revival in the middle ages. Tr. by Edw. M. Hulme. New York, Knopf, 1923.   D

GESSMANN, GUSTAV W. Die Geheimsymbole der Chemie und Medecin des Mittelalters. Eine Zusammenstellung der von den Mystikern und Alchymisten gebrauchten geheimen Zeichenschrift, nebst einem kurzgefassten geheimwissenschaftlichen Lexikon. Graz, Im Verlage des Verfassers, 1899. 67 p.   D, I

GHIL, RENÉ. Les dates et les œuvres; symbolisme et poésie scientifique. Paris, Crès [1923] *B'*

GILSON, ÉTIENNE HENRY. The philosophy of St. Thomas Aquinas; authorised translation from the 3d rev. ed. of 'Le thomisme.' Translated by Edward Bullough; edited by Rev. G. A. Elrington. Cambridge [Eng.] Heffer, 1924. *B*

GLOVER, TERROT REAVELEY. The conflict of religions in the early Roman empire. 3d ed. London, Methuen [1909] *J*

GOBLET D'ALVIELLA, EUGÈNE FÉLICIEN ALBERT, *comte*. La migration des symboles. Paris, Leroux, 1891. *J*

—— The migration of symbols, with introduction by Sir George Birdwood. London, Constable, 1894. *J*

—— Croyancés, rites, institutions. Paris, Geuthner, 1911. 3 vols. *J*

—— Lectures on the origin and growth of the conception of God as illustrated by anthropology and history. London & Edinburgh, Williams & Norgate, 1892. *J*

—— The contemporary evolution of religious thought in England, America, and India. Trans. by J. Moden. New York, 1886. *J*

GOLDSMITH, ELIZABETH EDWARDS. Life symbols as related to sex symbols; a brief study into the origin and significance of certain symbols which have been found in all civilisations, such as the cross, the circle, the serpent, the triangle, the tree of life, the swastika, and other solar emblems, showing the unity and simplicity of thought underlying their use as religious symbols; with more than 100 illustrations. New York & London, Putnam's, 1924. *F, J, K*

GÖRRES, JOHANNES JOSEPH VON. Die christliche Mystik. Neue aufl. in fünf Bänden mit einem Sach- und Namenregister. Regensburg, Manz [1879-80] 5 vols. *D*

GOUGAUD, LOUIS. Devotional and ascetic practices in the middle ages. London, Burns & Oates [1927] *D*

GOURMONT, RÉMY DE. Dante, Béatrice et la poésie amoureuse; essai sur l'idéal féminin en Italie à la fin du XIIIᵉ siècle. Paris, Mercvre de France, 1922. 78 p. *A, G*

—— Le latin mystique; les poètes de l'antiphonaire et la symbolique au moyen âge. Préface inédite de l'auteur. Frontispice de Maurice Denis, ornements de Roger Deverin. Paris, Grès, 1922. *D, E*

GRAF, ARTURO. Miti, leggende e superstizioni del medio evo. Torino, Loescher, 1892-93. 2 vols. *G, H*

—— Roma nella memoria e nelle imaginazioni del medio evo. Torino, Loescher, 1882. 2 vols. *G*

GRANDGENT, CHARLES HALL. Dante. New York, Duffield, 1916. *A*

—— Discourses on Dante. Cambridge, Harvard university press, 1924. *A*

HAIG, JAMES. Symbolism; or, Mind, matter, language as the elements of thinking and reasoning and as the necessary factors of human knowledge. Edinburgh & London, Blackwood, 1869. *B, C, K*

HARNACK, ADOLF *i.e.* CARL GUSTAV ADOLF. The expansion of Christianity in the first three centuries. Tr. and ed. by James Moffatt. London, Williams & Norgate; New York, Putnam's, 1904-05. 2 vols. *G, J*

HARRIS, WILLIAM TORREY. The spiritual sense of Dante's Divina commedia. New York, Appleton, 1889. *A, B*

HAURÉAU, BARTHÉLEMY. Histoire de la philosophie scolastique. Paris, Pedone-Lauriel, 1872-80. 3 vols. *B*

HAUVETTE, HENRI. Dante; introduction à l'étude de la Divine comédie. 2. éd., rev. Paris, Hachette, 1912. *A*

HEADLAM, CECIL. The story of Chartres; illustrated by Herbert Railton. London, Dent, 1902. *G*

HEATH, S. H. The romance of symbolism. London, Griffiths, 1909. *B', K*

HERVIEUX, LÉOPOLD, Les fabulistes latins depuis le siècle d'Auguste jusqu'à la fin du moyen âge. Paris, Firmin-Didot, 1893-99. 5 vols.

HINKLE, Mrs. BEATRICE (MOSES). The re-creating of the individual; a study of psychological types and their relation to psychoanalysis. New York, Harcourt, Brace [1923]   C, D, J, K

HIRN, YRJÖ. The Sacred shrine; a study of the poetry and art of the Catholic church. London, Macmillan, 1912. (Swedish ed. 1909). Bibl. pp. 555-70.
                                                                          D, E, F

HOLLINGWORTH, HARRY LEVI. Meaning and the psycho-physical continuum. Journal of philosophy, psychology and scientific method, 20: 433-41, 1923.   C, K

HOOP, J. H. VAN DER. Character and the unconscious; a critical exposition of the psychology of Freud and Jung. Authorized translation by Elizabeth Trevelyan. London, Trübner; New York, Harcourt, Brace, 1923.   C, K

HOPPENOT, J. Le crucifix dans l'histoire et dans l'art, dans l'ame des saints et dans notre vie. [Nouv. éd.] Lille, Paris, Société de Saint-Augustin, Brouwer [1902]   D, E, F, G

—— La messe dans l'histoire et dans l'art, dans l'ame des saints et dans notre vie. Paris, Brouwer, 1906.   D, E, F, G

HORNEFFER, AUGUST. Symbolik der Mysterienbünde. München, Reinhardt, 1916. (2. ed. Prien, Anthropos Verlag, 1924.) Bibl. pp. 239-44.   D, K

HÜGEL, FRIEDRICH, freiherr VON. The mystical element of religion as studied in Saint Catherine of Genoa and her friends. London, Dent; New York, Dutton, 1923. 2 vols.   B, C, D

HUGONIN, Mgr. Prolegomena to the works of Hugh of St. Victor. PL, 175.   B, D

HUIZINGA, JOHAN. Herfsttij der middeleeuwen; studie over levens- en gedachten-vormen der veertiende en vijftiende eeuw in Frankrijk en de Nederlanden. Tweede herziene druk. Haarlem, Willink, 1921.   F, G

—— The waning of the middle ages, a study of the forms of life, thought and art in France and the Netherlands in the xivth and xvth centuries. London, Arnold, 1924.   F, G

HULME, FREDERICK EDWARD. The history, principles and practice of symbolism in Christian art. 2d ed. London, Sonnenschein; New York, Macmillan, 1892.
                                                                          F, K

HUSENBETH, FREDERICK CHARLES. Emblems of saints: by which they are distinguished in works of art. 3d ed. edited by Augustus Jessopp. Norwich, Printed for the Norfolk and Norwich archæological society by Goose, 1882.   F

INGE, WILLIAM RALPH. The philosophy of Plotinus; the Gifford lectures of St. Andrews, 1917-1918. London, New York, Longmans, Green, 1918. 2 vols.
                                                                          B, D

—— Neo-platonism. ERE, 9: 307-19.   B, D

JAMESON, Mrs. ANNA BROWNELL (MURPHY). Sacred and legendary art. Boston, Houghton, Mifflin, 1893. 2 vols.   F, G

—— Legends of the monastic orders as represented in the fine arts. Forming the second series of Sacred and legendary art. 5th ed. London, Longmans, Green, 1872. 2 vols.   F

—— The history of Our Lord as exemplified in works of art: with that of His types; St. John the Baptist: and other persons of the Old and New Testament. Commenced by the late Mrs. Jameson. Continued and completed by Lady Eastlake. 3d ed. London, Longmans, Green, 1872. 2 vols.   F

JENNINGS, HARGRAVE. The Rosicrucians, their rites and mysteries; with chapters on the ancient fire- and serpent-worshipers, and explanations of the mystic symbols represented in the monuments and talismans of the primeval philosophers. London, Hotten, 1870. (3rd ed. greatly revised and enlarged. London, Nimmo, 1887. 3 vols.)   J

JONES, KAREL HENDRIK EDUARD DE. Das antike Mysterienwesen in religionsgeschichtlicher, ethnologischer, und psychologischer Beleuchtung. Leiden, Brill, 1909.   *C, D, E, J*

JOURDAIN, ELEANOR FRANCES. A study in the symbolism of the Divina commedia. Shaldon, Speight, 1902.   *A*

JUNDT, AUGUSTE. Histoire du panthéisme populaire au moyen âge et au seizieme siècle. Strasbourg, Sandoz & Fischbacher, 1875.   *B, D*

JUNG, CARL GUSTAV. Wandlungen und Symbole der Libido. Wien, Deuticke, 1912.   *C, D, J, K*

—— Psychology of the unconscious; a study of the transformations and symbolisms of the libido, a contribution to the history of the evolution of thought. Authorized translation, with introduction, by Beatrice M. Hinkle. New York, Moffat, Yard, 1916.   *C, D, J, K*

—— Psychologische typen. Zürich, Rascher, 1921.   *C, K*

—— Psychological types, or, The psychology of individuation. Trans. H. Godwin Baynes. London, Trübner; New York, Harcourt, 1923.   *C, K*

KAHN, GUSTAVE. Symbolistes et décadents. Paris, Vanier, 1902.   *B'*

KAMPERS, FRANZ. Mittelalterliche Sagen vom Paradiese und vom Holze des Kreuzes Christi in ihren vornehmsten Quellen und in ihren hervorstechendsten Typen. Köln, Bachem, 1897.   *G, J*

KATTUM, FRANZ XAVER. Die Eucharistielehre des heiligen Bonaventura. Münich, Datterer, 1920. 54 p.   *B, D, E*

KEICHER, OTTO. Raymundus Lullus und seine Stellung zur arabischen Philosophie. *Beiträge*, 7: 4-5, 1909.   *B, C, D*

KELLER, LUDWIG. Die heiligen Zahlen und die Symbolik der Katakomben. Berlin, Weidmann, 1906. 38 p.   *F*

KELSEN, HANS. Die Staatslehre des Dante Alighieri. Wien und Leipzig, Deuticke, 1905.   *A, G*

KEMP WELCH, ALICE. Beast imagery and the bestiary. *Nineteenth century and after*, 54: 501-9, 1903.   *G*

KEYSSLER, JOHN G. Dissertatio de cultu solis, Freji et Othini. (In Schedius, Elias: De diis Germanis, Halae, Crugius, 1728. p. 759-90.)   *J*

KIRCHER, ATHANASIUS. Arithmologia, sive de Abditis numerorum mysteriis. Rome, Varesii, 1665.   *D*

KNAPP, JULIET LEE. Symbolistic drama of today. *Poet lore*, 32: 201-33, 1921.   *B, I*

KNIGHT, RICHARD PAYNE. An inquiry into the symbolical language of ancient art and mythology. Privately printed, 1818. Reprinted and pub. by E. H. Barker. London, Black & Armstrong, 1836.   *F, J*

—— The symbolical language of ancient art and mythology. An inquiry. A new ed., with introduction, additions, notes tr. into English, and a new and complete index by Alexander Wilder. New York, Bouton, 1876.   *F, J, K*

—— A discourse on the worship of priapus. London, 1865.   *J*

KRAUS, FRANZ XAVER. Geschichte der christlichen Kunst. Freiburg im Breisgau, Herder, 1896-1908. 2 vols. in 3.   *F*

—— Dante, sein Leben und sein Werk, sein Verhältniss zur Kunst und zur Politik. Berlin, Grote, 1897.   *A, F, G*

KRAUSE, ERNST LUDWIG. Die Trojaburgen Nordeuropas, ihr Zusammenhang mit der indogermanischen Trojasage von der entführten und gefangenen Sonnenfrau (Syrith, Brunhild, Ariadne, Helena), den Trojaspielen, Schwertund Labyrinthtänzen zur Feier ihrer Lenzbefreiung. Nebst einem Vorwort über den deutschen Gelehrtendünkel. Mit 26 Abbildungen im Text. Glogau, Flemming, 1893.   *J*

KRETZMANN, PAUL EDWARD. The liturgical element in the earliest forms of the medieval drama, with special reference to the English and German plays. Minneapolis, 1916.   *E, G*

KREUSER, JOHANN PETER BALTHASAR. Christliche Symbolik. Brixen, Weger, 1868. F

KROLL, JOS. Die Lehren des Hermes Trismegistos. *Beiträge*, 12: 2-4, 1914. I, J

LABRIOLLE, PIERRE CHAMPAGNE DE. History and literature of Christianity from Tertullian to Boethius. Translated from the French by Herbert Wilson; with introductory foreword by His Eminence Cardinal Gasquet. New York, Knopf, 1925. B, D, G

LAJOLO, GREGORIO. Simboli ed enigmi danteschi. Rome, Casa ed. Navionale Roux e Viarengo, 1906. Vol. I. A

LANDROIT, JEAN FRANÇOIS ANNE THOMAS. Le symbolisme. 4. ed. Paris, Palmé, 1891. J

LANDRY, BERNARD. La notion d'analogie chez Saint Bonaventure et Saint Thomas d'Aquin. Louvain, 1922. 68 p. Thesis. B, D, K

LANG, ANDREW. Myth, ritual, and religion. London, Longmans, Green, 1887. 2 vols. J

LAUCHERT, FRIEDRICH. Geschichte des Physiologus. Strassburg, Trübner, 1889. I

LEASE, EMORY B. The number three, mysterious, mystic, magic. *Classical philology*, 14: 56-73, 1919. J

LEBRUN, PIERRE. Explication littérale, historique, et dogmatique des prières et des cérémonies de la messe suivant les anciens auteurs. Liege, Tutot; Paris, Desprez, 1777-78. E

LECLÉRE, ALBERT. Le mysticisme catholique et L'âme de Dante. Paris, Bloud, 1906. A, D

LEDUC, DÉSIRÉ CAMILLE. The liturgy of the Roman missal. English translation from the French of Dom Leduc and Dom Baudot. London, Burns Oates & Washbourne [1925] E

LEGG, JOHN WICKHAM. Ecclesiological essays. London, Moring, 1905. Contains a treatment of medieval ceremonial. E

LEGGE, FRANCIS. Forerunners and rivals of Christianity, being studies in religious history from 330 B.C. to 330 A.D. Cambridge [Eng.] University press. 2 vols. J

LEISEGANG, HANS. Die Begriffe der Zeit und Ewigkeit in späteren Platonismus. *Beiträge*, 13: 4, 1913. B

LENORMANT, FRANÇOIS. Chaldean magic: its origin and development. Translated from the French. With considerable additions by the author, and notes by the editor William R. Cooper. London, Bagster, 1877. J

LEUBA, JAMES HENRY. The psychology of religious mysticism. London, Trübner; New York, Harcourt, Brace, 1925. C, D

LÉVY-BRUHL, LUCIEN. Primitive mentality. Authorized translation by Lilian A. Clare. London, Allen & Unwin; New York, Macmillan [1923] C, J

LIHARŽIK, FRANZ. Das Quadrat die Grundlage aller Proportionalität in der Natur, und des Quadrat aus der Zahl Sieben die Uridee des menschlichen Körperbaues. Wien, Herzfeld & Bauer, 1865.

LITHABY, W. R. Architecture, mysticism, and myth. New York, Macmillan, 1892. D, F, J, K

LOISY, ALFRED FIRMIN. Les mystères païens et le mystère chrétien. Paris, Nourry, 1914. D, E, J

LOOMIS, ROGER SHERMAN. Celtic myth and Arthurian romance. New York, Columbia university press, 1927. G, H, J, K

LOT, *Mme.* MYRRHA (BORODINE). La femme et l'amour au XIIᵉ siècle, d'après les poèmes de Chrétien de Troyes. Paris, Picard, 1909. G

LOWEY, HEINRICH. Die mystischen Bezeichnungen Jesu Christi als Siloë, Schilloh, und Piscis, insbesondere die Bezeichnung der christlichen Opferfeier als Missa. Paderborn, Schöningh, 1888. D. K

LUNGO, ISIDORO DEL. Dal secolo e dal poema di Dante: altri ritratti e studi. Bologna, Zanichelli, 1898. *A*

LUTZ, EDUARD. Die Psychologie Bonaventuras, nach den Quellen dargenstellt. *Beiträge*, 6: 4-5, 1909. *B, C, D*

LUYCKX, BONIFAZ A. Die Erkenntnislehre Bonaventuras. *Beiträge*, 23: 3-4, 1923. *B, D*

MABILLON, JEAN. De Liturgica Gallicana. *PL*, 72. (App. ad opera S. Germani.) *E*

MACKENZIE, DONALD ALEXANDER. The migration of symbols and their relations to beliefs and customs. London, Trübner; New York, Knopf, 1926. *J*

MAETERLINCK, MAURICE. Ruysbroeck and the mystics, with selections from Ruysbroeck. Tr. by Jane T. Stoddart. London, Hodder & Stoughton, 1894. *B, D*

MÂLE, ÉMILE. L'art allemand et l'art français du moyen âge. Paris, Colin, 1917. *F*

—— L'art religieux de la fin du moyen âge en France; étude sur l'iconographie du moyen âge et sur ses sources d'inspiration; 250 gravures. Paris, Colin, 1908. *D, E, F*

—— Religious art in France, XIII century; a study in mediaeval iconography and its sources of inspiration; tr. from the 3d ed. < rev. & enl. > by Dora Nussey; with 190 illustrations. London, Dent; New York, Dutton, 1913. *D, E, F*

—— L'art religieux du XIIIᵉ siècle en France; étude sur l'iconographie du moyen âge et sur ses sources d'inspiration. Nouv. éd., rev. et cor., illustrée de 127 gravures. Paris, Colin, 1902. *D, E, F*

MALINOWSKI, BRONISLAW. Myth in Primitive Psychology. New York, Norton, 1927. Other works of interest. *C, J*

MALVEZZI, ALDOBRANDINO. Saggio sul misticismo cristiano. Bologna, Zanichelli, 1906. *D*

MANDONNET, PIERRE FÉLIX, ed. Siger de Brabant et l'Averroïsme latin au xiiiᵐᵉ siècle. 2. éd. rev. et augm. Louvain, 1908-11. *B*

MANNING, BERNARD LORD. The people's faith in the time of Wyclif. Cambridge [Eng.] University press, 1919. *E, G*

MARÉCHAL, JOSEPH. Études sur la psychologie des mystiques. Bruges, Beyaert. 1924- *C, D*

MARIE, AUGUSTE. Mysticisme et folie. (Étude de psychologie normale et pathologique comparées.) Paris, Giard & Brière, 1907. *C, D*

MARTIGNY, JOSEPH ALEXANDRE. Étude archéologique sur l'Agneau et le bon Pasteur; suivie d'une notice sur les Agnus Dei. Paris, Didron, 1860. *F*

MARTINO, PIERRE. Parnasse et symbolisme (1850-1900). Paris, Colin, 1925. Bibl. pp. 217-8. *B'*

MATTHEWS, WASHINGTON. Navaho legends. Collected and tr; with introduction, notes, illustrations, texts, interlinear translations, and melodies. Boston & New York, Houghton, Mifflin, 1897. *J*

MEADE, GEORGE ROBERT STOWE. Echoes from the gnôsis. London, Benares, 1906-1908. *J*

MERCER, JOHN EDWARD. *bp. of Tasmania*. Alchemy, its science and romance; with 4 illustrations. London, S.P.C.K.; New York, Macmillan, 1921. *I*

MILLET, GABRIEL. Recherches sur l'iconographie de l'évangile aux xivᵉ, xvᵉ et xviᵉ siècles, d'après les monuments de Mistra, de la Macédoine et du Mont-Athos, dessins de Sophie Millet; 670 gravures dans le texte et hors texte. Paris, Fontemoing, 1916. *F*

MÖNCHEMEIER, REINHARD. Amalar von Metz, sein Leben und seine Schriften; Ein Beitrag zu theologischen Litteraturgeschichte und zu Geschichte der lateinischen Liturgie im Mittelalter. Münster i. W., Schöningh, 1893. *B, E*

MOHLBERG, LEONHARD, *in religion* CUNIBERT. Radvlph de Rivo, der letzte Vertreter der altrömischen Liturgie. Louvain, Bureaux du Recueil, 1911-   E

MOLSDORF, WILHELM. Christliche Symbolik der mittelalterlichen Kunst. Leipzig, Hiersemann, 1926.   F

MOORE, CLIFFORD HERSCHEL. The religious thought of the Greeks, from Homer to the triumph of Christianity. 2d ed. Cambridge, Harvard university press, 1925.   J

MOORE, EDWARD. Studies in Dante. First series: Scripture and classical authors in Dante. Oxford, Clarendon press, 1896.   A

—— Studies in Dante. Second series: Miscellaneous essays. Oxford, Clarendon press, 1899.   A

—— Studies in Dante. Third series: Miscellaneous essays. Oxford, Clarendon press, 1903.   A

—— Studies in Dante. Fourth series: Textual criticism of the 'Convivio' and miscellaneous essays. Oxford, Clarendon press, 1917.   A

MOREY, CHARLES RUFUS. The origin of the fish-symbol. *Princeton theological review.* 1910-12. 8: 93 ff, 231 ff, 401 ff: 9: 268 ff: 10: 278 ff.   F, J

MORISON, JAMES AUGUSTUS COTTER. The life and times of Saint Bernard, abbot of Clairvaux, A.D. 1091-1153. London & New York, Macmillan, 1889.   D

MORRISSEY, HUGH. The fish symbol. (In Lattey, Cuthbert, *ed.:* Catholic faith in the holy Eucharist. 1923. pp. 199-215.)   E, F

MOSHER, JOSEPH ALBERT. The exemplum in the early religious and didactic literature of England. New York, Columbia university press, 1911.   G

MOTT, LEWIS FREEMAN. The system of courtly love studied as an introduction to the Vita nuova of Dante. Boston & London, Ginn, 1896.   A, G

MÜLLER, H. F. Dionysos. Proklos. Plotinos. Ein historischer Beitrag zur Neupla-tonischen Philosophie. *Beiträge,* 20: 3-4, 1918.   B

MÜLLER, KARL OTFRIED. Introduction to a scientific system of mythology. English trans. from the German original by J. Leitch. London, Longmans, 1844.   J

MÜLLER, WILHELM MAX. Egyptian [mythology]. Indo-Chinese [mythology] by Sir James George Scott. Boston, Marshall Jones, 1918.   J

MURARI, ROCCO. Dante e Boezio. Bologna, Zanichelli, 1905.   A, B

MURRAY, MARGARET ALICE. The witch-cult in western Europe; a study in an-thropology. Oxford, Clarendon press, 1921.   J

MYER, ISAAC. Qabbalah. The philosophical writings of Solomon ben Yehudah ibn Gebirol, or Avicebron, and their connection with the Hebrew Qabbalah and Sepher ha-Zohar, with remarks upon the antiquity and content of the latter, and translations of selected passages from the same. Also, An ancient lodge of initiates, tr. from the Zohar, and an abstract of an essay upon the Chinese Qabbalah, contained in the book called the Yih King; a translation of part of the mystic theology of Dionysios, the Areopagite; and an account of the con-struction of the ancient Akkadian and Chaldean universe, etc. Accompanied by diagrams and illustrations. Philadelphia, Pub. by the author, 1888.
      B, D, I, J

NARDI, BRUNO. Sigieri di Brabante nella Divina commedia e le fonti della filo-sofia di Dante. Firenze, Giuseppe, 1912.   A, B

NEILSON, WILLIAM ALLAN. The origins and sources of the Court of love. Bos-ton, Ginn, 1899.   G

NICOLE, PAUL. Anthropologie religieuse, Deus Sol. (In Société d'anthropologie de Paris. Bulletins et Mémoires. Paris, 1902. ser. 5, v. 3, pp. 325-33.)   J

NIEUWBARN, M. C. Church symbolism; a treatise on the general symbolism and iconography of the Roman Catholic church edifice. Trans. from the Dutch by the Rev. John Waterreus. London, Sands, 1910.   F

NOETLING, FRITZ. Die kosmischen Zahlen der Cheops-pyramide, der mathe-matische Schlüssel zu den Einheits-Gesetzen im Aufbau des Weltalls berechret. Stuttgart, Schweizerbart, 1921.   D, I, J

NUTT, DAVID, *ed*. Popular studies in mythology, romance and folklore. A series of inexpensive monographs by various scholars. London, Nutt, 1899-
G, H, J

OESTERLEY, WILLIAM OSCAR EMIL & GEORGE HERBERT BOX. A short survey of the literature of rabbinical and medieval Judaism. London, S.P.C.K.; New York, Macmillan, 1920. *D, I*

OGDEN, CHARLES KAY, & IVOR ARMSTRONG RICHARDS. The meaning of meaning; a study of the influence of language upon thought and the science of symbolism; with an introduction by J. P. Postgate, and supplementary essays by B. Malinowski, and F. G. Crookshank. London, Trübner; New York, Harcourt, Brace, 1923. *B, C, K*

OLCOTT, WILLIAM TYLER. Sun lore of all ages; a collection of myths and legends concerning the sun and its worship. With 30 full-page illustrations and several drawings. New York & London, Putnam's, 1914. (Representative of modern theosophical interest.) *J*

OLGIATI, FRANCESCO. The key to the study of St. Thomas from the Italian; with a letter of approbation from His Holiness Pope Pius XI, translated by John S. Zybura. St. Louis, Mo. & London, Herder, 1925. *B*

O'NEILL, JOHN. The night of the gods; an inquiry into cosmic and cosmogonic mythology and symbolism. London, Quaritch, 1893-97. 2 vols. *J*

ORR, MARY ACWORTH. Dante and the early astronomers. London, Gall & Inglis [1914] *A, I*

OSMOND, PERCY HERBERT. The mystical poets of the English church. London. S.P.C.K.; New York, Macmillan, 1919. *D*

OSMONT, *Mme*. ANNE. Le mouvement symboliste. Préface de M. Ernest Raynaud. Paris, Maison du livre, 1917. *B'*

OSTLER, HEINRICH. Die Psychologie des Hugo von St. Viktor. Ein Beitrag zur Geschichte der Psychologie in der Frühscholastik. Münster, Aschendorff, 1906. *B, C, D*

OTTERLOO, A. A. VAN. Johannes Ruysbroeck; een bijdrage tot de kennis van den ontwikkelingsgang der Mystiek. 's-Gravenhag, Belinfante, 1896. *B, D*

OTTO, RUDOLF. The idea of the holy; an inquiry into the non-rational factor in the idea of the divine and its relation to the rational. Translated by John W. Harvey. London, New York, Oxford university press, 1923. *B, D*

OVIDIO, FRANCESCO D'. Nuovi studii danteschi. Ugolino, Piero della Vigna, i simoniaci, e discussioni varie. Milano, Hoepli, 1907. *A*

—— Studii sulla Divina commedia. Milano-Palermo, Sandron, 1901. *A*

OZANAM, ANTOINE FRÉDÉRIC. Œuvres complètes, avec une préface par M. Ampère. 2ᵉ ed. Paris, Lecoffre, 1862-65. 11 vols. Vol. V contains a study of the sources of the Divine comedy. *A, G*

—— Dante and Catholic philosophy in the thirteenth century; tr. from the French by Lucia D. Pychowska, pub. for the Cathedral library reading circle. New York, Cathedral lib. assoc., 1897. *A, B*

PACHEU, JULES. De Dante à Verlaine (études d'idéalistes et mystiques). Paris, Plon, Nourrit, 1897. Dante as related to the French symbolist school.
A, B, D

PAINE, LEVI LEONARD. The ethnic trinities and their relations to the Christian trinity; a chapter in the comparative history of religions. Boston & New York, Houghton, Mifflin, 1901. *J*

PARIS, GASTON BRUNO PAULIN. La littérature française au moyen âge (xiᵉ-xivᵉ siècle) 3. éd., rev., cor., augm. et accompagnée d'un tableau chronologique. Paris, Hachette, 1905. *G*

—— Mediaeval French literature. London, Dent, 1903. *G, H*

PASCOLI, GIOVANNI. Minerva oscura: prolegomeni: la costruzione morale del poema di Dante. 2. ed. Livorno, Giusti, 1917. *A*

PASSERINI, GIUSEPPE LANDO, *conte*. Dante (1265-1321) Note biografiche e storiche. Milano, Caddeo [1921] *A*

PATTERSON, FRANK ALLEN. The Middle English penitential lyric; a study and collection of early religious verse. New York, Columbia university press, 1911. *D, G*

PATTERSON, LEONARD. Mithraism and Christianity; a study in comparative religion. Cambridge [Eng.] University press, 1921. *J*

PEERS, EDGAR ALLISON. Spanish mysticism; a preliminary survey. London, Methuen [1924] *D*

PFEIFFER, FRANZ, *ed*. Deutsche Mystiker des vierzehnten Jahrhunderts. Leipzig, Göschen, 1845-57. 2 vols. *B, D*

PICK, BERNHARD. The Cabala; its influence on Judaism and Christianity. Chicago, Open court pub. co., 1913. *B, D, J*

PIETROBONO, LUIGI. Dal centro al cerchio; la structura morale della Divina commedia. Turin, Soc. ed. internazionale, 1923. *A*

PIPER, FERDINAND. Mythologie und Symbolik der christlichen Kunst von der ältesten Zeit bis in's sechzehnte Jahrhundert. 1. bd. Mythologie. Weimar, Landes, 1847-51. 2 vols. *F*

PISCHEL, RICHARD. Der Ursprung des christlichen Fischsymbols. (Berlin. K. preuss. Akad. d. Wissensch. Sitzungsberichte 1905, pp. 506-32.)

POST, CHANDLER R. Medieval Spanish allegory. Cambridge, Harvard university press, 1915. *G*

POULAIN, AUG. The graces of interior prayer, trans. from the 6th ed. of Graces d'oraison, by L. Y. Yorke-Smith. London, Kegan Paul, 1910. *D*

POURRAT, PIERRE. La spiritualite chretienne. 2 vols. v. 2: Le moyen age. 1921. *B, D*

—— Christian spirituality. London, Burns, 1922-24. 2 vols. *B, D*

PRATT, JAMES BISSETT. The religious consciousness. New York, 1906. *C*

PROBST, JEAN HENRI. La mystique de Ramón Lull et *L'art de contemplacio*. Étude philosophique. Münster i.W., Aschendorff, 1914. *Beiträge*, 13: 2-3. *B, D*

PROTO, ENRICO. L'Apocalissi nella Divina commedia; studi sul significato della visione del Paradiso terrestre [Purg. xxvii-xxxiii] in relazione alle dottrine etiche, politiche e religiose di Dante. Napoli, Pierro, 1905. *A*

RAGON, JEAN MARIE. La messe et ses mystères comparés aux mystères anciens. ou complément de la Science initiatique. 3. ed. Paris, Denter, 1882. *E, J*

RANK, OTTO. Der Mythus von der Geburt des Helden. Versuch einer psychologischen Mythendeutung. Leipzig und Wien, Deuticke, 1909. 93 p. *C, J*

—— The myth of the birth of the hero; a psychological interpretation of mythology. Authorized translation by Drs. F. Robbins and Smith Ely Jelliffe. New York, Nervous and mental disease pub. cò., 1914. *C, J. K*

RAYNAUD, ERNEST. La mêlée symboliste (1870-[1910]) portraits et souvenirs. Paris, La Renaissance du livre, 1920-[192-?] 3 vols. *B'*

RÉCÉJAC, E. Essai sur les fondements de la connaissance mystique. Paris, 1897.

—— Essay on the bases of the mystic knowledge. Tr. by Sara Carr Upton. New York, Scribner's, 1899. *C, D*

REDGROVE, HERBERT STANLEY. Alchemy: ancient and modern, being a brief account of the alchemistic doctrines, and their relations, to mysticism on the one hand, and to recent discoveries in physical science on the other hand; together with some particulars regarding the lives and teachings of the most noted alchemists. With 16 full-page illustrations. 2d and rev. ed. London, Rider, 1922. *D, I*

—— Bygone beliefs, being a series of excursions in the byways of thought. London, Rider, 1920. *D, I*

REITZENSTEIN, RICHARD. Die hellenistischen Mysterienreligionem nach ihren Grundgedanken und Wirkungen; vortag ursprünglich gehalten in dem Wissenschaftlichen Predigerverein für Elsass-Lothringen den 11. november 1909. 2. umbearb. aufl. Leipzig, Teubner, 1920. D, J

RIBERA, JULIAN. Origenes de la filosofia de Raimundo Lulio. (Homenaje a Menendez y Pelayo, v. 2, 191. Madrid, Suarez, 1899.) B, D

RIBET, JÉRÓME. La mystique divine distinguée des contrefaçons diaboliques et des analogies humaines. Paris, Poussielgue, 1895-1903. 4 vols. D

RIBOT, THÉODULE ARMAND. Essai sur l'imagination créatrice. Paris, Alcan, 1900. B, C

—— Essay on the creative imagination. Tr. from the French, by Albert H. N. Baron. Chicago, Open court pub. co., 1906. B, C

RICKLIN, FRANZ. Wish fulfillment and symbolism in fairy tales. Authorized translation by Dr. Wm. A. White. New York, Nervous and mental disease pub. co., 1915. 90 p. C, J, K

RIVERS, WILLIAM HALSE RIVERS. Medicine, magic, and religion; the FitzPatrick lectures delivered before the Royal college of physicians of London in 1915 and 1916. With a preface by G. Elliot Smith, F.R.S. London, Trubner; New York, Harcourt, Brace, 1924. J

ROGERS, ELIZABETH FRANCES. Peter Lombard and the sacramental system. New York, 1917. B, D, E

ROHNER, ANSELM. Das Schöpfungsproblem bei Moses Maimonides, Albertus Magnus und Thomas von Aquin. Ein Beitrag zur Geschichte des Schöpfungsproblems im Mittelalter. Münster i. W., Aschendorff, 1913. B

ROLBIECKI, JOHN JOSEPH. The political philosophy of Dante Alighieri. Washington, D. C., Catholic university of America, 1921. A, B, G

RONCA, UMBERTO. Cultura medioevale e poesia latina d'Italia nei secoli xi e xii. Roma, Società Laziale, 1892. 2 vols. B, G

ROSSETTI, DANTE GABRIEL. Dante and his circle, with the Italian poets preceding him (1100-1200-1300) a collection of lyrics, tr. in the original metres. A new ed., with preface by William M. Rossetti. London, Ellis & Elvey, 1900. A

ROUSSELOT, PAUL. Les mystiques espagnols: Malon de Chaide, Jean D'Avila, Louis de Granade, Louis de Leon, Ste Thérèse, S. Jean de la Croix et leur groupe. Paris, Didier, 1867. D

ROUSSELOT, PIERRE. Pour l'histoire du problème de l'amour au moyen âge. Münster, Aschendorff, 1908. G

ROWBOTHAM, JOHN FREDERICK. The troubadours and courts of love. London, Sonnenschein; New York, Macmillan, 1895. List of authorities, pp. 315-317. G

SABATIER, PAUL. Vie de S. François d'Assise. 22. éd. Paris, Fischbacher, 1899. D

SAINTSBURY, GEORGE EDWARD BATEMAN. The flourishing of romance and the rise of allegory. New York, Scribner, 1897. G

SANCTIS, FRANCESCO DE. Quattro saggi danteschi. Nuova edizione per cura del prof. Francesco Moroncini. Napili, Morano, 1903. A

SANTI, ANTONIO. L'ordinamento morale e l'allegoria delle Divina commedia. Milan, Sandron, 1923-24. 2 vols. A

SAUER, JOSEPH. Symbolik des Kirchengebäudes und seiner Ausstattung in der Auffassung des Mittelalters, mit Berücksichtigung von Honorius Augustodunensis, Sicardus und Durandus. Mit 14 abbildungen im text. Freiburg im Breisgau, Herder, 1902. E, F

SAUNIER, MARC. La légende des symboles, philosophiques, religieux et maçonniques. Paris, Sansot, 1911. B, F

SCARTAZZINI, GIOVANNI ANDREA. Enciclopedia dantesca. Milano, Hoepli, 1896-1905. 3 vols. A

—— A handbook to Dante. Tr. from the Italian, with notes and additions, by Thomas Davidson. Boston, Ginn, 1887. Bibl. pp. 1-15. A

SCHAEFER, THEODOR. Ueber die Bedeutung der symbolischen Kultusformen des Judentums und des Christentums. Berlin, Mittler, 1909.   E, F, K

SCHAFF, DAVID SCHLEY. History of the Christian church. The middle ages. New York, Scribner, 1907-10. 2 vols. (Being v. 5, pts. 1-2 of his Hist. of the Christian church.)   B, E

SCHAFF, PHILIP. Literature and poetry. New York, Scribner's, 1890. Contains studies on Dante and on certain mediæval hymns.   G

SCHEFTELOWITZ, ISIDOR. Das Fischsymbol in Judentum und Christentum. Archiv. für Religionswissenschaft, 14: 1-53, 321-92, 1911.   J

SCHELLENBERG, ERNST LUDWIG. Die deutsche Mystik, illustriert nach den Originalen zeitgenössischer Meister. Berlin-Lichterfelde, Bermühler [1919]   D

SCHLESINGER, MAX. Geschichte des symbols; ein versuch. Berlin, Simion, 1912.   B, C, K

SCUDDER, VIDA DUTTON. Le morte Darthur of Sir Thomas Malory, a study of the book and its sources. London, Dent, 1921.   D, H

SEDGWICK, HENRY DWIGHT. Italy in the thirteenth century. Boston & New York, Houghton, Mifflin, 1912. 2 vols.   A, G

SEYMOUR, WILLIAM WOOD. The cross in tradition, history, and art. New York & London, Putnam's, 1898. Bibl. pp. xix-xxx.   F, G

SHARPE, A. B. Mysticism: its true nature and value with a translation of the "Mystical theology" of Dionysius, and of the letters to Caius and Dorotheus (1, 2 and 5). London, Sands; St. Louis, Mo., Herder [1910]   D

SILBERER, HERBERT. Problems of mysticism and its symbolism; tr. by Smith Ely Jelliffe. New York, Moffat, Yard, 1917. On psycho-analysis, alchemy, mysticism, and use of symbolism in Masonry.   C, D, I, K

SMITH, ARTHUR LIONEL. Church and state in the middle ages; the Ford lectures delivered at Oxford in 1905. Oxford, Clarendon press, 1913. 4 p.   G

SOMMER, HEINRICH OSKAR. Studies on the sources, 'Le Morte Darthur.' See vol. 3 of his edition; listed under Malory.   H

STEINER, RUDOLF. La mystère chrétien et les mystères antiques. Traduit de l'allemand et precédé d'une introduction par Edmond Schuré. Paris, Perrin, 1908.   E, J

—— Die Mystik im Aufgange des neuzeitlichen Geisteslebens und ihr Verhältnis zur modernen Weltanschauung. Stuttgart, Kommende tag a.-g. verlag, 1923.   D

—— Mystics of the renaissance and their relation to modern thought, including Meister Eckhart, Tauler, Paracelsus, Jacob Boehme, Giordano Bruno, and others. Authorized translation from the German by Bertram Keightley. New York & London, Putnam's, 1911.   D, I

—— The way of initiation; or, How to attain knowledge of the higher worlds. London, Theosophical pub. soc., 1908. Translated by Max Gysi.   D

—— Initiation and its results: a sequel to The way of initiation. London, Theosophical pub. soc., 1909.   D

STORCH, ALFRED. The primitive archaic forms of inner experiences and thought in schizophrenia; a genetic and clinical study of schizophrenia. Tr. by Clara Willard. New York & Washington, Nervous and mental disease pub. co., 1924.   C, D, J, K

STREET, OLIVER DAY. Symbolism of the three degrees. New York, Doran [1924]   D

STRZYGOWSKI, JOSEF. Origin of Christian church art, new facts and principles of research. Tr. O. M. Dalton & H. J. Braunholtz. Oxford, Clarendon press, 1923. Bibl. pp. 253-259.   F

STUDER, PAUL, & JOAN EVANS. Anglo-Norman lapidaries. Paris, Champion, 1924.   G, I

SWETE, HENRY BARCLAY. Church services and service-books before the reformation. New York, S.P.C.K., 1896.   E

SYMONS, ARTHUR. The symbolist movement in literature. Rev. and enl. ed. New York, Dutton [1919] Bibl. and notes, pp. 331-365.   B′

TAYLOR, ALFRED EDWARD. Platonism and its influence. Boston, Marshall Jones [1924]   B

TAYLOR, HENRY OSBORN. The classical heritage of the middle ages. New York. Columbia university press, 1901. Bibliographical appendix, pp. 359-389.   B

—— The mediaeval mind; a history of the development of thought and emotion in the middle ages. 3d (American) ed. New York, Macmillan, 1919. 2 vols.   B

THORNDIKE, LYNN. A history of magic and experimental science during the first thirteen centuries of our era. New York, Macmillan, 1923. 2 vols. Contains bibliographies.   I

THOULESS, R. H. An introduction to the psychology of religion. New York, Macmillan, 1925. Contains a discussion of the psychological elements in mysticism.   C, D

TORRACA, FRANCESCO. Studii danteschi. Napoli, Perrella, 1912.   A

TOYNBEE, PAGET JACKSON. Dante Alighieri, his life and works. [4th ed.] New York, Macmillan, 1910.   A

—— Dante studies and researches. London, Methuen, 1902.   A

TYRWHITT, RICHARD ST. JOHN. The art teaching of the primitive church; with an index of subjects, historical and emblematic. Pub. under the direction of the Committee of general literature and education appointed by the Society for promoting Christian knowledge. London, S.P.C.K. [1874?]   F

UNDERHILL, EVELYN. Mysticism; a study in the nature and development of man's spiritual consciousness. London, Methuen [1911]   D

—— The mystic way; a psychological study in Christian origins. London, Dent: New York, Dutton, 1913.   D

—— Ruysbroeck. London, Bell, 1914.   B, D

VALERIO, R. Stazio nella scala mistica della Divina commedia. 1906   A, B, D

VALLGORNERA. Theologica mystica D. Thomae. Turin, Marietti, 1890. First edition, Barcelon, 1662.   B, D

VERNON, Hon. WILLIAM JOHN BORLASE-WARREN-VENABLES. Readings on the Paradiso of Dante, chiefly based on the commentary of Benvenuto da Imola. London, Macmillan, 1900. 2 vols. (2d ed. 1909.)   A, B, D

—— Readings on the Purgatorio of Dante, chiefly based on the commentary of Benvenuto da Imola. 3. ed. revised. London, Methuen [1907]   A, B

—— Readings on the Inferno of Dante, based upon the commentary of Benvenuto da Imola and other authorities, with text and literal translation. With an introduction by Edward Moore. 2d ed., entirely re-written. London, Methuen [1906] 2 vols.   A, B

VOLKMANN, LUDWIG. Iconografia dantesca; the pictorial representations to Dante's Divine comedy, rev. and augm. by the author, with a preface by C. Sarolea. London, Grevel, 1899.   A

VOSS, JOHANN HEINRICH. Antisymbolik. Stuttgart, Metzler, 1824-26. 2 vols.   J

VOSSLER, KARL. Die philosophischen Grundlagen zum "süssen neuen Stil" des Guido Guinicelli, Guido Cavalcanti und Dante Alighieri. Eine Studie. Heidelberg, Winter, 1904.   A, B

WAITE, ARTHUR EDWARD. Azoth, or, The star in the East, embracing the first matter of the magnum opus, the evolution of Aphrodite-Urania, the supernatural generation of the Son of the Sun, and the alchemical transfiguration of humanity. London, 1893.   D, I

—— The doctrine and literature of the Kabalah. London, Theosophical pub. soc., 1910.   B, D

—— The hidden church of the Holy Graal. London, Rebman, 1909.   *D, H*
—— Lamps of western mysticism; essays on the life of the soul in God. London, Trübner; New York, Knopf, 1923.   *D*
—— A new encyclopædia of freemasonry (ars magna latomorum) and of cognate instituted mysteries: their rites, literature and history, with sixteen full-page plates and other illustrations. London, Rider, 1921. 2 vols.   *B, D*
WALL, OTTO AUGUSTUS. Sex and sex worship (phallic worship); a scientific treatise on sex, its nature and function, and its influence on art, science, architecture, and religion—with special reference to sex worship and symbolism. St. Louis, Mosby, 1922.   *J*
WARING, JOHN BURLEY. Ceramic art in remote ages; with essays on the symbols of the circle, the cross and circle, the circle and ray ornament, the fylfot, and the serpent, showing their relation to the primitive forms of solar and nature worship. London, Day, 1874.   *F, J*
WARREN, FREDERICK EDWARD. The liturgy and ritual of the ante-Nicene church. London, S.P.C.K., 1897.   *E*
WATKIN, EDWARD INGRAM. The philosophy of mysticism. New York, Harcourt, 1920.   *B, D*
WAUTIER D'AYGALLIERS, ALFRED. Ruysbroeck the Admirable; authorized translation by Fred Rothwell. London & Toronto, Dent; New York, Dutton, 1925.
          B, D
WEBBER, F. R. Church symbolism, an explanation of the more important symbols of the Old and New Testament, the primitive, the mediaeval and the modern church. Introduction by Ralph Adams Cram. Cleveland, J. H. Jansen, 1927.
          E, F
WEDEL, THEODORE OTTO. The mediæval attitude toward astrology, particularly in England. New Haven, Yale university press, 1920.   *I*
WELSH, ROBERT ETHOL. Classics of the soul's quest. New York, Doran [1923]
          D
WENTZEL, HANS. Symbolik im deutschen Volkslied. Marburg, 1915.   *G, J*
WESTCOTT, WILLIAM WYNN. An introduction to the study of the Kabalah. 2d ed. London, Watkins, 1926. (1st ed., 1910)   *D, J*
—— Numbers: their occult power and mystic virtue. Being a résumé of the views of the Kabbalists, Pythagoreans, adepts of India, Chaldean magi, and mediæval magicians. London, Theosophical pub. soc., 1890.   *D, I, J*
WESTON, JESSIE LAIDLAY. From ritual to romance. Cambridge [Eng.] University press, 1920.   *G, H*
—— The legend of Sir Gawain; studies upon its original scope and significance. London, Nutt, 1897.   *H*
—— The legend of Sir Lancelot du Lac; studies upon its origin, development, and position in the Arthurian romantic cycle. London, Nutt, 1901.   *H*
—— The quest of the Holy Grail. London, Bell, 1913. Bibl. pp. 155-157.   *H*
WESTROPP, HODDER M. & CHARLES STANILAND WAKE. Ancient symbol worship. Influence of the phallic idea in the religions of antiquity. With introduction, additional notes and appendix by A. Wilder. New York, Bouton, 1875.   *J*
WHITTAKER, THOMAS. Macrobius, or, Philosophy, science, and letters in the year 400. Cambridge, Cambridge university press, 1923.   *I*
WICKSTEED, PHILIP HENRY. Dante & Aquinas; being the substance of the Jowett lectures of 1911. London, Dent; New York, Dutton, 1913.   *A, B*
—— *tr.* The early lives of Dante, translated. London, Chatto & Windus; Boston, Luce, 1907.   *A*
—— From Vita nuova to Paradiso; two essays on the vital relations between Dante's successive works. Manchester, University press; London, New York, Longmans, 1922.   *A, B*
—— The reactions between dogma & philosophy illustrated from the works of S. Thomas Aquinas; lectures delivered in London and Oxford, October-December 1916. London, Williams & Norgate, 1920.   *B*

WISLICENUS, HUGO. Die Symbolik von Sonne und Tag in der germanischen Mythologie. Mit Beziehung auf die allegemeine Mythologie. 2. ausg. Zürich, Schabelitz, 1867.　　　　　　　　　　　　　　　　　　　　　　　　*J*

WITTE, JOHANN HEINRICH FRIEDRICH KARL. Essays on Dante, (being selections from the two volumes of "Dante-forschungen") selected, tr. and ed. with introduction, notes and appendices by C. Mabel Lawrence, B.A. and Philip H. Wicksteed, M.A. London, Duckworth, 1898.　　　　　　　　　　　*A*

WRIGHT, THOMAS. Essays on archæological subjects, and on various questions connected with the history of art, science and literature in the middle ages. London, Smith, 1861. 2 vols.　　　　　　　　　　　　　　　*F G, I*

WULF, MAURICE MARIE CHARLES JOSEPH DE. Histoire de la philosophie médiévale; précédée d'un aperçu sur la philosophie ancienne. Louvain, Institut supérieur de philosophie, 1900.

—— Philosophy and civilization in the middle ages. Princeton, Princeton university press, 1922.　　　　　　　　　　　　　　　　*B*

—— Mediaeval philosophy illustrated from the system of Thomas Aquinas. Cambridge, Harvard university press, 1922.　　　　　　　　　*B*

YARKER, JOHN. Notes on the scientific and religious mysteries of antiquity; the gnosis and secret schools of the middle ages, modern Rosicrucianism, and the various rites and degrees of free and accepted masonry. London, Hogg, 1872.　　　　　　　　　　　　　　　　　　　　　　　　*B, D, J*

YOUNG, KARL. The dramatic associations of the Easter sepulchre. Madison, 1920.　　　　　　　　　　　　　　　　　　　　　　　　*E, G*

ZEREGA-FOMBONA, A. Le symbolisme francais et la poesie espagnole moderne. Paris, Mercvre de France, 1919. 84 p.　　　　　　　　　　*B'*

ZINGARELLI, NICOLA. Dante. Milano, Vallardi [1899-1904]　　　　*A*

INDEX

Action, *see* Contemplation and action.

Adam, *see* Christ and Adam.

Aeneas, 65, 179, 294 n. 156, 311.

Albertus Magnus, 150, 271, 276, 319, 440, 444, 460.

Alchemy, 437 ff.

Alexandria, 136, 244 ff., 253 ff., 263 ff.

Allegorical method, *see* Fourfold method; Scriptural interpretation. *See especially* 263 ff., 278 ff.

Allegory, definition of, 9, 278 ff., 500; political, *see* Political allegory of the *Commedia;* second level of fourfold interpretation, 19, 63, 95-98, 260, 263, 270-271, 468-469.

Ambrose, 21, 268-269, 324, 340, 507, 511.

Anagoge, 19, 56 ff., 95-98, 270-271, 468-469.

Analogy, 364, 439, 490 n. 7. *See also* Symbolism; Reality and expression.

Andreas Capellanus, 512.

Angelic intelligences, 62, 88.

Animal symbolism, 116 ff., 139-140, 163 ff., 194 ff., 338, 421.

Annunciation, 296, 405.

Annus Canicularis, 167. *See also* Sirius, the Dogstar.

Antaeus, 197, 307.

Apollinarian heresy, 407.

Arian controversy, 144 ff., 335, 367.

Aries, 120, 161, 407.

Aristotle and Aristotelianism, 360, 361, 431. *See also* Scholasticism.

Arthuriad, *see* Grail legends.

Ascension, 84 n. 208, 235, 293, 301, 407.

Association, 13 ff. *See also* Symbol, definition of; Symbols, association of.

Astrology, 48 ff., 53 ff., 62, 66, 121, 220, 496.

Astronomy (medieval), 33 ff., 59, 189, 191, 220, 482-483.

Athanasius, 137, 144 ff., 149, 367.

Augustine, 21, 147, 149, 268-269, 334, 340, 341, 419, 424, 502 ff.

Augustinian philosophy, 152, 349 ff., 361 ff., 390, 502 ff.

Avarice, *see* Cupidity; *also Gravezza.*

Avaricious and prodigal, in Hell, 176, 298; Terrace of, 223 ff., 232.

Averroism, 51, 361-362.

Babylonian thought, *see* Sun in Babylonian thought.

Beatific Vision, 63, 93-94, 95, 166, 316, 365 ff., 391, 400, 407, 447.

Beatrice, 30, 35-37, 39, 56, 82, 89, 90, 92-93, 98-99, 163, 168-171, 185-187, 199, 210-211, 222, 226 ff., 229, 234 ff., 296, 319, 324, 329 ff., 379, 388, 428-430, 435, 493, 513; and Lady Philosophy, *see* Lady Philosophy; and Nine, 30-31, 95, 98-99, 237, 285, 325-326, 394, 467, 470; in the Pageant, 229, 319 ff.; and Virgil, 98, 467-469, *also* 168 ff., 227.

Ben del l'intelletto (Good of the intellect), 70 ff., 102, 177, 183-185, 190, 197. *See also* Choice.

Bernard, 92-93, 271.

Bestiary, 162, 421.

Body of Christ, *see* Christ, fourfold Body of.

Boethius, 341 ff., 362, 503.

Bonaventure, 61, 356, 362.

Bread of angels, 75, 233, 314, 322 n. 247, 329 and n. 272, 377-379, 415 n. 47, 432, 442.

Cacciaguida, 64-66, 86, 161.

Can Grande della Scala, 29, 76, 167, 208 n. 373, 311, 327, 470. *See also* Political allegory of the *Commedia;* Deliverer.

Cassian, John, 270, 498.

Cathedral, symbolism of, 398 ff., 403 ff., 465. *See also* Mass and mass symbolism.

Cato, 203 ff.

Cerberus, 184, 382.

Charon, 382.

Choice, 53, 55-56, 195, 196, 244. *See also Ben del l'intelletto;* Human will and natural law.

Christ, and Adam, 62, 217, 305 n. 187a; Divine and human nature of, 41, 70, 72, 98, 102, 465 ff., 469 ff., *also* 287 ff., *see also* Duality; fourfold body of, 69, 74, 77, 81, 83, 282, 286-287, 294, 297, 314, 321, 405; Head of Humanity, 63, 69 and n. 154, 288; life of, 67 ff., 291 ff., 298 ff., 300-301, 305, 407, *see also* Annunciation; Cross; Crucifixion; Incarnation; Passion; Logos, *see* Logos; as Radiance, 144 ff., 254, 276, 288, 335, *see also* Light (wisdom) element in Trinity; Redeemer, 165, 288-289, 309, 310, 317, 334, *see also* Deliverer; Empire